Law and Christianity in Latin America

This volume examines the lives of more than thirty-five key personalities in Latin American law with a focus on how their Christian faith was a factor in molding the evolution of law in their countries and the region.

The book is a significant contribution to our ability to understand the work and perspectives of jurists and their effect on legal development in Latin America. The individuals selected for study exhibit wide-ranging areas of expertise from private law and codification, through national public law and constitutional law, to international developments that left their mark on the region and the world. The chapters discuss the jurists within their historical, intellectual, and political context. The editors selected jurists after extensive consultation with legal historians in various countries of the region looking at the jurist's particular merits, contributions to law in general, religious perspective, and importance within the specific country and period under consideration. Giving the work a diversity of international and methodological perspectives, the chapters have been written by distinguished legal scholars and historians from Latin America and around the world.

The collection will appeal to scholars, lawyers, and students interested in the interplay between law and religion. Political, social, legal, and religious historians among other readers will find, for the first time in English, authoritative treatments of the region's essential legal thinkers and authors. Students and others who may not read Spanish will appreciate these clear, accessible, and engaging English studies of the region's great jurists.

M.C. Mirow, Professor of Law, Florida International University, Miami, Florida, USA.

Rafael Domingo, Spruill Family Professor of Law and Religion, Emory University, Atlanta, Georgia, USA; Álvaro d'Ors Professor of Law, University of Navarra, Pamplona, Spain.

Law and Religion

The practice of religion by individuals and groups, the rise of religious diversity, and the fear of religious extremism raise profound questions for the interactions between law and religion in society. The regulatory systems involved, the religious laws of secular government (national and international), and the religious laws of faith communities, are valuable tools for our understanding of the dynamics of mutual accommodation and the analysis and resolution of issues in such areas as: religious freedom; discrimination; the autonomy of religious organizations; doctrine, worship, and religious symbols; the property and finances of religion; religion, education and public institutions; and religion, marriage, and children. In this series, scholars at the forefront of law and religion contribute to the debates in this area. The books in the series are analytical with a key target audience of scholars and practitioners, including lawyers, religious leaders, and others with an interest in this rapidly developing discipline.

Titles in this series include:

Christianity and Private Law
Edited by Robert F. Cochran, Jr. and Michael P. Moreland

Law and the Christian Tradition in Italy
The Legacy of the Great Jurists
Edited by Orazio Condorelli and Rafael Domingo

Tax Law, Religion, and Justice
An Exploration of Theological Reflections on Taxation
Allen Calhoun

For more information about this series, please visit: www.routledge.com/Law-and-Religion/book-series/LAWRELIG

Law and Christianity in Latin America

The Work of Great Jurists

Edited by
M.C. Mirow and Rafael Domingo

Routledge
Taylor & Francis Group
LONDON AND NEW YORK

Produced by the Center for the Study of Law and Religion, Emory University

First published 2021
by Routledge
2 Park Square, Milton Park, Abingdon, Oxon OX14 4RN

and by Routledge
52 Vanderbilt Avenue, New York, NY 10017

Routledge is an imprint of the Taylor & Francis Group, an informa business

British Library Cataloguing-in-Publication Data
A catalogue record for this book is available from the British Library

Library of Congress Cataloging-in-Publication Data
Names: Mirow, Matthew C. (Matthew Campbell), 1962- editor. | Domingo, Rafael, 1963- editor.
Title: Law and the Christian tradition in Latin America : the work of great jurists / edited by M.C. Mirow and Rafael Domingo.
Description: Milton Park, Abingdon, Oxon ; New York, NY : Routledge, 2021. | Series: Law and religion | Includes bibliographical references and index.
Identifiers: LCCN 2020041208 (print) | LCCN 2020041209 (ebook) | ISBN 9780367896416 (hardback) | ISBN 9781003020257 (ebook)
Subjects: LCSH: Church and state--Latin America. | Ecclesiastical law--Latin America. | Law--Latin America. | Religion and law--Latin America. | Christianity and law.
Classification: LCC KG580 .L39 2021 (print) | LCC KG580 (ebook) | DDC 342.808/52--dc23
LC record available at https://lccn.loc.gov/2020041208
LC ebook record available at https://lccn.loc.gov/2020041209

ISBN: 978-0-367-89641-6 (hbk)
ISBN: 978-0-367-70748-4 (pbk)
ISBN: 978-1-003-02025-7 (ebk)

Typeset in Galliard
by Deanta Global Publishing Services, Chennai, India

Contents

Contributors

Ezequiel Abásolo, Professor of Legal History, University of Buenos Aires, Argentina, and Professor of Legal History, Pontifical Catholic University of Argentina, Buenos Aires, Argentina.

Jorge Adame Goddard, Professor of Law, Panamerican University, Mexico City, Mexico.

Fernán Altuve-Febres, Professor of Law and Legal History, and President of the Peruvian Society of History, Lima, Peru.

Juan Bosco Amores Carredano, Professor of Latin American History, University of the Basque Country, Vitoria, Spain.

Kif Augustine-Adams, Ivan Meitus Chair and Professor of Law, J. Reuben Clark Law School, Brigham Young University, Provo, Utah, USA.

Juan Cianciardo, Professor of Law and Legal Philosophy, University of Navarra, Pamplona, Spain.

Robert J. Cottrol, Harold Paul Green Research Professor of Law and Professor of History and Sociology, George Washington University, Washington, DC, USA.

Óscar Cruz Barney, Researcher, Instituto de Investigaciones Jurídicas, National Autonomous University of Mexico, Mexico City, Mexico.

José de la Puente Brunke, Professor of History, Pontifical Catholic University of Peru, Lima, Peru.

Rafael Domingo, Spruill Family Professor of Law and Religion, Emory University, Atlanta, Georgia, USA; Álvaro d'Ors Professor of Law, University of Navarra, Pamplona, Spain.

Marcelo Fernández Peralta, Professor of Legal Theory, Catholic University of Cuyo, and Congress University, San Juan, Argentina.

Alfredo de J. Flores, Professor of Legal Methodology, Federal University of Rio Grande do Sul (UFRGS), Porto Alegre, Brazil.

Juan Carlos Frontera, Professor of Legal History, University of El Salvador, and Professor of Legal History, University of Buenos Aires, Buenos Aires, Argentina.

Cristóbal García-Huidobro Becerra, Professor of Legal History, Pontifical Catholic University of Chile; Head of the Department of Law and Professor of Legal History, University of Santiago de Chile, Santiago, Chile.

Carlos García-Soto, Professor of Legal History, Monteávila University, and Professor of Administrative Law, Central University of Venezuela, Caracas, Venezuela.

Alejandro Guzmán, Professor Emeritus of Legal History, Pontifical Catholic University of Valparaíso, Chile.

Brian Hamnett, Professor Emeritus of History, University of Essex, United Kingdom.

Peter V. N. Henderson, Professor Emeritus of History, Winona State University, Winona, Minnesota, USA.

Eduardo Herrera Andrade, Associate Director of the Enterprise and Humanism Institute, University of Navarra, Pamplona, Spain.

Francisco Javier Infante Martin, Associate Professor of Law, Pontifical Catholic University of Chile, Santiago, Chile.

Viviana Kluger, Tenured Lecturer and Researcher, University of Buenos Aires; Deputy Director and Researcher, Instituto de Investigaciones de Historia del Derecho, Buenos Aires, Argentina.

Santiago Legarre, Professor of Law, Pontifical Catholic University of Argentina; and Research Fellow, Consejo Nacional de Investigaciones Científicas y Técnicas de Argentina, Buenos Aires, Argentina.

Abelardo Levaggi, Professor Emeritus of Legal History and Legal Methodology, University of El Salvador, Buenos Aires; retired Professor of Legal History, University of Buenos Aires, Argentina.

Raúl Madrid, Professor of Jurisprudence, Director of Law and Technology Program, Pontifical Catholic University of Chile, Santiago, Chile.

Álvaro R. Mejía-Salazar, Professor of Law, Universidad Andina Simón Bolívar, Quito, Ecuador; and Member of National Academy of History of Ecuador, Quito, Ecuador.

M.C. Mirow, Professor of Law, Florida International University, Miami, Florida, USA.

Hernán Alejandro Olano Garcia, Professor of Legal History and Vice President of La Gran Colombia University of Bogotá, Colombia; Member of the Colombian Academy of Jurisprudence, Bogotá, Colombia.

Agustín Parise, Associate Professor of Law, Maastricht University, Maastricht, the Netherlands; Director of Scientific Studies, International Association of Legal Science, Paris, France.

Rogelio Pérez-Perdomo, Professor of Law, Metropolitan University of Caracas; Member of the National Academy of History, Caracas, Venezuela.

José Ernesto Pimentel Filho, Professor of Legal History, Federal University of Paraíba, João Pessoa-PB, Brazil.

Susana T. Ramella, Professor of Institutions and Legal History, National University of Cuyo, Mendoza, Argentina.

Juan Carlos Riofrío Martínez-Villalba, Professor of Jurisprudence and Human Rights, Strathmore University, Nairobi, Kenya; Fellow, Center for the Study of Law and Religion, Emory University, Atlanta, Georgia, USA.

Juan Pablo Salazar Andreu, Research Professor, Popular Autonomous University of the State of Puebla, Puebla City, Mexico.

Martín Santiváñez Vivanco, President and Professor of Law, University of Saint Ignatius of Loyola (USIL), Lima, Peru.

Paul Sekscenski, Former Analyst, US Department of Labor, Washington, DC, USA; Independent Scholar, João Pessoa, Brazil.

Márcio Ricardo Staffen, Professor of Law, University of Vale do Itajaí, Brazil.

Víctor M. Uribe-Uran, Professor of History and Law and Chair, Department of History, Florida International University, Miami, Florida, USA.

Gustavo Adolfo Vaamonde, Professor of Theory and Method of History, Central University of Venezuela, Caracas; Member of the National Academy of History, Caracas, Venezuela.

Cristián Villalonga Torrijo, Assistant Professor of Law, Pontifical Catholic University of Chile, Santiago, Chile.

John Witte, Jr., Robert W. Woodruff Professor of Law, McDonald Distinguished Professor of Religion, and Director, Center for the Study of Law and Religion, Emory University, Atlanta, Georgia, USA.

Foreword

In an impressive series of writings over the past two decades, M.C. Mirow has brought Latin American law and legal history to brilliant light and life for the English-speaking world. His work ranges over five centuries—from the first Spanish colonial encounters with the New World to the latest legal and constitutional movements in the countries of the region. His works covers a five-thousand-mile long land mass—from the southern tips of Chile and Argentina to the northern edges of the colonial Spanish North American empire in Florida, Louisiana, and New Mexico. And his work cuts across various types of Latin American law—public, private, penal, and procedural laws set out in customs, codes, conventions, and constitutions that together govern the 650 million people living in this vast region of the world. Particularly Professor Mirow's signature titles *Latin American Law: A History of Private Law and Institutions in Spanish America* (Texas, 2004; 2009) and *Latin American Constitutions: The Constitution of Cádiz and its Legacy in Spanish America* (Cambridge, 2015) are standard English texts on Latin American law, which he presents in historical, comparative, biographical, and cultural perspectives. Important for this volume have been Mirow's careful documentation of the pervasive influence of Catholic teachings on Latin American law and politics over the centuries, and his call for legal historians to focus on the "neglected factor" of "individual experience in legal change."

Over the past three decades, Spanish legal historian and jurist, Rafael Domingo has brilliantly opened and integrated the worlds of ancient Roman law, Christian canon law, and modern civil law, which he has been drawing into a robust new theory of global law and religion. Professor Domingo has published more than one hundred articles and twenty-five books, including signature recent titles on *The New Global Law* (Cambridge, 2010), *God and the Legal System* (Cambridge, 2016), *Great Christian Jurists in Spanish History* (Cambridge, 2016), *Roman Law* (Routledge, 2018), *Great Christian Jurists in French History* (Cambridge, 2019), *Christianity and Global Law* (Routledge, 2020), and *Law and the Christian Tradition in Italy* (Routledge, 2020). He, too, has been working hard to build new legal, cultural, and religious bridges between Spain and its Latin American progeny, between the modern Anglo-American common law world and the Latin American civil law world, and between Catholics and Protestants, and European and Indigenous traditions in Latin America. Significantly, Domingo has published more than two hundred op-eds in Spanish and Latin American newspapers and has been interviewed more than forty times on CNN/Spanish edition on cardinal law and religion themes.

In this volume, these two great scholars have combined their talents and toolboxes to tell the story of law and Christianity in Latin America. While alert to earlier colonial times when Spanish and Portuguese law and religion dominated this region, the editors have focused their study on the nineteenth and twentieth centuries when independent nations were born and flourished. While taking note of a wide range of factors that have shaped the development of Latin American law, they tell this story through a series of thirty-seven biographical case studies commissioned from three dozen leading scholars in and on Latin America.

The chapters range from Juan Germán Roscio, a central figure in Venezuelan independence, to Carlos Alberto Menezes Direito, a prolific Brazilian jurist who strove to bring religious perspectives into both public life and law. Between these two bookends, readers learn about the lives and legal contributions of such codifiers as Andrés Bello, father of the Civil Code of the Republic of Chile. They encounter legal visionaries of the emergent modern Latin America, like Augusto Teixeira de Freitas, drafter of the Brazilian Esboço de Código Civil and Dalmacio Vélez Sarsfield, drafter of the Argentinian Civil Code. Also included are compelling studies of pacific revolutionaries like the Cuban priest Félix Varela; peace negotiators like José Bernardo Couto y Pérez; and the great Catholic martyr of social justice reform, Archbishop Oscar Romero. Other chapters introduce hitherto neglected legal scholars across the continent who helped with nation-building and legal development in their home countries.

Two important legal movements dominated the development of modern Latin American law: constitutionalism and codification. Early constitutions were modeled in part on the French and United States constitutions. These new Latin American constitutions formally eradicated traditional aristocratic privileges and institutions as well as the hierarchical categorization of persons into Indians, priests, merchants, and others. In their place, the constitutions formally enacted new legal systems, executive and legislative political bodies, and independent courts based on the principles of equal citizenship under the law and separation of powers. Despite these lofty constitutional aspirations, however, inequality, illegality, and political corruption have intermittently plagued the region.

Many modern Latin American countries adopted and adapted French civil, commercial, penal, civil procedural, and criminal procedural codes, and their concomitant principles of economic liberalism and legal positivism. Other European codes, too, born in part of Enlightenment liberalism and German historical jurisprudence had an influence—including notably the Prussian Civil Code and the Bavarian Penal Code. Many later Latin American countries looked for legal inspiration from their neighbors, too, rather than from across the Atlantic. For example, the Chilean Civil Code of 1855 by Andrés Bello, and the Argentine Civil Code of 1870 by Dalmacio Vélez Sársfield were highly influential in many other countries of Latin America and the Caribbean. So was the Esboço de Código Civil, the Brazilian draft civil code of 1865 by Augusto Teixeira de Freitas.

Latin America was founded not only as a set of Spanish and Portuguese colonies that eventually became nations, but also as a powerful new set of ecclesiastical provinces of the Roman Catholic Church that have remained formally in place to this day. The Catholic Church, however, has changed dramatically over the last five centuries, including in Latin America, which has been an important laboratory for such experimental movements as liberation theology and an important advocate for the changes eventually enacted by the Second Vatican Council 1962–1965. Particularly these latter reform ideas rendered the Church a critical actor in the process of legitimation and formation of the new nations, new political orders, and new legal systems, while remaining a fundamental institution of education, social welfare, and peacebuilding in the region. Especially after the reforms of the Second Vatican Council, the Church also became a powerful advocate of religious freedom and human rights.

Throughout Latin American history, the Church's influence was not only direct and institutional, but also indirect in shaping the culture, education, and values of the legal and political leaders and the people. And that influence can be seen poignantly in the lives and work of almost every one of three dozen figures featured herein. These were men of both faith and law, whose legal and political work was an expression and embodiment of a pervasively Catholic world view. These Christian values have continued to influence Latin American legal systems and actors, even though most of the modern secular legal documents no longer contain specific references to Christian sources or teachings.

Over the past half-century, the law, culture, and religion of the United States have also had a strong influence in Latin America. Notably influential have been the legal realist movement in American legal education; the growing interdisciplinary study of law and society, law and economics, and law and religion; and strong new constitutional and cultural perspectives on free trade, contractual freedom, social equality, human rights, freedom of speech, and religious freedom for all. Particularly these latter constitutional freedoms have transformed Latin America into a new mission field for American Protestant missionaries who have established a large number of new churches in the region.

Latin America has to face many serious challenges in the twenty-first century. Failure of national governance, institutional corruption, drug and sex trafficking, profound social instability and persistent inequality, poverty, violence, environmental exploitation, unemployment, and uncertainty in millions of families are some of these challenges. Each new form of pathos has added further wounds to a region still struggling to come to terms with ancient and deep scars produced by the Spanish conquest and Inquisition, the genocide of Indigenous peoples, and the active participation of the region in the trans-Atlantic slave trade well into the nineteenth century. At this fundamental level, Christianity and other faiths can and must continue to offer comfort and healing, restitution, and reconciliation, as well as continued reforms of the law on the books and the law in action.

This volume is the first such comprehensive history in English of law and Christianity in Latin American history. It is part and product of a multivolume series on great Christian jurists in world history, presenting the interaction of law and Christianity through the intellectual histories of a thousand legal figures from the past two millennia. Commissioned by the Center for the Study of Law and Religion at Emory University—where Professors Mirow and Domingo are senior fellows—each volume in this series focuses on a specific country, region, or era and samples the life and work of a score or more of its greatest legal minds over the centuries. These figures include not only civil and canon lawyers and judges but also theologians, philosophers, and church leaders who contributed decisively to legal ideas and institutions, or who helped create landmark statutes, canons, or cases. Thus, familiar Christian jurists like Gratian, Grotius, Blackstone, Story, Kuttner, and Scalia appear in this series, but so do Augustine, Isidore, Aquinas, Calvin, Barth, Maritain, and Romero. This approach is not intended to deprecate institutional, doctrinal, social, or intellectual histories of law, nor will it devolve into a new form of hagiography. It is, instead, designed to offer a simple method and common heuristic to study the interaction of law and Christianity around the world over the past two millennia.

Columbia University Press opened this series in 2006–07 with a three-volume work on *Modern Christian Teachings on Law, Politics, and Human Nature*, featuring nearly thirty modern Catholic, Protestant, and Orthodox Christian figures. Cambridge University Press has new titles on great Christian jurists in the first millennium, as well as in English, Spanish, French, Lowlands, and American history. Routledge has taken up the Italian, Nordic, Welsh, Russian, and Polish stories; Mohr Siebeck the German story; and Federation Press the Australian story. Forthcoming titles will cover great Christian jurists in the history of Scotland, Ireland, Austria, Switzerland, Greece, and, eventually, various countries and regions in Eastern Europe, Central Eurasia, the Middle East, Africa, and Asia.

It has been a joy for me to work with Professors Mirow and Domingo, and to learn from the powerful company of Latin American scholars whose work they have orchestrated and assembled in this hefty volume. I thank them for their ingenuity, expertise, and patience in building this impressive scholarly achievement. This volume was made possible by a generous gift from the FUNCIVA Foundation whose philanthropy is helping to build new scholarly bridges between the Spanish-speaking and English-speaking worlds of law and Christianity. The editors join me in extending our deep gratitude to the benefactor for this generous gift. I also join the editors in their kind acknowledgments and thanks to the many colleagues who contributed so generously to this project and volume, notably Gary Hauk, Anita Mann, and Amy Wheeler in our center.

It is a delight to publish this volume and several others in the distinguished Law and Religion series edited by one of the world's preeminent scholars of law and religion, Professor Norman Doe. Professor Doe and his many colleagues in the Cardiff Centre for Law and Religion have been vital trans-Atlantic allies with the Emory Center for the Study of Law and Religion. On behalf of our Emory Center, I extend my deep thanks for their leadership in this expanding global field of interdisciplinary legal study, and for their partnership with us in publishing this and parallel volumes on law and Christianity. Finally, I express warm thanks to Alison Kirk and her colleagues at Routledge for taking on this volume and applying their usual standards of excellence in their editing, production, and marketing.

John Witte, Jr.
Director, Center for the Study of Law and Religion
Emory University

Introduction

M.C. Mirow

Individuals and legal history

Legal change is often the underappreciated product of individual effort. Nonetheless, some transformative moments of legal change are commonly associated with individual names—Tribonian, Gratian, Bartolus, Accusius, Pothier, Portalis, Bello, Savigny, Blackstone, Madison, Llewellyn. Individuals and their writings have been instrumental in the path of the law. In keeping with this observation, it seems that the recent turn in legal history toward, or the reawakening of, biography and bibliography is appropriate.[1]

In 2005 I argued that individual experience has been a neglected aspect of legal change in Latin America.[2] New laws rely on the stuff of their creators, and even transplants rely on gardeners. Legal change emanates from intellectual steps taken in one person's mind. Thus, it is not surprising that where a jurist takes religious faith seriously, those beliefs, attitudes, and views become part of the core individual experience that shapes the jurist's views of law and its application in the world. In many ways, the present volume is an excitingly refined and full response to this concern raised more than fifteen years ago about legal change in a region I have studied for many years. I am grateful for the opportunity to be so closely involved in an exploration of this fundamental idea about legal change.

This book is a contribution to the biographical trend in scholarship through a project (now spanning many volumes and regions of the world) led by Professor John Witte Jr., Director of the Center for the Study of Law and Religion at Emory University. Since 2017, the center has published collections on jurists from England, Spain, France, Italy, Germany, and North America,[3] as well as two volumes serving as chronological and intellectual bookends: one on Christian jurists of the first millennium, and the other on the relationship between Christianity and global law.[4] The goal of this project is to explore the rich interaction between law and Christianity by examining the life and work of selected individuals whose contributions to law and legal development are widely recognized by lawyers, judges, and scholars as signal and lasting. Each study within these volumes on jurists attempts to apprehend the important relationship of individual faith and public contribution through law. These jurists served, in some ways, as conduits of Christian thought to the legal and social reality in which they practiced and shaped law. For the individuals studied in this volume, some excavation of the private world of their faith was often required to understand the public fruits of their beliefs.

Unlike the other volumes in this collection that address jurists in individual countries, this work takes a regional approach for all the countries of Latin America. Ensuring some representative selection across countries of the region was an important consideration. This volume on Christian jurists in Latin America examines the lives of thirty-seven personalities in Latin American legal history and, in particular, how their Christian faith was a factor in molding the evolution of law in their countries and the region.

The jurists studied here include twenty-three who worked predominantly in the nineteenth century and fourteen from the twentieth century. Each chapter discusses the jurist within his intellectual and political context. The editors were aware that this volume may be the first source in English for authoritative and scholarly treatments of many of these jurists. Few surveys of the history of Latin American law have been published in English, and these tend to focus more on doctrinal developments, essential sources and texts, and institutions, rather than the many individual actors who shaped the course of law in the region. Moreover, the availability of fine studies of colonial Latin American law in English has increased in recent years, and scholarship on *derecho indiano*, Spanish colonial law, has run deep and wide for nearly a century. A volume on jurists from the nineteenth and twentieth centuries thus makes a new contribution by bringing these influential jurists to the attention of the English-speaking world.

The contributors are committed to our belief that Latin America offers an important geographic region for scholarly attention for several reasons. First, this assembly of studies contributes significantly to our ability to understand the work and perspectives of jurists and their effect on legal development in individual countries and the region. Second, the region has a rich religious tradition, mostly associated with Roman Catholicism, from the colonial period to the present. Many jurists included here took their faith seriously and appropriated their religious convictions into their work in law as teachers, scholars, judges, and officials. Third, the individuals selected for study during the national period of Latin America's countries exhibit wide-ranging areas of expertise, from private law and codification, through national public law and constitutional law, to international developments that left their mark on the world. A reader of the volume from cover to cover will have gained rich insights into the legal development of the region that will supplement whatever can be gathered about sources, laws, and institutions of the region during this period. Most important, a frequently overlooked aspect of legal change or continuity in Latin America will become apparent—namely, the roles that Christianity and Christian belief played in legal development in the region.

Within the orbit of biographical legal studies, this volume on Latin America in the nineteenth and twentieth centuries has the further advantage of continuing the work of the volume on Spanish jurists. As Rafael Domingo and Javier Martínez-Torrón concisely explain in the Spanish volume, "Religion, not law, has been the true engine of Spanish culture."[5] Thus, by colonial extension, religion—and particularly Roman Catholicism—serves as a fundamental impetus or foil for political, legal, social, economic, and cultural change in this region.

The Church and law in Latin America

Several major stages during the independence and subsequent republic periods of Latin American countries presented new sets of challenges in the relationship between Church and state in the region. First, during the earliest period studied here, the Church was reluctant to recognize independence movements, and on achieving independence, new countries asserted their claims as the legitimate heirs to the carefully crafted Royal Patronage of the Catholic Church between the papacy and the Spanish Empire. Second, the failure to recognize fully this new relationship led to a long period of negotiations between Latin American countries and the Roman Catholic Church to establish accepted relationships that addressed fundamental questions of ecclesiastical appointments, finances, property, and status within the republics. Such questions were often worked out on the national level, and many of the jurists studied here contributed to settling these vexing questions. Third, as republics moved politically towards a form of liberalism that tended to include anticlericalism, the Church faced a substantial loss of power in the public square. Liberal reforms often included the nationalization of church property. Some Christian jurists studied here decried these developments and sought intellectual or political arguments against excessive liberalism. Fourth, in the twentieth century, Christian jurists attempted to construct appropriate responses to unbridled capitalism, socialism, and communism through their understanding and application of Catholic social doctrine. In this period, concern for those in poverty led some church officials and clergy to speak out for those where were not heard in the traditional political arenas.

The Royal Patronage and colonial law

Before the period studied in this book, the relationship between the Church and secular authorities was governed by a complex and carefully negotiated set of principles established in *derecho indiano*, or Spanish colonial law. The key aspect of this relationship was a delegation of authority and activities from the Church to the Spanish Empire that became the crown's Royal Patronage (*Patronato Real*) of the Church. Based on practices established from the Crusades, the "reconquest" of the Spanish peninsula, rights granted to Portugal in Africa, and the Spanish crown's evangelization in new territories, this collection of rights included the collection of tithes and the right to present bishops. In the early and mid-sixteenth century, Spain was granted universal patronage in the Indies and the right to change ecclesiastical jurisdictions.[6] Christian evangelization justified the Royal Patronage. The Americas presented new legal questions about the status of Indigenous peoples and their place in the Church, in the Spanish polity, and in law. Spanish theologians and canonists debated these questions and ultimately decided that Indigenous people had intellects and souls capable of permanent conversion to Christianity, an essential finding to justify the evangelical underpinnings of the Spanish enterprise in the Americas.[7]

Collecting the Church's revenues, controlling the appointment of high church officials, and filtering correspondence and information between the Americas and Rome were economic and political powers guarded jealously by the crown. The Royal Patronage limited the ecclesiastical jurisdiction in several ways, including moving testamentary causes to royal courts and providing avenues of appeal that hindered direct access to Rome.[8] Secular courts reviewed ecclesiastical judgments, taxed ecclesiastical corporations, and executed financial obligations on church officials, and such controls existed at local levels as well.[9]

These rights were woven into main sources of *derecho indiano*, including the *Ordenanzas del Patronazgo* (*The Ordinances of the Patronage*, 1574) and the first book of the *Recopilación de las Leyes de las Indias* (*The Compilation of Laws of the Indies*, 1680).[10] Despite the unusual quality of these rights in the crown, they were accepted and standard aspects of Spanish colonial law and an essential part of the legacy of *derecho indiano* in which Latin American jurists of the nineteenth and twentieth centuries were schooled.

The Royal Patronage was not the only lasting aspect that continued into the legal and political world of nineteenth- and twentieth-century Latin America. Spanish law and *derecho indiano* long recognized particular jurisdictional and substantive rights associated with particular favored groups in society. These collections of special rights or privileges were called *fueros*, and a *fuero* might attach to individuals with a particular status, such as the military, or to a particular town or region through the king's reward for special service. In the context of law and religion, and in Latin America, the ecclesiastical *fuero* was particularly important. It provided special substantive rules and jurisdictional advantages for individuals who successfully asserted the privilege. While the *fueros* were better developed and exercised in peninsular Spain, they and their application were part of the *derecho indiano* and made their way to the American provinces.

Independence

Establishing Roman Catholicism as the religion of the state, the Spanish Constitution of 1812, the Constitution of Cádiz, had wide application in the Spanish American provinces loyal to the royal government in Spain. This constitution, so often associated with liberalism, contains in its prologue the invocation: "In the name of God Almighty, Father, Son, and Holy Spirit, author and supreme legislator of society."[11] The Constitution of Cádiz established elected representative bodies at various levels of government, limited the power of the king, asserted individual property and contractual rights, reflected modern trends in protecting the criminally accused, removed seigniorial structures, and did away with tribute payments and forced labor by Indigenous people.[12] Furthermore, a minority of liberals at the Cortes hoped that the new constitution would welcome a new era of religious toleration.[13] Nonetheless, the Constitution of Cádiz was grounded in a Roman Catholic worldview; as one constitutional scholar has written of this constitution: "In reality, the whole text of the Constitution was saturated with strong religious overtones."[14] It did not significantly modify the state's management of the Royal Patronage of the Church.

The regency and the Spanish Cortes quietly took up the Royal Patronage, and this transfer of power appears to have been accepted by the American deputies in Cádiz, although at least one deputy objected to this continued exertion of power over the Church.[15] This constitution maintained the king's Royal Patronage of the Church "to present all bishoprics and all ecclesiastical dignitaries and benefices under the Royal Patronage of the church, at the proposal of the Council of State."[16] With tacit recognition of the Royal Patronage, the Constitution of Cádiz vested the Supreme Tribunal with jurisdiction to "hear all disputed matters pertaining to the Royal Patronage of the church" and "to hear appeals removing cases from ecclesiastical courts to royal courts."[17] Thus, this influential document in Latin American constitutionalism continued the exercise of the Royal Patronage by the king and nation.[18]

The lack of effective Spanish control and the eventual rebellion by American provinces led to independence. As towns, regions, and provinces moved toward autonomous control and independence—though often in the name of Ferdinand VII in light of his captivity and the vacant Spanish throne—new institutions asserting independence assumed the traditional powers of the king in relationship to the Church. They claimed to take up the sovereignty of the king, and this included the Royal Patronage.[19] New states required new constitutions, and these documents necessarily had to address questions of the Royal Patronage and the ecclesiastical *fuero*. These new constitutions were often the product of a Catholic Creole population that continued extant social, political, religious, and economic views consistent with their peninsular Spanish counterparts of the time.[20] For example, an early ephemeral example of Mexican independence constitutionalism, the Constitution of Apatzingán of 1814, maintained Roman Catholicism as the official state religion, and only Roman Catholics had political rights. Apostates and heretics lost citizenship. Freedom of the press was ensured only to the extent that expression was consistent with Roman Catholicism.[21] Similarly, in 1824 the Federal Constitution of the United States of Mexico maintained the favored status of Roman Catholicism.[22] Independence constitutions did not necessarily include a break with Rome and its religious authority.

National consolidation, liberalism, and conservatism

On gaining independence and passing through often unsettled and violent decades, the new governments of the region sought to consolidate power and institutionalize rule through constitutions. New private law could wait; public law and its supporting documents garnered immediate attention. Attempts to place the Church in new constitutional republican structures yielded wide variation. Some leaders sought to uphold the traditional place of the Church in political organizations and society; other leaders sought to crush its perceived economic, social, and political power. Moves to limit the Church and its influence were often linked to liberalism as a political philosophy or as a political movement. Each country has its own trajectory through these competing interests. One way to limit clerical power and privilege was to abolish the ecclesiastical *fuero*. Without the *fuero*, clerics were citizens and subject to the same rules, tribunals, and punishments as equal citizens under new constitutional provisions of citizenship and equality. In legal structures that maintained the ecclesiastical *fuero*, the Church and the clergy continued to hold and to exercise certain rights that pertained to their status and function. These were political decisions, and, broadly speaking, such decisions ran along liberal or conservative lines.

Liberalism and liberal thought in Latin American, and conversely conservatism and conservative thought, were not monolithic concepts but varied from time and place within the region. Liberalism advanced a number of ideas, including rights for the criminally accused, individual property as an absolute right, the freedom of contract, the nonintervention of the state in the economic affairs of the nation, and freedom of conscience. Liberalism asserted the equality of laws, the rationality of codes, the abolition of *fueros* based on individual status or territory, and unified systems of courts applying the same law to every member of the nation. In public law, it was aligned with constitutionalism, the separation of powers, limitations on the power of the executive or king, popular representation, and representative electoral bodies.

Liberalism's rationalism and association with Freemasonry often led to harsh and violent attacks against the Church and anticlerical stances against ecclesiastical officials and their privileges. Nonetheless, in the Spanish and Latin American contexts, liberalism was often consistent with a privileged position of the Catholic Church, and clergy were often an important voice in advancing liberal educational and philosophical approaches to government, constitutionalism, and law. Often associated with the birth, rise, and spread of Spanish liberalism, the Constitution of Cádiz, maintained a privileged status for Roman Catholicism and the ecclesiastical *fuero*. Thus, liberal reforms were not always linked to anticlericalism or religious tolerance. In the context of this constitution, liberalism could uneasily reside with Catholicism, monarchy, and nationalism.[23] Nonetheless, toward the middle of the nineteenth century, and particularly as liberalism and conservatism were manifested in political parties, liberalism made a clear break from the possibility of coexistence with Roman Catholicism and a special status for the clergy.

In relation to the Church, liberals, often in the context of establishing national constitutions, had to consider a range of social, legal, and religious institutions and practices, including religious individuals, ecclesial institutions, education, voting, civil registers, marriage laws, cemeteries, the national patronage of the Church, the ecclesiastical *fuero*, and the place of the Church in the constitution.[24] For example, liberal imposition of civil registries for births, marriages, and deaths led to varied responses at different layers of society from the laity and the lower clergy to the highest levels of the ecclesiastical and state hierarchies.

The place of religion and the Church was contested not only in the arena of public law. In fact, the quotidian aspects of life, such as birth, marriage, and death, were subject to jurisdictional battles. Some individuals and jurists viewed these events as religious or, in the case of marriage, sacramental, and thus properly within ecclesiastical control. There was extensive historical practice to justify this position. Other individuals and jurists believed these were matters of civil law to be controlled by the state without letting the Church have a say in such important matters. Similar heated disputes arose concerning divorce and the inheritance rights of children born out of wedlock. One could not draft a civil code without facing important choices on these issues. Indeed, considering that these issues touched every life, such determinations may have been of great impact and deeply experienced by the average citizen.

Conservatism also encompassed a somewhat shifting set of principles and positions, depending on time and place. Conservatives tended to value historical continuity with Spain in matters of religion, culture, education, society, and politics. With elitist aspects, conservatism valued a strong senate, strong executive and military powers that might guide and maintain economic progress and social order, limitations on suffrage, the incorporation of moral improvement and perfection in society, and the protection of private property—this last element shared with most liberals. Conservative constitutions sought to build political institutions and actors around unified, often Roman Catholic, ideas of the good and the improvement of the society and the nation.[25]

In an unexpected twist of interests, conservatives seeking to establish the absolute freedom of the Church and its institutions argued against the historical legacy of Spanish continuity. They asserted that the Royal Patronage was unique to the Spanish crown, and that the independent nations were not the successors to the imperial control of the Church. Liberals, however, found themselves arguing in favor of colonial continuity in relationship to the Royal Patronage; Spanish imperial control and supervision of the Church equated to national control of the Church, as the independent nations of Latin America were the successors of Spanish royal rights.

The case of Mexico is illustrative of the oscillation between liberal and conservative regimes that many countries of the region experienced in the nineteenth century. In 1836, Spain and the Vatican recognized Mexican independence. The Church enjoyed the support of Antonio López de Santa Anna during the years leading up to the Mexican Reform of 1854 and the economic and social secularization ushered in by Benito Juárez. The Constitution of 1857 subjugated religion to federal power.[26] Reforms following the Constitution of 1857 nationalized church property, established civil marriage and civil registers, suspended religious holidays, secularized hospitals and other charities formerly run by the Church, and dismantled religious communities.[27] Under Porfirio Díaz the Church was tolerated, but during the 1910s the Church was placed under national control. The Mexican Constitution of 1917 removed the legal personality of the Church and effectively removed any collective constitutional rights that could be exercised to protect it.[28] There were many other swings promoting and suppressing the Church in the course of these centuries in Mexico. The few chronicled here indicate the difficulties faithful individuals, and some of the Mexican jurists studied in this text, must have endured. Furthermore, even under liberal regimes, the Church and its individuals were powerful, often hidden, voices for legal and political change.[29]

If the liberal and revolutionary triumphs of Mexico illustrate one possible outcome in the relations between church and state during the nineteenth and twentieth centuries, Colombia's late-nineteenth-century movement called the Regeneration and the Colombian Constitution of 1886 illustrate a reaction to a firmly liberal regime under the Constitution of 1863 and a long-lasting conservative triumph. Reacting to earlier liberalism in Colombia, the Constitution of 1886 reinstated Roman Catholicism as a moral guiding force in politics and society. It permitted censorship of the press. Through a related concordat with the Roman Catholic Church in 1887, the Church was placed in control of education, civil registries, and cemeteries.[30] Colombia, however, was to experience extreme and violent oscillations between liberals and conservatives in the twentieth century.[31]

Some leaders throughout Latin America argued for freedom of religion and sought to place this freedom into constitutional form in the nineteenth century. These efforts were not to create religiously plural and openly tolerant societies. Instead, such positions were advanced to support the commercial and trading capacity of countries that sought to make their ports and major cities more welcoming places for foreign merchants and traders who might not be Catholic. For example, Argentine constitutionalist Juan Bautista Alberdi, who equated governing with populating, sought to attract, in his mind, "beneficial" immigrants who might bring trade and capital to the country, even if they were not Roman Catholic.[32] In the nineteenth century, more than fifteen Latin American countries had constitutional provisions permitting the freedom of public worship, but such constitutional protections might be quickly swept away by new regimes favoring Roman Catholicism and subduing the public display of other religions.[33]

Slavery and the status of enslaved humans presented fundamental legal and moral questions in nineteenth-century Latin America. While some voices arguing for the abolition of slavery and the dismantling of the international trade in enslaved humans were heard in the Spanish Cortes, the Constitution of Cadiz, and the Cortes did not abolish slavery. The independent countries of Latin America moved toward the extinction of such practices through laws of free birth, and in the mid-nineteenth century, countries of the region—such as New Granada, Ecuador, Argentina, Venezuela, and Peru—abolished slavery.[34] Religious analyses and theological positions informed discussions about slavery and race in the region.

The twentieth century and the rise of the social

The Mexican Revolution and the Mexican Constitution of 1917 placed the state over the Church and extended supervision of religious affairs under its provisions. For example,

> Article 130 gave federal authorities an exclusive jurisdiction in religious affairs, prohibiting Congress from establishing or prohibiting any religion, placed determinations of civil status within civil authorities, removed the legal personality of churches, gave local legislatures the power to determine the number of priests and ministers in each state, required members of religious orders to be Mexican by birth, prohibited religious officials from voting, removed official recognition from seminary studies, prohibited religious publications from commenting on political affairs, prohibited political meetings in religious buildings, and prohibited religious officials from inheriting unless the bequest came from a family member within the fourth degree, among other restrictions and prohibitions.[35]

Religious ceremonies were prohibited in public places, and religious corporations and ministers were prohibited from running primary schools.[36] These provisions created a new level of subordination of the Church to the state that sparked the Cristero Rebellion in Mexico and led to a protracted period, from the mid-1920s to the early 1930s, in which supporters of the Church battled anticlericalists. Many priests were expelled or murdered, and churches were plundered.

The Mexican Constitution of 1917 espoused new revolutionary principles and new perspectives on property and labor. Its provisions dealing with working conditions, fair wages, worker organization, land, the nationalization of natural resources, and petroleum rejected liberalism and ushered in new ideas of "the social" in the region. Because this constitution issued from a uniquely Mexican revolution, it did not serve as a regional model in these aspects as much as one might have thought. Nonetheless, it informed ideas of how governments and law should respond to poverty; the abuse of individuals and property in industrial and agricultural contexts was paramount in the twentieth century.

Although bolstered by European secular sociological thought from thinkers like Léon Duguit, much of Latin America's turn toward the social was the product of Christian thought. Neoscholastics examining Thomist writing on property, work, and human beings found established theological support to challenge the harshness of liberalism's absolute positions on property and contract. The Church provided another line of highly influential sources in this field when it directly faced the problems of capitalism and socialism through the encyclicals *Rerum Novarum* (1891) and *Qudragesimo Anno* (1931). Under contemporary European scholarship or Roman Catholic social doctrine, or both, constitutionalists and legal drafters appropriated these new approaches into their work. These new perspectives paved the way for improved working conditions and wages, collective bargaining through unions, and land reforms that redistributed agricultural and urban property to broad sections of society. Many of the regions' constitutions have adopted social approaches to labor, property, and contract founded on the secular sociological analyses imported from Europe, the religious positions advanced by neoscholastics and the encyclicals, or a combination of these.

Latin American political liberalism of the nineteenth century was recast into a narrower economic liberalism in the twentieth century. José Antonio Aguilar Rivera's analysis is instructive:

> If during the nineteenth century the constitutional aspect of liberalism was hegemonic, what happened in the twentieth century was that political liberalism was eclipsed by a different authoritarianism. Although individual liberties and democracy are from the beginning incompatible with dictatorships, the free market was not. Thus, in the countries of the Southern Cone, liberalism was reduced to one of its components, the economic.[37]

The broader program of liberalism was narrowed to economic liberalism, a form of neoliberalism that had direct effects on the peoples and economies of Latin America without carrying with it the full range of issues or positions associated with traditional liberalism. Indeed, in some contexts, this form of economic liberalism has been adopted by conservatives and conservative parties in the region.

Recent history

In the latter part of the twentieth century, Latin American countries experienced populist, authoritarian, and democratic regimes. The Church has almost always been called in to support, to mediate, or to resist governments, depending on the moment and the country. Military and authoritarian governments have trampled human rights, and some have been held accountable on the world stage for their horrific acts. As some countries moved to authoritarian, military, or dictatorial regimes, the Church's response has been mixed—sometimes engaging in worrisome complicity or willful blindness, and other times holding officials and governments to task.

Bishops' conferences in Medellín, Colombia (1968), and Puebla, Mexico (1979), and the rise of and responses to liberation theology led the Church, clergy, and laity to focus their efforts on people, individuals, and their poverty and suffering at the hands of repressive and unresponsive governments. While extensive work was done on the individual and local level, this commitment to a "preferential option for the poor" required moving forward on national and international fronts. From the national sphere, the Church expanded its repertoire of tools and actions to protect human dignity leading to a greater participation in international law and human rights—areas pursued by several of the jurists studied here.

Latin America today contains approximately forty percent of the world's Roman Catholics. Protestant Christianity has grown substantially in the region since the 1960s.[38] The Catholic Church and other Christian denominations continue to have direct and active influence in the politics and legal decisions of the day.

The jurists

All of the developments outlined above have necessarily shaped the accepted discourse of legal history in the region. The triumph of liberalism in the region during much of the nineteenth and twentieth centuries meant that some influential jurists are only now seeing the light of day as important national figures. Politics, rather than history, have kept some jurists hidden for decades. Jorge Adame notes that this was the case for Clemente de Jesús Munguía Núñez, bishop of Morelia and a fierce defender of the rights of the Catholic Church in Mexico during the 1850s.[39] Brian Hamnett similarly observes of Teodosio Lares that he has "been virtually forgotten in the historiography."[40] Hamnett's explanation for Lares's neglect may be expanded to cover many of the jurists studied in this volume:

> The obvious explanation for the neglect, as in the case of other Mexican figures, is the persistence in liberal and revolutionary historiography of throwing the focus, and moral approval, on their own principal leaders and, thereby, blotting their critics or opponents out of the picture.[41]

Viviana Kluger recounts that because Uruguayan codifier Tristán Narvaja was not a liberal, the School of Jurisprudence at the University in Montevideo debated at length whether to send his widow an official letter of condolence, and his contributions were underappreciated.[42] Agustín Parise notes that, for similar reasons, the life and work of Argentine jurist José Manuel Estrada have not been fully explored.[43] Thus, for many jurists, this volume serves as a contribution to correcting political biases that have guided the history and legal history of the region for decades, even centuries.

If political biases have led to the exclusion of jurists from the gaze of legal historians, a word on our selection process seems appropriate. First and foremost, we sought jurists whose lives and works would contribute to the underlying search for connections between faith and law in Latin America. We had a sense of some jurists who should absolutely be included, but our expertise was substantially limited by the geographical and temporal scope of the project. We turned to leading experts in the field throughout the region and sought their advice on who must be included in such a work. There was a great deal of discussion and culling; to some extent, the thirty-seven individuals studied here must be seen as *representative* jurists rather than as a definitive or comprehensive list of the most influential jurists in the region. Readers may of course ponder why one jurist was included and another excluded. Regrettably, for the nineteenth and twentieth centuries, we were unable to select any Latin American women whose legal influence and its relationship to personal faith would necessitate inclusion in this study. We remind our readers that no living jurist was considered for inclusion; we hope that a future volume on the twenty-first century will be more inclusive on many fronts. The construction of this volume reflects the lack of opportunity and the biases present in nineteenth- and twentieth-century Latin America.

Consistent with the practices of the other volumes in this series, we have defined the term "jurist" broadly to incorporate those who contributed to the development of law within the region, regardless of their strict identity as lawyer, judge, or professor. Some jurists appear for their philosophical, theological, moral, or intellectual contributions to legal development. Most were trained in law and viewed the world as lawyers. Others entered the legal world without traditional legal training. For example, Félix Varela, professor of constitutional law and author of one of the first books on the subject, had no formal legal training.[44] There are several other similar examples in these pages.

We also took care to ensure that different disciplines within law are represented in this volume. Some jurists pondered the political aspects of establishing new republics, international recognition, and constitutions and their content. Other jurists addressed essential questions of private law, such as the suitability of *derecho indiano* within national legal systems, codification, and regionally harmonized civil law. Still others advanced tailored legal changes in response to political and economic shifts or addressed the profound challenges of economic and racial inequality and human rights. Some jurists addressed canon law and the unique qualities it gathered in the Americas as shaped by the Spanish colonial patronage of the Church. These and other aspects informed our selection process as well.

After jurists were selected, we sought authors to write about each individual. Our experts come from Latin America, Europe, and the United States, and each author has a particular interest in, expertise on, or affinity for their subject. The expertise of these authors led the editors to ask them to write freely with their own approach to the jurists they study and present. While all authors were encouraged to provide essential biographical information and an overview of the scholarly production of each jurist, the authors selected their own paths and tone through the legal and spiritual lives of their subjects. These chapters should be read as rigorous essays on the life, work, and spirit of these jurists rather than as uniform encyclopedic entries. In our view, each chapter is enriched by the individual and often personal approach each author brings to the subject.

Many jurists included in this volume exhibited a wide range of interests and activities in public life. In the cosmopolitan legal centers of Latin America, it was not (and is not) unusual to find individuals who, in addition to practicing, teaching, and writing about law, also served in elected positions, advised government, drafted legislation and constitutions, established institutions, commented in newspapers and journals, and conducted international affairs. This is not exclusively a nineteenth-century phenomenon. The Brazilian Carlos Alberto Menezes Direito is the last jurist studied in this volume. As Robert Cottrol informs us, Menezes Direito was a member of the federal judiciary, a justice of the Supreme Federal Tribunal, a voice for the study and application of human rights, a professor of constitutional law and church doctrine, and a productive writer.[45] Menezes Direito serves only as an example of the multifaceted contributions that the jurists studied here made to law, government, and society.

Some jurists left important or surprising contributions in other fields. For example, Óscar Cruz Barney properly mentions the Mexican writer and diplomat José Bernardo Couto y Pérez's *Dialogue on the History of Painting in Mexico* (1872) and its insights on colonial Mexican religious art.[46] As Ezequiel Abásolo notes, the first two books written by Argentine constitutionalist Juan Bautista Alberdi were on music and a method for the art of playing the piano.[47] The flourishing of such multiple competencies was not exclusively the product of Latin America's nineteenth-century expansive notions of culture and education. In the twentieth century, too, as Santiago Legarre reveals, the Argentine constitutionalist Germán José Bidart Campos was an accomplished poet and, in 1977, published a book of poems including "sonnets in honor of the Virgin Mary."[48]

Thus, a broader reading of "jurist" seems particularly suited to Latin America, where service as a lawyer or judge was only one facet of a complex set of public activities in which skilled and trained individuals undertook what they were called to do at specific moments and throughout their lives. Proper training, formation, and personal faith often guided these jurists to undertake monumental tasks of national, regional, and world importance. For many of these jurists, gratitude for their individual good fortune and education, patriotic loyalties, and faith in God led to a sense of inescapable duty to establish, to reform, and to improve legal structures, ideas, and texts of lasting importance. Such perspectives and callings led them to defend the poor, to establish and to support human rights, and to battle for—and in one instance to die for—those oppressed through the injustices of the state.

Many of these jurists had important experiences outside Latin America and the Spanish-speaking world. Latin American jurists were not isolated from the rest of the legal world or even from the common law. In the independence period, many jurists were forced abroad by political winds. For example, Alejandro Guzmán reminds us of Andrés Bello's formative and trying residence in London for nearly two decades.[49] Those years clearly shaped the work and thought of one of Latin America's greatest codifiers. Rogelio Pérez Perdomo, in his study of Venezuelan independence thinker Juan Germán Roscio, reminds us that Roscio traveled in 1817 to Philadelphia, where he published his best-known work, *The Triumph of Freedom over Despotism*.[50] Javier Francisco Infante Martin notes the profound impact of Mariano Egaña's five years (from 1824 to 1829) in England, France, Russia, Spain, and the Netherlands on his views of government and the importance of a strong executive power in Chile.[51] Bartolomé Herrera, according to Altuve-Febres Lores, was transformed by his years in Italy, particularly in Rome.[52] Ezequiel Abásolo calculates that constitutionalist Juan Bautista Alberdi "spent more time abroad than in his native Argentina."[53] As a resident in Chile, Uruguayan codifier Tristán Narvaja spent time with his relative Gabriel Ocampo and, as Viviana Kluger observes, became familiar with Andrés Bello's efforts on the civil code.[54] Peter Henderson informs us that Ecuadorian president Gabriel García Moreno was moved toward a greater Catholic faith, the centerpiece of his political agenda, during his three years in Paris.[55] As Juan Bosco Amores reports, the international travels of Cuban educator and politician Antonio Sánchez de Bustamante through Europe, where he visited and met with international lawyers, contributed greatly to the thought of this Latin American pioneer of international law, author of the Bustamante Code, and judge of the Permanent Court of International Justice.[56] José de la Puente Brunke mentions José de la Riva-Agüero's year and a half in Europe, then another stay in Europe of eleven years, and even a two-year circumnavigation of the globe with stops in California, Asia,

Europe, and various countries of Latin America.[57] Cristián Villalonga notes the impact of Chilean academic and lawyer Pedro Lira Urquieta's trip during his mid-thirties to Belgium, Germany, and Italy.[58] Juan Carlos Riofrío Martínez-Villalba credits Bishop Juan Larrea's many international trips as a youth for the jurist's cosmopolitan and informed worldview, and his many years in Rome were both educationally and spiritually transformative.[59] These Latin American jurists often gathered important experiences abroad, and their international travels changed their views of the world, of their faith, and of the law. They developed their legal ideas in dialogue with other jurists, thinkers, theologians, and politicians.

Some jurists moved from their countries late in life. For example, the doyen of Colombian civil law, Fernando Vélez Barrientos, presented here by Victor Uribe-Uran, channeled his earnings from a successful career to move his family first to Manchester, England, then to Paris; he died in Rome.[60] Martín Santiváñez Vivanco reveals that with extensive duties at the United Nations, Peruvian diplomat Víctor Andrés Belaúnde spent his last decades in New York, where he died.[61] Even those who did not travel engaged with and confronted a panoply of European and American sources in their work. Latin American legal thought was not monolithic. Individual approaches were often unique and guided by the happenstance of particular teachers, sources, places, and moments in each jurist's experiences and studies. We must not forget the importance of chance in legal development.[62]

Faith and law

These studies reveal different levels of explicit engagement with faith. As Rogelio Pérez-Perdomo beautifully illustrates, the life and independence activity of Venezuelan politician and editor Juan Germán Roscio were guided by his religious beliefs and profound Catholic faith. Roscio's forceful writings for independence not only were grounded in religious and theological arguments but also borrowed the religious genres of confession and catechism.[63] Personal faith guided Chilean constitutionalist Mariano Egaña as he maintained the position of the Catholic Church as the official religion of the republic in his Constitution of 1833, a text that was to guide Chile politically for nearly a hundred years.[64] Javier Francisco Infante Martin ties Egaña's religious education and frequent attendance at Mass to his understanding of the republic's patronage of the Catholic Church and of the fundamentally religious aspects of civic virtue necessary in a republic.[65] Óscar Cruz Barney concludes that the diplomat and constitutionalist José Bernardo Couto y Pérez's "moral formation within the Catholic tradition and culture contributed to his vision of independent Mexico."[66] Thus, many jurists studied here openly and publicly displayed their faith in relation to their political convictions about newly independent republics and their legal underpinnings.

Similarly, in Mexico, where tensions between liberal and conservative visions of the state were perhaps their most fierce, Juan Nepomuceno Rodríguez de San Miguel's political and legal projects are found by Juan Pablo Salazar Andreu to have been remarkably consistent and cohesive. Rodríguez de San Miguel declined public roles of national import because the liberal government was at odds with his hopes for the religious and political trajectory of Mexico. Indeed, Rodríguez de San Miguel's defense of the Church and its assets, the place of the Church in Mexican government, and even his lasting and impressive scholarly contributions to Mexican law are related to his conservative Catholic formation and view of the Mexican republic.[67] Kif Augustine-Adams tells us that Mexican writer, professor, and politician Manuel Herrera y Lasso's "defense of Catholicism at the beginning of the Cristero Rebellion (1926–29) cost him dearly."[68] Exiled to Cuba for two years, he later helped to found Mexico's PAN party, whose platform sought to follow Catholic social doctrine on labor and wealth.[69] The studies of Mexican jurists presented here will shed light on the political and religious conflicts that have shaped the country's legal development over the past two centuries.

Other jurists led the Church to the center of political and public life. Ecuadorian president Gabriel García Moreno sought to establish a Catholic nation in the 1860s. Peter Henderson demonstrates García Moreno's decisive steps in this direction through his recruitment of Jesuits for public instruction, his careful negotiations of a concordat with the Holy See in 1861, and his drafting of the region's most deferential constitution to the Church, the Ecuadorian Constitution of 1869.[70] Eduardo Herrera and I explore the thought of Colombian scholar, journalist, poet, and philosopher Miguel Antonio Caro Tobar and the way his religious thought was tied to the Regeneration Movement and the conservative Colombian Constitution of 1886.[71] Caro sought to apply "Christianity to society."[72] By guiding the Regeneration and establishing key constitutional aspects of Colombia, Caro was an essential figure in consolidating the republic.[73]

Agustín Parise explores how, in Argentina, José Manuel Estrada co-founded the country's Catholic political party and served as its first president. Estrada constructed political, religious, and intellectual links between Catholicism, republicanism, and freedom in his opposition to the country's prevalent liberalism.[74] Nonetheless, as Cristóbal García-Huidobro succinctly strikes a truth for many of these jurists and their worldview, under the new republics "being a good citizen meant being a good Catholic."[75] What this meant exactly was subject to scrutiny by our jurists. For example, Márcio Ricardo Staffen chronicles Brazilian poet and philosopher Tobias Barreto's later critique of Brazilian Catholicism for its departure from Roman Catholicism.[76]

Latin American jurists worked in the trenches of the uneasy relationship between the Roman Catholic Church and the republics as heirs of the colonial patronage of the Church. Peter Henderson's study of Gabriel García Moreno accurately portrays the importance of this topic: "The debate about the Catholic Church's proper role in the newly independent Latin American republics in the early to mid-nineteenth century proved to be the most contentious issue dividing Liberals from Conservatives."[77] Brian Hamnett explores the tireless work of Teodosio Lares, author of a Mexican commercial code, to advance the interests of the Church in Mexico during the tumultuous political and governmental shifts in Mexico during the 1850s and 1860s. His complex negotiations to defend the powers of the Church led him to official positions within the Second Empire of

Maximillian, who took an unexpected turn against reestablishing the position and property of the Church. After 1867, with a liberal regime in place, Lares was unable to recover politically from his close association with the empire.[78] Similarly, Abelardo Levaggi discusses numerous actions by Argentine lawyer and politician Dalmacio Vélez Sarsfield in his long career as adviser and official to define the scope of the Church's authority in the appointment of bishops, ecclesiastical courts, convents, tithes, and expropriation of church property. Often remembered for his work on the Civil Code of 1869, Vélez left an important work on religious matters, his *Relations of the State with the Church in Early Spanish America* (1854).[79]

Jurisdictional tensions between Church and state arose in the context of private law. Juan Carlos Frontera notes Eduardo Acevedo's approach to marriage in his draft civil code for Uruguay during the late 1840s and early 1850s, when any settling of the issue in civil law left some in society with strong objections.[80] Viviana Kluger places Tristán Narvaja's Uruguayan Civil Code of 1868 into the context of the drafter's religious formation and faith to explain this code's substantial deferral to the Catholic Church and its institutions in matters of marriage and divorce.[81] As Hernán Alejandro Olano García and I report, Panamanian statesman and writer Justo Arosemena addressed marriage within a draft bill for religious freedom and, while in London, wrote a study of the law of marriage in the United Kingdom.[82] Gustavo Adolfo Vaamonde noted that Venezuelan jurist Julián Viso's proposals for reform in the 1850s included controversial provisions for religious freedom with the aim of repopulating the country's war-ravished countryside with Europeans and North Americans.[83] Other jurists studied here dealt with questions of marriage, its religious and civil aspects, the proper location of registries of civil status, and divorce.

Such ideological, religious, and political struggles continued in the twentieth century. Martín Santiváñez Vivanco describes Peruvian constitutionalist and internationalist Víctor Andrés Belaúnde this way: "First and foremost, he was a Christian realist, a down-to-earth man of faith."[84] This approach served Belaúnde throughout his later life, both in his advocacy for the Church during Peru's "firmly anti-Catholic Assembly" leading to the Constitution of 1933 and in his extensive work for the United Nations, including his service as president of the General Assembly.[85] José de la Puente Brunke notes that in a similar spirit, José de la Riva-Agüero brought his Catholic perspectives to challenge the newly adopted provisions of the Peruvian Civil Code. Riva-Agüero, in the words of de la Puente, expressed his concerns that "the Civil Code of 1936 weakened family, property, and religion in dealing with the 'foundations of the nation' that had to be consolidated."[86] Belaúnde and Riva-Agüero demonstrate the way that Catholic jurists raised forceful objections to developments they viewed as harmful to the Church and the country within the traditional spheres of both public law (as expressed in constitutional text) and private law (as found in the civil code).

Alvaro Mejía-Salazar describes the Ecuadorian diplomat and writer Julio Tobar Donoso as an "archetype of devout Catholics." Tobar Donoso applied his deep faith and learning to extensive writings on history, the Church, and law, with particular emphasis on Catholic social doctrine when he turned to issues of labor and property.[87] Consistently linking Catholicism with the Ecuadorian nation, he negotiated the accord between Ecuador and the Holy See in 1937 that governs relations today, helped to found the Catholic University of Ecuador, and led its law faculty for decades. He also served as a justice of the Supreme Court of Justice of Ecuador for twelve years.[88] Mejía-Salazar at one point concludes of Tobar Donoso that "it was impossible for him to separate his faith from his profession."[89]

Similarly, in Argentina, Tomás Casares's faith, as surveyed by Juan Cianciardo and Marcelo Fernández Peralta, underpinned his efforts for popular Catholic education through the creation of courses on Catholic culture that intellectually led to the foundation of the Catholic University of Argentina. Credited with renewing Catholic thought in Argentina during the twentieth century, Casares brought his religious perspectives to his legal philosophy and to his eleven years as a justice of the Argentine Supreme Court. As a justice, Casares was frequently in the minority, issuing eighty-five dissents and twenty-two solo opinions.[90] According to Cianciardo and Fernández, the "concept of dignity, as a consequence of humanity being created in the image God, was central to Casares's decisions."[91] Twentieth-century jurists were no less strident than their nineteenth-century counterparts in speaking their faith in societies and governments that did not welcome such perspectives.

Many twentieth-century jurists studied here were guided in their juridical, economic, and political thought by the Catholic Church's social doctrine found in papal encyclicals, including *Rerum Novarum* (1891) and *Quadragesimo Anno* (1931), papal responses to industrialization and socialism. For example, Cristián Villalonga writes of the Chilean jurist Pedro Lira Urquieta that his "relentless reflection on law and social affairs constitutes, to a great extent, a particular form of engagement with Catholicism after *Quadragesimo Anno* (1931)."[92] Lira's writings made frequent use of the Church's social teachings, and he served on the law faculty and as dean at the Catholic University of Chile for much of the middle of the twentieth century.[93] Lira, as Villalonga tells us, lived a life of "constant piety" and sought, in Lira's own words, "to translate his moral ideals into the law."[94]

Argentine constitutionalist and political theorist Arturo Sampay incorporated, as Susana Ramella reports, a learned neoscholasticism and a full understanding of Catholic social doctrine to his work as jurist and drafter of key provisions of the Peronist Argentine Constitution of 1949.[95] Similarly, Venezuelan president Rafael Caldera was drawn to the field of labor law by his interest in the application of the Church's social doctrine to the problems of workers in his country.[96] Carlos García Soto observes that, as a politician, professor, and constitutional drafter, Caldera "made an effort to unravel the core of the social doctrine of the Catholic Church," which he studied "since his days at the university and for his entire life."[97]

In a uniquely personal analysis of the life and work of the doyen of Argentine constitutional law of the twentieth century, Germán José Bidart Campos, Santiago Legarre notes that he remained "deeply faithful to his Christ-informed conscience," even through controversy and public criticism.[98] Influenced by the social teaching of the Church, Bidart was a pioneer in human rights.[99] Similarly, Robert Cottrol notes that at the end of the twentieth century, Brazilian jurist Menezes Direito's "reason to fight social, political, economic, racial, and cultural discrimination" was informed by his understanding of the Church's social doctrine expressed in the 1970s and 1980s. Menezes Direito's social commitment was, in his own view, a natural product of his Catholic faith.[100]

For other jurists found here, authors had to search extensively to find inklings of faith and Christianity surfacing in their public works or writings. These jurists were necessary for this book because of their high stature in the region. A book of Latin American jurists must include Andrés Bello, Juan Bautista Alberdi, and Augusto Teixeira de Freitas, for example. Even for Alberdi, whose anticlericalism and openness to freedom of conscience were evident, Ezequiel Abásolo uncovered not only Alberdi's recognition that Argentina was deeply Catholic but also Alberdi's embrace of Christian convictions.[101] Alfredo de J. Flores reminds us that Brazilian jurist Teixeira de Freitas wrote a study of the Eucharist; Flores places the religious practices of the jurist in his later life into the context of his professional disappointments and personal losses.[102]

Latin American jurists include priests, bishops, and saints. We must remember that the Catholic Church defended the Spanish monarchy in the Americas and broadly defended the Crown against independence movements in the region.[103] Nonetheless, Catholics called for independence in various forms and through various means. Certain of God's calling, Félix Varela, an intellectual leader of Cuban independence, was ordained a priest at the earliest possible moment.[104] After their various nations achieved independence, many jurists sought reconciliation with the Holy See through political and intellectual action.

Chilean bishop Justo Donoso was the region's preeminent canonist and, as García-Huidobro informs us, wrote a pathbreaking work on the unique attributes of canon law in the Americas while noting its unexpected formation under both customary practices and royal or republican authority. This work, *Institutions of American Canon Law* (1848), was written during a period of unsuccessful diplomacy between Chile and the Holy See in the first half of the nineteenth century.[105] Raúl Madrid examines Chilean jurist and bishop Rafael Fernández Concha as that country's preeminent legal philosopher and theologian of the nineteenth century in the intellectual battle against liberalism.[106] Peruvian bishop Bartolomé Herrera, as discussed by Fernán Altuve-Febres Lores, influenced his country's political thought and constitutional texts.[107]

Bishop Clemente de Jesús Munguía Núñez wrote the most important study of natural law in nineteenth-century Mexico, and Jorge Adame Goddard establishes Munguía as *the* intellectual leader in defending the rights of the Church during the reform period. Munguía created a fascinating constitutional crisis (later resolved) when, on his elevation to bishop, he publicly answered, "I do not swear," to a required oath that included his acceptance of the Mexican state's assertion of its patronage of the Church.[108] Ecuadorian bishop Juan Larrea was a prolific commentator on the civil code and author of nearly countless scholarly works on law and on the humanities. Juan Carlos Riofrío Martínez-Villalba describes Larrea's scholarly efforts to change the country's civil law, improve its constitutional provisions, and advanced human rights.[109]

The greatest sacrifice of faith levied against civil authority told in these pages is found in the work of St. Óscar Romero, "a Christian martyr for the gospel of social justice," in the words of Rafael Domingo.[110] Romero's advocacy for the voiceless poor was the fruit of his profound and consistent faith as he "defended human rights and social justice in a country wounded by political, military, and paramilitary crime."[111]

Numerous leading jurists of the region included individuals with priestly vocation, ecclesiastical office, and even official recognition of sanctity. Unlike many contemporary societies, the societies on which these jurists left their impact did not view such distinctions as impediments to acting in the public secular sphere, teaching law, writing legal treatises, and suggesting legal reform.

These jurists read, considered, and digested European or global trends in intellectual or political perceptions and appropriated and adapted them to their Latin American contexts. This means that Catholic beliefs and methods worked their way into notions of the Enlightenment, liberalism, and social thought. In Latin America, as in Spain, religion and Catholicism shaped and moderated the Enlightenment and liberalism, although both movements were officially prohibited by the Church. For example, Rogelio Pérez-Perdomo, commenting on Juan Germán Roscio, states, "The Spanish Enlightenment was Catholic, and there is every reason to think that Roscio shared these ideas, given his use of orthodox Catholic thinkers."[112] Thus, these jurists addressed the abolition of slavery, racial discrimination, and the protection of human rights from Christian perspectives. For example, Gustavo Adolfo Vaamonde recounts that Venezuelan jurist Julián Viso "did not resolve the great question of the day in Venezuela, the issue of slavery. While Viso acknowledged the rights of man, he referred to slavery as an established institution in Venezuela."[113] Victor M. Uribe-Uran explores Colombian jurist Fernando Vélez Barrientos's rejection of slavery as a "barbaric institution" and his position that no compensation should be afforded former slaveholders, because their actions violated human rights.[114] Ernesto Pimentel and Paul Sekscenski explore Brazilian lawyer Heráclito Sobral Pinto's deep religious faith as an ultraconservative Catholic. These beliefs guided him to his human rights work for many clients who were victims of state oppression and, fascinatingly, whose political or social views were in complete opposition to his own.[115]

Conclusion and *gracias*

The jurists studied here represent a remarkable range of legal interests and talents. Guided by their faith, they faced opposition and personal challenges as they sought to shape the laws and institutions of their countries, their regions, and the world. Personal faith and religious belief were constitutive aspects of these jurists' individual experiences; they often worked in conversation with the fundamental texts of theology and canon law in addition to the many standard works of civil and constitutional law. This volume thus makes a sound contribution to understanding not only the impact of Christianity, particularly Roman Catholicism, in effecting legal change in Latin America but also the influence of individual jurists within the legal history of the region. They worked in conversation with each other and with jurists from around the world. Additionally, they worked in conversation with their ideological and political opponents, and with the societies and governments in which they lived. We hope that this volume will continue scholarly discussion of the ways that religious belief and personal faith shape legal change, especially in the context of Latin American law.

As editors, Rafael Domingo and I thank Professor Norman Doe, Director of the Centre for Law and Religion at Cardiff Law School and editor of the Law and Religion Series at Routledge, for his confidence in this project and his support to bring the work of our contributors to fruition.

We thank John Witte Jr. for his continued encouragement and support of this work. This book would not have come about without his personal and institutional guidance and perseverance. Gary S. Hauk has provided patient, detailed, and elegant editorial suggestions and solutions as we grappled with various challenges in the preparation of the manuscript. We thank him and the Center for the Study of Law and Religion at Emory University for lending us his gifts in editing and English. Routledge has been an exceptional partner in publishing this book. We thank Alison Kirk and Emily Summers at the press.

I add my thanks to my wife, Angela Mirow. Beyond her personal support of my efforts in this project, she contributed materially to the translation of several chapters, discussed questions of terminology, and helped with many questions of Spanish along the way.

We would be remiss not to extend our special thanks and admiration to the authors of each chapter for their efforts and patience. The preparation of this volume coincided with the global pandemic of COVID-19. We lost only a few contributions to unexpected challenges, delay, or illness. All involved with this project experienced, at the very least, the delays and inconveniences of finding and checking sources, setting pen to paper, and revising drafts in a world of necessary quarantines and restrictions. While we are keenly aware of the physical hurdles presented, we must also acknowledge the psychological and emotional tolls that impede creative work, deep thought, and glittering prose. Rafael Domingo and I thank all who surmounted these obstacles to produce the book you now hold.

Notes

1 Serge Dauchy et al., *The Formation and Transmission of Western Legal Culture: 150 Books That Made the Law in the Age of Printing* (Cham: Springer, 2016); Rafael Domingo, ed., *Juristas Universales*, 4 vols. (Madrid: Marcel Pons, 2004).

2 M.C. Mirow, "Individual Experience in Legal Change: Exploring a Neglected Factor in Latin American Codification," *Southwestern Journal of Law and Trade in the Americas* 11 (2005): 301–21.
3 Orazio Condorelli and Rafael Domingo, *Law and the Christian Tradition in Italy: The Legacy of Great Jurists* (Abingdon: Routledge, 2020); Mark Hill and Richard H. Helmholz, eds., *Great Christian Jurists in English History* (Cambridge: Cambridge University Press, 2017); Olivier Descamps and Rafael Domingo, eds., *Great Christian Jurists in French History* (Cambridge: Cambridge University Press, 2019); Rafael Domingo and Javier Martínez-Torrón, eds., *Great Christian Jurists in Spanish History* (Cambridge: Cambridge University Press, 2018); Daniel L. Dreisbach and Mark David Hall, eds., *Great Christian Jurists in American History* (Cambridge: Cambridge University Press, 2019); Mathias Schmoeckel and John Witte Jr., eds., *Great Christian Jurists in German History* (Tübingen: Mohr Siebeck, 2020).
4 Rafael Domingo and John Witte Jr., eds., *Christianity and Global Law* (London: Routledge, 2020); Philip L. Reynolds, ed., *Great Christian Legal Thinkers in the First Millennium* (Cambridge: Cambridge University Press, 2019).
5 Domingo and Martínez-Torrón, "Introduction," in Domingo and Martínez-Torrón.
6 Ricardo Levene, *Manual de historia del derecho argentino*, 5th ed. (Buenos Aires: Depalma, 1985), 58–59; John F. Schwaller, *The Church and Clergy in Sixteenth Century Mexico* (Albuquerque: University of New Mexico Press, 1987); John F. Schwaller, "The Ordenanzas del Patronazgo in New Spain, 1574–1600," in *The Church in Colonial Latin America*, ed. John F. Schwaller, ed. (Wilmington: SR Books, 2000), 49–69.
7 Mirow, *Latin American Law*, 13; M.C. Mirow, "Juan Solórzano Pereira," in Domingo and Martinez-Torrón.
8 Abelardo Levaggi, *Manual de historia del derecho argentino* (Buenos Aires: Depalma, 1987) 2:34–35; Levene, 60, 121; José Luis Soberanes Fernández, *Los tribunales de la Nueva España* (Mexico City: Universidad Nacional Autónoma de México, 1980) 148–49, 159–60.
9 Jorge Adame Goddard, "Asimilación y rechazo en México del sistema de relaciones entre la iglesia y el estado contemplado en la Constitución de Cádiz," *Anuario Mexicano de Historia del Derecho* 22 (2910): 61–65.
10 M.C. Mirow, *Latin American Law*, 48.
11 M.C. Mirow, *Florida's First Constitution, The Constitution of Cádiz*, 15.
12 Mirow, *Latin American Constitutions*, 31.
13 Ibid., 62.
14 Joaquín Varela Suanzes-Carpegna, "El Constitucionalismo español y portugués durante la primera mitad del Siglo xii (un estudio comparado)," in *Visiones y revisions de la independencia Americana: La independencia de América, la Constitución de Cádiz y las constituciones iberoamericanas*, ed. Izaskun Álvarez Cuartero and Julio Sánchez Gómez (Salamanca: Ediciones Universidad de Salamanca, 2003), 21.
15 M.C. Mirow, *Latin American Constitutions*, 104, 120.
16 Constitution of Spain (1812), Art. 171(6); Mirow, *Florida's First Constitution*, 37.
17 Constitution of Spain (1812), Art. 261(7) and (8); Mirow, *Florida's First Constitution*, 47.
18 Mirow, *Latin American Constitutions*, 120.
19 Ibid., 25.
20 Ibid., 24.
21 Ibid., 134–35.

22 Ibid., 142–43.
23 Rafael Estrada Michel, *Monarquía y nación entre Cádiz y Nueva España: el problema de la articulación política de las Españas ante la revolución liberal y la emancipación Americana* (Mexico City: Editorial Porrúa, 2006), xxxv.
24 Mirow, *Latin American Constitutions*, 146.
25 Ibid., 187.
26 Ibid., 198.
27 Ibid., 183.
28 Ibid., 198.
29 Peter Lester Reich, *Mexico's Hidden Revolution: The Catholic Church in Law and Politics since 1929*. Notre Dame, IN: University of Notre Dame Press, 1995.
30 Mirow, *Latin American Constitutions*, 153–54.
31 Ibid., 216–20.
32 Ibid., 199.
33 Brian Loveman, *The Constitution of Tyranny: Regimes of Exception in Spanish America* (Pittsburgh: University of Pittsburgh Press, 1993), 372–73.
34 Mirow, *Latin American Constitutions*, 100.
35 Ibid., 209.
36 Ibid., 209–10.
37 José Antonio Aguilar Rivera, *La geometría y el mito: Un ensayo sobre la libertad y el liberalismo en México, 1821–1970* (Mexico City: Fondo de Cultura Económica, 2010), 141.
38 Pew Research Center, "Religion in Latin America: Widespread Change in a Historically Catholic Region," November 13, 2014, https://www.pewforum.org/2014/11/13/religion-in-latin-america/.
39 Chapter 12.
40 Chapter 8.
41 Ibid.
42 Chapter 16.
43 Chapter 21.
44 Chapter 3.
45 Chapter 37.
46 Chapter 7.
47 Chapter 11.
48 Chapter 35.
49 Chapter 2.
50 Chapter 1.
51 Chapter 4.
52 Chapter 9.
53 Chapter 11.
54 Chapter 16.
55 Chapter 17.
56 Chapter 24.
57 Chapter 26.
58 Chapter 31.
59 Chapter 36.
60 Chapter 23.
61 Chapter 25.
62 I owe this observation to Alan Watson.
63 Chapter 1.
64 Chapter 4.

65 Ibid.
66 Chapter 7.
67 Chapter 10.
68 Chapter 27.
69 Ibid.
70 Chapter 17.
71 Chapter 22.
72 Ibid.
73 Ibid.
74 Chapter 21.
75 Chapter 5.
76 Chapter 20.
77 Chapter 17.
78 Chapter 8.
79 Chapter 6.
80 Chapter 13.
81 Chapter 16.
82 Chapter 15.
83 Chapter 18.
84 Chapter 25.
85 Ibid.
86 Chapter 26.
87 Chapter 29.
88 Ibid.
89 Ibid.
90 Chapter 30.
91 Ibid.
92 Chapter 31.
93 Ibid.
94 Ibid.
95 Chapter 32.
96 Chapter 33.
97 Ibid.
98 Chapter 35.
99 Ibid.
100 Chapter 37.
101 Chapter 11.
102 Chapter 14.
103 Chapter 5.
104 Chapter 3.
105 Chapter 5.
106 Chapter 19.
107 Chapter 9.
108 Chapter 12.
109 Chapter 36.
110 Chapter 34.
111 Ibid.
112 Chapter 1.
113 Chapter 18.
114 Chapter 23.
115 Chapter 28.

References

Adame Goddard, Jorge. "Asimilación y rechazo en México del sistema de relaciones entre la iglesia y el estado contemplado en la Constitución de Cádiz." *Anuario Mexicano de Historia del Derecho* 22 (2010): 57–74.

Aguilar Rivera, José Antonio. *La geometría y el mito: Un ensayo sobre la libertad y el liberalismo en México, 1821–1970.* Mexico City: Fondo de Cultura Económica, 2010.

Carmagnani, Marcello, ed. *Constitucionalismo y Orden Liberal: América Latina, 1850–1920.* Turin: Otto Editore, 2000.

Condorelli, Orazio, and Rafael Domingo. *Law and the Christian Tradition in Italy: The Legacy of Great Jurists.* Abingdon: Routledge, 2020.

Cottrol, Robert J. *The Long Lingering Shadow: Slavery, Race and Law in the American Hemisphere.* Athens: University of Georgia Press, 2013.

Dauchy, Serge, Georges Martyn, Anthony Musson, Heikki Pihlajamaki, and Alain Wijffels, eds. *The Formation and Transmission of Western Legal Culture: 150 Books That Made the Law in the Age of Printing.* Cham: Springer, 2016.

Descamps, Olivier, and Rafael Domingo, eds. *Great Christian Jurists in French History.* Cambridge: Cambridge University Press, 2019.

Domingo, Rafael, ed. *Juristas Universales*, Vol. 4. Madrid: Marcel Pons, 2004.

Domingo, Rafael, and Javier Martínez-Torrón, eds. *Great Christian Jurists in Spanish History* Cambridge: Cambridge University Press, 2018.

Domingo, Rafael, and John Witte Jr., eds. *Christianity and Global Law.* London: Routledge, 2020.

Dreisbach, Daniel L., and Mark David Hall, eds. *Great Christian Jurists in American History.* Cambridge: Cambridge University Press, 2019.

Estrada Michel, Rafael. *Monarquía y nación entre Cádiz y Nueva España: el problema de la articulación política de las Españas ante la revolución liberal y la emancipación Americana.* Mexico City: Editorial Porrúa, 2006.

Hill, Mark, and Richard H. Helmholz, eds. *Great Christian Jurists in English History.* Cambridge: Cambridge University Press, 2017.

Joaquín Varela Suanzes-Carpegna. "El Constitucionalismo español y portugués durante la primera mitad del Siglo xii (un estudio comparado)." In *Visiones y revisions de la independencia Americana: La independencia de América, la Constitución de Cádiz y las constituciones iberoamericanas*, edited by Izaskun Álvarez Cuartero and Julio Sánchez Gómez, 13–51. Salamanca: Ediciones Universidad de Salamanca, 2003.

Levaggi, Abelardo. *Manual de historia del derecho argentino*, Vol. 3. Buenos Aires: Depalma, 1986, 1987, 1988.

Levene, Ricardo. *Manual de historia del derecho argentino.* 5th ed. Buenos Aires: Depalma, 1985.

Loveman, Brian. *The Constitution of Tyranny: Regimes of Exception in Spanish America.* Pittsburgh: University of Pittsburgh Press, 1993.

Mirow, M.C. *Florida's First Constitution, The Constitution of Cádiz: Introduction, Translation and Text.* Durham: Carolina Academic Press, 2012.

Mirow, M.C. "Individual experience in legal change: Exploring a neglected factor in latin american codification." *Southwestern Journal of Law and Trade in the Americas* 11 (2005): 301–21.

Mirow, M.C. "Juan Solórzano Pereira." In *Great Christian Jurists in Spanish History*, edited by Rafael Domingo and Javier Martínez-Torrón, 239–57. Cambridge: Cambridge University Press, 2018.

Mirow, M.C. *Latin American Constitutions: The Constitution of Cádiz and Its Legacy in Spanish America*. Cambridge: Cambridge University Press, 2015.

Mirow, M.C. *Latin American Law: A History of Private Law and Institutions in Spanish America*. Austin: University of Texas Press, 2004.

Pérez-Perdomo, Rogelio. *Latin American Lawyers: A Historical Introduction*. Stanford, CA: Stanford University Press, 2006.

Pew Research Center, "Religion in Latin America: Widespread change in a historically catholic region," November 13, 2014, https://www.pewforum.org/2014/11/13/religion-in-latin-america/.

Reich, Peter Lester. *Mexico's Hidden Revolution: The Catholic Church in Law and Politics since 1929*. Notre Dame: University of Notre Dame Press, 1995.

Reynolds, Philip L., ed. *Great Christian Legal Thinkers in the First Millennium*. Cambridge: Cambridge University Press, 2019.

Schmoeckel, Mathias, and John Witte Jr., eds. *Great Christian Jurists in German History*. Tübingen: Mohr Siebeck, 2020.

Schwaller, John F. *The Church and Clergy in Sixteenth Century Mexico*. Albuquerque: University of New Mexico Press, 1987.

Schwaller, John F. "The Ordenanzas del Patronazgo in New Spain, 1574–1600." In *The Church in Colonial Latin America*, edited by John F. Schwaller, 49–69. Wilmington: SR Books, 2000.

Soberanes Fernández, José Luis. *Los tribunales de la Nueva España*. Mexico City: Universidad Nacional Autónoma de México, 1980.

Part I

Nineteenth-century jurists

1 Juan Germán Roscio (Venezuela, 1763–1821)

Rogelio Pérez-Perdomo

Biographical introduction

Juan Germán Roscio (born at San Francisco de Tiznado, Venezuela, on May 27, 1763, and died at Cúcuta, Colombia, on October 3, 1821) was a major civil actor in Venezuelan independence and one of the top jurists and political thinkers of his time. He came from a modest family. His father, Cristóbal Roscio, was a military officer from Milan who entered the service of the Spanish monarchy. Settling in Venezuela, he acquired a cattle ranch near San Francisco de Tiznado, today Estado Guárico, and married Paula María Nieves, the daughter of an indigenous (Indian) woman and a Spaniard. In the language of Spanish American social stratification, Roscio's father was a *blanco de orilla* and his mother a *mestiza*, or mixed-raced person. Her mother's sister married a *pardo*, and Roscio had cousins who were *pardos.*[1] Roscio's own mixed background was evident in his physical appearance, but as his parents were married, he was legally classified as white. Nevertheless, he was considered socially far inferior to white creoles, Spanish America's highest social class. According to the strict rules of racial stratification of the time, the family's relation with *pardos* did not taint his blood but socially confirmed him as a person of lower class.

At age eleven, Roscio was sent to Caracas under the protection of the social philanthropist Doña María de Luz Pacheco, the daughter of the Count of San Javier, one of the most important families in the Caracas aristocracy. Roscio quickly distinguished himself by his intelligence and disciplined work habits. This powerful family's protection undoubtedly helped Roscio gain entrance to the Universidad de Caracas, an institution that required students to be "old Christians of pure blood," and that was attended by *mantuanos*, the creole white elite of the country.[2] There, Roscio became a *bachiller en cánones* (BA in canon law) in 1790, and a *doctor en cánones* in 1794. He also became a *doctor en derecho civil* (doctor in civil law) in 1800. He won distinguished intellectual awards both at the Universidad de Caracas and in the Academy of Public and Spanish Law, an institution that functioned in Caracas for several years at the turn of the century.

In 1798 Roscio became professor of Roman law at the Universidad de Caracas, a surprising appointment because his doctorate was in canon law. But Roscio had already established his status as a scholar. He was recognized as an *abogado* (lawyer) by the Audiencia de Caracas (the highest court in colonial Venezuela), a title that required specialized training. He had also applied to become a member of the Colegio de Abogados. A public corporation of great social and political importance in colonial Venezuela, the Colegio had some similarities with a bar association. Membership in the Colegio was necessary for professional practice, but it was also important as a sign of social prestige. The title of lawyer and membership in the Colegio conferred honor on the person. The Colegio required the applicant to pass the test of "pure blood," and for this purpose, it examined baptismal certificates, and high-ranking witnesses had to declare that they knew the family to be honorable and its members to be old Christians of pure blood.

In response to Roscio's application, the Colegio first dragged its feet. In 1798 Roscio urged them to decide the issue. He acknowledged that his grandmother was Indian but argued that Indians were free vassals of the Spanish Crown, equal to white Spanish subjects. The Colegio's board rejected the application but did not address the issue of Indian equality. Instead, it ruled that his father's pure blood quality was not proven. Later the board obtained another copy of the baptismal certificate for Roscio's mother and found discrepancies with the certificate that Roscio had provided earlier. The certificate produced by Roscio made no mention that his grandmother was Indian. The Colegio's board suspected fraud and therefore excluded Roscio in perpetuity.

They also officially communicated to the Audiencia their suspicion that Roscio was subversive and probably involved in the vast conspiracy against the Spanish monarchy uncovered that year in Venezuela (the *conspiración de Gual y España*). One of the conspirators' philosophical pillars was a declaration of equality along with a translation of the French Declaration of the Rights of Man and of the Citizen (1789), a key subversive document at that time. Roscio responded in 1799 with an impassioned written plea in which he reaffirmed his loyalty to the Spanish Crown and repeated his argument for equality of Indians always based on Spanish legislation and well-known Spanish authors. The Fiscal de la Audiencia (the highest prosecutor of the country) did not find anything subversive in Roscio's writing, which probably led to the dismissal of this accusation. Roscio did not attack the Colegio's decision in the Audiencia, but both parties demanded satisfaction because of the offenses proffered by the other party. No decision appeared in the documentation published by Héctor Parra Márquez.[3] In 1805 a new board of the Colegio, examining new documents, accepted Roscio as a member.

Roscio continued to ascend the Caracas colonial hierarchy. In addition to his position as professor of Roman (or civil) law, he became interim Fiscal de la Audiencia. During the crisis in colonial society caused by Napoleon's invasion of Spain, the abdication of the Spanish kings, and the appointment of Joseph Bonaparte as king of Spain, Roscio became a member of the Junta Suprema de Gobierno (Supreme Board of Government) in April 1810 and also served as the minister of foreign affairs. He was elected deputy to the Constituent National Assembly in 1811. He actively participated in drafting the most important documents of the First Republic, including the Act of Independence, the Manifesto of Venezuela to the World, and the Federal Constitution—the last written completely by Roscio.

In 1812 the First Republic collapsed, and royalists took power. They imprisoned Roscio and sent him to Spain with the expectation that he would be executed. Instead, the Spanish authorities decided to imprison him in Cádiz and later sent him to a prison in Ceuta. He escaped in 1815 and, after several incidents, arrived in Jamaica in 1816.

In 1817 Roscio traveled to Philadelphia, where he published *El triunfo de la libertad sobre el despotismo. Es la confesión de un pecador arrepentido de sus pecados y dedicado a desagraviar en esta parte a la religión ofendida por el sistema de las tiranía.* This is certainly his best-known work, frequently known by its short title: *The Triumph of Freedom over Despotism.* In 1819 he participated in the Congreso de Angostura and was an editor of *Correo del Orinoco*, the main periodical of independence proponents. In 1821, as the acting vice president of Colombia, he traveled to Cúcuta to take part in the constituent Congress of Colombia. He died there in October of that year, at age fifty-eight. Relatively late in life, he had married a liberal Spanish woman, and they had a daughter.

Intellectual and political contribution

Roscio was enormously appreciated and influential in his time. Simón Bolívar and Andrés Bello, among many others, wrote about him with great respect. Bello called him *Padre y maestro de la libertad* (father and teacher of liberty). Even José Domingo Díaz, a royalist writer who saw only vices and monsters among the independence leaders, recognized virtues in Roscio. According to Díaz, Roscio was "a lawyer of great credit whose behavior had a singular contrast of virtues and vices: disinterested, sober, modest, wrathful, ambitious, hypocritical, false, and ungrateful."[4] His preeminence and clear liberal position brought him the difficulties of imprisonment and exile previously mentioned.

Reactions to his writings over time show his broad influence and the strong hostility to his message in some quarters. *The Triumph of Freedom over Despotism* was edited several times in the nineteenth century: 1817, 1821, and 1847 in Philadelphia; and 1824, 1828, and 1857 in Mexico. In Mexico, his editor was Benito Juárez, who considered this book his bedside reading. The Inquisition ordered its destruction, and documentation shows that it was burned by the executioner in Caracas in 1818. A previous work, *Patriotismo de Nirgua y abuso de los reyes*, was originally published by the *Gaceta de Caracas* and as a booklet in 1811. Both publications disappeared at that time as a consequence of repression. But there was an edition in Cartagena in 1812, another in Lima in 1822, and yet others in Caracas in 1824 and 1875. The 1811 booklet reappeared in the Archivo de Indias in Seville in the twentieth century. Roscio's *Catecismo religioso-político contra el real catecismo de Fernando VII*, published in Maracaibo in 1821, was lost, and we know only its abridged content from a summary in the *Correo del Orinoco*.

By the mid-twentieth century, Roscio's work experienced a revival of interest. His complete works were published in Caracas in three volumes in 1953, and several scholars focused their attention on his work. Nevertheless, the editors of the complete works (which include letters and many documents from Roscio) chose to exclude Roscio's legal writings from his conflict with the Colegio de Abogados de Caracas. The probable reasons for this exclusion will be discussed later. Roscio is today considered a major intellectual of the early nineteenth century, a civilian hero of the Latin American independence movements, and an early liberal thinker.

Equality and new ideas

Roscio's writings in his conflict with the Colegio de Abogados are of great importance to understanding the evolution of his thinking and his later work. The first document was addressed to the Colegio itself in 1798, and the second to the Audiencia of Caracas in 1799. They were published as a whole by Parra Márquez in his *Historia del Colegio de Abogados de Caracas.* Roscio's writings are a rarity and provide a unique window into law practice at the time.

Lawyers and judges of the late eighteenth century did not produce extensive writings, and we therefore know little about which authors they were reading or how lawyers argued their cases. On the contrary, Roscio's writings are erudite. They show Roscio to be an exceptionally well-informed legal scholar and provide an example of the argumentation topoi that a lawyer could use. They also reveal the literature available in the colonial era and the ideas that penetrated the intellectual circles of colonial society. In addition, Roscio's writings of 1798 and 1799 contain autobiographical details that provide information regarding the gratifications, challenges, and limitations of a lawyer and legal scholar of his time.

The central intellectual theme of these two documents is equality. Roscio argues that American indigenous people are free vassals of the Spanish crown, and that they are equal to white Spaniards. Roscio's arguments are based in part on *derecho indiano* (Spanish colonial law for the Americas), which is consistent on this matter from the beginning of the Spanish colonization in the sixteenth century. Roscio was very familiar with this literature, but in addition, he gave arguments based on theology and political theory. Roscio handled theological literature with ease. Christ and Christianity recognize the equality of humans: we are all God's children. In political terms as well, equality is recognized. When people entered into the social contract, they did not choose individuals to govern based on who was the whitest or tallest, but who was more virtuous or more intelligent. Roscio provided many historical examples from ancient times to illustrate that it was not one's birth but rather one's behavior and effort that cause men to acquire these qualities. For example, biblical Joseph—a Jewish slave—was chosen by the Pharaoh to rule his people; Cicero had an obscure birth, and so on. Thus, Roscio did not base his arguments only on legal rules: theological and political arguments were also relevant.

The argument for equality seems obvious today, but in Spanish America (and Spain) of the Old Regime, society's basic tenet was inequality. There were noblemen and commoners, there were white, black, Indian, and various combinations:

mestizos, *pardos*, *mulatos*, *zambos*, and so on. Legal and social rules were specific for each group. Each had requirements regarding appropriate dress, their place in the church, whether they could use a sword or a wig, and how a member of a particular group should be punished. As the eighteenth century drew to a close, however, equality or inequality became a central social and political issue. In Spain, Enlightenment writers argued against the prejudices of the nobility. But in Venezuela, arguing for equality had a certain subversive tone. As we have seen, this led the board of the Colegio de Abogados to ask the Audiencia to investigate Roscio as possibly involved in the recent *Gual y España* conspiracy, a grave suspicion that could have produced terrible consequences for Roscio.

Roscio's vast and varied knowledge is surprising today. Was it exceptional? In its scope, it was not. What we know of lawyers' libraries shows them to have been interested in religious and historical matters, but Roscio's erudition seems exceptional. At the time, when there were no public libraries in Caracas and books were not abundant, Roscio possessed a large personal library—an important investment and a sign of distinction. In 1810 Roscio made a public offer to create the first public library of Caracas,[5] offering "1000 volumes…in the most usual languages of Europe." This offer certainly reveals much about his interests and scholarly vocation.

Politics and theology

In 1811 Roscio published two important documents: *The Manifesto to the World* and the *Patriotism of Nirgua and Kings' Abuses.*[6] The first work was unsigned, but his authorship is not questioned. Both documents present the same constitutional, theological, and historical arguments to justify the independence of Spanish America from Spain. Based on the constitution of the monarchy, both Charles IV and Ferdinand VII lost their legitimacy because of their conflict and dealings with Napoleon. Therefore Spanish America, Roscio argued, did not have to recognize them or Joseph Bonaparte as kings. In addition, Roscio explained that it is not sinful to live without a king, but it is sinful to live without law. He justified a republican regime on theological and historical grounds. He even justified tyrannicide, referencing Wycliffe and the Spanish scholastics ("the Jesuits") to explain how religion had been improperly used to justify monarchical absolutism.

The aforementioned *Triumph of Freedom over Despotism* is a longer book. It consists of 465 pages in the edition of Roscio's complete works. Ugalde argued convincingly that Roscio composed it between May 1814 and December 1815, mostly while he was a prisoner in Ceuta. His envisioned public was Spanish, and Ugalde found that the book is dominated by the polemic of Spanish religious theory.[7] There are no references to the Spanish American fight for independence, except for a brief mention in the introduction. Nevertheless, we know, from Roscio's letters and the will he drafted at that time, that Spanish American independence was his main concern.

The first thing to note is that Roscio chose the writing style of a confession, an old resource in the Catholic tradition going back to St. Augustine. As the title indicates, Roscio presented himself as a sinner who had accepted the divine power of kings. But a careful reading of sacred texts, and other reading and reflection, had convinced him that the doctrine of the divine origin of royal power is contrary to true religion. The style is a powerful literary resource employed by Roscio to address the religious public to explain the reasons for his conversion. He argues with abundant biblical arguments that true religion is compatible with liberalism and a republican regime, while monarchical absolutism is a distortion of Catholic orthodoxy.

Roscio was convinced that the most effective theoretical ground for liberalism and the independence of Spanish America was religious. He thought that the primary mistake of liberally minded promoters of independence was their assumption that they could replace theology by philosophy or modern rationalist thinking. Doing so, they left a good part of the population in the hands of religious preachers that supported absolutism. Institutionally, the Catholic Church was a strong ally of the Spanish absolute monarchy, and priests served as the monarchy's instruments of propaganda. The battle between liberal republicanism and monarchical absolutism therefore had to be fought with theological arguments. This is the central theme of the book, and the arguments are consequently biblical and evangelical. There are also references to the political thought of that time—equality, the rights of men, social contract, and so on—but these references are brief and peripheral; they are not central to the book.

The importance of Roscio's themes and arguments must be evaluated within their historical context. In January 1816, Pope Pius VII published the encyclical *Etsi Longissimo Terrarum*, calling on Spanish Americans to submit to "Our dearest son in Jesus Christ, Ferdinand, your Catholic King." Roscio had probably already written the *Triumph of Freedom over Despotism* and decided to publish it. The Pope's encyclical did not dissuade him. Roscio did not avoid intellectual fights, not even with the Pope.

Issues of interpretation

Modern scholars offer varied explanations for the roots of Roscio's thinking, an important issue for the history of ideas. Richard M. Morse perceived in Roscio the persistence of medieval Catholic thinking in Spanish America;[8] Augusto Mijares pointed to Rousseau and Mariana as influential authors;[9] Willwoll and Ugalde see the influence of both Suárez and Rousseau;[10] Luis Castro identified arguments and metaphors that could reveal the reading of Locke.[11] Even in his early writings, Roscio argued by using the ideas of the state of nature, natural rights, and social contract, but there are no references to Locke or Rousseau. In contrast, he frequently cited *derecho indiano* and authors like Benito Feijóo, Antonio Xavier Pérez y López, Luís António Verney (Barbadiño), and Juan Francisco De Castro, all part of the Spanish eighteenth-century Enlightenment. It is important to be aware that there was a Spanish Enlightenment, through which modern ideas penetrated into Spain without questioning Catholicism. In particular, the idea of equality and the criticism of nobility and birth privileges were present in eighteenth-century Spain. The Spanish Enlightenment was Catholic, and there is every reason to think that Roscio shared these ideas, given his use of orthodox Catholic thinkers. This is probably the reason the Fiscal de la Audiencia de Caracas did not find any subversive ideas in Roscio's writings. There is also reason to believe that Roscio expected justice from the king of Spain and that his expression of loyalty to the king was completely sincere.

In *The Triumph of Freedom over Despotism*, Roscio made indirect references to Rousseau, and Luis Castro's 1991 analysis of Locke's influence is convincing. Roscio, an omnivorous reader, knew the modern literature, probably after 1809, but he cited Wycliffe, Mariana, and "the Jesuits." He wanted to ground his arguments in religion, not in philosophy. For this reason, he concentrated on the Bible as a main source. Guillermo T. Aveledo Coll counted three hundred biblical quotations in the work, including ninety-seven from the New Testament.[12] Roscio went directly to biblical texts. Even if he clearly knew St. Augustine (he imitated his style of confession) and many other theologians, his argumentative interest was supported by the Bible. This was an authority that could not be rejected and could be very effective with Roscio's envisaged readers.

Behind the differences in interpretation of Roscio's work lies a basic lack of appreciation for the ways modern thought penetrated Spain and Spanish America. Spanish scholastics of the sixteenth and seventeenth centuries formulated many of the new ideas of the period. Francisco de Vitoria's *De Indis* had explained the natural rights of American Indians and accepted their basic equality with Europeans. Vitoria, Francisco Suárez, Fernando Vázquez de Menchaca, and other scholastics are mentioned by Hugo Grotius as his inspiration in *De Jure Belli*. Roscio, as professor of Roman or civil law, used Arnold Vinnius's edition of Justinian's Institutes. In this edition, entire paragraphs of Grotius are included, converting the text to an expression of rationalist natural law. Of course, Vinnius's text was *Elementa iuris naturae et gentium, castigationibus ex Catholicorum doctrina*, or expurgated of theological mistakes, but this did not affect the character of diffusion of the natural law ideas.[13] Roscio was familiar with the idea of the social contract and natural rights even before he could have read Locke and Rousseau, prohibited authors (but nevertheless read by some people) in Spanish colonial dominions.

We must also understand the resistance of the Colegio de Abogados to admitting Roscio, and their reading of his argument for equality as subversive. The lawyers were *blancos criollos*, white creoles, the elite of the colonial society. They were selective about admitting new members and strictly regulated members' behaviors to preserve the honor of the group. For example, the board of the Colegio had to approve the marriage of a lawyer, because the Colegio wanted to prevent any marriage that would diminish the position of a Colegio member. Similarly, a lawyer was sanctioned if he played cards with *pardos*. Roscio clearly did not have the high social status the Colegio required. As noted earlier, in contemporary terms his mother was half Indian; his father was a *blanco de orilla*. Considered even worse in his society, Roscio had uncles and cousins who were *pardos*. He could have argued that he was legally white, and in fact he did do so, but *en passant*. We can understand that his main argument was equality, but this was unacceptable to individuals imbued with the sense of their own social privilege. Moreover, the argument of equality coming from Roscio's mouth was an additional irritant. The Colegio could not accept a lesson from a *parvenu*; on the contrary, they saw him as deserving punishment.

Times were changing, and time cures all injuries; in 1805 Roscio became a member of the Colegio. When the time for independence came and equality was declared, Roscio and people like Miguel José Sanz and Francisco Espejo, distinguished members of the Colegio, and even the Marquis of Toro and his cousin Simón Bolívar, were active and friends on the side of independence. They all became equal citizens, even though some probably were more equal than others. Roscio's ability to speak in the language of monarchists and to destroy their theological arguments led to his persecution and the repression of his writings. As Díaz put it, his virtues (his knowledge and capacity to argue) were extreme, but they were used for the worst purpose: to destroy the theological grounds for absolute monarchy. The Holy Inquisition had a powerful reason to order the destruction of his work.

As mentioned, Roscio's important legal writings in his fight with the Colegio de Abogados were not included in his complete works. In his prologue to the *Complete Works*, Mijares points out the reason for the exclusion: they had been recently published by Parra Márquez in his history of the Colegio de Abogados de Caracas.[14] This reason is not very convincing, however. Different papers of his were included, even though they had not been previously published. Additionally, the legal writings were not a separate publication but part of a book on the Colegio de Abogados.

I suggest another reason for the exclusion: Mijares comments on Roscio's confession at the beginning of the *Triumph of Freedom over Despotism*. Mijares explains the confession as a literary resource because he did not find that Roscio was ever "servile," the word that Roscio and his contemporaries used to designate conservatives who accepted absolutism. Mijares reads Roscio's legal writings and comments on his argument for equality. According to Mijares, Roscio was familiar with modern thinking, and Mijares traces Rousseau's influence on Roscio in the argument for equality. But Roscio kept silent about his loyalty to the Spanish monarchy. This is a more probable reason for exclusion. Republican ideals were better served by presenting Roscio as committed to liberal and republican ideas from the very beginning.

An alternative explanation for Roscio's thinking is that Roscio was sincere in his confession. He served as Fiscal de la Real Audiencia, and he was harsh with the widow of conspiracy leader José María España, applying the severe Spanish rules on crimes of *lèse majesté*. He shared the common mistakes of the conservative Catholic thinking and political absolutism of his education, but arduous reflection and reading led to the *Triumph of Freedom over Despotism*. He explained his method: he analyzed carefully the Vulgate Bible, the official Catholic translation of the Bible, and searched its political texts. For this purpose, he did not examine the Vulgate for its religious content. He was a Catholic and did not want to question religion. He wanted, rather, to question the political meaning that late commentaries had assigned to these texts. He found that royal absolutism and the theory that royal power comes directly from God were not justified. On the contrary, sacred texts showed the role of the people in establishing political power.

God is, of course, the first cause (*causa primera*) of any political power. But God does not act directly on this matter; rather, God acts through the people. Thus, the people are the second cause (*causa segunda*).[15] This scholastic distinction became central to Roscio's political theory. In the *Triumph of Freedom over Despotism*, we find today a modern explanation of democracy and the rule of law, but an explanation based on biblical texts. The legislative power is supreme because it represents the people; legislation must be the expression of the general will of the people. Freedom is natural for human beings, and any restriction of freedom must follow legitimate steps.

More difficult to explain is the unequal impact of Roscio's work. Except for the *Patriotismo de Nirgua*, edited as part of a collection of volumes related to the independence of Venezuela in 1875, no other edition of Roscio's work was published in nineteenth-century Venezuela. On the contrary, the *Triumph of Freedom over Despotism* was edited three times in Mexico between 1824 and 1857. Ugalde explains the difference: while in Mexico the Catholic Church remained powerful and was monarchical, in Venezuela bishops and priests accepted the republican regime.[16] There was no need for Roscio's works in Venezuela, while he became important for the liberal cause in Mexico. Thus, for Benito Juárez, Roscio was fundamental reading.[17] In Venezuela, Roscio could be safely ignored. In addition, the emphasis placed on the military aspect of the independence movement and the protagonist role given to Bolívar dimmed Roscio's and other similar intellectuals' place in the conception of the new republic.

To understand this Catholic approach and its limits, it is important to read Roscio's other fundamental political texts drafted with other early republican intellectuals: the *Acta de la independencia de Venezuela* (July 1811) and the first Venezuelan Constitution (December 1811). Both documents defined Venezuela as a Catholic republic. Freedom of religion was guaranteed in a limited way. In colonial times, heterodoxy had been a crime. The new republic allowed private adherence to other religions and eliminated the special privileges of ecclesiastics (*fuero eclesiástico*). The *fuero*'s extinction was a polemical decision and produced the only dissenting opinions on the constitution. Roscio favored the extinction of the ecclesiastical *fuero*, but the republic had to remain Catholic. The big issue, of course, was the place of God (and the Catholic Church) in the republic and the limits of tolerance. It is in the context of this discussion that we have to understand Roscio's place in Latin American legal, political, and religious thinking.[18] Roscio was a Catholic liberal thinker. We can understand why his book became so important for Benito Juárez and anathema for the Holy Inquisition.

We should not judge Roscio, the Constitution of 1811, or the declaration of independence by our present standards. Although making some general references that implied that African people were also equal, Roscio never condemned slavery. This was not his fight. He never said a word on the equality of women, but this was not perceived as a problem in his time. Nonetheless, our consideration of present-day issues under Pope Francis can help our understanding of Roscio. In the early nineteenth century, as today, there were several strains of Catholic thinking. Roscio made an important contribution to an understudied area of thought—liberal Catholicism in the political realm. He was fundamental to the separation of the Catholic religion (and the Catholic Church) from monarchical absolutism. He also bolstered the place of the republic as the appropriate regime for the new nations of Spanish America. This was no small feat.

Notes

1 For racial connotations, this paper follows the language of colonial Spanish America. Aboriginal Americans are "Indians." *Blanco de orilla* denoted a recent immigrant from Europe. *Pardo* was a dark-skinned person generally with some mixing of African blood. "White creoles" were the descendants of conquerors and first colonizers. White creoles had most of the land and, together with the "peninsular whites" (royal functionaries), formed the upper class.
2 Pérez-Perdomo, *Los abogados de Venezuela*.
3 Parra Márquez, *Historia del Colegio de Abogados de Caracas*, vol. 1.
4 Ugalde, *El pensamiento teológico-político de Juan Germán Roscio*, 78.
5 Roscio, *Obras completas*, 2:13–14.
6 Ibid., 41–83 and 85–102.
7 Ugalde, *El pensamiento teológico-político de Juan Germán Roscio*.
8 Morse, *El espejo de Próspero*.
9 Mijares, "Prólogo," in Roscio, *Obras completas*, vol 1.
10 Willwoll, *Sesquicentenario de Juan Germán Roscio*; Ugalde, *El pensamiento teológico-político de Juan Germán Roscio*.
11 Castro Leiva, *De la patria boba a la teología bolivariana*.
12 Aveledo Coll, *Pro religione et patria*, 283.
13 Pérez-Perdomo, *Los abogados de Venezuela*.
14 Mijares, "Prólogo"; Parra Márquez, *Historia del Colegio de Abogados*.
15 Roscio, *Obras completas*, 1:63.
16 Ugalde, *El pensamiento teológico-político de Juan Germán Roscio*.
17 Miliani, "Juan Germán Roscio."
18 Aveledo Coll, *Pro religione et patria*.

References

Aveledo Coll, Guillermo T. *Pro religione et patria. República y religión en la crisis de la sociedad colonial venezolana (1810–1834)*. Caracas: Academia Nacional de la Historia y Universidad Metropolitana, 2011.

Castro Leiva, Luis. *De la patria boba a la teología bolivariana: ensayos de historia intelectual*. Caracas: Monte Ávila Editores, 1991.

Grases, Pedro. "Juan Germán Roscio." In *Obras*, edited by Pedro Grases, vol. 5. Barcelona/Caracas: Seix Barral, 1986.

Mijares, Augusto. "Prólogo." In *Obras completas*, edited by Juan Germán Roscio, Vol. 1. Caracas: Secretaría Décima Conferencia Interamericana, 1953.

Miliani, Domingo. "Juan Germán Roscio." In Juan Germán Roscio, *El triunfo de la libertad sobre el despotismo*. Caracas: Monte Ávila, 1983.

Morse, Richard M. *El espejo de Próspero. Un estudio de la dialéctica del Nuevo Mundo*. Mexico City: Siglo Veintiuno, 1982.

Parra Márquez, Héctor. *Historia del Colegio de Abogados de Caracas*, Vol. 1. Caracas: Imprenta Nacional, 1952.

Pérez-Perdomo, Rogelio. *Los abogados de Venezuela*. Caracas: Monte Ávila, 1981.

Pérez-Perdomo, Rogelio. *Roscio y el Colegio de Abogados de Caracas*. Caracas: Academia Nacional de la Historia, 2017.

Roscio, Juan Germán. *Obras completas*, Vol. 3. Caracas: Secretaría de la Décima Conferencia Interamericana, 1953.

Ugalde, Luis. *El pensamiento teológico-político de Juan Germán Roscio*. Caracas: Bid, 2007.

Willwoll, Guillermo Emilio. *Sesquicentenario de Juan Germán Roscio: Suárez-Rousseau-Roscio*. Caracas: Editorial Sucre, 1974.

2 Andrés Bello (Venezuela and Chile, 1781–1865)

Alejandro Guzmán

Childhood and advanced youth in Caracas

The Bello family

Andrés de Jesús María y José Bello López was born to Bartolomé Bello y Bello and Ana Antonia López Delgado toward the end of the Spanish Empire in America, in Caracas, the capital of the General Captaincy and Governorate of Venezuela. The first of three brothers and four sisters, he was baptized on November 29, 1781. The ancestral lines of both parents were of Canarian origin. His father was a lawyer by training and an amateur musician and was considered a good composer. He did not practice law, however; he was a government official, prosecutor of the Real Hacienda y Renta del Tabaco (royal treasury and tobacco income) in the province of Cumaná. His duties forced him to be frequently absent from the family home, and he died in 1804. Except perhaps for Andrés Bello's passion for music, which is no small accomplishment, his father seems not to have influenced the young man. Bello's maternal grandfather, Juan Pedro López, in whose house Bello was born, was a painter of great renown. Thus, the Bello family, though not part of the aristocracy, was not unknown in Caracas society.

Studies and friendships

Bello first studied in the convent of Las Mercedes. There, under the teaching of Fray Cristóbal de Quezada, between 1792 and 1796, he learned the elements of Latin and Castilian grammar. At the age of eleven, he read Calderón de la Barca and *Don Quixote* with attention. When Quezada died, in 1796, Bello entered the seminary of Santa Rosa, where he was cared for by the presbyter José Antonio de Montenegro. Bello's knowledge of Latin was so advanced that in 1797 he managed to pass the three prescribed courses of *Latinidad*, as they were then called. That same year, he enrolled in the Royal and Pontifical University of Caracas to study for a baccalaureate in arts (philosophy), a three-year program of study. He carried out his philosophy studies under the direction of Rafael Escalona, a priest, and although scholasticism prevailed, modern philosophy and natural science were part of the curriculum. Bello graduated in 1800, about the same time that he began to write his first poems.

During his stay in the seminary of Santa Rosa, Bello had established friendly relations with some children of the noble families of Caracas. His entrance in the university widened the circle of his acquaintances, and he worked, for example, with Simón Bolívar, for whom he acted as private instructor between 1797 and 1799. In general, Bello stood out from the studious youth of his time. He was admired for his advanced knowledge, natural talents, and modesty. This last quality, recognized during his maturity and old age, surely must have adorned him from his youth. A later testimony of Bolívar is eloquent in this respect: "I know the superiority of this contemporary of Caracas; he was my teacher when we were the same age; and I loved him with respect."[1] Toward the end of his university studies, Bello established a relationship with Alexander von Humboldt during Humboldt's scientific mission to Venezuela in the company of the Frenchman Aimé Bonpland. Bello served as a companion and guide during Humboldt's travels in the region.

Bello in public service and his first intellectual works

In 1802, Bello imitated his father and entered by competition into public service as the second official of the Government of Venezuela. Around the same year, he began studying the English language with the help of only a grammar text, just as he had learned French years before. As an exercise in English, he translated *An Essay on Human Understanding* by John Locke.

Bello rose quickly in the government, and in 1807 he was awarded the rank of honorary commissioner of war, equivalent in civil matters to the military rank of lieutenant colonel. In 1808 he was appointed political secretary of the Central Vaccine Board. In the same year, he was commissioned to write the official newspaper *La Gazeta de Caracas*, published by the recently introduced printing press. In 1809 he was already the first official of the interior. In that same year, he projected the publication of a magazine that would be called *El Lucero*, but it never saw the light. He also wrote a summary of the history of Venezuela, to be part of a major publication called *Calendario manual y guía universal de extranjeros en Venezuela para el año de 1810* (*Manual calendar and universal guide for foreigners in Venezuela for the year 1810*), the first book published in Venezuela, precisely in that year.

The revolution for independence

Meanwhile, events rushed forward in Europe in a way that would have an unexpected impact on Bello's life. In mid-July 1808, Vicente Emparan, the Captain General of Venezuela, received two issues of *The Times* of London and commissioned Bello to translate them into Spanish. Through them, news arrived of the amazing changes in the Spanish monarchy: the abdication of Charles IV and his heirs to the throne of Spain, the confinement of the royal family in the interior of France, and the ascension of Joseph Bonaparte. The nervous and hurried council called by Emparan to discuss these events and to adopt a response did not, however, directly mention the English news. Nonetheless, a few days later a French naval officer brought the official documents for Captain General Emparan. The French officer had participated in the advent of the new king and appeared before Emparan. Bello translated these documents, and the new reality had to be accepted. The captain general summoned a meeting of notables, which, pressed by a spontaneous and tumultuous town meeting of citizens, was forced to proclaim fidelity to Charles's son, Ferdinand VII. Later European events, and particularly the French invasion of Spain, led to the fear that an invasion would be attempted in America. Following the Peninsular example, on April 19, 1810, a conservative Supreme Junta forced the resignation of Captain General Emparan and appointed Bello as an attaché to the Ministry of Foreign Affairs. Venezuela desired to obtain the support of England to prevent a French invasion of Venezuela, either by the upstart king Joseph Bonaparte or directly by his brother, Napoleon. Attempting to avoid a conflict with the Peninsular Regency Council, the junta dispatched a diplomatic mission comprising Simón Bolívar, Luis López Méndez, and Bello to the Court of St. James's.

The diplomatic mission to London

The commissioners arrived in London in July 1810. They and the English minister reached an agreement that Great Britain would provide maritime protection to Venezuela in the event of a French attack while defending the rights of the legitimate sovereign. Britain also urged Venezuela to maintain the best possible relations with the Regency Council and offered itself as a mediator to these ends.

Shortly afterward, however, in September 1810, the Regency Council declared Venezuela an insurgent and subjected it to blockade. Bolívar returned immediately to Venezuela; it was agreed that López Méndez and Bello would remain in London to defend and promote the Venezuelan cause. In 1812, the Regency Council sent an army to Caracas to depose the government of the junta and restore the previous order. As a result, the diplomatic position of Bello and López Méndez changed to that of rebels. Bello was expressly removed from his former position in the restored government and—unemployed and without resources—both men resigned themselves to remaining exiled in London, waiting for better times. For Bello, this took almost twenty years.

Toward maturity in London

Activities and marriages in London

The London years were financially difficult for Bello. In 1814, he married Mary Ann Boyland, a young woman of humble Irish origin in her twenties, with whom he had three children. One of them died at an early age, in 1821. Mary Ann also died that year, and Bello fell into great sadness and despair. In 1824, however, he married Elizabeth Dunn, also a young woman of twenty-three years and perhaps of low Irish descent, who in London gave him four more children. Later, in Chile, they would have another eight children. Elizabeth survived to the same age as her husband and died in 1873, never having mastered Spanish.

In London, Bello was employed to edit some manuscripts of the English philosopher Jeremy Bentham (1748–1832). Bello attained this position on the recommendation of James Mill, father of the future philosopher John Stuart Mill. The elder Mill provided Bello entrée into radical political circles. Bello was also commissioned to correct the Spanish translation of the Scío Bible (a Spanish translation from the Vulgate by the bishop of Segovia, Felipe Scío de San Miguel). Bello offered private classes in French and Spanish and was the preceptor of Lord Hamilton's children when Hamilton was deputy secretary of foreign affairs in England. In the last phase of his stay in London, Bello acted as secretary of the legation of Chile, between 1822 and 1824, and that of Colombia, as the Bolivarian state comprising Venezuela, Nueva Granada (present-day Colombia), and Quito (Ecuador) was called between 1825 and 1829.

Friends and relationships

London gave Bello the opportunity to meet Spaniards and Latin Americans who lived there as exiles. Spaniards were mostly exiles from the restored absolutist government of Ferdinand VII; Latin Americans were exiles who had pressed for independence at home. In London he first met his countryman Francisco de Miranda, in whose house he lived immediately upon arrival. Bello continued in the city, even after Miranda left at the end of 1810 to return to Venezuela and intervene in the independence process. Through José María Blanco White, Bello met Fray Servando Teresa de Mier, a Mexican priest, who would participate in the future independence of his homeland. In 1813, Bello also had contact with the Chilean Francisco Antonio Pinto, the future president of his country. Bello represented Pinto before the English government and cultivated their friendship until Pinto's death.

Bello also met the Guatemalan Antonio José de Irisarri, who was serving the Chilean government as a diplomatic representative. Pinto and Irisarri had met as exiles in London during the period of the Spanish restoration in Chile, called the Reconquista in the historiography of Spain. When Chile strengthened its independence and constituted a republican government, Irisarri returned to represent it in England. In 1820, he commissioned Bello to study the educational system of Lancaster, and Bello fulfilled this task with a thorough report. Two years later, Irisarri obtained the appointment of Bello as interim secretary of his mission. In 1824, however, Irisarri was replaced in his diplomatic role by the Chilean Mariano Egaña, with whom Bello also established a relationship, beginning with reciprocal antipathy at first and later developing into a deep and enduring friendship. Egaña's admiration for Bello would be decisive in Bello's transfer to Chile, when the president of that republic was Egaña's former friend Pinto. Other friendships dating from Bello's London years were those with José Antonio Álvarez Condarco, the first head of the Chilean naval mission in London, and with José Miguel de la Barra, an outstanding man of culture, who was to be the first dean of the Faculty of Humanities of the University of Chile.

Bello met many other leading individuals during his long stay in London, including Spaniards Bartolomé José Gallardo and Vicente Salvá, both notable scholars, bibliophiles, and philologists, and the latter an important publisher. He also gained the acquaintance of Juan García del Río from Río de la Plata, the poet José Joaquín Olmedo from Colombia and Quito, and Vicente Rocafuerte, a future president of Ecuador, who would promulgate the Civil Code of Bello in his country. Bello also met José Fernández Madrid of Colombia, who held the presidency of his country, and with the Spanish writer José Joaquín de Mora, whom he met again in Chile, albeit under tense circumstances.

Studies and intellectual works

Bello's activity in London included some literary tasks in association with the Hispanic-American intellectuals he knew. For example, in 1820, with Antonio José de Irisarri, Bello edited the politically oriented magazine *El Censor Americano*, aimed at defending

Spanish America's independence and the monarchic constitutions of the resulting new states. Only one issue was published. In 1823, Bello and Juan García del Río published a magazine called *Biblioteca Americana o Miscelánea de Literatura, Artes y Ciencias* (*American library or miscellany of literature, arts, and sciences*), of which only the fascicles of the first volume and one of the second appeared. A new magazine by both editors was the *American Repertory*, which published four volumes between 1826 and 1827. These two publications contain original scientific and literary works by different authors, including Bello, as well as news and critical articles. The adjective "American," used in the title of both, gives sufficient account of their general objective: they intended to illustrate the opinion of Hispanic Americans while promoting knowledge of Continental Europe. By the second decade of the century, Bello was participating in enterprises conceived mainly for the first purpose. This facet of his intellectual work had already matured, and he would continue in this vein for the rest of his life, with the purpose of educating Hispanic-American citizens and fostering a Hispanic-American culture in the dismembered countries of the former monarchy.

Bello in Chile

Arrival in Chile

Andrés Bello and his family, with furniture, nearly four hundred books, and notes and manuscripts, arrived in Valparaíso on June 25, 1829, after a trip of more than four months, which at that time required passage around the stormy Cape Horn. The travelers still had to withstand mule-drawn coaches to Santiago, over hilly dirt roads, probably muddy and full of ruts. It is not fanciful to conceive the horror that these travelers would have felt, especially in constrast to the panorama offered by the then-small port of Valparaíso.

Mariano Egaña, who remained in London to attend to his diplomatic mission, had alerted his father, Juan Egaña, a lawyer, literary intellectual, and hero of Chilean independence, about the arrival of Bello and his family in Chile. Mariano Egaña had asked his father to house the Bellos until they found their own accommodations, so Bello at least did not enter Santiago without a place for his family to stay. He arrived with the promise of an appointment as assistant senior officer of the Ministry of Finance. That appointment was part of the offer made in London by Mariano Egaña to Bello to encourage his move to Chile, and Bello thus arrived with some form of employment.

State of the country on Bello's arrival

Bello's chosen country had been described by Bolívar as an "ocean of anarchy."[2] In the Republic of Chile, since the resignation in 1823 of the supreme director of the state, Bernardo O'Higgins, politics had not gone as expected. Following the constitution issued in 1818 under O'Higgins, three more written constitutions and a set of constitutional laws all had organized on paper a failed federal state. Twenty-three governments had come and gone. Just months after Bello arrived in Chile, a civil war broke out, and another soon followed.

On one hand was the group of liberals, derogatorily nicknamed *pipiolos* (from the Latin *pipio*, "chick"), to denote their political infantilism and inexperience in public affairs. Members of this group came from the small middle class of professionals traditionally excluded from government and senior administration—those other than lawyers. They managed to impose the charter of 1828 and elect President Pinto to sustain the government. There was also the upper-class group, which had promoted the Chilean War of Independence and ruled the country, even under O'Higgins. This group had substantial wealth in agriculture and was more socially influential. Liberals also derogatorily called this group "wigs," alluding to the Old Regime fashion of wearing powdered wigs, as an indication of their supposed love of the old.

To these two main groups was added that of the O'Higginists, eager to see the return of the Liberator to the government from his exile in Peru. The *estanqueros* (tobacconists) were led by Diego Portales and consisted of practitioners of high trade completely alien to political life. This group came from the failing concessional tobacconist business. They sought the institution of a stable and powerful regime, capable of maintaining public order. In this desire, the *estanqueros* agreed with the wigs and the O'Higginists, an alliance that proved natural against the weakness and ineptitude of the *pipiolo* government.

There was also the group of federalists, led by José Miguel Infante, an over-the-top ideologue. This group desired a federal government. Although it managed to impose this structure by means of singular laws in 1826 and 1827, those laws were not put into effect. This failure discredited the federalists' ideology and weakened their numbers. The *pipiolos* repudiated federalism on the occasion of the 1828 charter, so this regime also viewed the federalists as enemies. In the midst of these divisions, and subject to relentless opposition, President Pinto resigned his post on July 16, 1829, a few weeks after Bello's arrival, aggravating the political situation and putting the government of Francisco R. Vicuña, Pinto's lawful successor, at great risk.

Bello's first months in Chile were therefore not quiet. But the worst was yet to come. The conditions of public life soon deteriorated further after the illegal election of the vice president of the republic for the *pipiolos*. This led first to an O'Higginistt military uprising, supported by the wigs and *estanqueros*, and then to a civil war.

Presidential elections were due; under the Constitution of 1828, a vice president could serve only provisionally. The candidate of the victors in Lircay was General Joaquín Prieto Vial, commander of the first insurgent troops, who assumed the presidency on June 18, 1831. After an initial reluctance, Portales agreed to and probably decided Prieto's candidacy. It was a masterpiece of politics. A military man, Prieto had fought in the wars of independence and was the victor in Lircay. With familial roots in the southern city of Concepción, he held old O'Higginist sympathies. He pleased his fellow soldiers, many of whom had fought at Lircay, but who now had to be removed from the temptation to intervene in politics. Prieto also satisfied the desires of the Liberator's supporters without installing the Liberator, O'Higgins, himself. In short, this fulfilled the ambitions of the aristocracy of the old southern families that were usually displaced by the elite of Santiago. For others, Prieto gained favor by his loyalty and honesty, his absence of greater ambitions, and his moderate intellectual autonomy, combined with the vicarious respect and fear for him gained through Portales's support. Portales convinced everyone around him that Prieto was his selected and even anointed president of the republic.

Originally envisaged for 1836, work to reform the Constitution of 1828 accelerated, and a convention was convened in October 1831, producing a new text, the Constitution of 1833, which lasted until 1925. Little of the previous constitution survived in the new one. The new regime profoundly changed its implementation, endowing the president of the republic with great powers and a term lasting five years, with the possibility of immediate reelection for one time.

Formalized with the election of Prieto in 1831 and the issuance of the Constitution in 1833, the new regime gained almost universal acceptance. Opposition was only timid or nascent in these years, which moved forward under the watchful eye of Diego Portales.

First jobs

Within weeks of Bello's arrival in Chile on July 13, 1829, President Ruiz-Tagle appointed him senior auxiliary officer of the Ministry of Finance according to Mariano Egaña's proposal in London. The reality of his duties set in, and in April 1830, Bello was appointed consultant and secretary in the Ministry of Foreign Affairs, Justice, and Worship. In June 1834, he was promoted as a senior officer of that ministry, a kind of deputy minister of the division, or undersecretary in the current nomenclature. He left government service in 1855 for retirement. From the first moment he entered public administration, he inspired Chile's international politics and gave legal form to the country's relations with other states.

On February 1, 1830, Bello was commissioned to lead the College of Santiago, which, under the patronage of Diego Portales and his group, had started operating in early 1829. The college soon rivaled the Liceo de Chile, run by José Joaquín de Mora, a former acquaintance of Bello's in London. The Liceo de Chile also had begun operating in 1829 and was seen as an educational establishment inspired by the *pipiolas*. This affiliation was one of the reasons that moved Portales and his friends to found another institution more in keeping with his ideas. The director of the new college was an energetic priest named Juan Francisco Meneses, but when he assumed a ministry in the new government, Bello was appointed to replace him. Bello also gave lessons in natural law and *ius gentium*, or international law, as well as a subject that he created, the rather theoretical and law-oriented "universal law course," based on the ideas of Jeremy Bentham.

In February 1831, Mora was expelled from the country on the order of Portales, who could no longer tolerate the Spaniard Mora's corrosive and ingenious criticism of the new government. The Liceo de Chile closed its doors shortly after April 25, 1831, and a few months later, the College of Santiago, which no longer had a reason to exist, ceased operation.

Mora went to Peru and then Bolivia, where he also carried out educational activities and advised the supreme protector, Andrés de Santa Cruz, while Bello did the same in Chile with Portales, the enemy of the Bolivian ruler. Thus, Mora acquired new reasons to loathe Bello and Chile. Returning to Spain, Mora entered the Royal Spanish Academy. Many years later, probably with the quarrels of 1830 long forgotten, Bello praised Mora and his best-known work, *Spanish Legends*, in *El Araucano* (1840).[3] Mora also later praised Chile's stability and cultural progress, which he attributed in part to Bello, whom he described as a "great jurist and a deep literary man." In an ideological analysis of Bello's *Castilian Grammar*, Mora said that the work could be "considered as one of the most precious jewels of modern philology." Thus, in the course of their careers, these two intellectuals, who both had contributed much to the cultural order, ended up completely reconciled. This reconciliation was achieved at a distance; they never saw each other again after Mora left Chile.

With Portales's support, a state newspaper, *El Araucano*, was established in September 1830 to propagate government action. It included legislation such as decrees, laws, and drafts of legislative projects, but it did not serve as an official journal. Since 1823, a *Bulletin* of laws, government orders, decrees, and rules had served to publish these texts officially to the public. On September 17, 1830, Bello was appointed editor of *El Araucano*, along with Manuel José Gandarillas, and he remained the editor from 1835 until 1853, when he left public office.

The influence of this newspaper was felt immediately. Without prejudice to its governmental functions, that is, of reporting on and defending the government's actions, the paper began to act as a source for general culture and news. Bello was in charge of writing sections on foreign news. Using newspapers of diverse origins and his extensive knowledge of languages, Bello reported cultural and scientific information. Gandarillas was in charge of national, especially political, news.

In the columns of *El Araucano*, Bello stirred up issues that he was interested in seeing discussed and resolved. These issues included codification of the law and reform of the administration of justice, the obligation of the judges to provide explanations for their sentences, the adoption of the decimal metric system, aspects of literary property, the reform of the mortgage system, and the latest scientific and technical developments. He promoted literary criticism, theater, and music, and he wrote about how Spanish should be spoken and written and about the need to educate citizens.

The College of Santiago having closed its doors in 1831, Bello continued to offer lessons in natural law, *ius gentium*, and international legislation in his home beginning in April 1832, and soon began teaching Roman law as well. From 1834 on, he extended his teaching to Latin and Spanish grammar and literature. His students were young people who would later distinguish themselves in various areas of national life. Bello's private teaching ceased in 1843, when the University of Chile opened.

In 1843 Bello published anonymously his *Institutions of Roman Law* from his lessons on Roman law. For his lessons on *ius gentium*, Bello was guided by his manuscripts, most likely written during his stay in London. He published these in Santiago in 1833, under the title *Principios de derechos de gentes* (*Principles of the Law of Nations*) and later re-edited them for publication in Chile with the modernized title *Principles of International Law*.

The beginnings of legal codification

In July 1831, the government of Fernando Errázuriz, of which Diego Portales was minister of the interior, sent the senate a message aimed at promoting a draft to establish a procedure for codifying civil, commercial, criminal, and procedural law. The task was to be assigned to a "literary person of recognized experience," with Bello in mind. The project, however, suffered criticism and much delay in the senate and ended up being scrapped in the Chamber of Deputies. Meanwhile, Portales, sometime between 1831 and 1834, and on his own initiative and without waiting for a law to address the matter, ordered or begged Bello to start privately drafting a civil code. For the remainder of the 1830s, Bello completed a project on successions of property on death and another on obligations and contracts. He also drafted a preliminary title, of which there would be no public notice until the beginning of the following decade. In the meantime, he edited several articles on codification in *El Araucano*, through which he prepared public opinion for the work that would be done officially after 1840.

Bello's bachelor's degree in canon and civil law

The criticisms raised in response to the government's proposed project on codification in 1831 focused on two aspects of Bello's background—his nationality and his lack of a degree in law. Bello therefore began to legitimize himself and his work before others who were susceptible, critical, jealous, and envious. Some stated that Bello was incapable of undertaking Chilean codification because he did not have an academic degree in law and was a foreigner. In 1832, however, the government passed a law that granted Chilean nationality to Bello. In 1836, the University of San Felipe, having verified Bello's sufficiency of knowledge in the field, conferred on him the degree of baccalaureate in canon and civil law. At that time, the bachelor's degree was the only certification required to practice law in Chile (no licentiate was required). For a man of study, he needed only the academic, rather than the professional, degree. Nonetheless, many years later, in 1863, the newly constituted Santiago Bar Association made him an honorary member of the institution to signify that they considered him one of their own.

Still, rumors persisted against Bello. Some suggested that he was not as talented as he claimed; that his poetry was mediocre; that he had an obsequious character toward the powerful, whose favor he sought permanently. Criticisms included that he was proud in front of his inferiors, whom he even avoided greeting, and that he was animated by a great greed for money. Such attacks were entirely unwarranted.

New jobs

In March 1832, Bello was appointed to two public bodies. On one hand, he was appointed to the Board of Education, whose task was to monitor the education offered in the country's schools and to propose to the government their plan of studies. At that time, the main educational establishment in Chile was the National Institute, founded in 1813. It taught basic, middle, and higher education, but did not grant academic degrees that were within the competence of the University of San Felipe. The university, however, lacked teaching functions. In his new position, Bello intervened to reform higher education. In fact, he made a decisive intervention in the formulation of the new curriculum of the National Institute approved that year, 1832.

On the other hand, in that same year, Bello was appointed to the Book Censorship Commission to censor books imported from abroad. Paradoxically, in articles published in *El Araucano* in 1833 and 1834, Bello himself criticized this activity and unsuccessfully advised that it be suppressed. Censorship was abolished only much later, in 1878.

In addition to his increasing formal duties, Bello's other tasks mounted, and he was placed in charge of writing all kinds of documents. Thus, for example, he was entrusted with writing the annual accounts of the president of the republic to the National Congress on its opening days. Furthermore, Bello did not neglect his personal research. For example, in 1835, he published a work on the orthology and metrics of Spanish.

Bello as senator

Making use of its *de facto* power to direct the elections of senators and deputies, the government decided to incorporate Bello into the senate in 1837 by inviting him to present his candidacy, which resulted in the expected successful outcome. His designation-election, which was not legally incompatible with his position as a senior officer of the Ministry of Foreign Affairs, had to be renewed in the following periods until 1864. By then, the health of the aging Bello no longer allowed him to exercise his duties. He died the following year.

Bello never systematically presented a theory of legislation, but his various writings reveal his thought about the aims and nature of legislation and how these ideas were reflected in his work as a legislator. Leaving aside the most visible and important of all sources, the Civil Code, one recalls that the first law in which Bello intervened, as editor of the text proposed by President Prieto, was promulgated on July 25, 1834, on the ability of foreigners to execute a testamentary will in Chile. Foreigners faced various obstacles to doing this effectively; as a way of attracting them, the government decided to promote this draft legislation by Bello, who demonstrated broad liberalism in his approach. The regulation of the senate, approved on August 31, 1840, was also Bello's work.

Bello proposed three laws organizing two codification and review commissions, to which the code of 1855 is directly linked. The same happened with the law of November 19, 1842, creating the University of Chile; and with that of September 6, 1844, concerning marriage of non-Catholics in Chilean territory. He took an active part in the discussion of the law of August 8, 1849, which regulated the fate of land gained from recession of the sea. Bello wrote important laws on privileges, mortgages, and credit priority, of October 31, 1845, and October 25, 1854; the second is the direct antecedent of the Civil Code's provisions on the same subject. He also penned the law of July 14, 1852, disentailing *mayorazgos* (entailed estates). His draft legislation on the retroactive effect of the laws influenced the law of October 7, 1861, on the same subject. Bello also wrote the regulations for the registry of real estate of June 24, 1857, which are actually a decree with the force of law issued by the president of the republic through the authorization given him by article 695 of the Civil Code.

Bello as rector of the University of Chile

In 1839, Mariano Egaña, the minister of justice, adopted a measure that would have vast consequences. Basing his action on a claim by the rector of the University of San Felipe, the always combative priest Juan Francisco Meneses, against the National Institute, Egaña decreed that the old institute was extinguished and replaced by the University of Chile. This was actually only a change in name as a pretext to reorganize the institution. For the moment, things continued as before, and Meneses continued as rector until the legislation contemplated in the decree was issued. Despite the protests of the doctors' cloister, Egaña did not revoke the measure.

The Royal University of San Felipe de Santiago de Chile was founded by King Felipe V and honored his name. It was established in 1738, but its effective activity dates to 1758. Its teaching functions experienced ups and downs during the colonial era, but it always maintained competence to confer academic degrees through its own examinations. It comprised faculties of theology, canons and laws, arts (philosophy), and medicine. In 1813 the national government definitively withdrew its teaching activities and placed them in the hands of the National Institute. The university, however, maintained its jurisdiction to grant degrees, although, after 1823, it began to grant them after exams taken at the institute rather than in the university. University activities declined substantially. The need for reform was evident, and Egaña was well suited to undertake this reform.

Legislation on the university, written by Bello, was issued in 1843. The University of Chile came under the rule of a rector assisted by the University Council, consisting of the general secretary and the deans of the five faculties of theology, law, mathematics, medicine, and philosophy and humanities. The council conferred the degrees. The faculties were composed of academic members, at first appointed by the government but later selected by each faculty. Teaching functions were not attributed to the university, which remained based in the National Institute, although examinations for degrees had to be submitted to commissions of the respective faculty that granted them. The law entrusted the university with the "cultivation of letters and sciences in Chile." Consequently, Bello conceived the institution as an organic set of academies—the faculties—charged with cultivating and disseminating knowledge. In 1879, the university recovered its teaching function.

Despite Meneses's attempts to keep the office of rector, Bello was appointed rector of the University of Chile. On September 17, 1843, at the official inauguration ceremony, Bello delivered a speech designed to influence the activity of the institution for many years. His speech is a masterpiece of classical academic oratory; it employed thoughtful flowing structure, and Bello's language demonstrated linguistic perfection at the height of its style. It was unmistakably crisp, elegant, pure, and harmonious. Bello served as rector of the university until the end of his days, in 1865, and during his leadership the institution flourished and more than fulfilled its mission.

The codification of law as a public activity

In 1840, Senator Bello presented a bill aimed at the creation of a Legislation Commission of the National Congress, composed of senators and deputies and responsible for codifying civil law. Unlike what had happened at the beginning of the previous decade, this time the motion received universal acquiescence. Bello and Mariano Egaña were appointed members of the commission by the senate. During the previous decade, Bello had advanced such projects considerably, and he now presented them gradually to the commission for discussion, review, and approval. Between 1840 and 1845, a preliminary title and sections addressing inheritance and obligations and contracts, which were published in *El Araucano*, were dispatched. Meanwhile, Bello, with great discipline, did not abandon his personal intellectual work. In 1841 he published his analysis of the development of of Castilian grammar, and in 1843 and 1844 he published ten articles on philosophy in the magazine *El Crepúsculo*. These articles became part of his book *Philosophy of Understanding*, published in complete form posthumously in 1881.

During the second half of 1845, the commission stopped its work, and Bello had to continue the work alone. In 1846 he reissued the revised sections on inheritance in one volume, and in 1847 the section on obligations and contracts in another. Over the following five years he continued drafting the still-missing parts of the project.

Bello's occupations were numerous by then. He had to attend to his positions as a senior officer of the Ministry of Foreign Affairs, rector of the University of Chile, senator, and editor of *El Araucano* in addition to dispatching the multiple pieces of advice and documents that the government incessantly ordered him to produce. He also continued his personal literary activity. Thus, for example, in 1846 he published the second edition of a Latin grammar. The first edition of this work had been written by Bello's son Juan, who died in 1845, and Bello introduced such substantial changes that the book has been considered his. In 1847 he published a grammar of the Castilian language destined for use in the Americas, a masterpiece of linguistics of his time and an enduring work to the present. In 1848 he published a cosmography, and by 1849 he was writing *Principles of Roman law*, an early follower of German legal historicism, which he never completed. To all of this must be added his usual articles for *El Araucano*, even though in the second half of the 1840s his health was very poor. Under such circumstances, the delay suffered in his work of codification since 1847 is understandable.

Despite these extensive activities, at the end of 1852 Bello delivered the finished draft of the Civil Code to the government for printing at the beginning of 1853. President Manuel Montt created a Project Review Commission and selected a number of legal experts as members, including Bello and several judges. The commission finished its work in the second half of 1855 and produced a revised draft that the government printed the same year for presentation to the National Congress. Almost without reservation, without examining the draft's articles, both chambers gave their approval as a whole. President Montt promulgated the law approving the Civil Code on December 15, 1855, with its effective date of January 1, 1857. Meanwhile, in May 1856, the definitive edition of the new code saw the light of day under Bello's supervision, about twenty years after Diego Portales had first encouraged him to undertake privately this writing. It was a work that would be celebrated around the world.

Private life

The Bello family enjoyed a relaxed life in Santiago, in stark contrast to the shortcomings of their situation in London. After spending some time in the Santiago residence of Juan Egaña when they arrived in Chile, Bello and his family settled in a rented house on Santo Domingo Street, between the current Miraflores and MacIver. He then moved permanently to a large house he purchased on

Cathedral Street, between Teatinos Street and the current Amunátegui. The house was located near Santa Ana parish, which Bello joined.

Bello typically rose early and worked at home until mid-morning. He then divided his time between the Ministry of Foreign Affairs and the university rectory. In the afternoons or in the evenings, he attended the senate when it was in session. As he did not usually sleep easily, he would continue working until late at night. Meals then were at different hours, and apart from breakfast there was a midmorning lunch, after which Bello left home to attend to his jobs; after a dinner around five in the afternoon, he could take a short walk through the Alameda de Las Delicias. Bello was fond of a good and abundant table and liked to smoke cigarettes. He even wrote a poem titled "Tobacco." Portales, as a merchant who had greater access to cigarettes, would send them from Valparaíso. In his spare time, Bello was happy to listen to music, especially transcriptions of opera pieces, which his daughters performed on the piano. He loved animals.

During the summers, the family moved to Valparaíso, about one hundred kilometers from Santiago. They were often the guests at Admiral Manuel Blanco Encalada's farm, or of José Antonio Álvarez Condarco, whom Bello met in London. They also stayed at property owned by Mariano Egaña in the town of Peñalolén, near the capital, where they built a large house (preserved to this day). Egaña provided the house with a large amount of furniture personally purchased in Europe, where he also acquired statues and fountains to decorate the gardens. Nonetheless, Bello worked during this season as well.

There are several oil paintings and daguerreotypes of Bello at various moments of his adulthood and old age. Through them, one forms the impression of a correct, distinguished, and pleasant face, not devoid of good looks.

The last years

By 1845, Bello had begun to suffer from various diseases, some serious, and his ailments continued into the following decade. They did not prevent him from concentrating on the final phase of drafting the Civil Code, although they delayed his progress. These diseases, however, forced him to diminish his formal obligations. In 1853, when he was seventy-three years old, he retired from the *El Araucano*. In 1855 he left the Ministry of Foreign Affairs. He could leave this position in part because the government enacted a law thanking him for the Civil Code and paying him a life salary in his post as chief officer of the ministry. He remained in the senate until 1864 and as rector of the university until his death in 1865. He had tried to step down in 1857, when he suffered an attack of paraplegia that caused a disability in his movement, but this attempt was not successful.

During this period, Bello lived in his house, where he was allowed to gather the University Council. He was completely lucid, kept his dedication to study, wrote his literary works, and maintained his abundant correspondence. He usually spent eight or nine hours a day in his personal library. He was also visited by his disciples, friends, admirers, and foreigners passing through Santiago. In 1851, the Royal Spanish Academy appointed him an honorary academic, and in 1861 he was bestowed an individual membership as corresponding foreigner, a newly created category. In 1864 he received appointment as an international arbitrator to resolve a dispute between the United States of America and Ecuador, and in 1865 a similar appointment in a dispute between Colombia and Peru. Given his advanced age and the state of his health, he declined both designations

On September 1, 1865, Bello became ill with bronchitis, and his condition worsened over the following weeks. In the midst of delirium, he perceived verses of the *Iliad* and *Aeneid* written in the curtains of his bed. He died at dawn on October 15, 1865. His death produced universal mourning in Santiago and throughout the country. It was estimated that ten thousand people attended his splendid funeral—chartered by the state—a sign of the deep respect and affection that all strata of Chilean society had for him. Funeral speeches eulogized his high personal qualities, the supreme value of his work, and the national and continental significance of his teaching. It is not often that the natural hyperboles usually resorted to on such occasions are in fact not exaggerated but deserved praise, faithful to reality and exactly descriptive of the life and work of the deceased. This was the case for Bello. The Chilean historian of the Pacific War, Gonzalo Bulnes, left a testimony of the private feeling caused by Bello's absence, when he recounted accompanying his father, former President Bulnes, to pay a final tribute to the deceased. President Bulnes said to his son: "I have brought you to see Mr. Bello, although dead, because in your life you will be honored to have been close to him."[4]

Notes

1 Bolívar, *Cartas del Libertador* 7:127–28.
2 Ibid.
3 Bello, "Spanish Legends, by José Joaquín de Mora," in Bello, *Obras completas de don Andrés Bello*, 9:337–48.
4 Jaksic, *Andrés Bello*, 260.

References

Bello, Andrés. *Obras completas de don Andrés Bello*, Vol. 15. Santiago: Pedro J. Ramírez and Rafael Jover, 1881–93. A second edition in 27 vols has been issued: Caracas: La Casa de Bello, 1981–84.

Bolívar, Simón. *Cartas del Libertador*. Caracas: Fundación Vicente Lecuona, 1969.

Jaksic, Iván. *Andrés Bello: The Passion for Order*. Santiago: Editorial Universitaria, 2001.

3 Félix Varela y Morales (Cuba, 1788–1853)

M.C. Mirow

Introduction

Félix Varela y Morales was an eminent Cuban intellectual of the nineteenth century. He was an educator, philosopher, deputy, writer, and public thinker, known as the man "who taught Cubans to think."[1] Above all, he was a priest, and this vocation guided his life and work.[2] Called to serve God at an early age, Varela was ordained in 1811 and died in poverty, having dispensed his goods for the benefit of the poor. Although he spent his last thirty years in exile, Cuba remained his homeland. Havana, Saint Augustine, Madrid, New York, and a second period in Saint Augustine were chronologically the cities of his life, and they witnessed a continuity of service, academia, publication, politics, and faith. He spent brief periods in Seville and Cádiz. Varela is widely recognized as a precursor of Cuban independence, and his influential activities continued into his years in exile in New York City. On March 6, 2012, the Congregation for the Causes of Saints permitted the cause for beatification to commence and, a few days later, declared Varela Venerable.[3] He taught constitutional law and was deputy for Cuba to the Spanish Cortes in his earlier years. These less-studied aspects of his life during the 1820s are the focus of this chapter. Here, Varela, a jurist and constitutionalist shaped by faith, is our topic.

Biographical information

Félix Varela was born in Havana, Cuba, on November 20, 1788, and baptized a week later.[4] His father, Francisco, was born in Spain and served as a lieutenant in the Spanish army; his mother, María Josefa, daughter of a lieutenant colonel, was born in Santiago de Cuba.[5] Both parents died before Félix was nine years old, and his upbringing was entrusted to his grandfather Brevet Colonel Bartolomé Morales y Remírez, who was the commander of the Cuban Third Battalion stationed at the Castillo San Marco in Saint Augustine, East Florida, then a province in the Spanish Empire.[6]

Varela received an excellent home education in Saint Augustine. Recent scholarship reveals that he did not attend the well-known school of Fr. Hassett, a famed educator that Spanish Governor Zéspedes had brought from Philadelphia to Saint Augustine. Varela may have received private instruction and guidance from the head of the school, Father Michael O'Reilly.[7] Despite his grandfather's hopes that Varela would join the military, he announced that he wished instead to serve Jesus Christ and to save souls.[8] His grandfather acquiesced, and Varela was sent to the Seminary of San Carlos, Havana.[9]

The intellectual tone of Havana was then set by Bishop Juan José Espada y Landa, who, with Governor Someruelos, brought many modern advancements to the city. Varela embraced Espada's approach. As a student, Varela attended lectures at the University of San Gerónimo, where Thomism reigned, and at his own Seminary of San Carlos, where faculty and students were open to newer avenues of thought.[10]

Varela spent the first decade of the 1800s enmeshed in study.[11] Preparing for his Bachelor of Arts degree, Varela studied traditional theological texts at the university and attended lectures at San Carlos on physics, ethics, logic, and metaphysics by luminaries of Havana's intellectual life of the early nineteenth century. Varela attained the Bachelor of Arts degree in 1806, and at age nineteen received his first tonsure and permission to wear clerical garb.[12] He received his Licentiate in Arts in 1807.[13] The following years led to the minor orders, the subdiaconate, and a Bachelor of Theology degree in 1808.[14] Shortly afterward, he received the Licentiate in Theology.[15] At some point, Varela began to study violin, became an accomplished musician, and promoted musical education and performance in Havana.[16]

With Bishop Espada's approval, Varela taught Latin and rhetoric at San Carlos as he prepared for ordination. He applied for and failed to attain more permanent teaching positions, but the process led to public awareness of his gifts. Varela was ordained a deacon in 1810 and, with dispensation for his young age so that his grandfather, now in Havana, could attend his ordination to the priesthood, he was ordained by Bishop Espada in the Cathedral of Havana on December 21, 1811.[17] A teaching position opened up for Varela when Fr. Bernard O'Gavan y Guerra, a central figure at San Carlos, was elected to represent Santiago de Cuba in the Spanish Cortes of 1810. Bishop Espada appointed Varela to a newly created professorship of philosophy at San Carlos, where Varela unabashedly promoted the modern learning of the nineteenth century.[18] Varela gave homilies on the reception of the Constitution of Cádiz of 1812 in Cuba and on the dispatch of the first set of constitutional deputies from Cuba to the Cortes in Cádiz.[19]

Varela also wrote. His first major work, a treatise on new philosophical ideas for seminary students, appeared in 1812, when he was in his mid-twenties.[20] A stream of writings followed that reflected his work as a teacher. In 1814, he produced two summary volumes on sciences, mathematics, and philosophy. During the 1810s, Varela prepared several different works on philosophy that eventually coalesced into his *Lecciones de filosofía* in three volumes, which was employed for teaching not only in Cuba but also in many areas of the Spanish-speaking world.[21]

Recognized for his progressive ideas and accomplishments, Varela was elected a member of the Royal Patriotic Society on January 24, 1817. Within the society, he focused on issues of public education.[22] In the world of Havana, he became widely known for his eulogies and encomiums of important figures, including King Ferdinand VII, during the 1810s. These public addresses displayed Varela's circumspection, honesty, and great skill in weaving a narrative of these lives that left his audience appreciative of the subject and impressed by the speaker. With the reestablishment of the Constitution of Cádiz in Cuba in 1820, Varela became the first professor of constitutional law in Cuba, wrote the first text on the Constitution in the Americas in 1821, and became a deputy for Cuba to the Constitutional Cortes in Madrid in October 1822.[23]

On the conclusion of the Cortes in Spain, political considerations led Varela to spend the latter half of his life in exile, from his arrival in New York City in 1823 until his death in Saint Augustine, Florida, in 1853.[24] In the second half of 1823, when Varela was serving as a Cuban deputy to the Cortes, Ferdinand VII regained absolute rule. Allied with liberals at the Cortes for his positions on autonomous rule of Spanish provinces in Latin America, the recognition of independence of Latin American republics, and the incapacity of Ferdinand VII to rule, Varela found his life in danger.

Varela fled to New York City, arriving there on December 15, 1823. In 1824, Varela relocated from New York to Philadelphia, where he remained for a short while. In Philadelphia, he published the first issues of *El Habanero*, a magazine that would address many aspects of Cuban politics, including reasoned arguments for Cuban independence from Spain.[25] For these reasons, the Spanish governor of Cuba labeled the magazine and its author subversive.[26] A royal court in Seville sentenced Varela and sixty-five other deputies of the Cortes to death with forfeiture of their property on May 11, 1825.[27] With the Cortes still on his mind in 1826, Varela published a Spanish translation of Thomas Jefferson's manual on parliamentary practice in the US Senate.[28]

Varela obtained proof of his ecclesiastical credentials in 1825 from Bishop Espada in Cuba. When Bishop Connolly granted Varela permission to serve as a priest in the diocese of New York, the entire diocese contained only about thirty-five thousand Catholics. The subsequent decades were also times of significant persecution for Catholics in New York, and Varela gained renown there as an apologist. From 1825 until his death, he served the parishes of New York City, including St. Peter's, St. James, and the Church of the Transfiguration, and he created an asylum for children of poor widows and widowers.[29] From 1826 to 1842:

> the Reverend Félix Varela led two lives. As devoted missionary pastor and erudite Catholic apologist, he became almost as illustrious in New York as he had been in Havana. And he continued to hold the torch for Cuban progress, proclaiming, like many of his compatriots, that love of one's country and service to her was a cradle-to-grave obligation.[30]

Varela was elevated to vicar general of the diocese of New York in 1829.[31]

Varela established several periodicals to spread Catholicism in New York and the United States. From 1846 to 1853, Varela, suffering from pulmonary illnesses, spent more time in the city of his youth, Saint Augustine, Florida, where he served as a priest.[32] Varela lived modestly, celebrated Mass when his health permitted, and received visitors in a room behind the parochial school assigned to him by the pastor.[33] He died on February 18, 1853, in Saint Augustine. Varela's library of over five hundred volumes was sold in New York in 1880. At his request, Varela's body was buried in a simple grave in Tolomato Cemetery in Saint Augustine.[34] A chapel dedicated to his memory was constructed in the same location with funds from Cuban patrons, and Varela's remains were transferred to the chapel on April 13, 1853. In 1911, Varela's bones were transferred to Cuba and placed in a marble urn in the Aula Magna of the University of Havana.[35]

This chapter focuses on Varela as legal scholar and constitutional actor by closely examining the content of his written work on the constitution and the activities he undertook as a constitutional deputy in Spain. Varela's work as a priest and as an intellectual voice for Cuban advancement and independence spanned nearly his entire life. His activities as professor of constitutional law, author of a constitutional treatise, and deputy in the Cortes are confined to the early 1820s.

Professor

Varela was an intellectual; he was at home in the classroom and laboratory.[36] He sought truth through observation and individual study and passed this fearless approach to knowledge along to his students. Although he is not remembered as a teacher of the hard sciences, Varela taught physics and chemistry, developed demonstrations, and conducted field trips.[37] He frequently taught philosophy and adopted Spanish instead of Latin as his language of instruction early in his career.[38] His students included some of the most eminent men of Cuba in the period.[39] A student encomium to the teachers of the seminary in 1815 praised Varela as an outstanding teacher.[40]

Varela taught constitutional law in the Seminary of San Carlos in Havana.[41] Spain and its territories entered its second constitutional period in 1820 when Ferdinand VII was obliged to submit to the Spanish Constitution of 1812, the Constitution of Cádiz.[42] The Constitution of Cádiz was promulgated again in Cuba.[43] Article 368 of the constitution required that all universities that taught ecclesiastical and political sciences must also explain the constitution.[44] With the backing of the Royal Patriotic Society of Havana, Bishop Espada planned the new academic position and the requirements to fill it at San Carlos.[45] Bishop Espada urged Varela to compete for the chair.[46]

Varela won and had only a few months to prepare the new course. Varela's student José Antonio Saco assisted in the preparation of the course, and Varela served in the position from January 18, 1821, when the chair was inaugurated, until April 1821, when he was named a deputy to the Cortes in Madrid.[47] When Varela was called to the Cortes, his student Nicolás Escobedo continued the course.[48] Through his teaching and writing, Escobedo continued Varela's work to publicize liberal constitutionalism in Cuba.[49] Saco continued to support Varela and his political and educational agenda. Another student of Varela's, Blas Osés y Pérez gained the chair of constitutional law at the Universidad Literaria de México on December 28, 1820.[50]

Varela's course, Political Economy and Constitutional Law, opened at San Carlos with 193 enrolled students and members of the public who crowded the doors and windows of the great hall of the college.[51] Contemporary political economy included general aspects of political science and public law, including the nation, sovereignty, representation, and rights.[52] Varela was not lukewarm about the new chair and its promise. In the inaugural lecture of the course, he stated:

> I would call this chair the chair of liberty, of the rights of man, of national guarantees, of the regeneration of illustrious Spain, the fount of civic virtues, the foundation of the great edifice of our happiness, that which for the first time has reconciled between us laws and philosophy, that is to say, that has made laws that curb both fanaticism and despotism, establishing and maintaining holy religion and wise government.[53]

This constitutional patriotism and fundamental understanding of Spanish constitutional principles and texts later led Varela to action as a deputy in the Constitutional Cortes in Madrid established under the Constitution of Cádiz.[54]

Varela's approach to the constitution in the classroom was to explain the articles of the constitution as found in the text. Nonetheless, he offered deeper discussions of constitutional and political terminology as well as the underlying ideas of the constitution. This led him to address broader topics, such as the nature of a constitution, sovereignty, the division of powers, the nature of representative government, elections, the legislative process, the king's veto, the nature of national and individual liberty, and rights and guarantees.[55] The course on constitutional law was short-lived. When Spain and Cuba returned to absolute royal rule under Ferdinand VII in 1823, the course was abandoned.[56] Varela's book on the constitution remained.

Observations on the political constitution of the Spanish monarchy, 1821

Varela's *Observaciones sobre la constitución de la monarquía española* (*Observations on the political constitution of the Spanish monarchy*) vies with Ramón Salas's *Lecciones de derecho público constitucional* (*Lectures on public constitutional law*), both published in 1821, as the first book on modern constitutional law in Spanish.[57] Like Salas, Varela adopted Gaetano Filangieri's idea of a peaceful revolution, a revolution that would change the political and social composition of the polity and nation without violence.[58] This concept, a cornerstone of Varela's constitutional thought, was consistent with his politically liberal and Catholic perspectives. Fernández Viciedo writes that Varela "not only expressed in his constitutional work a marked influence of Spanish liberalism but also of pre- and post-revolutionary French Enlightenment itself."[59] Varela's study of modern philosophy and political thought informed his approach to the Constitution.[60]

Portillo Valdés identified three major sources for Varela's course and book on constitutional law. The first was Benjamin Constant's *Principes de politique applicables à tous les gouvernements représentatifs et particulièrement à la Constitution actuelle de la France* (*Principles of politics applicable to all representative governments and particularly to the present constitution of France*). This work, published in 1815, was available after 1820 in a Spanish translation and, as noted by Jean-Baptiste Busaall, with significant expansion into liberal political theory and constitutional comparison by Marcial Antonio López.[61] The second of Varela's sources was Francisco Martínez Marina's constitutional history of Spain published in 1813, titled *Teoría de las Cortes o grandes juntas nacionales de los reinos de León y Castilla* (*Theory of the Cortes or the grand national juntas of the kingdoms of Leon and Castile*). To these, Varela added a third major source, the daily sessions of the Cortes. Varela supplemented these core studies with his already extensive knowledge of modern political philosophy.[62] Varela's study of the constitution was at the crossroads of many strands of contemporary constitutional thought incorporating and responding to the works of "Filangieri, Constant, Martínez Marina, and Bentham."[63] From these perspectives, Varela sought to explore the bases of the constitution not as a perfect document, but as an improvement from the prior situation and one offering a promising vehicle for a peaceful revolution.[64]

While Varela opted for an article-by-article discussion in the classroom, his book abandoned this method and took on broader thematic scope. The work itself consists of ten rigorous essays or observations on the text of the Constitution of 1812. These observations infrequently cited the text of the constitution, and Varela often skipped large areas of it to focus on what he believed to be most telling or important aspects. Varela was selective in his treatment. The text reveals the extent to which a Cuban priest and intellectual might embrace liberal ideas within the context of a deeply Catholic faith.

Varela examined sovereignty, liberty, and equality in the first two observations. Popular sovereignty was the basis of the constitution; Varela rejected the notion that sovereignty resided in the king as delegated by God. Although Varela recognized that all good comes from God, he warned that such "celestial doctrines" on the king's sovereignty had been subject to abuse.[65] He explained:

> Let us give, then, to Caesar what is Caesar's, which comes down to a temporal power conferred by peoples, and which no individual ought to disobey. Let us give to God what is God's, observing his holy law and the essential obligations of justice in whatever form of society, but never let it be said that a just and pious God has wanted to take away from men the rights that he himself gave them by their nature, and that setting up a tyrant, has made them slaves. Words of adulation are very different, but this is true religion.[66]

Reflecting on passages in the *Observations*, Fernández Viciedo concludes that Varela had a dual notion of sovereignty. Fernández Viciedo writes:

> At first, Varela recognizes an indivisible and unlimited aspect in the hands of society and in reference to the organization of government, but once this is formed, the same remains controlled by it [society], as a way to protect the freedom of the individual from the nation's power.[67]

The foundation of society for Varela was the nature of humanity and not the association of individual wills. Nonetheless, Varela was an early adopter of the notions of contract and pact in his discussions of the rise of sovereignty. He wrote of a mutual pact between the people and the supreme authority. In fact, following this line of thought, as a deputy in the Cortes, he voted for the incapacity of King Ferdinand VII to govern.[68]

This understanding of proper sovereignty led Varela to the ideals of liberty and equality. Liberty was expressed, for Varela, on national and individual levels, and he turned to Benjamin Constant and Montesquieu to provide definitions of the term. On the individual level, liberty implicated personal property, individual freedom, domestic freedoms, and many protections for criminal defendants consistent with Enlightenment principles and the principle of legality. On the national level, liberty meant a government of laws supporting equality, which, for Varela, was expressed in three forms: natural equality, social equality, and legal equality.[69] Slavery did not appear in his observations at this, the most natural point in his discussion. Indeed, one scholar writes, "The mere fact of avoiding mention in his work of any favorable reference to the concession of political rights to those called free people of color, would not have passed unnoticed by his contemporary *habaneros*."[70]

In the third observation, Varela defined "political constitution" in the context of political science, "the science containing the reciprocal rights of those who govern and those who are governed," according to Jacob Friedrich Bielfeld's definition adopted by Varela.[71] Varela addressed the division of powers in the fourth observation. A division of power among the representative (legislative), executive, and judicial branches of government was necessary to avoid despotism. After this general observation, and without much more explanation, Varela shifted to an extensive discussion of the king's veto within the constitutional system of enacting legislation.[72] By placing so much emphasis on the king's role in legislation, Varela excluded many broader considerations of the balance of powers. One finds almost no mention of judicial power, a cornerstone of modern balance of power analysis, although Varela later takes this up in the seventh observation.

The fifth observation addressed the unicameral legislative body established under the Constitution of Cádiz. Varela objected to the creation of legislative bodies in Spain defined by nobility or by estates, not only because he had practical concerns about the variability and complexity of the Spanish nobility but also because of his political concern for union and cohesion.[73] He wrote:

> We repeat, a thousand and one times, that everything directed toward giving preference to one class of individuals over the others brings disunion, and is a method contrary to the present state of Spain and to progress, which has brought light to her and to all nations.[74]

Deputies, impediments to serving as a deputy, and the various rights and limitations attached to deputies were the topic of the sixth observation. Varela also addressed the right of a deputy to be tried by the Cortes for crimes, and the restrictions on deputies arranging for jobs or pensions for their relatives. He also examined representation for elections and noted inconsistencies in the exclusion of black residents (*castas*) and foreigners from the electoral process.[75]

In the seventh observation, addressing the attribution of powers, Varela tackled the nature of the regency, the king's power to declare war and make peace, the power to impede communications of the Roman Catholic Church to the nation, the limitation of *fueros* (special jurisdictional privileges), and the judiciary. Concerning the king's power over war and peace under the constitution, Varela provided extensive lists of pros and cons, including several opinions from past deputies.[76] The power to review communications from Rome under the constitution was a complicated process, a modern restructuring of the king's right under the royal patronage of the Church in colonial times. The constitution gave the king the following power:

> To allow to circulate or to retain conciliar decrees and pontifical bulls with the consent of the Cortes if they contain general dispositions; hearing the Council of State if they deal with particular or governmental matters; and, if they contain contested matters, sending his notice and decision to the Supreme Tribunal of Justice so that they are resolved in accordance with law.[77]

Varela observed that while this right to review and distribute the communications of the Church in the nation fundamentally was a right of the king as executive, the constitutional process complicated matters and even created problems in the proper allocation of power among the various branches of government.[78]

Varela also addressed judicial power in the seventh observation. Courts were constitutionally prohibited from any other business than deciding cases. He noted the prohibition of trials under courts established by commission rather than those created under constitutional authority. Similarly, the constitution revoked *fueros* that were common in colonial Spanish law. Now, only the military and ecclesiastical *fueros* continued under the constitution; everyone was subject to the same law in the same court. Varela discussed appellate structures in elaborate detail and noted the odd possibilities that a few appellate judges might overrule a greater number of judges in lower tribunals.[79]

Municipal and regional governments were the topic of the eighth observation. Varela noted that the nature of these institutions was administrative and not representative. Only the Cortes were representative; municipal and provincial government was an extension of the executive power. The eighth observation also addressed public education, a topic provided for in the constitution itself.[80]

The ninth observation examined disparate sections of the constitution. Varela questioned the presence of aspirational or hortatory language in the constitution that could not be reduced to positive law, such as the requirement to love one's country.[81] He also briefly examined classes of individuals who did not have the rights of citizens, such as those who were bankrupt, domestic servants, and minors. Varela noted the provision for freedom of the press and the requirement of no reforms to the constitution for eight years. Similarly, the tenth and final observation addressed a few specific questions related to elections.[82]

Thus, Varela's *Observations* addressed an eclectic mix of topics and questions. The work is stronger on the institutional and structural aspects of the constitutional monarchy than it is on the protections offered to citizens and the expression of constitutional rights and guarantees. This is not surprising; the Constitution of 1812 offered no list or declaration of individual or human rights. The positive rights offered to residents and citizens were scattered throughout the text, so it is not strange that Varela did not address these together.

Varela's use of the debates is noteworthy. First, this method of explaining the constitutional text shows that Varela had carefully considered this important source. Passages from the debates not only shed light on various articles and their meaning but also must have informed Varela on the style and form of intervention at the Cortes. Second, Varela considered explanatory passages from a number of luminaries at the Cortes of the early 1810s. In Varela's exposition of the Constitution, he referred to or quoted José Mejía Lequerica (New Granada), José Miguel Guridi y Alcocer (Tlaxcala), Agustín Argüelles (Asturias), the Conde de Toreno (José María Queipo de Llano, Asturias), José Espiga (Cataluña), Vicente Morales Duárez (Peru), and Felipe Aner (Cataluña), among others. Mejía Lequerica, a botanist from Quito, was a leader of the liberal American group of deputies and served as head of a commission of American deputies.[83] Argüelles and the Conde de Toreno were among the liberal and young faction of the deputies at the drafting of the constitution.[84] Argüelles, Duárez, and Espiga (another noted liberal) were on the influential drafting committee for the constitution; Argüelles and Espiga wrote the Introduction (*Discurso Preliminar*) to the constitution, a guiding work used to justify and interpret the text.[85] In the Cortes, Mejía Lequerica argued for the inclusion of blacks as political actors.[86] Guridi y Alcocer had advocated for the inclusion of blacks in the representative polity and the abolition of slavery.[87] On the other hand, Morales Duárez rejected black citizenship in the Cortes in 1811.[88] And Felipe Aner alleged that American deputies sought to include black citizenship merely to augment the region's political power.[89] Varela used passages from deputies with varying political standpoints and convictions to interpret the constitution and the issues it raised.

Varela's study of the constitution exposed fundamental themes excavated by someone with his training, interest, and faith. National sovereignty was created by God to ensure an ordered political system of freedoms and obligations. Representative institutions at the provincial and municipal levels reflected the necessary community to construct an effective government. Varela was conscious of attempts by peninsular Spaniards to limit the voice and vote of American Spaniards. He understood the document and its aims in its complex and transcontinental context. The constitution provided a structure of weights and counterweights to repel despotism and to dampen human passions leading to unfavorable results in government. Even the king's veto under the constitution was understood in this light. And the underlying Catholicism of the Spanish nation asserted in the constitution supported this view. Varela's reading of the constitution was filtered through his faith and his advanced philosophical understanding.[90]

Varela's work on his *Observations* provided an excellent background for his service in the Cortes as a deputy. He had considered the underlying philosophical and political structures of the document. Varela's frequent citation of many deputies from the Cortes that drafted the constitution indicated that he had worked through the main interpreters of the work and was familiar with their contributions and perspectives. Nonetheless, the *Observations* must be considered a preparatory work to Varela's engagement at the Cortes. There is surprisingly little overlap between his systematic exposition of highlights of the constitution in the *Observations* and the topics that led to Varela's contributions at the Cortes.

Deputy in the Cortes

Varela established his local expertise in the constitution through his course and his book. It was not surprising when he was selected to represent Cuba at the Spanish Cortes in Madrid. Bishop Espada supported Varela's service as deputy, and the course on the constitution was turned over to Nicolás Escobedo; Varela's philosophy duties were taken up by José Antonio Saco.[91] Other deputies elected to represent Cuba were Tomás Gener y Bohigas, Leonardo Santos Suárez, and José de las Cuevas.[92] A former student of Varela's, Felipe Poey y Aloy, studied law in Spain at this time and was in contact with his teacher.[93]

Varela spent about two and a half years in Spain. He arrived in Cádiz on June 7, 1821, and departed Europe from Gibraltar on October 26, 1823. He attended the Cortes as they fled French forces from Madrid, to Seville, and to Cádiz.[94] Varela carried with him and developed three extensive plans for the Cortes on the government overseas provinces, on recognizing the independence of American provinces, and on gradually extinguishing slavery.[95]

As chronicled by biographer Fidel Rodríguez, procedural objections and technicalities plagued Varela's full participation at the Cortes until the end of 1822.[96] Although elected for the 1822–23 session, Varela was not seated, because the Cortes annulled his election in Cuba for irregularities raised by political opponents. Varela was successfully reelected in November 1821, but notice of this reelection and accompanying documentation was delayed. Additional required papers were lost in a shipwreck on their way to Spain. After months of waiting for the appropriate paperwork and certifications, Varela, with Gener and Santos Suárez, was sworn in as deputy and given his seat in the Cortes on October 3, 1822.[97]

Despite the delay of more than a year in his admission to the Cortes, Varela used the time wisely. He attended the sessions as a member of the public, observed the nature of debate, joined political discussions that spilled out of the legislative sessions, and read widely in preparation for his duties. He worked informally with the other Cuban deputies to advance the interests of his region.[98]

Through the independence of American provinces, financial constraints, and the difficulties of travel to the Cortes, the representation of overseas regions was substantially limited. Although fifty-nine deputies from overseas participated in the 1820–21 legislative sessions, by the time Varela was seated, only a handful of overseas deputies represented Cuba, Puerto Rico, and the Philippines.[99] Varela distinguished himself at the Cortes through clear and reasonable advocacy of his positions, and he spoke on a wide range of topics.[100] Varela made notable contributions to the Cortes in the areas of overseas provincial government, the recognition of independent former colonies, the Church, and education. Although he had prepared to address the extinction of slavery, he did not present these plans to the Cortes.

Government

Varela was appointed to a commission to prepare a political and economic structure for provincial governments that developed into a plan for decentralized self-government for Cuba and other, similar territories.[101] The commission included Santos Suárez (Havana), José María Quiñones (Puerto Rico), Manuel Sáenz de Vizmano (Philippines), and two peninsular deputies. This plan was the natural outgrowth of the work the Cortes had already completed on a plan of government for the provinces of the peninsula and adjacent islands.[102] The commission sought a responsive and responsible system of governance that stressed the well-being of the colony over the enrichment of royal officials.[103] The 189 articles addressed all aspects of the governor, the provincial deputations, and municipal government. The plan included the ability of representatives to remove a governor for cause and of local authorities to suspend the application of peninsular legislation that would be a poor fit to the particular colonial circumstances.[104] This aspect of colonial suspension, or noncompliance, had a substantial history in the colonial *derecho indiano*.[105] The plan also included public education; agricultural, commercial, and industrial development; public works and the administration of public funds; and health and sanitary planning. Varela shepherded this project through the required readings of the proposed legislation and the twelve substantive debates held on its provisions from March 15 to May 30, 1823.[106] As French troops reestablished Ferdinand VII's power in 1823, the project was under detailed and final consideration by the Cortes when they were disbanded.[107]

Independence

The rebellion and independence of overseas provinces were constant political facts of the first decades of the nineteenth century, and the Cortes sought to address these challenges to Spain's sovereignty. In January 1822, before Varela was able to participate fully in the Cortes, the deputies considered a plan to send commissions to the Americas to determine the present state of unrest and the political desires of provinces. Deputies debated at length and considered a plan to recognize independence where it was already established, to cease hostilities, to establish a lasting peace, and to continue fruitful commerce through a federation of states.[108]

Another report drafted by Varela urged independence for prior colonies and incorporated his approach that independence should result from a peaceful, reasoned process rather than armed revolution.[109] Varela urged the Cortes to recognize that many former colonies in the Americas had passed the tipping point to independent republics. Recognizing these countries' independence, Spain should then build new economic alliances through international law.[110] Independence was widely debated in the final months of the Cortes as they sat in Cádiz while French troops swept through Spain. In the beginning days of August 1823, the commission on overseas provinces suggested commissions to discuss treaties to regularize relationships between Spain and newly independent countries. Though informed by his earlier plan, Varela's efforts failed, and the regular session of the Cortes was closed on August 6, 1823. A few days later, Varela published a long statement in a newspaper explaining his thought on independence in light of the actions of the Cortes.[111]

Church

Although the Constitution of Cádiz provided for Roman Catholicism as the official religion of the state, the Cortes of the 1820s had done much to dissipate the privileged position of the Church in Spanish society. The Cortes abolished the Inquisition and suppressed the Jesuits, monasteries, convents, and religious orders as popular anticlericalism spread. Some clergy openly supported an absolute monarchy against the constitutionalists. Nonetheless, in this atmosphere, Varela sought to harmonize his religious faith and vocation with the constitution and its institutions.[112] Rodríguez wrote:

> It is important to note that in Cuba, ecclesiastics like Bishop Espada and Fathers Varela, O'Gavan, Justo Vélez, and others of their group were considered liberals and were enthusiastic promotors of the reform of studies and the Enlightenment that included at the same time support of the Constitution.[113]

Such beliefs usually also encompassed the abolition of slavery; the advancement of science, education, technology, and agriculture; free trade; and the promotion of material, intellectual, and spiritual well-being. Nonetheless, when the Cortes moved against the Church with legislation undermining its independence and material support, Varela as priest and deputy experienced a serious conflict.[114]

Once seated as a deputy, Varela worked on numerous legislative proposals and drafts related to the Church. For example, in his first contributions as a deputy, on October 11, 1822, he worked on the role of chaplains in the military. He spoke on vacancies of bishops resulting from their anti-constitutional activities. Varela unsuccessfully spoke at length to support a proposal that would not diminish the ecclesiastical *fuero*. He addressed the financial relationship between the Church and the state, and the faculty of American bishops during the war with France.[115] Varela brought his faith in the institutional church to the debates and protected its interest against the position of anticlerical deputies in the Cortes.

Education

Varela's educational expertise led him to advance educational reform and, particularly, a plan for Cuba that included the elevation of the seminary in Havana to a university. On May 14, 1822, Varela presented his plan for public education to the Cortes. Through this plan and supporting documents, Varela argued that the Dominican University of San Jerónimo, also in Havana, was less equipped to take on the functions of a modern university than the seminary because it lacked scientific facilities and taught in a scholastic method. A description of the state of education in Havana supplemented this proposal. Legislative interest continued in the educational condition of Cuba, and in June 1822, an extensive questionnaire was dispatched to Cuba to determine the institutional, financial, and intellectual climate of the country with the creation of a national university there in mind. Varela took part in addressing these questions. In the legislative session of 1823, Varela was appointed to the commission on public education, where he addressed education at all levels. The cause for the university moved forward in the sessions held in Seville.[116]

Slavery

Varela lived in cities where enslaved humans and their suffering were a constant presence. He, however, had no enslaved humans or servants. His parents and grandparents held enslaved humans who were freed either during his relatives' lives or at their deaths.[117] Slavery and the trafficking of enslaved humans were issues in the Cortes that had drafted the Constitution of Cádiz more than a decade before Varela arrived in Madrid, but at the time it was closely tied to Cuba and its political and economic power within the empire.[118] Wealthy Cuban slaveholders, the financial reliance of the Cortes on American wealth to repel invasion, and concerns of violent racial uprisings were deciding factors in maintaining slavery within the Constitution of Cádiz at its drafting.[119]

Varela's plan called for compensation for slaveholders, a broader agricultural base, the assimilation of formerly enslaved humans into Cuban society as salaried workers, and the increase of Cuba's white population to create a racial balance on the island.[120] Varela's hopes for the extinction of slavery and of slave traffic were at odds with the commercial and agricultural powers Varela represented in Havana, whose fortunes were built on enslaved humans.[121]

In the 1820s, slavery came before the Cortes in many different ways. For example, when considering the draft criminal code before Varela was seated as a deputy, the Cortes had to consider the provisions for violations of a ban on slave trading, a topic greatly affecting Cuba. In April 1821, the Cortes discussed slavery in a session held in secret because of the sensitivity of the matter, making little headway. Similarly, in December 1822 the Cortes considered responses to Spain's treaty with England extinguishing the slave trade and Spain's lax enforcement of the treaty requirements. Although this might have been a propitious time for Varela to introduce his plan for the gradual extinction of slavery, he withheld his proposals. In fact, by the time Varela's service in the Cortes ended and he fled Cádiz for Gibraltar in 1823, he had never presented his plan for the gradual extinction of slavery. Scholars have debated whether this inaction was the product of his perceived allegiance to those in Cuba who supported slavery, an unfinished agenda stifled by the long delay of his admission into the Cortes, his assessment of political realities, or some other reason.[122]

In the Cortes generally

Varela was a skilled speaker in the Cortes, where he moved fellow deputies with his measured, studied, and respectful oration. Varela took up various activities and topics at the Cortes. He worked with other American deputies to remove Cuba and Puerto Rico from the impact of general legislation that might be harmful to the interests of overseas provinces. The American deputies also sought rules beneficial to the islands in matters such as trade.[123]

Varela's main interventions were at odds with the political and economic moments experienced by Cuba and Spain as a whole. In the decades leading up to the Cortes of 1822, Cuba had made a decided turn toward modern plantation economy undergirded by enslaved humans to fulfill colonial production for the Spanish Empire.[124] The abolition of slavery certainly ran counter to this vision. Furthermore, his notions of substantially autonomous rule for provinces and the recognition of the independence of Spanish American colonies to establish beneficial commercial and trade relationships were most likely based too much on realistic observations of the present situation rather than the peninsular hopes of maintaining economic and colonial structures of past decades. His interventions to protect the Church and its prerogatives also went against the general trends, although he provided clarity and considered action by the Cortes through his advocacy. Public education was less contentious, and here Varela's contributions were valued and often in tune with the spirit of the Cortes.

Conclusion

Varela is best known as an intellectual precursor to Cuban independence and as a compassionate and charitable priest who shaped Catholicism in New York during the middle decades of the nineteenth century. A third, and less studied, facet of Varela was his work in law and constitutionalism during the 1820s. Varela's teaching and writing broke new paths in this field. His intellectual mastery of the Constitution of Cádiz led him to apply this knowledge in the Spanish Cortes, where he took on massive projects in colonial governance and education while making substantial contributions to ecclesiastical matters, relations between the constitutional state and the Church, and debates about independence of former colonies. He was unfortunately unable to advance his projects to extinguish slavery. As teacher, writer, and politician, Varela was constantly shaped by his faith as a Roman Catholic priest. He saw each activity as imbued with a spiritual purpose to improve humanity and alleviate its suffering through modern principles of constitutional law. When the political and constitutional project of the Cortes disintegrated into royal absolutism, Varela, exiled in New York City, turned to those in spiritual need, the immigrant Catholics of his adopted city, and to those in political need, his fellow Cubans. In the most important things, Féliz Varela acted consistently throughout his entire life.

Notes

1 McCadden and McCadden, *Félix Varela* 1. De Céspedes attributes this to José de la Luz Caballero, who wrote "he was the one who taught us first to think." José de la Luz Caballero, *Gazette of Puerto Principe*, May 2, 1840, as cited in De Céspedes, "The Life, Thought, and Significance of Father Félix Varela."
2 Rodríguez, *Profundidad*, 103.
3 Paglia, *The Faith of Father Varela.*
4 McCadden and McCadden, 1.
5 Ibid., 1; Rodríguez, *La inquietud*, 122–27.
6 McCadden and McCadden, 2; Rodríguez, *Profundidad*, 87.
7 Ibid., 73, 75–76.
8 McCadden and McCadden, 6; Rodríguez, *La inquietud*, 106.
9 McCadden and McCadden, 6; Rodríguez, *Profundidad*, 92.
10 McCadden and McCadden, 11, 13.
11 Rodríguez, *Profundidad*, 106–29.
12 McCadden and McCadden, 13–14.
13 Rodríguez, *Profundidad*, 132–33.
14 McCadden and McCadden, 2.
15 Rodríguez, *Profundidad*, 141–42.
16 Rodríguez, *La inquietud*, 46–48; Rodríguez, *Profundidad*, 223–30.
17 McCadden and McCadden, 15, 17; Rodríguez, *Profundidad*, 162–67.
18 McCadden and McCadden, 17, 21–23.
19 Portillo Valdés, "Estudio preliminar," xix, xxii.
20 Varela, *Institutiones philosophiae eclecticae.*
21 McCadden and McCadden, 24–25. The work saw several editions: McCadden and McCadden, 70.
22 Ibid., 29–30; Rodríguez, *Profundidad*, 212–22.
23 McCadden and McCadden, 31–34, 41.
24 Ibid., vii.
25 Ibid., 49, 54–56.
26 Portillo Valdés, "Estudio preliminar," xxii–xxiii.
27 McCadden and McCadden, 59, 60–63.
28 Hernández Travieso, 342–43.
29 McCadden and McCadden, viii–ix, 68, 72–104.

30 McCadden, "The New York-to-Cuba Axis," 382.
31 McCadden and McCadden, 78.
32 Ibid., 112–13, 120–30.
33 Ibid., 129–33. For Varela's modest sources of income and his charitable expenditures see Rodríguez *La inquietud*, 112, 116–17.
34 Ibid., ix, 133, 138, 141.
35 Ibid., 142–45, 155–56.
36 Ibid., 17; Rodríguez, *La inquietud*, 383–84.
37 McCadden and McCadden, 20–21, 26–27.
38 Fernández Viciedo, 37.
39 McCadden and McCadden, 27; Rodríguez, *Profundidad*, 203–04; Valdés Domínguez, *Los antiguos diputados*, 225.
40 Valdés Domínguez, 278–82. For Varela's qualities as a teacher see Rodríguez, *Profundidad*, 255–60.
41 McCadden and McCadden, vii; Rodrígucz, *Profundidad*, 264–74.
42 Mirow, *Latin American Constitutions*, 113–15.
43 Mirow, "The Constitution of Cádiz in Cuba and Florida," 194–211.
44 Portillo Valdés, "Estudio preliminar," vii. For an English translation of the Constitution of Cádiz, see Mirow, *Florida's First Constitution.*
45 Varela, *Observaciones*, 5.
46 Portillo Valdés, "Estudio preliminar," xxii.
47 Ibid., xxii.
48 Fernández Viciedo, 36.
49 Pelegrín Taboada, *Shades of Liberalism*, 134.
50 Rodríguez, *La inquietud*, 384, 192, 273.
51 McCadden and McCadden, 35.
52 Portillo Valdés, "Estudio preliminar," xii.
53 Varela, *Observaciones*, 3.
54 McCadden and McCadden, 38.
55 Varela, *Observaciones*, 4–5.
56 McCadden and McCadden, 53.
57 Portillo Valdés, "Estudio preliminar," viii, xviii. Portillo Váldez provides a fruitful analysis and comparison of these works in Portillo Valdés, "Estudio preliminar," ix–xl.
58 Ibid., xiii.
59 Fernández Viciedo, 53.
60 Portillo Valdés, "Estudio preliminar," xix.
61 Ibid., xxiii. Busaall, "Constitution et *gouvernement de modernes*," cited in Portillo Valdés, "Estudio preliminar," xxiv.
62 Portillo Valdés, "Estudio preliminar," xxiii.
63 Ibid., xxv.
64 Ibid., xxv–xxvi.
65 Varela, *Observaciones*, 13.
66 Ibid., 14.
67 Fernández Viciedo, 46.
68 Ibid., 41, 43–44. This was the vote on June 11, 1823, to move the Cortes from Seville to Cádiz over the king's objection. Those supporting the move were later found guilty of lèse majesté and sentenced to death. Rodríguez, *La inquietud*, 20–424, 427.
69 Varela, *Observaciones*, 17–20.
70 Fernández Viciedo, 47.
71 Varela, *Observaciones*, 21.
72 Ibid., 25, 28–35.

73 Ibid., 37–39.
74 Ibid., 39.
75 Ibid., 47–48, 50, 53–55, 56–59.
76 Ibid., 61–72.
77 Constitution of Spain (1812), Art. 171(15), Mirow, *Florida's First Constitution*, 37.
78 Varela, *Observaciones*, 66–67.
79 Ibid., 67–72.
80 Ibid., 73–75.
81 Ibid., 79; Constitution of Spain (1812), Art. 6, Mirow, *Florida's First Constitution*, 16.
82 Varela, *Observaciones*, 79–85.
83 Mirow, *Latin American Constitutions*, 77, 96.
84 Ibid., 39–40, 51.
85 Ibid., 40, 56–57.
86 Ibid., 95–96.
87 Ibid., 96–99.
88 Ibid., 7.
89 Ibid., 95.
90 Portillo Valdés, "Estudio preliminar," xxvi–xxxvix.
91 McCadden and McCadden, 38; Rodríguez, *La inquietud*, 149–52; for Varela's short address on departing Havana, see Valdés Domínguez, 287.
92 McCadden and McCadden, 39; Rodríguez, *La inquietud*, 149; Valdés Domínguez, 18, 223.
93 Rodríguez, *La inquietud*, 27.
94 Ibid., 21.
95 Ibid., 22, 51, 540–54; see also Maza Miquel, 243–63.
96 Rodríguez, *La inquietud*, 36, 49–50, 62, 64–68, 132–34, 138–39, 154, 184–85, 195–96, 198–203, 207, 220–21, 244–45, 264, 274–75.
97 Ibid., 24, 49–50, 275–77.
98 Ibid., 36, 76, 220, 232–33, 271.
99 Ibid., 199–200.
100 McCadden and McCadden, 41.
101 Ibid., 41.
102 Rodríguez, *La inquietud*, 336–37, 359.
103 McCadden and McCadden, 42; Rodríguez, *La inquietud*, 362.
104 McCadden and McCadden, 42; Rodríguez, *La inquietud*, 398–99.
105 Mirow, *Latin American Law*, 235–37.
106 Rodríguez, *La inquietud*, 374–77, 393–99 (in Seville), 405–06 (in Seville), 413–16 (in Seville).
107 McCadden and McCadden, 43, 47–49.
108 Rodríguez, *La inquietud*, 170–76.
109 McCadden and McCadden, 43.
110 Ibid., 43; Portillo Valdés, "Estudio preliminar," xxxix.
111 Rodríguez, *La inquietud*, 458–71, 534–37.
112 Ibid., 82–85.
113 Ibid., 87.
114 Ibid., 88, 93, 201–02
115 Ibid., 284, 291–92, 352–55, 371–72, 409, 453.
116 Ibid., 94, 221–28, 255–60, 365, 397.
117 Ibid., 115; Rodríguez, *Profundidad*, 65, 174–75.
118 Rodríguez, *Profundidad*, 157–60.
119 Mirow, *Latin American Constitutions*, 95–101.

120 McCadden and McCadden, 46; Rodríguez, *La inquietud*, 52–53.
121 Rodríguez, *La inquietud*, 52, 162–63.
122 Ibid., 163–68, 177, 333–34, 475–80, 501.
123 Ibid., 302, 311–12, 317, 321, 349, 400–01, 445.
124 Portillo Valdés, "Estudio preliminar," xx.

References

Busaall, Jean-Baptiste. "Constitution et *gouvernement de modernes* dans l'Espangne du Triennat Libéral, concepts juridiques et modèles politiques." In *La Guerre d'Indépendence dans les révolutions espagnoles du XIXe siècle (1808–1875)*, edited by Jean-Philippe Luis and María Cruz Romero Mateo. Clermont-Ferrand: Université Blaise Pascal, 2008.

De Céspedes García-Menocal, Carlos Manuel. *The Life, Thought, and Significance of Father Félix Varela*. New York: Fordham University, January 27, 2005.

Fernández Viciedo, Yuri. "Félix Varela Morales y el Origen de la Enseñanza del Constitucionalismo en Cuba (1818–1824)." *Revista de Historia del Derecho* 47 (2014): 33–57.

Gay Calbó, Enrique. "El Padre Varela en las Cortes Españolas, 1822 y 1823." *Revista de la Universidad de La Habana* 14 (1937): 109–29.

Hernández Travieso, Antonio. *El Padre Varela: Biografía del Forjador de la Conciencia Cubana*. Miami: Editorial Universal, 1984.

Ibarra Cuesta, Jorge. *Varela el precursor: un estudio de época*. Havana: Editorial de Ciencias Sociales, 2004.

Maza Miquel, Manuel Pablo. *Por la vida y el honor: el presbítero Félix Varela en las Cortes de España 1822–1823*. Santo Domingo: Instituto Pedro Francisco Bonó, 2000.

McCadden, Joseph J. "The New York-to-Cuba Axis of Father Varela." *The Americas* 20, 4 (1964): 376–92.

McCadden, Joseph J., and Helen M. McCadden. *Félix Varela: Torch Bearer from Cuba*. 2nd ed. San Juan: Ramallo Bros., 1984.

Mirow, M.C. *Florida's First Constitution, The Constitution of Cádiz: Introduction, Text, and Translation*. Durham, NC: Carolina Academic Press, 2012.

Mirow, M.C. *Latin American Constitutions: The Constitution of Cádiz and Its Legacy in Spanish America*. Cambridge: Cambridge University Press, 2015.

Mirow, M.C. *Latin American Law: A History of Private Law and Institutions in Spanish America*. Austin: University of Texas Press, 2004.

Mirow, M.C. "The Constitution of Cádiz in Cuba and Florida." In *The Rise of Constitutional Governments in The Iberian Atlantic World: The Impact of the Cádiz Constitution of 1812*, edited by Scott Eastman and Natalia Sobrevilla Perea, 194–211. Tuscaloosa: University of Alabama Press, 2015.

Navia, Juan M. *An Apostle for the Immigrants: The Exile Years of Father Félix Varela y Morales (1823–1853)*. Salisbury, MD: Factor Press, 2002.

Paglia, Vicenzo. *The Faith of Father Varela and His Path to Sainthood*, March 21, 2016, https://nccfcommunity.org/the-faith-of-father-varela-and-his-path-to-sainthood/.

Pelegrín Taboada, Ricardo. *Shades of Liberalism: Lawyers and Social, Political and Legal Transformations in Nineteenth Century Cuba*. Unpublished PhD dissertation, Florida International University, Department of History, Miami, FL, 2018.

Portillo Valdés, José María. "Estudio preliminar." In Félix Varela y Morales, *Observaciones sobre la Constitución política de la Monarquía Española* , vii–xl. Madrid: Centro de Estudios Políticos y Constitucionales, 2008.

Rodríguez, Fidel E. *Félix Varela: Profundidad Manifesta I: Primeros Años de Vida del Padre Félix Varela Morales: Infancia, Adolescencia, Juventud (1788–1821)*. Miami: Ediciones Universal, 2007.

Rodríguez, Fidel E. *La inquietud del tiempo: El diputado Félix Varela Morales en las Cortes españolas (1821–1823)*. Madrid: Editorial Verbum, 2018.

Valdés Domínguez, Eusebio. *Los antiguos diputados de Cuba y apuntes para la historia constitucional de esta isla*. Havana: Imprenta El Telegrafo, 1879.

Varela, Félix. *Escritos políticos*. Havana: Editorial de Ciencias Sociales, 1977.

Varela, Félix. *El Habanero: papel político, científico y literario*. Miami: Revista Ideal, 1974.

Varela, Felix. *Institutiones philosophiae eclecticae*, Vol. 2. Havana, 1812.

Varela y Morales, Félix. *Observaciones sobre la Constitución política de la Monarquía Española*, edited by José María Portillo Valdés, vii–xl. Madrid: Centro de Estudios Políticos y Constitucionales, 2008.

4 Mariano Egaña (Chile, 1793–1846)

Javier Francisco Infante Martin

Introduction

Some men live their entire lives under the same political system. Their perspectives on legal, social, economic, and religious matters never vary. Others live exactly the opposite; they change viewpoints many times throughout tumultuous days. Mariano Egaña was in the latter group, and he became one of the main agents of change during his time.

His vast knowledge of law, history, and political economy, in its classical sense, led him to become one of the most controversial figures of his time as well as one of the most powerful men during the transition period that followed the South American Wars of Independence. At his peak, he designed a political system that would shape Chilean politics and structures for almost a century and would survive a civil war, three wars against foreign states, and several minor revolts. Even after the Chilean Civil War of 1891, between a strong executive and Congress, long after Egaña's death, his constitution was not amended, proving that it only needed to be otherwise interpreted to become a useful tool in the new parliamentary regime. Even after the revocation of Egaña's constitution, many of its provisions were replicated in the new Constitutions of 1925 and 1980.

The importance of individuals like Egaña during the independence period is key to understanding their contributions to Chilean legal development. His work lacked the intellectual consistency of other luminaries of the period. For example, José Miguel Infante made lasting contributions to liberal and federal ideas. Manuel de Salas, and even Egaña's father, Juan, shaped the country's civic-aristocratic republicanism model. Nonetheless, Mariano Egaña shaped the new political system that would emerge after the war. A strong supporter of a conservative political regime, he opposed first the authoritarian regime under Bernardo O'Higgins, then the federal model promoted by José Miguel Infante and other liberals, and finally the liberal regime set up under the Constitution of 1828 that was defeated in battle in 1829. During all of these events, he served as an authoritative voice of the conservative movement, serving as minister and Supreme Court prosecutor. Despite his strong conservative ideas, many inherited from the colonial period as well as from his early education, he had one feature that distanced him from others on the same political bench: his pragmatism and capacity for concretizing his discourse and ideas into political and legal institutions. Unlike his father, Mariano managed to make his constitutional opinions an undisputed reality and accepted political fact: authoritarian rule survived under a republican structure.

This chapter explores Egaña's intellectual formation and the varying positions he held during his active years. Egaña managed to take advantage of those positions to install his political ideas and form them into political institutions. Such ideas included his opposition to the abolition of slavery or the federal regime, and his support of the constitutional process that led to the Constitution of 1833 and the position of the Catholic Church inside that scheme.

A brief biography

Mariano Egaña was the eldest son of Chilean-Peruvian jurist Juan Egaña and his wife Victoria Fabrés, the latter with solid roots in Chilean aristocracy. Juan Egaña was one of the founding fathers and intellectuals of Chilean independence, as well as the drafter of the Chilean Constitution of 1823 and three other constitutional projects.[1] Thus, Mariano Egaña received a strict and detailed education as a child under the direct tutelage of his father.[2] He then received his law degree in 1809 from the Real Universidad de San Felipe, and, at eighteen years old, was admitted to the bar in 1811, just in time to participate in the first moments of the Wars of Independence.

During the first stage of independence, Egaña worked as secretary for the interior in 1813. This position led to his captivity and confinement in the Juan Fernández Islands when the Spanish Restoration took place between 1814 and 1817. Those were hard years for Egaña, who was accompanied by his father. His exile ended only after the definitive triumph of Chilean independence in 1817.

After his return to Chile, Egaña was appointed as a law clerk (*teniente asesor letrado*) for the Santiago Intendancy, a position created during the Bourbon reforms in the final years of the colonial period. He provided legal assistance to the local governor and served as a judge in financial and other matters.[3] Egaña was then appointed minister for the interior and foreign relations (*Ministro del interior y de relaciones exteriores*) before being appointed plenipotentiary minister to the United Kingdom, France, Russia, the Netherlands, and Spain.[4] He returned to Chile in 1829 and was again appointed minister for the interior and Supreme Court prosecutor (*Fiscal de la Corte Suprema*), a position he held until his death. Nonetheless, his most important role was probably as a member of Congress (*diputado*), a position to which he was elected in 1831. As deputy, Egaña became involved in the initial process for the reformation of the Constitution of 1828, which finally ended in the Constitution of 1833. In this role, Egaña exercised substantial influence and shaped Chilean institutions until 1925 and, in a less direct manner, the present day.

Beyond these appointments, Egaña was one of the few intellectuals to shape the first years of the new republic.[5] He defended many ideas that were later labeled as conservative, although his inspiration may as well have been liberal or at least enlightened, as one can see throughout his works. This fact is especially visible in his approaches to the role of the Church in the institutional framework of the constitution and in the Church's interactions with the government.

Egaña's thought was the product of two main influences. First was the education he received from his father, who dedicated himself to his son's intellectual formation. The second was Egaña's long residence in the United Kingdom, a period that left an imprint on his political thought, to the point of earning him the curious nickname Lord Callampa (Lord Mushroom) among his contemporaries—alluding to his admiration of constitutional monarchies.[6]

Juan Egaña took extreme care in the education of his sons and daughters, and Mariano, the eldest, received special attention. Juan Egaña had acquired one of the greatest libraries in Chile, comprising works that covered the classics to the Enlightenment and even included some censored authors. As a lawyer, Juan Egaña had a special predilection for the classical world—Roman law, culture, literature, and philosophy. He had a truly humanistic spirit, which he tried to transmit to Mariano, creating a personalized educational program and materials to teach him Latin in a different way than the classic books on the subject.[7] Unlike his father, Mariano Egaña was not a prolific writer of monographs. Juan Egaña was aware of his legacy as an author; the publication of his complete works speaks for itself. Mariano, in contrast, wrote legal and political opinions in newspapers, judicial reports, legal advice, and private and official letters. Much of his written work, such as his reports as Supreme Court prosecutor, remains to be published. Many of his private and official letters have already been published, giving historians privileged access to his inner thoughts and convictions.

Egaña died in 1846, and he was posthumously awarded public recognition from official authorities. President Manuel Montt, in a letter to Egaña's daughter, described him as "a wise and profound legislator, honest officer, dominated by a burning love for the Motherland, a distinguished statesman and indefatigable citizen in promoting public well-being."[8]

The ideas of a Catholic founding father

Egaña's complete intellectual heritage has yet to be studied, although the influence of his father is evident in many parts of his constitutional works, provoking debate on the origins of Egaña's political inspiration. According to his most recent biographer, Enrique Brahm García, Egaña's thought incorporated his fervent Catholicism, his authoritarian perspective on politics, and his mistrust of democracy—a view that is supported by historical consensus.[9] Fernando Campos Harriet, following Alberto Edwards, also emphasizes the father–son heritage but highlights Egaña's pragmatism when comparing him with his father.[10]

Egaña's academic formation and early politics were also profoundly shaped by his personal experience in Europe as plenipotentiary minister. He was appointed in 1823 by the new government led by Ramón Freire, perhaps in acknowledgment of Egaña's role in the fall of O'Higgins. Even though he became an absent figure of Chilean politics during his time in Europe, his extensive letters demonstrate how his views on the theory of government, the vision of his own country, and even his father's political positions varied during those five years. His central ideas, and thus the pillars of his political work, were the installation of the notion of political virtue into the republican system, the overcoming of political anarchy, the consecration of a stable government, and the establishment of reliable governmental functions in the executive branch.

Political virtue and the republic of merit

In one of his first letters to his father while on diplomatic mission, Egaña was a sharp critic of the Chilean debt and the method of paying it off by means of a tobacco monopoly. After definitive independence was accomplished in 1817 by the Argentinian general José de San Martín, the Chilean government presided over by Director O'Higgins agreed to finance and support the continuation of liberation, projecting it toward Peru, the last crucial stronghold of Spanish forces in the Southern Hemisphere. For that purpose, Chile entered into a loan from English bankers to finance a liberating expedition of naval forces led by San Martín and Lord Thomas Cochrane and composed of Argentinian, Chilean, and English soldiers and officers. After the convulsive years that followed O'Higgins's renunciation of the directorship, Chile stopped its payments on the loan. Instead, in 1824, a monopoly was given to private entrepreneurs who would have exclusive right to sell tobacco, tea, liquors, and playing cards. In exchange, the holders of the monopoly assume the obligation of paying the foreign debt.

The merchants were José Manuel Cea and Diego Portales. Portales was destined to be, in a few years, one of the leading architects of the political institutions under the Chilean Constitution of 1833, and thus a close collaborator with Egaña. Nonetheless, Egaña, in a letter of 1825, did not hesitate to criticize the plan and its participants:

> They take walks and laugh in social gatherings, and toast to the health of the government they know so well: they have the right to be considered with the courtesy that in Chile is dispensed to bad people, with preference to the good ones...It is not possible to serve such a country.[11]

This anecdote illustrates one of Egaña's significant concerns in politics and governance: his preference for the higher offices of the state to be filled by virtuous political citizens. A full appreciation of Egaña's constitutional model requires the study of other facets of his intellectual background and his political experiences before joining the Constituent Assembly of 1831.

Order in the house

After Egaña´s departure to Europe, Director Ramón Freire initiated a new military campaign to end, once and for all, the presence of Spanish troops in the Chilean south. Even though in 1824 the Chilean government was installed throughout the territory, the Chiloé Islands remained under Spanish rule. Thus, Freire took command of the troops and headed south to the Chiloé Islands.

Egaña's career as a diplomat in Europe probably moved his mind in the direction of favoring a more authoritarian political regime. According to Jaime Eyzaguirre, Egaña "achieved a great perspective because of his time in Europe as a diplomatic agent of the Chilean Government (1824–29). He then was able to appreciate in England the discredit that Chile was harvesting because of its [political] disorganization."[12] Edwards agrees with Eyzaguirre, stating that Egaña's years in England were decisive in the construction of his political views.[13]

The embarrassment Egaña suffered in England because of Chile's political dysfunction led to his support of an energetic executive, following the example of the British Government and constitutional monarchy, and building on the political foundations inherited from his father.[14] Vasco Castillo, however, has observed, "the solution proposed by Mariano Egaña points towards the strengthening of the executive power to face the dangers of a vicious populace."[15] By doing this, according to Castillo, Egaña took a different path than his father, who trusted virtue to be the cornerstone of the political system.[16] Egaña chose to endorse a robust presidential model, echoing the ideas of the central political figure of those years, Minister Diego Portales. Góngora goes one step further, and views Egaña's tendency towards a stable government—a "portalian" idea—as the only solution in a country with no political virtue.[17] In a letter to his father, Egaña listed all the causes of the political disorder that was suffocating Chile: "Chile has lost as much as a country can lose…the complete ruin of public morality; a delay in education; the fact of letting the citizens become used to a life without [political] institutions."[18]

The culmination of his argument was that democracy, as a system, could not promote the political conditions for a virtuous political community: "This democracy, father, is the worst enemy of [Hispanic] America, and for many years it will cause it many disasters," thus enforcing his idea of an authoritarian regime as the most suitable for the new American countries. In his perspective the "essence of public liberties" was to be sustained by two simple rules:

> 1) That laws are approved and contributions are decreed by a sufficient number of representatives of all the social classes, and 2) that judges enjoy the most complete independence and safety while in office…[and] all other power must be trusted to the moral or physical person that administers government.[19]

One must remember that Egaña was a lawyer. Indeed, at one point his friend Diego Portales mocked him for being a supporter of the rule of law, habeas corpus, and the right to be considered innocent until proven guilty. As Portales wrote:

> the good fellow [ironically] of Mr. Mariano has answered me not by a letter, but by a report, not a report but a treatise, about the nonexisting faculty

> that a government may have to detain suspects only because of their political affiliation...In summary: by following the judgment of jurist Egaña, facing the threat of an individual to overthrow the authority, the government must stay arms crossed, while, as he points, he [the individual] is not surprised in flagrance.[20]

The relationship between Egaña and Portales improved during the establishment of the authoritarian republic, and Egaña would align himself with Portales as the main supporter of a strong executive.[21] The lawyer in Egaña would tend to prevail in some matters, exposing him to the critics of politicians like Portales. While the latter had a more pragmatic approach to obtaining political results, Egaña placed his trust in the legal mechanisms with a fundamental respect for the constitution and other political civil rights and guarantees. He was, above all, a true believer in constitutional order and the rule of law. An excellent example of this can be found in his participation as one of the drafters of the Constitution of 1833 in the Constitutional Committee to which he was elected.

Once the Constitutional Committee was installed, Egaña submitted his own draft as a basis for the work of the committee. Many of the articles contained in it were adopted in the final version of the constitution. An important example is what has been identified as the "Golden Rule of Chilean public law," contained in Article 160 of the Constitution of 1833. It states:

> No officer or person or gathering of people can attribute to themselves, not even under the pretext of extraordinary circumstances, other authority or rights than those expressly granted by the laws. Any act in contravention to this article is invalid.

As Eduardo Soto has noted, this rule has no real precedent in any Chilean or foreign rule, and thus it was probably inspired by the works of Egaña's father and his own local political experience.[22] This rule, a mainstay of Chilean constitutional structure, has survived the political process through the years and was reproduced in the Constitution of 1925 (Article 4) and the current Constitution of 1980 (Article 7).

All of Egaña's political ideas rested firmly on the classical principles of politics, of which his father was probably the principal contemporary exponent. From this perspective, political strength rests on civic virtue, and virtue is supported by tradition, public morality, and education.

The rule of law was of vital importance in Egaña's political ideas. A strong executive was needed, but it also had to be supported by definite laws and entrenched in the political tradition of the country. In one of his letters to his father from France, Egaña wrote of his fascination with French political institutions that were sustained in laws supported by traditions: "Laws are nothing without traditions, even when they are the result of greater knowledge and civilization."[23]

Supporting a strong executive, one must establish the standard appropriate for a republican regime, argued Egaña. Some historians have characterized Egaña as a monarchist. Manuel Carrasco, for example, states that, with respect to the powers of Congress during the constitutional process of 1831, Egaña sustained ideas far from a republican model:

> Impregnated with monarchist ideas, he wanted to make of the Senate a sort of [British] House of Lords or Roman Senate, which represented the interests of the church and some kind of territorial nobility.[24]

Ricardo Donoso, less radical in his judgment, wrote that Egaña's years in Europe led him to "look with deep sympathies on the constitutional monarchy."[25]

Recent studies suggest a more reasonable option. Even though Egaña was an admirer of the British and French political systems, he was also a supporter of the republican model. He admired these other countries not for their political models but instead for the political guarantees they ensured. Bernardino Bravo, in his study of the Constitution of 1833, asserts that the powers of the president "are as wide as the ones that used to belong to the governor-capitan general-president during the colonial period, and even superior in many points to the ones of the king himself."[26] Enrique Brahm García is more cautious. For him, "the critics of Mariano Egaña, both his contemporaries as well as historians, accused him of being monarchical...The truth being said, these critics have some reason."[27] Others highlight the ambiguous character of the presidency.[28] Finally, others like Simon Collier read Egaña in what I think is the right approach: "Mariano Egaña...never considered a reversal to monarchy, either an absolute or constitutional kind."[29]

Whatever opinion historians may have on the true spirit of the Constitution of 1833 and, subsequently, the inspiration of Egaña's constitutional thought, the question must be viewed in historical context. Egaña was born during colonial rule but distanced himself from unconditional loyalty at a young age. He then suffered the consequences of the absolutist Restoration and even participated in the ending of the O'Higgins government, widely accepted as authoritarian. His subsequent experience as a diplomat coincided with what many Chilean historians have named a period of anarchy. Both experiences were decisive in his political inclinations, explaining his subsequent preference for a robust authoritarian regime.

Again, two letters manifest his views on the Chilean political process. In one letter, Egaña wrote to his father, Juan: "Believe me, my father, that such is the sad notion of Chile in Europe's concept, that I am ashamed that anyone may recognize me in the street."[30] In a second letter, Egaña mocked the federalist ideas circulated by leading political figure José Miguel Infante and the consequences these ideas had on the lack of political leadership: "No obstacles, my father, in the most intrinsic faculty of government, which is the appointment of its subordinates. Otherwise, we will have the *Republic of Infante.*"[31]

Egaña's views were not monarchical but were perhaps authoritarian and centralist, given his experiences. In any case, they were republican, given the content of the Constitution of 1833. Even when, as historians have noted, the president gathered almost every essential political power into his hands, it is also true that the same constitution was later applied, after a few nonsubstantial modifications, to a parliamentary regime (1891–1925). Even before then, Congress had gained continuous power through the years, having, since its origin in 1833, essential capabilities such as the annual approval of the national budget.[32] Although the mainstream historiography has repeated many times that the presidential regime better fits the "national spirit,"[33] it is only fair to assume that those involved in the Wars of Independence were not open to the adoption of a monarchy.[34]

Mariano Egaña and the Catholic Church

Egaña's religious beliefs did not necessarily live harmoniously with his political ideas but submitted to them. He was a strong supporter of the authoritarian republic from a temporal perspective. He was a firm and uncompromising advocate of the privileges he considered inherent to the civil government, including the patronage of and control over the Catholic Church.

Egaña received a complete Catholic education from his family and was very strict in his devotion, attending Mass frequently.[35] His convictions were never an obstacle to his role as a public servant. Nonetheless, like his father, he had no problem with the idea of Catholicism being the official religion of the state, as established in the Constitution of 1833.

Egaña's recognition of Catholicisim as the state religion followed both the colonial tradition and the influences of his father, whose constitutional works included the same position on this issue. Juan Egaña's views may be interpreted as placing the state above the Church. Many see a contradiction between the enlightened ideas that allegedly inspired Egaña and a staunch conservatism in line with monarchical and colonial social structures. The correct approach, however, is found in the context of the author. Egaña, in agreement with republicanism, considered the term "republic" in its classical sense: a political regime, opposed to monarchy and sustained in specific values, mainly civic virtue. One must also not forget the political role of the Catholic Church under Bourbon reformism.[36] Civic virtue, another inheritance from his father's tutelage, had a close relationship to the Catholic Church and religious education. During colonial rule, Catholicism was the only religion allowed, and the Crown was its main protector. The logical consequence was to consider the new republican government as the continuation of the Crown in all its prerogatives over the Church, such as the patronage and tithe collection. There was also the indirect influence over certain public duties performed traditionally by the Church, such as running of schools and hospitals. Furthermore, since religious education was the basis of all morality, private or public, the Church held the most important position in the formation of the virtuous citizen. Hence a correlation between religion and enlightenment had a political role in the formation of the new republic.

Despite this symbiotic relation, Egaña's main pillar of the new political regime was a strong and almost omnipresent government. Therefore, in any possible conflict between the power of the state and the prerogatives of the Catholic Church, Egaña took the side of the state.

A good example of his siding with the state occurred in 1832. The episcopal office of the Diocese of Concepción had been vacant since 1816, and Ignacio Cienfuegos had served as the administrator for a long time. Cienfuegos was a central political figure and—though a principal supporter of federalism and, therefore, of the alleged anarchy of the previous years—an undisputed patriot. Because of the long period without a proprietary bishop, President Prieto proposed, using his right to do so, Ignacio Cienfuegos as the Chilean state candidate for the position of bishop of Concepción, to which the Holy See agreed.

Nonetheless, when the papal bull arrived in Chile, it avoided any mention of the Chilean government's proposition, appointing Bishop Cienfuegos as a *motu proprio* decision of the pope. As prosecutor of the Supreme Court, Egaña had the duty to inform the government of any providence given by a foreign state—the inherited *exequatur* procedure. Even when the response was in favor of the Chilean proposition, Egaña's position was to reject it, since it ignored the patronage prerogatives of the Chilean state.[37] His opposition to the bull was ignored, and the government finally recognized the appointment made by the Holy See with some variation. This event and Egaña's position perfectly illustrate the reasoning behind his regalism. Diego Barros, however, later qualified Egaña's position on the obedience of the Church to the civil government as "intransigent and immovable."[38]

Whichever opinion one may have on Egaña's position concerning the role of the Church in the new republic, he always stood for the primacy of the rule of law, whoever was involved. This was a clear expression of one the fundamental aspects of Chilean republicanism: equality before the law.

Conclusion

As Julio Heise has noted, Egaña perhaps "dreamed of a government in the style of King Charles III,"[39] the archetype of political despotism in the Spanish Empire. It is, however, hard to sustain the belief that Egaña dreamed of a monarchy. A man of his time, and aware as he was of the political and social context, he probably recognized that republicanism was the only viable solution for the political chaos that followed independence. There is no reference that implies any open support of his for a Chilean monarchy for Chile. As one of the principal and most influential people of his time, Egaña would not consider the idea of losing the political liberties obtained after independence at both the national and local levels. Egaña was an enthusiast of political tradition and political stability, and his views on monarchy must be understood from a republican perspective: a complete democracy in a new political community would result in chaos and misrule, and thus an energetic executive, surrounded by prestige and unquestionable political power, was the temporary solution. From Egaña´s perspective, republicanism was the correct choice, but a modest republicanism, so that the political structures that until then had ensured the political, judicial, and religious control by enlightened and trusted residents of the capital would not suffer any modifications. In the end, he proposed a unique form of republican monarchy.

The position of the local church in this context is a good example. Despite his personal religious views, Egaña, as a statesman, would endorse only decisions that confirmed the patronage of the state over the Church, especially considering the public role of the Church in the republican structure. He believed in a church at the service of the state, and a state protecting the true faith. Thus, republican patronage was the only logical solution to be pursued by the new government he designed, a position that finally triumphed and lasted until the Chilean Constitution of 1925.

Notes

1 Javier Infante, *Antiguo régimen e ilustración en Juan Egaña: estudios sobre gobierno, justicia, guerra y hacienda* (Santiago: Ediciones Bicentenario, 2017).
2 José Santiago Melo, "Don Mariano Egaña," in *Galería Nacional o colección de biografías y retratos de hombres célebres de Chile*, ed. Narciso Desmadryl (Santiago: Imprenta Chilena, 1854), 2:89.
3 There were three intendancies in Chile. From north to south: Coquimbo, Santiago, and Concepción.
4 Santiago Melo, "Don Mariano Egaña," 92.
5 He was one of the main sponsors of the Universidad de Chile, a new institution designed to replace the colonial Real Universidad de San Felipe. Diego Barros Arana, *Historia general de Chile*, vol. XVI, *Organización de la república 1820 a 1833 (continuación)* (Santiago: Editorial Universitaria, 2001), 243. After this new institution was inaugurated, he became the first dean of the law school. Egaña´s university became a beacon of light for the more disadvantaged portions of Chilean society, although it was later overshadowed by other universities.
6 His admiration for the British constitutional regime is not as evident in the mainstream historiography. Enrique Brahm García, *Mariano Egaña: derecho y política en la fundación de la república conservadora* (Santiago: Editorial Bicentenario, 2007), xiv.
7 Javier Infante Martin, "Juan Egaña contra la nación de comerciantes. Educación, religión y ciudadanía en la formación republicana," *Revista de Historia del Derecho* 48 (July–Dec. 2014): 75–98.
8 Santiago Melo, "Don Mariano Egaña," 99.
9 Brahm García, *Mariano Egana* , xiv–xv.
10 Fernando Campos Harriet, *Historia constitucional de Chile: las instituciones políticas y sociales* (Santiago: Editorial Jurídica de Chile, 1977), 358. Alberto Edwards states that Egaña was "the son of the more theoretical of the classics, of the most incorrigible of the dreamers, of the author of the inquisitorial and academic Constitution of 1823." Alberto Edwards, *La organización política de Chile* (Santiago: Editorial del Pacífico, 1943), 118.
11 Mariano Egaña and Juan Egaña, *Cartas de don Mariano Egaña a su padre, 1824–1829*. With an introduction by Anyceto Almeyda (Santiago: Editorial Nascimento, 1948), 105.
12 Jaime Eyzaguirre, *Historia de las instituciones políticas y sociales de Chile* (Santiago: Editorial Universitaria, 1979), 96.
13 Edwards, *La organización política de Chile*, 118.
14 Barros Arana brilliantly summarizes Egañas point of view:

"[While] progressive in the administration, empassioned by intellectual culture and determined to spread it, he was contained in his role as reformer because of his attachment to traditional concerns, and by his political principles propitious to the constitution of a fair and just government, but strong and vigorous enough to make itself respected if needed. The conservation of public tranquility and the ordained functioning of the state justified, in Egaña's opinion, the sacrifice of some liberties which can only be enjoyed in more advanced nations." Barros Arana, *Historia general de Chile XVI*, 216.

15 Vasco Castillo, *La creación de la República. La filosofía pública en Chile 1810–1830* (Santiago: Ediciones LOM, 2009), 191.
16 Cf. Infante, *Antiguo régimen e ilustración en Juan Egaña.*
17 Mario Góngora, *Ensayo histórico sobre la noción de estado en Chile en los siglos XIX y XX* (Santiago: Ediciones Universitarias, 1986), 75.
18 Egaña and Egaña, *Cartas de don Mariano Egaña a su padre*, 253–54.
19 Ibid., 263.
20 Diego Portales to Antonio Garfias, December 6, 1834, in Diego José Víctor Portales, *Epistolario*, ed. Carmen Fariña Vicuña (Santiago: Ediciones de la Universidad Diego Portales, 2007), 589.
21 Portales also mistrusted democracy. In one of his most famous letters, he states that

> "The democracy that the deluded preach so much, is an absurdity in countries like the [Hispanic] Americas, full of vices and where citizens lack all virtue, as is it necessary to establish a true republic…The republic is the system to be adopted. But do you know how I understand it for these countries? A strong, centralized government, whose men are true models of virtue and patriotism, and so guide them through a path of order and virtue. Once they have become moralized, let the true liberal government [rise], completely free and full of ideals, where all citizens take part."

Diego Portales to Mr. Cea, March 7, 1822, in Portales, *Epistolario*, 9. On this point, the similarity between Portales and Egaña is obvious.

22 Eduardo Soto Kloss, "La regla de oro del derecho público chileno," *Revista de Estudios Histórico-jurídicos* XV (1992–93): 354.
23 Anyceto Almeida, *Cartas de don Mariano Egaña a su padre*, 296–97.
24 Manuel Carrasco Albano, *Comentarios sobre la Constitución política de 1833* (Valparaíso: Imprenta y Librería del Mercurio, 1858), 93.
25 Ricardo Donoso, *Las ideas políticas en Chile* (México: Fondo de Cultura Económica, 1946), 98.
26 Bernardino Bravo Lira, "La constitución de 1833," *Revista Chilena de Derecho* 10, no. 2 (May–Aug. 1983): 322.
27 Brahm García, *Mariano Egaña*, 124.
28 For example, Francisco Zúñiga Urbina states: "The Constitution of 1833 did not strictly adjust to the presidential regime; but neither did it follow the parliamentary regime of England. There were adopted dispositions from both [models], with a presidential preponderance." Francisco Zúñiga Urbina, "La Constitución conservadora de 1833 y la vision crítica de Juan Bautista Alberdi," *Revista de Derecho Constitucional* 23 (May–Dec. 2010): 314.
29 Simon Collier, *Chile. La construcción de una República 1830–1865: política e ideas* (Santiago: Ediciones de la Universidad Católica de Chile, 2005), 172.
30 Anyceto Almeida, *Cartas de don Mariano Egaña a su padre*, 119.
31 Ibid., 267.
32 Eyzaguirre even writes that the "Constitution was built on reasonable checks and balances." Jaime Eyzaguirre, *Fisionomía histórica de Chile* (Santiago: Editorial Universitaria, 1996), 128.

33 "[They] created, then, the constituents of 1833, a supreme chief of the nation molded in memory of the colonial structure. Nothing could be more in accordance to the country's idiosyncrasy than what was [its] tradition." Alberto Edwards, "La constitución de 1833," *Revista Pacífico* 5 (May 1913): 596.
34 Ibid., 598.
35 Brahm García, *Mariano Egaña*, 181.
36 As has been highlighted in other works, one of the main pillars of Bourbon Reform, especially under King Charles III, was the assignment of a new role to the Church, almost as a branch of the new *administración*, following French Bourbon experiences as Gallicanism. This idea of a national church, even though it never settled in the Spanish Empire, reinforced the prerogatives that the Crown had over the Church—most evident in the expulsion of the Jesuits in 1767—and was later projected into the new independent countries. For the Chilean case, see Lucrecia Enríquez Agrazar, "La iglesia y la crisis monárquica," in Fernando Silva Vargas and Juan Eduardo Vargas Cariola, eds., *Historia de la República de Chile Volumen 1: El fin de la Monarquía y los orígenes de la República (1808–1826)* (Santiago: Zig Zag, 2013), 712.
37 Ricardo Montaner Bello, *Historia diplomática de la independencia de Chile* (Santiago: Editorial Andrés Bello, 1961), 394.
38 "[Egaña was] as prosecutor of the Supreme Court, and after that as senator, minister and member of the State Council, an indefatigable defendant of civil government prerogatives, the reason why the members of the clergy looked at him with an attitude very similar to hatred." Barros Arana, *Historia general de Chile* XVI, 112.
39 Julio Heise González, *150 años de evolución institucional* (Santiago: Editorial Andrés Bello, 1979), 57.

References

Barros Arana, Diego. *Historia General de Chile*, Vol. 16, *Organización de la república 1820 a 1833 (continuación)*. Santiago: Editorial Universitaria, 2001.

Brahm García, Enrique. *Mariano Egaña: derecho y política en la fundación de la república conservadora*. Santiago: Centro de Estudios Bicentenario, 2007.

Bravo Lira, Bernadino. "La Constitución de 1833." *Revista Chilena de Derecho* 10, no. 2 (1933): 317–29.

Campos Harriet, Fernando. *Historia constitucional de Chile: las instituciones políticas y sociales*. Santiago: Editorial Jurídica de Chile, 1977.

Carrasco Albano, Manuel. *Comentarios sobre la Constitución política de 1833*. Valparaíso: Imprenta del Mercurio, 1858.

Collier, Simon. *Chile. La construcción de una República 1830–1865: política e ideas*. Santiago: Ediciones de la Universidad Católica de Chile, 2005.

Donoso, Ricardo. *Las ideas políticas en Chile*. Mexico City: Fondo de Cultura Económica, 1946.

Edwards, Alberto. "La Constitución de 1833." *Revista Pacífico* 5 (1913): 593–604.

Edwards, Alberto. *La organización política de Chile*. Santiago: Editorial del Pacífico, 1943.

Egaña, Juan, and Mariano de Egaña. *Cartas de don Mariano Egaña a su padre, 1824–1829*. With an introduction by Anyceto Almeyda. Santiago: Editorial Nascimento, 1948.

Enríquez Aagrazar, Lucrecia. "La Iglesia y la crisis monárquica." In *Historia de la República de Chile volumen 1: El fin de la Monarquía y los orígenes de la República*, edited by Fernando Silva and Juan Eduardo Vargas, 711–25. Santiago: Zig Zag, 2013.

Eyzaguirre, Jaime. *Fisionomía histórica de Chile*. Santiago: Editorial Universitaria, 1996.

Eyzaguirre, Jaime. *Historia de las instituciones políticas y sociales de Chile*. Santiago: Editorial Universitaria, 1979.

Góngora, Mario. *Ensayo histórico sobre la noción de Estado en Chile en los siglos XIX y XX*. Santiago: Ediciones Universitarias, 1986.

Heise González, Julio. *150 años de evolución institucional*. Santiago: Ediciones Andrés Bello, 1979.

Infante Martin, Javier. *Antiguo régimen e ilustración en Juan Egaña: estudios sobre gobierno, justicia, guerra y hacienda*. Santiago: Ediciones Bicentenario, 2017.

Infante Martin, Javier. "Juan Egaña contra la nación de comerciantes. Educación, religión y ciudadanía en la formación republicana." *Revista de Historia del Derecho* 48 (2014): 75–98.

Montaner Bello, Ricardo. *Historia diplomática de la independencia de Chile*. Santiago: Editorial Andrés Bello, 1961.

Portales, Diego José Víctor. *Epistolario de Diego Portales*. Edited by Carmen Fariña Vicuña. Santiago: Ediciones de la Universidad Diego Portales, 2007.

Santiago Melo, José. "Don Mariano Egaña." In *Galería nacional o colección de biografías y retratros de hombres célebres de Chile*, edited by Narciso Desmadryl, Vol. 2, 87–100. Santiago: Imprenta Chilena, 1854.

Soto Kloss, Eduardo. "La regla de oro del derecho público chileno." *Revista de Estudios Histórico-Jurídicos* XV (1992–93): 333–58.

Toribio Medina, José. *Historia de la Real Universidad de San Felipe*. Santiago: Imprenta Universo, 1928.

Zúñiga Urbina, Francisco. "La Constitución conservadora de 1833 y la vision crítica de Juan Bautista Alberdi." *Revista Mexicana de Derecho Constitucional 23* (2010): 307–27.

5 Justo Donoso Vivanco (Chile, 1800–68)

Cristóbal García-Huidobro Becerra

Introduction

For much of its history as part of the Spanish colonial empire, Chile was one of the most distant provinces of the Spanish Crown, and it played a marginal role within the imperial economy. Additionally, the presence of hostile Indigenous peoples (the Mapuches) along the southern border of the country drained economic and military resources for their containment, which placed a heavy burden on the imperial treasury. Nonetheless, from a military point of view, Chile's strategic position in South America was vital to the security of the viceroyalties of Peru and the Río de la Plata. Chile served as a barrier against possible invaders, especially one of Spain's closest competitors for imperial hegemony, Great Britain. It was perhaps this motive that led the Spanish Crown to invest in the development of such a distant and backward outpost. From the mid-eighteenth century on, the reforms implemented by the Spanish Bourbons in their American domains sought to increase the power of the Crown, to strengthen imperial bureaucracy, to stimulate the economy, to make tax collection more efficient, and to invigorate the power of the state through a gradual process of administrative centralization. Chile was no exception to these reforms.

The country's sparse population, primarily dispersed in the countryside, exacerbated the colony's economic backwardness. It was for this reason that, as early as 1715 and before other parts of the empire, a policy of founding cities was established in Chile. After seventy-five years, this policy had led to the development of more than twenty-five urban settlements. Along with the new cities came the opening of new markets and growth in interurban trade, which increased the demand for more agricultural products. Likewise, increased commercial exchange led to a gradual improvement in the collection of taxes by the colonial authorities. The rate of this fortunate cycle was accelerated by an increase in the production of cereals, especially wheat, owing to the demand for these products in the Peruvian market.[1]

This series of events led the Spanish Crown to promote a second reformist stage in Chile. It was now time to develop the infrastructure and colonial administrative institutions. For example, addressing the lack of an institution of higher education, in 1747 the Royal University of San Felipe in Santiago became a reality, through a *real cédula* (royal order) of Philip V, followed by the creation of institutions of secondary education.

To strengthen the judiciary, the colonial administration created two new courts—a tribunal of commerce and another with jurisdiction over mining. Indeed, the reformist momentum did not stop there. The foundation of the Contaduría Mayor, which handled the accounts of the kingdom in addition to the construction of roads, bridges, and other public works that facilitated communications and transportation, became the symbol of the renewed interest of the Crown in one of its most distant and backward territories.

Chile entered the nineteenth century with a robust bureaucracy and a growing infrastructure. Perhaps underdeveloped in comparison to more prosperous provinces within the empire, Chile slowly thrived in various ways thanks to the Bourbon reforms. Unavoidably, however, Chile had to suffer the full weight of the crisis of the Spanish monarchy. The Napoleonic invasion of Spain opened the way for the struggle for national independence in Chile, the construction of the republic, and its consolidation as a viable state. These were the crossroads in the country where Bishop Justo Donoso Vivanco was born. He lived in a country in transition, from the *ancien régime* to modernity, paraphrasing François Xavier Guerra.

The War of Independence, nothing less than a civil war, counterposed two conflicting ideological models that were complicated to reconcile. Nevertheless, despite the struggle for independence, essential parts of colonial institutions endured into the republic. Donoso's life and works were shaped by and contributed to Chile's historical framework. Lawyer, priest, and canonist, he dedicated his life to safeguarding the rights of the Church in a hostile political environment. He struggled, however, to build bridges between civil and ecclesiastical authorities at a time when concord between Church and state was fundamental to the tranquility of the country. Given the disruptions that ensued from changes in the political regime, such harmony was threatened.

Three unsuccessful diplomatic missions, between 1823 and 1850, sought to lay the foundations for a settlement between the Chilean Church and the civil administration after the expulsion from Chile of Monsignor Juan Muzi, the apostolic vicar of the pope, in 1824 and the subsequent exile of Monsignor José Santiago Rodríguez Zorrilla, the bishop of Santiago, the following year. The inclination of the Holy See to defend the monarchy in Spanish America did not improve the situation. The tension and strain were evident. For example, the papal brief *Etsi longissimo terrarum*, issued by Pius VII, urged the faithful to "uproot and completely destroy the disgraceful plagues of riots and seditions that the enemy planted in those countries of America subject to the Catholic king of Spain."[2]

Some years later, Pope Leo XII continued the defense of the monarchical cause, even after the independence armies were victorious. In his papal brief of 1824, *Etsi iam diu*, the pope attacked the supporters of the rupture with Spain, accusing them of having plunged the continent into a fratricidal war. In addition, Leo condemned the ideas defended by the supporters of independence:

> In consequence, we cannot help but regret bitterly, observing the impunity with which the debauchery and the license of the wicked run; already noticing how the spread of incendiary books and pamphlets spreads and spreads, in which both powers, ecclesiastical and civil, are depressed, despised, and attempted to be made hateful; and, finally, watching out for those cabals that are formed in the gloom of darkness, in the manner of devastating locusts from a dark well.

He continued, paraphrasing the prophet Jeremiah: "We have waited for peace, but no tranquility has come; we have waited for the time of healing, but only horror has come; we have relied on the time of health, but only disturbance has occurred."[3]

Although relations between the Church and the new Spanish American states were not at their best, both state and ecclesiastical authorities needed each other if they wanted to subsist in this brave new world of independent nations. There, governments inspired by the ideologies of liberalism and the Enlightenment—doctrines openly condemned by the Church—faced ruling the population of countries which saw, in the Church and its shepherds, the logical link between them and God.

In these complicated circumstances, Justo Donoso became a central figure. As a priest, he had no problem reconciling his ecclesiastical work with his loyalty to the republic. Being a good citizen did not have to be in open contradiction with being a good Catholic, but quite the opposite: being a good citizen *meant* being a good Catholic. Therefore, evangelizing, educating, and instilling morals in the population meant, in the eyes of Donoso and other members of the clergy—many of them convinced republicans—collaborating with the consolidation of republican institutions. Moreover, given the link that existed between Church and state in Chile, being a priest also meant being a state official. Therefore, being a good citizen and a good priest also entailed the obligation to be a competent official at the service of the republic. Donoso was committed to this project. His devotion to the service of God resulted in devoted and loyal service to the republic and its interests.

Biographical information

Donoso was born in Santiago de Chile, on July 10, 1800, the son of Juan de Dios Donoso and Gertrudis Vivanco. His father, a merchant of means, wanted to introduce Justo into his profession. The young Donoso, however, never showed great interest in his father's way of living; he preferred reading, the arts, and prayer.

In 1816 he entered as a novice in the Recoleta Dominica of Santiago and continued his studies in the same monastery. There, his religious vocation became stronger, and at the end of his secondary education he decided to become a priest. Five years after this decision, on November 3, 1822, the Bishop of Santiago, José Santiago Rodríguez Zorrilla, ordained him as a priest. In October 1824, the apostolic vicar of His Holiness, Monsignor Juan Muzi, granted Donoso a rescript of perpetual secularization, permitting him to live in the world outside the Dominican order.[4]

Between 1827 and 1828, Justo Donoso toured the provinces of Aconcagua and Coquimbo as a missionary, serving in Sotaquí as a vicar to the priest of that parish, his brother Francisco. In 1829 Donoso took charge of the parish of Talca, where he stood out for his inclinations towards rural missions and spiritual exercises.

In 1840 he was summoned to Santiago to teach theology at the Conciliar Seminary, and in 1843 he was appointed rector of the same school. Although his religious work was the mainstay of his efforts, he began to work in legal sciences and journalism. In 1825 he became the editor and publisher of a newspaper titled *El Pensador Político-Religioso*, devoted to defending the rights of the Catholic Church in Chile. Later, he would serve as editor of two weekly papers written in the epistolary format: *Cartas de Ciriaco a Eristanes* and *Cartas de Teófilo a Cristófilo.*[5] In April 1843, however, by order of the archbishop of Santiago, Manuel Vicuña, Donoso oversaw the creation of *La Revista Católica*, the official press organ of the archdiocese, as its first director. *La Revista Católica* became an instrument to counteract the opinions of some parts of Chilean society increasingly inclined towards secularist policies and very critical of the Church and its relationship with the Chilean state.[6]

By 1844 Donoso presented himself for the corresponding examinations to become a lawyer. He was subsequently appointed a member of the faculty of theology of the University of Chile by President Manuel Bulnes. That same year, the Chilean Government proposed to the Holy See the creation of the bishopric of Ancud, a newly created diocese in the Chiloé Archipelago. Donoso assumed the bishop's seat in 1845. His work in that diocese was arduous. He organized its administration, made pastoral visits, founded a seminary, began the construction of the city's cathedral, gathered a synod of the priests of the diocese, and established the parishes of Chacao, Dalcahue, Lemuy, and La Unión.

In 1852 Donoso was presented to the Holy See to assume the dignity of bishop of La Serena, and he was formally appointed to the position in 1853. In La Serena, he had the same zeal and commitment he displayed in Ancud. He founded a series of parishes in the province, ordered the construction of buildings for the conciliar seminary, and contributed to the establishment in the diocese of the Sisters of the Sacred Heart, the Sisters of the Good Shepherd, and the Sisters of Charity (Hermanas del Sagrado Corazón, Hermanas del Buen Pastor, and Hermanas de la Caridad).

Justo Donoso also participated significantly in the political sphere. He was elected to the Chamber of Deputies, representing Chiloé, for the period 1852 to 1855; but he seems not to have joined the assembly, since he had then been transferred from Ancud to the bishopric of La Serena. He was elected senator for the 1855–64 legislature and was a member of the Permanent Commission of Ecclesiastical Affairs. He was also Minister of Justice, Worship, and Public Instruction from September 18, 1861, to January 1862, in the first ministerial cabinet of President José Joaquín Pérez Mascayano, while serving as bishop of La Serena. Donoso died in La Serena as bishop of that diocese on February 22, 1868.[7]

Contributions to the development of canon law

In the prologue of his *Instituciones de Derecho canónico americano*, Donoso explained the usefulness and necessity of writing a manual of canon law from the Spanish American perspective. There, the bishop reflected on the legal and administrative situation of the Church in Spanish America, making the necessary counterpoint with the status of the Church in Europe. According to Donoso, the evolution of legal institutions in Spanish America differed considerably from the rest of the Catholic world. The characteristics of Spanish American canon law, added to the educational status of the region's clergy, considered by Donoso as deficient, made the examination of the development of canon law in the region pertinent for American clergy.

Evangelizing the New World

The arrival of Europeans in the New World and the dynamic nature of Catholicism of the Counter-Reformation gave new vigor to the Church. The new territories became an opportunity for the Church to expand its teachings in the lands that the explorers of the late fifteenth century had claimed for European powers. This missionary enterprise required a partner. In the case of Spanish America, the Crown was willing to play that role, but the price would be high. By the *Inter caetera* bull of 1493, granting Spain sovereignty over much of the new territory, Pope Alexander VI had imposed on Spain the duty of evangelizing the New World. The bull *Universalis Ecclesiae* of July 1508 would additionally organize not only the mode of evangelization but also the nature of the *patronato*, or Royal Patronage of the Church, which would exert royal authority over the Church.[8]

In general terms, over time Spanish monarchs had the final word regarding the organization of the Church in America, leading them to become de facto vicars of the pontifical authority. The Holy See was unable to prevent this situation from becoming a common and accepted practice. Indeed, the Laws of the Indies granted the Catholic Church substantial protection by the Spanish Crown. However, this did not prevent the civil authority from greatly asserting its ecclesiastical prerogatives in both economic and administrative matters. Nevertheless, the pope reserved his inherent powers in cases of strictly religious matters, so that Catholics in Spanish America were not separated from the main body of the Church.[9]

In time, the Spanish monarchs managed to obtain from the pope greater privileges regarding the administration of the Church in America. They based the necessity of those privileges on the protective function provided by the Crown and its asserted need for proper political control over the Church. Because of this, the Laws of the Indies granted the Catholic Church a particular position in the government and regulated its functions, especially in the ecclesiastical government. Nevertheless, the status and privileges of the Church could never become an obstacle for civil authorities. This, then, was the origin of the *patronato indiano*, the Royal Patronage of the Spanish colonial Church.[10]

With the advent of Bourbon reforms, the Crown sought to increase its centralized control. By 1735, Philip V ordered the formation of an advisory board dedicated to compiling the scattered legislation dealing with the Crown's *patronato* to obtain a complete picture of the power of the Crown in relation to the Church. The legal protection of the Church, however, was conceived by the Bourbons in a different way than by their predecessors. Now, the *patronato* was considered an inherent attribute of the king, emanating from his sovereignty by divine right. This idea departed from the notion, sustained since the sixteenth century, that the privilege was part of a gracious concession granted by the authority of the Apostolic See. This new conception, known as "regalism," became the dominant doctrine until Spanish American independence.

With the rise of regalism after 1737, relations between the Crown and the Holy See were governed by a system of concordats. These legal instruments sought to balance the royal claims of the Bourbons and the prerogatives of Rome. The first concordat, subscribed by King Philip V and Pope Clement XII, was replaced in 1753 by a new one signed by King Ferdinand VI and Pope Benedict XIV. As a result of this new concordat, the state reaffirmed its dual role of patron and defender of the Church. At the same time, the Church became an essential tool for the government's pretensions. Thus, the union between the Church and the state was maintained even after the revolution for Spanish American independence.[11]

Independence in Chile and the crisis of the union between Church and state

Although Chile had consolidated its independence by the early 1820s, an essential part of the clergy remained faithful to the Spanish Crown, especially the high clergy in the most populous cities. Nonetheless, the idea of independence found support among a significant group of ecclesiastics willing to spread among the faithful not only the word of God but also the revolutionary cause. Indeed, once the triumph of independence was secured, the Chilean Church was freed from the control exercised by the Spanish colonial authorities. It maintained its logical bond of dependence and obedience to the Apostolic See in Rome.

The new scheme of relations between Church and state was structured on the new republican administration's continuation of the *patronato*. While proclaiming Catholicism as the official religion of the state, the new republic considered itself the political heir of the Spanish Crown and its established prerogatives over the Church.[12] The Holy See rejected these claims of the Chilean Government since the authority over the Church granted by the *patronato* corresponded to only the monarch's prerogative. Therefore, when Chile broke its ties with Spain, the Church was freed from its links with the state. Nevertheless, the Apostolic See had no means to deter the Chilean authorities from applying a new arrangement, and therefore the Church remained subject, under protest, to civil authorities.

Thus, the groups closest to the clergy assumed that the modus vivendi between the Church and the state in Chile should always occur in the face of "a government made up of Catholics, who think, feel, and act Catholic."[13] Although the government recognized the primacy of Catholicism over any other religion, it did not escape the civil authorities' discomfort that irregularities in relations with Rome persisted. Indeed, the position of public authority remained diffuse concerning ecclesiastical affairs and the scope of the power of the pope in matters of religious government in Chile.

During the first government of Ramón Freire (1823–26), an attempt was made to give the Chilean Church a "national" character by getting the Holy See to end the administrative dependence of the Chilean bishoprics on the Archdiocese of Lima, in Peru. Notwithstanding this approach, the question of who should obey the archbishop of Lima in controversies between the state and the Church in Chile remained unresolved. The absence of a concordat between the Republic of Chile and the Holy See made it challenging to elucidate such parameters to establish accepted methods for the resolution of possible conflicts.

There were various attempts to resolve this problem. With this goal in mind, a diplomatic mission headed by Monsignor José Ignacio Cienfuegos went to Rome. The Holy See also sent an apostolic mission led by Monsignor Juan Muzi to Chile, but this effort unfortunately failed and ended prematurely with the expulsion of Muzi from the republic.[14] These actions reinforced among Chilean officials the idea of the purported supremacy of the state over the Church. Moreover, in case of conflict, the government considered its demand for open support from the national clergy legitimate. The Holy See and the Chilean Church condemned this position and refused to officially recognize the Chilean Government's position on the issue. This stance was accepted *de facto*, however, since resistance could bring greater evils to the Church.[15]

Despite such protests, relations between the Church and the state in Chile operated during the first half of the nineteenth century under the following scheme. The state demanded loyalty and awarded civil and religious offices to priests who demonstrated their public patriotism and commitment to the state. The Catholic Church submitted to secular control and enjoyed primacy and exclusivity as the official religion of the state. This was a reconfiguration of the royalist structure of patronage now under the Republic of Chile.[16] Because of the social influence the Church exercised in the community, the state kept the Church as its ally and subordinate, maintaining the conception that the social body was a Catholic society or Church, a mixture of a lay community and clergy, as synonymous with the entire nation.[17]

A clergy cultivated in religious and legal matters: Donoso's two great publications

Donoso was constantly concerned about the education and preparation of the clergy to face the challenges that pastoral work imposed on them. Bishop Donoso also wanted to ensure that parish priests had the necessary knowledge in law to exercise their work as state officials, given the system that existed with the Church. For this purpose, in 1844 he published his first book, *Manual del párroco Americano* (*Manual of the American parish*).[18] In its prologue, Donoso noted the importance that:

> those called to carry out the parish ministry study pastoral theology with assiduous concentration, and that part of the ecclesiastical and municipal legislation details and determines in particular the prerogatives, faculties, and duties of pastors of the church.[19]

This activity was of paramount importance because parish priests were considered state officials in keeping baptism records and the dates of births, marriages, and deaths.

The *Manual* was Donoso's first contribution to the pastoral work of priests. It also provided the essential elements of canonical and ecclesiastical law that parish priests faced in their work. In its nineteen chapters and two appendices, the text runs from the most basic definitions—such as the origin of the phrase "parish priest" and its statutory interpretation—to the creation, union, and division of parish territorial jurisdictions, and the rights of the parish as a legal institution, among other subjects. Likewise, the work covers more complicated matters related to the legal and canonical sustenance of churches and expounds on the papal bulls of Pius V, Clement XI, and Benedict XIV, as well as related provisions from the Council of Trent. It also touches relevant matters from the administrative point of view, such as parish priests' character as direct representatives of the bishops, something *sui generis* in American canon law.

On a more practical level, several pages address the issue regarding the records that the parish priest must keep, their format, the certifications he can isssue, and the management of his archives. Finally, the *Manual* also refers to all aspects of the sacraments, their importance, their formalities, and the rites that should accompany them. The work exhorts the exemplary conduct that the parish priest must have with his congregation.

Donoso's first book reveals his model for teaching ecclesiastical and canon law. He employs direct and straightforward language. He constantly reminds the reader of the particular circumstances of Spanish American dioceses under a series of canon and civil rules arising from the old relationship between the Spanish Crown and the Holy See. Finally, the work demonstrates his permanent pedagogical interest in a manner of instruction that is best suited to the essential work of the parish priest.

An excellent complement to the seminal work of the *Manual* was his *Diccionario teológico, canónico, jurídico, litúrgico, bíblico* (*Dictionary of theology, canon law, law, liturgy, and the Bible*), published in 1855.[20] Although he began writing this while he was bishop of Ancud, Donoso saw it published the year he took office as bishop of La Serena. In its first pages, Donoso explains the plan of the work and its objectives:

> The same desire to cooperate in the realization of the important work of the general instruction in the religious, legal, and moral sciences which moved me to publish the *Manual del párroco americano*, moves me now to offer it to the studious youth. The epigraph of this writing indicates, of course, the subjects on which it is written: dogmatic and moral theology; the canon law and discipline of the church; civil jurisprudence; the liturgy or science of the sacred rites and ceremonies of the church and the history of its main festivities; sacred scripture, the books that compose it, its authors; etc.[21]

The *Diccionario* is a lengthy collection of definitions on different topics, which, in its four volumes, alphabetically covers theological, legal, and biblical aspects. In this sense, again, Donoso seeks to contribute to religious formation but expands his audience to the laity, approaching matters that typically would be unknown to persons with no connection to the ecclesiastical world.

Regarding the legal definitions in the book, one finds both canon and secular law. An essential part of the definitions found in the dictionary comes from the *Instituciones de Derecho canónico americano* (*Institutes of American canon law*), a book Donoso published in 1848. Nevertheless, he indicated that he made specific updates in his *Diccionario* due to modifications introduced by "common law in force in Spanish America, created by express privileges emanating from the Apostolic See, of legitimate customs, conciliar decrees, and statutes dictated in accordance with the demands and special circumstances of these churches."[22] This comment implied not only that there were revisions of canonical norms throughout the text but also, given the *patronato*, that it was necessary to define the scope of civil laws and norms that supported the observance of canon law mandates. Moreover, Donoso proposed that the work's definitions fell into four major legal categories: people, property, procedure, and crimes and penalties. Regarding civil law, Donoso resorted to the doctrine of the Spanish laws still in force in America, and of course in Chile.[23]

Instituciones de derecho canónico americano

In 1848, while serving as bishop of Ancud, Donoso published his most famous and thoughtful work on canon law. After several years of work and adapting some elements of his *Manual del párroco*, Donoso published *Instituciones de Derecho canónico americano*.[24] With eight editions between 1848 and 1909, this work became a particularly important contribution to the study and teaching of canon law.[25]

In *Instituciones*, Donoso highlights the importance of the study of legal regulations for their historically positive influence on the development of legislation in the Western world. Moreover, the intimate connection between civil and ecclesiastical law, primarily in the countries of Spanish America in which colonial legislation was still in force, was another reason to study canon law.[26] In the prologue of the *Instituciones*, Donoso gives a brief historical reflection on the importance of canonical norms in the development of the law and their influence on the Spanish legal system in America. Indeed, from the provisions of the councils of the Visigothic kingdom of Toledo to the *Siete Partidas* of Alfonso X and the legislation contained in the *Recopilación de Leyes de Indias* (1680), the contributions of the Catholic Church were undeniable.

Donoso intended not only to prove the influence of canon law but also to recapitulate a position advanced in his *Manual*, namely, the distinctive character of Spanish American canon law. On this point, Donoso reflected:

> Anyone among us who undertakes the study of canon law...goes into a chaos of darkness and confusion...All the general theories and doctrines based on clear texts of canon law are studied, and yet, when practically the opposite happened in America, one is convinced: either that one does not understand what one reads, or that among us all the rules are violated.[27]

Thus, Donoso attempted to explain the particularities of Spanish American canon law as the product of a special relationship between the Church and the Spanish Crown, as well as with the republican states that succeeded it. Through the force of these customs, Spanish American canon law emerged as a unique legal system. Legal texts emanating from the Apostolic See were supplemented and even modified by customs or the provisions of local ecclesiastic councils. Furthermore, the influence of regalism exercised through the *patronato*—the privileges granted by the pope and even by the concordats signed between the Holy See and Spain—accounted for the unique legal situation of the Church in America.

The work is structured in four parts, following the model set by Gaius in his *Institutes*. The first part, called "isagogic book," is an introduction to the rudiments of canon law. It begins with the analysis of an "ecclesiastical society," highlighting its perfect and independent character in relation to temporal authority. This part continues to analyze the notions and classifications of canon law and general and particular ecclesiastical councils. It then delves into the sources of canon law: constitutions and pontifical rescripts, custom, and the "ancient law" of Greco-Latin traditions. There is also "new" law originating in Gratian's *Decretum* and the *Decretals* of Gregory IX. The development of the new law is further examined in the norms dictated by the Council of Trent and the concordats signed by Spain and the Holy See. The last section of the introductory part addresses general principles of canon law and its technical words, formulas, citations, and abbreviations.

The other three parts of the *Instituciones* follow the order Donoso borrowed from Justinian's *Institutes*: persons, property, procedural law, and penal law. The second part treats natural and legal persons. Here, Donoso contrasts Roman law with canon law to study the condition of the clergy in America. Finally, he also explores quite extensively the entire hierarchy of the Catholic Church: the pope, cardinals, pontifical legates, bishops, and parish priests. The third part treats the property and economy of the Church. Nonetheless, Donoso also includes commentaries regarding the sacraments and their regulation, indulgences, the celebration of religious festivals, the worship and veneration of the saints, and matters relating to fasting and abstinence. The fourth and final part of the *Instituciones* deals with judicial procedures, ecclesiastical crimes, and penalties. This part also addresses issues relating to canonical jurisdiction and those subject to it, what type of cases fall under the jurisdiction of ecclesiastical courts, and crimes, penalties, and ecclesiastical censures.

The *Instituciones* was undoubtedly a modern work for its time, considering the arc of subjects that it encompasses, including the *ius commune* and colonial and republican canon law. In that sense, Donoso chose a model of systematic organization of canonistic study inaugurated by Pablo Lancelotti in the sixteenth century, through his work *Institutiones juris canonici* and later adopted in canonistic literature such as the first Code of Canon Law of 1917.[28]

Donoso's contributions are not merely methodological. His analysis of the existence of Spanish American canon law, as the result of the close cooperation between Church and state, generates a critical turning point. Donoso frequently highlights the particularity of Spanish American canon law as distinct from European canon law. He sought to emphasize the specific conditions of the legal relations between state and Church in America to understand the theoretical and practical implications of how the two institutions interact. This interaction implied a tension between the two powers, forcing the ecclesiastical and secular authorities to face a dilemma: either the state exercises sovereign authority over the Church, or the Church defends its prerogatives against the overreaching of the state. Nonetheless, Donoso proposed a third way, based on the harmony of both powers. A Catholic state, with a Catholic population, needs the Church to maintain this nature. Thus, the study of canon law in a Catholic state is essential to laying the foundations of the country's political and legal institutions as a minimum moral condition of sovereign and institutional existence.

Final considerations: Church and state

Donoso's *Instituciones* effectively describe and analyze most aspects of Spanish American canon law. Directly discussing the sources, Donoso clarifies the differences between the regulations governing universal ecclesiastical institutions and those explicitly created by and for Spanish America.

The book also adopts an antiregalist character, a persistent approach in his study of canon law. Donoso consistently emphasizes the character of the "perfect society" of the Church, which transcends the problems of secular norms. Likewise, Donoso reaffirms the independent character of the Catholic Church regarding earthly authorities, despite the pact of protection between the Spanish Crown and the Apostolic See. Therefore, Donoso himself, in veiled form, criticized the position of the governments of the Spanish American republics regarding their claim to be heirs of the *patronato* initially held by the king of Spain, as monarch and Christian prince.[29]

It is not strange that Justo Donoso chose to criticize this position through a book on canon law. On one hand, the Church and the state were united constitutionally, considering the parish priests as state officials whose salaries were determined through legislation of the annual budget. On the other hand, there was a more important reason to explain Donoso's stance. He belonged to a generation of priests who, apart from their ministry, had studied and even practiced as lawyers. Rafael Valentín Valdivieso, archbishop of Santiago from 1848 to 1879, practiced for almost a decade as a lawyer before being ordained a priest in 1834. Joaquín Larraín Gandarillas, a bishop *in partibus* and director of the seminary of Santiago, also studied law before becoming a priest. He was a staunch promoter of the independence of the Church. Moreover, Larraín was closely tied to the creation of the Conservative Party in 1857, whose political platform included the end of the *patronato* and questions about the freedom of education. Several other names could be added to the list of figures from this particularly influential generation in pastoral, legal, and political fields: Ramón Ángel Jara, who, like Justo Donoso, would be bishop first of Ancud and then of La Serena; and José Alejo Eyzaguirre and his nephew José Ignacio Víctor Eyzaguirre, both lawyers and defenders of the rights of the Church.

Thus, from the second half of the nineteenth century on, a generation of priests emerged who were fervent and convinced republicans and patriots, and who defended the independence of the Church from the state. They considered the arrangement between the Church and state as favorable for the dissemination of the teachings of the Catholic Church. Nonetheless, they were conflicted when faced with the assertion of secular authorities to assume the financing of the Church, because this gave government officials a voice and vote regarding Church administration, and these officials demanded obedience to the supreme authority of the republic.

Through his books, Justo Donoso tried to explain the complex relationship between secular and religious authorities in the Spanish American world, something no one had yet achieved. First, Donoso identified the historical parameters of this relationship, whose roots were deeply embedded in colonial law and extended to the republican era. This is the main contribution of his early books. Second, Donoso tried to build bridges between the secular and the spiritual spheres, seeing in the Church and its laws a way to contribute to the development of the state. In this way, he sought to enhance the social and moral education of the population while defending the autonomy of the ecclesiastical authority concerning the state as the right way to maintain necessary harmony. Therefore, Bishop Donoso concluded that a thorough and meticulous study of the development and history of the Church's legal institutions in Spanish America provided more precise guidance on how the union between church and state should work.

Justo Donoso also used several works written by Italian authors who were not often merely canonists—usually mixing instead law and history as a method for approaching its subjects. An intellectual heir to eighteenth-century colonial thought, Donoso also makes extensive use of works on Church history in which the use of law is limited. This practice comes from the relevance the Catholic Enlightenment gave to history, eager for the creation of a positive theology. Furthermore, the importance of custom as a source of canon law, which was necessarily based on actual events in the past, should not be forgotten.[30]

As a bishop, senator, and minister, Donoso was a state official, but that did not diminish his defense of what he considered the acquired rights of the Catholic Church in Chile. To him we owe the first comprehensive study of canon law in Spanish America and Chile, and therefore his work became the foundation for the proper formation of priests and the laity at a time when both civil law and canon law were part of the same legal system. Indeed, the study of Donoso's work not only allows us to internalize the essential elements to understand the cumulative and historical interaction between canon and secular law, but also serves as a witness to the history of Chile and its institutional development over almost three hundred years.

Notes

1 Barbier, *Reform and Politics in Bourbon Chile: 1755–1796*, 189–94.
2 Promulgated in 1816. See https://w2.vatican.va/content/pius-vii/it/documents/breve-etsi-longissimo-30-gennaio-1816.html accessed on May 20, 2019.
3 https://w2.vatican.va/content/leo-xii/it/documents/breve-etsi-iam-diu-24-settembre-1824.html. Accessed on May 20, 2019.
4 Prieto del Río, *Diccionario biográfico del clero secular de Chile, 1535–1918*, 190.
5 Salinas, "Justo Donoso Vivanco (1800–1868)," 39.
6 Silva Castro, *Prensa y periodismo en Chile (1812–1956).*
7 Magallanes, *Biografía del Iltmo. Señor Obispo de La Serena doctor D. Justo Donoso.*
8 Bejarano Almada, "Las bulas alejandrinas: detonantes de la evangelización en el Nuevo Mundo."
9 Guzmán and Vio, *Don Francisco de Paula Taforo y la vacancia arzobispal de Santiago*, 151ff.
10 García Gutiérrez, *Apuntes para la historia del origen y desenvolvimiento del Regio Patronato Indiano hasta 1857*; and Felipe Westermeyer, "Confesionalidad del Estado," 446.
11 Cárcel Ortiz, *Historia de la Iglesia en la España contemporánea*, 56; and González Fuertes, "La cámara de Castilla y el Real Patronato (1733–1759)," 85–86.
12 Valencia Avaria, *Anales de la República de Chile*, vol. 1.
13 Guzmán and Vio, *Don Francisco*, 17.
14 See Barros Borgoño, *La misión del vicario apostólico don Juan Muzi*; and Hendricks, "The First Apostolic Mission to Chile."
15 Nevertheless, these claims subsequently were condemned in the *Syllabus*, since they concerned "the destruction of the rights of the Church; it concerns the destruction of its independence…This proposition amounts to the omnipotence, the absolute despotism of the civil power." See Fabres, *Obras completas de José Clemente Fabres*, 11:35.
16 Oviedo Cavada, *La misión Irarrázaval en Roma 1847–1850*, 26–38.
17 Pike, "Church and State in Peru and Chile since 1840." For another insight, see Retamal and González, "El gobierno chileno y el concepto misionero del Estado (1829–1861)."
18 Donoso, *Manual del párroco americano.*

19 Ibid., 3.
20 Donoso, *Diccionario teológico, canónico, jurídico, litúrgico, bíblico.*
21 Donoso, *Diccionario*, 1:v.
22 Ibid., 1:viii.
23 The civil and criminal codes came into force only in 1857 and 1875, respectively. Regarding this matter, see Westermeyer, "Derecho indiano y Derecho patrio"; and Peña, "Las raíces histórico-culturales del derecho penal chileno."
24 Donoso, *Instituciones de Derecho canónico americano.*
25 The versions of the *Instituciones* were published in Valparaíso (1848), Paris (1854, 1863, 1868, 1876, 1885), Santiago (1861), and Freiburg im Breisgau (1909).
26 Donoso, *Instituciones*, 1:8.
27 Donoso, *Instituciones*, Vol.1 p. 10.
28 Merello, "El derecho de presentación en un canonista chileno," 458.
29 Ibid., 459.
30 Dougnac, "La producción canonista italiana," 171.

References

Araneda Bravo, Fidel. *Historia de la Iglesia en Chile*. Santiago: Ediciones Paulinas, 1986.

Barbier, Jacques. *Reform and Politics in Bourbon Chile: 1755–1796*. Ottawa: Ottawa University Press, 1980.

Barros Arana, Diego. *Un decenio de la historia de Chile (1841–1851)*, vol. 2. Santiago: IHPUC, 2003.

Barros Borgoño, Luis. *La misión del vicario apostólico don Juan Muzi. Notas para la historia de Chile (1823–1825)*. Santiago: Imprenta La Época, 1883.

Bejarano Almada, María de Lourdes. "Las bulas alejandrinas: detonantes de la evangelización en el Nuevo Mundo." *Revista del Colegio de San Luis* 6, no. 12 (2016): 224–57.

Cárcel Ortiz, Vicente. *Historia de la Iglesia en la España contemporánea: Siglos XIX y XX*. Madrid: Ediciones Palabra, 2002.

Collier, Simon. *Chile: La construcción de una república 1830–1865*. Santiago: Ediciones de la Universidad Católica de Chile, 2005.

Collier, Simon. "Religious Freedom, Clericalism, and Anticlericalism in Chile, 1820–1920." In *Freedom and Religion in the Nineteenth Century*, edited by Richard Helmstadter. Stanford, CA: Stanford University Press, 1997.

Donoso, Justo. *Diccionario teológico, canónico, jurídico, litúrgico, bíblico*, Vol. 4. Valparaíso: Imprenta de El Mercurio, 1855.

Donoso, Justo. *Instituciones de Derecho Canónico Americano*, Vol. 2. Valparaíso: Imprenta y Librería de El Mercurio, 1848.

Donoso, Justo. *Manual del párroco americano o instrucción teológico-canónico-legal, dirigida al párroco americano, y particularmente al chileno sobre sus derechos, facultades y deberes, y cuanto concierne al cabal desempeño del ministerio parroquial: obra útil a los párrocos, confesores y demás eclesiásticos*. Santiago: Imprenta del Progreso, 1844.

Donoso, Justo. *Representación que hacen a la H. Cámara de Senadores el Iltmo. y Rmo. Sr. Arzobispo de la Metrópoli de Santiago de Chile Dr. Don Rafael Valentín Valdivieso, e Ilustrísimos Señores Obispos sufragáneos de La Serena y Concepción acerca del Código Civil*. Santiago: Imprenta de la Opinión, 1857.

Dougnac, Antonio. "La producción canonista italiana en dos pensadores hispanoamericanos de comienzos del siglo XIX: El chileno Justo Donoso y el peruano Francisco de Paula González Vigil." *Revista Chilena de Historia del Derecho* 24 (2013–14): 15–189.

Fabres, José Clemente. *Obras completas de José Clemente Fabres*, Vol. 11. Santiago: Imprenta Cervantes, 1909.

García Gutiérrez, Jesús. *Apuntes para la historia del origen y desenvolvimiento del Regio Patronato Indiano hasta 1857.* Mexico City: Ediciones Jus, 1941.

González Fuertes, Manuel Amador. "La cámara de Castilla y el Real Patronato (1733–1759): de la prepotencia a la impotencia." *Brocar* 25 (2001): 75–107.

Guzmán Rosales, Miguel, and Octavio Vio Henríquez. *Don Francisco de Paula Taforo y la vacancia arzobispal de Santiago: 1878–1887.* Santiago de Chile: Universidad Catolica, Instituto de Historia, 1964.

Hendricks, Frances. "The First Apostolic Mission to Chile." *Hispanic American Historical Review* 22, no. 4 (1942): 644–69.

Krebs, Ricardo. *La Iglesia de América Latina en el siglo XIX.* Santiago, Ediciones de la Universidad Católica de Chile, 2002.

Krebs, Ricardo, et al. *Catolicismo y laicismo. Las bases doctrinarias del conflicto entre la Iglesia y el Estado en Chile 1875–1885.* Santiago: Ediciones Nueva Universidad, 1979.

Magallanes, Valentín. *Biografía del Iltmo. Señor Obispo de La Serena doctor D. Justo Donoso.* Santiago: Imprenta del Ferrocarril, 1871.

Merello, Italo. "El derecho de presentación en un canonista chileno del siglo XIX: Justo Donoso Vivanco." *Revista de Estudios Histórico-Jurídicos* 23 (2001): 457–67.

Oviedo Cavada, Carlos. *La misión Irarrázaval en Roma 1847–1850.* Santiago: Instituto de Historia, Pontificia Universidad Católica de Chile, 1962.

Peña, Silvia. "Las raíces histórico-culturales del derecho penal chileno." *Revista de Estudios Histórico-Jurídicos* 7 (1982): 289–314.

Pike, Fredrick. "Church and State in Peru and Chile since 1840: A Study in Contrasts." *American Historical Review* 73, no. 1 (1967): 30–50.

Prieto del Río, Luis Francisco. *Diccionario biográfico del clero secular de Chile, 1535–1918.* Santiago de Chile: Imprenta Chile, 1922.

Retamal, Julio, and Javier González. "El gobierno chileno y el concepto misionero del Estado (1829–1861)." *Historia* 5 (1966): 197–214.

Salinas, Maximiliano. "Justo Pastor Donoso Vivanco (1800–1868)." *Anales de la Facultad de Teología* 31 (1980): 38–64.

Sánchez, Marcial. *Historia de la Iglesia en Chile*, Vol. 2. Santiago: Editorial Universitaria, 2009.

Silva Castro, Raúl. *Prensa y periodismo en Chile (1812–1956).* Santiago: Ediciones de la Universidad de Chile, 1958.

Valencia Avaria, Luis. *Anales de la República de Chile*, Vol. 1. Santiago: Editorial Andrés Bello, 1986.

Westermeyer, Felipe. "Confesionalidad del Estado, real patronato y derecho canónico indiano en las Cortes de Cádiz." *Revista de Estudios Histórico-Jurídicos* 38 (2016): 445–70.

Westermeyer, Felipe. "Derecho indiano y Derecho patrio en las memorias de los ministros de Justicia de Chile (1839–1873)." *Revista de Estudios Histórico-Jurídicos* 33 (2011): 533–81.

Williams, Edward. “Secularization, Integration, and Rationalization: Some Perspectives from Latin American Thought.” *Journal of Latin American Studies* 5, no. 2 (1973): 199–216.

Woll, Allen. “For God or Country: History Textbooks and the Secularization of Chilean Society, 1840–1890.” *Journal of Latin American Studies* 7, no. 1 (1975): 28–43.

6 Dalmacio Vélez Sarsfield (Argentina, 1800–74)

Abelardo Levaggi

Introduction

Dalmacio Simón Vélez Sarsfield, the most notable Argentine jurist of the nineteenth century, was born in Córdoba del Tucumán on February 18, 1800. His parents, natives of the same province, were Dalmacio Vélez Baigorri, a man of vast culture who had an insatiable love of reading, and Rosa Sarsfield Palacio, of Irish descent. The younger Dalmacio's baptismal date of September 19 was preserved in the Cathedral of Córdoba.[1]

His father died when Dalmacio was only four months old. His mother taught him notions of religion, and he received a Catholic education at the School of the Convent of Saint Francis. His early education was under the tutelage of lay brother Tomás de los Dolores, a person of austere virtue.[2] Vélez studied at the School of Montserrat until he was fourteen years old, and then attended the School of Arts, where a student "becomes imbued with that religious and moral teaching he receives in classrooms."[3] Both schools depended on the greater University of San Carlos. He graduated in 1818 with the titles of both Bachelor and Master of Philosophy and had sworn to "defend publicly and privately our blessed Virgin Mary, who was conceived without original sin, from the first moment of her natural being."[4]

The teaching of law at the University of Córdoba followed the traditional method, based on *utrumque ius*—both Roman law and canon law. Vélez, as a law student in 1818 and 1819, was initiated into the knowledge of Church law through the *Institutionum Canonicarum Libri IV* of Joannis Devoti, the official text used by the professor, although we do not know who the professor was. Once Vélez completed his basic studies, he obtained the title of Bachelor of Law in July 1820. Economic need, a consequence of his father's death and his mother's poverty, did not allow him further formal education.

He did his forensic practice in the office of the adviser to government, José Dámaso Gigena. This practice was requisite to registration as a lawyer. The certificate he received at the end of the practice stated that he was credited with "uncommon talents, and a tireless desire to advance in knowledge and skills."[5] With three months of practice and an examination result of "sufficient," he began his practice, always in Córdoba, in December 1822. That year, as capitular advocate of the poor, he made his first steps toward a specialization in canonical affairs. He exercised that office "not just to execute the obligations attached to it, but [to use] everything that could instruct [him] in these matters by attention to the many affairs—civil, criminal, or canonical—before the curia."[6]

Vélez's canonical education was shaped by his reading of works on religious themes and critical notes and comments to the *Decretales* of the humanist Jacques Cujas, an author that he never abandoned.[7] Several books of public ecclesiastical law and some canonists were among his library as we know it today. Vélez's *Catalogue* contains the following books: *Instituciones del Derecho canónico*, by Domingo Cavalario (París, 1846); *Máximas sobre recursos de fuerza y protección*, by José de Covarrubias (Madrid, 1785); *Manuel de droit public écclésiastique français*, by André-Marie Dupin (Paris, 1845); *De regio patronatu Indiarum*, by Pedro Frasso (Madrid, 1775); *Examen crítico de los discursos sobre una constitución religiosa considerada como parte de la civil*, by Gregorio Funes (Buenos Aires, 1825); *Sacrae Rotae Romanae decisiones, et summorum pontificium constitutiones recentissimae*, by Cardinal de Luca (Venice, 1759); *Cursus iuris canonici. Hispani et indici*, by Pedro Murillo Velarde (Madrid, 1791); and *De la souveraineté dans l'église*, by J.B.C. Picot (Paris, 1873). Moreover, one finds the *Corpus iuris canonici, constitutiones*, by Clemente V (Lyon, 1606) and works in accordance with canon law. Vélez's library contained no classical authors of treatises.[8]

Settlement in Buenos Aires; member of the Constituent Congress of 1824; performance at the University; and Unitary Party affiliation

A few months after completing his practice in 1823, Vélez was transferred to Buenos Aires, where he settled and lived most of his life. The Chamber of Justice, presided over by Manuel Antonio de Castro, a prestigious jurist and politician from the province of Salta, examined Vélez and incorporated him in the Registry of Attorneys in December 1823. Two days later, Vélez married his niece, Paula Piñero—through a waiver of kinship—with whom he had a daughter, Vicenta.[9] His wife died in December 1831, and in 1834 Vélez married Manuela Velázquez, a relative of Paula, with whom he had three children: Constantino, Aurelia, and Rosario.[10]

In Buenos Aires, Vélez was intensely active. He maintained a friendly relationship with Manuel Antonio de Castro, the governor of Córdoba, as Vélez was assistant adviser to the government. Castro introduced him to the Unitary Party. Vélez began his public service at age twenty-four as a representative for San Luis to the Constitutional Congress meeting in Buenos Aires. Emphasizing his solid expertise in the area, he joined the Committee of Finance.

The constitution was approved in December 1826, and Vélez had to present it to the government of the province of San Juan. On the way there, he learned that the *caudillo* Facundo Quiroga had invaded the province, so Vélez refrained from entering the province and mailed Quiroga the constitution. A decade later, this opponent would be one of his main clients.[11]

In 1826, Vélez was also appointed professor of economic policy at the University of Buenos Aires, a position that he held until February 1829. Apparently, he gave only a few lessons, but as a professor he acquired the title of doctor and used that title ever afterward.[12]

Vélez opened his law firm in 1828. By the end of the following year, however, when the Federalist Party leader Juan Manuel de Rosas was elected governor, Vélez left the city and took refuge at his wife's farm in Arrecifes. Because of his status as a leader of the provincial Unitary Party, he was forced to leave Buenos Aires, and for eleven months he remained in Córdoba, separated from his family, until he managed to return. In the village of San Nicolás de los Arroyos he met with his wife and daughter, though his wife died shortly afterward.[13]

At the beginning of 1832 Vélez settled once again in Buenos Aires, where he resumed the practice of law. His law firm was one of the most prestigious in the city. As a lawyer, he was an *ex officio* member of the Theoretical and Practical Academy of Jurisprudence. In 1837, however, he lost this status because he was unable to show that he was "notoriously addicted" to the cause of the federation. Between 1834 and 1835, Vélez edited important pedagogical works on law: *Instituciones de Derecho real de España*, by José María Álvarez; *Prontuario de práctica forense*, by Manuel Antonio de Castro; and *Institutiones juris ecclesiastici*, by Franz Xaver Gmeiner (Xaverius Gmeinerius), an Austrian theologian of Febronian ideas. The first edition of these *Institutiones* was published in German in 1779. They were reissued in Buenos Aires because the professor of canon law, Eusebio Agüero, adopted them as a text and did not make copies. The volume printed in Buenos Aires in Latin does not clarify the details of Vélez's participation. Joaquín V. González wondered whether Vélez edited, annotated, or corrected the text. According to José María Mariluz Urquijo, it is likely that Vélez's contribution was limited to deleting most of the information relative to Germany.[14] Whatever his participation, there is no proof that he shared the heterodox ideas of the author, which tended toward supporting the Reformation. Various types of royalist perspectives were then asserted, and Vélez's royalist features borrowed from traditionalists and moderates rather than from enlightened royalists.

The Argentine government and the right of patronage

In 1834 Vélez was one of the law professors convened to weigh in on the bull that Pope Gregory XVI had issued *motu proprio* two years earlier, which did not recognize the right of patronage for the governor of Buenos Aires. The pope promoted Mariano Medrano from the apostolic vicariate of Buenos Aires to titular bishop of Aulon *in partibus infidelium*, with the right of succession to the Diocese of Buenos Aires in case of its vacancy. The majority of judges, theologians, and law professors convened by the government—thirty-nine in total—joined the royalist opinion of the public prosecutor of state, Pedro José Agrelo. Vélez's opinion stood alone in respecting the rights of the Church and aspiring to establish balance and harmony between the two powers. If the Catholic Church had been only one church among others in the nation, the question of patronage would not have arisen. Adhering to the principle of religious freedom, Vélez stated that "laws that determine the relations of men with their creator do not need the protection of any power, and even less protection bought very dearly by the arrogation of the Church's governance through direct means of domination."[15] Vélez referred to the governance of the Church by the ecclesiastical hierarchy as needing to protect subjects, a responsibility that would have included a justified right of patronage, as long as its conditions remained.

The interested powers, the Church and the state unilaterally, had to set limits, although Vélez thought that they "must negotiate the acquiescence of the sovereign," whose powers had a necessary reference. He advised that the government should act in the meantime in the sense of Agrelo's propositions, because that was the will of the nation. Medrano's bulls deserved approval and public distribution because they had been previously presented by the diocesan bishop, although unsuccessfully so.

Vélez saw nothing unusual in the conduct of the pope, who always exercised his authority this way. Vélez did not deny the right of patronage but indicated how to obtain it. Although Vélez's expressions seem contradictory, his fundamental idea was that of the bilateral feature of the patronage. The remedy was a concordat, finally attained by an agreement with the Holy See in 1966.[16]

The government acted in accordance with Vélez's opinion. By a decree in March 1834, it gave currency to the bulls "as if" the bishop "had been appointed and presented in form" and because it was the first case that had occurred since independence.[17]

Adviser to Governor Rosas

In 1840 the persecution by Governor Juan Manuel de Rosas of his opponents worsened. Fleeing this danger, Vélez took refuge in Arrecifes and then, in February 1842, in Montevideo, where he continued to practice law and to translate Virgil's *Aeneid* from Latin into Spanish. He became an expatriate, and the province embargoed all his property.[18]

Some of his friends who were related to Rosas interceded in 1846, so that Vélez could return to Buenos Aires. The disembargo of his property took almost two years. He reopened his law firm, and it regained its earlier prestige. Rosas himself requested his advice several times, although Vélez continued to be a member of the Unitary Party despite retiring from political activity.[19]

One of the opinions Vélez drew up at the request of the governor became the germ of the book Vélez published in 1854 with the title *Relaciones del Estado con la Iglesia en la antigua América Española* (*Relations of the state with the Church in early Spanish America*). Rosas was concerned that the pope had appointed a coadjutor with the right of succession unless the sovereign had presented it. Vélez put forth two hypotheses: the first, which was unrelated to the case, was that the bishop *in partibus infidelium* (in parts where there were unbelievers) was destined to a position of service not endowed with any benefit; the second hypothesis, applicable to Monsignor Mariano José de Escalada, was that an auxiliary appointed to serve with a proprietary bishop would have benefits.

The solution to the first hypothesis was that the supreme pontiff was unable to appoint a bishop *in partibus* without the introduction or consent of the sovereign when the appointee was intended to serve as papal nuncio or papal vicar in apostolic ministry, or would not have a benefit in a church with a patron. The second solution, according to the greatest number of canonists, was that the bishop *in partibus*, to be appointed auxiliary of a church with a patron, should be presented to the pope by the sovereign of the state. Accordingly, the opinion presented by Vélez to Rosas was that the designation of Escalada as a coadjutor or auxiliary bishop was not valid because it lacked the requisite presentation by the patron.[20]

Although the work received some criticism, it was supported by Bishop León Federico Aneiros, who recognized its "rare wealth of knowledge."[21] He associated it with the "unique powers" held by the kings of Spain in the American Church under the "great and extraordinary circumstances" of the colonization of the Americas by Spain. Historical perspective endeavored to interpret the past based on these events. Aneiros acknowledged that the pope had acted wisely under the circumstances, which had prevented the creation of bishoprics and the Church's establishing itself as the sole ecclesiastical regime.

Since 1492, the relation of the Church with sovereigns in the Americas had lacked legal precedents and ecclesiastical customs. The origins of the rights of popes, kings, and people were difficult to determine. Through concessions and papal privileges, the sovereigns dictated civil laws to rule America. This doctrine was shared by almost all sixteenth-century jurists, but Vélez perceived a change in circumstances and the desirability of modifying the law. The statesman looked to the jurist to chart new directions. Vélez expressed adherence to the Catholic Church in the following categorical terms:

> The state should seek to protect the Catholic Church not as a foreign or political protection, nor only as provided in the Constitution of Buenos Aires [of 1854] that has been limited to say "the state pays for its worship, and all residents are obliged to respect it," but [must provide] broader protection for the propagation of [the church's] doctrines, the conservation of its institutions, and support for its authorities and mandates. The church meets an overall worthy and high need. There is an interest that is bigger, more general, than the religious interest. None therefore has more rights to the protection of the government in the country.[22]

In 1850 Rosas turned again to Vélez to consult about a juridical-ecclesiastical problem, which this time arose in the Banda Oriental del Uruguay (present-day Uruguay). The territory was part of the Diocese of Buenos Aires, and its bishop, Benito Lué y Riega, had died in 1812. Since then, and as a result of lack of communication with Rome, the ecclesiastical government of the Banda Oriental was temporarily in charge of the priest of the Metropolitan Church of Montevideo, Dámaso Antonio Larrañaga. When the political independence of Uruguay was declared in 1830, the provisional president, Juan Antonio Lavalleja, asked the pope to declare an ecclesiastical separation of the dioceses. In a brief of August 1832, considering that the appointment of Medrano as the bishop of Buenos Aires did not include the República Oriental del Uruguay, the Holy See raised Larrañaga to the rank of apostolic vicar with jurisdiction in Uruguay.

When a civil war began in 1835, Reds (Unitaries) occupied Montevideo, and Whites (Federalists) occupied the provinces. Larrañaga, in the provinces, delegated his functions relative to Montevideo to the priest Lorenzo Antonio Fernández, with the title of provisor and general vicar. Red authorities wanted to get rid of an enemy apostolic vicar, Larrañaga, residing in the provinces. They called for separation. In August 1847, the internuncio in Rio de Janeiro invested Fernández with the dignity of apostolic vicar for Montevideo, the same function that Larrañaga exercised for the entire country.

Larrañaga died in 1848, and the White government feared that the Holy See would extend the jurisdiction of the Unitary Fernández to the rest of the country. This was indirectly done by the internuncio in Rio de Janeiro, when he appointed Fernández to succeed Larrañaga. President Manuel Oribe, declaring the "national church" headless, designated the priest Manuel Rivero as ecclesiastical provisor in the provinces. Rosas, apparently *motu proprio*, consulted with Vélez.

Vélez's response was an extensive memorial sent to Rosas in May 1850. Vélez expounded on the substantive law and procedure. He reiterated the thesis of the originality of American ecclesiastical law. The new government enjoyed the same rights and privileges as the kings of Spain. The Roman curia should not create dioceses or rule them without agreement of the patron against the state's inheritance of royal Spanish law.

The method of governing the American churches through apostolic vicars failed. What was tolerable in the early days of the revolution no longer sufficed when the European powers recognized the independence of the young republics. In the absence of an ecclesiastical chapter that ruled in sees without a head, the metropolitan performed these duties; these functions rested with the bishop of Buenos Aires. Another motive in his favor was that both churches remained united, without canonical separation. Therefore, it was the prelate of Buenos Aires who had to assume the administration of the Banda Oriental (Eastern Side) Church with prior permission and license from the Banda Oriental Government. The effective exercise of jurisdiction would be delegated to a general vicar at the pleasure of that government.

The opinion of Vélez was more political than legal and more royalist than his former opinion. It is likely that he wanted to please Rosas, his main benefactor. Oribe was not persuaded and did not follow the advice. The arrival of the papal envoy, Lodovico Besi, to the Río de la Plata gave him the possibility of dealing as a valid interlocutor. Besi appointed Apostolic Vicar Rivero for the duration of the division. After the civil war, the internuncio in Rio de Janeiro returned the full jurisdiction to Fernández.[23]

After Rosas: advice on Church affairs

Following Rosas's defeat in the battle of Caseros in February 1852, Vélez returned to political activity with great fervor. He was one of the most outstanding personalities of the Unitary Party, although not everyone forgave his relationship with Rosas. He founded and, for months, directed the famous *El Nacional* newspaper, identified with the politics of the port city of Buenos Aires. Despite being from Córdoba, he challenged the agreement of the governors of San Nicolás de los Arroyos, which legitimized the inauguration of General Justo José de Urquiza, provisional director of the Confederación Argentina. It caused the separation of Buenos Aires and its organization as an independent state.

In Buenos Aires, Vélez was provincial deputy from 1852 to 1853, and again from 1855 to 1856; minister of government from May 1856 to May 1857, and from May to November 1859; provincial senator from May 1857 to May 1859; and government adviser from January 1855 to May 1856, and May 1857 to September 1858. In addition, he negotiated peace treaties with the Confederación Argentina and held several judicial and administrative roles. As minister of government, he participated with Edward Acevedo in the drafting of the Code of Commerce.

As government adviser, he opined on canonical and public ecclesiastical issues. One of the most important opinions was that of 1855, on the provision of the Diocese of Buenos Aires following the death of Mariano Medrano in April 1851, when Rosas still ruled the province. In March 1854, the executive branch presented to the pope, as new proprietor, Auxiliary Bishop Mariano José de Escalada for canonical institution. Pius IX appointed him without mentioning the civil presentation. Escalada immediately requested the passing or *exequatur* of the bull with certain reservations, including the formula of the oath, considering that it was opposed to the laws of God and the Church.

Prosecutor Juan Andrés Ferrera challenged the apostolic letters because they did not refer to the presentation. Vélez ruled that the rights of government provision remained in force, which was certainly recognized by law. Although he regretted the lack of a concordat that regulated the relations between the two powers, he admitted that, according to the traditional prudence practiced by both, a status quo provided for such a lack.

Although the bull that appointed Escalada did not refer to the patronage, the rescript that accompanied it, addressed to the executive branch, said that the appointment was made under its "postulation," words that had to be interpreted as "solemn," and Vélez alluded to the canonical provision in its "mystical meaning," a concept that by its polysemy Vélez could use to disarm the prosecutor's interpretation.

He advised the granting of the *exequatur* for preserving "good harmony with a power so high for us as the supreme pontiff." Refusal would perhaps incite him to foster greater doubts. Escalada would render the oath of law to the minister of foreign affairs, the clerk of government, and two witnesses. The capitular vicar and the ecclesiastical chapter, who installed him in the diocese, would then be notified.

Vélez did not consider Escalada's resistance admissible, because it implied the repeal of many established laws that were still in force. It justified Vélez's lament about the state of the provincial Church and emphasized the dignity of his conduct. The voice of the bishop "is always peaceful, always in good faith, always the sincere expression of the Shepherd, who only seeks the good of the Catholic people."[24]

Prescribed by the Law of the Indies,[25] the formula of the oath could not be changed. Vélez advised the government to request the opinion of scholars and respectable churchmen about this question, and the issue was resolved according to this advice."[26] Escalada presented the papal brief regulating the functioning of the ecclesiastical courts. Prosecutor Rufino de Elizalde challenged it with exaggeratedly royalist and Josephinist arguments. At points he denied the pope the primacy of jurisdiction in the Church and the power to transfer jurisdiction to the state.

Vélez, in turn, developed his ideas of papal primacy.[27] He agreed with the prosecutor that the brief should be retained but in other arguments found "anti-Catholic doctrines which cannot pass in silence." Papal supremacy was not declared expressly in the ecclesiastical constitution. Vatican I would do this a few years later, but the idea was already established in the Laws of *Partidas*.[28] This source affirmed that papal supremacy was

> one of the principles vital to the church, a divine institution, because the church is one, and there is no church where a portion is mission, or a portion without the supremacy of the Holy See. Even if the right of the papal supremacy were not defined solemnly in its entirety by the church, the doctrine had already established itself, and the supreme pontiff exerted it...All this does not detract from the supremacy of the pope when the needs or convenience of the church require it. If the mission that Jesus Christ gave to the Apostles continued in the episcopate, it was given to all of them together as a single individual. To be legitimate, the power of the episcopate must recognize the unity of the church and its visible head imposed by its founder.

The right of the political power to participate in the creation of the ecclesiastical courts was derived from the competence attributed to it by civil law. Civil authority was obligated to comply with ecclesiastical decisions and to assist the ecclesiastical authorities economically, and the ecclesiastical authorities were to ensure the right to patronage. The pope had accorded that right to all the governments of Europe and America. Otherwise, civil tribunals would have denied the effect of ecclesiastical resolutions.[29]

As minister of government, Vélez described Rosas's decree of April 1834 unfavorably, noting that it organized the ecclesiastical courts "without the consent of or notice to the sovereign pontiff, destroying earlier known spiritual jurisdictions, and creating others than those created by His Holiness and the sovereign of the state." Escalada denied the validity of that decree.[30]

The establishment in Buenos Aires of the Congregation of the Irish Sisters of Mercy, dedicated to education and hospital care, prompted jurists' warnings. If the sisters wished to found a convent or "religious place," they had to apply for permission from the temporal power. After the unfavorable reaction of the bishop, the nuns, backed by the same prelate, asked the government for permission to settle. Vélez issued a clear opinion that opened the door to all religious communities wishing to settle in the country. A juridical person, he said, is:

> a moral being that has rights and special obligations that can be created only by law and not by a particular string of individuals. In all times, from paganism to the Law of the Indies, moral or juridical persons have needed the consent of the supreme authority of the state for their birth and existence. They will have no privileges or exceptions...and then their religious association will be in perfect harmony with all legislation in the country. Through free association, they do not need any authorization to begin filling the religious purposes that have been proposed. But this kind of association, the only kind agreeable to the people, is quite different from a convent.[31]

Another matter that Vélez explained in *Relaciones* concerned the abolition of tithes in Buenos Aires by a provincial law of December 1822. Tithes were almost the only income of the Church. This law determined that the religious objectives to which the tithes were intended would be served instead through state funding. All goods that were not in the immediate service of worship were under the exclusive control of the government. Moreover, the chaplaincy and pious memorial gifts of the cathedral revenues passed to the government. Since then, the state treasury has funded the ecclesiastical department.

This concept was extended in the senate:

> the government...said it would provide for the expenses of worship and brought to the treasury all the properties belonging to the cult. How is the cult, Catholics will ask. There has been worship, churches have been abandoned, and ecclesiastics are dying of hunger. The government has forgotten them completely, and thus it happens whenever the communal interests have relied on governments.[32]

In the Buenos Aires Chamber of Deputies, Vélez added that the Church has never needed the protection of the government—whether a miserable salary or an immediate dependence on it. Of this reliance, Vélez noted, "this degrades the church."[33]

In 1865 the governor of Santa Fe, Nicasio Oroño, planned the expropriation of the Franciscan Convent of San Lorenzo to found a rural school. The plan was questioned by the national government, which denied him this power. Oroño sought the opinion of Vélez, whose response was forceful, unlike the usual lines of moderate and respectful thought. The governor's letter is not known, and Vélez's bluntness was most likely in response to the way the problem was presented to him. He encouraged the governor not to give up. He considered that, if for any reason the friars would triumph, the nation would go backward and subordinate itself to the will of the ecclesiastical power.

On the right of the friars, Vélez established that "the moral community is a creation of law. If the law grants the quality of civil person capable of owning goods, the law can withdraw the concession that it granted when the social interest demands it."[34] If they lacked their own incomes and lived on alms, they did not have any right to the property of the convent. All concession that the province granted them would be merely gratuitous.[35]

Vélez's suggestion would be correct in a hypothesis regarding dissolution of a juridical person, but that was not the case at hand. The project of expropriating a convent rested on the recognition of the order's right to property, which was to receive a fair compensation. The discussion was reduced to whether the cause alleged by the governor justified the exceptional measure, and whether the province had the constitutional authority to apply it.

The triumph of the Confederación over Buenos Aires in the battle of Cepeda in 1859, and the subsequent signing of the Pact of San José de Flores, forced Buenos Aires to rejoin the Confederación with recognition of the right to examine the national constitution and, where appropriate, propose amendments. In February 1860, in Buenos Aires, the assembly was constituted to review and to make possible amendments to the constitution. Vélez was a member of the drafting commission to propose amendments.

When the conflict resumed in 1861, the Confederación was decisively defeated in the battle of Pavón, and the capital was moved from Paraná to Buenos Aires. In May 1862, Vélez accepted the representation of Córdoba in the senate. In October, President Bartolomé Mitre named him finance minister, a position in which he served until September 1863.

Editor of the Civil Code; death; adherence to Catholicism

By the Decree of October 1864, Vélez received the commission to draft the Civil Code, which he concluded in July 1869. "To make this work," he said to the minister of justice:

> I have absolutely closed my studio, without continuing or accepting the defense of any important cause, and I have devoted to this work all my studies, all my time. Only in this way have I been able to advance the project.[36]

Vélez´s Catholicism is engraved in the Code, particularly in the declaration of the Church as a legal entity of necessary existence and the Catholic religion as a "state religion," even though it was only so in the province of Buenos Aires, not in the nation as a whole. However, he brought this particular arrangement to the constitution. He allowed bequests in favor of the testator's soul and provided for canonical marriage or, in any case, religious marriage. He said in the note to Article 147, with Savigny's words, that "when the priest asks the consorts whether they promise love and fidelity until death, and the consorts make this promise...they are meant to know the Christian rules of marriage and to live according to them."[37]

Concerning the civil marriage law of Santa Fe, Vélez opined in 1867, that:

> if only the will of the people were law, it would knock [aside] the customs, the morals, [and] the religion of those habitants. The text of this law clearly proves that it was sanctioned because of hatred to the Catholic Church's prescriptions.[38]

Vélez worked on the draft of the Civil Code when his friend Domingo Faustino Sarmiento succeeded Mitre in the presidency of the nation. Sarmiento appointed Vélez minister of the interior, which he served between October 1868 and May 1871, when he resigned from public service because of a gradual deterioration of his health. In December 1871, a newspaper said: "Doctor Vélez was, he no longer is. He lived in the past; today he vegetates."[39] He died on March 30, 1875, at midnight, with Catholic attention during his last hours. The president of the nation, Nicolás Avellaneda, bid farewell to his remains and exclaimed: *"Tandem quiescit!"*—"Finally he rests!"[40]

Conclusion

There are no known acts of Vélez's devotion or public profession of Catholicism. With an awareness of his belonging to the Catholic Church, he was faithful in his teaching and ideas. Despite being surrounded by an environment hostile to the Church, he held it in very high regard for the services that it offered to society.

In the era of national organization, with its strong agnostic imprint and extremes that rose to the level of hatred and violence, Vélez did not share the convictions of the age. Nevertheless, his opinions were respected for their knowledge and wisdom. Two qualified witnesses support the assertion that he was a Catholic jurist. Around 1855, the Holy See, in the instructions given by the apostolic delegate Marino Marini, expressed that Vélez demonstrated "great religiosity" and "moderation."[41] For his part, Archbishop Uladislao Castellano of Buenos Aires defined him as a "believer," "irreproachable," a man who practiced "the life of the home," and "when he came near the end of his existence, he spontaneously called to a priest."[42] Although with some hesitation, Vélez represented, in the midst of an environment dominated by heterodoxy, an expert jurist in canon law and public ecclesiastical law of essentially Catholic ideas.

Notes

1 Oliva Vélez, "Dámaso Simón Dalmacio Vélez Sarsfield."
2 Castellano, "La biografía," 1.

3 *Diario de sesiones de la Cámara de Diputados del Estado de Buenos Aires 1856–58*, Session of December 21, 1856.
4 Martínez Paz, *Dalmacio Vélez Sarsfield*, 14; Torres. *Dalmacio Vélez Sarsfield*, 40.
5 Levaggi, *Dalmacio Vélez Sarsfield, jurisconsulto*, 14.
6 Martínez Paz, *Dalmacio Vélez Sarsfield y el Código Civil argentino*, 8–22 and 374–86; Cháneton, *Historia de Vélez Sarsfield*, 20–27; Torres, *Dalmacio Vélez Sarsfield en la Universidad y su correspondencia en Córdoba*, 19–48; Levaggi, *Dalmacio Vélez Sarsfield, jurisconsulto*, 13–14.
7 Dellaferrera, "Dalmacio Vélez Sarsfield, canonista," at 49.
8 *Catálogo de la Biblioteca Dalmacio Vélez Sarsfield*; Díaz Bialet, *El derecho romano en la obra de Vélez Sarsfield*, 1:60.
9 Cháneton, *Historia*, 40 and 583; Levaggi, *Dalmacio Vélez Sarsfield, jurisconsulto*, 14–15.
10 Cháneton, *Historia*, 55–62 and 105, note 28; Levene, *Historia del Derecho Argentino*, 10:566 76; Levaggi, *Dalmacio Vélez Sarsfield, jurisconsulto*, 16.
11 Levene, *Historia*, 558–59.
12 Cháneton, *Historia*, 77–80; Levaggi, *Dalmacio Vélez Sarsfield, jurisconsulto*, 15.
13 Levaggi, *Dalmacio Vélez Sarsfield, jurisconsulto*, 15.
14 Cháneton, *Historia*, 55–62; Levene, *Historia*, 566–76; Mariluz Urquijo, "Las Instituciones de Derecho Eclesiástico de Gmeiner"; Levaggi, *Dalmacio Vélez Sarsfield, jurisconsulto*, 16.
15 Levaggi, *Dalmacio Vèlez Sarfield, jurisconsulto*, 62.
16 *Memorial ajustado de los diversos expedientes seguidos sobre la provisión de obispos en esta Iglesia de Buenos Aires*, 96–100.
17 Legón, *Doctrina y ejercicio del patronato nacional*, 257–82.
18 Risolía, "Contribución al estudio del embargo y desembargo de los bienes de Vélez Sarsfield"; Levaggi, *Dalmacio Vélez Sarsfield, jurisconsulto*, 16.
19 Levaggi, *Dalmacio Vélez Sarsfield, jurisconsulto*, 17.
20 Ibid., 53–54; Legón, *Doctrina y ejercicio*, 283–90.
21 Levaggi, *Dalmacio Vélez Sarsfield*, 55–57.
22 Vélez Sarsfield, *Relaciones del Estado con la Iglesia*, 280.
23 Saldías, *Papeles de Rozas*, 2:38–53; Magariños de Mello, *El gobierno del Cerrito*, 460–61; Levaggi, *Dalmacio Vélez Sarsfield, jurisconsulto*, 65–67.
24 Levaggi, *Dalmacio Vélez Sarfielfd, jurisconsulto*, 69–70.
25 Partidas I.8.1.
26 Vélez Sarsfield, *Escritos jurídicos*, 307–14; Levaggi, *Dalmacio Vélez Sarsfield, jurisconsulto*, 69–70.
27 Levaggi, *Dalmacio Vélez Sarfield, jurisconsulto*, 71.
28 Partidas I.5.4.
29 February 23, 1858. Vélez Sarsfield, *Dictámenes en la Asesoría de Gobierno del Estado de Buenos Aires*, 144–50; Levaggi, *Dalmacio Vélez Sarsfield, jurisconsulto*, 71–72.
30 April 30, 1857. The solution was delayed. Monsignor Escalada, by decree of December 17, 1866 (approved by National Executive on April 22, 1867), held the ecclesiastical jurisdiction. It ratified the existing order and organized the second instance. The decree was reproduced in the newspaper *El Judicial* (Buenos Aires, March 22, 1867). See Levaggi, *Dalmacio Vélez Sarsfield, jurisconsulto*, 72.
31 Vélez Sarsfield. *Escritos jurídicos*, 319–22; Bruno, *Historia de la Iglesia en la Argentina*, 10:294–300; Levaggi, *Dalmacio Vélez Sarsfield, jurisconsulto*, 77–78.
32 Levaggi, *Dalmacio Vélez Sarfield, jurisconsulto*, 78.
33 Vélez Sarsfield, *Relaciones del Estado*, 256–57. *Diario de sesiones…1858*: 129. *Diario de sesiones…1856*, session of October 24, 1856: 13.
34 Levaggi, *Dalmacio Vélez Sarfield, jurisconsulto*, 87.

35 July 5, 1865. Congreso Nacional, *Diario*, 632–33. Levaggi, *Dalmacio Vélez Sarsfield y el derecho eclesiástico*, 254–60, and Levaggi, *Dalmacio Vélez Sarsfield, jurisconsulto*, 85–86.
36 Levaggi, *Dalmacio Vélez Sarfield, jurisconsulto*, 173.
37 *Código Civil*, note art. 147.
38 Levaggi, *Dalmacio Vélez Sarsfield, jurisconsulto*, 319.
39 "Cambio de Ministerio," *El Nacional* (Buenos Aires, December 15, 1871), 1.
40 Cháneton, *Historia*, 269.
41 Bruno, *Historia de la Iglesia*, 376.
42 Castellano, "La biografía," 1.

References

Allende, Guillermo L. "Cicerón y Vélez Sarsfield." *La Ley*, 1083–88. Buenos Aires, 1990-A.

Aneiros, Federico. "Derecho Público Eclesiástico, por el Dr. Dalmacio Vélez Sarsfield." In *La Religión. Periódico Teológico-Social*, Vol. 1, 493. Buenos Aires, 1854.

Bruno, Cayetano. *Historia de la Iglesia en la Argentina*, Vol. 10. Buenos Aires: Editorial Don Bosco, 1975.

Cámara de Diputados del Estado de Buenos Aires. *Diario de sesiones de la Cámara de Diputados del Estado de Buenos Aires (1856–58)*. Buenos Aires: Imprenta Americana, 1857–60.

Carbia, Rómulo D. "El Derecho Público Eclesiástico de Vélez Sarsfield. Su origen y su verdadero valor." *Nosotros* 13, no. 33 (1919): 98–101.

Castellano, Uladislao. "La biografía." In *Vélez Sarsfield (Número único). Publicado en honor del ilustre jurisconsulto con motivo de la inauguración del monumento erigido a su memoria por la Municipalidad de Córdoba*. Córdoba: La Moderna, 1897.

Catálogo de la Biblioteca Dalmacio Vélez Sarsfield. Prologue by Enrique Martínez Paz. Córdoba: Universidad Nacional de Córdoba: Biblioteca Mayor, 1940.

Cecarelli, S. M. "Enfrentamientos con la Iglesia en Santa Fe. El Convento de San Lorenzo y los cementerios (1867)." *Revista Histórica* 6, no. 16 (1990): 97–127.

Cecarelli, Silvana Mabel. "El primer matrimonio civil en Argentina." *Revista Histórica* 6, no. 17 (1991): 83–163.

Cháneton, Abel. *Historia de Vélez Sarsfield*. Reedition. Buenos Aires: EUDEBA, 1969.

Congreso Nacional. *Diario de sesiones de la Cámara de Diputados. Año 1902*, Vol. 1. Buenos Aires: Congreso Nacional, 1902.

Dellaferrera, Nelson. "Dalmacio Vélez Sarsfield, canonista." *Revista de Historia del Derecho* 29 (2001): 27–49.

Díaz Araujo, Enrique. *Consideraciones sobre Vélez Sarsfield y su obra*. Mendoza: Universidad de Mendoza, 1971.

Díaz Bialet, Agustín. *El derecho romano en la obra de Vélez Sarsfield*, Vol. 1. Córdoba: Universidad Nacional de Córdoba, 1949.

El Solo Sumo Pontifice. *Memorial ajustado de los diversos expedientes seguidos sobre la provisión de obispos en esta Iglesia de Buenos Aires, hecha por el solo Sumo Pontífice sin presentación del Gobierno*. Buenos Aires: Imprenta Argentina, 1834.

Frías, Pedro J. "Vélez Sarsfield y el Derecho público eclesiástico: ayer y hoy." *Archivum* 20 (2001): 41–51.

García, Manuel R. E. A. *Juicios críticos sobre el proyecto de Código Civil argentino.* Buenos Aires: Jesús Menéndez, 1920.

Gmeinerius, Xaverius [Franz Xaver Gmeiner]. *Institutiones juris ecclesiastici methodo scientifica adornatae.* Buenos Aires: Typographia Reipublicae, 1835.

Kaufmann, José Luis. *La presentación de obispos en el patronato regio y su aplicación en la legislación argentina.* Buenos Aires: Editorial Dunken, 1996.

Legón, Faustino J. *Doctrina y ejercicio del patronato nacional.* Buenos Aires: J. Lajouanne y Cía., 1920.

León, Pedro. "Ideologías atribuidas al Codificador." In *Homenaje a Dalmacio Vélez Sarsfield. Bicentenario de su nacimiento (1800–2000)*, Vol. 1, 53–64. Córdoba: Academia Nacional de Derecho y Ciencias Sociales de Córdoba, 2000.

Levaggi, Abelardo. *Dalmacio Vélez Sarsfield y el derecho eclesiástico.* Buenos Aires: Perrot, 1969.

Levaggi, Abelardo. *Dalmacio Vélez Sarsfield, jurisconsulto.* Córdoba: Facultad de Derecho y Ciencias Sociales, Universidad Nacional de Córdoba, 2005.

Levaggi, Abelardo. "La Iglesia y sus relaciones con el Estado [1810–1914]." In *Nueva Historia de la Nación Argentina*, Vol. 3, 313–44. Buenos Aires: Academia Nacional de la Historia/Editorial Planeta, 2000.

Levaggi, Abelardo. "Religiosidad de Dalmacio Vélez Sarsfield." *Archivum* 26 (2007): 143–48.

Levene, Ricardo. *Historia del Derecho Argentino*, Vol. 10. Buenos Aires: Editorial Kraft, 1958.

Magariños de Mello, Mateo J. *El gobierno del Cerrito. Colección de documentos oficiales de los poderes del gobierno presidido por el brigadier general Don Manuel Oribe. 1843–1851*, Vol. 2. Montevideo: Siglo Ilustrado, 1948–54.

Mariluz Urquijo, José María. "Dalmacio Vélez Sarsfield: tradición y modernidad." *Revista de Historia del Derecho* 29 (2001): 13–26.

Mariluz Urquijo, José María. "Las Instituciones de Derecho Eclesiástico de Gmeiner." *Revista del Instituto de Historia del Derecho* 1 (1949): 38–42.

Martínez Paz, Enrique. *Dalmacio Vélez Sarsfield y el Código Civil argentino.* Facsimile reedition. Córdoba: Academia Nacional de Derecho y Ciencias Sociales de Córdoba, 2000.

Martínez Paz, Enrique, ed. *Dalmacio Vélez Sarsfield. Político y jurista. Escritos y discursos.* Buenos Aires: Editorial América Unida, 1927.

Molinari, Diego Luis. "Bases y formación del espíritu jurídico de Dalmacio Vélez Sarsfield." *Anales de la Facultad de Derecho y Ciencias Sociales* 20 (1919): 333–39.

Molinario, Alberto D. "La ley santafesina de matrimonio civil." *Anales de la Facultad de Ciencias Jurídicas y Sociales de la Universidad de La Plata* 23 (1964): 191–261.

Oliva Vélez, Pedro C. "Dámaso Simón Dalmacio Vélez Sarsfield. Aportes para su biografía." *Revista Notarial* 789 (1971): 1433–57.

Risolía, Marco Aurelio. "Contribución al estudio del embargo y desembargo de los bienes de Vélez Sarsfield." *Revista del Instituto de Historia del Derecho Ricardo Levene* 24 (1978): 225–41.

Ruiz Guiñazú, Enrique. "La estirpe intelectual de Vélez." *Revista del Instituto de Historia del Derecho* 11 (1960): 190–211.

Saldías, Adolfo. *Papeles de Rozas*, Vol. 2. La Plata: Talleres Gráficos, 1907.

Tonda, Américo A. *La Iglesia argentina incomunicada con Roma (1810–1858). Problemas, conflictos, soluciones.* Santa Fe: Editorial Castellví, 1965.

Torres, Félix A. *Dalmacio Vélez Sarsfield en la universidad y su correspondencia en Córdoba*. Córdoba: Universidad Nacional de Córdoba, 1997.

Vélez Sarsfield, Dalmacio. *Derecho público eclesiástico. Relaciones del Estado con la Iglesia en la Antigua América Española*. Buenos Aires: J. A. Bernheim, 1854.

Vélez Sarsfield, Dalmacio. "Dictamen sobre la ley santafesina de matrimonio civil." *Revista de Legislación y Jurisprudencia* 4 (1870): 191–201.

Vélez Sarsfield, Dalmacio. *Dictámenes en la Asesoría de Gobierno del Estado de Buenos Aires*. Buenos Aires: Instituto de Historia del Derecho Ricardo Levene, 1982.

Vélez Sarsfield, Dalmacio. "Escritos jurídicos." In *Colección de Textos y Documentos para la Historia del Derecho Argentino*, 11. Buenos Aires: Abeledo-Perrot, 1971.

Vélez Sarsfield, Dalmacio. *Relaciones del Estado con la Iglesia*. Buenos Aires: Librería La Facultad, 1919.

Zorraquín Becú, Ricardo. "La formación intelectual de Vélez Sarsfield." *Revista del Instituto de Historia del Derecho Ricardo Levene* 15 (1964): 156–78.

7 José Bernardo Couto y Pérez (Mexico, 1803–62)

Óscar Cruz Barney

Introduction

During the first decades of the nineteenth century, Mexico developed lasting processes of formation and integration of political and ideological positions. Opposition formed between liberalism and conservatism, federalism and centralism, and monarchy and republic. Great jurists participated in these processes not only from a legal point of view but also with their contributions to the world of culture, art, and literature. This is the case of José Bernardo Couto y Pérez, whose moral formation within the Catholic tradition and culture contributed to his vision of independent Mexico. This chapter addresses the jurist's family origin, his training, his participation in government tasks, and his contributions within both the legal literature and the culture of Mexico.

José Bernardo de Couto y Pérez was born in the city of Orizaba in the state of Veracruz, Mexico, in 1803.[1] Son of Blas Antonio de Couto and María Antonieta Pérez, he had one brother, Juan Crisóstomo de Couto Pérez. José Bernardo married his niece, María Piedad de Couto y Minón, a descendent of José Domingo de Couto Ibea, the first Prior del Consulado de Comercio de Puebla—that is, president of the guild and commercial court of Puebla.[2] After studying humanities and law at the Colegio de San Ildefonso, José Bernardo obtained his degree on August 9, 1827. He taught international public law and joined the Ilustre y Nacional Colegio de Abogados de México in 1846, becoming its rector in 1858.

Couto was adviser to the Commercial Court of Mexico City in 1841, 1850,[3] and 1852.[4] He was a member of the legislature of the State of Veracruz in 1828 and participated in ten national congresses.[5] He was a regular member of the Council of Representatives from 1841 to 1843, which meant recognition of his intellectual and political worth. He was a senator for the class of farmers of Veracruz and later for the capitalists and merchants. He collaborated with President José Joaquín Herrera as his minister of justice from August 14 to October 19, 1845, and was commissioned to initiate peace negotiations with the United States of America during the war in 1847. He was a minister of the Supreme Court of Justice in 1851.

Couto belonged to the Academy of Law and Political Economy, the Academy of Language, the National Academy of the Three Noble Arts of San Carlos, and the Mexican Association of Geography and Statistics, among other associations and academies. In Spain he was appointed academic of the Real Academia Española de la Lengua.

A disciple of the liberal José María Luis Mora, Couto adopted moderate liberal ideas.[6] He became a "necessary man in all the great political, legal, and diplomatic matters of the country."[7] He died on November 11, 1862, in Mexico City, and was buried in the Pantheon of San Fernando; his remains were later exhumed and placed in the high chancel. The library of the Ilustre y Nacional Colegio de Abogados de México has borne his name since its inauguration on October 19, 2011.

Important for assessing Couto's contributions to Mexican law was his membership in and subsequent presidency of the Government Council of the Department of Veracruz, a council created during the republic of Félix Zuloaga. From this council, together with Juan Nepomuceno de Vértiz y Delgado and José María Andrade, on June 15, 1858, he sent to the Minister of the Interior, Luís Gonzaga Cuevas, their draft of the *Estatuto Orgánico Provisional de la República*. Unknown to Mexican historical literature until quite recently, this *Estatuto* was a foundational document in Mexican constitutionalism. The topic of the *Estatuto Orgánico Provisional de la República* was a matter for Secretary Gonzaga Cuevas, who was sure to have participated in its drafting. Couto's participation in drafting the *Estatuto* was essential, and he was its first signer.

Written work

Couto wrote legal, artistic, and biographical works. He was the author of various collaborations in the *Diccionario Universal de historia y de geografía*[8] of Manuel Orozco y Berra. A little later, Couto published his *Discurso sobre la constitución de la Iglesia* (*A discourse on the constitution of the Church*).[9] It condemned a dictatorial government that attempted to involve itself in internal matters of its citizens. In this context, one notes a change in Couto's actions and politics, moving from the moderate liberal party to the conservative party. Couto's discourse displays his legal scholarship and his knowledge of ecclesiastical matters and canon law.

His final report, or *discurso*, as rector of the Ilustre y Nacional Colegio de Abogados de México was published in 1860.[10] He also published two very important opinions: "Dictamen dado al tribunal mercantil de esta capital por su asesor Lic. D. José Bernardo Couto, sobre si puede el reo en el juicio ejecutivo invertir el orden de la ejecución, señalando bienes raíces antes que muebles"[11] and "Dictamen del Lic. D. José Bernardo Couto, asesor del tribunal mercantil, sobre la subsistencia y jurisdicción del mismo tribunal, después de establecido en la nación el sistema de gobierno general."[12] Both in his speech and in his opinions on commercial matters, José Bernardo Couto reflected his vision of the law and the need, especially in his opinions, to keep the commercial jurisdiction separate from the civil jurisdiction.

In 1872 he published his celebrated *Diálogo sobre la historia de la pintura en México* (*Dialogue on the history of painting in Mexico*), in which he refers to many works that form the Mexican school of painting. This book is considered his defining work, in which "he reveals the delicate artistic sense of the author and the profound research effort he made to write about a matter that no one else had addressed previously."[13] The *Diálogo* reflects his idea of education and the need to leave something lasting and positive for future generations. It presents the glorious past of Mexican painting and predicts a bright future. It also offers an extremely important insight into the religious art of New Spain. In 1898, Couto's collected works were published in the Library of Mexican Authors.[14]

Major themes and contributions

> [Couto] lived during a time when thinking men felt overwhelmed by events and there was notable pessimism about the situation of the country. However, many of his contemporaries, and even Couto himself, passionately sought if not solutions at least actions that would ease the torment and total destruction.[15]

This call to action in Couto's life was revealed at particular moments. Although Couto's activities were varied and important, three great moments in national life merit particular attention: the peace negotiations with the United States after the War of 1846–47, the drafting of the *Estatuto Orgánico Provisional de la República* (Provisional Organizational Statute of the Republic) of 1858, and the rectorship of the Ilustre y Nacional Colegio de Abogados de México.

The war between Mexico and the United States and the Guadalupe Hidalgo Treaty

In the mid-1840s, in addition to the problems presented by the incursions of the United States into Mexican territory, internal rebellions continued to emerge. President James Polk of the United States attempted the annexation of Texas and the territories of New Mexico and California. At first, he offered to buy these territories, but when the Mexican Government refused, war ensued. General Zachary Taylor led the invading US army in its incursion into Mexican territory. On the Mexican side, General Mariano Arista crossed the Río Bravo (Rio Grande) to confront Taylor's men on April 25, 1846. This confrontation served as a pretext for Polk to ask Congress to declare war. Mexico did not declare war until after the occupation of Matamoros (May 18, 1846) and Taylor's continued advances into the interior of the country. Mexico declared war on July 7, 1846, although the government had been previously authorized to repel the aggression. Polk apparently sought a war sufficient only to secure the desired territories and to obligate Mexico to recognize those conquests. Nonetheless, prosecution of the war extended to the occupation of the capital of the republic.

On the Pacific coast, the ports of Mazatlán and La Paz fell, and from them the US forces left for upper California, which they occupied on January 13, 1847.

Santa Fe fell in August 1846, and San Diego in December of the same year. Taylor took Monterrey in September and Saltillo in November. In Veracruz another front was opened with General Winfield Scott at the head of the US troops. The port, with General Juan Morales in charge, was bombarded from March 22 to 29, when it surrendered after a heroic defense and the transfer of command to General José Juan Landero.[16]

Santa Anna retook power on March 21 and decided to leave the capital to fight the invader; General Pedro María Anaya remained as provisional president. In April, Santa Anna was defeated in the battle of Cerro Gordo, and one month later, Scott entered Puebla without much resistance. The US government appointed Nicholas Trist as envoy to negotiate peace with Mexico. In spite of his differences with Scott, he soon contacted the Mexican authorities to initiate negotiations, but with little success.

In August, Scott marched toward Mexico City and engaged General Valencia, who was defeated at the Battle of Padierna on August 20, 1847. That same day, Churubusco fell, after one of the most difficult battles for Scott. Subsequently, in the early days of September, Molino del Rey, under the command of General Antonio de León, fell to the US forces. From there, the invading army went to the Castillo de Chapultepec, where Nicolás Bravo and around eight hundred defenders were located, among whom was a group of cadets from the military school. The Castillo de Chapultepec fell and, days later, Mexico City suffered the same fate, even though the inhabitants of the capital contributed to its defense. By September 16, 1847, the US flag was waving in the National Palace. Santa Anna resigned as president, succeeded by Manuel de la Peña y Peña, who assumed the position on September 23 and moved the government to the city of Querétaro.

Under these circumstances, Couto was assigned the most important commission in Mexican history. With José Joaquín Herrera, Ignacio Mora Villamil, and Miguel Atristain, he initiated the first peace negotiations with the United States. Accepting the designation of negotiator on August 27, 1847, Couto indicated:

> Persuaded that in the unfortunate situation the republic finds itself, no Mexican could refuse to provide the services that the public authority requests of him, I accept the indicated commission and I will report immediately to receive the instructions the supreme government wishes to give me.[17]

The difficult negotiation was soon suspended on September 6 in view of the demands of the United States. The talks were resumed in November by Couto, together with Miguel Atristain and Luis Gonzaga Cuevas, leading to the eventual signing of the treaty.

Nicholas Trist initiated the negotiations with the Mexican Government in January 1848. Mexico ceded California and New Mexico—excluding Sonora, Chihuahua, and Baja California—in exchange for an indemnity of fifteen million pesos. The treaty was signed in Guadalupe Hidalgo on February 2, 1848, was received by Polk on February 19, and was approved by the US Senate on

March 10, 1848.[18] The war was over, and Mexico had lost more than half of its territory.[19]

The Provisional Organizational Statute of the Republic of 1858

Couto favored Mexico as a republic built on Catholic values.[20] He asserted that Catholicism was the largest and most beautiful plan for association ever seen on Earth.[21]

During the struggle between liberals and conservatives in Mexico in the 1850s, Interim President Félix Zuloaga established a government council on January 25, 1858.[22] Couto was a member of the council for the Department of Veracruz and later its president. On June 15, 1858, the government council, with Couto as president and Juan Nepomuceno de Vértiz y Delgado and José María Andrade as secretaries, sent to the secretary of the interior, Luis Gonzaga Cuevas, the draft of the Provisional Organizational Statute of the Republic. The draft had been previously approved by the Council of State. This document was unknown in Mexican historical legal literature and was not published in any of the important collections of Mexican legislation such as those of Arrillaga, Dublán, or the Mexican Archive.[23] Félix Zuloaga apparently did not transmit it to his supporters and followers, although they knew of its existence.[24]

The Provisional Organizational Statute of the Republic was within the jurisdiction of the secretary of the interior, and one may speculate that Secretary Cuevas participated in its drafting. Regarding the work on the *Estatuto*, Couto refers to a conversation with José Joaquín Pesado, a member of the government council, in which Pesado expresses his concerns about the *Estatuto*, a work of the greatest interest, which Pesado would promote in the council.[25] The *Estatuto* provides a window into Couto's thoughts on the republic, government, Mexican society, and the political moment of his country.

The *Estatuto* begins in the name of God and is divided into six sections and forty-six articles. In the first section, the statute offers a catalog of fundamental rights and obligations toward the country arising from the ideas proclaimed on achieving independence. Article 1 establishes that the public law of the Mexican nation is based on three guarantees proclaimed in Iguala in 1821: religion, independence, and union.[26]

Important for our purposes, Couto sought to maintain the country's religious unity. Religious intolerance, found in early Mexican constitutional documents—such as the Plan de Iguala, the Córdoba Treaties, and the 1824, 1835, 1836, 1843 and 1847 constitutions—was reestablished. The religion of the state was Catholic, as professed by the Roman Catholic Church. The nation did not permit the exercise of any other religion in its territory.

Catholic values inserted in the *Estatuto* can be clearly identified. The *Estatuto* contains certain basic rights and principles such as:

Liberty. In Mexico every person is born free and can never be enslaved. Anyone who is a slave outside of the country would be free upon entering Mexican territory. Any attempt to introduce slavery in Mexico would be considered a crime against the fundamental laws of the state.

Due process. No one can be imprisoned except by a written order of a competent authority. Anyone who is imprisoned has the right to demand a copy of the order for imprisonment, signed by the public officer that executed it, except in the case of *delito infraganti* (in flagrante delicto), in which case any person can detain offenders and take them to the authority.

Principle of nonretroactivity of the law. A penalty can be imposed only by the decision of a competent judge and after legal process in which the offender has been heard and his defenses received.

Prohibition of cruel and unusual punishments; prohibition of torture. The penalties of confiscation of property, disgrace of relatives, or mutilation may not be imposed for any crime. Nor may any kind of torture be used in pretrial investigations, even tortures that could have effects other than loss of life, nor may those condemned to die be denied the time necessary to receive religious support or to give testimony.

Inviolability of private property and proportionality in taxes. Property is inviolable, whether belonging to private individuals or to civil or religious corporations. The authority may not deprive anyone of what he has legally acquired, nor impede him from its use and enjoyment, nor demand anything more than the payment of taxes or levies for the public revenue corresponding to each individual or corporation, in proportion to what he possesses, and always proceeding according to general rules.

Expropriation. Expropriation may be carried out only after a resolution by the legislature, with payment to the owner, in cash, for the full value of the property, appraised by experts appointed by both parties; and with indemnity, in the same form, for any resulting damages.

Obligations of the inhabitants. All the inhabitants of the republic are obligated to obey its laws, to respect and to obey its magistrates of the law, and to contribute to the public revenue.

Obligations of Mexicans. Mexicans are also obligated:

1. To defend the country.
2. To do other acts of public service that the laws require.
3. To have unwavering loyalty to the nation, even when residing outside its territory.

Legal status of foreigners. Foreigners passing through and residing in the republic are under the safeguard of the law of nations and under the protection of the national laws.

The points described above reflect Couto's vision of freedoms and fundamental rights. They reflect the formation and thinking of the jurist. The impact of the statute was limited by the disappearance of the Central Republic with the installation of the Second Mexican Empire.

The rectorship of the Ilustre y Nacional Colegio de Abogados de México

At the end of May 1758, a group of lawyers in Mexico City, headed by attorney Baltasar Ladrón de Guevara y Espinosa de los Monteros, the "American Ulpian,"[27] requested and obtained from both the viceroy and the Real Audiencia of New Spain permission to meet with other New Spain attorneys to discuss the founding of a *colegio* for the mutual support and dignity of lawyers.[28] This permanent establishment, through the contributions of its members, would help lawyers and their families and would manage other aspects of professional activity.[29] Authorization for the foundation of the Colegio was granted by Charles III through the royal order (*real cédula*) of June 21, 1760. The Colegio was granted the title of *Ilustre*, and it was admitted under royal protection.[30] The creation of the Ilustre y Real Colegio de Abogados de México was part of an extensive task of organizing the legal profession undertaken by Charles III in the Hispanic world under the auspices of the Enlightenment and the spirit of the guild.[31] The patron saints of the Colegio were, first of all, the Virgin of Guadalupe, followed by San Juan Nepomuceno, San Juan de Dios, and San Andrés Avelino.

One of the aspects of greatest interest regarding the Ilustre y Real Colegio de Abogados in the colonial period is the political role of some of its members in the years of the War of Independence.[32] From the confrontation between the city council of Mexico City and the Real Audiencia in 1808 until the triumph of the Army of the Three Guarantees and of Agustín de Iturbide in 1821, several lawyers of the Colegio were on the front line of the events. These included Francisco Primo de Verdad y Ramos, Juan Francisco de Azcárate, Carlos María de Bustamante, and José Miguel Guridi y Alcocer, to mention just a few.

With independence, the Colegio decided to join the independent country and adopt the name of Ilustre e Imperial Colegio de Abogados de México—Mexico having been born into independence on September 27, 1821, as the Mexican Empire under Agustín de Iturbide, or Agustín I. The Colegio appeared before the Provisional Board to pledge its oath of independence in the session of October 9, 1821.

On the fall of the empire and the establishment of the republic, the name of the Colegio changed to that of Ilustre y Nacional Colegio de Abogados de México, which remains to this day, since through a decree of April 16, 1823, it was ordered that every establishment, office, and any others that carried the name "Imperial" must change it to "National."

Bernardo Couto joined the Ilustre y Nacional Colegio de Abogados de México on January 25, 1846, when José María Jiménez was rector. At that time, members of the Colegio included exceptional lawyers such as Andrés Quintana Roo (minister of the Supreme Court of Justice), José María Bocanegra (retired minister of the Supreme Court of Justice and former rector of the Colegio), Crispiniano del Castillo (senator of the republic), Manuel de la Peña y Peña (former president of the republic, former president of the Supreme Court of Justice, and subsequently rector of the Colegio), José Hilario Elguero (deputy of the General Congress), Pedro Escudero y Echánove (future codifier of Mexican civil law), Juan José Flores Alatorre (retired minister and former rector of the Colegio), Mariano Yáñez (deputy of the General Congress and future codifier of Mexican civil law), José María Lacunza (deputy to the Congress and future codifier of Mexican civil law), José María Lafragua (senator and future codifier of Mexican criminal law), Antonio Martínez de Castro (deputy to the General Congress, future minister of justice, and codifier of Mexican criminal law), José María Zamacona (future codifier of Mexican criminal law), and many others. In 1848 Mariano Otero would join the Colegio.

Couto was appointed in 1858 to be rector of the Colegio for the period 1858–59. He succeeded José Gabriel Sagaseta, who was rector from 1852 to 1858. The report of Couto's first term was published in 1860 by the Press of Ignacio Cumplido. He had the enormous fortune of being rector of the Colegio on its hundredth anniversary.[33] He would be reelected for a second term, which concluded in 1862.

In his first report, Couto asked God to guide the Colegio to purposes always good and dignified, with development and prosperity. The prayer must have worked, because the rector on the second term could present a history of the Colegio with grander and better achievements. The rectorship of Bernardo Couto was followed by that of another great jurist, José Fernando Ramírez. The library of the Ilustre y Nacional Colegio de Abogados now bears the name of José Bernardo Couto, in recognition of his work as a jurist and builder of independent Mexico.

Couto was an exceptional character in nineteenth-century Mexico. His commitment to education, culture, and law were remarkable, all imbued with his formation and Catholic convictions, within an idea of the nation and a pride essential for the formation of the country.

Notes

1 See Mayagoitia y Hagelstein, "Los rectores del Ilustre y Real Colegio de Abogados de México," 475. See also Noriega Elio, "Los grupos parlamentarios en los Congresos mexicanos," 1810 y 1857; and Morineau, "Couto y Pérez, José Bernardo."

2 Cruz Barney, *El Consulado de Comercio de Puebla*.

3 That year he published "Dictamen dado al tribunal mercantil" and "Dictamen del Lic. D. José Bernardo Couto."

4 Cruz Barney, *Historia de la jurisdicción mercantil en México*, 165.

5 His enormous political activity can be seen in Costeloe, *La República central en México, 1835–1846*.

6 Ricardo Couto, *Homenaje a don José Bernardo Couto*, 11.

7 Ibid.

8 Press of F. Escalante, Librería de Andrade, Mexico City, 1854.

9 Mexico City, Edición del Diario de Avisos, Press of Vicente Segura, 1857.

10 J. B. Couto, *Discurso que en la elección de oficios del Ilustre y Nacional Colegio de Abogados de México*.

11 In *Variedades de jurisprudencia*, vol. 1.

12 Ibid.

13 Ibid., 17.
14 J. B. Couto, *Obras del doctor D. José Bernardo Couto.*
15 Gutiérrez Haces, "Estudio Introductorio."
16 Bauer, *The Mexican War 1846–1848,* 248–53.
17 R. Couto, *Homenaje*, 12.
18 Soberanes and Vega, *El Tratado Guadalupe Hidalgo.*
19 Ibid.
20 Acle Aguirre, "Amigos y aliados," 222.
21 J.B. Couto, *Discurso sobre la constitución de la Iglesia*, 140.
22 Arrillaga Basilio, *Recopilación de leyes,* 13–16.
23 Cruz Barney, *La República central de Félix Zuloaga.*
24 I acquired the original manuscript in a book auction a few years ago, and after determining its nature, importance, and content, I published the facsimile of it in the Institute of Legal Research of the UNAM.
25 Document 944, Fondo XVII-3, CEHM.
26 Carbonell, et al., *Constituciones históricas de México.*
27 Mayagoita y Hagelstein, "240 años del I. y N. Colegio de Abogados de México," 609.
28 Mayagoitia y Hagelstein, "Don Manuel Ignacio Beye de Cisneros y Quijano."
29 Mayagoitia, "Los rectores," 267.
30 Cruz Barney, "El Ilustre y Nacional Colegio de Abogados de México. 250 años de colegiación de la abogacía"; and Cruz Barney, "250 años del Ilustre y Nacional Colegio de Abogados de México."
31 Barcia Lago, *Abogacía y ciudadanía*, 431.
32 Cruz Barney, "Los abogados y la independencia de México."
33 I had the privilege to be president of the Colegio on its 250th anniversary.

References

Acle Aguirre, Andrea. "Amigos y aliados: José Bernardo Couto (1803–1862) y José Joaquín Pesado (1801–1861)." *Historia Mexicana* 61 (2011): 163–230.

Arrillaga Basilio, José. *Recopilación de leyes, decretos, bandos, reglamentos, circulares y providencias de los supremos poderes y otras autoridades de la República Mexicana.* México: A. Boix, 1864.

Bauer, Jack. *The Mexican War 1846–1848.* New York: Macmillan, 1974.

Carbonell, Miguel, Óscar Cruz Barney, and Karla Pérez Portilla, compilers. *Constituciones históricas de México.* 2nd ed. Mexico: Porrúa, 2004.

Costeloe, Michael P. *La República central en México, 1835–1846. Hombres de bien en la época de Santa Anna.* Translated by Eduardo L. Suárez. México: Fondo de Cultura Económica, 2000.

Couto, José Bernardo. "Dictamen dado al tribunal mercantil de esta capital por su asesor Lic. D. José Bernardo Couto, sobre si puede el reo en el juicio ejecutivo invertir el orden de la ejecución, señalando bienes raíces antes que muebles." In *Variedades de jurisprudencia o colección de diversas piezas útiles para ilustración del derecho, Tercera Parte del Semanario Judicial*, Vol. 1. México: Press of J. M. Lara, 1850–55.

Couto, José Bernardo. "Dictamen del Lic. D. José Bernardo Couto, asesor del tribunal mercantil, sobre la subsistencia y jurisdicción del mismo tribunal, después de establecido en la nación el sistema de gobierno general." In *Variedades de jurisprudencia o colección de diversas piezas útiles para ilustración del derecho, Tercera Parte del Semanario Judicial*, Vol. 1. México: Press of J. M. Lara, 1850–55.

Couto, José Bernardo. *Discurso que en la elección de oficios del Ilustre y Nacional Colegio de Abogados de México, celebrada el 29 de enero de 1860 leyó el Rector Dr. D. José Bernardo Couto.* México: Press of Ignacio Cumplido, 1860.

Couto, José Bernardo. *Discurso sobre la constitución de la Iglesia.* México: Edición del Diario de Avisos, Press of Vicente Segura, 1857.

Couto, José Bernardo. *Obras del doctor D. José Bernardo Couto.* México: Imp. de V. Agueros, 1898.

Couto, Ricardo. *Homenaje a don José Bernardo Couto, Rector en el Primer Centenario.* Presentación de Francisco Javier Gaxiola. México: Ilustre y Nacional Colegio de Abogados de México, Librería de Manuel Porrúa, 1961.

Couto, Ricardo. *José Bernardo Couto.* Prologue by Leonardo Pasquel. Mexico City: Editorial Citlaltepetl, 1961.

Cruz Barney, Óscar. "250 años del Ilustre y Nacional Colegio de Abogados de México." In *De leyes e historia. Homenaje al 250 aniversario del INCAM y a los 45 años de la Universidad Anáhuac México Norte*, edited by F. Anaya Ojeda and J. Ordoñana Martínez, 53–84. Mexico City: Ed. Porrúa, Ilustre y Nacional Colegio de Abogados de México, Universidad Anáhuac, 2010.

Cruz Barney, Óscar. "Los abogados y la independencia de México." In *Juicios y causas procesales de la independencia mexicana*, edited by Francisco Ibarra Palafox, 323–45. Mexico City: Instituto de Investigaciones Jurídicas, UNAM, 2010.

Cruz Barney, Óscar. *El Consulado de Comercio de Puebla. Régimen jurídico, historia y documentos, 1821–1824.* Mexico City: Instituto de Investigaciones Jurídicas, UNAM, 2006.

Cruz Barney, Óscar. "Don José Bernardo Couto y Pérez y la formación del Estado Mexicano." In *Los abogados y la formación del Estado mexicano*, edited by Óscar Cruz Barney, Héctor Fix Fierro, and Elisa Speckman Guerra, 517–41. Mexico City: Instituto de Investigaciones Jurídicas, Instituto de Investigaciones Históricas, Ilustre y Nacional Colegio de Abogados de México, 2013.

Cruz Barney, Óscar. *Historia de la jurisdicción mercantil en México.* Mexico City: Instituto de Investigaciones Jurídicas, UNAM, Ed. Porrúa, Universidad Panamericana, 2006.

Cruz Barney, Óscar. "El Ilustre y Nacional Colegio de Abogados de México. 250 años de colegiación de la abogacía." *Lecturas Jurídicas.* Mexico City: Universidad de Chihuahua, Faculty of Law, V period, Special Edition, September 2010.

Cruz Barney, Óscar. "José Bernardo Couto y Pérez." In *Leyes y Letras*, edited by Luis Martí Mingarro, 605–8. Madrid: Ed. Rasche, Unión Internacional de Colegios y Agrupaciones de Abogados, 2014.

Cruz Barney, Óscar. *La República Central de Félix Zuloaga y el Estatuto Orgánico Provisional de la República de 1858.* Mexico City: UNAM, 2009; 2nd edition, Porrúa, 2011.

Gutiérrez Haces, Juana. "Estudio Introductorio." In José Bernardo Couto, *Diálogo sobre la historia de la pintura en México*, México: Consejo Nacional para la Cultura y las Artes, Col. Cien de México, 1995.

Mayagoita y Hagelstein, Alejandro. "240 años del I. y N. Colegio de Abogados de México." *Revista de Investigaciones Jurídicas* 24 (2000): 609–12.

Mayagoitia y Hagelstein, Alejandro. "Don Manuel Ignacio Beye de Cisneros y Quijano, Rector del Ilustre y Real Colegio de Abogados de México." *Ilustre y Nacional Colegio de Abogados de México A.C. Mecanismo de Comunicación* 1, no. 2 (2010).

Mayagoitia y Hagelstein, Alejandro. "Los rectores del Ilustre y Real Colegio de Abogados de México: la primera generación (1760–1783)." In *Carrera, linaje y patronazgo. Clérigos y juristas en Nueva España, Chile y Perú (siglos XVI–XVIII)*, edited by Rodolfo Aguirre Salvador, 267–315. Mexico City: CESU, UNAM, Plaza y Valdés, 2004.

Morineau, Marta. "Couto y Pérez, José Bernardo." In *Enciclopedia jurídica mexicana*, Anuario 2005. Mexico City: Instituto de Investigaciones Jurídicas, UNAM, 2005.

Noriega Elio, Cecilia. "Los grupos parlamentarios en los Congresos mexicanos, 1810 y 1857. Notas para su estudio." In *El poder y el dinero. Grupos y regiones mexicanos en el siglo XIX*, edited by Beatriz Rojas, 120–140. Mexico City: Instituto Mora, 1999.

Soberanes Fernández, José Luis, and Juan Manuel Vega Gómez. *El Tratado Guadalupe Hidalgo en su sesquicentenario.* Mexico City: Instituto de Investigaciones Jurídicas, UNAM, 1998.

8 Teodosio Lares (Mexico, 1806–70)

Brian Hamnett

Introduction

Teodosio Lares, an active jurist and significant political figure in his time, is one of those extraordinary figures in Latin American history who have been virtually forgotten in the historiography. Even so, he appears at crucial junctures in Mexican political life during the 1850s and 1860s. The obvious explanation for the neglect, as in the case of other Mexican figures, is the persistence in liberal and revolutionary historiography of throwing the focus, and moral approval, on their own principal leaders and, thereby, blotting their critics or opponents out of the picture. Lares, however, was no reactionary. Despite evident co-operation with General Antonio López de Santa Anna's last regime in 1853–55, General Miguel Miramón's conservative regime in 1860, and Emperor Maximilian of Habsburg's Second Mexican Empire of 1863–67, Lares managed to preserve a distinct political identity on the unstable middle ground between conservatism and radical federalism, and between clericalism and liberal secularism. He constantly remained a dedicated reformer of the judicial system. In the decades following Mexican independence from Spanish rule in 1821, the new republic desperately needed a revision of its legal system, updating or superseding colonial law, and in accordance with social and economic realities.

Biographical information

Lares originated from Asientos de Ibarra in the state of Aguascalientes. From 1836 to 1850 he was closely associated with the Literary Institute of Zacatecas, where he became director. In 1848, he was elected deputy for Zacatecas in the National Congress, the beginning of a long political career. He was elected to the senate in 1851.

The political position of Lares has proven difficult to ascertain, both in his day and in the historiography. He seemed to stand somewhere between moderate liberalism and conservatism in the period between 1851 and 1867. From 1853, Lares was clearly influenced by the ideas of Lucas Alamán, former minister, historian, and founder of the Conservative Party in 1849. Both of them saw the Santa Anna dictatorship as the only recourse for stabilizing the country in the aftermath of military defeat in the war with the United States in 1846–47 and in the face of widespread rural rebellions. Lares agreed with the view, expressed in Alamán's letter of March 23, 1853 to Santa Anna, that the Catholic religion provided the only remaining bond of unification among the diverse peoples of the Mexican Republic.[1] However, we do not find Lares among the ardent proponents of monarchy as the solution to Mexico's problems, despite Alamán's inclination in that direction. Lares was prepared to rally to the empire in 1863, like many other leading figures, under the belief that it could bring together moderate opinion, protect the Church, and provide a vehicle for reform and stability, avoiding the extremes of radical liberalism and federalism. Lares sought to continue his reforms of the judicial system, begun ten years earlier. For his acceptance of employment under the empire, the victorious liberals in 1867 branded him a traitor.

Lares and the judiciary

Lares demonstrated his concern for judicial reform by presenting a series of fourteen lessons on Administrative Law at the *Ateneo Mexicano* in Mexico City in 1851 and published in the following year by the well-known liberal publisher, Ignacio Cumplido. These highlighted outstanding issues that required resolution. One of them concerned the legal definition of properties possessed by Indigenous communities, an anomaly arising from the lapse of colonial law at independence. Corporate and community property-ownership had been recognized under the Hispanic Laws of the Indies, codified in 1681 (*Recopilación de las Leyes de los Reinos de Indias*), but, even before independence, a tendency towards privatization had been growing and would reach its climax during the Liberal Reform period. In the specific case of the Indian quarters (*parcialidades*) of San Juan and Santiago in Mexico City, Lares argued for sustaining the legal right of communal property ownership.[2]

The lectures also highlighted the ambiguous relationship between the executive and the judicial powers in the liberal constitutional system, founded upon the separation of powers and deriving from the Spanish Constitution of 1812. The federal system, dating from the Mexican Constitution of 1824, restored in 1846 after the collapse of a centralist experiment initiated in 1835, had, in his view, further exacerbated the problem. He sought to regulate this anomaly in a series of laws directed towards the administration of justice, the centerpiece of which was the Law for the Regulation of Contention in Policy Administration. This law proved, in the long run, to be the most significant contribution which Lares made to the development of Mexican jurisprudence. Its models were the Spanish law of 1845 and the French law of 1851.

From April 20, 1853, until August 12, 1855, Lares was Santa Anna's secretary of justice, ecclesiastical affairs, and public instruction. Alamán supported his candidature for this post, and, after Alamán's death, on June 2, 1853, Lares became the leading figure in the administration. He supported Santa Anna's abandonment of the Constitution of 1824 and the federal system and dissolution of the state legislatures in April. One of Lares's first actions was to control the press through a series of tight regulations designed to cool down the political polemic, which he saw as a prime cause of division in the country and a threat to religious orthodoxy. The principle introduced was registration of all publishers' names and addresses with the authorities and the imposition of fines for violations of the new law. Publishers were to be held responsible for what their writers and editors produced. Government authorities were to examine every text. Similarly, all booksellers were to have government license or be put out of business.[3] Alamán's influence seems to have been behind this law, which was modeled on the French Organic Law of February 17, 1852.[4]

The *Ley para el arreglo del contencioso administrativo* of May 25, 1853, intended to reduce the intervention of the judicial power in the process of implementation of policy by the executive power. The law sought to remove obstacles which were arising from appeals to the courts by private individuals, groups, or corporations seeking to block the application of government policy in their own interest. This law established the idea of *lo contencioso administrativo* in Mexican jurisprudence.[5] The authoritarian implications of this law, although envisaged by Lares as a tightening of rules, incensed liberals of the succeeding Reform era. They did not rescind the law, however, but simply allowed it to lapse.

Lares was able to secure implementation of this law, because no constitution was in place at the time, and no legislative bodies were in existence during the dictatorship. The law formed part of a process of establishing a distinct Mexican legal system to supersede Spanish colonial law. The Spanish monarchy had been ruled by the *Novísima Recopilación* of 1805, which was a renovation of the *Nueva Recopilación* of 1567, founded upon the *Ordenanzas Reales* of the Kingdom of Castile dating from 1480. With the development of liberal constitutionalism in the Hispanic world, beginning with the Cádiz Constitution of 1812 and followed by the Mexican Constitution of 1824, new principles, institutions, and practices were introduced alongside these older compilations. Specific declarations of political rights in 1812 accompanied the separation of powers and the fundamental liberal principle of equality before the law; federal structures were established in Mexico after 1824.

When the federal constitution was restored in 1846, an *Acta de Reforma* in May 1847, influenced by the moderately liberal political thinker, Mariano Otero, contained in Article 25—a new legal process known as the *juicio de amparo*, which would come to have transcendent significance in Mexican jurisprudence. It was a procedural law empowering the courts to oversee enforcement of laws by government officials.[6] This procedural authority, however, raised the question of the relationship of the judicial power to the executive. The objective of the Lares Law was to resolve this dilemma by introducing the new category of "law of administrative contention." He therefore had to define what was meant by the specifically administrative: public works; contracts; patents; issues concerning agriculture, commerce, and industry; matters involving national revenues; social welfare; conditions in textile workshops; alignment of streets; maintenance of roads, canals, dykes, waterways and water deposits; and issues arising from opposition to improvements and innovations.[7] Lares intended to strengthen the executive power in a period of challenge from all sides and de-politicize recourse to *amparo*.

The Lares Law provided prior recourse in writing to the authority responsible for the action contested, expressing the reason for complaint. If no redress resulted within fifteen days through this process of administrative contestation, then, as a last resort, recourse might be made through the judicial process. This law sought to strike a balance between executive authority and private rights.

Simultaneously, Lares issued a series of laws determining the structure and operation of the judiciary. The 454 articles of the Law for the Regulation of the Administration of Justice on December 16, 1853, established the hierarchy of courts, reaching up to the Supreme Tribunal of Justice from the base level of local and district courts of the first instance through the secondary and superior courts of the departments of the central system of government. The law delineated the relation between the courts and the executive power. Under this law, the Supreme Tribunal of Justice would consist of fifteen sitting members, plus a further fifteen ancillary members (eleven *numerarios* and four *supernumerarios*), appointed by the executive power.[8] The Law Concerning the Responsibility of Justices, on December 27, 1853, dealt with procedure, irregularities, and abuses (including bribery, unwarranted influence, and absenteeism) and established the procedure for the training of members of the legal profession.[9] These laws completed the process of centralizing the administration of justice. After the fall of Santa Anna in August 1855 and the restoration of federalism, this law was abrogated by the liberal group around President Juan Álvarez. Benito Juárez, Minister of Justice, restructured the Supreme Court and the hierarchy of courts in his Law for the Reform of Judicial Administration, issued on November 23, 1855, generally known as the *Ley Juárez*.[10] The Law of May 25, 1853, concerning administrative contention, was left on the shelf, to be reclaimed at a later time. The federal Congress enabled the *Ley de Amparo* in 1882 to become part of the amendment to Article 107 of the Constitution of 1857.

During the middle of the nineteenth century, several Spanish American republics adopted commercial codes designed to supersede colonial laws: Colombia in 1853, Argentina in 1862, Chile in 1867. Mexico was part of that pattern. Lares drafted the commercial code of May 1, 1854, based on the French code of 1807 and, in part, the Spanish code of May 30, 1829. The focus of the Mexican code, however, lay on the judicial aspects of trade. The intention was to replace the *Ordenanzas* of Bilbao of 1560 (though originating in 1429), which Philip II (1556–98) made applicable to the entire Hispanic monarchy, and the New Ordinances of 1737, which Philip V (1700–46) did likewise. These older provisions had provided commercial and maritime legislation and regulations for contracts and for the organization of trading bodies. The new codes would bring them up to date. The Lares code was the first attempt in Mexico to formulate a new commercial code that corresponded to the economic conditions of the time. It was abandoned, however, with the collapse of Santa Anna's rule and formally repealed in 1856 by the liberal administration, which objected to the inclusion of the privileges (*fueros*) of specific corporations. Until a new commercial code could be compiled, commercial practice reverted in part to the *Ordenanzas* of Bilbao or to the Lares code, as the states in the federal system decided.[11]

The French intervention in Mexico (1862–67) forced the Juárez administration, a coalition of moderate and radical liberals, to abandon Mexico City in 1863. This situation enabled the establishment, first, of a regency and, subsequently, the Second Mexican Empire, when a new coalition of forces took power—moderates, conservatives, clericals, and monarchists. Lares returned to the center of politics. The imperial regime in 1863 restored, on principle, the Lares commercial code of 1854 and appointed a committee to develop responses to it. The first two volumes of this new commercial code appeared in print in 1866. However, the empire collapsed in the following year. This ensured the definitive ending of Lares's career in politics. The commercial code, however, survived until superseded by the federal commercial code of 1884 (revised in 1889), modeled on the Italian commercial code of 1882.[12]

Lares and the Catholic Church

Lares believed in maintaining the Catholic Church as the established religion of the Mexican state. He remained a close friend and ally of Archbishop Pelagio Labastida of Mexico and Bishop Clemente de Jesús Munguía of Michoacán. They were the two principal opponents of the Liberal Reform Laws of 1855–60 and the federal Constitution of 1857, which removed reference to Catholicism as the religion of the state. Even so, Lares served the Second Empire, which, in 1865, proclaimed religious toleration, in accordance with morality and law. Under Maximilian, he cooperated with moderate liberals such as José Fernando Ramírez and Manuel Siliceo, and generally sought accommodation between Church and state. Like these liberals, Lares remained skeptical of the advantages of federalism in an impoverished and divided country, in which the central government found it difficult to assert its authority.

In 1851, Senator Lares joined Alamán and Bernardo Couto, another prominent conservative, in lobbying on behalf of Munguía, the choice of Pope Pius IX (1846–78) for the bishopric of Michoacán, to be allowed by the civil authority to take possession of the diocese. The origin of the problem was that Munguía, opposed to the intervention of the civil power in ecclesiastical affairs, had refused, at the ceremony of institution, to swear the required oath to the Constitution of 1824, in which one clause appeared to authorize this. President Mariano Arista, however, allowed the consecration to proceed in Morelia Cathedral on January 18, 1852.[13] Deepening conflict followed in that state between its radical liberal and anticlerical governor, Melchor Ocampo (in office June 1852 to January 1853), and local clergy over parish dues.

In his report of February 14, 1852, to the Arista administration, Lares dealt with the long-standing problem of the relationship between the religious orders and the diocesan bishops. In the diocese of Oaxaca, where the Dominican order had been strong for most of the colonial era, the provincial wanted to appoint his own candidates to certain parishes in the diocese, even though the general trend in the later colonial period had been towards the replacement of members of religious orders as parish priests by secular clerics not in religious orders and under the direct authority of the diocesan bishop. Lares recommended the exclusion of the provincial from the process of selection of parish priests, which should be the preserve of the bishop. Lares rested his case on the Law of March 22, 1829, which affirmed appointment under canon law and in accordance with ecclesiastical custom, making allowance, nevertheless, for the civil power's faculty of exclusion. In the Oaxaca context, the provincial might pass a list of no more than three potential candidates to the bishop, who would make the decision and then refer it to the civil power. The bishop would then invest the selected candidate. This practice was designed to ensure harmony between the ecclesiastical and the civil powers, as was usually the case between Governor Benito Juárez (1847–52) and Bishop Antonio Mantecón. Lares's position was upheld by the Arista administration on February 23, 1852.[14]

When the Holy See proposed to send an official visitor to examine the condition of the religious orders in Mexico, the idea was met with resistance from the regular clergy. The papal Secretary of State, Cardinal Giacomo Antonelli, appointed Munguía, the bishop closest to Pius IX in sentiment, to be this visitor. Accordingly, Lares issued a decree on May 10, 1855, that all authorities should support the visitor in his actions. The ulterior purpose behind the visitation was to ascertain the actual condition of the orders, which were held to be in a poor state and low in numbers, with a view to reforming them before the civil power took a decision to do so unilaterally. With the Santa Anna regime on the point of collapse, Lares asked Munguía, on August 6, 1855, to suspend the visitation.[15]

Excellent relations with Murguía explained Lares's support for the bishop's reform program in the diocese of Michoacán in 1853–55. This included the foundation of a girls' school in Zamora and a diocesan seminary in Morelia, designed exclusively for the training of priests, in order to improve their quality. To that end, Lares granted Munguía use of the former Jesuit College of San Francisco Javier, where the state legislature, dissolved by Santa Anna, had previously met under the federal system. The seminary opened on January 16, 1855. In September 1853, Lares facilitated the reestablishment of the Society of Jesus in Mexico, offering the San Gregorio College in the capital as their place of residence.[16]

The Holy See, concerned to continue the process of reconstituting the Catholic Church in Mexico following the disruption in the aftermath of independence from Spain, authorized the creation of a new bishopric for San Luis Potosí in November 1854. This came into being when Lares was also secretary for ecclesiastical affairs. The bishopric would consist of sections of the three dioceses of Michoacán, Guadalajara, and Mexico. As minister of public instruction, Lares on May 31, 1853, upheld observance of the Catholic religion as the prerequisite for teachers in primary schools, and on January 28, 1854, he specified that the Christian religion was to be taught in all schools. Lares issued a general plan of studies on December 19, 1854, establishing the hierarchy of progression from primary education to six years of secondary education and university with four faculties: philosophy (which included physical and natural sciences and mathematics), medicine and pharmacy, jurisprudence, and theology. This plan did not survive the Liberal Reform, which produced its own plan.[17]

From April 1853, the Santa Anna administration aspired to negotiate a concordat with the Holy See, in order to settle outstanding issues, such as the questions of national government patronage over the Church, claimed by right of inheritance from the Spanish Crown. These questions extended to appointments to episcopal office and the role of the Church in public education. The proposed concordat would be negotiated between Manuel Larráinzar, Mexican minister in Rome, and the Holy See. Munguía, however, remained suspicious. In his view, the Mexican Church, which had been tightly controlled by the Spanish metropolitan government before 1821, should be as closely connected to Rome as possible, in order to maintain a unity of doctrine and purpose. He feared the intrusion of the civil power on the grounds that, in its own interests, would seek to put obstacles in the way of this intimacy. For that reason, he sent a confidential letter to Cardinal Antonelli on May 1, 1855, advising against a concordat. His worst fear was that increased separation from Rome would lead the Church to disaster. As far as we are able to say, it does not appear that Lares knew of this confidential letter, since he complained of the Holy See's reluctance to speed up negotiations for the concordat. However, by that time, Santa Anna had resigned on August 12.[18]

Lares reappears in politics in Miramón's conservative administration as minister of justice once again from April 13 until December 14, 1860, during the last stage of the Civil War of the Reform (1858–61). One French observer described him as a clerical, more concerned with the interests of the Church than with those of the state. The liberal army entered Mexico City on December 25. Juárez resumed power in the city in January 1861 and restored the federal Constitution of 1857 and the Reform Laws of 1855–60.

Lares and the Second Empire

Responding positively to the French intervention, which forced the Juárez administration out of Mexico City for a second time, Lares presided over the Assembly of Notables of July 8–10, 1863, which invited the Archduke Maximilian of Habsburg to accede to the Mexican throne, vacant since the abdication of the first emperor, Agustín I (Iturbide), in March 1823.[19] In the meantime, a regency council consisting of Juan Nepomuceno Almonte, Mariano Salas, and Archbishop Labastida would oversee the country. The regency entrusted the exercise of the executive power in November 1863 to a provisional superior governing board under the presidency of Lares. This made the key relationship at the apex of politics that between Lares and the archbishop, since the principal outstanding issues, inherited from the Juárez administration, were the future of the nationalized ecclesiastical properties and, more generally, relations between Church and state. Napoleon III, who had sponsored the French intervention in the expectation of transforming Mexico into a client state in Meso-America, and Marshall Achille Bazaine, the French military commander, both favored the maintenance of the

Reform Laws, in the hope of rallying moderate opinion to the empire. Such a view threatened to provoke the ecclesiastical hierarchy into outright opposition. Lares was caught in the middle.

This delicate situation deteriorated, when Bazaine, hostile to conservatives and the clergy, instructed the regents, on November 7, to direct the courts to handle cases arising from the transfer of ecclesiastical properties to their new owners. The archbishop saw this order as tantamount to recognizing the Nationalization Law of 1859. He appealed to Lares to declare Bazaine's instruction null and void. However, on December 15, Bazaine declared that the Reform Laws would be upheld. Eleven days later, the ecclesiastical hierarchy protested the regents' maintenance of the Nationalization Law and its ratification of transactions ensuing from it. On December 30, the Supreme Court supported the hierarchy's opposition to the regents' action. Furthermore, the court declared the Superior Governing Body to have superior status to the regency in the issuing of decrees.

A tense relationship developed between the clergy and the French military authorities by the end of 1863. The Supreme Court wrote the regents on December 31, 1863, and January 7, 1864, denouncing the Reform Laws as an aberration—unjust and invalid. Bazaine's response was to dissolve the Supreme Court. The arrival of Maximilian and Carlota in June 1864, however, failed to improve the situation. The emperor brought into government a range of talents, among whom the principal figures were moderate liberals.

Lares, however, remained in a key position. On December 4, 1864, he was appointed, along with Munguía, to the newly established eight-man Council of State under the presidency of Larráinzar. Practically half the council consisted of moderates, rather than conservatives.[20] After the papal nuncio, Monsignor Pietro Francesco Meglia, arrived in Mexico City on December 7, 1864, he quickly discovered that Maximilian's position on the Church question corresponded more to the French and moderate liberal positions than to that of the clericals and conservatives. At the same time, the emperor inherited the traditional Habsburg policy of keeping the Church subordinate to the monarchy. The nuncio presented the pope's letter to the emperor, calling for the nullification of the Reform Laws and the reversal of liberal policies towards the Church so that it could have full liberty from state control. Maximilian opposed all of that, although he revived Santa Anna's former policy of seeking a concordat with Rome. The bishops protested the emperor's policies on December 29, 1864, and upheld the position of the pope.[21]

Lares, as a councilor of state, became a central figure in the imperial government's negotiations with the papal nuncio concerning a concordat between Church and state. After December 28, the imperial government's position became clear: it favored the maintenance of Catholicism as the protected religion of the state but also toleration for other Christian denominations. The emperor, however, was to exercise the same rights of patronage over the Church as the Spanish monarchs in the colonial era. The Church was to transfer to the state all rights relating to ecclesiastical properties nationalized in 1859. The pope and the emperor together would determine which of the religious orders extinguished under the liberal republic were to be restored, and the clergy would receive salaries from the state, as in the France of Napoleon I. This position might be described as both Catholic and liberal, though one opposed by Pius IX and his representative in Mexico. It was far from any idea of a Catholic state. Both Labastida and Munguía profoundly opposed the subordination of the Church, as they saw it, to the imperial government and deplored the degree of distancing of the Mexican Church from the Holy See that these proposals entailed.[22] Meglia rejected all the proposals. The rift between Church and state further worsened when Maximilian, despairing of the nuncio, decided to take matters into his own hands. The imperial decree of December 28 confirmed the purchases of ecclesiastical property. Labastida and Munguía went into complete opposition to the imperial government. Maximilian, who regarded the latter as the leading figure in the clerical opposition, expelled him from Mexico on March 26, 1865, and the nuncio departed for Rome on May 27.

In effect, from December 1864 through the course of 1865, Maximilian's government ratified the Reform Laws. Use of the privilege of the royal permission (*pase regio*) blocked publication of Pius IX's *Syllabus of Errors* of December 8, 1864, in Mexico. The pope's document condemned the notion that the Church should accommodate the position of liberal governments and that the civil power had a right to exercise control over the Church, that is, exactly what Maximilian had been trying to do. The imperial decree of April 10, 1865 guaranteed religious toleration. The new ministry, constituted in April, had prominent moderate Liberals, such as José Fernando Ramírez (at foreign relations since July 1864), Juan de Dios Peza (war), and Manuel Siliceo (education). Lares remained in position on the Council of State.[23]

To the horror of Lares, a definitive breach between the empire and the Holy See seemed imminent. The emperor, who saw Lares closer to his own position, came to regard him as an indispensable link holding together the component elements of the imperial regime. Lares, Pedro Escudero y Echánove (Minister of Justice), and the Empress Carlota struggled in vain to avoid the collapse of ecclesiastical support for the empire.[24] Before leaving for an imperial visit to Yucatán with Carlota at the beginning of November 1865, Maximilian, appointed a new regency council, consisting of Almonte, Bazaine, and Lares.

As relations between Maximilian and the French command deteriorated in Mexico during 1866 and Napoleon III's position in Europe became precarious, the French emperor decided on the withdrawal of his forces. This made the position of Lares, regarded as a calming influence, even more indispensable. The three moderate liberal ministers left the government on March 3, as Maximilian recognized the necessity of bringing the conservatives back into the political and military leadership.[25] He still remained hopeful of the prospect of negotiating a concordat with Rome. On July 16, the emperor appointed Lares to be minister of justice, a position he would hold until March 18, 1867, when the empire entered its final crisis. Lares held the presidency of the Council of State from October 6, 1866, until March 19, 1867. It appears that the prime condition Lares made for accepting the office of minister of justice was that the government should abandon its previous policies towards the Church.[26] On August 31, Maximilian appealed to Archbishop Labastida to help find a resolution of the Church–state problem. Little time remained, however. Prominent conservatives like Tomás Marín (interior) and Larráinzar (finance) joined Lares in a new ministry. Count Émile de Kératry, an intimate of Bazaine, described the ministry as consisting of *les réaccionnaires*.[27]

Maximilian held a high opinion of Lares, who, he hoped, would give cohesion to the government. As he explained to the conservative, Ignacio Aguilar y Marocho:

> This person, who possesses a legitimate influence acquired through distinguished service in the great offices of state, also has solidly established bonds of friendship with the senior clergy. No one would be better than he to direct the final negotiations with the bishops for the purpose of concluding a concordat on the bases which have been established in Rome between the special mission and the Holy See.[28]

This hope, however, remained wishful thinking on the emperor's part. Nevertheless, he believed that Lares's position as virtual intermediary with the bishops would be able to steer a course that could sustain political liberties without compromising the position of the Catholic religion.[29] By September 1866, the government consisted mainly of conservatives, enemies of the previous moderate liberal ministers, hostile to the French army, and welcoming the return of Generals Miramón and Leonardo Márquez to Mexico.[30]

Napoleon III and Bazaine urged Maximilian to abdicate and leave Mexico while he still could. Lares, however, intervened on October 20, 1866 to beg the emperor to remain, or else the entire ministry would resign. The emperor ultimately decided to pass the final decision to his Council of Ministers. On January 14, 1867, a Junta of Notables, meeting for that purpose under the presidency of Lares, urged Maximilian to remain, but by a majority of only one vote out of total of thirty-three members. According to Kératry, Lares and Márquez persuaded Maximilian to take personal command of the imperial army and make a last stand in the pro-conservative city of Querétaro, regardless of Bazaine's reservations concerning the military position.[31] Lares and Bazaine bitterly conflicted, on January 25–27, 1867 over the timing of the French army's evacuation from Mexico, which Lares believed to be in the autumn of that year. Bazaine, preparing the final evacuation for February, angrily called this calumny and broke off all further contact with the imperial government.[32]

Maximilian wrote to Lares on February 9, expressing the hope that the departure of French troops would bring peace and unity to the country, although the opposite was happening. Increasing loss of territory to the republican army made the holding of the desired elections impossible.[33] Maximilian left Mexico City with an escort under Márquez. They reached Querétaro on February 18 to join Miramón and General Tomás Mejía, the principal commanders of the imperial army. From Querétaro, Maximilian appointed Lares, Lacunza, and Márquez to the regency council in Mexico City on February 20. Márquez, on that day and the next, wrote urgently to Lares, as head of government in the capital, to dispatch a convoy with extra artillery. With the capital already surrounded by republican irregular bands, Lares replied that it would be too risky to remove the Hussars from defending the capital to escort the equipment, which would, in any case, not be adequate. There were no funds left in the treasury. Márquez replied that Querétaro could not risk sending a column out to meet the equipment in transit. Nevertheless, he praised Lares's dedication: "Señor Lares, with his characteristic exactitude and great activity, had arranged everything on the spot and replied to me on the 24th."[34] On March 18 and 19, Lares was removed from both the ministry of justice and the presidency of the Council of Ministers. He remained, however, president of the Supreme Tribunal of Justice and was appointed a substitute for the new president of the ministry, Santiago Vidaurri, when Maximilian constituted another regency on March 20. The emperor replaced Vidaurri with Lares on May 11, with Lacunza and Márquez as the two coregents. Four days later, Querétaro fell, and Maximilian, Miramón, and Mejía became republican captives subject to trial. Right to the end, the emperor's confidence in Lares never wavered.[35]

After the execution of Maximilian, Miramón, and Mejía in June 1867 in Querétaro, the liberal newspaper *El Globo* published, on January 7, 1868, a list of the "traitors" who had collaborated with the empire: Lares, Almonte, Joaquín Velázquez de León, Aguilar y Marocho, Marín, and three others. Perhaps because of sympathy with Lares's judicial experience and competence, Juárez, a fellow lawyer and a skilled manipulator of the law, pardoned Lares in November of that year.[36]

Conclusion

Lares occupied a shifting middle ground at a time of social tension across the country and polarization between conservatives and radical federalists. His closeness to the episcopate differentiated him from other moderates and explained his concern for the position of the Church in relation to the civil power. He does not appear to have been either a dedicated monarchist or partisan of the idea of a Catholic state. He was prepared to work with Santa Anna for a stronger central and executive power and later with Maximilian in the hope that the empire would provide unity and stability for the country. He was wrong on both accounts. In those regimes, Lares promoted negotiations for a concordat between the Mexican state and the Holy See, even though Bishop Munguía feared that such a course would expose the Church to increasing intervention by the civil power. Lares was a meticulous reformer of the judicial system, with remarkable attention to detail, as his laws issued in 1853 demonstrated. He sought to redress the anomalies and contradictions in Mexico's laws, inherited, in part, from the corporate juridical structure of the Spanish-colonial *ancien régime* and, in part, from the liberal constitutional system deriving from the Spanish Constitution of 1812 founded on the principle of equality before the law. To this should be added the Mexican federal Constitution of 1824, founded upon the principle of shared sovereignties with an uncertain balance both between central and provincial power, and among the divided executive, legislative, and judicial powers. Despite his significant contributions to the development of Mexican jurisprudence, his political mistakes accounted for his subsequent eclipse.

Notes

1 González Navarro, *Anatomía del poder en Mexico (1848–1853)*, 363–64, 394–96, 403–04. The two liberal newspapers, *El Monitor Republicano* and *El Siglo XIX* differed: the former said Lares was a conservative and the latter a liberal. See Vázquez Mantecón, *Santa Anna y la encrucijada del Estado*, 15, 37–38, 44. See also Mijangos y González, "El pensamiento religioso de Lucas Alamán."
2 Lira González, "El contencioso administrativo y el poder judicial en México a mediados del siglo XIX," 621–34.
3 Dublán Lozano, *Legislación mexicana*, 6:369. Suárez de la Torre, *Constructores de un cambio cultural*, 240. The publisher José Mariano Lara, a supporter of the regime, continued to flourish.
4 Vázquez Mantecón, *Santa Anna y la encrucijada del Estado*, 201–03, 220. The French law aimed to regulate the political and social content of newspapers. It placed the press under police supervision, obliged newspaper owners to make a large deposit of fifty thousand francs as a guarantee of conformity, and imposed a stamp duty on each number, thereby leading to an increase in the price of newspapers. It gave the Ministry of the Interior the power to appoint or dismiss editors. See Plessis, *De la fête impériale au mur des fédérés, 1852–1871*, 24–25.
5 Dublan y Lozano, *Legislación mexicana*, 6, Law of May 25, 1853, 416–18: see, for instance, Article 13, "Los tribunales judiciales no pueden proceder contra los agentes de la administración, ya sean individuos o corporaciones, por crímenes o delitos cometidos en el ejercicio de sus funciones, sin la previa consignación de la autoridad administrativa."
6 Tena Ramírez, *Leyes fundamentales de México*, 442–77. Zamora, et al., *Mexican Law*, 84. For the colonial antecedents, see Owensby, *Empire of Law and Indian Justice in Colonial Mexico*, 20–21, 51–52.
7 Dublán y Lozano, *Legislación Mexicana*, 6, Law of May 25, 1853, 416–18. Lira González, "Lo contencioso administrativo, ejemplo difícil para el constitucionalismo mexicano," 300–11.
8 Lira González, "Administrar Justicia sin Constitución," 118–20.
9 Dublán y Lozano, *Legislación Mexicana*, 6, Law of December 27, 1853 (66 articles), 881–90.
10 Arnold, *Política y justicia*, 151–55, 159–61.
11 Mirow, *Latin American Law*, 51, 156, 160. Means, "Mexico's Commercial Law, 1854–1884."
12 Zamora, et al., *Mexican Law*, 84–86, 448–49.
13 Mijangos y González, *The Lawyer of the Church*, 145.
14 Connaughton, *Construcción de la legitimidad política en México*, 250.
15 Mijangos, *The Lawyer of the Church*, 193–95.
16 Ibid., 200–01, 203–04.
17 Vázquez Mantecón, *Santa Anna en la encrucijada del Estado*, 78–93.
18 Mijangos, *The Lawyer of the Church*, 202–04.
19 Tamayo, *Benito Juárez* (*BJDOCS*), 13:709, 713.
20 Centro de Estudios de Historia de México (CEHM), Fondo IX-1, leg. 3, no. 291, J. Velázquez de León (Minister of State) to Ignacio Aguilar y Marocho

(Minister to the Holy See), Mexico City December 11, 1864. "El Pájaro Verde," 3, no. 12, p. 1, January 17, 1864.
21 Galeana de Valadés, *Las relaciones Iglesia-Estado*, 108–10.
22 Galeana, *Las relaciones Iglesia-Estado*, 106–07.
23 CEHM, "Diario del Imperio," 1, no. 83, Mexico City April 10, 1865.
24 Galeana, *Las relaciones Iglesia-Estado*, 119–27, 144.
25 Kératry, *Maximilien*, 174–75, 200. Galeana, *Las relaciones Iglesia-Estado*, 170–71.
26 Galindo y Galindo, *La gran década nacional*, 3:522. He described Lares as the "friend and agent of Archbishop Labastida."
27 Kératry, *Maximilien*, 174–75, 200. Galeana, *Las relaciones Iglesia-Estado*, 170.
28 CEHM, Fondo IX-1, no. 832, Maximilian to Ignacio Aguilar y Marocho, Chapultepec August 18, 1866.
29 CEHM, Fondo XXIII, Archivo de General Almonte (1854–1871), docs. 1–74: Maximilian to Almonte (in Paris), no. 61, Chapultepec August 18, 1866; no. 65, Maximilian to Almonte, Chapultepec September 20, 1866.
30 Galindo y Galindo, *La gran década nacional*, 3:523, 526.
31 *BJDOCS*, 2:704–06. Kératry, *Maximilien*, pp. 200, 221–23, 343, 346, 350. Blumberg, *The Diplomacy of the Mexican Empire*, 239–41.
32 Archivo General de la Nación, Segundo Imperio legajo 9, Lares to French representatives, Mexico City, January 25, 1867; Bazaine to Lares, Mexico City, January 27, 1867.
33 *BJDOCS*, 2:709–17.
34 *BJDOCS* 9:710–11, Maximilian to Lares, Querétaro, February 9, 1867; Lares to Maximilian, Mexico City, February 10, 1867. Leonardo Márquez, *Manifiestos. El Imperio y los Imperiales)*, rectifications by Angel Pola (Mexico City: F. Vázquez editor, 1904), 117–20.
35 Márquez, *Manifiestos*, 77–81. Blumberg, *The Diplomacy*, 257–59.
36 *BJDOCS*, 13:709–13.

References

I have not had the opportunity to study the Teodosio Lares Papers (1833–64) in the Nettie Lee Benson Library, Latin American Collection, at the University of Texas, Austin, where the greater part of the documents refers to the years 1863–64.

Archivo General de la Nación [AGN], Mexico City, Ramo de Segundo Imperio.

Arnold, Linda. *Política y justicia. La Suprema Corte mexicana (1824–1853)*. Mexico City: Universidad Nacional Autónoma de México, 1996.

Blumberg, Arnold. *The Diplomacy of the Mexican Empire, 1863–1867*. Malabar, FL: Robert Krieger, 1987.

CEHM (Centro de Estudios de la Historia de México). Fondo 9–1, leg. 3; Fondo 23, docs. 1–74 (1854–71). "Diario del Imperio," 1 (1865). "El Pájaro Verde," 3 (1864).

Connaughton, Brian. *Construcción de la legitimidad política en México*. Mexico City: Universidad Autónoma Metropolitana/UNAM/El Colegio de México, 1999.

Dublán, Manuel, and José María Lozano. *Legislación mexicana. Colección legislativa completa de la República Mexicana con todas las disposiciones expedidas para la*

Federación, el Distrito y los territoriales federales, Vol. 52. Cambridge: Cambridge University Library, DVD-ROM, 2004. Original imprint: Mexico City: Imprenta del Comercio, 1876–1912. Compiled by Mario Téllez González and José López Fontes.

Galeana de Valadés, Patricia. *Las relaciones Iglesia-Estado durante el Segundo Imperio.* Mexico City: Universidad Nacional Autónoma de México, 1991.

Galindo y Galindo, Miguel. *La gran década nacional, 1857–1867. Relación histórica de la Guerra de Reforma, intervención extranjera y gobierno del archiduque Maximiliano*, Vol. 3. Mexico City: Facsimile edition, FCE/Instituto Cultural Helénico, 1987 [Tipografía de la Secretaría de Fomento, 1904–1906].

González Navarro, Moisés. *Anatomía del poder en México (1848–1853).* Mexico City: El Colegio de México, 1977.

Hamnett, Brian R. "La Iglesia católica en México y el desafío liberal, 1855–1876. Aspectos metodológicos e historiográficos." In *Religiosidad e Historiografía. La irrupción del pluralismo religioso en América Latina y su elaboración metódica en la historiografía*, edited by Hans-Jürgen Prien, 169–85. Frankfurt am Main: Vervuert, 1998.

Kératry, Émile de. *L'Élévation et la Chute de l'Empereur Maximilien. Intervention française au Mexique (1861–1867).* Paris: A. Lacroix, Verboeckhoven et Cie, 1867.

Lira González, André. "Administrar Justicia sin Constitución. Continuidades e innovaciones bajo la dictadura de Santa Anna, 1853–1855." In *Los caminos de la Justicia en México*, 115–40. Mexico City: Suprema Corte de Justicia Nacional, 2010.

Lira González, Andrés. "El contencioso administrativo y el poder judicial en México a mediados del siglo XIX. Notas sobre la obra de Teodosio Lares." In *Memoria del 11 Congreso de Historia del derecho mexicano (1980)*, edited by José Luis Soberanes Fernández, 621–34. Mexico City: UNAM, 1981.

Lira González, Andrés. "Lo contencioso administrativo, ejemplo difícil para el constitucionalismo mexicano." In *La ciencia del derecho procesal constitucional mexicano. Estudios en homenaje a Héctor Fix-Zamudio en sus cincuenta años de investigador*, edited by Eduardo Ferrer MacGregor and Arturo Zadívar Lelo de Larrea, Vol. 12, 289–319. Mexico City: UNAM, 2008.

Means, Robert C. "Mexico's Commercial Law, 1854–1884." *Boston College International and Comparative Law Review* 2, no. 2 (1978–79): 299–335.

Mijangos y González, Pablo. *The Lawyer of the Church: Bishop Clemente de Jesús Munguía and the Clerical Response to the Mexican Liberal Reforma.* Lincoln: University of Nebraska Press, 2015.

Mirow, M.C. *Latin American Law: A History of Private Law and Institutions in Spanish America.* Austin: University of Texas Press, 2004.

Owensby, Brian. *Empire of Law and Indian Justice in Colonial Mexico.* Stanford, CA: Stanford University Press, 2008.

Plessis, Alain. *De la fête impériale au mur des fédérés, 1852–1871.* Paris: Éditions du Sueil, 1973.

Tamayo, Jorge L., ed. *Benito Juárez, Documentos, discursos y correspondencia* [*BJDOCS*], Vol. 15. Mexico City: Secretaría del Patrimonio Nacional, 1964–1970. See especially volumes 2, 9, and 13.

Tena Ramírez, Felipe. *Leyes fundamentales de México.* Mexico City: Porrúa, 1964.

Vázquez Mantecón, Carmen. *Santa Anna y la encrucijada del Estado. La dictadura (1853–1855).* Mexico City: FCE, 1986.

Zamora, Stephen, et al. *Mexican Law.* New York: Oxford University Press, 2004.

9 Bartolomé Herrera Vélez (Peru, 1808–64)

Fernán Altuve-Febres Lores

Biographical introduction

Bartolomé Herrera Vélez was born in a modest Christian home in Lima on August 24, 1808. He was the legitimate son of Manuel Herrera and Paula Vélez Rodríguez, and when he was barely five years old he and his younger brother, Juan Gualberto, lost their parents and were left in the care of their maternal uncle, Luis Vélez. When Luis also died, Herrera was left under the care of his teacher, the priest Manuel Pedemonte, who, observing his intelligence, paid for his education at the prestigious Colegio de San Carlos. Herrera's first biographer, Raphael María Taurel, tells us:

> After finishing his courses, Dr. Herrera graduated from college as a teacher and from the faculty of theology at San Marcos University at the age of twenty. He was drawn to the faculty of jurisprudence. But because he was studying philosophy, his superiors saw the need to reward him for his exemplary conduct and his remarkable achievement. To use his talents for the good of the school, they entrusted him with the teaching of the above-mentioned class and of mathematics.[1]

In 1831 Herrera was assigned to Huanuco to reorganize the national school of that city, and then returned to San Carlos, where he was promoted to vice-rector and regent of theology and arts (under this rubric were included philosophy, mathematics, and physics). At the end of 1831, he was ordained a priest by Bishop Orihuela, and in 1834 he was assigned his first parish, in Cajacay, in the province of Cajatambo in the mountains of Lima. In a biographical note, Alfredo Leubel explains Herrera's remarkable pastoral work:

> In that curate, Dr. Herrera lived in retirement, committing himself to the performance of his duties as parish priest, and to the establishment of schools for the Christian education of children. He was struck shortly afterward by that peculiar disease of the sierra known as [Peruvian] warts [Carrion's disease], and had just come out of a long convalescence when the archbishop called him to serve as secretary for the visitation of the diocese. This was

> only done in Lima, because an illness that attacked the archbishop prevented him from travelling around his diocese. In 1837, Dr. Herrera returned to his parish in Cajacay, after having been, in Lima, part of the board that was appointed to examine the constitution of that year, in which the immunities and the sovereign authority of the church were unknown; and soon afterwards he was attacked again by warts, being forced to ask for a coadjutor and go down to be cured.[2]

In 1840, the young parish priest was transferred to Lurin. While on this mission, he was summoned to deliver the sermon at the funeral of the president of the republic, Marshal Agustín Gamarra (1792–1841), held on January 4, 1842. In this brilliant oratorical piece, Herrera highlighted the importance of the *caudillo* and his courage in the battle stopped only by his death. But the president's death, Herrera pointed out, was not only tragic, but also a punishment for Peru for so many years of disorder, chaos, and small ambitions; thus he exclaimed: "The secret party spirit had usurped the love of the country; and the country that is visible only to the hearts that pay him the tribute of love did not exist for many." In the face of this punishment, Bartolomé Herrera made his "call to order," and to avoid sins against the homeland of disobedience and anarchy, he supported the defense of authority.

On his return to Lurin, in October 1842, he received a visit from General Francisco Vidal, who was passing through on his way to the capital to take over the government. Vidal was surprised by Herrera's intelligence and appointed him rector of the Colegio de San Carlos in Lima. It was then that Herrera was able to initiate a true educational reform that was summarized by his disciple José Antonio de Lavalle with these words:

> The work of Dr. Herrera as such, in the nine years that he was in charge of that establishment, cannot be studied in the narrow pages of a newspaper: it is enough to say, that he established a new system of education, changing completely the plan, the texts, and the doctrines of teaching: that he himself wrote some of those and taught philosophy, political economy, natural rights, constitutional law, people's rights, canon law, and theology; [that he] established the most severe discipline by deploying the most vigorous energy, united to the most sagacious forms, and formed a great number of very useful disciples, who have subsequently occupied the highest positions of the state and have shone in the forum, the magistracy, the chair, the church, the military, and letters.[3]

Nearly twenty-five years after the proclamation of Peru's independence, the government of General Ramón Castilla summoned the wise rector of the Colegio de San Carlos to deliver the sermon in the *Te Deum* for that anniversary. This is how he came to perform his most important piece of oratory, which had the purpose of defining the Peruvian nation that God and history had formed at the same time. Thus, he postulated the political rights that should govern it.

The sermon was divided into three parts: (a) the introduction, (b) "I have formed you," and (c) "my servant you are Israel, do not forget me." In the introduction, Herrera thanks the Almighty for the independence of Peru. Furthermore, he points out that the country had found peace in the legal regime after anarchy, and that the Lord was the author of this well-being.

In the second part of the sermon, Herrera recounts the history of Peru, through which Providence had guided the formation of the new state. Herrera speaks of the Inca empire, which, on the basis of God's laws, prepared the fertile land for the Gospel that Spain would bring—Catholic Spain, of the true faith, chosen by God for that work, and not another people fallen victim to the Protestant rebellion. The work of the Motherland is in her children, who reached the age of being able to govern themselves and demanded their right; the grieving mother opposed this, but the energy of the children was imposed by the divine will, which granted freedom. In the last part of the sermon, Herrera analyzes the points on which the freedom of Peru and the Peruvians rests. This freedom was freedom within Christian morality.

This speech produced an immediate shock and almost a year of journalistic controversy between the former defenders of "popular sovereignty" and the new promoters of the "sovereignty of intelligence." The importance of this debate launched Herrera into political celebrity.

> It is interesting to note how, despite the violence, reactions to Herrera's ideas were perfectly tolerated and even politically supported by the fact that Herrera was elected deputy for Lima and even served as president of the chamber of deputies. When General José Rufino Echenique became president of the republic in 1851, he first appointed a single minister general, José Crisóstomo Torrico, but later Echenique handed over the portfolios of justice, instruction, worship, and foreign relations to Bartolomé Herrera and also entrusted him, on an interim basis, with the portfolios of government, police, and public works. It was the minister of justice who encouraged the drafting and later promulgated the first Peruvian civil code.[4]

When Herrera finished his work as minister of state in 1852, he was sent as a plenipotentiary to the courts of Italy—Turin, Naples, and the Holy See—receiving in the last of these the highest praise from Pope Pius IX and Cardinal Antonelli. In the words of another of his biographers, Monsignor Pedro García Sanz, "The sight of Rome, of that ark of faith, knowledge, and all Christian virtues, made such a wonderful impression on Dr. Herrera that it purified the man and sanctified the priest."[5]

On his return to Peru, the ultraliberal revolution of 1854 broke out, which produced a radical constitution in 1856. That same year, a conservative counterrevolution broke out in the city of Arequipa, which put the new government of Marshal Ramón Castilla in check.

In 1859, Herrera again was elected to Congress with a majority of his supporters. He was appointed bishop of Arequipa and had to leave the constituent assembly to take possession of his diocese, but his friends and disciples sanctioned the conservative constitution of 1860, which would be the longest in the country, lasting sixty years.

About this important episcopal work, Monsignor García Sanz wrote in 1873:

> After nearly four years of such heroic episcopal work, perhaps more than because of the very painful illness that afflicted him for some years, he passed, poor in worldly wealth but rich in merit, to a better life, helped with all the consolations of our Holy Mother Church, and grieved by all those who had the joy of treating him and esteem him, that all was one, on August 10, 1864, at the age of fifty-six, when the Fatherland and the church promised each other even more happy events of their talents, virtues, and singular labor.[6]

Sovereignty of the intelligence

Herrera was one of the most important figures in the political culture of nineteenth-century Peru, but, as Fernando de Trazignies Granda has rightly noted, he also stood out in its legal culture, because the master of San Carlos managed to "offer a new philosophy of law." In this sense, Trazignies explains the relevance of Herrera as an ingenious thinker as well as a contradictor of the philosophical legal ideas of the eighteenth century still in vogue in the Peru of his time. He effectively confronted the old ideas because he managed to invest:

> the order of novelty and to present as new that which is a critique from the traditional point of view of liberal ideas that were considered novel or revolutionary in their time. But it is not a simple return to the past and to tradition; Herrera offers us a renewed tradition…In this sense, it is truly a "new" legal philosophy; it is the tradition that reappears after the liberal boom; it is a "neotraditional" attitude…with a markedly conservative character.[7]

This objective seems to have been among his plans since he began his rectorship at the Convictorio Carolino, because in his 1843 speech to the minister of Instruction, reporting on the state of the school, he said:

> I must declare in honor of the college that I find the natural sciences to be in a remarkable state of advancement. As far as morals are concerned, they call for an indispensable reform, the study of the law of nations, and that of the philosophy of the human spirit. I am going to teach a course in this last science myself, taking advantage of the abundance of light that Scotland and France have poured on it.[8]

The school that came from Scotland and developed in France is none other than eclecticism or doctrinism, which was a current of rationalist thought that surfaced during the post-Napoleonic Restoration (1814–30), and which was consolidated especially during the July Monarchy (1830–48). The purpose of this eclectic school was to reconcile the ideas of tradition of the old regime with the ideas of freedom of the new regime. Herrera therefore opposed what was understood as the guiding principles of both absolutism and liberalism, the force and the will respectively, to sustain the supremacy of common sense or the judgment of reason.

The two remote inspirers of eclecticism were the Viscount of Chateaubriand—who accepted the reality of a new postrevolutionary order but sought to preserve the greater magnitude of that past which signified the greatness of the monarchy—and Benjamin Constant—who, without breaking with the monarchical tradition, sought to extend bourgeois liberties. In the middle of these two thinkers were the representatives of eclecticism, among whom Royer Collard, François Guizot, and Victor Cousin stood out as the most notable.[9] The last of these, Cousin gave rise to what would be the most important distinction between eclectic thought, or doctrinaire liberalism, and ideological or revolutionary liberalism, which, following Voltaire and Rousseau, affirmed that reason was a work par excellence of the will and freedom of the individual. Although both currents are based on rationalist philosophy, "ideologues" held that the "judgment of reason" was a voluntary act, while "doctrinarians" considered that an act of reason was determined independently of the will and only under the protection of its own logical foundations.

It is from the difference between both liberalisms that Herrera decided on the strategy of opposing, to the voluntarist rationalism of the radicals, the anti-individualist rationalism of the doctrinaire ones, but without forgetting his commitment to Catholicism when remembering that:

> Royer Collard…is regarded as the founder of French rationalism, which we profess in philosophy, but from which in religion we are, and the priests are, as far removed as the revealed truth is from its absolute negation.[10]

Herrera made this decision because he was aware that liberal republics were an irreversible fact in Latin America, and, within this adverse political context, he had to try to use the most suitable means to achieve a rebirth of the natural order. In a note to his sermon of July 28, 1846, he explained:

> Just as God made use of Plato's philosophy to show the affinity of reason with the truth of the Gospel, which came to lift man out of pagan sensuality, so now, for the revival of Christianity in those who have fallen into a more clumsy gentility than the old one, He makes use of the same design, of spiritualistic or rational philosophy, and thus gives the priesthood a help that is not out of the order of nature.[11]

In this same sermon, Herrera proceeds to question the fundamental principle of voluntarist liberalism, referring to the notion of popular sovereignty that Benito Laso described as "political dogma" during the controversy that followed that intervention in the Cathedral of Lima. In the subsequent debate, Herrera answered his antagonist Laso on July 30, 1846, explaining his intention:

> In the sermon I gave on the day of the anniversary of our independence, I tried to destroy two errors: (1) [the error] that it is a disgrace for America to have fallen under the power of sixteenth-century Spain; (2) the error of popular sovereignty in the sense it is commonly given, and which so openly opposes the right to freedom.[12]

In place of the error of sovereignty born from the general will, Herrera proposes a new interpretation of sovereignty as an alternative, inspired originally by the theory that François Guizot had sustained in a pamphlet titled *De la souverainité* (1822), which explained sovereignty of the general reason. According to sovereignty of reason, power was to be vested in the most able men, who, through proper representative government, were to select such men in mutual revelation and self-recognition. Guizot himself had thought that this selection should be made by intermediate classes, or groups of moral or spiritual interest from which he allowed himself to speak of the need to form a "government of the spirits."

In this sense, Jan Goldstein[13] has observed that the censorial bourgeoisie led by Guizot proposed corporate and anti-individualist policies as a barrier to the possible irruption of social movements, moving away from a "liberalism against the state" and postulating a "liberalism from the state." For the doctrinarians the only two forms of democratic access were culture and wealth, so it is understood that for these thinkers the diffusion of education was seen as a social policy, while Guizot invited citizens to participate in politics with his famous phrase "enrich yourselves."

But this formula responded to the social reality of France, which had a powerful bourgeoisie, and where there was a strongly centralized institutionality very much influenced by Montesquieu's division of powers, something Guizot accepted almost religiously. Therefore, when the political ideas of the eclectics were received in other countries, their proposals had to be substantially adapted to other realities. In the case of Spain, the theses of the French doctrine reached the Spanish language in 1837, thanks to the famous *Lessons in Political Law* by the young Juan Donoso Cortés, but under a different notion; thus was born the sovereignty of the intelligence.

As Rodrigo Fernández Carvajal has brilliantly noted, the latter notion abandons the idea of a representative government in order to grant to the "legitimate aristocracies" the right to command by means of a "power that is not divided but unique, because of the intelligence that is embodied in them."[14] From this we can conclude that the sovereignty of reason proposed by Guizot changes its functionality in the sovereignty of intelligence of Donoso Cortés, because for the latter, "It is not, as in French doctrines, the theoretical crowning of the division of powers, but an anchor to hold on to in order to build and consolidate power, when it hardly exists."[15] Therefore Fernández Carvajal concludes that "the doctrine of the sovereignty of intelligence and the unity of power are fused into a single enthusiasm—the intelligent—which history claims is the monarchical power by which society becomes a person."[16]

Nineteenth-century Peru showed the same picture of anarchy and disorder as contemporary Spain. That is why Mario Alzadora Valdés writes:

> Herrera knew that Peru needed an elite...when the power of the nobility was diminished, there was nothing left but the charismatic power of a political class, according to Max Weber's terminology—that is, based on a selection by intelligence and the aptitude to command.[17]

Hence the rector of San Carlos borrowed from Donoso Cortés the famous doctrine of the sovereignty of intelligence, which gave the right of command to what Herrera called "the aristocracy of knowledge, created by nature."[18] The doctrine of the unity of power, as also seen in his words, tells us that:

> one must not lose sight of the fact that sovereignty is one because its end is one; and that if it were divided into fractions, which would act in a discordant and unbound way, that would not preserve unity, nor would there be sovereignty, if the end of it were reached.[19]

Now, the doctrine of the unity of public power that Herrera embraced did not imply the disappearance of differentiated functions within the exercise of this power, which should be well ordered so as not to obstruct each other and harm the institutions. In this sense, he explains:

> It is commonly divided into four powers: legislative, judicial, executive, and conservative. For in every orderly society there must be laws, and government according to them, and judgments according to them also, in the disputes of private individuals; and finally, since public power is thus divided, it must be prevented from being invaded and from clashing with each other... the conservative.[20]

The conservative power

Benjamin Constant wrote his most important contribution to political law in 1814, *Reflexions sur les Constitutions et les garanties avec une enquisse de la Constitution*, which we know as *Cours de politique constitutionnelle.* This text was widely quoted by Herrera in *Las Notas al Compendio del Derecho público interno y externo*, published in 1845 and 1848 "for the use of the Colegio de San Carlos." Herrera relied on the Portuguese translation of Constant's work by Silvestre Pinheiro Ferreira, one of the most important disseminators of Constant's constitutional doctrine in the Portuguese language, through whom Constant's remarkable influence was introduced into the public law of Brazil and its Imperial Constitution of 1824.

For Joaquín Varela Suanzes, the most relevant contribution of Constant's constitutional theory is his doctrine of neutral power, which he outlined during the

Consulate—that is, during a republican regime; he followed Emmanuel Sieyès but gave his thought a very personal slant.[21] Sieyès had also proposed during the Consulate to create a neutral power by means of a collective body called the *colleges des conservateurs*, which would designate the consuls and defend the balance between the institutions of the state, while simultaneously proposing a *jury constitutionaire* to control the constitutionality of the laws.

Constant recognized that the seed of his doctrine on neutral power was in the work of an Anglophile monarchist, Count Clermont Tonnerre, who during the days of the 1789 assembly had mentioned for the first time a “royal power” other than executive power. On the other hand, we must bear in mind that Carl Schmitt has recalled that the remote source of these conservative institutions is to be found in seventeenth-century republican England, especially in James Harrington’s ideas about the bodies called Conservators of Liberty and Conservators of the Charter. Explaining the meaning of real or neutral power, Daniel Soria Luján says:

> This royal power, which resided in the monarch, had the purpose of watching over the harmonious development of the other powers, preventing any of them from exceeding their powers to the detriment of the others; that is to say, maintaining the balance between these powers. For this reason, in relation to state powers, the king’s prerogative constituted for Constant a “neutral power,” which was not an active but a passive power. On the other hand, he criticizes the fact that this power is granted to the legislative or the executive, since they would later degenerate into arbitrariness and despotism, respectively.[22]

The fourth power was definitely taken over by French publicists from the practice of the British regime in order to introduce it into their constitution and thus try to overcome the drawbacks of Montesquieu’s theory of the three powers. It was generically called the conservative power, but if we do a more detailed analysis, we find evidence that it was presented under three different modalities. It appeared first as a “tribune power” in the writings of Sieyès, with a collegiate conformation, and it was understood as a power to defend and protect the constitution from any possible violation. Second, it was a “neutral power” with a passive character, owing to which the head of state acted only as an arbitrator when the powers were exceeded. Benjamin Constant was the postulator of this modality and described it as “the key to the organization.” Finally, the third modality was that of a “real power” of an active nature as outlined rudimentarily by Count Clermont Tonnerre, where the head of state was to moderate the regular functioning of the institutions. The German doctrine, whose exponents included Krausists like Heinrich Ahrens, called it the “inspective power.”

Under these influences, Silvestre Pinheiro devised for the Bragança monarchy a new power made up of three members called the Supreme Council of Constitutional Inspection and Censorship, which would bring together in one body the powers of arbitration and control of the constitution in the manner of

Constant. The Brazilian Constitution of 1824 followed this suggestion in part and thus formed an active fourth power, but it made it unipersonal and was called the "moderating power," ruling that:

> the key to the entire political organization is delegated privately to the emperor, as supreme head of the nation, and his first representative, so that he may unceasingly veil the maintenance of the independence, balance, and harmony of the most political powers.[23]

The case of Spain was different because the concept was first influenced by Sieyès and not by Constant, and that is why the Cortes of Cádiz accepted the interpretation of the conservative power as a collegiate body in the form of the Permanent Deputation in the Constitution of 1812. This body was to watch over the observance of the charter and the laws and therefore defend them, and this is from whence the idea of forming a collegiate conservative power to control constitutionality came. This line of thought was maintained in Peru until the middle of the nineteenth century, and that is why Daniel Soria Luján writes, "Consequently, the Council of State of the Charter of 1839, especially between the years 1845 and 1851, had an eagerness to become an inspecting body of all the powers of the state."[24]

Herrera, however, as we have seen, was a protagonist in the politics of those years and did not share the idea of a collegiate conservative power. Furthermore, he was dedicated especially to controlling the president, which is why, when he drew up his draft constitution in 1860, he gave the Council of State a merely consultative role:

> The Council of State is, in my project, a body destined to enlighten the government and to serve as a guarantee of success in administrative measures. The powers given to it by the 1839 Constitution were not in line with that destiny, which is the true purpose of the Council of State; the executive branch could not have sufficient confidence in those who were to be its accusers, nor could they be confident in accusing the president of the republic, with whom they had often been accomplices.[25]

For this reason, in his notes to the Pinheiro Compendium, Herrera highlighted the Franco-Portuguese doctrine, pointing out that:

> The conservative power is destined to prevent the other powers from going beyond the limits set by constitutional law...This led Constant to conceive of the need to create a power entirely different from the other three: essentially impartial and neutral, and lacking the means to tyrannize.[26]

And that is why he was troubled:

> In our republican constitutions, this power, distinct from the other powers, is missing. This neutral and entirely conservative power. Each of the three powers has conservative attributes...each one is limited when exercising

> authority over the others. But there is one who does not feel this influence, and it is in fact unlimited: this power is that of the Congress...[which] is the public power that has sufficient means to ensure the practice of law in this part, confronting Congress when it wants to trample on everything to enforce an act of arbitrariness or to consummate perhaps a revolution...Here is a deplorable vacuum, which should be filled in the constitutions of Spanish America so that it can truly be called free.[27]

This "deplorable void" Herrera tried to fill with his project of constitutional reform, giving the senate, the Chamber of Deputies, or the president the competence to solve conflicts according to the case, but subtly highlighting the presidency as a moderating power over what he calls the administrative, legislative, and judicial powers. This was in response to the fact that the rector of San Carlos considered the president—although he is not called sovereign—to be the expression of the unity of sovereignty because:

> he too represents the unity of public authority, which is well perceived in the case of international disputes. And even outside this case, the president is the one who enforces the laws and the judicial sentences. It can be said that, while there is order in the republic and harmony among the authorities at whose head the president is, no provision is fulfilled, but that ordering its execution is the essential act of sovereignty.[28]

In this vein, Herrera understood it to be natural that the president should rise above the legislature, not because of the supremacy of the presidentialist form of government, but as a constitutional defender of sovereign unity.

The organic democracy

Generally, it has been thought that organicist or corporate juridical-political theories have been proper only to Plato's classic thought, to the Stoics, or to Christian Thomism, which saw the community as a republic and influenced Hispanic traditionalism. But Gonzalo Fernández de la Mora[29] demonstrated the existence of an organicist tendency within the purest nineteenth century demoliberalism, specifically in the work of Karl C.F. Krause and his disciples, who were very close to the corporate vision of the social order held by traditionalist thinkers. In that sense, the Spanish scholar explains:

> Krausist organicism and traditional Spanish corporativism agree on the following theses: (a) Society is not a situation to which man voluntarily accedes through a social contract...; (b) there is no such thing as man in isolation but only man within one or more groups; (c) between the family and humanity there is a series of intermediate bodies; (d) these intermediate bodies, such as the municipality or the guild, have their own autonomy, and the state must respect this; (e) the mission of the state is subsidiary, and it can only assume

> those functions that are not effectively carried out by the intermediate bodies; (f) the interests of the various social groups must be represented in the political bodies.[30]

Due to these convergences of thought, the conservatives of Latin America accepted with greater sympathy some recognized liberals, such as Heinrich Ahrens—a student of Krause and author of *Cours de Droit Naturel* (1839)—as well as the father of English positivism, Herbert Spencer—author of *The Social Organism* (1860)—since they did not break openly with a social order that the Latin American conservatives defended by tradition. This acceptance is understandable because in the mid-1840s, Herrera himself introduced Ahrens's thought to the Colegio de San Carlos when teaching natural law. Under the intellectual protection of this author with clear liberal roots, Herrera could argue in favor of a political order that valued intermediate bodies without having to resort to traditionalist authors.

Apart from the French traditionalists and the German Romantics, the organicist ideas of the social order also influenced doctrinaire liberals, such as Royer Collard, who reacted philosophically against the absolute individualism of the Enlightenment. Such doctrinaire liberals asserted that society had never been composed of isolated individuals but was based on natural or accidental associations,[31] and these thinkers therefore believed in the formation of spontaneous bodies with initiative for the improvement of the representative regime.

From all of the above, we can understand why not only the conservatives but also the Peruvian liberals welcomed corporate ideas, as can be seen in the electoral program of the Progressive Club of 1851[32] that was prepared by professors of the Guadalupe school, where they were said to teach the "true Ahrens." That document, whose authors include a disciple of Herrera, Pedro Gálvez, raises an organicist conception of society, formed from social subjects with different associative purposes. Its only difference from the conservative conception was that it made corporatism egalitarian and not hierarchical. Thus it is evident that by the 1850s, Ahrens's organicism had a very relevant presence in the Peruvian political culture, a situation that was consolidated from 1860 on thanks to the influence of Ahrens on the *Dictionary of Peruvian Legislation* by the Krausist jurist Francisco García Calderón Landa.

To understand the success of Ahrens's thinking, we must understand that, as A.L. Sánchez Marín puts it, "the essential concept from which it starts is that of the organism." Nature is an "organism in which all things, center and parts, determine each other." Consequently, human society appears as an organically articulated structure. In the idea of an organism, this philosopher finds the informing principle of social life: "The great social organism will comprise a set of systems and particular organisms, each of which has its own activity and special purpose."[33]

Sánchez Marín concludes:

> From what has been said so far, it can be seen that for this author, there are two types of relationships, one that affects the person in the totality of his

> or her purposes, and another that takes the person in one of his or her main purposes.

The result for Ahrens is obvious: "(he) recognizes in each member of the social order its double quality as member of the political order and as an order of human culture," and this double quality or condition has for him an important political projection in the configuration of the public representation. These two conditions, for Ahrens, "must find a conforming expression in the system of election and representation." The logical result of this duality demands bicameralism:

> The general or national representation, to reflect this internal organism of society in its two kinds of groups, must be the product of a double system of election, and be divided into two assemblies or chambers, resting on different principles, of which one, which we will call first, would represent the spheres of complete life or the great centers of life located in varying degrees, and constituted lastly by the provinces…The second chamber, on the contrary, would be formed by election in the various orders of culture or, as it is said, of social interests…More specifically, the first of these assemblies would be elected by the provincial representatives, appointed in turn by the municipal ones, and the second chamber would be composed of the representatives appointed by each cultural or interest sector, and there could be delegates from the political groups in both chambers.[34]

Around 1860, Ahrens's usefulness in both political and legal philosophy was widely consolidated, and Herrera turned to him again when he wrote his brilliant draft Constitution of 1860 to propose an organic democracy that would restore a balance between the old social institutions and the new political ideas that had been fractured by the two civil wars between 1854 and 1858.

This is why Herrera, now the bishop of Arequipa, in designing the legislative power he wished to present to the Constituent Congress, adopted the Ahrens concept of two levels of representation. In the "Preliminary Note" to his project, he writes:

> Thus, as the Chamber of Deputies represents the variable interests and new ideas, the Senate must represent the permanent interests of all social classes, the eternal principles of law, and the fixity of institutions. This is the fate of the Senate in any good political organization.[35]

This senate, destined to serve as a good political organization, Herrera establishes with thirty members divided into various classes, where three senators are to be elected from each of the careers or professions by the citizens. These classes included, for example, the political profession, the treasury, the magistracy, the clergy, and the army and the navy. Herrera here specifies:

> If someone gets angry with the word class…believing that I establish privileged classes, I hope that, little by little, his spirit will calm down, he will perceive that I do not establish, but that I recognize, the existence of the

> classes or professions that, independently of my will, exist in Peru as in every nation; and that the privilege must be very far from my mind when I attempt for all classes to be represented, and that none is better represented than another.[36]

For all that, he concludes:

> There can be no more democratic thinking, no more just thinking. A Senate formed in this way may well be entrusted with a good deal of conservative power, and some of the powers of Congress, the exercise of which is often necessary for the conduct of public business. On many occasions, when Congress is not in session, that is why I thought it would be convenient for the Senate to be a permanent chamber.[37]

Herrera's constitutional project, which, according to José Pareja Paz Soldán, "was distinguished by its conciseness, by its sober and elegant wording, and by its legal sense," had as its most important achievement to defend the relevance of the social order within the political institutions and to postulate for the first time in history a corporate chamber, or functional senate, as Víctor Andrés Belaúnde would call it in the 1931 Constituent Assembly, but doing so under the protection of the very philosophical foundations of its detractors. For as Gonzalo Fernández de la Mora has well noticed:

> The first great theoretician of organic democracy is Ahrens, and those who have succeeded him in this sociopolitical line are more or less indebted to him. The corporativisms of the second third of the twentieth century in Europe do not have their speculative roots in German Romanticism or French traditionalism, as is often mistakenly believed, but in the school of Krause.[38]

Natural law

In the 1840s, Herrera engaged in an intense debate with Peruvian liberalism, which was extremely influenced by a theoretical Jacobinism. In this context, the writings of Heinrich Ahrens were a valuable aid "to reestablish the lost secular 'order' of Peru," thanks to the political-social conception of Ahrens, who understood the community as an organism and whose vision was compatible with the traditional social order. But beyond the political–social plane, the field that helped Herrera most in his purpose of restoring order was the conception of law to which Krause and his disciples gave enormous importance. As could be seen from Ahrens's *Course on Natural Law*, Krause and his followers had a monistic vision of law—that is, for this school there was no extreme distinction between natural law and positive law. In this sense, Krausian *iusnaturalism* was intended to overcome the dualism of natural law and positive law on the bases of an ideal law:

> In such a way that what was positive law had to be natural law as well, insofar as both had the same object. However, [*iusnaturalism*] also recognized the difference that in natural law, the law appears as an invariable and intangible principle, not realized in time, while the positive one was its practical realization.[39]

Now, as we can see, natural law was an ideal for Krausism, that is, Krausism does not define natural law and relativizes its content, but it recognizes the value and existence of natural law, even if it is "intangible." Very different was the position of Jeremy Bentham and his utilitarian school, who distinguished themselves by wanting to maximize social utility in a similar way as legislators should do by creating and modifying positive laws for the benefit of the majority. In his *Fragment on Government* (1776), Bentham shows that for him, utilitarianism was a tool of legislative reform because of his "theory of law as mandate," by which the only important thing is the will of the legislator—that is, only positive law has value. It is understood here because Bentham criticized the idea of a natural right, considering the idea of moral rights (that is, rights not founded on a legal norm) as "nonsense," and the concept of natural rights as "nonsense on stilts."[40]

It is therefore not strange that the followers of the earliest European liberalism were so enthusiastic about the father's postulates of utilitarianism. In America, admiration for this idea took hold very early among the revolutionaries for independence. In 1802, Benthan had become taken with Francisco de Miranda and had correspondence with other heroes, such as Simón Bolívar, to whom he offered himself as a possible writer of the codes of the new republics. Bentham's ideas were also disseminated in higher education very soon, both in Spain and in Latin America. The University of Salamanca was the Hispanic academic scene where English utilitarianism was first embraced, and its most important protagonist was Ramón de Salas, author of the *Lessons in Constitutional Public Law*. In Peru, this ultraliberal influence was so important that Domingo Garcia Belaunde writes:

> It is interesting to note that the first book printed among us on constitutional law, in 1827, is that of Ramón de Salas (1753–1837), a professor from Salamanca, who published in 1821 the first Spanish manual on the subject the first in the order of time—which was reprinted in Lima.[41]

From the above, one can understand why, when Herrera entered the rectorship of the Colegio de San Carlos, he immediately replaced the text of Salas with Ahrens's *Course on Natural Law*, and in the context of a liberal republic like Peru, he managed to marshal a liberalism of quality against a Jacobinism of quantity.

As we have seen, because the Krausists recognized the existence of a natural right, although they did not give it a specific content, Herrera, by personally dictating the course of natural law, was able to give it a context, and this was Christian natural law. That is how he taught that "The first truth that we establish in our lessons of natural law, and which we suppose to be admitted as an unquestionable principle, by all who have greeted that science, is: that the only source of rights is nature."[42] He adds:

> The conformity of beings with their end, in which the truth of existence consists, is a rational necessity, a demand that reason inevitably perceives after it discovers the nature of a being and its end, and this is what is called natural law.[43]

He argues that:

> there is the right denied by Bentham, there is a law other than the will and human interests, which obliges the will and protects the interests by governing them. He who promulgates it is the reason: he who imposes it is God.[44]

Finally, he concludes:

> Without the idea of this necessary and divine law, it would be impossible to understand human laws and their binding force: while recognized, the idea of human law is clear and complete. If we have that rule of conduct dictated by God, and if societies are subject to it and must take the indispensable measures to ensure its observance, they can express it, determine it and point out punishment to the violators.[45]

In this way, the natural Christian right in the Thomistic tradition of late scholasticism filled the Krausian *iusnaturalism* with content and directly confronted that "protopositivism" that constituted Bentham's ideas.

This anti-Bentham concern can also be seen when students are warned in the *Notes to the Compendium of Internal and External Public Law* of Silvestre Pinheiro Ferreira:

> Before we begin to turn away, as we need to do in these notes, from some of Mr. Pinheiro's doctrines, we must show him our respect… (but) he carried with him a fragment of the body that left a heavy and dismal fragment that sometimes made him shipwrecked. We are talking about Bentham's selfish principle. It is our grave duty to point out this risk to our students; and only such serious consideration could overcome the shyness we experience in placing our reflections alongside the thoughts of such a distinguished writer.[46]

When Bartolomé Herrera left politics in 1861 to devote himself to his episcopal ministry in Arequipa, he found the time to write his remarkable and little-known *Treatise on Theodicy* for the use of the diocesan seminary of San Jerónimo. The philosopher Antonio Pintor Ramos explains:

> The term theodicy has a curious and little-known history. This neologism jumped to publicity when, in 1710, Leibniz published his *Essay of Theodicy on the Goodness of God, the Freedom of Man and the Origin of Evil.* The term was so foreign to the German philosopher's contemporaries that it was curious that some readers—and not always bad readers—believed that, since the work was published without an author's name, "Theodicy" (Theodysseus) was the pseudonym under which Leibniz was hiding. Although the term was not completely lost, it did not become generally known until 1836, when the French philosopher Victor Cousin managed to introduce it into academic programs under the name Leibnizian of Theodisea.[47]

However, the new theodicy of Cousin retained only the name of Leibniz, because while Leibniz sought a study on the justice and justification of God, Cousin sought to formulate a rational treatise on God.

The Polish philosopher Bogumil Jasinowski, in *The Problem of Natural Law in Its Philosophical Sense* (1967), explains to us that since natural law is essentially metaphysical, it is very closely linked to the problems that theodicy plants. This is so because, while theodicy saves the concept of God as absolute being and good, natural law is its reflection in trying to save what is properly human before the threat of human weakness.

In consequence, by posing Herrera's theodicy as a defense of God and the nature of creation in the traditional line of *theologia naturalis scholastica*, as César Félix Sánchez Martínez has shown,[48] one is brought towards the full consecration of Christian natural law and therefore should categorically affirm, in the words of Miguel Ayuso, "what is the doctrinal nature of the thought of those authors that I had used in law courses in order to temper the radicalism of the teaching of public institutions in Peru after the emancipatory revolution."[49]

That is why Herrera explained that: "Cousin, founder and head of the eclectic school of France, has made great efforts to purge himself of the pantheistic label. But he has not retracted the many passages in his works that have brought him that blemish."[50] In the same vein, for Arhens, Herrera stated, "Arhens, a Belgian philosopher, whose works circulate among us like those of Cousin, is also a pantheist. While he condemns Spinoza's doctrine, Schelling's, Hegel's, and other pantheists, he actually holds that of the latter."[51]

This was the definitive demarcation from the eclecticism and Krausism that he had used as a dialectical instrument against Jacobinism and its theodicy, thus resulting in his last legacy of defense of the faith and the natural Christian right. As he was so often heard to say in the pulpit:

> Save me from betraying you and my country by indulging the tumultuous passions of the crowd, whom you have imposed on me the duty to warn and lead by the path of health; save me from strengthening the ungodly thought that nations are outside the rule of God's law.[52]

Notes

1 Taurel, "Biografía del Señor D. D. Bartolomé Herrera."
2 Leubel, *El Perú de 1861.*
3 Lavalle, "Bartolomé Herrera."
4 Trazignies, *La idea del derecho*, 97.
5 García y Sanz, *Biografía del Illmo. Sr. D. D. Bartolomé Herrera.*
6 Ibid.
7 Trazignies, *La idea del derecho*, 97.
8 Herrera, *Escritos y discursos*, 1:40.
9 Varela Suanzes, "El Liberalismo francés después de Napoleón," 37–38.
10 Herrera, *Escritos y discursos*, 1:97, note 24.
11 Ibid., 1:96, note (d).
12 Ibid., 1:105–06.
13 Goldstein, *The Post-Revolutionary Self.*
14 Fernández Carvajal, "Las constantes de Donoso Cortes," 82.
15 Ibid.
16 Ibid., 85.
17 Alzamora Valdez, "El Pensamiento de Bartolomé Herrera."
18 Herrera, *Escritos y discursos*, 1:131.
19 Ibid., 2:31, note 3.
20 Ibid., 2:30, note 3.
21 Varela Suanzes, "Principios de política y otros escritos de Constant."
22 Soria Luján, "La defensa política de la constitución del Perú en el siglo XIX."
23 Scantimburgo, O Poder Moderador.
24 Soria Luján, "Defensa política."
25 Herrera, *Proyecto de Constitución.*
26 Herrera, *Escritos y discursos*, 2:100, note 25.
27 Ibid., 2:101, note 25.
28 Ibid., 2:57, note 10.
29 Fernández de la Mora, *Los teóricos izquierdistas de la democracia orgánica.*
30 Fernández de la Mora, "El Organicismo Krausista," at 183.
31 Diez del Corral, *El Liberalismo doctrinario*, 266.
32 Loayza, "El Club progresista y la coyuntura electoral de 1849–1851."
33 Sánchez Marín, "Representación orgánica."
34 Ibid.
35 Herrera, *Proyecto de Constitución.*
36 Ibid.
37 Ibid.
38 Fernández de la Mora, "Organicismo Krausista," 119.
39 Almoguercs, "Derecho natural krausista y derecho natural escolástico."
40 Bix, *Diccionario jurídico de teoría jurídica.*
41 García Belaunde, "Bartolomé Herrera, traductor de Pinheiro Ferreyra."
42 Herrera, *Escritos y discursos*, 2:6, note 1.
43 Ibid., 2:14, note 2.
44 Ibid.
45 Ibid., 2:4–15, note 2.
46 Ibid., 2:8, note 1.
47 Pintor Ramos, "La Teodicea de Rousseau," at 101.
48 Sanchez, "En defensa de Dios."
49 Ayuso, *Bartolomé Herrera y la Contrarrevolucion.*
50 Herrera, *Tratado de Teodicea*, No. 86.
51 Ibid., No. 88.
52 Herrera, *Escritos y discursos*, 1:72.

References

Almogueres, Joaquín. "Derecho natural krausista y derecho natural escolástico." *Baja palabra. Revista de filosofia* 2, no. 17 (2017): 229–52.

Altuve-Febres, Fernán, ed. *Bartolomé Herrera y su tiempo: [Actas del Congreso Internacional Conmemorativo del Bicentenario del Natalicio de Bartolomé Herrera (1808–2008)].* Lima: Sociedad Peruana de Historia, 2010.

Alzamora Valdez, Mario. "El Pensamiento de Bartolomé Herrera." *Mercurio Peruano* 279 (1950): 203–22.

Ayuso, Miguel. "Bartolomé Herrera y la Contrarrevolucion." In *Bartolomé Herrera y su tiempo*, edited by Altuve-Febres, 112–18.

Bix, Brian H. *Diccionario jurídico de teoría jurídica.* Mexico City, 2009.

Diez del Corral, Luis. *El Liberalismo doctrinario.* Madrid: Centro de Estudios Constitucionales, 1984.

Fernández Carvajal, Rodrigo. "Las constantes de Donoso Cortes." *Revista de Estudios Políticos* 95 (1957): 75–108.

Fernández de la Mora, Gonzalo. "El Organicismo Krausista." *Revista de Estudios Políticos. Nueva Epoca* 22 (1981): 99–184.

Fernández de la Mora, Gonzalo. *Los teóricos izquierdistas de la democracia orgánica.* Madrid: Plaza & Janes, 1985.

García Belaunde, Domingo. "Bartolomé Herrera, traductor de Pinheiro Ferreyra." In *Bartolomé Herrera y su tiempo*, edited by Altuve-Febres, 133–41.

García y Sanz, Pedro. *Biografía del Illmo. Sr. D. D. Bartolomé Herrera, dignísimo Obispo de Arequipa, y Oda elegiaca escrita por P. E. con motivo de su fallecimiento.* Lima: Tip. La Sociedad, 1873.

Goldstein, Jan. *The Post-Revolutionary Self: Politics and Psyche in France, 1750–1850.* Cambridge, MA: Harvard University Press, 2005.

Herrera, Bartolomé. *Escritos y discursos*, Vol. 2. Lima: Biblioteca de la Republica, 1929.

Herrera, Bartolomé. *Proyecto de Constitución.* Lima: Imprenta de José Masías. 1860.

Herrera, Bartolomé. *Tratado de Teodicea.* Arequipa: Universidad de San Agustín de Arequipa, 1872.

Lavalle, José Antonio. "Bartolomé Herrera." In *El Perú Ilustrado.* Lima: P. Bacigalupi, January 18, 1890.

Leubel, Alfredo G. *El Perú de 1861.* Lima: Imp. del Comercio, 1861.

Loayza, Alex. "El Club progresista y la coyuntura electoral de 1849–1851." In *Historia de las elecciones en el Perú. Estudios sobre el gobierno representativo*, edited by Cristóbal Aljovín de Losada and Sinesio López, 395–424. Lima: Instituto de Estudios Peruanos, 2005.

Pintor Ramos, Antonio. "La Teodicea de Rousseau." *Cuadernos salmantinos de filosofía* 5 (1978): 101–34.

Sánchez, César Félix. "En defensa de Dios: escolástica, eclecticismo y polémica en el Tratado de Teodicea (1872) de Bartolomé Herrera." Thesis. Universidad de Piura, 2015.

Sánchez Marín, A. L. "Representación orgánica." *Razón española* 112 (2002): 133–53.

Scantimburgo, João de. *O Poder Moderador. História & teoria.* São Paulo: Livraria Pioneira Editore, 1980.

Soria Luján, Daniel. "La defensa política de la constitución del Perú en el siglo XIX." *Revista de Estudios Histórico-Jurídicos* 23 (2001): 525–45.

Taurel, Raphael M. "Biografía del Señor D. D. Bartolomé Herrera." In *Obras Selectas del Clero Peruano*, Vol. 2. Paris: Librería de A. Mézin, 1853.

Trazignies, Fernando. *La idea del derecho en el Perú republicano del siglo XIX*. Lima: Pontifica Universidad Católica del Perú, 1982.

Varela Suanzes, Joaquín. "El Liberalismo francés después de Napoleón." *Revista de Estudios Políticos* 76 (1992): 29–43.

Varela Suanzes, Joaquín. "Principios de política y otros escritos de Constant." *Historia Constitucional* 3 (2002): 287–94.

10 Juan Nepomuceno Rodríguez de San Miguel (Mexico, 1808–77)

Juan Pablo Salazar Andreu

Introduction

Mexico after independence was characterized as a society looking for order, justice, and identity. Overwhelmed by Western Enlightenment ideas that permeated part of the population and fostered the formation of illustrious men who defended ideological currents of varying stripes, the intellectual movement in general sought to create a nation with its own identity. One of these illustrious intellectuals was Juan Nepomuceno Rodríguez de San Miguel.

The attempt to identify the thought of Rodríguez de San Miguel requires some relevant biographical data, such as the social and political context of his day, his legal training and activity as a public servant, his legacy in many documents of law, and some writings he published in the confrontation between liberals and conservatives. Rodríguez de San Miguel was an eminent man of his time who had a way of acting consistently with his beliefs. These beliefs helped him to identify legal problems and propose solutions in the context of a Catholic *iusnaturalism* with a strong tendency to reinforce the royalty and conservative stances.

Biographical background

Juan Nepomuceno Rodríguez de San Miguel grew up in the context of a still-developing Mexico, in which various social tendencies that often worked against his own formation would later draw his criticism. Thus, it is important to investigate his origins in their social and political context.[1]

His person

Born in Puebla de los Ángeles on April 6, 1808, Juan Nepomuceno Rodríguez de San Miguel was baptized in Holy Church Cathedral. His parents were the *mayorazgo* (firstborn with rights over inheritance) Juan Rodríguez de San Miguel y Zambrano and Juana Mori García Huesca.[2] From the records, one may presume that he lived most of his life in Mexico City, although his family and professional ties also kept him close to the city of Puebla. His basic education began at the age of three, and at the age of twelve he entered the Colegio de Minería, in the Academy of Fine Arts, where his tutor was Gregorio Mier y Terán.[3]

Rodríguez de San Miguel became a brilliant lawyer, but he also held positions in the executive, legislative, and judicial branches of the Mexican Government. He also had a career in teaching in the first chair of sacred canons (1832) and international public law (1833). Throughout his life, he staunchly defended his views of the person, society, and the state—views characterized by strong but elegant substance, full of coherence, and always grounded in law. Rodríguez de San Miguel died in 1877, leaving a legacy shaped by the legal methodology of compilation of laws, a trend that competed with the French-style codification advocated by the liberals of the time.

Social and political context

The society that was taking shape in the Mexico of the nineteenth century was marked by the contrasts of different ways of understanding life and social institutions—as well as how to develop an extensive territory, whose population was always searching for an identity as a country. Rodríguez de San Miguel lived and left his influence as a jurist during this time of social change. Growing up with the ideas of a Catholic society under the rule of the Bourbon dynasty, he received during his basic and advanced education a very strong and conservative formation. Analyzing the society of his time, he exposed those phenomena that, from his Catholic perspective, were problematic for the new nation, offering proposals to change what he considered was wrong and defending what worked, all while using legal instruments and argumentations.

The ideas of his day were those of a society that had found its most basic institutions protected by a Catholic ideal, which defined the concepts and the actions of a good person, family, and citizen. Against these established mores, liberal ideas proposed the autonomy of the person and the invitation to seek one's own happiness through scientific knowledge founded on empiricist, rationalist, and critical thought. These different ways of thinking confronted each other in the landscape of the new nation, each justifying each in its own way and by its own epistemic criteria the need for a society supervised by social institutions defined by either regalism, Catholicism, or secularism. It was the liberal currents, after a direct and violent affront to the conservatives, that would end up defining the course of the Mexican nation, based above all on the scientific method and subsequent Mexican positivism.

The ideologies of the conservatives and liberals proposed and created different political institutions according to whichever group in turn led the young nation. This alternating leadership finally defined the legal norms that, throughout a violent nineteenth century, would shape a Mexican state with both liberal and conservative political constitutions. The justifications that the respective conservative and liberal sides advanced gave rise to constant political struggle, which resulted in the loss of much of the national territory, foreign interventions, and an imperial government under the emperor Maximilian.

There was a close relationship between these national political facts and the life of Rodríguez de San Miguel. He served as a public servant in the roles of legislator-constituent; national, state, and federal judge; and litigator of various causes. What is perhaps outstanding about this jurist—more than his possessing legal scholarship that no one of his time doubted—was the coherence between his thinking and his action on the political and juridical level. Always faithful to his ethical convictions, his religion, and his national obligation, he defended his causes with solid arguments, presenting a real and strong option for the basis of a Mexican republic that would preserve the traditions of the Catholic religion. He turned to a compilation of laws based on a coherent epistemology that would bring together tradition and novelty, while undertaking his public service with the highest standards of technical quality and professional commitment.

Training

Rodríguez de San Miguel was a notable lawyer who litigated issues of various kinds, especially civil and commercial law. Additionally, however, he drew on his knowledge of canon law to write many articles in defense of the prerogatives of the Catholic Church, its patrimony, and the religion it professed—which, in his opinion, was the key to the social cohesion that his country needed.

Law degree

Rodríguez de San Miguel's trajectory, in terms of his legal performance, was long and prodigious, as he had a practical understanding of the whole of the legal system—not only because of his study and his performance of functions in the various areas of government, but also because of the constant litigation of matters throughout his life. He studied jurisprudence in 1827, performing his professional practices with the judge Pedro Galindo, the magistrate Manuel de la Peña y Peña, as well as with José Mariano Marín.[4] During his preparation as a jurist, Rodríguez de San Miguel received recognition as a prominent "citizen of the State of Mexico" and was appointed as a member of the Academy of Legislation and Political Economy of Mexico City. After graduating in 1832, he taught in the first chair of sacred canons, and in 1833 he enrolled in the National Bar Association of Mexico and became, for a brief time, a professor of international public law.[5]

Columnist

As mentioned, Rodríguez de San Miguel had a very strong social and political perspective of the Catholic Church as the institution in which every Mexican citizen should find identity. In this sense, he exercised his intellectual acuity and his facile pen to present his ideas in various articles of the newspaper *La Cruz*. The newspaper had a religious inclination and had been established to disseminate traditional doctrines and defend Catholic positions and ideas.[6]

Some of his most relevant writings consisted of a defense of the clergy against liberal-tinged ideas: "Considerations on the true character and spirit of the statements of clergy reform, their corruption, and wealth" (August 7, 10, and 13, 1848); and "Dissertation on freedom of religion in the Mexican Republic" (July 31, 1848), in which he defends the idea that in Mexico only the cult of the Catholic religion should be allowed in the face of the freedom of other cults and rituals. With these positions, it is clear that the ideological tendency of his scholarship was the same that he always defended and argued with the highest technical rigor, using his preferred epistemic method. In the same way, he used these views to clarify those social, political, and legal institutions that must remain, those deserving of reforms, and, finally, those that are useless and must be phased out.

Activity as a public servant

In public service, Rodríguez de San Miguel worked in all three government branches with discipline and technical rigor as well as great skill in the legal dimensions of various areas of law. He was senior officer of the Municipal Secretariat of Mexico City (1833); participated in the Board of Directors of the National Amortization Bank (1837); was the syndic of the city council in 1838; served as attorney general of the nation, an office that he resigned to return to private practice in 1853; and was a member of the commissions to arrange the administration of justice and codification of the law. In 1858 he was councilor for the government of Félix María de Zuloaga, and he belonged to the assembly of notable advocates for a moderate monarchy in Mexico.[7]

In the legislative branch, he was a member of the advisory board for legislation in 1838–40 and in the Legislative Assemblies of 1842 and 1853; he also participated in the ordinary and extraordinary Constitutional Congresses of 1843. He was a senator for Puebla until 1853. After the promulgation of the Constitution of 1857 he was elected deputy, but he declined this role for reasons of ideological conscience in terms of religious tolerance, because the Constitution of 1857 was a liberal one.[8]

In the judiciary, he served as magistrate of the court in the period 1838–40; during the Second Mexican Empire, he was a magistrate of the Supreme Court of Justice, an office that he resigned on ideological grounds, when he opposed alienation of the property of the Church.[9]

Between 1842 and 1853, he worked in the private area as a conciliator and quadrennial examiner of the Illustrious and National Bar Association of Mexico, attorney for San Andrés and San Juan de Dios hospitals, and fiscal defender of chaplaincies and charitable works of the archdiocese appointed by the archbishop of Mexico, a charge he later resigned for health reasons.[10]

Jurist

Rodríguez de San Miguel had great command of the science and use of law, thanks to constant study and analysis, which are both evident in each of the legal works that he developed through his professional life. He established himself as one of the most complete jurists of the nineteenth century, an assertion that can be verified with the analysis of his articles and legal papers, which show his integral knowledge of civil and canon law theory, norms, and interpretation. He even used a specific methodology of codification attached to the standards of the Justinian tradition, in clear contradiction to the French codification, which would eventually be framed in the national legal system that led to Mexican positivism.

Legal legacy

With regard to Rodríguez de San Miguel's legacy in the realm of legal doctrine, it is important to consider the political and legal context in which he lived. The period was marked by confrontation between liberals and conservatives—the former adhering to ideals of the Enlightenment, which had begun in the West in the previous century but had obvious repercussions in the Mexican national context. The conservative thinking of Rodríguez de San Miguel, however, led him to act in defense of the national legal and political customs formed by a combination of Castilian, Spanish, colonial American, and Mexican legislation, with a strong interest in the preservation of many of the Catholic Church's prerogatives.

Rodríguez de San Miguel's commentary on Joaquín Escriche's *Diccionario razonado de legislación civil, penal, comercial y forense* (*Reasoned dictionary of legislation and jurisprudence*)—which will be analyzed later— served to contrast the liberal ideas of Escriche with the quotes of the conservative Rodríguez de San Miguel. The ideological dispute of these enlightened men is perfectly shown here. As for Rodríguez de San Miguel's *Pandectas hispano mexicanas*, it represents the complete knowledge that its author had about the substantive law that regulated the Mexico of his time. The methodology he used to systematize this work corresponds to the codification seen as a compilation of laws from different sources in order to understand the origin of the various legal institutions that were, and still are, applied to the national context.

Curia filípica mejicana is a clear example of Rodríguez de San Miguel's deep knowledge of due-process law. In this work, he specifies the various jurisdictional processes applicable in Mexico in civil, commercial, and criminal law, as well as various reforms that, in his time and according to his conception, would have been prudent to apply for improving the administration of justice.

The great variety of writings and articles in which the ideas of such an illustrious thinker can be found show the evolution of his way of thinking in the study of eighteenth-century thought, as he moved from being first a royalist and then a conservative to meet the liberal ideas imported from Europe. Rodríguez de San Miguel defended a conservatism in the manner of Edmund Burke, and he specifically advocated for a natural right of the Catholic Church, with a legal system based on a canonical–civil structure and rules sanctioned in Castile, Spain, New Spain, and Mexico. In the same way, he supported a constitutionalism based on a moderate monarchy or a centralized republic in which civil and religious competences are the core of the state with a codification adequate to ensure balance. The function of the law, according to this perspective, was to conserve national institutions and to adapt them to new needs. Thus, Rodríguez de San Miguel used a legal methodology of codification similar to that proposed by Francis Bacon (1561–1626).

Political context

As already mentioned, the political tendencies of the nineteenth century proposed different forms of state to meet the needs of balancing government institutions with changing legal demands. The ideas in which such tendencies found their basis came from England, France, and the United States and were the product of revolutionary movements that defined new forms of society based on the paradigm of scientific knowledge. The implied reconfiguration of social, political, and legal institutions on many occasions broke with the old and familiar forms of power—which the wave of new ideas could no longer legitimize. Various ideological currents were formed to defend the old customs, with some modifications, as well as to propose new institutions that charted a new course in the activity of the state. This was a time that pitted conservatives against liberals. In New Spain, before the creation of the Mexican nation, these ideological streams also flowed into society, causing the effervescence of social movements that began a new episode in the struggle for power.

With the creation of the Mexican state and the promulgation of the Constitution of 1824, the First Federal Republic was born, defended by the newly created liberal current. Faced with this situation and the progress of the political agenda that sought the formation of a secular state and the disentailment of ecclesiastical property, a new intellectual front arose to defend the traditional institutions that had defined New Spain, especially in terms of the Catholic Church and its assets.

The various confrontations between liberals and conservatives were developed in all areas of society. In the legal field, both sides wrote liberal and conservative constitutions. But it was in the military field where the opposition reached its climax, with the beginning of a civil war that caused the imposition of a Mexican empire—which, although sought by the conservatives, paradoxically made use of institutions of a liberal court.

The political issue was decided in favor of the liberals, who, in the last third of the nineteenth century, established a political system based on the sociological paradigm of positivism, which would also permeate the legal field with codifications of Austrian and French design. This reduced legal reality to a positive norm created by the scientific process of a legislative power prepared for the complex work of codification.

Rodríguez de San Miguel staunchly defended his moral, social, political, and legal convictions against a massive political reality of which he did not approve. In the face of the idea of a Mexican state, he advocated for a limited monarchy and, subsequently, a centralized republic. In the face of the idea of secularism, he defended the tradition of the Catholic religion, arguing in favor of a state that had Catholicism as a single religion. In the face of the disentailment of ecclesiastical goods, he defended the moral, social, and public function of the Church. In the face of a codification based on positivism, he advocated for the traditional compilation of laws, synonymous with national identity and culture.

Legal context

When Mexico arrived at independence, legal science had to deal with some intellectual novelties: Spanish doctrine was radically renewed, bringing into practice liberal thought and its postulates about what was considered legal according to constitutionalism, the rule of law, and codification, among others institutions and characteristics.[11] In the previous context:

> It went from simple reprints of Spanish legal books in Mexico to its complete redevelopment in the light of Mexican law, but without "cutting the umbilical cord" of Spanish doctrine, which was also logical, because during that first century of life, independent Spanish colonial law continued to be applied in the absence of a legal system of [Mexico's] own.[12]

The mismatch between the legislation of New Spain and that of Mexico provoked confusion, which was understood as the opportunity to consolidate the variants of codification. The idea of generating Mexican codes that systematized the order and the law according to the constitution was the trend of the time. To do so, it was necessary to fight for the method on which the new legalism would be based and, with that, the system that would regulate the legal life of Mexican society.

About his works

Some of Rodríguez de San Miguel's important works may be analyzed by means of quotations that epitomize their thought and the transcendence that it has had for the national juridical reality.

The Reasoned Dictionary of Civil, Criminal, Commercial, and Forensic Legislation

Written by the jurist Joaquín Escriche y Martín (1784–1847), this dictionary was published in Paris in 1831. Of a doctrinal type, it included legislation, jurisprudence, and doctrine.[13] In 1837 Rodríguez de San Miguel added to this work annotations in the form of quotations that would enrich it by showing a clear difference between the liberal and conservative currents. As for the nature of the work, María del Refugio González notes that part of the richness of the writing consists of the contrast of these ideas through the words of the respective contributors:

> The work of Escriche and the annotations of Rodríguez de San Miguel are representative of currents of thought that have the same origin, but that in

> the end were contrary. The first reflects the liberal ideas which were those of its author, whereas the notes and additions of [Rodríguez de San Miguel] reflect the enlightened and traditionalist mentality of the annotator in an openly conservative position.[14]

Thus, the idea that the jurist had in mind was to "adapt the work of Escriche to the institutional and legal reality of the Mexican nation, in full conservative restoration."[15] With this, he reinforced through juridical doctrine the project of a nation that from his perspective was worth building.

The method that Rodríguez de San Miguel used to adapt the institutional and legal reality of Mexico at that time was through quotations:

> I resolved therefore to put the quotations of the law, of some authors and notable people, the main novelties introduced by Mexican laws, and some poor notes of mine, which I have offered not with the idea of challenging but in the exercise of freedom. One can say that one does not perceive things in the same way as others yet leave the doctrine intact. I am not satisfied that the reader will incline toward the one that best suits him.[16]

Within the adaptations made by Rodríguez de San Miguel, filling in what he considers to be "unforgivably missing," he points to notions about religion, usury, and the interest of money. Here, in the words of María del Refugio González, "the Mexican author deployed his erudition and extensive knowledge of the norms and doctrine of civil and canon law that supported the legal order in New Spain."[17] Among the many authors on whose work he based his own are: Agustín Barbosa, Juan del Castillo Sotomayor, Diego de Covarrubias y Leyva, José Marcos Gutiérrez, Juan Gutiérrez, Johann Gottlieb Heineccius, Gregorio Mayans y Siscar, Juan Sala, Francisco Salgado de Somoza, and Juan Solórzano Pereyra. He also drew upon his own works, for example the *Manual de providencias económico políticas* (*Handbook of economic political measures*) of 1834 and *La vindicación de los que se dedican a la abogacía* (*The vindication of those dedicated to lawyering*) of 1835.[18] Finally, it should be pointed out that due to the transcendence of Escriche's work, it has been published since its first version in more than thirty-five editions, many of them with the annotations of Rodríguez de San Miguel.[19]

Las Pandectas Hispano-Mexicanas

This work can be considered the most representative of Rodríguez de San Miguel's output, because it shows the legal current to which he belonged and, likewise, the methodology he used to compile the various Castilian, Spanish, and Mexican laws. The work has two editions: the first, of 1839–40, printed in the office of Mariano Galván Rivera in three volumes; the second, of 1852, elaborated in the library of J.F. Rosa in three volumes.

Rodríguez de San Miguel called the work *Pandectas* as an allusion to the original Greek meaning of a universal compilation like the Justinian's *Digesta seu* Pandectae[20] and his objective was "to form this collection from the ancient law, complementing that with what had been dictated by the national governments."[21]As for his method, Rodríguez de San Miguel refers to Francis Bacon and the methodology he suggested:

> 1. Omit all useless and outdated objects. 2. Of the antinomies, or things in opposition, adopt the most well founded and abolish their counterparts. 3. Of identical things, which are reiterations of each other, leave one instead of all, which seems more perfect. 4. Discard laws that do not resolve issues and are the occasion of disputes. 5. Reduce to short terms what is verbose or redundant.[22]

Part of the position that Rodríguez de San Miguel had on legal issues—"on the need for good legislation in society, and its state in ours"—becomes clear when he legitimizes, from the regal virtue of Alfonso X of Castile, the prudence he showed in recognizing the principles of justice that do not vary. In this sense, Rodríguez de San Miguel criticizes the positivist posture of codification cuts off historical roots. Thus, his position toward natural law was one of understanding the existence of principles and values of justice, which in essence must be the basis for creating norms of law; this requires the idea of respect for both traditions and legal customs, and the rejection of foreign novelties that lack roots in society.

An example of the critique of positivist-type codification is his argument for the efficiency of the *Siete Partidas* in terms of the administration of justice. This was a Castilian statutory code first compiled during the reign of Alfonso X of Castile (r. 1252–84), with the intent of establishing a uniform body of normative rules for the kingdom. It was later established in New Spain as a main source of law. The *Pandectas*, then, were the legal expression of an idea of codification based on the compilation of customary and natural law as opposed to the positivist codification of the French liberal court.

Curia Filípica Mejicana

Juan Luis Soberanes Fernández calls Rodríguez de San Miguel "the famous Mexican jurist of the nineteenth century"[23] and writes, "It is essential to know the background of our procedural and mercantile rights, which also has the merit of being a Mexican book, which, without despising the Spanish inheritance, knew how to cultivate the foundations of a self-doctrine."[24] Its origin goes back to the book *Curia Philippica*, printed in Lima in 1617 together with the book *Labyrintho de comercio terrestre y naval* (*Labyrinth of terrestrial and naval commerce*), which were authored by Juan Hevia Bolaños and gathered into a single volume under the title of *Curia Philippica* in 1644.[25] "Curia" refers to the forum or public place where justice is administered, and "Philippica" honors King Philip III, then monarch of Spain.[26]

In his work, Rodríguez de San Miguel specifies what, in his opinion, should be changed in various existing procedures.[27] He touches on the reform of jurisdictions, mayors, judges of the first instance, the courts of second and third instance, the courts for criminal cases, the executive trial, summary judgments, criminal trial, and asylum. As for the judges of first instance and the increase of their workload (to consider small claims), caused by the abolition of mayoral positions, he specifies that what must be done is to increase the number of judges in proportion to the number of cases.[28] Speaking about the tribunals of second and third instance, he says, "This part of the republic is on the same level as the others, and therefore has in the order of the judiciary a superior court in charge of second and third instances."[29]

On jury trials for criminal cases, Rodríguez San Miguel opposed them and considered them an institution suitable only in civilizations "in which enlightenment and morality are found in a degree of great elevation."[30] It is possible to appreciate his conservative position when, on this topic, he expresses distrust of innovations:

> The universal cry that has risen against those who must administer it [the jury trial]—especially in the criminal branch, because one does not see the punishment of as many crimes as are committed—is not a motive for the complete destruction of old practices and the adoption of theories new and unknown. Whether to correct the defects that suffer from those, delete much useless paperwork, or multiply the number of judges, establish a real police, subjected entirely to the judiciary, and justice will be administered straight and promptly, without having to expose oneself to the serious drawbacks of innovations.[31]

As can be seen with the *Curia Filípica*, Rodríguez de San Miguel knew the objective law that served to materialize the substantive rights of both private and public law; this is evident in his compilation of legislation that allowed various actions to be initiated for claiming subjective rights or for defense in criminal matters. Not only that, but along with the laborious work of litigation he also served as judge and understood the ontology of the process, so he criticized the procedural institutions of his time and proposed various reforms, understanding that it was necessary to preserve what worked and modify what caused failures that were translated into social discontent, so fashionable in the independent period of Mexico.

Conclusion

In reviewing the life and writings of Juan Nepomuceno Rodríguez de San Miguel, one can notice that, both in his thinking and in his public life, he was always consistent with his moral convictions, which he at all times defended. Beyond that, however, his critique of the liberal forms of his time was one he made with the conviction of the necessity to identify the moral, social, political, and legal institutions that could lead to the ideal of generative cohesion that the nascent Mexico demanded, thus nurturing the political and economic stability that the nation craved. Regardless of the fact that he was eventually overcome by those liberal institutions, the advances he made for the society in which he lived are unquestionable. The legal reference to his name and his works survives in editions throughout the history of Mexico. In this way, the rational Catholic debate concerning natural law that he defended, supported by the immense bibliography that he marshaled for proof, as well as his legal methodology of compilation of laws, are aspects of legal science that cannot pass unnoticed. This is, by the way, one more of his great contributions to the Mexican legal system.

Finally, it is necessary to understand the conditions in which a person unfolds, the beliefs he holds, the way in which he argues them, and the way in which he lives them. If it is about coherence in thinking and doing, Rodríguez de San Miguel is the example of an eminent jurist who knew how to live up to the turbulent moments of his time, synonymous with rigor of substance and form, with a clear methodology on the ways of grounding a philosophy at the service of the state and society, taking the way of legal rules. Much good would be done in recognizing the coherence of his ideas, regardless of the epistemological criterion of absolute truth, always so elusive and difficult to assimilate.

Notes

1 Sánchez Santos, "Biographical notes," 2.
2 González Domínguez, "Juan N. Rodríguez de San Miguel, Mexican conservative jurist," 235.
3 Ibid.
4 Ibid.
5 Ibid., 235–36.
6 González Domínguez, *Juan N. Rodríguez de San Miguel*, 113.
7 Ibid., 236–37.
8 Ibid.
9 Ibid.
10 Ibid.
11 Rodríguez de San Miguel, *Curia filípica mejicana*, p. x.
12 Ibid.
13 Escriche, *Diccionario razonado*, 12–13.
14 Ibid., 20.
15 Ibid., 25.
16 Ibid., 22.
17 Ibid., 25.
18 Ibid., 30-49.
19 Ibid., 49–54.
20 Ibid., xxxi.
21 Ibid.
22 Ibid., xxxi–xxxii.
23 Rodríguez de San Miguel, *Curia filípica mejicana*, xii.
24 Ibid.
25 Ibid., vii.
26 Ibid.
27 Ibid., 564–71.
28 Ibid., 566.

29 Ibid., 567.
30 Ibid.
31 Ibid.

References

Cruz Barney, Óscar. *Historia del derecho en México.* 2nd ed. Mexico City: Oxford University Press, 2012.

Escriche, Joaquín. *Diccionario razonado de legislación civil, penal, comercial y forense. Con citas del derecho, notas y adiciones por el licenciado Juan Rodríguez de San Miguel*, edited by María del Refugio González. Mexico City: UNAM-IIJ, 1993.

González Domínguez, María del Refugio. "Juan N. Rodríguez de San Miguel, jurista conservador mexicano." In *Estudios jurídicos en homenaje a Marta Morineau*, Vol. 1, *Derecho romano. Historia del derecho*, edited by Nuria González Martín. Mexico City: UNAM, 2006.

González Domínguez, María del Refugio. *Juan N. Rodríguez de San Miguel, jurista conservador mexicano (1839–1863).* Compiled and with an introduction by María del Refugio González. Mexico City: UNAM, 1992.

Lira, Andrés. "La Facultad Económico-Coactiva, 1837–1899: Una Aportación del Régimen Unitario al Orden Republicano en México." *Estudios* 105 (2013): 121–133.

Lorente, Marta, and Jesús Vallejo, eds. *Manual de historia del derecho.* Valencia: Tirant Lo Blanch, 2012.

Pampillo Baliño, Juan Pablo. *Historia general del derecho.* Mexico City: Oxford University Press, 2008.

Rodríguez de San Miguel, Juan Nepomuceno. *Apuntamientos del informe, que por parte de la testamentaría de D.J.M. Floreo, hizo el lic. J.N. Rodríguez de San Miguel en el Tribunal de Circuito de México, en la vista del recurso de denegada apelación del fallo pronunciado en el Juzgado de Distrito, en el juicio de alcabalas, instaurado por el denunciante D.M. Nava contra la expresada testamentaría.* Mexico City: J.M. Lara, 1859. José María La Forge collection. Bar code 51530. Topographic location 4 1 01 01 03.

Rodríguez de San Miguel, Juan Nepomuceno. *Curia filípica mejicana. Obra completa de práctica forense: conteniendo además un tratado íntegro de la jurisprudencia mercantil.* Foreword by José Luis Soberanes Fernández. Facsimile edition of 1st edition of 1858. Mexico City: Porrúa, UNAM-IIJ, 1991.

Rodríguez de San Miguel, Juan Nepomuceno. *Informe ó alegacion en derecho, que por el Convento de Carmelitas de la ciudad de Querétaro, y en apoyo de la jurisdicción del Ordinario Metropolitano, hizo el lic. J. Rodriguez de San Miguel, ante la…Suprema Corte de Justicia, en la vista del recurso de fuerza introducido por el M.R.P. Provincial del Carmen [Angelo María de San José], sobre no tocar al ordinario conocer de la enajenación de la hacienda de Chichimequillas.* Mexico City: collection José María La Forge, 15789_04-41010102, 1852.

Rodríguez de San Miguel, Juan Nepomuceno. *Pandectas hispano-mexicanas.* 4th ed. Mexico City: UNAM-IIJ, 1991.

Sánchez Santos, Trinidad. "Biographical notes of some distinguished Mexicans. Mr. Lic. D. Juan Rodríguez de San Miguel." *El Nacional*, Mexico, Sunday, May 24, 1885, vol. 7, no. 112, p. 2.

Santillán Ramírez, Iris Rocío. "El control social de las mujeres a través de las leyes." La Colonia en México. *Alegatos: Revista Jurídica de la Universidad Autónoma Metropolitana* (Mexico, January–April 2018). Https://www.academia.edu/36780343/El_control_social_de_las_mujeres_a_trav%C3%A9s_de_las_leyes._La_Colonia_en_M%C3%A9xico.

11 Juan Bautista Alberdi (Argentina, 1810–84)

Ezequiel Abásolo

Introduction

Intellectual, humanist, journalist, musical expert, and, in truth, almost a polymath, Juan Bautista Alberdi was, above all, a lawyer, vibrant and lively, arrogant in his expressions, and great in many of his intuitions. A man of his time, he continues to project an influence to the present day. In this regard, one can note that from the restoration of the Argentine constitutional order, in 1983, to the present, the Supreme Court of Justice of the nation has reported on more than one hundred occasions of its trials with decisions that have been based on his work.

As in the lives of other, comparable Hispanic-American personalities, the biography of the brilliant jurist from Tucumán was marked by more than one contrast. As a consular figure helping to direct the Argentine course through the nineteenth century, he barely resided in his country as an adult. Of the half-century of life that he enjoyed after his graduation as a doctor of law from the University of Córdoba, he remained in his homeland for little more than seven years. Throughout his life, he spent more time abroad than in his native Argentina: forty-nine years out of eighty-four. On the other hand, the man who rightly has been considered the primary intellectual responsible for the national constitution of 1853 held almost no relevant public positions in Argentina. He was neither president, nor a minister of executive power, nor a judicial magistrate, nor a constituent representative. He barely became a national legislator in the twilight of his life, serving on some other occasions as a diplomat and as a second-order administrative figure. As I have already noted, however, Alberdi was first of all a lawyer of intense and successful forensic action. Thus, one can understand why lawyers of the Argentine Republic celebrate their profession on August 29, the anniversary of the birth of our hero.

A biography like Alberdi's—rich in nuances, intellectual twists, and original contributions—cannot be reduced to a list of trips, public functions, forensic tasks, and works destined for publication. What I offer here, then, is a synthetic chronology of his professional and intellectual activity. I then move to a re-creation of the most significant aspects of his life as a lawyer, which offers the opportunity to dialogue with some constants that identify him successively as a student, a professional of the forum, and a statesman. Given the nature of the volume in which this narrative is framed—a collection of essays about Latin American Christian jurists—I do not deal here with all of Alberdi's life and contributions, nor do I focus on the topics that are usually of greatest interest to historiographers. Rather, I refer to his promotion of the Argentine constitution and, especially, to his profile as a lawyer. Finally, I draw on the direct Alberdian sources available and suggest a bibliography of classic and recent works.

Biographical information

Formed by a life experience intensely embedded in the shocks and triumphs of nineteenth-century Argentina, Alberdi's personality exceeds the narrow framework of a particular nation-state. An authentic South American figure, he traveled almost half of the vast continent personally, including visits to Lima and Rio de Janeiro. If Buenos Aires and Montevideo were the cradles of his legal training, Valparaíso was the happy setting of the full deployment of his intellectual and professional activity.

Juan Bautista was born on August 29, 1810 in San Miguel del Tucumán, at that time a small town of about four thousand inhabitants and the center of a district of another twenty thousand souls. He was the son of Salvador Alberdi, born in Biscay, and Josefa Aráoz, from Tucumán, a member of an influential and traditional Creole family, who had an exceptional literary inclination. Unfortunately, Josefa died five months after the birth of Juan Bautista. Alberdi's father, a liberal merchant who spoke French and admired Rousseau and Raynal, served after 1803 as a deputy of the Buenos Aires Consulado in Tucumán.[1] A friend of the lawyer and patriot general Manuel Belgrano, Salvador Alberdi received Rioplatense citizenship in 1816 and died in 1822. Two years later, the young Alberdi was awarded a scholarship to complete his secondary studies in the City of Buenos Aires, in the newly established College of Moral Sciences. Soon, however, he abandoned formal education and entered work as a dependent in a trading house. In these circumstances, he began to love reading, while his uncle taught him Latin. Alberdi managed to return to school, where he befriended Miguel Cané, in whose house he boarded.

In 1830, after completing his secondary studies, he began his higher education in law at the University of Buenos Aires. Two years later he published *El espíritu de la música* (*The spirit of music*) and *Ensayo sobre un método nuevo para tocar el piano con la mayor facilidad* (*Essay on a new method of playing the piano most easily*). In 1834, after a visit to his homeland, he wrote *Memoria descriptiva sobre Tucumán* (*Descriptive report of Tucumán*). During that same year, he obtained his degree in law, not in Buenos Aires but in Córdoba. However, he returned to Buenos Aires, the capital, where he attended the Academia de Jurisprudencia, although he never succeeded in registering as a Buenos Aires lawyer. In 1835, he released his first work, in which he displayed his legal ability: it is the *Respuesta al voto de América* (*Response to the vote of America*), in which he replies to Rivera Indarte. Under the guidance of Esteban Echeverría, Alberdi began reading French Romantic authors. In 1837 he published the *Fragmento preliminar al estudio del derecho* (*Preliminary fragment of the study of law*). During that time he also attended the Salón Literario and became a member of the Generación de la Joven Argentina. He collaborated on the newspaper *La Moda* and became editor of the fifteenth symbolic word of the *Dogma Socialista* of Echeverría, a work in which the fundamental principles that animated the young people who yearned for the definitive organization of the country were synthesized in fifteen words.

Overwhelmed by the direction established in the dictatorial government of Juan Manuel de Rosas, in 1838, like many other Argentines, Alberdi emigrated to Montevideo. There he accompanied general Juan Galo de Lavalle as his secretary at the beginning of his campaign against the Argentine dictatorship. Among other tasks, Alberdi wrote the Uruguayan declaration of war against the government in Buenos Aires. In 1840 he managed to enroll as a lawyer in the Montevideo forum, and from that moment he shared the practice of law with that of journalism. In 1843 he made his first trip to Europe.

On his return to the New World in 1844, Alberdi decided to settle in Chile, where an important colony of Argentine emigrants had settled. He went first to the capital, Santiago, and then, after a brief experience in the south of the country, ended up settling in Valparaíso. During his stay there, in addition to successfully practicing law and journalism, he published several legal contributions in which he applied his deep knowledge of positive law.

Thus, among other works, in 1846 his *Manual del escritor, del impresor y del jurado* (*Manual of the writer, printer, and jurist*) appeared, and two years later he produced not only an interesting collaboration of a hundred pages referring to the organization of the Chilean courts, but also the *Manual de ejecuciones y quiebras* (*Manual of judgments and bankruptcy*). By the end of the 1840s, his frequent contact with the successful model of Chilean authority (linked to the empire of the 1833 Portalian constitution), as well as the formidable South American repercussions of the 1848 European revolutions stirred in him—as in almost all Argentine exiles—the most extreme manifestations of their transformative ideas. Thus, as Dardo Pérez Guilhou observes, the most conservative features of his political-legal personality were consolidated.[2]

After the defeat of the dictatorship of Juan Manuel de Rosas by Justo José de Urquiza in the Battle of Caseros, on May 1, 1852, Alberdi wrote his most significant and influential work, *Bases y puntos de partida para la organización política de la República Argentina* (*Bases and starting points for the political organization of the Argentine republic*), in which he reconciles the concerns and proposals of the federal and unitary factions, until then in conflict. He sent the work to General Urquiza, who received it with enthusiasm. In later editions, Alberdi incorporated a constitutional project for the country. This material was specially considered by the Argentine constituents who approved the Constitution of 1853.

The triennium between the beginning of 1852 and the beginning of 1855 was intense. It was possibly the most fruitful and relevant period of his profuse intellectual public life. Jorge Mayer states that at that time, "his voice had conquered a consecrated authority." After publishing his *Bases* in 1852 and discussing the matter with Domingo Faustino Sarmiento, toward the end of 1853 he published his *Estudios sobre la constitución de 1853* (*Studies on the constitution of 1853*), and in the middle of the following year his *Examen de la Constitución Provincial de Buenos Aires* (*Examination of the provincial constitution of Buenos Aires*). Months later, he drafted his *Sistema Económico y Rentístico de la Confederación Argentina* (*Economic and revenue system of the Argentine Confederation*), which he delivered to the press by the beginning of 1855.

President Urquiza appointed Alberdi as the Argentine chargé d'affaires to the United Kingdom and France in 1854, and he later became plenipotentiary minister in those countries as well as in Spain and Rome. With the change of the national political landscape after the battle of Pavón, in 1861, Alberdi lost his status as a diplomat, but he decided to remain in Europe as a private individual. During these years, he maintained an intense correspondence. In 1868, he published a critique of the civil code project prepared by Dalmacio Vélez Sarsfield. Two years later Alberdi wrote his essay *El crimen de la guerra* (*The crime of war*), which remained unpublished until his death. In 1874 he published *Peregrinación de Luz de Día, o, Viaje y aventuras de la verdad en el Nuevo Mundo* (*Pilgrimage of the light of day, or travels and adventures of truth in the New World*). Returning to Argentina in 1879 to serve as a national deputy for the district of Tucumán, he fulfilled this function until the conflict that concluded with the federalization of the City of Buenos Aires was unleashed, in 1880. The following year he published *La República Argentina consolidada* (*The consolidated republic of Argentina*) and returned to settle in France. Nominated to serve as the Argentine ambassador to Chile, he declined for health reasons and was appointed instead as the immigration commissioner, replacing Carlos Calvo. Alberdi died in Neuilly-sur-Seine, France, on June 19, 1884.

Training and intellectual references

Some recent studies have drawn attention to the traditional character of the legal thinking and intellectual framework of Alberdi.[3] This should not surprise us, as he was a jurist of a time of transition, when the weight of the past coexisted daily with the present. However, he did take into account several innovations of his own time. Thus, for example, by the mid-1830s, at the end of his university studies, Alberdi decided to expand his previous university education. He did it under the guidance of Juan María Gutiérrez and Esteban Echeverría. As Alberdi himself would remember years later:

> By Echeverría, who had been educated in France, during the Restoration, I had the first news of Lerminier, Villemain, Victor Hugo, Alexandre Dumas, Lamartine, Byron, and everything that was then called Romanticism, as opposed to the old classical school. In college I had studied the philosophy of Condillac and Locke. The reading of Helvecio, Cabanis, Holbach, Bentham, and Rousseau had absorbed me for years. To Echeverría I owe the evolution that took place in my spirit with the readings of Victor Cousin,

> Villemain, Chateubriand, Jouffroy, and all the eclectics from Germany, in favor of what was called spiritualism.[4]

In university classrooms, Alberdi drew on the standard knowledge of the Spanish American lawyer of his time—that is, the *ius commune* and Spanish law, to which he sometimes added illustrations from the Laws of the Indies and national regulations. Presumably—though the relevant concrete documentary evidence is missing—Alberdi's initial contact with legal studies were carried out under the directives of the influential text *Prontuario de práctica forense* (*Record of forensic practice*) by Manuel Antonio de Castro.[5] On the other hand, as a student of the recently established University of Buenos Aires, he received lessons from authors unknown in the region, such as Jeremy Bentham. What his formal higher education provided was a solid traditional legal formation, thanks to his passage, along with fellow students and friends like Miguel Cané and Manuel Quiroga de la Rosa, through the jurisprudence classrooms of the Spanish professor Rafael de Casagemas.[6] In that environment, the young Alberdi began to exercise one of his most frequent roles: that of a merciless critic of more or less exhausted intellectual authorities. It is not surprising that the initial targets of his sharpness were stale Castilian commentators such as Gregorio López and Antonio Gómez, or some other more or less contemporary authorities, such as the Guatemalan José María Alvarez. His early differences with Bentham, who was taken as an oracle by the illustrious Rivadavians, tell us a lot about the originality and courage of young Alberdi's judgment.[7]

In the course of an autobiographical essay, Alberdi gives us valuable complementary information about the initial process of building his intellectual references. "However varied the phases have been because my life has passed," he explains, "the form that my intelligence has preserved during it came from its first period, spent in my country. It was, of course, that of my education. But my education was not done only at the university." He continues explaining the diverse and eclectic collection of texts that were then integrated into his horizon of references:

> More than all this they contributed to forming my spirit, the readings of the authors, which I must name, to complement my first education. My favorite readings for many years in my early life were the best-known works of the following authors: Volney, Holbach, Rousseau, Helvecio, Cabanis, Richerand, Lavatter, Buffon, Bacon, Pascal, La Bruyere, Bentham, Montesquieu, Benjamin Constant, Lerminier, Tocqueville, Chevallier, Bastiat, Adam Smith, J-B. Say, Vico, Villemain, Cousin, Guizot, Rossi, Pierre Leroux, Saint Simon, Lamartine, Destutt de Tracy, Victor Hugo, Dumas, P.L. Couvier, Chateaubriand, Mme. De Stael, Lamenais, Jouffroy, Kant, Merlin, Pothier, Pardessus, Troplong, Heinecio, El Federalista, Story, Balbi, Martínez de la Rosa, Donoso Cortés, Capmany. It is seen from this catalog that I did not frequent Spanish authors much; not so much for the anti-Spanish concerns, produced and maintained by the war of our independence, but by the

> philosophical direction of my studies. In Spain, I did not find a philosopher like Bacon and Locke, or political philosophers like Montesquieu, or jurists like Pothier.[8]

On the other hand, when some time had elapsed and Alberdi became more interested in the people's rights, he turned to Grotius, Vattel, Alberico Gentili, Wheaton, Andrés Bello, Lieber, and Bluntschli.[9] Here we find a trait of the Alberdian personality: his inexhaustible curiosity, which did not diminish with the years. In this way, Alberdi incorporated to the end his usual references to Laboulaye; to Fustel de Coulanges and his great book *The Ancient City* of 1864; to Herbert Spencer; and to Paul Leroy-Beaulieu, and his study titled *Les Guerres contemporaines (1853–1866)*.[10] In short, Alberdi was not only a connoisseur of traditional Spanish American law who learned at the university and in practice, but also a writer abounding in contemporary European legal and philosophical expressions, especially French and Italian ones.

Intellectual personality

Alberdi the statesman and Alberdi the jurist coexisted with Alberdi the lawyer. The skillful operator in the forum knew and criticized the interpretive cunning of the old curial styles. With the sagacity of genius, he knew how to condense in his writings the synthesis of scholarly authors, which he interspersed with original seminal ideas, local practices, and various social moods. Endowed with a superior and simultaneously pragmatic intellect, he aspired to achieve, before anything else, as he made clear in his *Elementos de Derecho público provincial* (*Elements of provincial public law*), "practical results" with the application of his criticisms and doctrines.[11] Without becoming a writer of treatises—something that he himself did not claim—it is possible to identify several habitual, more or less permanent, features of his intellectual production.

Arrogant on more than one occasion—sometimes to the point of confessing bluntly that his analyses have been elaborated "on the fly"—he uses and abuses irony.[12] For example, along with false flattery, he applies irony again and again throughout his controversy with Vélez Sarsfield about the future Argentine civil code. He says he was surprised to find in the code, among other things, that the Brazilian jurist Augusto Teixeira de Freitas had been "dethroned in the predilection of the Argentine code writer to Caius, Tronchet, Portalis, Meleville," many famous European classical and contemporary jurists. One of his best-achieved arguments results when he reasons that if "the Argentine code is the work of Brazilian politics rather than Argentine politics," while "the political father of that Code is [Argentine] General [Bartolomé] Mitre [Martínez], [then] Don Pedro II [emperor of Brazil] is the grandfather."[13]

Possessing gifts of communication and synthesis, Alberdi's intellect has a predilection for schemas, intended not only for his own study and the exercise of his journalistic activity but also as a support for his forensic activity. This is demonstrated by the synoptic picture that accompanies his defense of José León, accused of the murder of Guillermo Lavergne in 1842.[14] Similarly, hours before presenting for his law degree in Córdoba, he showed one of his evaluators "the synoptic chart that, by way of study, I had made of the third law book, to use it as an aid in navigating the course of the exam."[15] As for the features of Alberdian rhetoric, it is distinguished by a remarkable capacity for expression, and by the abundance of visual evocations, rich images, and multiple metaphors. In the fine and delicious description of the Piedmontese forum he offers in *Veinte días en Génova* (*Twenty days in Genoa*, 1843), Alberdi says a lot about the eloquence he likes to display in his own oratory. He explains:

> I am far from preferring, against the crude nakedness of a conscientious and logical discourse, the frivolous and pedantic rascal with unfounded words or energy…[I sympathize with] the simple and reserved self-restraint and grace of bearing, of style, with which they enhance and recommend, I will not say the countenance but, the very background of the discourse, whatever the place in which it is pronounced. One can and should demand of the forensic word the elegance with which the mathematician Zussane wanted to expose geometry itself, based on the fact that the elegance of exposure gives relief and transparency to the body of truth. In addition, why dress the thought with a rude and unkempt tunic, in the enclosure where the lawyer and the judge are obliged to wear a bright and black robe?[16]

Constants of Alberdian thought

Already during the nineteenth century, Manuel Bilbao and Arturo Reynal O'Connor, responsible for the first publication of Alberdi's *Obras Completas*, highlighted his "powerful intelligence" and his thought "endowed by nature" for "assimilating modern ideas."[17] Besides the fact that the style of these editors can appear foreign to us today, there is no doubt about the aptness of their description. A man of contrasts and contradictions, he was sympathetic to a peculiar and debatable historicism, insofar as he affirmed that "we have no history, we are from yesterday."[18] On the other hand, he occasionally recognizes that Argentina:

> has two original laws in the absence of one, as the nation has two stories: one that begins with the conquest implemented by our European race and by its victorious installation on the American soil; another that begins and develops with the republic, independent of all power concerning Spain.[19]

Alberdi shared a simultaneous concern to achieve civilization and progress, which he identified with non-Spanish Europe and with liberalism. In this way, he affirmed that "freedom is a machine that, like steam, requires for its handling English machinists of origin"; and that "Europe will bring us its new spirit, its habits of industry, its practices of civilization, with the immigration it sends us."[20] As for his early anti-Hispanicism, in the *Fragmento preliminar al estudio del Derecho*, he assures that if "we owe to Spain [our] chains, to France we owe

[our] freedoms."[21] Concordantly, he is convinced that the happy establishment of a new legal regime in the country will require overcoming the difficult obstacle represented by "the accumulation of fragments that still remain of the old" Spanish regulatory framework, which he associates, plainly, with tyranny.

Paradoxically, his anti-Hispanicism owes much to Peninsular writing. Notably, one author he emulated, the caustic Spanish critic Mariano José de Larra, published some of his best journalistic contributions under the name of Fígaro, and the young Alberdi adopted as his own pseudonym that of Figarillo.[22] Among the many expressions of his anti-Hispanicism was a case in Montevideo in June 1842, when he described the Laws of the Indias as "disgraceful," and a quarter of a century later denounced the same laws as designed to leave out the foreigner.[23]

Regarding his liberalism, on the other hand, one should remember what can be considered his intellectual testament—a conference titled, significantly, "The Omnipotence of the State is the Denial of Individual Freedom." Held in the classrooms of the University of Buenos Aires on May 24, 1880, as part of the presentation of degrees, the occasion offered Alberdi an opportunity to synthesize his attachment to this ideology. Declaring himself an enemy of "societies that expect their happiness from the hand of their governments," while "expecting something that is contrary to nature," Alberdi says that "states are rich by the work of their individuals, and this work is fruitful because man is free, that is, owner and lord of his person, of his property, of his life, of his home."[24]

A jurist by training and temperament, in his constitutional reflections he shows a formidable gravitation toward the theoretical principles of the liberal economic science of his time, embodied in the work of authors such as the Englishman David Ricardo. In this way, in his introduction to the *Sistema económico y rentístico*, he begins by stating that "the Argentine federal constitution contains a complete system of economic policy, insofar as it guarantees by strict provisions the free action of labor, capital, and land."[25]

Expressing his complex temperament, Alberdi integrates into his considerations a deep Christianity with a marked anticlericalism, a position that led him to reproach the author of the Argentine civil code who had ceded a part of the sovereignty of the Argentine Republic to "the hands of the king of Rome, Supreme Pontiff of Catholics."[26] This passage explains, at least partially, why some faithful reproached him for his openness to freedoms of conscience and cults. Even more, others arrived at the point of denouncing these liberal positions as heretical. Although he admitted that Argentina was "without a doubt deeply Catholic," he also warned that this condition did not result from any constitutional mandate but derived from the "direct and free election of [Argentina's] children, by tradition, by education, by vocation."[27] While the ecclesiastical hierarchy and its normative production provoked in him rejection, perhaps because of his Masonic affiliation, perhaps because of his inherent anti-Spanish bias, or perhaps for both reasons, the truth is that he simultaneously embraced Christian convictions. Thus, he underscores in an 1852 letter to Bartolomé Mitre that his *Bases* "are not mine because neither the writer nor the deputy makes bases: God makes them" and is the one who "gives each people its constitution or way of being normal, as he gives to each man."[28] Fifteen years later, in 1867, in *El crimen de la guerra*, he states that "Christian morality is the morality of today's civilization par excellence," that "the Gospel is the right of people," and that modern man "is the man of Jesus Christ."[29] On the other hand, in 1874, within the framework of that work in which he reconciles fantasy and satire—*Peregrinación de luz de día*—he makes his *Don Quixote* character say that wise legislators "know how to be mere copyists of God, when they make laws which are already made and write codes that govern the world without being written," while "society is the work of God."[30]

As was common among his contemporaries in the Río de la Plata basin, Alberdi usually practiced eclecticism, a trend that can be seen in his constitutional proposal of the state form, with which he intends to reconcile centralism with federalism. Pragmatic and original, Alberdi presents himself as a man of solutions rather than problems, and a skilled student of the best of the public spirit. Thus, in presenting his book *Bases* to General Justo José de Urquiza, in a letter dated in Valparaíso in May 1852, Alberdi says: "in it, there is nothing of mine but the work of weakly expressing what belongs to good common sense" and "the experience of our country."[31] Such a mood was also shared in those days by Domingo Faustino Sarmiento, the ardent Sanjuanino, sometimes friend, and sometimes enemy of Alberdi, who, when he learned about Alberdi's great intellectual contribution, wrote to him that "his constitution is a monument: it is you the legislator of good sense in the forms of science."[32]

The derivation of Alberdi's pragmatism is that he imagines the post-tyranny constitution not as a text "definitive" but as something "of transition," provided with "a mission of circumstances, not to be forgotten. It is intended to fill in a certain number of needs and not all. It would be unwise to aspire to satisfy all the needs of the republic at once."[33] For him, also, "as before we placed independence first, today we must put there free immigration, freedom of trade, railroads, industry without hindrance."[34] In short, "the population of the Argentine Republic, today deserted and lonely, must be the great and primary end of its constitution for long years."[35] To reach this goal, Alberdi understood that the fundamental norm must be original. If it is not, it is simply bad "because it must be the expression of a special combination of facts, of men, and of things, it must essentially offer the originality that affects that combination in the country to be constituted."[36]

Attitude toward the Code

In terms of the law, Alberdi soon perceived the enormous distance that separated his generation from the previous one, and the antiquity that overwhelmed the most reputable Spanish jurists, from the legendary Gregorio López to the contemporary (in his view admirable) Joaquín de Escriche.[37] "Openness to Lerminier and his fiery pages," Alberdi confessed, "made in my ideas the same change that Savigny's book had worked in his."

> I stopped conceiving the legal world as a collection of written laws. I found that it was nothing less than the moral law of the harmonious development

> of social beings; the very constitution of society, the mandatory order in which the individualities that constitute it are developed. I conceived the law as a living phenomenon that was necessary to study in the organic economy of the state. In this way the science of law, like physics, had to become experimental; and thus charged with interest and animation that it did not have in the written texts, nor in abstract doctrines.[38]

One can understand, then, why, in the opening of his early work *Fragmento preliminar al estudio del Derecho*, he decided to reproduce that part of law 13, title 1, *partida* 1, in which it is assumed that knowledge of the laws is not limited to remembering its letters, but rather consists in unraveling its understanding.[39]

Convinced that "the law is one for the entire human race, by virtue of the very unity of the human race," as he writes in *El crimen de la guerra*,[40] Alberdi undergirds his thinking with the idea that there is an intimate and intense relationship between the thought of the jurist and the social reality of his surroundings. He argues: "Laws, like rivers, are adjusted in their course to the nature of the soil in which they make their way."[41] A topic that concerned him was the law in its everyday use and its codification. In this category of ideas, and beyond any strict forensic interest, the statesman Alberdi was concerned about the status of civil law as organic law of the constitution. In this regard, throughout his *Bases*, he affirms that it would be:

> precise, then, that the civil laws of processing and commerce be modified and conceived in the sense of the same tendencies that must preside over the constitution, of which, in the last analysis, the various branches of private law are nothing other than organic laws.[42]

In his criticism of the Civil Code of 1868, he returned to the same matter and affirmed that "civil laws are nothing but organic laws of the provisions of the national constitution, which enshrine the natural rights on which civilians, the family, and society are founded."[43] He also assumed that private law must respond to the "economic needs of this era." A relentless critic of the colonial past, he never tired of pointing out the opposition between the old civil law of the Indies and the new liberal economic system sought by the Argentine Constitution of 1853.[44] On the other hand, to promote the codification of private law in Argentina at that time, when, according to his (debatable) point of view, the country was transitioning to an "unknown and new life in its organic structure,"[45] in his *Sistema económico y rentístico* he applied sociological and historicist criteria to ensure that the codes are "the expression of society, the image of its social status, which essentially results from the combination of three orders of fact, namely: moral facts, political facts, and economic facts."[46] Likewise, Alberdi alluded to Savigny's own words, according to which "a code must contain only the principles from which the decisions of the specialties emanate, because the law, like geometry, subsists on fundamental and fruitful points." To be faithful to his principles, Alberdi then considers that the

Argentine code must receive "the Hispano-American revolution about the family and civil society."[47]

Regarding the "civil constitution" of a country, Alberdi is concerned, in short, with the "spirit of the code," that is, the code

> considered in its relations with the reason that has determined its composition, with the method that presided over its work, with the sources and models by which the author has been inspired, with the government system of the country in which it should be applied, with the commercial vocation of the peoples of La Plata, with its nature and historical character, and, finally, with the political moment of its elaboration and sanction.[48]

Hence, he inclined to reject adapting "the old colonial law" to the fashion of the nineteenth century. Faced with the proposals for the code, he advocated, on the contrary, as the "most convenient" for Argentines, the "partial and prompt reforms" of legislation and defense of the judicial role. Thus, in his *Bases*, he proclaims that "the law, the constitution, the government, are empty words, if not reduced to facts by the judges who, ultimately, make them become reality or not."[49] In his *Carta para formar a un abogado* (*Letter to train a lawyer*), dated in Valparaíso in April 1850 and addressed to Lucas González, he assigned to jurisprudence the condition of being "the logic itself considered under a certain aspect."[50] In his *Bases*, similarly, he gives jurisprudence the mission of satisfying "great means of improving and correcting laws without repealing or changing them."[51] However, he does not fail to express his reservations against the traditional argumentation methods used by jurists. Thus, he clarifies that:

> if it is true that the comment is a supplement to the legislation and a means of providing stability for the preservation of its text, it can also be the means of compromising and misplacing it due to a fundamental error in the comment system.

In an analogous sense, he strongly affirms in his *Estudios sobre la Constitución de 1853*, that "any unnecessary interpretation…and every interpretation that makes the law say the opposite of what it literally says is ruinous of law and justice."[52]

Notes

1 Mayer, *Alberdi y su tiempo*, passim.
2 See Pérez Guilhou, *El pensamiento conservador de Alberdi*.
3 See Sadler. On the survival of the traditional legal culture, see Abásolo, *Bastante Más que "degradantes andrajos de nuestra pasada esclavitud."*
4 J.B. Alberdi, *Escritos póstumos*, 15:295.
5 On the importance of Manuel Antonio de Castro, see Abásolo.
6 See Leiva, "Las lecciones de derecho civil."
7 Alberdi, *Obras Completas*, 1:137.

8 Alberdi, *Escritos póstumos,* 15:308–09. On the initial formation of Alberdi, see Laclau, "Las influencias filosóficas," and Ghirardi, *La filosofía en Alberdi.*
9 Cf. Alberdi, *Escritos póstumos*, vol. 2, passim.
10 Alberdi, *Obras Completas*, 8:166.
11 Ibid., 5:56.
12 Ibid., 7:81.
13 Ibid., vol. 7:96 and 127
14 Ibid., 2:25.
15 Alberdi, *Escritos póstumos*, 15:281.
16 Alberdi, *Obras Completas*, 2:289.
17 Ibid., 1:vii and xii.
18 J.B. Alberdi, *Obras Completas,* vol. 1, 139.
19 Ibid., 7:102.
20 Ibid., 3:87.
21 Ibid., 1:131.
22 Ibid., 1:xvii.
23 Ibid., 7:113.
24 Ibid., 8:161.
25 Ibid., 3:144.
26 Ibid., 7:98.
27 Ibid., 7:115 and 116.
28 Ibid., 3:443.
29 Alberdi, *Escritos póstumos*, 2:9.
30 Alberdi, *Obras Completas*, 7:16.
31 Gianello, *Bases*, p. 16.
32 Letter form Sarmiento to Alberdi. D.F. Sarmiento letter, September 16, 1852, Yungay, Alberdi, *Obras Completas*, vol. 4, 135.
33 Alberdi, *Obras Completas*, 3:525.
34 J.B. Alberdi, *Obras Completas*, vol. 3, 403.
35 Ibid., 3:451.
36 Ibid., 3:394.
37 Ibid., 3:346.
38 Ibid., 1:103.
39 Ibid., 1:99.
40 Alberdi, *Escritos póstumos*, 2:34.
41 Alberdi, *Obras Completas*, 7:95.
42 Ibid., 3:439.
43 Ibid., 7:105.
44 Ibid., 3:440.
45 Ibid., 4:245.
46 Ibid.
47 Ibid., 7:87 and 82.
48 Ibid., 7:80 –81
49 Ibid., 3:440.
50 Ibid., 3:344.
51 Ibid., 5:149.
52 Ibid., 5:195.

References

Abásolo, Ezequiel. *Bastante más que "degradantes andrajos de nuestra pasada esclavitud." Fragmentos sudamericanos de la pervivencia de la cultura jurídica indiana durante el siglo XIX.* Buenos Aires: Instituto de Investigaciones de Historia del Derecho, 2014.

Alberdi, Juan Bautista. *Bases.* Edited by Leoncio Gianello. Santa Fe, Argentina: Castellvi, 1957.

Alberdi, Juan Bautista. *Escritos póstumos*, Vol. 16. Buenos Aires: J.B. Alberdi, 1900–01.

Alberdi, Juan Bautista. *Obras Completas*, Vol. 8. Buenos Aires: La Tribuna Nac., 1886–87.

Ghirardi, Olsen A. *La filosofía en Alberdi.* 2nd ed. Córdoba: Academia Nacional de Derecho y Ciencias Sociales de Córdoba, 2000.

Laclau, Martín. "Las influencias filosóficas en el pensamiento de Juan Bautista Alberdi." *Revista de Historia del Derecho* 41 (2011): 139–161.

Leiva, Alberto David. "Las lecciones de derecho civil de Rafael de Casagemas (1932–1833)." *Revista de Historia del Derecho* 17 (1989): 445–545.

Mayer, Jorge M. *Alberdi y su tiempo.* Buenos Aires: Eudeba, 1963.

Mirow, M.C. "Bases y puntos de partida para la organización política de la República Argentina." In *The Formation and Transmission of Western Legal Culture: 150 Books that Made the Law in the Age of Printing*, edited by Serge Dauchy, Georges Martyn, Anthony Musson, Heikki Pihlajamäki, and Alain Wijffels, 367–370. Cham: Springer, 2016.

Pérez Guilhou, Dardo. *El pensamiento conservador de Alberdi y la Constitución de 1853. Tradición y modernidad.* 2nd ed., corrected and expanded. Mendoza: Editorial de la Universidad Nacional de Cuyo, 2003.

Sadler, Mélanie. "Los discursos alberdianos o la gran plasticidad del orden jurisdiccional tradicional." *Revista Historia y Justicia* 7 (2016): 121–156, online at http://journals.openedition.org/rhj/805.

12 Clemente de Jesús Munguía Núñez (Mexico, 1810–68)

Jorge Adame Goddard

Introduction

The jurist and bishop Clemente de Jesús Munguía is an important figure in Mexican history who has not had the recognition he deserves. He has been associated with the Conservative Party—the defeated party—which in official Mexican history has been considered not as an opposition party in a democratic regime but as an enemy party of Mexico, favorable to foreign interests. In recent years this perspective has been overcome, and it is now easier to undertake scholarly study of Clemente de Jesús Munguía's person and his work. The most complete biography of Munguía is by Pablo Mijangos y González, *The Lawyer of the Church*,[1] from which I have benefitted greatly in this biographical note.

Munguía's life of only fifty-eight years may be divided into three distinct periods. The first (1810–40) is the time of formation, especially as a jurist, which ends when, after successfully practicing the profession, he decides to renounce it and ask for admission to the priesthood. The second period (1841–51) is his work as a priest, aimed at improving the intellectual and moral training of young people entering the seminary of Morelia. His success in this task led to his appointment as rector of the seminary in 1843. The third period (1852–68), with the greatest impact on Mexican public life, includes the years as bishop (consecrated in 1852), during which he sought to have the Mexican political order recognize the Church's freedom.

His life as layman, citizen, and lawyer (1810–40)

Clemente de Jesús Munguía was born in 1810, the same year that the revolution for the independence of Mexico began. This coincidence foreshadowed a life agitated by changing political circumstances. He was born on November 21, in Los Reyes,[2] a town of about three thousand inhabitants near the city of Zamora, in the west of the Intendencia de Valladolid, later called the State of Michoacán. His father, Benito Munguía, was a retailer who had a grocery store in his home; Clemente's mother was María Guadalupe Núñez.

Munguía was the only son of this marriage. When he was six years old, his parents took him to Guadalajara to receive the sacrament of confirmation because the diocese of Michoacán was then vacant. A few days after returning to Los Reyes, his mother died. His father entered into a second marriage with Josefa Cárdenas, with whom he had another son, who died a few years later. Having lost his mother, and with no siblings, Munguía grew up as a lonely child.

His education was typical of children in that region. He attended the parish school, where he learned reading, writing, elementary arithmetic, Christian doctrine, and good customs. He lived in Los Reyes for the first fourteen years of life, and apparently nothing foreshadowed that he would stand out as a philosopher, jurist, and bishop.

The region suffered greatly during the independence revolution, and perhaps for that reason father and son moved to Zamora in 1824, as the first constitution that organized Mexico as a federal republic came into force. Apparently, his father returned to Los Reyes, but Munguía stayed to live in Zamora at the home of the Robles brothers—Francisco, who was a priest, and Toribio, a merchant; the plan was for Munguía to work as an employee of Toribio Robles's trade and thus learn the business.

Munguía's contact with Francisco Robles, however, opened his intellectual landscape, thanks to the good library in the priest's house. Through Francisco Robles, Munguía met Pelagio Antonio de Labastida y Dávalos, originally from Zamora, with whom he would have a lifelong friendship. Munguía's interest in books was evident to all who met him. Antonio de Labastida said that Munguía already showed, in those years in Zamora, that he was inclined to be a scholar.

Munguía spent six years in Zamora in commerce, but his interest in books was recognized by another priest, a friend of Francisco Robles, Ángel Mariano Morales, who was then rector of the Conciliar Seminary of Morelia. Moved by Munguía's fondness for study and by the intellectual capacity he recognized in him, Mariano Morales offered Munguía a scholarship to study at the Morelia Conciliar Seminary. Munguía was then nineteen years old, about four or five years older than the other young people entering that school, but age did not matter. He accepted the scholarship, and in February 1830 he moved to Morelia, where he would spend much of his life.

Shortly after Munguía entered the seminary to begin the study of humanities, his father died. Only in his twenties, Munguía was orphaned and without siblings. Thus, he focused his life on the seminary and the guidance provided by Mariano Morales.

Morelia was a legal city, a place where, mainly in the seminary, letters and the arts were cultivated, and where many intellectuals, priests, and politicians were formed who would later appear in national politics, such as Melchor Ocampo.[3] It was also the episcopal seat of the diocese of Michoacán, which then encompassed the states of Guanajuato and Guerrero and parts of the state of Mexico. Studies in the humanities included grammar, rhetoric, and Latin literature and were usually completed in five years, but Munguía completed this program in two years with excellent grades. He also complemented his training with the reading of Spanish classics such as Cervantes, Luis de Granada, and Jovellanos.

Another unforeseen change came to boost Munguía's intellectual training when Pope Gregory XVI appointed Juan Cayetano Gómez de Portugal bishop of Michoacán. Goméz de Portugal was interested in improving the formation of the priests in his seminary. The rector of the seminary, Mariano Morales, was appointed bishop of Sonora, and in 1833 the new bishop of Michoacán appointed a new rector, the priest Mariano Rivas, who undertook a major reform of the studies in the seminary and would be a very important influence on the intellectual development of Clemente de Jesus Munguía. The reforms introduced by the new rector aimed to update the content of the courses and corresponding readings to reflect the state of the sciences and philosophy of the nineteenth century.

After studies in humanities, Munguía began philosophy, which usually included logic, mathematics, general physics, metaphysics, and ethics. Munguía's performance was outstanding. In addition to recommending the reading of new books,[4] Rector Rivas encouraged Munguía to found and promote a literary academy, organized and directed by students, to improve their academic training. On November 10, 1833, at the closing of the academic year, Munguía announced the founding of the literary academy and gave a speech[5] indicating that he had assimilated the new ideas promoted by Rector Rivas. Munguía proposed that for the development of Mexico, social progress depended on education and knowledge.

After passing the philosophy courses, Munguía had to choose to study either theology to become a priest or jurisprudence to become a lawyer. Unlike his friend and seminary companion Pelagio Antonio de Labastida, who opted for the priesthood, Munguía opted for law. Rector Rivas appointed Munguía professor of Spanish grammar (1835), *belles-lettres* (1836), and Latin syntax (1838), an unusual honor for someone still only a student of jurisprudence.

He graduated from jurisprudence on May 19, 1838, passing his examination before the High Court of Justice of Michoacán. By then the political situation had changed. Mexico had entered a new centralist republic, under the presidency of Antonio López de Santa Anna, organized by a new constitution known as the Seven Constitutional Laws. Munguía began his professional life in public office: he was appointed a member of a primary education council[6] and district judge in Morelia.[7]

His good reputation as a speaker brought him an invitation to deliver a speech at the Independence Memorial Party on September 16, 1838.[8] It was an honor for a twenty-seven-year-old, as this occasion was taken by speakers to disseminate their political opinions. Munguía's speech is conciliatory and optimistic. He remembers independence as a great good of the Mexican nation, which foreshadowed its consolidation and progress, but notes that, after the first few years, the country entered a succession of conflicts that seemed unending. He believed that the cause of these conflicts was the tyranny of passions, that is, the inability of Mexicans at the time, and especially its rulers, to dominate and to direct their passions,[9] particularly the ambition for power. However, he thought it was still possible for the nation to reach its highest level if it could be constituted in a political regime that respected citizens' freedom and allowed the development of virtue and philosophy. He pointed out openly, at a time when Santa Anna was leading the first centralist republic, that Mexico should not restore an oppressive regime. This would violate the rights of human fraternity and natural law. He said it was necessary instead to give direction to the exercise of political power and to subordinate it to ethical and religious principles. Here, he already expressed the conviction of subordinating political power to natural law—that is, to subordinate power to ethics and religion. His speech was well received and also published the same year.

At the same time, in the company of his friend and fellow student Ignacio Aguilar y Marocho and his friend Estanislao Herrera, he opened a law firm. They attracted some important business. Some of Morelia's notables remembered Munguía's defenses in difficult cases. Morelia did not provide the opportunities these young lawyers sought, however, so two years later, in October 1840, they closed the office and opened another in Mexico City.

The legal life of the capital did not satisfy Munguía, according to his biographer Miguel Martínez,[10] who says that he was not accustomed to the practice of *chicanas* or *corruptelas*, nor to the ways of reasoning that prevailed then. But the capital offered him the opportunity to meet the intellectual elite of the time: Lucas Alamán, Manuel Carpio, Francisco Manuel Sánchez de Tagle, and the Jesuit Basilio Arrillaga. Munguía especially enjoyed the meetings in the Lateran Academy, where he delivered an entrance speech, which is not preserved, on the philosopher Peter Abelard. He met José Joaquín Pesado, Fernando Calderón, Ignacio Rodríguez Galván, Alejandro Arango y Escandón, Ignacio Ramírez, and other intellectuals through the Academy.[11]

In late 1840, Aguilar y Marocho decided to return to Morelia, and Munguía was left without his partner and alone with his friend and assistant Estanislao Herrera, who became ill in January 1841. Despite Munguía's assistance, Herrera died quickly. In April 1841, Munguía returned to Morelia, his stay in the capital having lasted only six months. The short period there proved decisive, because it led Munguía to become a priest.

Priest and rector of the seminary (1841–51)

Shortly after his return to Morelia, Munguía sought admission to the priesthood. His application simply stated that he sought this "for reasons of conscience."[12] The request was enthusiastically received by the rector of the seminary, Mariano Rivas, and by the Bishop of Michoacán, Gómez de Portugal, who dispensed with some formalities. After Munguía made a spiritual retreat, he was ordained a priest on May 10, 1841. From then on, he focused his life on the Morelia seminary, which, through the support of the bishop and the work of its rector, Mariano Rivas, had become one of the best and most progressive institutions of higher education in the republic. The seminary played an important role in the formation of clerics and lawyers who became important men in politics. Munguía returned as a full-time professor of jurisprudence. When Rector Rivas died in 1843, the bishop of Michoacán had no hesitation in appointing Munguía as the new rector. He remained in that position until being appointed bishop of Michoacán in 1851.

Munguía's years in the seminary, from 1841 to 1850, were years of great intellectual work and moral formation. One of his main concerns, shared with the former rector, was to form the character of seminarians so that they could direct and control their emotions. As part of the academic reform, efforts had been made to update the texts used in teaching. Munguía continued this task and prepared several texts. He published a *Gramática General* (*General grammar*, 1837);[13] then, for the rhetoric courses, he published *Estudios oratorios u observaciones críticas sobre algunos discursos de los oradores más clásicos antiguos y modernos* (*Oratorical studies, or critical observations on some speeches by the most classical, ancient and modern speakers*, 1841).[14] He made a revised and expanded edition (1849) of the *Elementos de gramática castellana* (*Elements of Castilian grammar*), by Joaquín de Avendaño, and also published an anthology of classical Spanish texts, with some of the author's studies, with the title of *Lecciones prácticas de lengua castellana* (*Practical lessons in the Spanish language*, 1845).[15] Both texts served to train seminarians in grammar and rhetoric. He wrote two other texts for the courses of theology—an exposition of Catholic doctrine and dogmas,[16] and a study in moral theology,[17] published after his appointment as bishop (1852). For philosophy, he published *Del pensamiento y su enunciación considerado en sí mismo, en sus relaciones y en sus leyes* (*On thought and its enunciation considered in itself, in its relations and in its laws*, 1852),[18] intended to replace the texts then in use. The title of this last work already shows one of the predominant characteristics of his thought: he was not an original author but an author of great syntheses that facilitated the comprehension of complex subjects.

Munguía was particularly interested in the reform of legal studies. In August 1843, when he was already rector, the General Plan of Studies of the Mexican Republic of President Santa Anna was published. This plan envisaged a reform of legal studies to reorganize the field in accordance with a systematic structure. The idea was to return civil and canon law back to their base of natural law. A few months before the publication of the national plan, Munguía wrote to Rector Rivas, requesting his authorization to write a book of jurisprudence, in which Munguía would compose all the legal matter, civil and canonical, beginning with metaphysical principles, which would give unity to the whole. The proposal would agree with the national plan. To this end, Munguía began to prepare another great work of synthesis, his *Curso de jurisprudencia universal* (*Course of universal jurisprudence*), to which he dedicated his efforts for several years.

In 1844 he published the first two volumes of the course of universal jurisprudence.[19] The first pages of the first volume presented the reasoned plan of the whole work. Munguía sought to present, in a "quick and compendious" way, "the general picture of the science of the jurisconsult, in the first principles, in ideological generation, in historical succession, and in the methodical ramifications and practical applications of all laws." The plan was to divide the work into two great treatises, one on divine law and the other on human law. The treatise on divine law was divided into three parts: one's obligations to God, those to oneself, and those to others. The human-law treatise would begin with a study on constitutional law, followed by civil law (that is, all laws published by the state), another on international treaties (political law), and another on legislation concerning relations of the state with the Church. From that plan, he published only one more volume, which he called *Del culto considerado en sí mismo y en sus relaciones con el individuo, la sociedad y el gobierno* (*On religion considered as itself and in its relations with the individual, society, and government*, 1847).[20]

The intention to compile all legal science into one work was extremely ambitious, and Munguía came to fulfill it in only a minimal way: the three published tomes covered only the first part ("human obligations to God") of the first treatise on divine law. Perhaps it was the publication of the new curriculum that led Munguía to reduce his project and write a text that would give students the knowledge of the first legal principles, so that they could, as the curriculum intended, structure all the legal knowledge presented to them.

In 1849, he published in Mexico the four volumes of his best-known work: *Del Derecho natural en sus principios más comunes y en sus diversas ramificaciones* (*On natural law in its common principles and in its various branches*).[21] He divided this work into a preliminary study of philosophical and theological content (142 pages of volume one), where he revealed his conception of natural law and the two means of knowing it, namely, natural reason and revelation. Because the first law commands one to love God above all things and one's neighbor as oneself, Munguía divides the whole work into three parts. The first deals with one's obligations to God (volume one, pages 142 to 213); the second, with one's obligations to oneself (volume two, pages three to 101) and the third, the most voluminous, with one's obligations to others (volume two, pages 113 to 377, and all of volume three [303 pages] and volume four [374 pages]). The first and second parts are a study of moral theology.

The third part is on law and is divided into six sections. The first deals with the obligations that all persons have with each other, regardless of their membership in a particular social group, such as obligations to respect the life and property of others. The second section contains a philosophical reflection on the nature of society, its origin, its essence, its fundamental qualities, and its means of action. The third section is about domestic society, that is, family. The fourth section, on civil society—i.e. national society or the state, as it was then called—occupies the entire third volume. Section five deals with the "political society," or the community of nations, and the last section, the sixth, deals with religious society, or the Church.

Munguía's main concern was the definition of the principles that govern the organization of social life in its different stages: family, nation, and community of nations. He focused his attention on the organization of civil life, in what we might call a rational constitutional right, derived from the very nature of the human being and of social life. I agree with Pablo Mijangos's assertion that the work is primarily constitutional law.[22]

The last part of the work regards the Church as a society, similar to the civil society and political society, which has all the features common to any society and which therefore constitutes a complete or "perfect society." This was the starting point in facing one of the great problems in Mexico, how to regulate relations between church and state. The last part of the work (almost one hundred pages) is dedicated to this subject.

Munguía's years as a priest and rector of the seminary had a profound influence. In the seminary he governed and led his students. The reform of the seminary not only was a renewal of the subjects being taught but also was mainly aimed at the human and ethical formation of students. Along with making necessary changes to the content of the subjects being studied and updating the texts being used, Munguía sought improvements in the material conditions of the seminary and took special care to form good habits or virtues in the community. The reforms made by Munguía and the previous rector were already moving in the direction subsequently recommended by Pope Pius IX's envoy inspecting the Mexican seminaries.[23]

Munguía's work on natural law was the most important on this subject published in Mexico in the nineteenth century. It was a fundamental work for those who sought a political and economic regime different from the liberal regime, and for those who wanted not a Catholic monarchy but a representative republic ordained according to Christian social ethics. The work also explained Munguía's approach to the relations of Church and state, in which he played a decisive role.

Bishop and defender of the Church (1852–68)

José Cayetano Gómez de Portugal, the bishop of Michoacán, died on April 4, 1850. Three days later, the ecclesiastics who formed the chapter of the cathedral of Michoacán unanimously elected to propose Clemente de Jesús Munguía as the new bishop.[24] This action was communicated to the government but, in the view of the federal government, the election was hasty, as the cathedral chapter had to first notify the government of the death of Bishop Gómez de Portugal and then send the governor a list of three candidates, from whom the government would choose the candidate to propose to the Holy See. The cathedral chapter then sent a list, but as one of the candidates stated that he was unwilling to accept appointment, the government requested more candidates and was three more names were given. These incidents already revealed the atmosphere of mutual mistrust, or at least lack of comprehension, between the civil rulers and the canons of Morelia. The federal government sent the list of candidates to the governors of the affected entities. Governor Juan Álvarez de Guerrero was the first in favor of Munguía. Álvarez would later lead the revolution of Ayutla, from which arose the Constitution of 1857 and the Reform Laws. Then the governor of Michoacán, who had been silent, also decided to support Munguía. Finally, President Herrera approved the nomination of the candidate on June 28, 1850.[25]

The federal government prepared Munguía's file and presented it to Pope Pius IX, through the representative of the Mexican Government in Rome, José María Montoya, who was in charge of obtaining the bull of Munguía's appointment. Montoya announced on October 16, 1850, that the pope had accepted Munguía as new bishop. The appointment bull arrived in Mexico on December 27, 1850. To complete the process, it was necessary for the bishop-elect to swear obedience to the constitution and the general laws of the republic and then to be consecrated bishop. The oath would take place at Morelia Cathedral on January 6, 1851, and would be administered by the governor of Michoacán, Juan Bautista Ceballos.

When the time came, the governor asked Munguía:

> Do you swear to obey the constitution and the laws of the United States of Mexico, and to accept, from now on, the new laws published in accordance with the patronage,[26] and the division of your diocese that the government should make in accordance with the Holy See?

Munguía replied, "I do not swear." The ceremony, of course, was suspended, and a political scandal arose.

Munguía expressed his reasons for not swearing in a letter he sent to the new president of the republic, Mariano Arista, on January 15. His refusal arose not from political reasons but from a judgment of conscience, in particular in relation to the obligation to accept the divisions of the diocese. In the manifesto to the nation that he published to explain his conduct,[27] Munguía said that he was not sure that the laws regulating the patronage, to which the oath referred, were the laws that would be published after Mexico concluded a concordat with the Holy See and thus obtained the right of patronage, rather than any other law intended to regulate a right of patronage not granted by the Holy See. This was the right of patronage defended by the liberals on the grounds that the Mexican state was a successor to the Spanish monarchy.

The incident was a sign of what would be one of Bishop Munguía's main tasks, to defend the Church's rights in the face of the liberal state. At the time, the question of the patronage—that is, of the rights or privileges that the state had or could have with respect to the life and organization of the Church—was fundamental. The Liberal Party, especially the radicals, wanted the preservation of the regime that the Church had in Mexico at the time of the last Spanish monarchs, those of the Bourbon dynasty. The Bourbons intended an absolute monarchy and exaggerated and abused the rights the Church had granted to the Spanish monarchs. These rights had been given in exchange for the monarchs' support of the work of evangelizing America. The Crown by this means enlarged its political power. Liberals saw in this system, which implied the subordination of the Church to political power, the appropriate mechanism for creating a state that subordinates the Church. For this reason, the Liberal Party repeatedly stated that the Mexican state, whatever its political form, was the successor to the Spanish monarchy and, therefore, had the same right of patronage that the Spanish monarchs had.

For their part, the bishops and a group of Catholic citizens wanted a change that would allow the Church to maintain its freedom from the new state. They rejected the Mexican state as the successor to the Spanish monarchs, because the new state was the fruit of a revolution and not a peaceful succession. They wanted an agreement or concordat with the Holy See in which, bilaterally, as in any treaty between two nations, both parties fixed the rules according to which they would establish their relations, would respect their respective areas of action, and would collaborate with each other. In principle, these defenders of the Church's authority were not opposed to granting some right of patronage in exchange for some cooperation, but they required that the patronage be the result of an agreement with the Holy See, and not merely a unilateral assertion that the right of patronage of the Spanish monarchs remained. On this important issue, the liberals wanted to keep the old, and the conservatives wanted to implement something new. When Munguía received an explanation that the patronage referred to in the swearing formula would be one granted by a concordat with the Holy See, he declared that he was willing to swear.

President Arista's first reaction to the refusal to swear was to refer the appointment bull to Mexico City. He sought to order, as if he had the power to order, the cathedral chapter of Morelia to dismiss Munguía, who was the vicar of the diocese. There followed a few months of controversy among detractors of Munguía, who accused him of provoking the government, and others who supported him, including the governor of Michoacán and notables from the region. After receiving the explanations of Munguía, the president agreed to repeat the swearing-in ceremony, which occurred almost a year after the first attempt, on December 22, 1851; the consecration as bishop took place at Morelia Cathedral on January 18, 1852.[28]

Munguía's refusal to swear was a clear manifestation of his position of rejecting the imposition of the Liberal Party on the Church and to push for a concordat establishing a new system of relations between the Church and the state. He expressed this intention in his first pastoral letter, issued in February 1852, in which he invited reconciliation and understanding. This conciliatory attitude could not last long, however, because a radical or "pure" liberal, Melchor Ocampo, assumed the governorship of Michoacán in May 1852, and he went on to develop an anticlerical program against the seminary and the Hospital of St. John of God. Munguía realized that the measures against the seminary and the hospital were not isolated acts but the first instances of a medium- or long-term anticlerical policy. He published a second pastoral letter, on July 31, 1852,[29] in which he warned that there were signs of further persecution against the Catholic religion. Soon afterward, the local legislature passed a law ordering that the state government had the right to demand from the Church the ninth part of all the tithes collected, as the Spanish monarchs had done. This created severe tension between municipal officials, who demanded payment, and the parish priests, who withheld it. With Ocampo's government began the open confrontation between Munguía and the liberals who intend to subordinate the Church. This battle occupied the last twelve years of his life.

It is not right to say that Munguía was a conservative in this fight, because both conservative governments and liberal governments faced the same problem. He opposed the anticlerical legislation and policy of Governor Melchor Ocampo

(1852) but also the draft of a concordat presented by Santa Anna to the Holy See (1855). He opposed the "reformist" legislation of the liberal governments of Presidents Comonfort (1855–57) and Juárez (1859–61), but also the measures and draft concordat of the French generals and Emperor Maximilian (1862–65). The main argument was always the freedom or independence of the Church with respect to political power.[30]

His position caused him to suffer unpleasant consequences. When he was just nineteen years old and a simple trade employee (1829), he was arrested by the prefect of Zamora, a member of the "York" Party—the radical Liberal Party—for protesting against the reelection of the governor of Michoacán, José Salgado. After the triumph of the Ayutla Revolution (1855), to which he gave his support, Munguía was continually blocked in his efforts. He was first harassed in Morelia, by the radical governor Miguel Silva, and had to move to Guanajuato in 1856. His criticism of the government of President Comonfort caused the governor of Guanajuato, in that same year, to order that Munguía be transported by armed guard to Mexico City, to be confined in the Coyoacán neighborhood and forbidden to leave its boundaries. There he remained during the three years of the so-called War of Reform (1858–60), in which he fought, among other things, for the freedom of the Church from the state. At the end of the war, with the victory of the radical Liberal Party, Munguía, along with other bishops, was exiled from the country (January 1861) and went to reside in Rome. He returned to Mexico in 1863 because the pope asked him to do so; by then he was weak and progressively losing his sight. Although he had already submitted his resignation, Pope Pius IX did not accept it and asked him to return to Mexico, where he arrived in September of that year. French generals then ruled as commanders of the invading army, and in June 1864 Emperor Maximilian arrived. Munguía strongly protested against the generals and the emperor for their actions against the rights of the Church, and Maximilian ordered him to leave the country in March 1865.[31] Munguía returned to Rome, and there opposed the draft of concordat submitted by the imperial government, because in his opinion, it did not guarantee the freedom of the Church.[32]

His doctrine on the relations between the Church and the state had already been formulated and published in the fourth volume (sixth section, third book) of *Del Derecho natural* (*On natural law*). This work viewed relations between the state and the Church from the perspective of two "perfect" societies—that is, societies that have all the constituent elements and essential characteristics of a society. The state, or civil society, and the Church, or religious society, were both perfect societies and remained on their own, without being dependent on the other; each had its own purpose—the temporal common good, which is the end of the state, and the common spiritual good or salvation, which is the end of the Church. Although they differed essentially, each had its own scope of action and means of action. The approach he made was modern and surpassed the vision of the former patronage, that is, that the Mexican state, as successor to the Spanish monarchy, would have the rights and privileges that the Holy See had granted them in compensation for the duties they assumed to support the evangelization of the new territories. Munguía's final point was the reciprocal independence of both societies, which, once recognized and assured, could, and should, give rise to collaborative agreements in common areas for the benefit of the Mexican people. Instead, the liberals raised the Church as a state-dependent society.

Munguía's doctrine on this subject was widely disseminated through a document he wrote, between 1856 and 1857, on the occasion of the so-called Juárez Law of November 23, 1855. This law suppressed the recognition of the exclusive jurisdiction of the Church, as well as that of the army, and reorganized the form of integration of the Supreme Court of Justice to be controlled by the president of the republic. Before this law, anticipating that it would be the beginning of a series of attacks against the Church, Munguía published his eighth pastoral letter, dated December 19, 1855, in which he announced that he would publish some "instructions" on how the faithful should deal with the state's abusive claims against the Church.

The bishop was not mistaken in anticipating that this law would be the beginning of a series of anticlerical measures. Soon afterward, the government nationalized assets of the archbishopric of Puebla, ordered the expulsion of the bishop of that diocese, Pelagio Antonio de Labastida, and published the law of confiscation (*desamortización*) of the assets of ecclesiastical and civil corporations. On February 5, 1857, Article 123 of the Constitution was promulgated as a statement that "It is exclusively for the federal powers to exercise, in matters of religious worship and external discipline, the intervention that law designates"—that is, the laws may regulate religious worship and the organization and external life of the Church.

The text announced in the eighth pastoral letter was published in April 1857, two months after the promulgation of the constitution, and was reprinted five times in the years of the religious conflict.[33] He wrote it when he was confined to Coyoacán. This letter earned him the recognition by both the bishops and the apostolic nuncio as the intellectual leader of the defense of the rights of the Church. [34]

From a short-term perspective, Munguía's struggle for the independence of the Church from the state may seem futile. The Liberal Party triumphed and took over political power from 1867 to 1911, with no adversary that could contest it. The Constitution of 1857, with its Article 123, as well as all the laws to which Munguía had severely objected (the Reform Laws) were in force; moreover, the reform principles contained in several laws were incorporated into the Constitution in 1873. Apparently Munguía did not win anything. But the fact is that the faithful of the Catholic Church, both laypeople and priests, bishops and religious, maintained the idea that the Church is independent of the state, so the liberal governments of the time had to stop applying these laws in order to govern. This set up a *modus vivendi* that allowed the liberal government to keep the laws in force, simply as a political flag, and left citizens and communities and associations of believers to live freely according to their faith. In the face of this reality, can it be said that Munguía's struggle was futile? Rather, it seems to me that the social reality configured was that of Munguía's proposal; a free Church and a free state were the most appropriate characterization of Mexican reality.

After Munguía's expulsion to Rome, he never returned to Mexico. His health worsened, and he died in Rome on December 14, 1868. Nearly thirty years later, in 1897, when political passions had subsided, his remains were transferred to Mexico and interred in Morelia Cathedral.

Notes

1 Mijangos, *Lawyer of the Church.*
2 See Martínez, *Monseñor Munguía*, 1:12; Munguía was baptized on the 23rd.
3 Bravo Ugarte, *Munguía*, 16, gives these other names of people who were important in that time as Munguías's companions: Juan B. Cevallos, Ignacio Aguilar y Marocho, José Guadalupe Romero, Antonio Florentino Mercado, Pelagio Antonio de Labastida y Dávalos, and José María Orozco.
4 Mijangos, *Lawyer of the Church*, 10, says that Rector Rivas moved Munguía to read "the works of Étienne Bonnot de Condillac and other authors of the French Sensualist School"; but Bravo Ugarte, *Munguía*, 15, states that, according to Miguel Martínez, Rector Rivas changed his mind about Condillac and proscribed all the books of that philosophical school.
5 The text of that speech has been preserved in Martínez, *Monseñor Munguía*, 150–59.
6 He was nominated as a member of the Junta Inspectora de Instrucción Primaria; he gave a critical speech about the conditions of primary education in Michoacán and published a little book about orthography; see Bravo Ugarte, *Munguía*, 24–25.
7 He was proposed for that position by the government of the state of Michoacán and designated by the federal government; he heard cases regarding public and military finances. See Bravo Ugarte, *Munguía*, 25.
8 See Munguía, *Discurso cívico.*
9 This idea seems to be taken from Cicero, *De re publica* (see, for example I.52 and V.1–2), a book with which Munguía was familiar.
10 Martínez, 561–69, cited by Mijangos, 22.
11 See Bravo Ugarte, 25–27.
12 General Archive of the Nation, Justice/Ecclesiastical, vol. 113, fol. 146, cited by Mijangos, 146.
13 See Munguía, *Gramática General.*
14 See Munguía, *Estudios oratorios.*
15 See Munguía, *Lecciones prácticas.* This book is referred to in his *Memoria instructiva.*
16 See Munguía, *Exposición de la doctrina Católica.*
17 See Munguía, *Estudios fundamentales.*
18 See Munguía, *Del pensamiento.*
19 See Munguía, *Curso de jurisprudencia.*
20 See Munguía, *Del culto considerado en sí mismo.*
21 See Munguía, *Del Derecho natural.* A facsimile edition, with an introductory study by Faustino Martínez Martínez, was published by the Supreme Court of Justice of the Nation and the National Commission on Human Rights, Mexico, 2005.
22 Mijangos, 95.
23 For details about his work in the seminary, see Bravo Ugarte, 29–37.

24 About Munguía's election and the events that followed, see Ornelas Hernández, "El obispo de Michoacán," 253ff.
25 See Mijangos, 137ff.
26 The Patronato (Patronage) was a set of rights that the Holy See had conceded to the Spanish monarchy in compensation for the support that the Crown gave to the evangelization of the New World. It was a general belief in political circles, mainly among liberals but also among some conservatives, that the Mexican Government had inherited those rights but not the obligations of supporting the evangelization. This erroneous belief was one of the main reasons for problematic relations between the Mexican state and the Catholic Church.
27 See Munguía, *Manifiesto.*
28 Ornelas Hernández, 253ff., says that the position of Munguía was only a way to pressure the liberal government; but he does not consider the problem, seen by Munguía, of giving recognition to the liberal proposal of a right of patronage without a new agreement with the Holy See.
29 See Munguía, "Segunda carta pastoral."
30 See references for a collection of his writings defending the freedom of the Church and criticizing the liberal legislation named: Munguía, *Defensa Ecesiástica.* This work is completed by another collection: *Sermones del Arzobispo de Michoacán Doctor Don Clemente de Jesús Munguía*, also in the references.
31 There are two protesting letters to the emperor signed by Munguía and Labastida y Dávalos, archbishop of México: *Exposición de los Ilmos. Señores arzobispos de México y Michoacán a S.M. el Emperador. Pidiendo la derogación de la ley de 26 de diciembre de 1865 sobre tolerancia religiosa*; and *Representación que los Illmos. Señores Arzobispos de México y Michoacán dirigen a S.M. el Emperador, pidiendo la derogación de las leyes de 25 de junio de 1856 y 13 de julio de 1859 y disposiciones concordantes, a que se refiere el Decreto de 26 de febrero de 1865, sobre revisión de todas las operaciones de desamortización y nacionalización de bienes eclesiásticos, ejecutadas a consecuencia de dichas Leyes.* Both letters are collected in *Miscelánea*, noted in the references.
32 See Mijangos, 224ff.
33 For an analysis of this document, see Adame, "La doctrina," 231ff.
34 Mijangos, 164.

References

Adame Goddard, Jorge. "El Derecho natural de Clemente de Jesús Munguía." In *Memoria del III Congreso de Historia del Derecho Mexicano*, 11ff. México: Universidad Nacional Autónoma de México, 1984.

Adame Goddard, Jorge. "La doctrina de Clemente de Jesús Munguía sobre las relaciones entre la Iglesia y el Estado." In *Por una Iglesia libre en un mundo liberal*, edited by Casas García, Mijangos, and Adame Goddard, 231ff. México: Universidad Pontificia de México y El Colegio de Michoacán, 2014.

Bravo Ugarte, José. *Munguía. Obispo y Arzobispo de Michoacán (1810–1868). Su vida y su obra.* México: Ed. Jus, 1967.

Casas García, Juan Carlos, Pablo Mijangos y González, and Jorge Adame Goddard, eds. *Por una Iglesia libre en un mundo liberal. La obra y los tiempos de Clemente de Jesús Munguía, primer arzobispo de Michoacán (1810–1868).* México: Universidad Pontificia de México y El Colegio de Michoacán, 2014.

Martínez, Miguel. *Monseñor Munguía y sus escritos.* Book 1. Mexico: José Mariano Lara, 1870; Books 1 and 2, Morelia: Fimax, 1991.

Mijangos y González, Pablo. *The Lawyer of the Church: Bishop Clemente de Jesús Munguía and the Clerical Response to the Mexican Liberal Reform*. Lincoln: University of Nebraska Press, 2015.

Miscelánea o sea Colección de Artículos extractados de algunos periódicos. Seguidos de algunos folletos sueltos. Mexico: Mariano Villanueva Press, 1865.

Munguía Núñez, Clemente de Jesús. *Del culto considerado en sí mismo y en sus relaciones con el individuo, la sociedad y el gobierno. O sea, tratado completo de las obligaciones para con Dios*. Morelia: Ignacio Arango, 1847.

Munguía Núñez, Clemente de Jesús. *Curso de Jurisprudencia universal o Exposición metódica de los principios del Derecho Divino y del Derecho Humano*, Vol. 2. Morelia: Ignacio Arango, 1844.

Munguía Núñez, Clemente de Jesús. *Defensa Eclesiástica en el Obispado de Michoacán desde 1855 hasta principios de 1858*, Vol. 2. Mexico: Vicente Segura, 1858.

Munguía Núñez, Clemente de Jesús. *Del Derecho natural en sus principios más comunes y en sus diversas manifestaciones, o sea, Curso elemental de Derecho natural y de gentes, público, político constitucional, y Principios de Legislación*, Vol. 4. Mexico: Imprenta de la Voz de la Religión, 1849. Facsimile edition, Mexico: Suprema Corte de Justicia y Comisión Nacional de Derechos Humanos, 2005.

Munguía Núñez, Clemente de Jesús. *Discurso cívico pronunciado el 16 de septiembre de 1838*. Mexico: I. Avila, 1838.

Munguía Núñez, Clemente de Jesús. *Estudios fundamentales sobre el hombre considerado bajo el triple aspecto de la religión, de la moral y de las leyes* y *Examen filosófico sobre las relaciones del orden natural y sobrenatural ya entre sí, ya con la perfección intelectual, moral y social de la especie humana*. Published in *Obras Diversas del Licenciado Clemente de Jesús Munguía, Obispo de Michoacán*. Second series. Mexico City: La Voz de la Religión, 1852.

Munguía Núñez, Clemente de Jesús. *Estudios oratorios u Observaciones críticas sobre algunos discursos de los oradores más clásicos antiguos y modernos*. Morelia: Ignacio Arango, 1841.

Munguía Núñez, Clemente de Jesús. *Exposición de la Doctrina Católica sobre los Dogmas de la Religión*. Mexico City: Tomás S. Gardida, 1856.

Munguía Núñez, Clemente de Jesús. *Gramática general o Aplicación del análisis a las lenguas*. Morelia: Juan Evaristo de Oñate, 1837.

Munguía Núñez, Clemente de Jesús. *Instrucciones Pastorales del Lic. Clemente de Jesús Munguía Obispo de Michoacán a los fieles de su diócesis. Precedidas de su octava Carta pastoral en que se les anuncia y propone los puntos que deben ser tratados en ellas*. Mexico City: Vicente Segura, 1857.

Munguía Núñez, Clemente de Jesús. *Lecciones prácticas de lengua castellana*. 1st ed. Morelia: Ignacio Arango, 1834; 2nd. ed., 1845.

Munguía Núñez, Clemente de Jesús. *Manifiesto que el Lic. Clemente Munguía, electo y confirmado Obispo de Michoacán por nuestro Smo. Padre Pío IX, dirige a la Nación mexicana, explicando su conducta con motivo de su negativa el día 6 de enero al juramento civil*. Morelia: Ignacio Arango, 1851.

Munguía Núñez, Clemente de Jesús. *Memoria instructiva sobre el origen, progresos y estado actual de la enseñanza y educación secundaria en el Seminario Tridentino de Morelia*. Morelia: Ignacio Arango, 1849.

Munguía Núñez, Clemente de Jesús. *Obras diversas del Lic. Clemente de Jesús Munguía, Obispo de Michoacán. Primera serie*, Vol. 3. Morelia: Ignacio Arango, 1851.

Munguía Núñez, Clemente de Jesús. *Obras diversas del Lic. Clemente de Jesús Munguía, Obispo de Michoacán. Segunda serie*, Vol. 2. Morelia: Ignacio Arango, 1852.

Munguía Núñez, Clemente de Jesús. *Del pensamiento y su enunciación considerado en sí mismo, en sus relaciones y en sus leyes.* Published in *Obras diversas del Lic. Clemente de Jesús Munguía, Obispo de Michoacán*, 1–3. First series. Morelia: Ignacio Arango, 1852.

Munguía Núñez, Clemente de Jesús. "Segunda carta pastoral." *La Voz de la Religión* 3: 7–14 (1852).

Munguía Núñez, Clemente de Jesús. *Sermones del Arzobispo de Michoacán Doctor Don Clemente de Jesús Munguía. Seguidos de una colección de documentos relativos a la defensa canónica de la Santa Iglesia, los cuales no figuran en la Defensa eclesiástica.* Mexico City: Mariano Villanueva Press, 1864.

Ornelas Hernández, Moisés. "El obispo de Michoacán, Clemente de Jesús Munguía. ¿Escándalo o provocación política?" In *El Estado laico y los derechos humanos en México: 1810–2010*, edited by Margarita Moreno Bonett and Rosa María Álvarez de Lara, Vol. 1, 253ff. Mexico City: Universidad Nacional Autónoma de México, 2012.

13 Eduardo Acevedo Maturana (Uruguay, 1815–63)

Juan Carlos Frontera

Introduction

The dawning of the nineteenth century found the region of the River Plate in the midst of widespread unrest. The pact between the Crown and the vassals was broken. The winds of revolution and independence stirred. Yet in 1806 and 1807, Spanish *creoles* repelled two invasions of Buenos Aires by Great Britain, and thus, through a militia led by ordinary men, the inhabitants of the western edge of the River Plate maintained their oath to the Spanish king. Montevideo and Buenos Aires were then small cities whose ports were their main sources of sustenance. Through trade, some of their merchants benefitted from belonging to the Spanish trading monopoly, while others claimed similar benefits even though they had not been granted such privileges officially. This difference led to strong clashes between those who benefitted from the system and those who did not. Some feared trade with foreign merchants; others took advantage of opportunities for smuggling.[1]

The creation of the Viceroyalty of the River Plate in 1776 brought advances through a combination of mercantilist and physiocratic ideas that led to substantial economic development. *Estancias* (landed estates) as economic units became important contributors to the region's production and, at the same time, the owners of these estates grew in political power.[2]

Into this period of change, Eduardo Acevedo was born on September 15, 1815, in the city of Montevideo. The town had begun its revolutionary process on February 28, 1811, with the so-called Cry of Asencio. Relations between the Oriental Strip (nowadays mostly Uruguayan territory) and Buenos Aires had not been positive following the Assembly of 1813. In 1815, the diplomatic mission of Buenos Aires to Ferdinand VII failed, and one year later, the United Provinces of the River Plate declared their independence from Spain. Shortly afterward, José de San Martín made his historic crossing of the Andes to liberate both Chile and Peru.

Despite Acevedo's brief life, he left his mark as a jurist, teacher, and legislator. His biographer, Jorge Peirano Facio, expressed the view that Acevedo was a typical, iconic figure of the nineteenth century. Acevedo lived during turbulent, fratricidal wars, yet always knew how to encourage sentiments against them. He embodied a passion for legal institutions, as he lived in an anarchic environment that led him to resist the arbitrary and narrow-minded power of the local creole leaders.[3]

Acevedo's grandfather, Tomás Álvarez de Acevedo, was born in 1753 in the town bearing his own surname in the province of León, Spain. Tomás had entered the University of Salamanca, where he graduated as a licentiate in both canon and civil laws. In 1775, Tomás Álvarez de Acevedo filled the position of prosecutor of the Royal Court (*Audiencia*) of Lima, to which he was promoted after holding the same office at the Court of Charcas.

Eduardo Acevedo's father, José Acevedo y Salazar, was born in Santiago de Chile and was considered a peninsular Spaniard because of his family origins and education. José settled in Montevideo by 1810 and died when Eduardo was still a child. José had studied law at the University of Valencia, where he served as president of the Academy of Public Law. In 1801, José earned the degree of doctor. The Governing Board of the Royal Company of the Philippines assigned him to the Americas after he completed further studies in London.[4]

Luis Goddefroy, Acevedo's maternal grandfather, a French seaman residing in Montevideo, adopted Acevedo after the death of his father and gave him the best education possible. In 1827, grandfather Luis sent the barely twelve-year-old Acevedo to Buenos Aires to complete middle-school studies. Acevedo entered the University of Buenos Aires in 1833 and graduated as a Doctor of Laws on August 6, 1836.

Acevedo's legal studies were influenced by a chair-holder at the University of Buenos Aires, Rafael Casagemas, a scholar who did not follow the teachings of the well-known Pedro Somellera. Casagemas adopted the more pragmatic orientations of the positivist school and instilled in his students a set of principles based on "the incomparable Bentham."

In keeping with Casagemas's reaction against Somellera, Acevedo substituted Somellera's text for that of José María Álvarez when he himself began teaching in Buenos Aires. Acevedo's lectures exerted a remarkable impact on his students, not so much because of their brilliant and novel content, but for their practical approach, moral stance, and even-handedness. In his classes, he sought to instill in his students a spirit of almost religious worship for law and justice, whose triumph would solve the problems affecting the countries around the River Plate. Important pieces of this solution were the consolidation of institutions, the codification of private law, and the statutory demarcation of the respective activities of political rulers and judges.[5]

After this period in Buenos Aires, Acevedo practiced law in Montevideo at a firm established by his grandfather Luis Goddefroy. One year after arriving in Montevideo, in 1840, Acevedo was appointed vice president of the Academy of Jurisprudence. During his time in the city, Acevedo married Joaquina Vázquez. He served as a public defender for poor defendants in Montevideo. In 1842, he was appointed a judge of criminal matters and temporarily served as an acting civil judge. The civil wars eventually caused him to move his law firm to Buenos Aires, where he was soon recognized as one of the most prestigious lawyers of his time.

The so-called Great War, one of the civil wars in Uruguay, happened between the years 1839 and 1851.

Acevedo was one of the founders of the Professional Association of Attorneys of Buenos Aires. In 1856 he was elected to the presidency of the Academy of Jurisprudence of Buenos Aires and was reelected in 1858. Acevedo thus knew life on both sides of the River Plate—in Buenos Aires and Montevideo.

Acevedo was a simple but distinguished man with attractive intellectual and moral qualities. With a broad forehead, framed by black hair and black sideburns that closed into a dense beard, he had an intelligent and detached look and a distant sweetness typical of idealistic spirits. He was good-natured and kind, while still shrewd in judging both people and general matters. Naturally even-tempered and noncompetitive, he did, however, adopt sternness in his principles, even though he would cool this temperament and let the errors of others pass.[6]

Acevedo died at the age of forty-eight in Montevideo. He had witnessed—and indeed had shaped in many ways—times of institutional organization, independence wars, civil wars, and the consolidation of Uruguay's national territory.

Legal works and instruction

As a lawyer, Acevedo wanted first and foremost to engage in the noblest and highest task of drafting rules of law to provide his country with a body of laws supporting its institutional life in a peaceful, harmonic, and civil manner.[7] For example, by the age of twenty-one, he had concluded one of his most important works, the Commercial Code for the Province of Buenos Aires. His scholarly legal work consisted of only a few superb publications. Although trained in law and legal scholarship, Acevedo was above all a man of action.[8] Convinced that law must be a way of life, he constantly fought to impose it. With a mentality set on law, Acevedo had little time to engage in research.

Acevedo's thesis on lawyers as a completion of his university studies, presented on September 6, 1836, was his most renowned work. Described as a lengthy research work and more serious than the theses of his time, it is characterized by its humanistic and historical insights. In this way, the work reflected Acevedo's upbringing, which informed his approach to all matters. This work shows Acevedo's great maturity as he focused on the apparent decline of the legal profession, the moral conditions that lawyers must meet, and the obligations they must be willing to assume.[9]

As Jorge Peirano Facio affirmed, Acevedo knew how to teach law even when universities and institutions of legal education were scarce. Despite the brevity of his life, Acevedo contributed substantially to legal education and legal development. His teaching activity was broader than his scholarly undertakings. Acevedo had an overriding tendency to seek the effectiveness of law. He sought to instill in others the practical effectiveness of legal rules rather than deep comprehension through scholarly research.

His teaching tasks and duties were conducted at the Academy of Jurisprudence.[10] Peirano Facio recalled an article published in *El Nacional* about Acevedo's time at the Academy of Jurisprudence of Buenos Aires. The article reported:

> By the time Acevedo took charge of studies at the Academy, the Spanish routine reigned there with omnipotent influence. The doctrine forged by the same old scholars and treatise writers was the law everyone was subject to, both indisputably and inarguably; hence, his first civic aim was to ignite in his disciples the yearning for research and to teach them how to turn to the very primary source of legal information—the law itself. Acevedo, who loves the science he has made his own lifetime profession, and to which he has devoted the full power of his intelligence, is communicative, fervent in his enthusiasm for the law, and meets all the conditions with which a master needs to be imbued.[11]

For civic instruction, Acevedo wrote a catechism of the Constitution in 1851, in which he explained the core points of Uruguay's constitutional regime, as had been done in Spain in 1812. Similarly, civic duty led him after the Peace of the Union, in 1852, to establish the Society of Friends of the Country in Uruguay.

Political activities and ministerial duties

In 1857 Acevedo's friends registered him on the list of candidates for deputies in the Department of Montevideo. He won the election, but he resigned from his seat in spite of the letter that Jaime Estrazulas, a remarkable Uruguayan citizen, wrote to Acevedo urging him to accept. Thus, the political plan to initiate Acevedo on the path to the presidency of Uruguay failed.

Two years later, however, actions resumed to advance Acevedo's candidacy for the presidency of the country. The results were poor because Acevedo wanted neither to be linked to the prevailing regime nor to strike a deal with local *creole* leaders. Acevedo reported a secondary reason why he could not accept the candidacy—because in Buenos Aires he was earning a better income than he could in Montevideo, and he had no other sources of income.[12]

Acevedo's candidacy for the presidency of the Uruguayan Republic was announced yet again in 1860. Acevedo requested that his name be withdrawn, but at the insistence of his friends, he stayed in the race. Although the political winds were blowing in his favor, local *creole* leaders running against him effectively countered them. The winning presidential candidate was Bernardo Berro, who quickly appointed Acevedo as the minister of government and foreign affairs. Acevedo accepted despite some qualms expressed by members of his family, who did not want to change their lifestyle in Buenos Aires.

The *bonaerense*[13] press expressed its sorrow on Acevedo's departure from their city. They were aware of the political hardship of Acevedo's new home, and they feared that his sacrifice in abandoning his life in Buenos Aires would become a futile undertaking.[14] The *porteños*, natives to the City of Buenos Aires, even prepared a farewell event in his honor—while Acevedo, always inclined to avoid this kind of acknowledgment, asked his steamer to set sail one hour earlier.

On his return to his hometown, he vigorously undertook his two ministries. No issue went unattended. His intense activity surprised his staff members, whom he required to report to their offices three hours earlier than had been their practice. Acevedo worked incessantly during the day from his office and after working hours in his private office. His actions were relentless.[15] To weaken the influence of *creole* leaders in the government, he broke up the political leadership in the command headquarters of the national police. He sought to raise departmental revenues.

In the appointment of ecclesiastical offices, the apostolic vicariate had become accustomed to authorizing appointments simply by communicating them to the government. In 1860 two decrees were issued by the executive power, and inspired by Acevedo, reestablished the constitutional doctrine that the vicariate had to obtain the government's approval before making any appointment, an approval granted by the executive power as patron of the Roman Catholic Church. Acevedo also established that the appointments of the *curia* were subject to acceptance by the executive. Some experts on Uruguayan history point out that this was the first recognition of the government's patronage in that country.[16]

In 1861 a parish priest refused to preside at the funeral of a man who purportedly had been a mason. The incident sparked a scandal. The Ministry of Government finally authorized the burial of the remains, which resulted in the vicariate's objection that this action violated canon, civil, and administrative law. The vicariate suspended the granting of burial licenses issued by parish priests until the corpse at issue was unearthed.

The government responded with a decree in April 1861, stating that it was contrary to public hygiene to take a corpse, sometimes in a state of putrefaction, to the Church for a Mass, because this conduct jeopardized the health of all present. That regulation provided that bodies had to be taken directly to cemeteries for burial, bypassing the Church. The conflict between the government and the vicariate led to social turmoil on the issue. After several days of clashes, the parties reached an agreement. If the vicariate would renew its blessing of cemeteries through the granting of burial licenses by priests, the government would not object to such an act in its religious or spiritual sense. The matter led to the secular government beginning to intervene in the cemeteries.[17]

Acevedo's work in both ministries led to an improvement in the country's international credit, an improvement that redounded to neighboring countries.[18] Indeed, shortly before Acevedo left the ministries, the country entered negotiations with Paraguay to boost trade between the two countries.[19]

By a decree on May 4, 1860 the Ministry of Government launched into measuring its territory and examining the ownership titles. The advisory committee for this project essentially had to determine promptly the extent of the country and its ownership. The ministry also established that occupants of public lands could reclaim them within a specified time period, and such action would bar other claimants. Those who reclaimed land were accepted by the government and would have a preemptive right to purchase it.[20]

Acevedo acted as minister of foreign affairs while Uruguay consolidated its independence. In 1860 the country came of age and joined the international community as a sovereign nation. Foreign delegations accepted that they were dealing with independent authorities. In this capacity, Acevedo faced claims from Brazil, France, England, Portugal, and Spain seeking to protect their nationals against the new legislation of Uruguay. In similar fashion, he also worked on settling debt from Anglo-French claims for the damages caused by war.[21]

One of Acevedo's major aspirations was to channel the energies of the country toward the future and suppress those factors that might drag the country backward and seriously harm public tranquility. For example, on March 30, 1861 a decree opened the country's doors through a simple administrative act to all who wanted to return. This action provided amnesty to all who had participated in subversive movements of the past. In the case of military chiefs, the government reserved the right to determine in which department they would live unless they chose the capital city. With the return of such individuals, political propaganda was also regulated. Many feared that with the return of those taking advantage of amnesty, their outdated ideas that had brought about so much violence might again gain circulation.[22]

Under the pressure of political turmoil, Acevedo left the ministry before the amnesty was discussed in the assembly. He did not want to participate in the conflict.[23] His work as the minister of government and foreign affairs was suddenly interrupted by a presidential decision in June 1861. Yielding to prevailing political pressures, the president decided to get rid of one of his ministers, Eduardo Acevedo. The reason was to end the conflict.[24]

Legislation

Acevedo's most outstanding work was legislative. Beyond his service as legislator, he was the main driving force behind pieces of legislation even when he was not an active member of the House. He wrote several drafts of codes both in Buenos Aires and in Montevideo and drafted several bills and decrees. This work reflected his belief that he should always provide his country with legislation when it was needed.

Peirano Facio affirmed that Acevedo's work did not have the dimension of either academic research or community outreach. Acevedo had an obsession to overcome—by law—the turmoil his communities were experiencing. This work underscored his yearning to institute the rule of law.[25]

His legislative works were many. In 1849, he drafted regulations for justices of the peace, which became effective in Miguelete in February of that year. In 1850, with Juan Francisco Giró and Juan María Reyes, he drafted a set of general regulations for public instruction of the states for free and obligatory public education. In 1850, he also drafted the regulations of secondary school and higher learning that would be a portent of the national education system of

Uruguay. In 1856, as a legislator, Acevedo promoted passage of the Mortgage Act, which constituted the first step in Uruguay to improve national legislation on this important issue. He supported the enactment of the Rural Code, and he drew up a plan for the reform of the military system and the penitentiary system.[26]

For fourteen months, the overwhelming work of the ministry filled all of Acevedo's working day and much of his night. With the profound disappointment caused by the unexpected ministerial crisis that led to Acevedo's ousting, his health became impaired. When he was performing public duties in Montevideo, his health grew alarmingly weaker. Life as a public official upset him. On the resumption of his peaceful life in Buenos Aires, his health recovered.

Throughout December 1861, Carlos Tejedor wrote to him from Buenos Aires and urged him not to remain hidden at home. It had already been six months since Acevedo had left the ministry, and his health, judging by Tejedor, was fully recovered. Iconic figures Vicente Fidel López, Diego Lamas, and Tristán Azambuya wrote to him with the same intentions. These latter individuals expressed their joy in 1862 when Acevedo was elected senator for the Department of Montevideo.

Acevedo's performance during a brief period of 1863, the last year of his life, was mainly represented by a bill that established an interpretation of the constitutional prohibition that superior military officers could not hold public office, in accordance with Article 25, paragraph 1 of the constitution. That particular prohibition did not include regular colonels and other major chiefs of the army unless they held a military command. Acevedo also worked on draft legislation on the entry of the military into the legislative body.

Among other initiatives, Acevedo studied the reorganization of universities through a commission of which he was a member. He also worked on various issues such as the reduction of postage costs, abolition of a passport exit from the state, and the need to inspect exports, mainly beef. In this last activity, Acevedo included cross-references to the work of Michel Chevalier on the United States. Ready to face some of the most important problems of economic and administrative life, Acevedo's own notes show that he was getting ready to play an active role in the senate. Poor health, however, cut these plans short.

Codification

Perhaps Acevedo's most outstanding legacy was his drafting of the Civil Code for Uruguay and the Code of Commerce for the Province of Buenos Aires. According to Peirano Facio, Acevedo poured his passion for the law and his extremely broad scholarly learning into these projects.[27]

Drafting of the Civil Code for Uruguay began in 1847, and by 1849, the work was completed just one month before the end of the Uruguayan Civil War (known there as "the Big War").[28] According to Peirano Facio, nobody doubted Acevedo's authorship of the draft of the Civil Code published in 1852, which did not finally become law. Another project included in the Uruguayan Civil Code was known as the "Narvaja Code," which differed from Acevedo's bill.[29]

Acevedo expressed the main features of this work in its preamble. He noted that the present state of Uruguay's legislation contained some confusion, gaps, and incoherence. These were hurdles that impeded the settling of legal disputes. Present legislative texts from different times led to a labyrinth of sources. Indeed, existing national legislation could easily be viewed from the perspective of the *Fuero Juzgo*.[30]

Regarding marriage, Acevedo mentioned that his proposal alarmed many experts who considered that marriage should be fully submitted to ecclesiastic jurisdiction. Acevedo responded that such an opinion was strange for present times, and that it also conflicted with the basic principles of law. He asserted that a religious sacrament should not be confused with a legal contract. The former should entirely remain subject to ecclesiastic jurisdiction, whereas the latter was proper to the civil one. He founded his opinion on that of Charles III, who could hardly be labeled a disciple of Voltaire. Acevedo reported that Charles III addressed this question in *The Pragmatics* of March 26, 1776, which limited the options for marriage for children in the royal family. Charles III stated that he entrusted the examination of this matter to a board of ministers charged with proposing the most convenient and fairest remedy in keeping with his royal authority and with civil contract and temporal effects, while leaving the ecclesiastic authority and canon provisions intact with respect to the value, subsistence, and spiritual effects of the sacrament of marriage.

Pope Benedict XIV faced a similar situation when the clergy of Belgium asked whether a marriage solemnized before a civil judge (sometimes a heretical judge) and consummated without performance of Catholic ritual should be approved. The Council of Trent, however, had mandated that marriage be contracted before a parish priest, or before any priest who may serve as the parish priest, and two witnesses. Benedict responded that even though it is the opinion of some theologians that marriage consists only of consent, the pope's opinion remained in the middle. Thus, the ecumenical synod had rendered voidable any marriages contracted outside Catholic ritual. As the Council of Trent was interpreted in Belgium, consent before a civil judge, even though sufficient for a civil contract of marriage, was not sufficient for sacramental marriage. Missionaries were thus sent to Belgium to instruct Catholics that after giving their consent before the civil judge, they should appear before a Catholic priest, who would provide them with appropriate nuptial blessings.[31] Indeed, the reviewing commission suggested the suppression of the chapter on civil marriage.

Acevedo's main approach was to keep present legislation effective insofar as it did not conflict with contemporary practice, keeping in mind the needs of the country. With this principle in mind, Acevedo stated that although some provisions should have been changed, their continuance presented no substantial danger. For even though they were not the best provisions, they did not conflict with the customs of the country and its constitutional principles. Originality in legislation for its own sake would open a chimera and lead to absurdity. He followed the thought of Raymond-Theodore Troplong that the best legislation is that which best adapts to the customs of a country, although it may not be the most faithful to the rules of logic.

Acevedo apologized for not consulting his professional peers. Although he held great respect for their opinions, both distance and circumstances prohibited such consultation. Hoping to be useful to his country, he desired their observations and was grateful to those who might help him improve his work. He hoped that by the time his work was discussed in the legislative chamber, it would have received the benefit of his friends' suggestions and their approval. However imperfect the draft, it might lead to a permanent improvement in national law.[32] Despite two attempts to pass the bill, however, the project did not move forward.

In 1856 some articles in the press reported activity in the Argentine Congress related to the enactment of Acevedo's Civil Code. They pointed out that codifications were similar across the world, with minor features characterizing each country. In this case, they advised the adoption of one of the two codes drawn up in the neighboring states, with modifications to account for local experience and condition.[33]

In June 1856, the Government of the Province of Buenos Aires entrusted Acevedo to draft a commercial code with the Argentine jurist Dalmacio Vélez Sarsfield, then minister of government of the province, who was also involved in the tasks of codification. In the notes submitting the bill, Acevedo and Vélez Sarsfield expressed that considering the applicable civil codes, it was impossible to draft a new commercial code. Commercial laws relied on the preexistence of civil laws, except for those rare provisions that are somehow grounded on rules that existed before the civil code. Acevedo and Vélez Sarsfield explained that they had prepared thirty provisions of the civil code to be inserted into the code wherever appropriate. With this action, the drafting of a civil code in harmony with the country's needs would be less difficult.

Acevedo and Vélez Sarsfield asserted that they had not introduced innovations into the received law of Buenos Aires. In their view, the case law was uniform across the nations with respect to the matters legislated in those thirty provisions, and they had done nothing but shape a code containing rules of law that were already in existence. The Commercial Code was enacted by the House of the Province of Buenos Aires in October 1859 and by the National Congress of Argentina in September 1862.

The Uruguayan Government did not want to fall behind. In a message dated February 25, 1859, the Government of Uruguay requested the General Assembly to enact the code drafted by Acevedo and Vélez Sarsfield. The Legislation Committee of the House of Deputies issued a very favorable report by mid-1861, and by a decree dated May 26, 1865, the interim government, led by General Venancio Flores, incorporated this code into the legislation of the Uruguayan Republic.

Acevedo's contribution to the Commercial Code for the Province of Buenos Aires was not recognized at first. A heated debate arose regarding attribution of authorship to the Argentine Vélez Sarsfield. The legal historiography points out, however, that the work was the product of co-authorship between Acevedo and Vélez Sarsfield.[34]

On the legal profession

Acevedo turned to law to serve the republic. He was well-prepared for this profession and believed deeply in law and the rule of law. The multitude of lawyers in the country brought discredit to the profession, because many lawyers lacked the requisite skills or other essential attributes for the practice of law. Lawyers could not earn a sufficient living from their work, and they criticized the professional failures of their colleagues while relying on dishonesty in attempting to find legal work. Many sought to practice law only for financial gain and never seriously considered the law as a vocation. Acevedo understood that the plethora of lawyers contributed to the discredit of the profession. He believed that all lawyers should have the same level of training and skill, and that the number of fair lawsuits was sufficient to provide financial support to all attorneys.

He added that the essential qualities of a lawyer ought to be both intellectual and moral. He understood that intellectual components of the law are so varied that it is not possible for any given lawyer to know them all. Yet any lawyer, he asserted, must have exacting notions of ideology to be able to perform according to a correct morality. And one must know history to understand the profound sense and spirit of laws.[35]

Conclusion

Eduardo Acevedo was one of the greatest jurists from the River Plate, and his work was not confined to his home country of Uruguay. He stood out as a brilliant codifier both there and in Buenos Aires. He skillfully and cautiously modernized law while maintaining the continuity of legal institutions and the customs and culture of the region of the River Plate.

Beyond being an eminent jurist, Acevedo was a prominent politician. Yearning for his country's recognition as an independent and modern nation, Acevedo faced a difficult task. Although on many occasions his contemporaries did not thoroughly understand his opinions and actions, Acevedo acted with consistency. He stated that every time he undertook a public office, he performed it with honesty, humility, and tenacity. Whenever he was thoughtlessly removed from the political arena, sometimes abruptly, he would soon afterward be approached to serve again in public life. He lived his intense, brief, and productive life to the fullest.

Notes

1 Floria, *Historia de los argentinos.*
2 Míguez, *Historia Económica Argentina.*
3 Peirano Facio, *La Obra jurídica de Eduardo Acevedo*, 3.
4 Peirano Facio, "El Codificador 'Eduardo Acevedo,'" 8.
5 Peirano Facio, *La Obra jurídica de Eduardo Acevedo*, 8.
6 Peirano Facio, "El Codificador," 7–30.
7 Peirano Facio, *La Obra jurídica de Eduardo Acevedo*, 3.

8 This was a characteristic of those times. University graduates were called on to render military service and governmental duty. That requirement favorably caused the Uruguayan codification processes to be eclectic, since it was not until the twentieth century that Uruguay began to have its own scholarly and academic school of law.
9 Peirano Facio, *La Obra jurídica de Eduardo Acevedo*, 5.
10 Lawyers had to undertake their university studies away from Montevideo, since there was no university in that city. Many went to Buenos Aires because of its proximity; that city had had its own university since 1821. The second stage of education, the practice of the legal profession, was then carried out in Montevideo at the Academy of Jurisprudence.
11 Peirano Facio, *La Obra jurídica de Eduardo Acevedo*, 6.
12 Acevedo, *Eduardo Acevedo años 1815–1863*, 237.
13 *Bonaerense* means "native to the province of Buenos Aires."
14 Acevedo, *Eduardo Acevedo años 1815–1863*, 246.
15 Ibid., 247.
16 Ibid., 249.
17 Ibid., 250–51.
18 Ibid., 263.
19 Ibid., 303.
20 Ibid., 293–95.
21 Ibid., 314–18.
22 Ibid., 289.
23 Ibid., 282.
24 Ibid., 328–32.
25 Peirano Facio, *La Obra jurídica de Eduardo Acevedo*, 7.
26 Ibid., 10.
27 Ibid., 10.
28 Acevedo, *Eduardo Acevedo años 1815–1863*, 338.
29 Peirano Facio, *La Obra jurídica de Eduardo Acevedo*, 11.
30 The *Fuero Juzgo* was a codex of Spanish laws enacted in Castile in 1241 by Ferdinand III. It is essentially a translation of the *Liber Iudiciorum*, formulated in 654 by the Visigoths.
31 Acevedo, *Eduardo Acevedo años 1815–1863*, 342–43.
32 Ibid., 338–45.
33 Ibid., 358–59.
34 Vélez Sarsfield did not help to calm the debate. In *El Nacional* on August 28, 1862, and in the debates held at the senate in the Federal Congress upon the nationalization of the Commercial Code, in August 1862, Vélez Sarsfield said that the legislation was his own work and that Acevedo's contributions were minor. Acevedo never spoke of the issue.
35 Acevedo, *Eduardo Acevedo años 1815–1863*, 424–75.

References

Acevedo, Eduardo. *Eduardo Acevedo años 1815–1863. Su obra como codificador, ministro, legislador y publicista*. Editada por G. Ramírez, A. Palomeque, and E. Azarola. Montevideo: Imprenta El siglo ilustrado, 1908.

Floria, Carlos Alberto, and César A. García Belsunce. *Historia de los argentinos*. Buenos Aires: El Ateneo, 1971.

Míguez, Eduardo. *Historia Económica Argentina desde la Conquista a la crisis de 1930*. Buenos Aires: Cúspide, 2008.

Peirano Facio, Jorge. "El Codificador Eduardo Acevedo." Text taken from the *Revista de la Asociación de Escribanos del Uruguay (1957)*, 175–92. Montevideo: Asociación de Escribanos del Uruguay, 1958.
Peirano Facio, Jorge. *La Obra jurídica de Eduardo Acevedo*. Montevideo: Ministerio de Instrucción Pública y Previsión Social, 1964.

14 Augusto Teixeira de Freitas (Brazil, 1816–83)

Alfredo de J. Flores

Introduction[1]

The consolidation of Brazilian law in the nineteenth century arose in the context of national independence from Portuguese domination (1822) and brought to the fore the relation between the principles and method of natural law (derived from the scholastic tradition received in Brazil in the period before independence) and the nineteenth-century model of legislation inspired by the Napoleonic Code. This process in Brazilian law brings us to Augusto Teixeira de Freitas,[2] an author who belonged to an era in the history of Brazilian law when national legislation was incipient and scientific approaches to law were almost nonexistent. With his acute perception of the reality of legal phenomena, especially in private law, he established a solid basis for national law in Brazil by defending several elements of the legal tradition of the *ius commune*.

This famous Brazilian codifier produced one of the most significant civil codes in Latin America in the nineteenth century, the *Esboço do Código civil* (*Outline of the civil code*). Through this and other works, his methods and intellectual taxonomy of law influenced the work of many jurists responsible for national and foreign legislation. As an initial example, one can mention Dalmacio Vélez Sarsfield, the Argentinian codifier who based his own project on the structure of the *Esboço*. Vélez's code continues to this day as the main civil legislation of Argentina—and a fundamental reference for the new Argentinian civil and commercial code of 2014. Furthermore, the work of Teixeira de Freitas also influenced Brazilian forensic practice during the Empire of Brazil (1822–89) and the beginning of the First Republic (1889–1930).

The relevance of this Brazilian intellectual is not to be reduced to the mere image of a successful lawyer in the nineteenth century. It should also be remembered that his *Esboço* is typically modern—considering the debate over codification at that moment—while taking into account the previous tradition of natural law as reflected in Portuguese national legislation of the time, which was the basis for the *Esboço*, and in the formal aspects of legal institutions derived from Roman law.

Biographical information[3]

The son of Felicidade de Santa Rosa de Lima Teixeira and Antonio Teixeira de Freitas Barbosa, Augusto Teixeira de Freitas was born on August 19, 1816 in the town of Cachoeira, a former captaincy of Bahia, in colonial Brazil. By order of Emperor Pedro I, his father was granted the title of Barão de Itaparica (Baron of Itaparica) on April 8, 1826, resulting in a significant improvement of his family's welfare and social status. Thanks to this title, young Augusto had some rare opportunities, such as receiving his basic education in his hometown.

From an early age, he demonstrated great aptitude for studies, particularly in Latin.[4] After completing basic education at age sixteen, he chose to study law. There were only two faculties of law in Brazil at the time, in Olinda and São Paulo. Perhaps because of the proximity to his hometown and the presence of several of his acquaintances, he opted to enroll in the School of Olinda in 1832, where he studied the first year of the course. At the end of that year, however, he suddenly made the decision to continue his studies at the Academy of Largo de São Francisco, in the city of São Paulo, where he began his second year of studies. Teixeira de Freitas attended the course for a certain time, possibly until the end of the fourth year, that is, from 1833 to 1835, and in this school his professors praised him for his dedication to study and his good grades. In the middle of 1835, perhaps because he had strongly criticized some professors, he returned to Olinda and received his degree on October 6, 1837. By then, he had married his cousin, Matilde Teixeira de Lima, and his father had died.

Looking for opportunities to establish himself in legal practice, Teixeira de Freitas moved to Rio de Janeiro, the capital of the empire. There, he could thrive in his studies and improve his acute logical views on legal subjects. He achieved significant success in his practice. His reputation as a brilliant lawyer spread among members of the profession, who reckoned him as one of the best attorneys in the country. This explains why, in 1843, he was invited,[5] along with other great lawyers of the capital, to be a founder of the Instituto dos Advogados Brasileiros (Institute of Brazilian Lawyers), which was the first association of its kind in the country. Thus, through the quality of his forensic work and his diligence in dealing with legal issues, Teixeira de Freitas exhibited a deep understanding of legislation and its mechanisms. In 1844, at the young age of twenty-seven, he received a seat as a referee on the Conselho de Estado (Council of State) from the Emperor Pedro II—a sign of great success for a lawyer at the time. In this position, Teixeira de Freitas gave legal advice on the most relevant governmental issues and was frequently consulted by the imperial court and by high-ranking officials. This gave him direct contact with ministers and counselors of the empire, excellent opportunities to display his legal and political acumen.

Teixeira de Freitas strengthened his friendship with the Minister of Justice of the Imperial Government, José Thomaz Nabuco de Araújo. In 1854, when the government declared the need for a compilation of the country's civil legislation, Teixeira de Freitas made preliminary contact with Nabuco de Araújo and showed his interest. The result was a contract,[6] signed on February 15, 1855, by both the counselor and the imperial government, by which Teixeira de Freitas would start elaborating new legislation for a period of five years. The work was completed in 1857 and was called the *Consolidação das leis civis* (*Consolidation of civil laws*).

On its completion, Teixeira de Freitas officially presented this work on December 4, 1858. The appropriate governmental commission gave its approval. The success of the work was a result of the author's earnestness and his spirit of absolute dedication to the project. He had worked alone in this enterprise of compilation, following Savigny's recommended method. In his books, the German jurist had stated that such a work requires a single mind to dominate every subject under study and to organize it according to scientific criteria. Therefore, Teixeira de Freitas believed it would be easier to achieve perfection by working alone. Despite this initial position, he appreciated constructive criticisms of his work, such as those published by counselor Antonio Rebouças, to which Teixeira de Freitas responded in later editions of the *Consolidação* in 1865 and 1876.

After success in this task, Teixeira de Freitas was naturally hired to codify Brazilian civil legislation. In the wake of the compilation's success, the government hired him on January 10, 1859, to begin drafting a civil code, allowing less than four years to complete the work. Judging from the deadline stipulated in the contract, he intended to utilize the studies made for the compilation, which could explain the short period set for the construction of the codified text.[7]

In fact, with his commitment, Teixeira de Freitas managed to elaborate a model civil code—a logical systematization of legal subjects that was nevertheless completely different from other codes of the period. It provided the structure for a new civil system, resulting from his research into its topics, especially by means of comparison with models already known at the time. For this reason, when he became acquainted with the Portuguese civil codification process, he elaborated his critique of the Portuguese-Brazilian jurist Antonio de Seabra and published his thinking as the *Nova apostilla á censura do Senhor Alberto de Moraes Carvalho* (*New marginal note to the criticism...*) in 1859. In this discussion over the project's systematization, Teixeira de Freitas developed a strong criticism of the work of the Portuguese codifier, justifying his position by highlighting the proximity between Portugal and Brazil.

Teixeira de Freitas's perfectionism not only was reflected in his new project but also resulted in delay in completing the draft. Despite this, he managed to publish the text in fascicles until 1865, when he was forced to present the final work before a commission specifically constituted by the government to examine the project. He titled the final text *Código civil—Esboço* (*Civil code—an outline*), which, later, was repeatedly quoted as *Esboço do Código civil.*

The commission began its revision on April 20, 1865. Regarding the initial part of the project, the "Preliminary Title," the examiners enumerated a list of critiques, demanding proper responses from Teixeira de Freitas to their objections. Because of such strong opposition, the jurist sought to demonstrate to Nabuco de Araújo that it would be best to close the activities of the commission, which was subsequently shut down on August 31 of that year.

This quarrel led the jurist to abandon the project, greatly resenting the criticisms of the examiners. Later, Teixeira de Freitas received correspondence from the minister of justice Martim Ribeiro de Andrada, dated November 20, 1866, seeking to involve Teixeira de Freitas again in the project. In response, on September 20, 1867, Teixeira de Freitas sent a famous letter,[8] in which he manifested an interest in continuing his work, but only if he could elaborate a new model, completely unprecedented in the history of codification: initially he would elaborate a code that ordered all essential legal elements—a *Código geral* (general code), as he called it. Furthermore, he would create another draft of a private law code, his *Código civil* (civil code).

Despite some favorable comments from government members on the innovative proposal, the new Minister of Justice, José de Alencar, rejected the idea. In fact, for a long time, Alencar had disagreed with Teixeira de Freitas's style of work, calling it "premature," even though he recognized the jurist's high reputation. Moreover, Alencar understood that Teixeira de Freitas had breached the contract for drafting the code, and Alencar concluded that the new proposal was unacceptable, as it would also incur expenses to the public treasury. Unfortunately, this denial served the interest of politicians who opposed Teixeira de Freitas. With such critiques of the codifier's work, Alencar managed to address the issue through the informal termination of the contract—to the point of putting aside the report made by the examination committee in June 1868, which had actually been favorable to Teixeira de Freitas's proposal. As the matter unfolded, and as the emperor remained isolated from the issue, Teixeira de Freitas became discouraged and lost faith in the cause.

Nevertheless, a few years later, a new Minister of Justice, Manuel Antônio Duarte de Azevedo, tried to solve the problem and summoned Teixeira de Freitas to a meeting on April 7, 1872. However, after listening the jurist's thoughts and complaints, Duarte de Azevedo was unable to reach an agreement, and on November 18, 1872, he officially terminated the contract, thereby burying the possibility of resuming the jurist's project. Teixeira de Freitas did not reconcile himself with this fact for the rest of his life.

Although defeated, Teixeira de Freitas authored the most relevant proposals of the time for drafting legislative texts—the *Consolidação* and the *Esboço*, both masterpieces of Brazilian legal science. Nonetheless, recognition was subdued; for example, the text of the *Consolidação* was widely used in legal practice but infrequently discussed. Restrictions on the use of the *Esboço* were much greater because it was not promulgated. It was cited only in academic works and in subsequent projects of other civil codes. In other words, appreciation and respect for Teixeira de Freitas's work came mostly from his publication of books. Nonetheless, to the present day, much of his academic work has not been the object of deeper scholarly reflection, including his more practical production, such as his reports prepared for the Council of State, still underestimated by historiography despite their relevance to the government of the time.

Some of his lesser-known books include commentaries on Portuguese legal classics. In addition, on procedural subjects Teixeira de Freitas published

Primeiras linhas sobre o processo civil (*First lines on civil process*), by Joaquim José Caetano Pereira e Sousa, in 1879–80, and *Doutrina das acções* (*Doctrine of actions*), by José Homem Corrêa Telles, in 1880. On civil topics, he published António Joaquim de Gouvêa Pinto's *Tratado dos testamentos e successões* (*Treatise of wills and successions*) and *Formulario dos contractos, testamentos, e de outros actos do tabellionado* (*Formulary of contracts, wills, and other notary acts*), both in 1881. Publishing these books granted the jurist a greater recognition in the Brazilian publishing market, especially among legal practitioners and students. Yet this did not prevent the erroneous idea, argued by commentators on his work, that these books would be of little intellectual value. In fact, they were distinct works, but did not fit into the sweep of the author's well-known legislative works, which had more elaborate levels of applied legal science.

The singular scenario of his legislative work in Brazil—the coexistence of social recognition on one hand and the political obstacles to the continuity of the *Esboço* on the other—did not interfere with the influence his works would have in South America—mainly thanks to Dalmacio Vélez Sarsfield. In fact, in the implementation of codes during the process of independence of South American countries, the Argentine Republic benefited from the profound influence of Teixeira de Freitas's projects, a fact confirmed by Vélez himself,[9] the jurist responsible for the Argentine Civil Code of 1869.

The Argentinian Code became the means for propagating Teixeira de Freitas's ideas in several Latin American countries in the nineteenth century. This was because Vélez used the system of the *Esboço* alongside several rules of the Brazilian civil code project in constructing its analogue in Argentina. Yet Vélez also made his own contribution, as he finalized what the Brazilian jurist had left unfinished, that is, the final part of the *Esboço*. Moreover, the relationship between the two South American codifiers was not restricted to intellectual projects. Such links were fostered by both governments at the time because of the alliance between Brazil and Argentina, especially during the Paraguayan War (1865–70), when the relation between the two countries had to be strengthened. Nonetheless, these connections were not restricted to politics: Teixeira de Freitas was flattered by the deference of Vélez and visited Buenos Aires in 1866, passing through Montevideo (Uruguay) and intending to stay in the region, as reported by local newspapers. In summary, Teixeira de Freitas faced a dilemma at the time: on one hand, the Brazilian government denied his project's continuity; on the other, there was direct support for his influence on the Argentinian text abroad,[10] thanks to the efforts of Brazilian diplomat Francisco Otaviano de Almeida Rosa, in international mediation.

Almost all commentators, both admirers and opponents of Teixeira de Freitas, have noted that during his final period, he suffered from gradual dementia, which would have affected his character and his ideas, as they saw the jurist becoming "an intolerant religious maniac." This image is distorted, as he suffered greatly from the frustrations brought on by the codification process. His personality was affected, certainly, yet it cannot be deduced that he had fully lost his mental faculties.[11] For instance, he showed great intellectual capacity up to his last book, *Vocabulario jurídico* (*Legal vocabulary*), published in 1883.

Attributing a state of madness to the Brazilian jurist does not follow if one considers all his works as presented in his own style and as contributions to the course of Brazilian legal science. Teixeira de Freitas's nonlegal works also support this conclusion. His religious *Córtice eucarístico* (*Eucharistic cortex*), published in 1871, confirmed his sentiment as a Roman Catholic, while in the text *Pedro quer ser Augusto* (*Pedro wants to be Augusto*), published in 1872, the author polemically counters the policies of Emperor Pedro II, who at the time intended to invite the Portuguese codifier Visconde de Seabra to create the Brazilian Civil Code. Such a stance in these works is different, but not strange; in fact, in the controversy of 1872, Teixeira de Freitas resumed the criticism of Seabra that he initially had made in the *Nova apostilla* of 1859, although he did not undertake a deep analysis of Seabra's legal system.

Unfortunately, after these moments, a great sorrow came to the lawyer's life when he lost his only son in 1883, Augusto Teixeira de Freitas Jr. This extreme grief may explain his delicate psychological situation sometimes described as madness. One month after his son's death, the jurist passed away, stripped of his glory, in the city of Niterói, in Rio de Janeiro province, on December 12, 1883. His funeral took place in the same city. In 1943, his remains were transferred to his native land, Bahia, during the celebration of the centenary of the *Instituto dos Advogados Brasileiros.*

The work of Teixeira de Freitas

Teixeira de Freitas's biography shows the relevance and contribution of the jurist to both Brazilian and universal legal history. In what follows, this chapter examines the role of his vision of legal subjects in the context of his time and works. Teixeira de Freitas may be viewed as a jurist inspired by Christianity and a defender of natural law. Here, this chapter examines two facets more closely: (1) the scientific-legal aspect of his work, and (2) the possible philosophical questions derived from his writings.

The scientific-legal aspect of his work

First and foremost, the specific value and usefulness of Teixeira de Freitas's works for Latin America stand out. Indeed, a vast collection of works by contemporary Romanists indicate Teixeira de Freitas's contribution to building unity in Latin American law, as demonstrated in the writings of Italian professors Sandro Schipani[12] and Pierangelo Catalano.[13]

This image of Teixeira de Freitas is supported by several observations. For example, in some writings, he reviews the work of Andrés Bello, the illustrious Venezuelan who wrote the Chilean Civil Code in the mid-nineteenth century. And, as already mentioned, the Brazilian expert influenced the work of Vélez Sarsfield. Judging by the relevance of Teixeira de Freitas's work in the history of Latin American codifications, he was largely responsible for the unity of civil legal doctrine in South America. This uniformity manifested itself in a general theory applicable to national laws, as can be seen in the legislative technique used in codifications of the period. Furthermore, from the perspective of legal science, criteria for constructing a juridical technique more adequate to the cultural context of Latin America are similar to elements of the thinking that appeared in the books of the Brazilian jurist.

This picture presented by Italian Romanists recognizes an important facet of Teixeira de Freitas's work: his influence on the elaboration of legal doctrine and his clear role in developing the national legal theory of the region. This recognition also finds support in the works of Brazilian authors. The twentieth-century legal theorist Francisco Cavalcanti Pontes de Miranda, in his *Tratado de Direito privado* (*Treatise of private law*), declares himself a disciple of Teixeira de Freitas's ideas and identifies him as the greatest jurist of the Brazilian Empire.[14]

Possible philosophical questions

Some philosophical questions emerge regarding Teixeira de Freitas's vision of legal technique, and at least three aspects should be emphasized. First is the need for a philosophical reading of legal phenomena. One cannot reduce reality to a theoretical hypothesis but must observe the historical interpretation suggested by Teixeira de Freitas. In this case, the jurist's various works manifest a conception of law that encompasses all spheres. More specifically, when the author writes on civil codification, he manifests a theoretical-philosophical conception which serves as the basis for technical enterprise; in addition, his vision of legal technique claims to present itself as a model of a truly scientific construction for a legal system.[15] The first philosophical question, then, concerns the extent to which the technique he used in his models of systematization of civil law corresponds to a rational ordering par excellence of this matter.

In this case, it is essential to mention that the codifying method is a kind of legal skill linked to the need for elaborating rules through legislation; in other words, it does not refer *prima facie* to a particular judgment about the application of law to concrete cases (as in judicial decisions) because it is directed toward a universal application (the generality of legislation). This scope is the first characteristic of codification, and Teixeira de Freitas acknowledged this in a particular and special way when seeking excellence in the construction of a civil legislative system;[16] he had the opportunity to perfect his model of legal technique in the process of developing his *Esboço*. For this reason, Teixeira de Freitas understood that legislative technique should always accompany the reality of phenomena, visualizing their own generality. He was also considered a *vir bonus, iuris peritus* (good man, expert in law), as he embodied in his own life the public and private virtues (kindness, honor, and self-denial) typical of Roman jurists; the jurist's admiration for Roman civilization becomes evident.[17]

The second aspect of his vision for legal technique worthy of emphasis is his logical accuracy in the elaboration of the *Esboço*. He intended to define the legal rules of the text according to the nature of each legal institution, organizing all civil institutions within a sole legal system embodied in the *Esboço*.[18] The perfection sought in the elaboration of the civil legal system would result from its author's precise legal technique.[19] This explains why Teixeira de Freitas was able to achieve excellence in this method to the point of supporting such a range of phenomena through the construction of linguistic and technical elements favoring harmony in human relations. This is an important key to the influence of his work on several other foreign codifiers.

The third aspect to be emphasized is his construction of the legal system based on the reality of legal relations, in the sense advocated by Savigny.[20] Teixeira de Freitas had read French translations of Savigny's works and offered a peculiar interpretation from the perspective of the classic legal tradition of the Iberian matrix. Nevertheless, it is necessary to remember that Teixeira de Freitas always sought to treat legal phenomena in a modern language,[21] particularly when he had difficulties building a set of concepts and rules in the process of civil codification.

It is possible to indicate points in which Teixeira de Freitas shows his understanding of the phenomena of law according to patterns defended by the authors of the classical legal tradition. Indeed, he defends the condition of the person in the *Esboço*, and the *nasciturus* (a Roman legal concept referring to the fetus) when he frames it in terms of a person yet to be born (the concept of *pessoa por nascer*, unborn person) in the text of his draft code. He shows without doubt that the unborn child has legal personhood like any other human being.[22]

Under Teixeira de Freitas's supervision, the work of elaborating the *Esboço do Código Civil* was a typically legislative task, in which one recognizes the nature of legal relations and institutions. The codification also included details of a legal phenomenology since the system was elaborated according to the legal technique of the time. Consequently, Teixeira de Freitas defined an idea of construction of a civil system in which practical legal knowledge prevails—and this concretized a legislative technique through its necessary link to the reality of legal relations.

Some inferences can be made from the philosophical questioning proposed by the work of Teixeira de Freitas, and these inferences can serve as a corollary for the consideration of his work. From a generic point of view, Teixeira de Freitas approached the thought of philosophical realism in its Aristotelian-Thomist connotation, incorporating an account of the Iberian scholastic tradition while maintaining the perspective of a constant dialogue with modern legal experience. In fact, the *iusnaturalistic* vision of that time had a traditional understanding of its connections to Roman law that valued the role of institutions and legal relations.[23] Teixeira de Freitas's *iusnaturalistic* discourse, embedded in a Christian and humanistic understanding of the world, embraced elements of scientific truth manifested in the legal history of rules and institutions.

Moreover, thanks to Teixeira de Freitas's realistic view of the applicability of classical philosophical notions in the construction of a properly modern legal system, the outcome for the Brazilian codification process was the approval of the code.[24] This fact is not usually emphasized in current research on the history of legal theory, especially because some authors of natural law understand that the classical legal view could be covered only by judicial application; however, as this debate offers a considerable amount of controversy, it must be approached elsewhere.

Conclusion

The four most important ideas of Teixeira de Freitas are the classification of civil institutions, the unity of private law, the concept of the general code, and the notion of the unborn person,[25] all of which are explained here in summary form.

First, Teixeira de Freitas developed criteria to classify civil institutions, which would be a constant focus of his legislative works, as stated in the *Consolidação* and the *Esboço*. Composed of a deep methodological structure, this point of the author's thinking is singularly portrayed in these works. He even modified his initial conceptions to classify all civil institutions according to some categories: the *Esboço* was divided into a *Parte Geral* (general part) and a *Parte Especial* (special part), and the latter into personal rights (obligations and family), real rights (the rights of property), and relations between both of the previous categories—an innovation at the time.

Second, the unity of civil law is manifested in the aforementioned letter of 1867. Here, while studying the civil system, Teixeira de Freitas acknowledged the existence of many intersectional areas between civil and commercial law and concluded that it was necessary to reestablish this unity in his *Esboço* by covering both subjects in a single system.

Third—and also linked to his proposal of 1867—the idea of a general code was the corollary of a "law of the laws," in the sense defined in an earlier era by Francis Bacon. Teixeira de Freitas explained that such a general code would encapsulate the essence of legal doctrine, guaranteed in a higher law. In fact, after this moment, the notion of the general theory of law in Western legal thought arose in accordance with the jurist's intuition.

Finally, the notion of the *pessoa por nascer* (unborn person) was a more particular aspect of his thought, but one that influenced the whole structure of the civil system, as an expression of the link between the reality of the facts and the civil legal technique. Not by chance, it is one of the most important concepts of his theory. It remains very present in Argentinian legislation through Vélez, although the concept was forgotten in Brazil in the parliamentary debates on the project elaborated by Clóvis Bevilaqua.[26] In Brazil, the concept continued to be ignored in the new Code of 2002, a project led by Miguel Reale.

Thus, Teixeira de Freitas contributed profoundly to legal science in Brazil, Latin America, and the world. He kept a fair balance between his commitment to natural law and the need for change in Brazilian law and legal institutions. His vision is reiterated in subsequent works in both Brazil and abroad that recognize him as undeniably the greatest of all Brazilian jurists.

Notes

1 I am grateful to Guilherme Tumelero Macedo, an undergraduate student at the Faculty of Law of Universidade Federal do Rio Grande do Sul, for his comments

on the translation and his attentive revision. I also thank the editors of this volume for reviewing the text.

2 The most relevant biographies on the Brazilian jurist are Vianna, *Augusto Teixeira de Freitas: traços biográficos*; and Meira, *Teixeira de Freitas: o jurisconsulto do Império.* These serve as a guide for the biographical considerations presented here.

3 See Flores, "Augusto Teixeira de Freitas."

4 Meira, *Teixeira de Freitas*, 27–29.

5 Ibid., 73–75.

6 For the full transcription of the letter, see Meira, *Teixeira de Freitas*, 94.

7 On the transition from the *Consolidação das Leis Civis* to the *Esboço do Código Civil*, see Meira, *Teixeira de Freitas*, 181–207.

8 For a reproduction of the letter, see Meira, *Teixeira de Freitas*, 352–56.

9 For further details on this relationship, see Meira, "Direito brasileiro e Direito argentino (Códigos comercial e civil)—influência do 'Esboço' de Teixeira de Freitas no *Projecto* de Vélez Sarsfield."

10 We should not forget the criticism of Teixeira de Freitas among Argentinian intellectuals. One of the strongest critiques towards Vélez's project was made by Juan Bautista Alberdi, who interpreted the use of the *Esboço* as part of a Brazilian project of political domination in the Rio de la Plata region. Cf. Vianna, *Augusto Teixeira de Freitas*, 265.

11 See Barahona, "O ocaso da razão jurídica."

12 For an explanation on the importance of the "Latin American system," see Schipani, "Sistemas jurídicos e Direito romano."

13 According to Catalano, in contemporary times, there are two traditions of legal thought: the Justinian tradition, which persists in the area of Iberian influence and is the basis of the Latin American system of Teixeira de Freitas; and the tradition of the European Pandectist school, which defined Western legal science. Faced with this separation, Catalano notes that, despite some abstraction in the concepts of the Latin American system, this system is actually connected to the concrete reality of human beings, especially when some things are read between the lines of the *Esboço*, such as the recognition of the existence of human beings conceived in the womb, the legal concept of the unborn person (*pessoa por nascer*), following the Roman–Iberian legal tradition within a modern context. See Catalano, *Diritto e persone*, 195–215.

14 Pontes de Miranda, *Tratado de Direito privado*, 1:xxiii.

15 For this reason, Teixeira de Freitas speaks of a rational systematization affirming that

> the division is the instrument of the analysis; but, after this, the differences and similarities of the observed entities or facts are known, the classification, the instrument of synthesis, distributes them, not in isolated series, but in upper and lower classes subordinated to each other, and forming a true system, which is not a simple arrangement and superposition, but a fabric, an aggregate of parts reciprocally united,

as can be seen in his critical book to the draft of the Portuguese Civil Code. See Teixeira de Freitas, *Nova apostilla á censura do Senhor Alberto de Moraes Carvalho*, 52 (Flores translation).

16 Some authors speak of perfectionism, such as Hahnemann Guimarães, who emphasizes this characteristic in the personality of Teixeira de Freitas, pointing to something positive in the method of work of the Brazilian civilian; see Guimarães, "Teixeira de Freitas—sua vida e sua obra."

17 Sampaio, "Teixeira de Freitas—sua vida e sua obra."

18 Since the *Consolidação*, Teixeira de Freitas was concerned with a specific form of organization, "to find, however, the limits of civil law." Teixeira de Freitas, *Consolidação das leis civis*, vii (Flores translation).

19 For this reason, Teixeira de Freitas sought to understand the essence of legal reality; indeed, his work would be

> to examine legislation in its own text without influencing others' opinions, to compare new and old laws with care, to measure accurately the scope and consequences of each and every one, that is the laborious process to be employed in order to know the living substance of the legislation.

Teixeira de Freitas, *Consolidação*, vii (Flores translation).

20 The concept of "legal relationship" comes from Savigny's theory. See Savigny, *System des heutigen Römischen Rechts*, 1:7–8.

21 This modern vision includes the important role of subjective rights in the legal system; see Teixeira de Freitas, *Nova apostilla*, 56–57.

22 Defined by Freitas in Article 53: "are unborn people who, although not yet born, are found, however, already conceived in the maternal womb": Teixeira de Freitas, *Código civil. Esboço*, fasc. 1, 59 (Flores translation).

23 According to philosophical realism, Massini recalls that the realistic view of law with a practical character of the legal phenomenon must be a legacy of Aristotelian and Roman thought. Massini, *Sobre el realismo jurídico*, 17–18.

24 For Teixeira de Freitas's explanation on the "nature of things" (*natureza das cousas*), see Teixeira de Freitas, *Nova apostilla*, 10.

25 For more details on the concepts of "person" and "unborn person" (*pessoa por nascer*) in Teixeira de Freitas, see Flores, *El concepto jurídico moderno de "persona."*

26 Bevilaqua, *Linhas e perfis jurídicos.*

References

Barahona, Henrique. "O ocaso da razão jurídica: a loucura de Augusto Teixeira de Freitas e a 'Questão Religiosa.'" In *Teixeira de Freitas e o direito civil*, edited by Roberto and Ribeiro, 25–42. Belo Horizonte: Initia Via, 2017.

Bevilaqua, Clóvis. *Linhas e perfis jurídicos.* Rio de Janeiro: Freitas Bastos, 1930.

Catalano, Pierangelo. *Diritto e persone. Studi su origine e attualità del sistema romano*, Vol. 1. Turin: Giappichelli, 1990.

Flores, Alfredo de J. "A noção de 'Consolidação das leis' na literatura jurídica brasileira da segunda metade do século XIX." In *Teixeira de Freitas e o direito civil*, edited by Roberto and Ribeiro, 104–26. Belo Horizonte: Initia Via, 2017.

Flores, Alfredo de J. "Augusto Teixeira de Freitas." In *Dicionário de Filosofia do Direito*, edited by Vicente de Paulo Barreto, 796–800. Rio de Janeiro: Editora Renovar; São Leopoldo: Editora Unisinos, 2006.

Flores, Alfredo de J. "Direito natural e codificação: atualidade do método realista clássico de Teixeira de Freitas." *Revista da Faculdade de Direito da UFRGS* 30 (2012): 7–26.

Flores, Alfredo de J. *El concepto jurídico moderno de 'persona': histórico y problematización.* Caracas: Livrosca, 2014.

Flores, Alfredo de J. "El proyecto de modernización del ideario liberal republicano en Brasil en cuestión: las ediciones de la 'Consolidação das leis civis' durante la 'República Velha' (1889–1930)." In *Derecho privado y modernización: América Latina y Europa en la primera mitad del siglo XX*, edited by Thomas Duve, María

Rosario Polotto, and Thorsten Keiser, 179–98. Frankfurt am Main: Max Planck Institute for European Legal History, 2015.

Flores, Alfredo de J. “La interpretación jurídica en Freitas: el sistema jurídico decimonónico y el realismo aristotélico-tomista.” *Ars Iuris* 39 (2008): 209–28.

Flores, Alfredo de J. “O papel de Teixeira de Freitas no contexto do pensamento jurídico do séc. XIX.” *Latin American and Caribbean Journal of Legal Studies* 1 (2006): 1–16.

Guimarães, Hahnemann. “Teixeira de Freitas—sua vida e sua obra.” *Revista Forense* 97 (February 1944): 253–55.

Massini, Carlos. *Sobre el realismo jurídico.* Buenos Aires: Abeledo-Perrot, 1978.

Meira, Sílvio. “Direito brasileiro e Direito argentino (Códigos comercial e civil)—influência do ‘Esboço’ de Teixeira de Freitas no Projecto de Vélez Sarsfield.” In *Estudos jurídicos em homenagem ao Professor Caio Mário da Silva Pereira*, edited by Hamilton de Barros e Moraes and Caio Mário da Silva Pereira, 345–90. Rio de Janeiro: Forense, 1984.

Meira, Sílvio. *Teixeira de Freitas: o jurisconsulto do Império.* 2nd ed. Brasília: Cegraf, 1983.

Meira, Sílvio. “Teixeira de Freitas e Pontes de Miranda—a audácia do pensamento.” *Revista de Direito Civil* 5, no. 16 (1981): 153–59.

Morais Filho, Evaristo de. “Teixeira de Freitas, a busca da perfeição e a dogmática jurídica.” *Revista Forense* 81, no. 291 (1985): 1–22.

Nacata Júnior, Edson Kiyoshi. “Personae—res—actiones: Direito romano e tradição romanística na construção do sistema de direito civil de Augusto Teixeira de Freitas.” In *Teixeira de Freitas e o direito civil*, edited by Roberto and Ribeiro, 54–103. Belo Horizonte: Initia Via, 2017.

Pereira, Aloysio Ferreira. “O uso brasileiro do Direito romano no século XIX. Papel de Teixeira de Freitas.” In *Augusto Teixeira de Freitas e il Diritto latino-americano*, edited by Schipani, 83–89. Padua: Cedam, 1988.

Pontes de Miranda, Francisco Cavalcanti. *Tratado de Direito privado*, Vol. 1. Rio de Janeiro: Borsoi, 1954.

Rangel, Alan Wruck Garcia. “O projeto de Teixeira de Freitas: um Código Civil antinapoleônico? Contribuição ao estudo do comparatismo jurídico no século XIX.” In *História do Direito. Entre rupturas, crises e descontinuidades*, edited by Arno Wehling, Gustavo S. Siqueira, and Samuel Barbosa, 165–83. Belo Horizonte: Arraes Editores, 2018.

Reale, Miguel. “Humanismo e realismo jurídicos de Teixeira de Freitas.” In *Augusto Teixeira de Freitas e il Diritto latinoamericano*, edited by Schipani, 11–18. Padua: Cedam, 1988.

Reis, Thiago. “Teixeira de Freitas, lector de Savigny.” *Revista de Historia del Derecho* 49 (2015): 181–222.

Roberto, Giordano Bruno Soares, and Gustavo Pereira Leite Ribeiro, eds. *Teixeira de Freitas e o direito civil: estudos em homenagem ao bicentenário (1816–2016).* Belo Horizonte: Initia Via, 2017.

Sampaio, Nelson. “Teixeira de Freitas—sua vida e sua obra.” *Revista Forense* 97 (1944): 257–63.

Savigny, Friedrich Carl von. *System des heutigen Römischen Rechts*, Vol. 1. Berlin: Veit und Comp., 1840.

Schipani, Sandro, ed. *Augusto Teixeira de Freitas e il Diritto latinoamericano.* Padua: Cedam, 1988.

Schipani, Sandro. "Sistemas jurídicos e Direito romano. As codificações do Direito e a unidade do sistema jurídico latino-americano." In *Direito e integração*, edited by José Paes Landim, 34–53. Brasília: Universidade de Brasília, 1981.

Teixeira de Freitas, Augusto. *Código civil—Esboço*. Rio de Janeiro: Typographia Universal de Laemmert, 1860–65.

Teixeira de Freitas, Augusto. *Consolidação das leis civis*. Rio de Janeiro: Typographia Universal de Laemmert, 1857.

Teixeira de Freitas, Augusto. *Consolidação das leis civis*. 2nd ed. Rio de Janeiro: Typographia Universal de Laemmert, 1865.

Teixeira de Freitas, Augusto. *Consolidação das leis civis*. 3rd ed. Rio de Janeiro: B. L. Garnier, 1876.

Teixeira de Freitas, Augusto. *Doutrina das acções, por José Homem Corrêa Telles. Accommodada ao fôro do Brazil por Augusto Teixeira de Freitas*. Rio de Janeiro: H. Garnier, 1880.

Teixeira de Freitas, Augusto. *Formulario dos contratos, testamentos, e de outros actos do tabellionado, por José Homem Corrêa Telles. Renova-se para o Brazil, até o corrente anno de 1881, o conhecido manual do tabellião, ou ensaio de jurisprudencia eurematica*. Rio de Janeiro: B. L. Garnier, 1881.

Teixeira de Freitas, Augusto. *Nova apostilla á censura do Senhor Alberto de Moraes Carvalho sobre o projecto de Codigo civil portuguez*. Rio de Janeiro: Typographia Universal de Laemmert, 1859.

Teixeira de Freitas, Augusto. *Primeiras linhas sobre o processo civil, por Joaquim José Caetano Pereira e Souza. Accommodadas ao fôro do Brazil até o anno de 1877 por Augusto Teixeira de Freitas*, Vol. 4. Rio de Janeiro: Typographia Perseverança, 1879–80.

Teixeira de Freitas, Augusto. *Tratado dos testamentos e successões, por Antônio Joaquim Gouvêa Pinto. Accommodado ao fôro do Brasil até o anno de 1881 por Augusto Teixeira de Freitas*. Rio de Janeiro: B. L. Garnier, 1881.

Teixeira de Freitas, Augusto. *Vocabulario juridico: com appendices. I–Logár, e Tempo; II–Pessoas; III–Cousas; IV–Factos*. Rio de Janeiro: B.L. Garnier, 1883.

Vianna, Manoel Alvaro de Souza Sá. *Augusto Teixeira de Freitas: traços biográficos*. Rio de Janeiro: Typographia Hildebrandt, 1905.

15 Justo Arosemena Quesada (Panama and Colombia, 1817–96)

Hernán Alejandro Olano García and M.C. Mirow

Introduction

A Panamanian who lived during the period of that country's union with Colombia, Justo Arosemena Quesada was a father of Panamanian nationalism. He was a statistician, politician, parliamentarian, economist, philosopher, jurist, diplomat, polemist, and journalist. He was also a nonpracticing Christian, convinced that "no civilized country today can dispense with religious tolerance, freedom of conscience, and the free admission of any honest and industrious foreigner."[1]

Despite being a radical liberal of the Golgotha wing of the Liberal Party, Arosemena had a deep moral sense, was respectful of human dissent, and presented a loyal and sensible opposition to conservatism. He was a great thinker and a prolific writer, focusing on the relationship of history, law, and society. He adopted a scientific approach to political and social problems with deep analysis. Some of his works were influenced by English positivism and Benthamist utilitarianism. Above all, his works

> studied the country as the colonial period left it, both from the physical point of view and from the moral and intellectual point of view, observing how the population was distributed, and what were its habits, customs, accomplishments, inclinations, and means of subsistence. [He studied] its level of popular education in the various regions of the republic, and its distance from the most advanced societies in culture and civilization.[2]

From childhood, he was curious and was an uncommon observer of people and things; he remembered facts and circumstances of even minor episodes. For this reason, he was fond of phrenology, that ancient psychological doctrine, according to which mental attributes were located in precise areas of the brain that correspond to the shape of the skull, and that revealed the aptitudes and character of people. He studied this practice in New York, where he was associated with the firm of Camacho, Roldán y Vengochea. In 1851, he decided to have the shape of his skull analyzed in a Dr. Fowler's office, from which it emerged that he had "intellectual faculties suitable for science and literature, and willingly to engage in either of these two studies."[3]

His essay "El Estado Federal de Panamá" ("The federal state of Panama") is perhaps the most important publication on the subject in Colombia, in which his conciliatory position and visionary work as a jurist stand out. He contributed to the drafting of numerous constitutional texts, in which he sought to moderate the impetus of his contemporaries—the fire of Tomás Cipriano de Mosquera, the tranquility of Aquileo Parra, and the achievements of Rafael Núñez.

The isthmian state of Panama was the region of the Colombian federation with the greatest world trade. It had the highest number of foreigners and the republic's two most important infrastructure projects of the nineteenth century: the Panama Railroad (1855) and the French Canal (1881). Panama was in close contact with world powers such as England, the United States, and France. These conditions led Arosemena to meditate deeply on the relationship between the region and the political center in the context of the relationship between the United States and Spanish America.

Considering the nature of Latin civilization, Arosemena concluded that its foundation was democracy. Arosemena put all of his energies at the disposal of the Panamanians as an expression of his collective sense of nationality. He was described as "the man of greatest intellectual and moral stature that the Isthmus has produced" and was known for his "irreproachable honesty, for the integrity of his character, for his powerful intelligence, and for his vast knowledge."[4] Arosemena was recognized for:

> defying and overcoming prejudices, defending his convictions without weakness, and his duties while rejecting the privileges and conventions of obsolete positions in the name of freedom and justice as fundamental postulates of his religion without dogmas.[5]

He was, without a doubt, a tireless thinker, who always spoke and wrote with fervent truth and justice. He did not suffer fools gladly.[6]

Biographical information

Justo Arosemena Quesada was born in Panama City on August 9, 1817, and died in the city of Colón on February 23, 1896. He was baptized with the names of José Justo del Carmen on August 11, 1817, by the rector of the cathedral, Fr. José Calvo, with Blas Arosemena and Manuela Quesada as his godparents. He came from one of the few notable families living in the city, along with the Vásquez de Gortayre, Caparroso, Icaza, Arze, and Soparda families. The Arosemenas, who had arrived from Bilbao in the seventeenth century, stood out among these leading families.

Justo Arosemena was the son of Mariano Arosemena, who had participated in the struggle for freedom against Spain in 1821, and was related to the Marquises of Negreiros mentioned by Ricardo Palma in his *Traditions*. Justo's mother, Dolores Quesada, was of illustrious descent, related to the founder of Bogotá, Gonzalo Jiménez de Quesada. Justo's siblings were Manuela, Mariano, Blas,

Carmen, Luisa, Martina, and Dolores. Arosemena was the grandson through the paternal line of Colonel Pablo de Arosemena, Knight of the Royal and Distinguished Spanish Order of Charles III and Martina de la Barrera. Through his maternal line, he was the grandson of Miguel de Quesada and Catalina Velarde. With Pablo de Arosemena as his godfather, Arosemena was confirmed on September 29, 1818 by the bishop of Panama, José Higinio Durán.

After learning English at a very young age, Arosemena was enrolled at the age of five in the elementary school of his city, under the care of Alfredo Baquerizo, an Ecuadorian. He then entered the Colegio de Panamá, a secondary school, where Canon Dr. Juan José Cabarcas was the rector. After a family disagreement about whether to continue his studies in England or in Bogotá, his mother said that divine providence wanted him closer, and he was sent to the Colegio Mayor de San Bartolomé in Bogotá, accompanied by his uncle Blas, who had just been elected a senator.

At San Bartolomé, he obtained the degree of Bachelor in Humanities and Philosophy in 1833, then entered the Central University, where he received, with the signature of Ezequiel Rojas, the diploma of bachelor of jurisprudence in 1836. These studies were preceded by:

> the approval of the literature classes, which included: Spanish and Latin combined, Greek, English, French, literature, fine arts, eloquence, and poetry. In addition, classes in philosophy also had to be approved: mathematics, geography, physics, logic, ideology and metaphysics, morals and natural law. To obtain the degree of bachelor of law, the following courses were required: Principles of Universal Legislation, Constitutional Law and Administrative Science, International Law and Political Economy, Civil Law, and Ecclesiastical Law.[7]

After graduating and returning to his city, Arosemena started working in Panama in the office of Dr. Esteban Febres Cordero, a prestigious lawyer in the courts of New Granada, Ecuador, Peru, and Chile—countries in which Febres Cordero had lived and practiced law. After practicing for fourteen months in that firm, Arosemena traveled to Cartagena and enrolled in the University of Magdalena and Isthmus, obtaining the degrees of Bachelor and Doctor of Jurisprudence on December 22, 1837. The respective diplomas were signed by Dr. Bernardo José Garay, rector of the university, and by the most senior examiners, Dr. Dionisio Araújo and Dr. Manuel del Río.

Arosemena was admitted to practice before the Magdalena Court of Justice, covering the provinces of Cartagena, Santa Marta, Mompós, Panama, and Veragua. He sought a court in his city, which was established on May 15, 1835, despite the fact that the judges of the Magdalena Court heard cases originating in Veragua and Panama until April 30, 1838, when the Court of Appeals of the Isthmus was formally installed.

On March 19, 1838, before Fr. Manuel de la Barrera, canon of the cathedral, Arosemena married Francisca Barrera, daughter of Lino de la Barrera and

Josefa Velarde. Mariano Arosemena, Joaquín Morro, and Manuel Velarde served as witnesses. After Francisca's death, Arosemena married again in 1858 to Luisa Livingston. It was not a happy marriage.

Arosemena was President of the Sovereign State of Panama, minister of foreign affairs, and Ambassador of the United States of Colombia to Peru, Venezuela, and France, and to the United States as resident minister. He called the United States a "land of wonders, but unfortunately also of contrasts." He was also president of the South American Congress, where he would expound his pan-Americanist ideas and the plan of continental integration dreamt by Simón Bolívar. Arosemena made proposals on numerous topics, including "commerce and navigation, rights of domiciled foreigners and the protection of foreigners' property, private international law, counselor relations, postal and telegraphic communications, and grievances and war."[8]

Arosemena was also a representative to the House between 1851 and 1852. He proposed numerous bills with great success in enacting them into law. These included proposals for public education, the decentralization of income and expenditure, establishing properties in the province of Panama, reforms related to sealed paper and coinage, relations with Peru, real property owned by the state, concessions to the Panama Railway, housing, the elimination of fortifications, a school for girls in Bogotá, judicial reforms, abandoned land, commercial courts, and the transfer of the walls of Panama to that city.

Particularly important for our purpose, Arosemena proposed a bill on religious freedom. Article 1 established that all religions were permitted under the same equal treatment. The only concession was in favor of Catholicism, established by the constitution. Religious functions of any religion would be celebrated within the temples or buildings for such use. The faithful should support their ministers and priests. Furthermore:

> for civil purposes, marriage must be contracted in New Granada under the terms established by law. For religious purposes, the contracting parties may celebrate marriage before or after signing the marriage contract, according to the rites of their respective religion.

Civil divorce could be decreed by the authorities only in Panama. The United States of Colombia permitted this in 1924 by Law 54 after Colombia separated from Panama.

Arosemena was a convinced abolitionist and received a prize from the Institute d'Afrique, the French abolitionist society. He was one of the great ideologues of the Colombian federation, acting as President of the National Convention of Rionegro in 1863 and a member of the commission of ecclesiastical affairs that removed the name of God from the constitutional preamble. At the end of the convention, President Tomás Mosquera offered him the portfolio of interior and foreign relations. Refusing this honor, Arosemena was appointed on June 6, 1863, as plenipotentiary minister of the United States of Colombia to the Republic of Peru and extraordinary envoy and plenipotentiary minister to Chile, Salvador, Honduras, Nicaragua, and Costa Rica.

His visionary activity took him to Chile from 1866 to 1868, and there he was the proxy of a company established in New York to build a telegraph line, which would extend through Bolivia, Peru, Ecuador, and Colombia, with Chile and Panama as its Pacific ends. The development of transportation led him to consider an expeditious route from the Atlantic to the Panamanian Pacific by way of a navigable channel or a transisthmian railroad. "Arosemena, however, believed that because no serious calculations had been made of the cost of a waterway or a road, it was necessary to determine beforehand how much both would cost."[9]

In July 1869 he was elected deputy to the Legislative Assembly of Panama and senator for the State of the Isthmus to the National Congress of 1870 and 1871. He also served on the committees for accounts, foreign affairs, and petitions.

In 1876 Arosemena settled in London, his favorite city. In 1877 he published there *La Revolución en Colombia* (*The revolution in Colombia*), and in 1878 the second edition of *Constitutional Studies.* In 1879, under the pseudonym Philanthropus, he published *The Institution of Marriage in the United Kingdom.* In this work, he stated:

> in the legal sense, the word *marriage* already indicates *legality* in the union between man and woman. It is unquestionable that the essence of such a union is founded in nature. The permanent union between a man and a woman, with the objects that the law attributes to marriage, constitutes it in substance, even without the intervention of civil law. Therefore, marriage has existed in all ages and at all times, whatever the formalities to which the law, religion, or custom may be subject. That is why the Christian Church has also tolerated clandestine marriages in which there was almost no other formality than the will of the contracting parties.[10]

Arosemena used this study to homologate his law degree to practice in Chile.

Longer works also addressed a variety of subjects. He wrote *Apuntamientos para la introducción a las ciencias morales y políticas por un joven Americano* (*Notes for the introduction of moral and political sciences for a young American*), published in 1840 in New York by Juan de la Granja, one of the first political science and sociology texts for Latin America. It included a synoptic plan of moral and political sciences. One circle, the practice of demarcated rules of conduct, was surrounded by a second circle, that of the strategies of the moral and political sciences. The core of the diagram represented the general norms (nomology), which in positivist philosophy is a branch of ethics that studies the historical and geographical transformations of moral ideals.

His "Examen sobre la franca comunicación entre los dos Océanos," from 1846, explored the possibilities of "a great canal that, by cutting the Isthmus in which we live in the most complete way, would allow all ships to communicate freely between the two oceans."[11] He provided a preliminary study, the probabilities of the great nations to undertake the work, the explorations to be done, the interest of commercial nations in the work, the interest of private entrepreneurs, the likelihood that the Granadian Government would carry out the work (he criticized the apathy of the congressmen), and the advantages of such a construction for the Istmeños, particularly for the provinces of Panama and Veraguas.

In 1849 Arosemena published *Principios de moral política* (*Principles of political morality*), written as a catechism with questions and answers. Here, Arosemena provided the foundations of his ethical doctrine and cautioned that with independence, the condition of free citizens was attained without an understanding of the concomitant rights and obligations associated with this new status. He also defined the art of morality in terms of dogmatic morality and experimental morality. Dogmatic morality, based exclusively on religious authority, was inherently an art; but because it was not based on science, it was not universal. It served only the members of their respective religions. Experimental morality, based on human nature and either science or art, was universal and served all people.

As a result of later reflection, in 1860 Arosemena published *El Código de moral fundada en la naturaleza del hombre* (*The code of morals based on human nature*), which he called a philosophical entertainment. This work, in the form of 253 apothegms, attempted to apply the idea that to govern is to moralize, and to moralize is to improve. The application of morals was impeded in prisons, which Arosemena called "meetings of corrupt men." He said that "prisons did not fulfill the main purpose of punishment to amend the offender," because inmates imbued with vice "excelled in brazenness and impertinence."[12] The application of morals was not limited to penal laws and institutions but also extended to moderation in religious sanctions and ordinary education to ensure proper behavior of people. Thus, Arosemena's moral program was extensive.

El Estado Federal de Panamá (*The federal state of Panama*, 1855) was a key work in the historical, juridical, political, and economic construction of Panamanian identity. Through this work, Arosemena became recognized as a father of the nation.

In keeping with his vision of American unity, Arosemena wrote *Estudios constitucionales sobre los Gobiernos de la América Latina* (*Constitutional studies on the governments of Latin America*, 1878), his most ambitious work, with three editions. Here, he critically examined Latin American constitutional law of the late nineteenth century and its limits in view of the integrationist possibilities it offered. According to one scholar, Arosemena distinguished among different varieties of political thought:

> [prescientific publicists], such as all the socialists from Plato to Fourier; those scientists with partial contributions, such as Aristotle, Saint Thomas Aquinas, Bodin, Hobbes, Locke, and Montesquieu; and finally, those properly scientific, such as Comte, Guizot, Mill, Laboulaye, Tocqueville, and Hildreth. Arosemena praises above all the works of Tocqueville, *Democracy in America*, and of Hildreth, *Theory of Politics*.[13]

In *Constitutional Studies*, Arosemena analyzed the constitutions of the Empire of Brazil, Chile, Argentina, Uruguay, Paraguay, Bolivia, Peru, Ecuador, the United States of Colombia, the United States of Venezuela, the United Mexican States,

Guatemala, El Salvador, Nicaragua, Costa Rica, Central America, and Haiti. He analyzed their backgrounds with general and particular observations. This detailed and critical work led him to conclude: "There is no doubt that, with the exception of Brazil and Chile, none of them has completely achieved, and most of them are still far from realizing, the great consortium of freedom and order."[14]

In 1864, as a diplomat, Arosemena published *Estudio sobre la idea de una Liga americana* (*Study on the idea of an American league*) to promote regional integration as a continuation of Bolívar's proposals at the Congress of Panama in 1826. For Arosemena, nothing was more natural than the idea of union by treaty among weak independent states sharing a common origin, language, religion, and customs, and situated together in territories bathed by the same rivers and seas. Working in competition and together in the development of their great resources, these countries might aspire to the highest civilization. At the end of the work, Arosemena, included a draft treaty in twenty articles to found the South American League.

This work was followed in 1870 by *Constituciones políticas de América Meridional* (*Political constitutions of South America*), one of the first works of comparative constitutional law of the continent. It included his draft of the Constitution of the State of the Isthmus of 1841. The work provided a sociological synthesis of the Hispano-American civilization, with all its inherent problems, as reflected in the constitutions in force in the ten independent states or nations of South America (Brazil, Paraguay, Argentina, Uruguay, Chile, Bolivia, Peru, Ecuador, Colombia, and Venezuela). With these sources in mind, Arosemena offered a succinct but complete history of the political changes, governments, and constitutions that each country had from independence to the present. He also commented on each constitution, discussing its main provisions and comparing them with the constitutional precedents of the same country and with the contemporary constitutions of the other countries.

Arosemena was also a civic leader and drafter of legislation. In 1868, he was contracted to write the Judicial Code of Panama, including the organization and procedures; to revise the Code of Commerce; to prepare a military code; and to codify all the laws in force on public administration. Together with Dr. Antonio del Real, Arosemena offered drafts related to the civil code, rural mining, the criminal code, judicial organization, civil prosecution, and criminal prosecution. In 1892, he drew up, on behalf of the Council of Panama, a draft contract for the construction of a proposed aqueduct and published, in *La Situación*, his famous studies *Moneda en el Istmo* and *Qué es un peso*? Two years later, in 1894, he drafted a contract for the Council of Colón (1894) on electrical lighting, and indeed much earlier, by 1855, had proposed that Bogotá and Panama have hydrogen-carbonate gas lighting. He founded a shipyard in Taboga, drafted the statutes of the Panama Chamber of Commerce, and made a valuable donation of his books to its library to celebrate the fourth centenary of the first Columbian voyage to America. For the governor of the department in 1894, he prepared an enlightened draft decree regulating the service of day laborers and contract workers as well as limiting the work of women and minors, governing strikes, and remedying accidents at work. Again in 1894, he formulated a draft Code of Police Law for the department.

In Caracas in the 1880s, Arosemena was appointed commissioner *ad honorem* to represent the State of Panama in the celebrations of the centennial of the Liberator, held in 1883. Then, arriving from New York in 1885, he served as fiscal visitor, railroad inspector, and government agent before the United Company of the Inter-Oceanic Canal. He also founded a bank in Caracas, with the help of Samuel Piza and Recaredo Villa, who contributed twenty thousand pesos. Likewise, Arosemena grappled with the twenty-four volumes of information proposed by Venezuela in 1881 to establish land boundaries with Colombia, and he was the architect of the Spanish arbitration award of Queen María Cristina in 1891, settling this dispute.

Arosemena died in Colón on February 23, 1896 of an enlarged heart. His body was wrapped in a national flag offered by Colonel Shaler, superintendent of the railroad, and taken by train to Panama City to be laid to rest in the cathedral. He was buried, on behalf of the National Treasury, at 4:30 PM on February 24, 1896.[15]

On November 19, 1898, two years after Arosemena's death, the Congress of the Republic of Colombia, motivated by the fact that Arosemena left his wife destitute, decided to grant "to the widow of Dr. Arosemena, resident in New York, a monthly pension for life of two hundred pesos in paper money, whose equivalent in gold will be paid by the Consulate General of the Republic." In another expression of gratitude, on December 20, 1906, the National Assembly of Panama, noting that Arosemena died poor, "with poverty which is the best aura of his public career," ordered an oil painting with his image for the Assembly. In addition to the portrait, the Assembly paid for the professional studies of his grandson Demetrio Fábrega Arosemena, who, for lack of money, had not been able to continue his studies in Bogotá. Finally, on the centenary of Arosemena's birth, the National Assembly decreed that August 9, 1917, would be a national holiday.

Statements reporting Arosemena's relative poverty were true. He was never wealthy, and his fortune was limited to a few thousand pesos earned as a lawyer. He invested in stocks and bonds, especially in official debts of some South American countries, such as Colombia, Peru, and Venezuela. He acquired Coibits Island from the nation, but he never realized financial gain from this unusual acquisition.

Jurist

Arosemena wrote, drafted, and proposed various forms of legislation and legal projects. Taken together, these reveal his skill as a legal thinker with a practical bent. Nonetheless, these works also reveal a jurist steeped in sound legal structures and a deep understanding of law. As a jurist, Arosemena exhibited a highly structured approach to legal concepts. For example, at the Convention of Rionegro in 1863, he provided the following taxonomy of rights:

Unlimited rights to be guaranteed by law:

I. Life.
II. Belief. Its derivative, religion.
III. Thought. Its derivative, expression, whose forms are: word, writing, and the press, must be correlated with discussion, teaching, and learning, respectively.

Rights that must be guaranteed by law with limitations:

IV. Peaceful assembly without weapons.
V. Association, except to commit crimes.
VI. Voluntary love among those past adolescence.
VII. Movement, except in cases of:
  (i) judicial arrest:
    (a) for a crime which is being tried or punished;
    (b) for civil liability;
  (ii) military arrest in time of war;
  (iii) sanitary arrest in time of epidemic:
    (a) requiring passports;
    (b) prohibiting communication altogether.
VIII. Production, except for public health.
IX. Employment, except through criminal actions.
X. Property as defined in the Civil Code:
  (i) of what is produced;
  (ii) of land; and without any political encumbrance other than:
    (a) general contributions;
    (b) moderate fines;
    (c) expropriation (with compensation) for public use.

Similarly, on another occasion, Arosemena turned his attention to the structure of law set out in a series of codes. For Panama as a state within Colombia under the constitutional act of February 27, 1855, he proposed the normative structure of several codes—a total of six—with several divisions. The work provided for cross-references and concordances among the codes, and provided an attractive method of normative classification. Codes three through six addressed civil law, criminal law, judicial proceedings, and miscellaneous provisions. Codes one and two merit closer attention to gain an idea of Arosemena as jurist.

The topics addressed in these codes are:

Code 1. Political laws. This code embraced the organization of public power, except for details of the judicial branch. His code consisted of seven laws, including the constitution, which, in a complete body of legislation, must take first place. The remaining six, like all the other laws, would rest entirely on the constitution. Here is the nomenclature of the laws of the political code, according to their linkage and gradual dependence: constitution of the state, territorial division, organization of the secretariat of state, elections of state officials, organization of the executive administration, organization of military forces, and the municipal regime.

Code 2. Fiscal laws. This code embraced the area of public finances and taxes in the following structure: the public treasury, import and export, income tax, sealed-paper tax, the registration of documents, income from state property, postal services, benefits, administration of the public treasury, salaries of state officials, and the examination of accounts.

Arosemena also established himself as an early proponent of national administrative law. He similarly proposed social legislation with rights and obligations among individuals, as members of the society were "susceptible to be damaged by selfishness, or by lack of probity."[16] A government should provide structures and agencies to promote the essential ends of society. In this field, Arosemena proposed the following divisions: the administration of civil and criminal justice; a moral police to prevent and stop crimes and to pursue and guard criminals; a physical police to prevent and lessen natural calamities that threaten an indefinite number of people; and public works, enterprises, or operations of common utility, which neither individuals nor private companies are willing or able to undertake on their own.

To improve the provision of such essential services, Arosemena proposed that the government establish a staff of responsible officials. For example, for Panama, Arosemena advocated the transfer of federal national power to the regional states in several instances, including popular elections, the administration of the public treasury, aspects of military forces, the establishment of punishment or clemency supported by the state, and activities of a lower order that are more or less remotely aimed at better provisions of essential services. These principles and structures are an example of the rich wealth of ideas that Arosemena had spread with enviable success among his contemporaries.

Constitutionalist

Arosemena was a protagonist in the Colombian constitutional process of the second half of the nineteenth century. He helped shape the Constitutions of 1853, 1858, and 1863. Despite his journalistic work and other writings, Arosemena had time to devote himself to drafting so many provisions that they could have filled an entire book of constitutional acts for the Colombian confederation. These were separately published under the pseudonym of "Fabio." These works were discussed in the Congress of 1856 and were proposed with Arosemena's signature and those of Senators Manuel Murillo Toro, Salvador Camacho Roldán, Tomás Cipriano de Mosquera, Félix Villa, Camilo Ordóñez, Santos Gutiérrez, and Guillermo Pereira. This proposal, although it did not pass, was undoubtedly the basis of the Constitution of 1858, a second stop toward federation, when the country took the name of Confederación Granadina.

Arosemena was the president of the Rionegro national convention for the Constitution of 1863, the Rionegro Constitution. The driving forces in Arosemena's constitutional thought were equity and equality. Equity, according to the Spanish Royal Academy, is "natural justice, as opposed to positive law,"[17] but how could this justice be imparted in the United States of

Colombia? Arosemena considered not only equity but also the ways in which the states must provide equal treatment and conditions for all. Each province had the freedom to handle its own decrees, but everything must accord with the constitution.

Thus, Arosemena upheld state sovereignty as an essential principle of the federation. This principle was recognized from the first line of the first article, which also provided that the sovereignty of the nation was formed by the union of states. Later, in his *Estudios Constitucionales* (*Constitutional studies*), Arosemena expanded on sovereignty within the federal system and stated, "The Constituent Assembly of Colombia was the representative of a noble, lofty and courageous people."[18] Arosemena described the power of each state and how it resolves problems internally. He also, however, recognized a power centralized in the general sovereignty, so that if a problem that was beyond the control of the federal state arose, the governmental entities of the United States of Colombia would step in and control the situation in a balanced and fair manner.

Many observations by Arosemena on the constitutional level referred to a common end, an "alliance and eternal pact between nations," but at the same time, he stated that this type of alliance would always have difficulties. There had not been a consensus on several articles of the proposed text. Seeking justice in the new arrangement, Arosemena stated that "the best combination in each country is that which gives peace, order, security, freedom, and progress in every sense."[19] Similarly, Arosemena wrote that the "independence of the nation without the freedom of the citizen is a joke."[20]

A main issue in the Constitution of 1863 was the definition of rights, which remained mostly unexercised and neglected during the fratricidal period of continuous wars that for twenty-two years afflicted Colombia until the advent of Regeneration in 1885. Arosemena was drawn to the Venezuelan constitution as a model of precision and elegant expression. As president of the National Convention, a senator and a supporter of justice, Arosemena was questioned for his preference for constitutions and treaties belonging to other states, whose fidelity was questionable. Nonetheless, he was open to these sources. By 1870, he had already made one of the most important analyses of comparative law in Latin America. For example, Arosemena found it relevant to compare foreign sources on the inviolability of human life. He wrote:

> According to the first paragraph of Article 15 of the Colombian Constitution, it seems that the entire guarantee consists of not decreeing the death penalty in the law, which we consider to be a double error, since in addition to the fact that life is threatened by individuals no less than by the government, capital executions that are not based on a legal sentence and which are so common in all civil wars throughout the world are outside the constitutional prescription.[21]

Even then, capital punishment was an aberrant act. Within the context of civil war, it had to be handled with great care; if not based on a legal sentence, it might be outside the scope of the constitution. Although very controversial, this issue was of great political relevance at the time and lasted in Colombia until the abolition of capital punishment with the constitutional reform of 1910. Therefore, in the face of the preponderance of a right to life, for Arosemena, "nothing is more dangerous in politics, as in any other science, and especially those that refer to human behavior, than not admitting a principle with all its consequences."[22] Indeed, as early as 1856, Arosemena had begun drafting a law that commuted the death penalty to a prison term of ten to fifteen years.

Arosemena also sought to define individual freedom, since the freedom of each person cannot begin where that of another person ends. In a conflict of rights, individual freedom must yield, so that the most important right prevails. For this reason, Arosemena was able to discuss many of the articles and subparagraphs of the constitution with great clarity. Thus, equality and equity prevailed in many of his remarks and were to bring about changes, some only achieved with the secession of Panama in 1903.

Arosemena sought modifications to the Constitution of 1863. For him, there was injustice in governing Panama from Bogotá. Likewise, five years after the constitution was issued on May 8, 1863, Arosemena reviewed the text and affirmed that in that constitution, "the liberal party, taking its honesty to an extreme that no one demanded of it, consigned entirely new, contradictory, and impractical principles."[23] The constitution had a long list of civil rights, but it omitted the means of realizing them, and therefore, while it conferred many rights, it did not actually give any guarantees.

Rafael Núñez and Miguel Antonio Caro later led a movement to overcome the catastrophic era of the Constitution of 1863 and were harshly criticized by Arosemena. The new Constitution of 1886, drafted by a national convention of delegates tailored to the president's interests, centralized the government of the republic and suppressed the federal states. As a result, states lost their own representation, and the government was merged with the executive power so that the president became synonymous with the government for his term of six years. The governors or heads of new sections were placed under the executive, which had broad powers in cases of foreign war or internal commotion that were easily concocted for the purpose of asserting authority. With the consent of congress, the executive was granted certain extraordinary powers, even in times of peace, for reasons of public convenience. The new constitution also gave the president the power to appoint judges of the Supreme and higher courts, who, for the first time in the constitutional history of the republic, were granted life tenure. It also permitted the election to congress of executive employees, which, together with the veto, more effective now than ever before, gave the president a preponderant influence in legislation.[24]

The new constitution reestablished fuller relations between Church and state, and permitted religious education for the young. It defined certain guarantees and maintained capital punishment. It subjected the printing press once again to the vagaries of government authorities or judges, and hindered the free public expression of opinion; in fact, newspapers that did not praise the government were suspended. Dissident citizens were deported without trial. All of these actions called into question the progress claimed by the Regeneration.[25]

Conclusion

Justo Arosemena was a remarkable jurist of the nineteenth century who, despite world travels and multiple interests, remained focused on his native region and state of Panama. His broad-reaching studies of morals, history, trade, regional integration, law, and comparative constitutionalism permanently changed Colombia, Panama, and the region. He was a jurist, constitutionalist, and drafter of legislation, and many of his proposals were adopted and aptly met the needs of the time. His interventions in constitutional debates and his diligent construction of constitutional provisions shaped Colombian constitutionalism.

Notes

1 Méndez Pereira, *Justo Arosemena*, 159.
2 Moscote and Arce, *La vida ejemplar de Justo Arosemena*, 162.
3 Méndez Pereira, *Justo Arosemena*, 543.
4 Asamblea Nacional de Panamá, Ley 41 de 1906.
5 Méndez Pereira, *Justo Arosemena*, 543.
6 Ibid., 548.
7 Moscote and Arce, *La vida ejemplar de Justo Arosemena*, 15.
8 Ibid., 327–28.
9 Ibid., 118.
10 Méndez Pereira, *Justo Arosemena*, 381.
11 Arosemena, *Examen sobre la franca comunicación entre los dos Océanos*, 44.
12 Moscote and Arce, *La vida ejemplar de Justo Arosemena*, 132.
13 González Marcos, *Derecho comparado al servicio de la democracia*, 1:20.
14 Ibid., 2:323.
15 Méndez Pereira, *Justo Arosemena*, 550.
16 Ibid., 218.
17 Real Academia Española, *Diccionario de la lengua española.*
18 Méndez Pereira, *Justo Arosemena*, 330.
19 Constitution of 1863.
20 Moscote and Arce, *La vida ejemplar de Justo Arosemena*, 300.
21 Constitution of Rionegro, 1863, p. 88.
22 Méndez Pereira, *Justo Arosemena*, 326.
23 Moscote and Arce, *La vida ejemplar de Justo Arosemena*, 314.
24 Ibid., 419–20.
25 Ibid.

References

Arosemena, Justo. *Apelación al buen sentido y a la conciencia pública en la cuestión "Acreencia Mejicana."* Bogotá: Imprenta de Echeverría Hermanos, 1857.

Arosemena, Justo. *Apuntamientos para la introducción a las ciencias morales y políticas por un joven americano.* New York: Imprenta de don Juan de la Granja, 1840.

Arosemena, Justo. *Código de moral fundada en la naturaleza del hombre. Juguete filosófico.* Bogotá: Imprenta de Echeverría Hermanos, 1860.

Arosemena, Justo. *El Estado Federal de Panamá*. Panamá: Asamblea Legislativa, 2003.
Arosemena, Justo. *Estudio sobre la idea de una Liga americana*. Lima: Imprenta de Huerta, 1864.
Arosemena, Justo. *Examen sobre franca comunicación entre los dos Océanos*. Bogotá: Imprenta de Cualla, 1846.
Arosemena, Justo. *Principios de moral política redactados en un catecismo y varios artículos sueltos*. Bogotá: Imprenta de Cualla, 1849.
Constitución de los Estados Unidos de Colombia (1863). *Constitución de los Estados Unidos de Colombia, con antecedentes históricos i comentarios por Justo Arosemena*. Le Havre: Imprenta A. Lemale Ainé, 1879. Available at https://babel.hathitrust.org/cgi/pt?id=hvd.32044059057455;view=1up;seq=94.
Elespectador.com. *La Constitución de Rionegro*. Available at https://www.elespectador.com/opinion/la-constitucion-de-rionegro-columna-449386
Gobierno de la República de Panamá. Available at https://www.asamblea.gob.pa/biblioteca/biografia
González Marcos, Miguel. *Derecho comparado al servicio de la democracia. Estudios constitucionales de los gobiernos de América Latina por Justo Arosemena: Propuesta de una lectura*, Vol. 2. Panamá: Asamblea Nacional de Panamá, 2009.
Méndez Pereira, Octavio. *Justo Arosemena*. Panamá: Imprenta Nacional, 1917.
Moscote, José Dolores, and Enrique Arce. *La vida ejemplar de Justo Arosemena*. Panamá: Departamento de Bellas Artes y Publicaciones—Ministerio de Educación, 1956.
Real Academia Española. *Diccionario de la lengua española*. 23rd ed. Version 23.3 online. Available at https://dle.rae.es

16 Tristán Narvaja (Argentina and Uruguay, 1819–77)

Viviana Kluger

Biographical introduction

Tristán Narvaja was a jurist, professor, theologian, and politician who was born in the present territory of the Argentine Republic and carried out all these activities in Argentina, Chile, and Uruguay. Although a productive scholar throughout his career, he is best known as the principal drafter of the Uruguayan Civil Code of 1868. He was born in the province of Córdoba on March 17, 1819, to Pedro Narvaja y Dávila and Mercedes Montelles. Although he was given the name of José Patricio Tristán Narvaja y Montelles at birth, he was called Tristán at confirmation and later adopted this name.[1]

He learned Christian values at home and was taught to read and write by his father.[2] At the age of eleven, he entered school at the Franciscans' Convent in Córdoba, where he began studies for the priesthood, subsequently receiving the tonsure and the minor orders. Nonetheless, apparently suffering from a serious lung condition, he requested a dispensation because of health reasons. He may also have felt called to letters and the law rather than to the priesthood.[3]

In 1836 he completed his studies in theology, canon law, and jurisprudence. He did not receive the major orders and thus changed universities. In 1837 he traveled to Buenos Aires and enrolled in two degree courses at the university: theology and jurisprudence. He first obtained a doctorate in theology with a thesis titled *De misterio infallibile Sanctissimae Trinitatis* (*The infallible mystery of the Holy Trinity*).[4] On December 12, 1839, after completing the three-year law-degree course, he submitted his doctoral thesis in law, titled *Abolición de la pena capital* (*Abolition of the death penalty*). According to Armando Pirotto, in his thesis Narvaja pursued a courageous and solid defense of the abolition of the death penalty, thus embracing the ideas advocated by Cesare Beccaria and Gaetano Filangieri.[5]

On completing the doctoral degree, Narvaja was required by university rules to take practice courses at the Theoretical-Practical Academy of Jurisprudence of Buenos Aires and work as an articled clerk in a law firm. In March 1840, Narvaja joined the law firm of José Zorrilla and enrolled at the academy. However, his unitarian political ideas, contrary to those of the regime of Juan Manuel de Rosas in Buenos Aires, led to his arrest. On his release, like many other countrymen, he emigrated to Montevideo, where he settled in 1840.[6]

During his stay in Montevideo, Narvaja strengthened his ties with jurists Eduardo Acevedo, Dalmacio Vélez Sarsfield, and Joaquín Requena,[7] the last of these entrusted some years later with drafting the Uruguayan Code of Civil Procedure. On November 26, 1840, Narvaja requested permission to enroll in the Theoretical-Practical Academy of Jurisprudence in the city of Montevideo, to which he was introduced by Requena and Acevedo. He took the entrance exam in December of that year, then lived in Montevideo before returning to Buenos Aires in 1843. From there he traveled to Bolivia and then settled in Chile.

During his stay in Chile, he paid frequent visits to his relative, jurist Gabriel Ocampo, who was then to take part in the drafting of Chile's civil code. Narvaja settled in the city of Copiapó, where he built a successful law practice and gained extensive experience in mining legislation. In Chile, Narvaja wrote a highly praised study on mining law. Most importantly, though, he was close to the preparatory works of Andrés Bello's Chilean Civil Code, which he began to admire as a model of legislation. He focused his attention on the works and controversies revolving around the preparation of Chile's Civil Code. Narvaja lived in Chile until late 1853, then moved to Montevideo, where he lived until his death.

On his arrival in Montevideo, Narvaja revalidated his law degree and on February 3, 1854, and took the oath to practice law. That same year, he married Joaquina Requena Sierra—Joaquín Requena's daughter—with whom Narvaja had a daughter, Mercedes. When Joaquina died in 1865, he married Umbelina Tapia y Sierra, with whom he had five sons: Manuel Tomás, Tristán Hilario, Alfredo, Ricardo, and Augusto.[8]

In 1868, in recognition of his contributions to Uruguayan legislation, in particular the drafting of the civil code, he obtained citizenship by means of a decree issued by Provisional Governor Venancio Flores.[9] Narvaja died in Montevideo on February 19, 1877, at the age of fifty-seven, leaving behind five children.[10]

Teaching

Narvaja was a professor of civil law at the Law School of Montevideo between 1855 and 1873, a member of the Jurisprudence Commission of the University of the Republic in 1855, and a member of the University Council in 1864.[11] He began his teaching career when he was appointed to the chair of civil and commercial law of the School of Jurisprudence on May 8, 1855. He held this chair for seventeen years, until 1872.[12] He taught civil, commercial, and criminal law. He taught the law of nations in the early years of this subject in law faculties, and he renewed the study methods of civil law. During his years as a professor, he fostered the study of political economics, theology, and criminal law.[13] While a professor, he prepared a seven-hundred-page work summarizing his lessons, but for financial reasons it was not published. Some of the students who received their legal education from him later became prominent figures in Uruguay.[14]

Judicial and political activity

In 1872 Narvaja became a member of the Higher Court of Justice, where he actively worked for more than three years.[15] In 1875 he entered parliament as a deputy for the Department of Durazno and held that position for three months. As a legislator, he was a person of few words and an enemy of long interventions. According to his contemporaries, he would be quiet for entire sessions and would engage in debates only when an important matter was at stake. Nevertheless, these traits did not prevent him from taking part in international-law issues. For example, he introduced for the first time in Uruguay the use of the reservation clause in favor of bordering states. He also spearheaded the enactment of the rural code and submitted numerous initiatives designed to amend or supplement Uruguayan legislation. These reforms addressed the subjects of judicial liability, the repeal of a law of 1874 regulating the legal profession, and the creation of a register of naval attachments and mortgages.[16]

His work as a deputy included the publication in 1875 of an article titled "La libertad de defensa y el ejercicio de la Abogacía" ("Freedom of defense and the practice of law").[17] He also drafted a set of mortgage laws—which, according to Zachariae, were the best to that date—that established a radical separation between mortgages and privileges.[18] He left his legislative position in August 1875, when he was appointed minister of government by President Pedro José Varela Olivera. He was provisional minister of the treasury and of foreign relations until February 1876, when he retired to private life.[19]

Publications

While he was a student at the Academy of Jurisprudence, Narvaja published in 1841 his first legal work, *Administración de justicia en la República Oriental del Uruguay* (*Administration of justice in the Oriental Republic of Uruguay*), which summarized all the judicial regulations and practices in force in Uruguay during that period.[20] With a perfect mastery of Latin, Narvaja also translated classical works that were published in *El Nacional* in 1842 and 1843 and that, according to Peirano, reveal the humanist education he received during his youth in his hometown, Córdoba.[21]

His work *Ley Hipotecaria y Graduación de Acreedores* (*Mortgage law and the priority of creditors*) appeared in 1864 and was published by the government together with Narvaja's commentary the following year.[22] Some years later, in 1867, Narvaja published his article "Cuestión de oportunidad" ("A question of opportunity"), which consisted of an argument submitted by Narvaja before the Higher Court of Justice concerning an award of court costs in a probate proceeding.[23]

In 1871, after he had drafted and defended his civil code, Narvaja wrote *Sociedad conyugal y las dotes* (*Marital partnership and dowries*). According to Peirano, this work is the fruit of Narvaja's intellectual and legal maturity as he veered away from the interpretive methods to which the great European jurists were confined. The book reveals his general knowledge of legal history, comparative law, and sociology.[24] In spite of his well-known Christian thought, Narvaja departed from the religious tradition when he deemed it proper, and in this regard, in his work on marital partnership, he criticized the abuse of canon law in establishing ownership of the dowry. Moreover, he disapproved of the oath, as he thought it could be used to violate legal prohibitions made on public policy grounds.[25]

The Civil Code of the Oriental Republic of Uruguay

Narvaja's most prominent work was the drafting of the Uruguayan Civil Code of 1868, through which the country gained entry into a new and modern legal world. His code was conceived in line with the codification movement that spread across Europe and the Americas.[26] When Narvaja drafted the code, the codes of Chile, Peru, and Bolivia had already been enacted, and Dalmacio Vélez Sarsfield was working on the code of the Argentine Republic.

In Uruguay, Eduardo Acevedo in 1852 had prepared a draft civil code. On March 20, 1866, Uruguayan President Venancio Flores issued a decree mandating that the same commission that had revised the commercial code—enlarged to include Uruguayan jurist Joaquín Requena—revise Acevedo's draft code for the purpose of enacting Uruguay's Civil Code. The commission began work on July 1, 1866, and finished twenty months later, in November 1867; however, it did not work directly on Acevedo's draft, as envisaged by President Flores's decree, but on another draft prepared by Narvaja, which was nevertheless based on Acevedo's work. The preparation of the draft code demanded a great deal of energy and work from Narvaja: he had to close his law practice for almost two years and abandon all activities other than his university chair. Once concluded, his draft code was submitted for governmental approval. It was enacted on January 22, 1868, and came into effect on January 1, 1869.[27]

Plan, method, and sources of the code

As far as the language and style of the code are concerned, Narvaja adopted a technique similar to that of the Chilean code. This resulted in a clear, direct, and flexible code that allowed it to remain in effect in Uruguay for almost a century without the need for extensive reforms or substantial restructurings. With respect to the code's sources, Narvaja was well acquainted with studies and research into Roman law, all the previously enacted codes, and the work of the commentators on the codes of France, Austria, Louisiana, Holland, Prussia, Baden, Württemberg, Sardinia, Portugal, and Belgium, among others.[28] In this regard, Narvaja took into account the ideas of the greatest interpreters of the Code Napoleon—such as Raymond-Theodore Troplong, Charles Demolombe, Frédéric Taulier, Charles Aubry and Frédéric Charles Rau, among others, as well as the work of Andrés Bello, Eduardo Acevedo, and Florencio García Goyena.

Narvaja's code, however, was not a mere compilation of sources, as he took Uruguay's legislation, customs, usage, and the particular needs of the country into account. Accordingly, he departed from the solutions adopted by other codes when they did not respond to Uruguayan reality. The result was an eminently eclectic civil code. Narvaja thus removed from his civil code topics frequently found in other codes. These included, for example, civil death, fiduciary substitution, imprisonment for debt, betrothal, the vendor's right to rescind a sale on the grounds of extraordinary injury, grace periods, *restitutio in integrum*, the appointment of guardians for spendthrift persons, the legal mortgage, the reservation of property in case of second marriage, and preemptive rights and rights of first refusal.

Narvaja's code did not include footnotes to its articles, as did Vélez Sarsfield's code for Argentina. Indeed, Narvaja was not amenable to publishing the text of the annotated code. From his perspective, the code was not a scholarly work but rather a set of imperative or prohibitive formulas. Thus, it had to be confined to the naked text, devoid of any annotations, as that of any other law; this helped maintain the coercive force that compelled compliance with the law.[29]

Nevertheless, a publication was envisaged containing the annotations and commentaries that had served as sources of the Uruguayan civil code. Narvaja himself had included these materials in a copy of the code he had given to his friend Ponce and in another copy he had left to his sons Ricardo and Manuel.[30] However, this work was not published. An article published by his son Ricardo suggests that such publication might not have been forthcoming because, as Narvaja was a university professor, he could provide detailed and lengthy explanations of the code during his classes. According to Ricardo Narvaja, the codifier compared, reviewed, and studied ancient law, modern codes, a vast number of scholarly works, state law, and foreign law. [31]

Other codes

While Narvaja is widely known for the Uruguayan Civil Code, he drafted other codes and laws that helped to shape Uruguay's legal structure as an independent state. In 1865 Narvaja was appointed to a commission tasked with amending the commercial code. He participated substantially in the amendment and submitted the relevant report to the executive. This code, which came into effect on July 1, 1866, amended two hundred and fifty articles of Acevedo's Code and contributed new doctrinal views. Narvaja's work updated older commercial legislation by abolishing imprisonment for debt and civil death, reinforcing respect for commercial transactions regarding interest and contracts, repealing the grace periods customarily granted by courts to debtors and usury laws, incorporating the provisions of the mortgage law, and, ultimately, aligning commercial law with the legal trends prevailing at the time.[32]

Narvaja also drafted a mining code enacted on February 5, 1868. This work called on all the experience he had gained when in the field in Chile. Although replaced in 1884, this code incorporated basic mining law principles, such as the eminent domain of the state over all of its mining fields.[33]

Christian thought

As a university student, Narvaja studied classical Spanish and Latin religious and theological works under his principal law teacher, Rafael Casagemas.[34] In this respect, his education was similar to that of other jurists, such as Vélez Sarsfield (with whom he always had a close friendship), Lisandro Segovia, Pedro Somellera, Gabriel Ocampo, and many others who had studied in Córdoba.[35]

Narvaja's Christian thought was reflected in the regulation of marriage in his civil code, an approach in line with the education he had received at home and deepened through his years in Córdoba and religious studies. Narvaja grounded the religious regulation of marriage in his conviction that it was not possible to sweep away religious beliefs so deeply rooted in society. His note to the title on marriage in his civil code had a similar approach to that taken by Vélez Sarsfield in Argentina.[36] Consequently, Narvaja closely linked ideas of family and marriage to religion and canon law, evincing in such code provisions his religious convictions and radically departing from the liberal ideas prevailing at the time.

Narvaja recognized the legal validity of religious marriage, did not accept civil divorce, and entrusted the record of marriages to parish registers—thus opposing the idea of the state being in charge of civil registration. In this respect, the message issued by the members of the codes commission—Manuel Herrera y Obes, Antonio Rodríguez Caballero, Joaquín Requena, and Tristán Narvaja—to Governor Venancio Flores on December 31, 1867, commented that most states in Europe kept registers in the hands of the Church. Even in those countries where Catholicism was no longer the state religion, legislators did not believe they would easily find more able and trustworthy persons to whom they could entrust the delicate functions of civil status officers.[37]

Narvaja's code established that marriage between Catholics could be contracted only in accordance with the canons of the Catholic Church, and that the power to determine the validity of a marriage between Catholics lay with the ecclesiastical authority. Consequently, all questions relating to marriage impediments and their dispensation were reserved to the ecclesiastical authorities.[38] In addition, mixed marriage, that is, a marriage between a Catholic and a non-Catholic Christian—which was authorized by the Catholic Church—was to take place in accordance with the practices established by the Catholic Church. Again, the power to make a determination as to the impediments to such marriages lay with Catholic Church officials, as was the case with marriage between Catholics.[39] Nonetheless, and unlike the Argentine codifier, Vélez Sarsfield, Narvaja provided for the case of marriage between non-Catholic Christians and between persons who did not profess Christianity. The civil effects of such marriages were addressed in a special section on the impediments to them and the corresponding civil certificates.[40]

With regard to divorce, Narvaja's civil code vested the ecclesiastical courts with the authority to grant the divorce or separation of spouses previously married by, or with the authorization of, the Catholic Church. Thus, his code did not admit absolute divorce, and it vested only civil courts with the power to regulate the civil effects of religious divorces, such as in matters of community property, alimony, and child custody.[41] Nevertheless, Narvaja provided for the situation of those having contracted marriage without the authorization of the Catholic Church. In these cases, he established a civil divorce proceeding with no dissolution of the bonds of marriage.[42] The Catholic Church was vested with the authority to declare the nullity of a marriage contracted in accordance with its canons.[43] A separate procedure was set forth for determining the nullity of civil marriages or marriages contracted without the authorization of the Church.[44]

With respect to civil status, Narvaja entrusted parish registers with all the evidence of the civil status of persons, and the civil status of non-Catholic individuals could be demonstrated by certificates issued by civil authorities.[45] In addition, these civil registers were to be used for documents relating to the birth of children of non-Catholic individuals, as entered by a competent justice of the peace.[46]

Controversies around the Civil Code

The code was at the center of a number of controversies. One concerned the authenticity of the text and asserted that the text published in 1868 did not match the originals. In this respect, the reviewing commission reported through its chairman, Don Manuel Herrera y Obes, at the request of the Chamber of Representatives in August 1869, that the originals had been destroyed during the printing of the code. Nonetheless, the report confirmed that the printed text was, in the view of the codification commission that had approved it, the same as the text contained in the original manuscripts. It was thus confirmed that the text was authentic; the enemies of the code were discredited. It was also argued that the code was not only riddled with defects but also unconstitutional because it had a retrospective effect. Therefore, some asserted that the courts should refrain from applying it.

Narvaja had virtually no allies in his defense of the scientific merit of his work. However, through a number of articles published in *La Tribuna*, he defeated his detractors, among whom was the Argentine lawyer and politician Vicente Fidel López.[47] López criticized Narvaja for the lack of originality of the code, as it resembled the Chilean code; for his failure to include precedents of his own; and for substantive issues such as the definition of the contract. Narvaja defended the code's originality and pointed out that it was very difficult to create a work and too easy to criticize it.[48] This controversy ended in 1870, when, according to Peirano, López was unable to respond to Narvaja's reasons.[49] Finally, Narvaja was also criticized, especially by liberals, for having left the regulation of marriage in the hands of religious authorities.[50]

Final considerations

Despite his recognition as an important historical figure in the mid-nineteenth-century River Plate region, Tristán Narvaja was not popular in his time. This could have been due to his conservative Christian thought, which did not fit well with the liberal ideas prevailing in Uruguay at the time. Narvaja thought the scant esteem shown by his contemporaries could be explained by the fact that he was not Uruguayan.

Notwithstanding his Christian thought, Narvaja departed from his religious ideas when he considered them inappropriate in certain circumstances, respected the ideas of others, and excused himself from acting in those opportunities in which he thought his Christian position could prejudice his colleagues or disciples. An example of this restraint was when the essayist, politician, and lawyer Ángel Floro Costa submitted his doctoral thesis attacking the principles of the Christian dogma on marriage. On that occasion, Narvaja refrained from giving his opinion on the thesis in order not to prejudice his disciple, not even with involuntary bias, and explained in the University Council the reasons for his decision, which he had thought of disclosing in private to the rector of the university, Fermín Ferreira.[51]

Peirano, on the other hand, attributes the scarce esteem Narvaja received in life to his being an unlikable character with a serious and surly countenance, who kept away from social life at a time when a dilettante attitude was one of the basic features of Montevidean elegance. Added to this were his political affiliation and his collaboration with, and sympathy for, the dictatorial governments of Venancio Flores and Pedro Varela. When Narvaja died, his enemies stated that he lacked the best virtue: that of being a liberal, a viewpoint to which he never adhered due to the lasting impact of his Christian education and settled beliefs.[52]

His death went unnoticed. The university in which he had been a professor for seventeen years, and whose council he had served as a member, hesitated before sending a letter of condolence to his family, alleging that his public actions did not warrant such a gesture. At the session of the University Council held on March 2, 1877, Rector Berinduague recalled Tristán Narvaja's death and proposed that a letter of condolence be sent to his family. Justino X. Jiménez de Arechaga argued that the proposition was not fair, as the public actions of Doctor Narvaja did not merit such deference. Antonio E. Vigil, successor to Narvaja in his chair, held that a letter should be sent, as that did not mean deifying him but simply lamenting his loss. Arechaga responded that Narvaja had had many defects and that every man should be excused for his defects, but defects had a limit—implying that Narvaja's had gone well beyond that limit. At that point, the rector proposed a vote on the issue. Carlos M. de Pena argued that a distinction had to be made between the politician, the University Council member, and the professor, and added that while he was an enemy, like no other, of the politician, he admired the professor, and therefore, he thought a letter of condolence should be sent to the family. Pedrales stated that Narvaja had served the university for a long time and that the letter did not need to make reference to the political problem. Finally, the issue was put to the vote, and it was resolved that a letter of condolence would be sent to the family of the codifier, with two of the council members voting against such decision.[53]

Narvaja was a valuable figure with an active involvement in the legal profession, university teaching, the legislature, and the political world. At his death, he left behind an important yet understudied corpus of legal work, the best known of which is the Uruguayan Civil Code of 1868, which made it possible for Uruguay to enter the legal modernity of the time. This code, while it was a reflection of the ideas circulating in other latitudes, did not lose sight of Uruguayan customs and needs. This trait has allowed it, with certain amendments, to remain in force until today.

Notes

1 Pirotto, "El doctor Tristán Narvaja."
2 Maiztegui Casas, "El Codificador Adusto."
3 Pirotto, "El doctor Tristán Narvaja," 62.
4 Peirano Facio, *Tristán Narvaja*, 26.
5 Pirotto, "El doctor Tristán Narvaja," 63.
6 Peirano Facio, "Semblanza de Tristán Narvaja," 101.
7 Pirotto, "El doctor Tristán Narvaja," 64–65.
8 Peirano Facio, "Semblanza de Tristán Narvaja," 101 and 105, 66, 106 and 108, 109–10.
9 De León, *Tristán Narvaja*.
10 Peirano Facio, "Semblanza de Tristán Narvaja," 126.
11 De León, *Tristán Narvaja*.
12 Peirano Facio, "Semblanza de Tristán Narvaja," 110–12.
13 Peirano Facio, *Tristán Narvaja,* 13.
14 Peirano Facio, "Semblanza de Tristán Narvaja," 112.
15 De León, *Tristán Narvaja*.
16 Peirano Facio, *Tristán Narvaja*, 73–85.
17 Narvaja, "Libertad de defensa."
18 Carve, "Apuntaciones biográficas," 13.
19 Peirano Facio, "Semblanza de Tristán Narvaja," 125.
20 Peirano Facio, *Tristán Narvaja*, 29.
21 Peirano Facio, "Semblanza de Tristán Narvaja."
22 http://liberalism-in-americas.org/258, last accessed on January 17, 2019.
23 Narvaja, *Cuestión de oportunidad*.
24 Peirano Facio, "Semblanza de Tristán Narvaja," 115.
25 Peirano Facio, *Tristán Narvaja*, Annex 6 and 169-–70.
26 Ibid., 9.
27 Ibid., 58–69.
28 Tristán Narvaja, *Fuentes, notas y concordancias*, xvii.
29 Ibid., xxviii–xxi, xiv.
30 Peirano Facio, "Semblanza de Tristán Narvaja," 110–11.
31 Narvaja, *Fuentes, notas y concordancias*, xxiii, introduction, xvi.
32 Peirano Facio, "Semblanza de Tristán Narvaja," 116.
33 Ibid.
34 Rafael Casagemas was appointed to the chairs of civil law and natural law and of law of the nations in 1832, both of which he held until 1857, with a brief interregnum in the latter chair by Valentín Alsina between 1834 and 1835. See Cutolo, *Nuevo diccionario biográfico argentino*, 28–29.
35 Peirano Facio, *Tristán Narvaja*, 31.
36 According to Pirotto, "El doctor Tristán Narvaja," 83.
37 Civil Code for the Oriental State of Uruguay, signed into law by the provisional government on January 23, 1868, and enacted by the Honorable Assembly on July 20, 1868 (Montevideo, Imprenta de La Tribuna, 1868), III.

38 Article 87.
39 Article 88.
40 Articles 90–100.
41 Articles 145–46.
42 Articles 148–71.
43 Article 172.
44 Articles 173–81.
45 Article 41.
46 Article 43.
47 Peirano Facio, "Semblanza de Tristán Narvaja," 118–19.
48 Pirotto, "El doctor Tristán Narvaja," 88.
49 Peirano Facio, "Semblanza de Tristán Narvaja," 118–19.
50 Pirotto, "El doctor Tristán Narvaja," 81.
51 Peirano Facio, "Semblanza de Tristán Narvaja," 107–08.
52 Ibid., 107.
53 Peirano Facio, "Semblanza de Tristán Narvaja," 107.

References

Carve, Luis. "Apuntaciones biográficas. Tristán Narvaja." *Revista de la Asociación de Escribanos del Uruguay* 57 (1971): 11–15.

Cutolo, Vicente Osvaldo. *Nuevo diccionario biográfico argentino (1750–1930)*. Buenos Aires: Editorial Elche, 1947.

De León, Marcelo. *Tristán Narvaja. Historias universitarias.* File prepared within the framework of the unpublished project directed by M. Blanca París de Oddone, Diccionario de Personalidades de la Universidad de la República 1849–1973. Available at http://historiasuniversitarias.edu.uy/wp-content/uploads/2017/10/Narvaja_Tristan.pdf (last accessed on December 28, 2018).

Maiztegui Casas, Lincoln. "El Codificador Adusto." *El Observador*, October 15, 2006 (10–11).

Narvaja, Tristán. *Cuestión de oportunidad.* Argument submitted by Dr. Tristán Narvaja before the Higher Court of Justice. Montevideo, 1867.

Narvaja, Tristán. *Fuentes, notas y concordancias del Código Civil de la República Oriental del Uruguay.* Montevideo: Tipografia y litografia Oriental, 1910.

Narvaja, Tristán. "La libertad de defensa y el ejercicio de la abogacía." Speech delivered by Dr. Tristán Narvaja at the session of the Chamber of Representatives held on July 9, 1875. *Revista de Derecho, Jurisprudencia y Administración* 2 (1895): 282–84.

Peirano Facio, Jorge. "Semblanza de Tristán Narvaja." *Revista de la Asociación de Escribanos del Uruguay* 57 (1971): 97–126.

Peirano Facio, Jorge. *Tristán Narvaja, un jurista rioplatense en tiempos de la codificación.* Buenos Aires: Instituto de Investigaciones de Historia del Derecho: Editorial Dunken, 2008.

Pirotto, Armando. "El doctor Tristán Narvaja." *Revista de la Asociación de Escribanos del Uruguay* 57 (1971): 60–96.

17 Gabriel García Moreno (Ecuador, 1821–75)

Peter V.N. Henderson

Introduction

Born to an elite family on December 24, 1821, Gabriel García Moreno grew up in Ecuador's principal seaport, Guayaquil, then a city of some twenty thousand inhabitants. The youngest of nine children, Gabriel proved academically precocious. His mother, Mercedes, a very devout woman, hoped he would choose a career in the Church. Although the family attempted to homeschool Gabriel, his obvious brilliance led Mercedes to ask the family's priest, Father Miguel Betancourt, to tutor young Gabriel. Astonished that the young man had mastered Latin in ten months, Father Betancourt urged that Gabriel be sent to Quito, the country's largest city and capital, to complete his education. Entering the Colegio San Fernando, García Moreno had every intention of eventually seeking a degree in theology at the University of Quito. At age seventeen, he even took minor orders and received the tonsure—the haircut of an acolyte.

A year later, he changed his mind. Whether his decision to forgo a career as a priest in favor of a degree in jurisprudence was because of a growing interest in politics or his recognition that he simply did not have the calling for the priesthood remains a matter of dispute. Throughout the remainder of his career, however, his religious devotion would be entangled with his pragmatic desire to shape Ecuador's laws in accordance with Catholic beliefs. Like most law graduates in nineteenth-century Latin America, García Moreno expected to serve his country as a politician rather than as a practicing attorney. On García Moreno's graduation in 1848, a friend noticed his growing interest in national matters and suggested that he write a book about Ecuador's history. "I prefer to make it," retorted García Moreno.[1]

His political profile broadened in the 1850s when he took up his vitriolic literary cudgel in defense of the controversial religious order of the Jesuits, a position that alienated him from Ecuador's liberal president. While exiled in Paris from 1853 to 1856, García Moreno experienced a rekindling of his faith. Chided by friends for not going to confession, he mended his ways, attended mass daily, and devoured a twenty-nine-volume work titled *Histoire Universale de l'Église Catolique*. Pope Pius IX's idea of ultramontanism, designed to strengthen papal leadership and reinvigorate the Catholic faith as a counterpoise to nineteenth-century liberalism, intrigued García Moreno, who saw the papacy as a potential ally in his efforts to reform the clergy and to construct the Catholic nation. By 1859, García Moreno's countrymen recognized him as one of the principal leaders of the conservative, pro-clerical faction of Ecuadorian politics.

The year 1859 marked Ecuador's near disintegration into four parts as the result of a regionally based civil war. When the liberal government inadvertently provoked a Peruvian invasion, García Moreno disavowed the actions of the liberals and rebelled with the backing of conservatives from the interior. By 1860 the country faced not only the Peruvian occupation of the south coast but also a four-way civil war between the liberal generals in Guayaquil, García Moreno and the conservatives in the northern and central highlands, and breakaway movements in the provinces in the interior south (Azuay) and the far south (Loja). After the Peruvians retreated and the tide of battle turned against the liberals, García Moreno persuaded the governments of Azuay and Loja to join him, but only after conceding that the provinces would retain considerable autonomy under a new constitution. Meanwhile, he had learned his limitations as a military commander and so persuaded independence hero Juan José Flores to lead the final assault on Guayaquil in September 1860. Now García Moreno faced the task of overcoming regionalism and uniting the nation. His solution would be to utilize the Catholic faith as the common denominator with which, he believed, all Ecuadorians could identify.

From García Moreno's perspective, very little went right during his first presidential term (1861–65). The federalist Constitution of 1861, designed to protect regional interests, essentially emasculated presidential powers. García Moreno's domestic agenda in part featured an ambitious modernization effort. To overcome topographical divisions caused by Andean geography, he proposed a modern road system and even a railroad that would unite the country physically and promote greater economic activity. But the lack of revenues, caused largely by the opposition of regional interests emboldened by the federalist constitution, hampered progress. For example, García Moreno wanted to use the *trabajo subsidiario* tax (levied on Indigenous men in lieu of labor requirements) to pay workers to build the National Road from Quito to Guayaquil; instead, municipalities insisted that the funds be spent on local projects and maintenance. García Moreno had more latitude with his "Catholic nation" project because the legislature authorized him to pursue a concordat (treaty) with the papacy.[2] But foreign entanglements—two wars with Colombia and ongoing troubles with Peru—sapped Ecuador's limited discretionary budget and prevented much progress. Constitutionally barred from reelection, García Moreno placed two unsatisfactory interim presidents in office. During these four years, he remained Ecuador's indispensable man by crushing the liberal exile invasion at the battle of Jambelí and leading recovery efforts in northern Ecuador following the devastating earthquake of 1868.

García Moreno's aspirations for a Catholic nation came to fruition during his second term (1869–75). His Constitution of 1869 provided the framework for the administration's policies and strengthened the president's authority. To imbue the next generation with Catholic principles, García Moreno invested heavily in a free parochial school system. In addition to primary schools, the government expanded the number of secondary schools and created several new institutions of higher learning, including the Polytechnic Institute as well as the College of Obstetrics. The lifestyles and practices of the adult generation proved harder to reform, but García Moreno attempted to punish moral turpitude such as public drunkenness, concubinage, and adultery.

The Catholic nation ideal also promoted contemporary technology to geographically unify the nation. First, the president proposed a network of six roads that would knit together all regions of the country and provide access to multiple ports. Of these highways, only the García Moreno Highway from Quito to Guayaquil was completed (with the final segment being a narrow-gauge railway). The new road reduced travel time between the two cities from a minimum of two weeks to four days. Supplementing the road system, the government strung telegraph wires to speed communications. As Ecuador's economy expanded, new lighthouses and improved port facilities helped increase traffic to Guayaquil, although the city retained its reputation as the "pesthole of the Pacific" because of its all-too-common yellow fever epidemics. Although cacao constituted Ecuador's primary export (and would do so until 1920), the country offered the world a fairly broad array of other natural products too.

In sum, García Moreno's achievements, especially during his second term, exceeded the accomplishments of any of his predecessors. But his government and laws based on Christian principles came at a cost. Liberals in particular anguished over the diminution of their liberties and political freedom. Because his fervid religiosity made him the iconic Catholic statesman, he was a polarizing figure and aroused significant antipathy from liberals throughout South America. Perhaps not surprisingly, then, he was brutally assassinated on August 6, 1875, four days before he would have been sworn in for his third term as president. So much did his work appeal to conservative Catholics, however, that over the next fifty years, several adherents mounted campaigns to have him declared a martyr and a saint.

The defense of the Jesuits

In 1767, Spain's King Charles III initiated a controversy about the Society of Jesus that would continue well into the nineteenth century by expelling the religious order from all of his possessions in Europe, Asia, and Latin America. Founded originally as a militant organization to restore Catholicism in those parts of Europe where the Protestant Reformation had seeded itself, the Jesuits later expanded their operations to Latin America and Japan. Unlike other religious orders, the Jesuits' superior general reported directly to the pope. Well educated and extremely devout, the Jesuits quickly gained a reputation as very successful businessmen, operating large *haciendas* throughout Latin America whose profits funded the Jesuits' schools and their missions along the frontiers of the empire in places like Paraguay, the Oriente of Ecuador, and upper California, the so-called Rim of Christendom.[3] Because the order demanded that its friars be well educated, Latin American elites enrolled their sons in Jesuit *colegios* and universities in many Latin American cities.

By the late eighteenth century, the monarchy's view of the usefulness of the Jesuits changed. First, as the Bourbon kings sought to regain more authority over their empire, they feared the independence of the Jesuits headquartered in Rome, unlike other religious orders housed within the Spanish domains. Second, enlightened monarchs like Charles III agreed with writers like Jean-Jacques Rousseau, who portrayed the Jesuits as reactionaries opposed to new ideas. Finally, rumors (later proven false) about the extraordinary wealth of the Jesuits aroused the cupidity of Latin Americans and the monarchy, which hoped to realize immense sums from the confiscation of Jesuit properties. By all accounts, Latin Americans were only impoverished by the loss of their best teachers, who returned to Europe, leaving vacancies in the educational system that would not be filled for years.

The debate about the proper role of the Catholic Church in the newly independent Latin American republics in the early to mid-nineteenth century proved to be the most contentious issue dividing liberals from conservatives. The Jesuits served both sides as a useful symbolic pawn in the argument. As probably the most religious country in South America (Simón Bolívar referred to it as a "monastery"), Ecuador prolonged the debate longer and more contentiously than elsewhere. The Jesuits stood at the heart of the controversy.

García Moreno's first contribution to Catholic jurisprudence in Ecuador was his advocacy for the Jesuits. In May 1850, the Colombian Government ordered their expulsion from the country, and the rabidly anticlerical general José María Obando executed the decree by forcing the Jesuits to march from southern Colombia to the port of Santa Marta in the north, where they had passage for Jamaica. However, they preferred exile in a Catholic land and took refuge on a British ship that conveyed them to Panama. Meanwhile, García Moreno, returning with his brother Pedro Pablo from a European business trip on July 19, 1850, encountered the Jesuits in Panama and offered to intervene on their behalf with the Ecuadorian Government. He argued that these educated Jesuits could contribute to the school system and by their good behavior help to clean up the rampant corruption prevalent among Ecuadorian monastic institutions. When Obando learned that the Jesuits intended to go to Ecuador, he protested and unsuccessfully urged the Ecuadorian Government to reject them, but Ecuador's devout civilian president agreed to grant them asylum. Subsequently, Obando conspired with Ecuadorian liberal general José María Urbina to overthrow the sitting government and expel the brothers.[4]

The plot eventually succeeded in September 1851, when Urbina's army swept the moderates from power. Almost immediately, Colombia's Minister to Ecuador, Jacobo Sánchez, published a diatribe and demanded the Jesuits' expulsion. García Moreno responded in kind in November with a sixty-two-page essay, titled "In Defense of the Jesuits," in which he attempted to refute each of Sánchez's arguments while simultaneously engaging in *ad hominem* attacks against the author. García Moreno reiterated the positive benefits Jesuits could provide as teachers and missionaries and denied they were political activists. He characterized the attacks of the Reds (as he called them), as "enemies of the Catholic faith." His strongest argument, made as a nationalist, pleaded that Colombia had no more right to dictate Ecuador's clerical policies than Ecuador did to insist that Colombia expel the Freemasons and socialists.[5]

Meanwhile, Urbina called for a constituent assembly to meet in the liberal stronghold of Guayaquil in July 1852. In his proclamation, Urbina pointed out that the liberal revolution promised to promote peace with Colombia, a strong signal that the topic of the Jesuits' presence in Ecuador would be subject to debate. Not surprisingly, the liberal delegates at the assembly (acting as the legislature) overwhelmingly passed a statute on October 2, 1852, expelling the Jesuits. Protests led by elite women, especially in the conservative highland cities, erupted. As the time designated for expulsion neared, García Moreno organized a petition in Quito which eight thousand people signed, requesting a delay. But the government remained adamant. A military force surrounded a Jesuit church in Quito and, on a rainy evening in November, escorted the brothers to Guayaquil.

Six days later, on November 21, García Moreno penned his final words on the matter in a two-page essay titled "Adios to the Jesuits." He made the case that a miscarriage of justice had occurred, claiming the Jesuits had been persecuted because they defended the Catholic faith. In addition, García Moreno underscored the disappointment of the people from the highlands, who appreciated the brothers' good deeds. Finally, he wished the brothers better luck, hoping that they would end up on peaceful and happier shores, as most of them intended to pursue their work in Peru.[6]

True to his word, a decade later García Moreno fulfilled his promise to bring back the Jesuits. The Constituent Assembly of 1861 authorized him to negotiate a contract for their return. After their previous experience, their superior general demanded guarantees before sending friars to Ecuador again. Two trusted envoys, Antonio Flores (future president, 1888–92) and Ignacio Ordóñez (later Bishop of Cuenca) negotiated the contract. The superior general insisted on restitution for the Jesuits' lost property so that the order would have sufficient funding to accomplish its missions. By the end of July 1863, he signed the contract, and several Jesuits made preparations to sail to Ecuador. Without hesitation, García Moreno approved the arrangement, knowing that Jesuits would serve as effective math and science teachers—the core of a more modern curriculum.

The Jesuits made significant contributions to secondary and post-secondary education during García Moreno's second term. The president's own interest in science led him to create several new specialized institutes. His pet project, the Polytechnic Institute, offered practical training in engineering, metallurgy, surveying, and architecture. Fortuitously, just as García Moreno launched the Polytechnic, Germany's "Iron Chancellor," Otto von Bismarck, expelled Jesuits who taught science from his country as part of his *Kulturkampf* program. Several of these exiles came to Ecuador, including Juan Menten, who oversaw the construction of the Astronomical Observatory in Quito; Teodoro Wolf, who authored a multivolume work on the geography and geology of Ecuador; and

Josef Kolberg, who wrote a narrative describing the Jesuit missionary effort in the Amazon. Each held faculty positions at the Polytechnic. However, the birth of the Polytechnic proved premature because the government's interest in the project dwindled after García Moreno's death, and preindustrial Ecuador could not offer much in the way of employment to these graduates.[7]

The concordat

Concordats in international law are specialized legal agreements between a given country and the Holy See. In the aftermath of the wars of independence, Latin American nations generally aspired to regularize the relationship between themselves and the papacy and settle issues of competing jurisdictions—which matters fell under the domain of the Church and which fell under the jurisdiction of the state. Governments like the liberal one in Gran Colombia (of which Ecuador was a part) claimed they had inherited the *patronato real* (Royal Patronage) in its entirety from Spain after severance of the imperial tie, and so asserted in the Patronage Law of 1824. That patronage power granted to the Spanish monarchs by Pope Julius II, in 1508, among other matters permitted the state to select high Church officials like bishops and archbishops who then would be formally approved by the Holy See. The papacy disputed the continuity of *patronato* and the legality of the Patronage Law of 1824, absent a formal concordat.[8]

Beginning in the 1850s, conservatives in Latin America enjoyed a resurgence of influence; therefore several such governments sought concordats. Pope Pius IX began negotiating concordats with Latin American countries in the 1850s: Bolivia signed the first such agreement in 1851, and Costa Rica and Guatemala followed suit the next year. These concordats presumed the exclusivity of the Catholic faith and restored other traditional privileges to the Church. Although Pope Pius conformed to a general formula for every concordat, each differed somewhat depending on national circumstances. Pope Pius hoped that Ecuador would respond favorably to the idea of a concordat because of its peoples' reputation for piety.

Not surprisingly, after the conservatives' victory in the civil war of 1859–60, they wanted to negotiate such an agreement. Delegates acting as the sitting legislature, once the Constitution of 1861 had been approved, authorized García Moreno to enter into this discussion. The language of the enabling statute, however, was ambiguous and later proved a bone of contention between liberals and conservatives.[9] On its face, the statutory language appeared to authorize the newly elected President García Moreno to negotiate the treaty and sign it on behalf of the republic before submitting it to Congress for ratification during the August 1863 session.

For his part, García Moreno sought the concordat for several reasons. First, on a policy level, he saw the Catholic faith as the cornerstone of Ecuador's national identity—the force that would unite all Ecuadorians in a common belief in a nation governed by Christian principles. Subsequently, many of his enemies and even modern historians have drawn the erroneous conclusion that he wanted

Ecuador to become a theocracy—a state governed by priests. Strictly speaking, these critics are completely incorrect. Rather, García Moreno advocated for a powerful secular executive to administer a modernizing state guided by moral, Catholic practices.

Second, García Moreno hoped that the concordat would empower the Church (with his assistance) to clean up the country's longstanding problem of clerical corruption caused by abuses of the *fuero*, or clerical privilege. Two of Ecuador's most famous eighteenth-century visitors, Jorge Juan Santacilia and Antonio de Ulloa, had detailed in their secret report the moral laxness of the clergy which continued unabated into the 1860s. García Moreno was determined to end this state of affairs: "The corruption of the clergy surpasses that of all other classes of society, but I am prepared to moralize the country and I am not afraid of the difficulties." Priests continued to seduce women in the confessional, including one abuser whom García Moreno accused of "imitating Byron's *Don Juan*." On more than one occasion police detained drunken monks who had abandoned their cloisters—all behaviors García Moreno found unseemly.[10] He initially believed that by granting the Church more independence regarding spiritual matters, it would reform itself and become his partner in his Catholic nation.

At the end of 1861, García Moreno ordered young Ignacio Ordóñez, the archdeacon of the Cuenca Cathedral and brother of one of his important political allies in France, to negotiate the concordat. He chose Ordóñez in part because he could fund his own travels, in part because he spoke French fluently, and in part because he was already in Europe hiring Christian Brothers and Jesuit educators for Ecuador. The envoy received nine specific instructions from the president. These instructions included allowing papal bulls to pass through to Ecuadorian clergy without interference by the state, clerical oversight of education, and a revision of the *fuero* eliminating appeals (*recurso de fuerza*) to Ecuador's secular courts while allowing secular courts to prosecute clergy for minor crimes. In addition, García Moreno proposed an end to the traditional *patronato real* but instead would allow the papacy to select Ecuador's bishops and archbishops while the government retained the right to reject a corrupt candidate. He also wanted to create three new dioceses as the constituent assembly had suggested. He requested the right to close convents that failed to follow the rules of their order and sought a compromise on tithe income and other church revenues. In sum, he "wanted the Church to have all the independence it needs to comply with its divine mission."[11] Above all, he insisted that the papacy grant him authority to end clerical corruption. García Moreno believed that these provisions would be consistent with the new role that Pius IX claimed for himself after 1848.

The revolutions of 1848 had stripped the papacy of its political role in central Italy. No longer did Italians believe, as some had in early 1848, that Pius IX could be the instrument of Italian unification. Pius's treatment at the hands of the revolutionaries (he felt so threatened that he fled Rome at night disguised as a priest) not only advanced his conservativism but also reconciled him to the idea that his role was now limited to being the spiritual leader of the Roman Catholic faith. As such, he pursued the idea of ultramontanism, namely, that his spiritual authority (and even infallibility) extended throughout the Catholic world.[12] García Moreno completely concurred and conceded the pope's complete authority in spiritual matters.

Ordóñez arrived in Rome in early 1862 and spent three months negotiating with Cardinal Giacomo Antonelli, the papacy's foremost diplomat. During this time, Ordóñez deviated significantly from García Moreno's instructions. For example, he abandoned García Moreno's idea that the papacy should have a free hand selecting Ecuador's bishops and archbishops, and instead proposed the *terna* system—whereby local clergy would propose three candidates for the office, the president would select one, and Rome would make the formal appointment. The draft agreement also stated that the pope, not civil authorities, would decide whether to create new dioceses. The question of tithe allocations remained to be decided later. Most importantly, the draft concordat did not address the process for reforming corrupt orders. On May 1, 1862, Ordóñez and Cardinal Antonelli signed the twenty-five articles, and Ordóñez returned to Ecuador to present it to García Moreno.

Even before Ordóñez arrived, he heard rumors that García Moreno had concerns about the negotiated draft because it contained no language specifying ways to implement reform. Almost immediately, the president ordered Ordóñez back to Rome bearing three letters outlining revisions to the draft agreement. Two of the letters addressed reforming the *fuero* system. First, García Moreno demanded that clergy who repeatedly violated their vows be stripped of their *fuero*. Second, the president requested that offending clergy be tried in civil courts if the local bishop agreed. Although the pope hoped for milder measures, García Moreno demanded tough penalties against reprobate monks as the best means of reducing immorality within the regular orders. The third letter asked the pope to confirm the legal title to confiscated Church property that citizens had bought during the liberal years, allegedly in order to salve their consciences. The Church, however, would be permitted to acquire new income-producing property to further its mission. The papacy agreed to these terms, and García Moreno signed the amended concordat in April 1863. García Moreno believed that by signing the concordat, he had complied with the procedural requirements of the enabling statute, and that Congress retained minimal amendment authority.[13]

The publication of the signed concordat brought howls of protest. Liberals and members of the Church hierarchy spoke against it for very different reasons. First, liberals like Guayaquil's Pedro Carbo thought that the agreement ceded too much influence to the Vatican. As the leading voice on the city's Municipal Council, he penned a text, "The Exposition," in May 1863, in which he laid out the liberals' objections to the concordat. He argued that the president procedurally exceeded his constitutional authority because the document called for congressional ratification of all international treaties *before* receiving the presidential signature. Carbo also argued that the concordat inappropriately delegated to the executive branch other powers constitutionally granted to Congress and the judiciary. Practically speaking, Carbo and his allies had no interest in helping García Moreno create the Catholic nation. Rather, they preferred the Church–state relationship embodied in the Law of 1824. Despite García Moreno's threat to resign if the concordat was not ratified, Congress insisted upon debating the document during the legislative session of 1863.

Simultaneously, members of the clergy also registered opposition to certain articles of the concordat. The hierarchy objected to the plan to create three new dioceses in the cities of Riobamba, Ibarra, and Loja. As the minister of war commented: "The high clergy objected (to the new dioceses) not for the love of the Holy Father, but to avoid the plan to reduce their salaries to a fixed and moderate one."[14] Because tithe income would remain constant, the creation of three new dioceses would transfer a portion of the income of the archbishop of Quito and the bishops of Guayaquil and Cuenca to the new bishoprics.

García Moreno quickly recognized that he needed to compromise. Therefore, he seized the initiative and, on August 22, penned a letter to Congress proposing six revisions. The most important of them proposed creating fixed fees for clerical services; redivided tithe income to benefit Ecuador; lessened the salaries of the existing episcopal sees so that new dioceses in Riobamba, Loja, and Ibarra could be funded; and suppressed any convents where fractious monks refused to follow their order's regulations. The apostolic delegate, Francesco Tavani, who had come to Ecuador to oversee the final implementation of the concordat, felt betrayed by García Moreno's proposed compromises. In turn, García Moreno now saw Tavani as an impediment to his reforms because Tavani insisted on retaining traditional *fueros* and opposed the creation of the new dioceses. As García Moreno explained to his leading diplomat, the revisions represented political expediency. Congress had sent word requiring these changes before formal approval, and so, lacking the votes, García Moreno acceded to its wishes. In the final draft, the Chamber of Deputies added another provision, outlawing the proposed practice of letting papal communications proceed directly to the Ecuadorian hierarchy without prior governmental approval.

García Moreno had misgivings about the prospects of renegotiating the reallocation of tithe money. "The odious issue of the tithe, in particular, might cause the pope to refuse further changes." Tired of wrangling with Congress and embroiled in the early stages of a war with Colombia (whose president, Tomás Cipriano de Mosquera, threatened to invade Ecuador in September 1863 to recreate the union of Gran Colombia and prevent Ecuador from reaching an agreement with the pope), García Moreno felt he had no choice but to agree to the revised concordat. "It is true I agreed to the reforms…but I accepted them because of the Colombian threat."[15]

In 1864, Antonio Flores traveled to Rome to meet with Cardinal Antonelli, who assented to the congressional revisions because they were identical to concessions recently granted to three Central American republics. Pope Pius and Cardinal Antonelli agreed with García Moreno's desire to purify monastic institutions by allowing the government to dissolve corrupt monasteries, because the archbishop of Quito still had not enforced discipline. Antonelli also supported García Moreno's objective of bringing the faith closer to the people by creating the new dioceses and more parishes, but insisted that each new diocese open a seminary to train priests and provide adequate funding for the bishop and the cathedral chapter. As García Moreno predicted, the tithe issue proved complex. The Vatican agreed to allow a committee of clergy and government officials to set the tithe ratio. In the meantime, Pope Pius generously granted Ecuador all of the tithe revenues from 1863 and 1864 to defray the costs of the Colombian War. Despite García Moreno's pessimism, the committee finally agreed to increase Ecuador's share of the tithe permanently from one-third to one-half, as Congress hoped.

Once the committee resolved the tithe issue, the creation of the new dioceses began in earnest. By creating new dioceses, García Moreno decentralized the Church hierarchy and thus permitted newly installed bishops like Ignacio Ordóñez (now ordained as the bishop of Riobamba) to assign more priests to rural parishes. New seminaries opened to supply priests to smaller communities. Before this reform, the majority of Ecuador's clergy lived in the country's three largest cities; afterward, Ecuadorians in smaller towns also heard the Mass and received sacraments. Making the sacraments available to more parishioners furthered the president's vision of creating the Catholic nation. Despite the opposition of liberals, who complained that Ecuador now had as many bishops as more populous Peru, the new bishoprics and their seminaries opened in 1865. Officially signed in April 1866, the concordat succeeded in decentralizing the Catholic Church and making the faith more accessible to Ecuadorians. The concordat stood as the most durable achievement of García Moreno's first term and constituted García Moreno's second major achievement as a Catholic jurist.

The Constitution of 1869

Gabriel García Moreno made his final contribution to Ecuadorian jurisprudence in January 1869, when he drafted an extremely conservative constitution to replace the moderate Constitution of 1861. During his tenure as special diplomatic envoy to Chile in 1866, he expressed his admiration for his host country, which, in the early nineteenth century, had been the most stable of Latin America's republics. García Moreno attributed the relative calm of Chilean politics to the effectiveness and durability of its Constitution of 1833. Although the wording of Ecuador's Constitution of 1869 would not precisely replicate the language of Chile's instrument, the principles would look very similar. García Moreno offered his proposed draft to the constituent assembly (comprised almost exclusively of his friends and allies), who adopted the draft with few changes. The assembly then submitted the proposed constitution to the electorate in the form of a plebiscite, which was overwhelmingly approved in July 1869.

The new constitution achieved two of García Moreno's long-term objectives: to strengthen the president's role, and to lay the foundation for a Catholic nation. First, it strengthened the powers of the executive branch of government, allowing an active president to exert authority over the entire nation while diminishing provincial autonomy. It also weakened the national legislature, limited municipalities' ability to retain tax revenues, and restricted citizens' personal liberties. As a consequence (particularly of the latter ideas), liberal critics dubbed the Constitution of 1869 the Black Charter.

First, the Constitution of 1869 strengthened the president's role. Reflecting back on Ecuador's post-independence history, García Moreno made the plausible case that constant political upheavals had disrupted almost all progress towards modernization. The solution, he believed, would be to create a government more like Chile's, where, between 1833 and 1860, presidents served essentially ten-year terms, then rigged the next election for a like-minded successor who would provide substantial continuity of policy. As its first step in this direction, Ecuador's Constitution of 1869 lengthened presidential terms to six years and allowed for immediate reelection (Article 56). The constitution charged the president with three primary responsibilities: to preserve order within the country; to assure the national security of the country; and to defend the constitution and the laws (Article 59). Article 60 provided more specificity: the president convened Congress, nominated Supreme Court justices, issued pardons, named the cabinet, directed diplomacy, oversaw the treasury, commanded the armed forces, and could declare a "state of siege" (martial law) in times of emergency.

Recall García Moreno's utter frustration with the Constitution of 1861, which had delegated significant powers to municipalities and hampered his efforts to undertake national projects such as road construction. The Constitution of 1869 removed these (literal) roadblocks. By granting the president the right to appoint provincial governors, *jefes políticos* (political chiefs, who administered cantons), and even the political lieutenants who presided over municipal councils, the executive could control regional officials and tax revenues (Article 60[5]). To maintain a watchful eye over the provinces, García Moreno required every governor to submit monthly accounts about political and economic activities within their province. In addition, provincial inspectors of education reported directly to the president. Even bishops occasionally informed the president about pressing issues. For the first time since the 1830s, Ecuador enjoyed a smoothly functioning bureaucracy that allowed Quito to respond to crises.

Article 19 diminished the role of the legislature. Congress met only every other year for sixty days. While Congress could impose taxes and negotiate loans, the president had the right to collect the money and allocate expenditures. Congress reviewed the budget and expenses when it met, but in practice the power of the purse lay with the executive branch. Congress could promote education and science and could legislate about uniformity of the coinage (Article 35). When the legislature was not in session, the Council of State (whose members the president named) served as the advisory body for the president (Article 69). Congress could pass statutes, but if the president vetoed the legislation in its entirety, the measure could not be brought up again until the next congressional session, two years hence (Article 41). If the executive vetoed portions of the law, Congress could adopt his suggestions and the statute would be approved. Otherwise, the proposed law could not be revisited for two years (Article 42). Likewise, the constitution hardly provided for an independent judiciary, because judges were elected for six-year terms with no lifetime tenure.

The firm hand of the executive branch also allowed the president to limit citizens' civil liberties. Not surprisingly, the Constitution of 1869 did not grant the broad spectrum of civil liberties commonly found in liberal constitutions. Although citizens could not be arrested without a warrant (Article 91) and enjoyed a presumption of innocence until proven guilty (Article 95), other commonly observed freedoms were limited. For example, the constitution guaranteed citizens free speech and a free press, "as long as religion, morality, and decency were observed" (article 102). Unarmed citizens could associate freely, but could do so only as long as they "respected religion, morality, and public order" (article 109). Other freedoms found in liberal constitutions were not enumerated in the Constitution of 1869 because, in García Moreno's view, they constituted a threat to public order.

Second, the constitutional provisions laid the foundations for the Catholic nation. The creation of a strong, centralized government that guaranteed orderly governance was not an end to itself but rather the means for creating the Catholic nation—García Moreno's other great project. Thus, consistent with the terms of the concordat, the state in partnership with the Church would act to expand educational opportunities and uplift the morality of those who transgressed against accepted societal beliefs. As a result, Ecuador would realize a sense of national identity in conformity with the will of the people.

Thus, not only did the Constitution of 1869 retain the colonial ideal of the exclusivity of the Catholic faith (Article 9), but Article 10 went further and made being Catholic a necessity for citizenship and suffrage, a most unusual requirement. In reality, this provision disenfranchised few people, as well over 99 percent of Ecuadorians were Catholic. (A tiny Jewish minority and a handful of Protestant businessmen and diplomats lived throughout the country.) More liberals were denied citizenship under Article 13 because they "belonged to a society prohibited by the church"—language that included the Freemasons. Otherwise, literate Ecuadorian males over the age of twenty-one (or eighteen if married) enjoyed the right to vote. Other provisions reflected the importance of the Church in Ecuadorian society. Article 7 required all citizens to respect religion. Unlike in liberal states, clergy played a role in government as one cleric served on the Council of State (Article 69).[16]

García Moreno believed that with free, mandatory, elementary education delivered by members of religious teaching orders who would inculcate the proper values into the next generation of citizens, he would lay the foundation for a durable Catholic nation. The president controlled the funding of education, oversaw expenditures, and supervised the provincial inspectors of education (Article 60[8] and 60[9]). To fulfill the mission of molding good Catholic youths, the administration paid to bring European friars and nuns who specialized in primary education to Ecuador. (Their arrival virtually eliminated the use of poorly educated Ecuadorian friars in the classroom.) The order of the Christian Brothers, founded in the seventeenth century, advocated the modern LaSalle method of instruction, where the teacher worked directly with students rather than using less well-trained monitors to do so. Likewise, the order of the Sisters of the Sacred Heart sent accomplished teachers to fulfill their vocation working with Ecuadorian girls. Education expenditures increased from fifteen thousand pesos before 1861 to over a hundred thousand pesos annually in the 1870s, in part because of García Moreno's commitment to education, in part because of enhanced revenues from expanding cacao exports, and in part from the reduction of military expenditures. The primary school system enrolled over thirty-two thousand pupils by the end of García Moreno's second term. Teachers not only offered a standard elementary school curriculum but also instructed students in religion, Christian doctrine, civility, and morality—all key values of the Catholic nation.

The president aspired to establish a primary school for boys and girls in each parish. To do so, the government had to locate a suitable building, equip it adequately (including a portrait of the Virgin Mary), and pay the teachers' salaries (always near subsistence level). To preserve girls' honor, separate school facilities had to be provided for them. Despite authorizing legislation, schools rarely existed on *haciendas*, where landlords preferred to keep charges working. Indigenous communities resisted mandatory education as well, because in their view the curriculum's intent was to hispanize them. To try to resolve this problem, García Moreno created a "normal" school (teachers' college) for prospective Indigenous teachers, but it never attracted many students. Despite the government's aspirations, it never had sufficient revenues to meet the demand for education. As a result, ordinary citizens continued to bombard the president's desk with petitions to fund more schools.[17]

Although García Moreno prioritized primary education, he also expanded secondary and post-secondary education. He funded secondary schools in all provincial capitals (most intended for boys, although some girls' schools opened). Although the government provided some scholarships, enrollments were limited effectively to higher-income families because students paid tuition, room, and board. Based on his personal experiences, García Moreno chose the Jesuit order to instruct secondary school boys. The president required each Jesuit instructor to bring scientific equipment with him to provide more science classes in the curriculum. Having visited Western Europe and the United States, García Moreno understood that technology would play an increasingly important role in Ecuador's modernization. For students continuing to postsecondary education, García Moreno opened several new schools in addition to maintaining the University of Quito. These post-secondary schools (the Polytechnic Institute, the College of Obstetrics [for women], seminaries, a military academy, a normal school, a trade school for artisans, as well as the Conservatory of Music and the School of Fine Arts) all offered practical education that would contribute to the nation-building project.

While the government designed the educational system to shape the malleable minds of the younger generation, the regime also attempted to improve the morals of the adult population. Morality crusades in Latin America dated back to earliest colonial times, but they found revived emphasis in García Moreno's second presidential term. Reforming adults' morality has never been easy. Two transgressions particularly concerned García Moreno: public drunkenness and sexual activities outside the bonds of matrimony. Statutes passed in 1870 criminalized both of these activities.

Public drunkenness has long concerned moral reformers up to the present. (The revolutionary Mexican government of the 1930s conducted a very active campaign against vice.) These campaigns often targeted Indigenous communities. Market days offered an occasion for men to imbibe, as did religious festivals where syncretized Catholic and Indigenous customs included drinking rituals. García Moreno changed market days from Sundays to prevent the spectacle of drunken parishioners. He and his governors attempted to end semi-religious holidays like Carnival, when vice manifested itself. Those convicted of public drunkenness paid fines or served terms in the municipal jail. In reality, however, elites who commonly drank to excess in the privacy of their own homes (such as United States Minister to Ecuador, Edward Rumsey Wing) faced no punishment other than the president's snide comments.

Concupiscence also troubled García Moreno's scruples. Indigenous couples in the highlands continued to practice trial marriages into the 1860s and beyond. Likewise, in Guayaquil and other coastal communities, where sexual mores were less stringent, couples of all economic and cultural backgrounds engaged in non-marital sexual activities. Lists of individuals charged with violating the sexual morality statute arrived on the president's desk each month. The fact that these lists continued to be lengthy until 1875 suggests the futility of trying to modify adult behavior.[18]

García Moreno's devotion to creating the Catholic nation manifested itself in other ways. For example, he dedicated Ecuador to the Sacred Heart of Jesus, a favorite cult of conservatives and Pope Pius IX. The cult stood for the redemptive power of Jesus's love and acted as a symbol for rejecting secular liberalism. With García Moreno's encouragement, Congress passed a statute in 1873 authorizing the cult's establishment, making Ecuador the first Latin America nation to embrace the Sacred Heart.[19] During the 1880s, successor presidents began constructing a large basilica in Quito dedicated to the cult. This final gesture by García Moreno reemphasized his belief that only the Catholic faith could bind the Ecuadorian people together into a nation.

Conclusion

García Moreno's political career intersected with legal issues at three critical junctures. His contributions qualify him as one of Latin America's great Christian jurists. First, as a persuasive advocate, he convinced a sympathetic president to accept exiled Jesuits from Colombia. García Moreno's writings ignited public outrage against their re-expulsion by a new liberal government, allowing for their return in the 1860s. Second, he negotiated a concordat with Pope Pius IX that allowed Ecuador to reestablish formal relations with the Holy See, reform corrupt monastic orders, and extend the Church's services to smaller and more remote communities. Finally, he drafted the Constitution of 1869, which allowed him to formulate policies to create a Catholic nation consistent with the values, as he perceived them, of the Ecuadorian people. Although after 1895 liberals reversed these accomplishments, García Moreno's skillful legal reform efforts made him stand tall as the leading Christian jurist in nineteenth-century Ecuador.

Notes

1 There are more than thirty biographies of García Moreno in multiple languages. The most comprehensive is Severo Gomezjurado's *Vida de García Moreno*. The most scholarly Spanish language biography is Luis Robalino Dávila, *Orígenes del Ecuador de hoy: García Moreno*. For an English language biography, see my *Gabriel García Moreno*. The quote is from Augustine Berthe, *García Moreno, presidente del Ecuador*, 1:101–06.
2 Henderson, "La Constitución de 1861," 47–69.
3 Bolton, *Rim of Christendom*.
4 Loor, *Jesuitas*, 16–35.
5 García Moreno, in Pólit Laso, *Escritos de García Moreno*, vol. 1, 3–98, and 99–101.
6 Loor, *Jesuitas*, 162–215.
7 Henderson, *Gabriel García Moreno*, 165.
8 King, "Ecuadorian Church-State Relations," 41-44.
9 King, "Ecuadorian Church-State Relations," 1-8; Bustos Videla, "Church in Ecuador," 55–85.
10 Henderson, *Gabriel García Moreno*, 69–71.
11 King, "Ecuadorian Church-State Relations," 122–27.
12 Kertzer, *The Pope Who Would Be King*.
13 King, "Ecuadorian Church-State Relations," 128–44, 161–67.
14 Daniel Salvador to Juan José Flores, August 22, 1863, BC/JJC (Banco Central, Fondo Jacinto Jijón y Caamaño), Libro 000167, #80.
15 García Moreno to Antonio Flores, February 10, 1864, in Loor, *Cartas de García Moreno*, vol. 3, 200.
16 Borja y Borja, *Las constituciones del Ecuador*, cxxiv, cxxvii–cxxviii.
17 Henderson, *García Moreno*, 153–74; Rodríguez, *The Search for Public Policy*, 82–84. For the demand for schools, "We see primary education as the foundation of public happiness and the future of families." Petition from parents and inhabitants of the parish of Atuntaqui to the Secretary of Gobierno, May 10, 1862, ANHG, (Archivo Nacional de Historia, Ministerio de Gobierno), Imbabura, (1862) #47.
18 List of prisoners for sex crimes, Governor Santisteban to Minister of the Interior, February 21 and September 5, 1872, AHNG, Guayas, #55 and 217.
19 President of the senate's report, October 8, 1873, contained in RDS (Records of the US Department of State) T-50, reel 13.

References

Berthe, Augustine. *García Moreno, presidente del Ecuador: Vengador y mártir del derecho cristiano*. Paris: Victor Retaux é Hijo Libreros Editores, 1892.

Borja y Borja, Ramiro. *Las Constituciones del Ecuador*. Madrid: Ediciones Cultura Hispánica, 1951.

Bustos Videla, César. "Church and State in Ecuador: A History of Politico-Ecclesiastical Relations during the Age of Gabriel García Moreno." PhD dissertation: Georgetown University, 1966.

Gomezjurado, Severo. *Vida de García Moreno*, Vol. 13. Cuenca and Quito: Various publishers, 1955–75.

Henderson, Peter V. N. *Gabriel García Moreno and Conservative State Formation in the Andes*. Austin: University of Texas Press, 2008.

Henderson, Peter V.N. "La Constitución ecuatoriana de 1861: el debate." *Procesos: Revista Ecuatoriana de Historia* 30 (2009): 47–67.

Kertzer, David I. *The Pope Who Would Be King*. New York: Random House, 2018.

King, William Martin. "Ecuadorian Church-State Relations under García Moreno, 1860–1864." PhD dissertation: University of Texas, Austin, 1974.

Loor, Wilfrido, ed. *Cartas de Gabriel García Moreno*, Vol. 4. Quito: La Prensa Católica, 1956.

Loor, Wilfrido. *Los Jesuitas en el Ecuador: su ingreso y expulsion, 1850–1852*. Quito: La Prensa Católica, 1959.

Pólit Laso, Manuel María. *Escritos y discursos de Gabriel García Moreno*, Vol. 2. Quito: Encuadernación Salesianas, 1923.

Robalino Dávila, Luis. *Orígenes del Ecuador de hoy: García Moreno*. Quito: Talleres Gráficos Nacionales, 1949.

Rodríguez, Linda Alexander. *The Search for Public Policy: Regional Politics and Government Finance in Ecuador, 1830–1940*. Berkeley: University of California Press, 1985.

18 Julián Viso (Venezuela, 1822–1900)

Gustavo Adolfo Vaamonde

Introduction

The life of nineteenth-century Venezuelan jurist Julián Viso had a personal dimension and an intellectual one. On the personal and professional level, Viso presents a biography of a prominent lawyer, professor, and diplomat who left lasting legacies in each area of his public life. On the intellectual level, we are fortunate to have his many proposals and projects as a law student, legislator, and educator. Together, these dimensions shed light on this leading Latin American intellectual and the complex formation, development, and consolidation of the juridical order and institutions in independent Venezuela.

Viso was born in 1822 in the city of Valencia, during the wars of Spanish American independence. The former Captaincy General of Venezuela is now part of Colombia.[1] Even though the patriot army had defeated the Spanish forces in the Battle of Carabobo, in 1821, monarchical authorities controlled several territories for two more years. Royalist guerrillas lingered until the early 1830s. Viso's childhood thus coincided with the movements of national liberation and the beginning of independent states in South America.

This leading Venezuelan experienced the nineteenth-century trials, tribulations, and successes of his new nation. As in other South American nations, the consolidation of independence and the establishment of new institutions were complex and, at many junctures, traumatic developments. Colombia was unable to maintain its precarious political stability once the last representatives of the Spanish monarchy departed. In 1830 Venezuelan legislators promulgated a new constitution that dissolved Colombia and established the new Venezuelan Republic. For almost three decades, the republic experienced relative tranquility while introducing liberal policies to consolidate its institutions. In 1858 the Long War, also known as the Federal War, shattered the peace when political actors—many of them hailing from the independence era—split into two factions. The war resulted in substantial loss of lives, infrastructure, and national wealth. While resolving the first major schism of independent Venezuela, the Peace Treaty of Coche of 1863 inaugurated an era of significant political instability, reflected in constant confrontations and protests known as revolutions. Armed violence became the regular means to act politically because the legal methods of political participation had not fully developed. These revolutions disrupted how the government and administration of justice worked until the first decade of the twentieth century.[2] Half a century of wars kept the new nation and the new state in distress. This history accounts for the difficulties that contemporaries faced when developing strategies and projects to achieve political, economic, institutional, and social stability in Venezuela.

The convulsed history of the nineteenth century framed how Viso envisioned his innovative legislative and educational policies to consolidate the new nation. His goal was to establish the social, legal, and constitutional foundations to build a country from its infancy. Thus, one of Viso's biographers called him "the founder of Venezuela's nationality."[3]

A family of lawyers

Julián Viso's parents were Antonio Viso and Josefa Antonia Berbén Arias. It was the second marriage for both of them. Antonio was a Spaniard who had arrived in Venezuela in the late eighteenth century.[4] His first marriage resulted in three children, including the well-known patriot presbyter José Félix Blanco. During the late colonial period, Antonio and one of his brothers were employed in the Royal Audiencia of Caracas. Established in 1786, this audiencia was the Spanish monarchy's highest tribunal or court of justice in the Captaincy General of Venezuela. Antonio held the positions of *procurador* and public defender.[5] His career highlights suggest that a broad spectrum of colonial society respected his legal acumen. Most notably, Antonio represented the leading men of color of late-nineteenth-century Caracas, including Diego Mejía Bejarano and Miguel José Landaeta.[6]

On February 10, 1795, Charles IV issued the controversial order of *gracias al sacar*. This order allowed vassals belonging to the *castas* (people of mixed races) to attain, for a fee, "licenses, exemptions, and prerogatives" previously limited to white vassals.[7] Venezuelan *pardos* (people of white and black ancestry) saw the order as a means to circumvent their stratified society, with Antonio representing their interests against the white elite. At the other end of the social and ethnic spectrum, Antonio Viso also provided legal representation to Francisco Espejo, the most noted colonial lawyer of his generation. In his role as the Royal Audiencia's prosecutor, Espejo led investigations to prosecute pro-independence movements in Venezuela in the late eighteenth century and early nineteenth century.[8] When Espejo himself joined the Spanish American rebels in 1810, Antonio defended him against a charge of sedition in 1812.[9]

Josefa Antonia Berbén Arias was born in the city of San Carlos, in the Province of Venezuela. Her father was Simón Berbén, a peninsular military man in Venezuela's Veteran Battalion. In 1772, he was a lieutenant stationed in the city of Caracas. Later, he worked as a scribe for colonial lawyers and as an administrator of the royal tobacco monopoly in San Carlos, where he founded a primary school. During the wars of independence, Berbén joined the patriot army.[10] In 1806 his daughter Josefa married José Ramón Azpurúa Peláez, a clerk of the prominent lawyer Juan Germán Roscio.[11] The couple settled in San Carlos, where Azpurúa Peláez assisted his father-in-law in the royal tobacco monopoly and later in his school. José Ramón and Josefa Antonia had three children: María del Carmen, Gertrudis Concepción, and Ramón, who was to become a famous politician, writer, diplomat, and biographer. During the Wars of Independence, Azpurúa Peláez became a cavalry officer in the patriot forces and died when fighting royalist guerrillas in 1814. The widowed Josefa Antonia relocated to the city of Valencia, where she married Antonio Viso. In addition to Julián, they had another son, Antonio.

Law and education surrounded young Julián, thanks to his father and maternal grandfather's activities. Tradition thus rooted his interest in law. He had remarkable siblings. His brother, Antonio Viso, was an influential economic adviser during the presidencies of Antonio Guzmán Blanco in the 1870s and 1880s. His half-brothers, José Ramón Azpurúa and José Félix Blanco, are still remembered for *Documentos para la historia de la vida pública del Libertador*, a monumental published collection of historical documents related to Venezuela. To have siblings who were leading public figures may have encouraged Viso's desire for study and research. Furthermore, Viso had social connections with the most distinguished families and the leading politicians in Valencia and Caracas. The siblings had significant commercial ties, a facet of Viso's life that is not yet well understood.[12]

Viso was a partner at the firm Azpurúa & Company, which focused on the "building and maintenance of public works that were subjected to competitive bidding by the government through provincial deputations."[13] This family connection provided Viso with some personal wealth as well as business and political opportunities that led him to develop legal, educational, and diplomatic skills and initiatives.[14]

The study and codification of law in Venezuela

Julián Viso distinguished himself foremost as a law student, lawyer, and legislator. His contributions set valuable precedents in Venezuela's institutional and legal history during its first decades. His legal study began at the University of Caracas in 1841. He soon demonstrated his interest and talent when focusing on the philosophy of law and the juridical doctrine of substantive and procedural rights. As a young student, along with his classmate Pedro Pablo del Castillo, Viso wrote *Código de Procedimiento Ilustrado: Con notas sobre Derecho español y doctrinas de pragmáticos* (*An illustrated code of procedure, with notes on Spanish law and pragmatic doctrines*). He apprenticed first in the law office of Doctor José de Jesús Paúl, *licenciado relator de la corte* (lawyer rapporteur of the court), and later continued to gain experience under José Nicolás Milano, chancellor of the Caracas superior court, and Doctor José Gil, Supreme Court Justice. Finally, in 1851, Viso attained the degrees of Bachelor, *licenciado*, and Doctor of Civil Law.[15] He was also granted the professional title of *abogado* (lawyer).

Viso's first professional position was as senior clerk in the Ministry of the Interior in 1853.[16] That same year, Viso made an impression in the legal field in Venezuela when offering to the executive branch to draft civil, penal, and procedural codes. His initiative addressed the pressing concern that Venezuela did not have such essential legislation more than two decades after gaining its independence. Despite the years since independence, Venezuela was still subject to a "confusing legal system."[17] Consequently, the courts used a diverse group of legal sources to address the nation's legal needs:

> First the national laws promulgated after 1810 were applied. Next, [they used] the Spanish law written for America, [and] later the Recopilación de Indias [Compilation of the laws of the Indies], Ordenanzas de Bilbao, de Intendencia y de Nueva España [Ordinances of Bilbao, the intendency, and New Spain]. In the third place, the aforementioned Ordinances and laws contained in the Recopilación de Indias, the Reales Cédulas [Royals Charters] after the Novísima Recopilación [Most recent compilation of Spanish law], fifth the laws of these Novísima Recopilación and, finally, the contents of the fuero Real, [Royal charter] in the Fuero Juzgo [Charter of procedural law] and in the Partidas [The Seven Partidas].[18]

The dependence on an assortment of now-foreign legal texts accounted for Viso's proposal to regulate society with specific national laws. On his own accord, he began to write a civil and a penal code along with codes of procedures in 1853. Although not sanctioning his proposal, Congress gave him a stipend of two hundred pesos a week to support his effort. The following year, the executive branch submitted Viso's completed civil code to Congress. This pioneering effort to codify civil law set a precedent in Venezuelan law. Viso explained his sources to President José Gregorio Monagas:

> The bases of my work are Justinian and Spanish legislation; the civil codes of France, the Two Sicilies, Sardinia, Holland, and Louisiana; the mortgage laws of Greece and Genoa; the jurisprudence established by various decrees of the Court of Cassation of France and the Supreme Court of Venezuela; the doctrinal writings of the grand authorities Pothier, Merlin, Favard de Langlade, Portalis, Pardessus, Zachariae, Savigny, and other Spanish practitioners and of Vidaurre, who dedicated his pen to the Republic of Peru.[19]

These sources indicate a considerable undertaking. In one comment, Viso highlighted the comparative nature of his contribution:

> it is absolutely not concerned with changing the substance of the current law, but only to elevate it to the height of the intellectual movement of the most advanced nations and to conclude the many divergences of some Spanish jurists on matters of law.[20]

Many contemporary scholars, nonetheless, deemed Viso's proposed codes as too conservative. Furthermore, he did not resolve the great question of the day in Venezuela—the issue of slavery. While Viso acknowledged the rights of man, he referred to slavery as an established institution in Venezuela and even determined punishments appropriate to various offenses by slaves. For these reasons, Congress did not approve Viso's proposals.[21]

Despite the initial failure, Viso persisted in his work to codify civil, penal, and procedural law in Venezuela. His efforts ran parallel to his duties in official positions. At the time, he was a senior clerk in the Ministry of the Interior. In 1855 the government appointed him interim minister in charge of the interior, "justice and foreign relations in the transition cabinet between the administration of José Gregorio Monagas and José Tadeo Monagas."[22] However, he lasted only a very short time in that position.

Employment in the central administration did not stop Viso's efforts to deepen his study of private law, a topic often the subject of his debates with noted lawyer Luis Sanojo in the journal *El Foro*. Between 1856 and 1860, Viso delved into the interpretation of juridical institutions in articles addressing sales contracts, inheritance, estate administration, creditors, mixed marriages, subsequent legitimation, evidence, contracts, retroactivity of laws, and *res judicata*.[23]

Political turmoil inspired Viso to continue his legislative proposals. In 1857, President José Tadeo Monagas attempted a constitutional reform to ensure his reelection. The reaction catalyzed a political movement, the March Revolution, that expelled the president from power and the country.[24] The interim president, Julián Castro, convoked a national convention in the city of Valencia, then the provisional capital. The convention sanctioned a new constitution on December 24, 1858. In the context of changing the fundamental law, Viso proposed a constitutional project published in the journal *El Foro* between March and May. The most controversial constitutional proposal centered on how to organize the state. The contemporary debates pitted federalism against centralism. In this regard, Viso argued:

> I did not believe it convenient…to adopt the form of a simple and pure confederation that becomes an eventual league of equal powers and absolutely independent, but instead [to adopt] the form of a national republic composed of several departments, which are dependent and subordinated to a general government established by them.[25]

In another text, he specified the vices of political centralism:

> [T]the idea of domination cannot fail to become generalized and vividly stimulated under a central regime, where government power extends to all the things it intends to direct, and where public offices and appointments allow the practice of systematically directed authority.[26]

Likewise, he was an advocate of federation as a form of organization of government: "We must establish local freedom, which is the most durable and strongest of public freedoms, because through the practice of communal or municipal life, citizens will rise to understand the state's most complicated activities."[27]

Innovative proposals, such as the law of direct, universal voting complemented his vision of a hybrid state organized in administrative departments dependent on a central power. The historian José Gil Fortoul described Viso's ideas as follows:

> The territory is divided into a federal district and five or more departments (imitating the system of 1821), the departments into the provinces, these into cantons, and those into parishes. Each department has its legislature, governor, and other employees, elected freely through the local sovereignty. Viso also proposes universal and direct elections, the elimination of a permanent military force, the abolition of imprisonment in civil and mercantile matters, the use of the death penalty only for premeditated murder with treachery, and religious freedom.[28]

Religious freedom was the most controversial issue. To uphold the state's official religion required onerous taxation, one of the heaviest obligations of Venezuelan citizens. Also, any notion of religious freedom highlighted the "liberal" tenet of religious tolerance that had been central to the Venezuelan state since 1830. The hope was to attract European and North American immigration to a countryside sparsely populated since the devastating Wars of Independence.[29] Even though Congress rejected his reforms, Viso's constitutional proposal enriched the debates in the National Convention of Valencia during the complicated juncture of 1857.

Yet another political revolution permitted Viso to push for the codification of law in Venezuela. In 1861 General José Antonio Páez arrived from New York to overthrow the government, imprison President Pedro Gual, and declare himself a dictator. The change of government ended the military conflict known as the Long War. One of the new president's concerns was the negative impact of incomplete legal codes. As one historian claimed:

> Changes were discouraging, and amid so many frustrations and delays of not moving along with necessary speed, codification could fulfill neither its early functions as a complement to the Constitution nor its function to share with the Constitution the changes that should have harmoniously originated in the Legislative Power. The time came when "just settling into power, General Páez ordered the creation of a commission to draft national codes, particularly the project of a civil code and a penal code." Indeed, it was General Páez's deliberate action that made the existence of a civil code possible to transform the legal regime of property, its dominion, possession, use, and enjoyment.[30]

In 1861 Viso was named to the legislative commission to create civil and penal codes. Other prominent members were lawyers Elías Acosta, José Reyes, Modesto Urbaneja, as well as Isaac J. Pardo and Fernando Antonio Díaz. On October 28, 1862, congress sanctioned Viso's new civil code.[31] On April 9 of the following year, it approved a penal code based on the Spanish code and a code of criminal procedure based on Viso's proposals.[32] His influence continued in another round of reforms when he joined a commission to draft the new civil code sanctioned on October 28, 1867.

Viso's intense lifelong study of judicial doctrine, the philosophy of law, and legislation allowed him to be the most influential promoter and drafter of codification in independent Venezuela. He drafted a constitution, four proposals for the civil code, three for the penal code, and three for codes of civil and penal procedures. Several presidents and congresses relied on him as a legislative leader during an era of political turmoil. Viso's efforts mirrored those of Andrés Bello, another Venezuelan and the drafter of Chile's Civil Code of 1855.

Other professional activities

Julián Viso was also an educator concerned about new generations of Venezuelans. His outstanding reputation as a teacher and professor led the government to name him the dean of the National School in Valencia in 1877, a position he held until 1880.[33] The appointment took place at a time of change for higher education. President Guzmán Blanco believed that the University of Caracas, the nation's most prestigious educational institution, had become the meeting point for his enemies and the source of political dissent. To counter the university's standing, the president elevated the national schools across the country by allowing them to issue university degrees equivalent to those in Caracas. The deans of the national schools were to be part of the new upper echelon of academia. Later in life, Viso was briefly the minister of public education in 1890.

His contributions to education expanded into preserving and disseminating Venezuela's history. Viso wrote a chronology of national history titled *Resumen histórico de Venezuela hasta 1823* (*Historical summary of Venezuela to 1823*), which was published in *El Primer libro venezolano de Literatura* in 1895.[34] He also promoted the establishment of a National Archive in Venezuela. His teaching, writing, and interest in history led him to become a founding member of the National Academy of History in 1888. This corporation aimed to study, disseminate, and protect the national historic heritage, a mission that continues one hundred and thirty years later.[35]

Another area in which Viso excelled was diplomacy. His first position in foreign affairs was as a representative of Colombia. In the nineteenth century, it was common for intellectuals, lawyers, and men of letters to represent countries other than their own. In 1868 he became the vice-consul of the United States of Colombia in Venezuela, and in 1869 the consul general of Colombia in Venezuela.[36]

The border disputes between the new republics of New Granada (modern-day Colombia) and Venezuela began with the dissolution of Gran Colombia. In 1833 commissioners Santos Michelena for Venezuela and Lino de Pombo for New Granada presented a joint border agreement, which was rejected by the Venezuelan Congress. Yet again, commissioners Fermín Toro and Joaquín Acosta achieved no tangible result in the mid-1840s. Negotiations recommenced only during the first government of President Antonio Guzmán Blanco. In preparation for these negotiations, the Venezuelan government established a team to examine the legal deeds and documents to be used to defend the national interests. On April 3, 1872, Viso became the plenipotentiary minister of Venezuela in the controversy over the limits between Colombia and Venezuela.[37] His skills were critical both in the research team and the arbitral proceedings to defend Venezuela's territorial claims. His first assignment was to hold preliminary talks with Colombia's representative, Aníbal Galindo.[38] In 1874 Viso compiled a valuable collection of historical documents supporting Venezuela's territorial claims. The documents, now housed in the General Archive of the Nation, were published in several tomes.[39]

In 1879 Viso was named minister of foreign relations. His mission was to conduct negotiations with Great Britain over the border dispute in the Guianan territory west of the Essequibo River. In 1882 he was named "the Republic's attorney and agent on the issue of the boundary with Colombia." Consequently, Viso and his family relocated to Madrid. Colombia and Venezuela chose King Alfonso XII, and later his widow Regent María Cristina, to arbitrate their longstanding border dispute. In the Spanish capital city, Viso outlined the arguments that supported Venezuela's objectives. In 1884 he was briefly in charge of the Venezuelan legation in Spain. Two years later, he returned home and, once again, was briefly both the minister of foreign relations and the president of the Supreme Court of the Federal District.[40]

Viso knew how to respond to change and how to apply his knowledge to create and to promote projects in all areas of public life. In the second half of the nineteenth century, his diverse activities took place when many attempted to consolidate the state's institutions and to implement, in practice, positivist ideas of progress in most public policies until the turn of the century. In 1890 Viso retired from public life. At the turn of the century, he died of a heart attack in his home in Caracas on July 20, 1900.

Conclusion

The first decades of the nineteenth century witnessed a turning point in Venezuela, with political changes paving the way for the country's independence from the Spanish monarchy. The republic began in earnest in 1830, when a new constitution put forth an accord that separated the Department of Venezuela from Colombia. The first stages of the nation's independent life were spent establishing institutions and designing and applying policies to rebuild a country devastated during the long, grueling wars of independence that lasted thirteen years. Viso was born into and grew up in these circumstances of historic import.

In the next half-century, Viso participated actively and decisively in the development and consolidation of institutions and the national identity of independent Venezuela. His contributions encompassed the realms of law, education, and diplomacy. Early on, this talented law student at the University of Caracas drafted proposals for civil, penal, and procedural codes that included the most avant-garde contemporary positions in legislation, doctrine, and jurisprudence from around the world. Throughout his professional and public life, Viso was a leading figure in the processes of codification that took place in Venezuela in the 1850s and 1860s. His passion for the study of the philosophy of law, legal doctrine, and legislation did not keep him from teaching; he was a school teacher and a professor. His outstanding performance gained him the prominent positions of the dean of the national school and minister of public education. Similarly, his knowledge of law and research skills allowed him to play a central role in Venezuelan diplomacy in the most highly sensitive areas of national borders. He was a minister of foreign relations, a general consul, the head of the Venezuelan Embassy in Spain, and part of the teams in charge of negotiating Venezuela's boundaries with Colombia and Great Britain.

Notes

1 Gran Colombia (1819–30) was a new, independent republic that encompassed the former territories of the Captaincy General of Venezuela, the Viceroyalty of New Granada, and the Presidency of Quito.
2 Some examples are the Blue Revolution (1868), the April Revolution (1870), the Legalist Revolution (1892), and the Revolution of the Liberal Restauration (1899). All of these political and armed movements led to changes of government in Venezuela. At the same time, other armed attempts to counter the leaders emerged from victorious revolutions.
3 Mijares, *Don Julián Viso*, 10.
4 Ibid., 39.
5 In her book, Adriana Hernández reconstructed Viso's genealogy. Hernández, *Jurisprudencia, liberalismo y diplomacia*, 36.
6 Ibid., 37.
7 See Troconis de Veracoechea, *Cédula de Gracias al Sacar*, 764.
8 Francisco Espejo was the royal prosecutor in the conspiracy of Gual y España in 1797, the French-inspired revolt in Maracaibo in 1798, the attempted invasion by Francisco de Miranda in 1806, and the proposal to establish a junta in Caracas amid the Napoleonic invasion in 1808. See Vaamonde, *Diario de una rebelión*, 315ff.
9 See Cira Naranjo de Castillo, "Espejo, Francisco," in Fundación Polar, *Diccionario de Historia de Venezuela*, 2:271.
10 Hernández, *Jurisprudencia*, 37.
11 Ibid. See also Carmen Naranjo, "Azpurúa Peláez."
12 As one biographer writes:

> The businesses that he pursued seemed destined to satisfy his and his family's basic needs, without ever becoming his primary interest, which was to develop his career as a lawyer, or to be more precise, as a legislator. His passion was directed towards the profession's academic angle, devoting himself to the study of the philosophy of law and the interpretation and improvement of law's more arcane issues. Even though the world of books and philosophy was his passion, it was not legislative activity that supported him financially, at least not exclusively…There were the businesses that he undertook with his half-brother Azpurúa; the agricultural holding of the hacienda La Isabelica, which he owned in Valencia; and the fees that he occasionally charged in his work as a litigator that allowed him to maintain his usual, comfortable standard of living.
> (Hernández, *Jurisprudencia*, 53–54)

13 Ibid., 54.
14 Ibid.
15 Ibid., 21.
16 Ibid.
17 Mijares, *Don Julián Viso*, 13.
18 Ibid.
19 Cited in Mijares, *Don Julián Viso*, 19 (translation M.C. Mirow).
20 Viso quoted in Guardia, "La Codificación Civil de Páez."
21
> As Viso's project acknowledged innate rights of man, the code fell into contradiction when it regulated the difference between free and enslaved people and referred to slavery as one of the Republic's institutions...He is called free he who is not a slave—in other words, the one who can act according to what he believes convenient, without being subjected to any owner who decides over his person and capacities...He is called a slave who is subjected to serve a certain person his entire life or one who acquires rights over him while he is not emancipated. The logic over the future of that society induced Viso to include slaves in his project and to establish the punishment that the master should apply to them. The master can punish correctionally his slave according to the quality of the offense or excess, but he cannot wound or hurt him with a punishment that causes grave concussion or effusion of blood...If the masters or their foremen exceed themselves in corrective punishment, they will be forced to sell the slave with a ban on repurchasing him, and the earnings will be directed to a manumission fund.
>
> (Ibid.)

22 Hernández, *Jurisprudencia*, 21.
23 On the development of the doctrine, see Sanojo and Viso, *Estudios escogidos.*
24 See Castillo Blomquist, *José Tadeo Monagas.*
25 Viso quoted in Mijares, *Don Julián Viso*, 57.
26 Viso, "Federación," 150.
27 Ibid., 151–52.
28 Ibid., 58.
29 Viso remarked on "the unbearable tyranny to force a citizen to support with his contributions a faith that is not his." Ibid.
30 Guardia, "La Codificación Civil de Páez." The quoted passage is from Plaza, *El último régimen del General José Antonio Páez*, 199.
31 Hernández, *Jurisprudencia*, 22.
32 Ibid.
33 Ibid., 24.
34 Mijares, *Don Julián Viso*, 63.
35 See Venezuela, Academia Nacional de la Historia, *Reglamento de la Academia Nacional de la Historia y Normas de procedimiento.*
36 Hernández, *Jurisprudencia*, 22–23.
37 Pérez, "Viso, Julián."
38 Hernández, *Jurisprudencia*, 22.
39 Mijares, *Don Julián Viso*, 42.
40 Hernández, *Jurisprudencia*, 25.

References

Castillo Blomquist, José. *José Tadeo Monagas: auge y consolidación de un caudillo.* Caracas: Monte Ávila Editores, 1991.

Fundación Polar. *Diccionario de Historia de Venezuela*, Vol. 4. Caracas: Fundación Polar, 1997.

Guardia, Amelia. "La Codificación Civil de Páez." *Sistema de Información Científica. Red de Revistas Científicas de América Latina y el Caribe, España y Portugal*, https://www.redalyc.org/html/1700/170018112007/ Revisado el 20/12/2018.

Hernández, Adriana. *Jurisprudencia, liberalismo y diplomacia: la vida pública de Julián Viso (1822–1900)*. Caracas: Instituto de Altos Estudios Diplomáticos "Pedro Gual"—Ministerios de Relaciones Exteriores, 1999.

Mijares, Augusto. *Don Julián Viso, 1822–1900*. Caracas: Ediciones de la Fundación Eugenio Mendoza, 1960.

Naranjo, Carmen. "Azpurúa Peláez, José Ramón." In *Diccionario de Historia de Venezuela*, edited by Fundación Polar, Vol. 1, 326. Caracas, 1997.

Pérez, Omar Alberto. "Viso, Julián." In *Diccionario de Historia de Venezuela*, edited by Fundación Polar, Vol. 4, 278. Caracas, 1996.

Plaza, Elena. *El último régimen del General José Antonio Páez, 1861–1863*. Caracas: Universidad Central de Venezuela, Facultad de Ciencias Jurídicas y Políticas, 2000.

Sanojo, Luis, and Julián Viso. *Estudios escogidos, seguidos de Ensayos Polémicos entre ambos autores. Selección y Nota Preliminar: Dr. Gert Kummerow*. Caracas: Ministerio de Justicia, 1959.

Troconis de Veracoechea, Ermila. "Cédula de Gracias al Sacar." In *Diccionario de Historia de Venezuela*, edited by Fundación Polar, Vol. 1, 764. Caracas, 1997.

Vaamonde, Gustavo Adolfo. *Oscuridad y confusión. El pueblo y la política venezolana del siglo XIX en las ideas de Antonio Guzmán Blanco*. Caracas: Universidad Católica Andrés Bello, Fundación Empresas Polar, 2004.

Vaamonde, Gustavo Adolfo. *Remedios para atajar el mal. Venezuela, 1730–1806*. Madrid: Ediciones 19, 2016.

Venezuela. Academia Nacional de la Historia. *Reglamento de la Academia Nacional de la Historia y Normas de procedimiento*. Caracas: Academia Nacional de la Historia, 2015.

Viso, Julián. *Alegato de Venezuela en su controversia sobre límites con Colombia*. Madrid: Sucesores de Rivadeneyra, 1883.

Viso, Julián. *Código de procedimiento, con notas sobre el derecho español y doctrina de los pragmáticos*. Valencia: Imprenta de N. Carrasquero, 1851.

Viso, Julián. "Federación. 1858." In *Textos fundamentales de Venezuela*. Edited by Rafael Arráiz Lucca and Edgardo Mondolfi Gudat, 147–52. Caracas: Fundación para la cultura urbana, 2001.

19 Rafael Fernández Concha (Chile, 1832–1912)

Raúl Madrid

Biographical introduction

Rafael Fernández Concha is probably the most outstanding Chilean theologian and philosopher of law of the nineteenth century. He was born in Santiago on October 25, 1833, to a family whose features outline rather well the future bishop's traits, especially his markedly devout character. He was the son of Pedro Fernández Recio and Rosa de Santiago Concha y de la Cerda, who both belonged to traditional aristocratic Chilean families, although his mother's lineage was more relevant than his father's. Rafael's parents had thirteen children beginning in 1823, among whom Domingo and Pedro were representatives of the Conservative Party. Domingo was a renowned national public figure: four times senator and economically involved in 1888 in founding the future Pontifical Catholic University of Chile, which has had a majorly significant role in the intellectual and cultural life of the country since then. In addition, he was a pioneer in Chilean viticulture, for he was the first person who received advice from French experts in bringing the first French strains to Santa Rita Vineyard, which he founded in 1880 in the town of Alto Jahuel.

Rafael's father, Pedro Fernández Recio, descended from an ancient Galician family. He was a lawyer, university professor, and Chilean representative. He participated in the sadly famous affair known as the "the question of the sacristan," during President Manuel Montt's government, by defending two canons who had appealed to the secular court to overturn an action by the senior sacristan of the cathedral.[1] In 1847 Fernández Recio was appointed to succeed Mariano Egaña[2] at the faculty of law of the University of Chile. On the death of his wife, in 1872, and as all of his children were adults, Fernández Recio requested ordination as a priest, asserting that he did so "to celebrate Holy Mass every day, which made me happy all my life."[3] He became a presbyter at the age of seventy-seven (1873) and at the same time published *Chilean Philothea*, or devout life. The illustrious public man died ten years after being ordained as a presbyter.

On the other hand, according to the chroniclers of the time,[4] Rafael's mother was the daughter of the Fifth Marquis of Casa Concha—former *oidor* (judge) of the Real Audiencia (Royal Court) during independence—and seems to have been a woman of great sanctity, an "outstanding matron for her piety and philanthropy."[5] She was also a member of the Charitable Society of Santiago, entrusted with building the main convent of the Good Shepherd Congregation. After her death, the children donated the residence to the congregation, later establishing the Rosa de Santiago Concha School in 1884 and the Church of Saint Peter.

At just nine years old, in 1843, Rafael Fernández Concha began his study of humanities at the Instituto Nacional (National Institute). Founded in 1813, the institute was key in the development of education in Chile. Its initial objective was to raise citizens to serve the country: defend it, lead it, make it bloom, and honor it. The institute's mission was to deliver intellectual and military education to all young people, regardless of their social origin or economic status, and to influence the conduct of society by spreading ideas from its classrooms until they became public convictions. Throughout the nineteenth century, the Instituto Nacional was the main center of secondary education in the country and the center of debate on questions of education. Here, Fernández Concha was Andrés Bello's student and obtained the highest grades.[6]

Following a family tradition, Fernández Concha later studied law at the University of Chile and graduated as a bachelor of law in 1855 by presenting a dissertation titled "*La facultad de testar y el artículo 1354 del Proyecto del Código Civil*" ("The capacity to make a will and Article 1354 of the draft Civil Code"). After analyzing this institution from the perspective of comparative positive law, he immediately addresses the philosophical field, asking whether testate or intestate succession is a natural right or not. As Hanisch says, "here we recognize the philosopher that he will be all his life. He disengages from illusion and delves into the essence of things as he aims at studying law from its causes."[7]

He graduated as a lawyer in 1856 and was elected an academic member of the faculty of law and political science in 1857. In 1856 he was appointed substitute professor of canon law at the University of Chile. The following year, due to the resignation of his cousin, Manuel María Güemes Fernández, he was appointed interim professor, and in 1863 he received the chair, which he held for ten years.[8] When Professor Antonio García Reyes died, a position as a member of the faculty became vacant, to which Fernández Concha acceded in 1857 after publicly reading a speech or dissertation on teaching law. He claimed that students should be given all the aspects of their specialty, particularly the place that law has in human sciences, and the principles that determine the just and the unjust. He thought that the jurist should be trained in philosophy of law because the jurist needs to nourish his spirit from the sources of thought. He stated that limiting oneself exclusively to experience narrows intelligence, making one unable to rise to the causes of legal norms. Referring to the idea of justice, he commented on what he considered wrong solutions—pantheism, skepticism, Bentham's utilitarianism, Smith's sympathy, Hutcheson's inner sense, or Kantian doctrine. Here we find the basis—what he would consider the introduction—of his future *Philosophy of Law*. The speech was so important that it would continue to be cited at the University of Chile a hundred years later.[9]

Relying on a number of sources, Hanisch says that Fernández Concha suffered a spiritual and religious crisis (between 1855 and 1857), known only after it had passed. He was both an open and critical spirit. He also brought his eagerness for constructive analysis to the field of faith. At that time, young people were disoriented between philosophical systems and the rise of secularism. "Many of his contemporaries lost their faith in their youthful years...Skepticism imbued the environment."[10] For Fernández Concha, reading Kant may have triggered this crisis. As he observed:

> If daring thinkers of the shadowy Germany have tried to create an absolute transcendental science, the radical impotence of their efforts has not been shown more clearly than in their absurd and pilgrim systems, which have only served to better reveal those limits.[11]

This reflection is probably why he focused on Greek thought, especially Plato and Aristotelian-derived scholasticism, in the work of its supreme representative, Saint Thomas Aquinas.

This spiritual crisis led him to embrace the priesthood, leaving earthly love, for he was in love with God and the Virgin Mary. He did not contemplate entering a regular community because he did not consider himself suitable for that type of communal existence. Thus, in 1859 he joined the Seminary of Santiago, whose rector was Joaquín Larraín Gandarillas, future first rector of the Catholic University to be founded in 1888. Fernández Concha was ordained a priest in January 1860. In January 1863 the archbishop of Santiago appointed him acting prosecutor, and later, in July, he became provicar. In December 1864 he was promoted to acting judicial vicar, and in March 1866 he was appointed provicar capitular until 1887, after Archbishop Valdivieso died. From that moment on, he did not have a position in the archiepiscopal curia; he dedicated himself to literary works and special commissions from the prelate. Between 1864 and 1874, an era when there were almost no newspapers in Santiago, Fernández Concha frequently wrote in the *Revista Católica* (*Catholic Magazine*), which was formally run by Archbishop Crescente Errázuriz. In fact, the actual directors were Larraín Gandarillas and Rafael Fernández Concha, who "very frequently wrote theological articles, extremely learned, but rather dense, as was everything that came out of his erudite pen."[12] He served in this position until the magazine was closed in 1874. When Archbishop Mariano Casanova reopened the magazine in 1892, he appointed Fernández Concha as its censor.

Fernández Concha was elected representative for Rancagua from 1870 to 1873. During this period, he joined the Permanent Commission of Ecclesiastical Affairs, but the records of his interventions remain unknown, as he seems to have limited himself to simply attending the sessions. He also participated in the Constituent Congress of 1870, whose objective was to reform the Constitution of 1833. In 1875 he was elected member of the faculty of theology of the University of Chile. His induction speech referred to morality as not independent from religion.

In 1889 he traveled to Europe and stayed in Barcelona, where he published his remarkable *Mystical Theology* the same year. He also visited Rome and the Holy See and returned to Chile in September 1890.

On May 24, 1893, Archbishop Casanova appointed him vicar general, and in July 1887 he was appointed to the commission in charge of organizing a diocesan synod to be held in 1895. Fernández Concha prepared the final wording of the code of ecclesiastical law for the governance of the diocese that was subsequently promulgated. At the request of the government of Chile, the Holy See appointed him Bishop of Epiphany on January 14, 1901. Due to his illnesses, Fernández Concha resigned the position of vicar general on December 16, 1901. Casanova tried to prevent him from leaving and gave him permission to rest, but Fernández Concha insisted, and his resignation was accepted on June 20, 1902. He had served the Church in government and in the curia for forty years.[13]

Fernández Concha was a tireless worker but was far from sullen or reluctant to engage in social relations. He highly appreciated friendship and enjoyed afternoon gatherings where the art of conversation was practiced, as in Europe. He did not participate in political quarrels, which annoyed some of his companions, but he was respected for his great intelligence and talent. He was rather a peculiar person: apprehensive in the extreme, very careful not to change anything in his daily life, and doing everything thoughtfully. He always ate the same food, which had to include a large piece of meat at every meal. He dreaded becoming ill.[14]

As to his appearance, he was extremely tall and thin; his head, ironically, was very small compared to his body, as if nature had resolved to manifest how great it was by putting so much into so little. He must have projected an ascetic and distant physical type, not so much because of his disdain for people but out of his deeply rooted abstraction, which might have been noticed in a gaze that was often thought cold beyond what it really was.

Fernández Concha died in Santiago, Chile, on October 13, 1912, from a stroke that caused him to fall next to the Church of National Gratitude. He was buried in the crypt of the cathedral a little before his eightieth birthday. The Chilean Government, through Minister Antonio Huneeus, expressed condolences, thanking Fernández Concha for the services he rendered the country.

Intellectual and theological work

Ayala attributes to Carlos Casanueva the statement that Fernández Concha "was endowed with the most extraordinary speculative talent that has ever been in Chile."[15] According to information traced from chroniclers such as Vicente García Huidobro and Crescente Errázuriz, he must have been a man of great contemplative ability, which led him to withdraw suddenly in the middle of meetings, or express contempt to the vicissitudes and circumstances of daily life, whether public or private. This led Errázuriz to describe him as a bad adviser in ordinary affairs and a bad boss, as he was:

> too attached to his ideas, impractical, underestimated public opinion excessively, and had little knowledge of men, as he barely lived in the real world. He was on the verge of being wrong at every moment, and his mistakes could be more fateful the more remarkable were his qualities of intelligence and heart and the greater tenacity he put into maintaining his opinions.[16]

However, it must be borne in mind that Fernández Concha and Archbishop Errázuriz had been engaged in a bitter dispute when the latter accepted the direction of *El estandarte católico* (*The Catholic Standard*) in 1874, because Fernández Concha was against mixing religion and politics, for which Errázuriz called him "rigid." Despite a polite manner, his personality could be seen as inflexible at first, as he was always in contact with abstract ethical and legal models. But there is no reason to think that a man whose intelligence was capable of delving into the essence of metaphysical and ethical principles was incapable of adjusting them to concrete circumstances. Rigidity seems more applicable to the kind of person Fernández Concha was not—a formalist. He was not actually rigid but scrupulous, which caused him many problems at the end of his life, when he had to bear a sickly zeal in fulfilling his duties as a priest and his administrative work in the Church.

In addition to a significant variety of articles and minor works—letters, speeches, newspaper articles, dissertations, and official documents—Fernández Concha produced four major works that are the pillars of his thought: *Derecho público eclesiástico* (*Ecclesiastical public law*), in two volumes published in 1872; *Filosofía del Derecho* (*Philosophy of law*) in two volumes published in 1881; *Teología mística* (*Mystical theology*) published in Barcelona in 1889; and his last great work, *Del hombre en el orden psicológico, religioso y social* (*On Man in the Psychological, Religious, and Social Order*) that appeared in 1900. Each merits brief and separate discusion.

Ecclesiastical public law

This book was originally a set of articles published in *Revista Católica* during 1872 that argued against liberal positions. The articles were consolidated and improved for publication into a single monograph, which aimed at guiding public opinion away from liberal secularism, very much in vogue in Chile at the time through the influence of European works. The book was republished in 1894 and omitted comments on the freedom of education in Chile, because disputes on this topic had been resolved by the turn of the century. In this second edition, Fernández Concha expanded the work, converting the chapter on religion in the natural order into a treatise, which went from the earlier nineteen pages to more than a hundred.

Of particular interest, chapter eight deals with morality. The author here introduces the philosophical topics that he will later develop in successive works. He explains, with seemingly voluntarist implication, that morality should be the love of God,[17] and he soon details it by stating that "if, as rational beings, God is our ultimate goal, it is clear that in order to act rationally, we must lead our actions towards Him."[18] In other words, God is loved as perfect; therefore, it is rational to make Him the object of the will. The author then develops the arguments against what he calls "independent morality," a "modern opinion" that separates morality from religion,[19] which is now known as the transcendent foundation of the objective moral order. This work does not explicitly verify his evolution from Suarezianism to Thomism, although one grasps this indirectly, as Fernández Concha follows the steps of Thomas Aquinas and separates himself from Suárez. Despite both Aquinas and Francisco Suárez being scholastic philosophers, there is a significant difference between them about the concept of law, since the former considered that law to be fundamentally an act of reason, while the latter seemingly taught that law pertained to the will.[20]

Mystical theology

This book is a truly masterful treatise, demonstrating a thorough knowledge of the most relevant authors who referred to union with God through contemplation.[21] It also offers a testimony of Fernández Concha's personal experience of the Holy Spirit in the sacrament of confession and in pastoral life. The treatise highlights the author's capacity for work and his comprehensive knowledge of the relevant sources. He had considered writing a second part of this book, which he never published, called *Practical Mystical Theology*. He was working on it when he died. Hanisch points out that "his wisdom is enormous and systematic. He does not make history, but places other people's ideas in the development of his own thought, and discusses them freely."[22]

In this work, Fernández Concha addresses exclusively the essence and nature of infused contemplation (without mentioning asceticism). For him, contemplation is an "extraordinary" path. He explains:

> There are two kinds of paths leading to the end of devout souls, which is the perfection of the spirit ciphered in the all-embracing union with the Supreme Good. On one hand, the ordinary path is based only on reason and faith and, therefore, available to everyone. On the other hand, the extraordinary one [Is] also based on certain experiences of the Divinity and of otherworldly spirits, and is a path that only some chosen ones follow. The former is the object of ascetic theology, the latter pertains to mystical theology.[23]

As noted, the author's object is infused contemplation in all its aspects, because it is the transcendent principle that works under the Holy Spirit. Studying it is the central object of the book.[24]

In addition, the work is grounded in scholasticism; he devotes a great effort to deciphering the most difficult questions of theology with the language of the Scholastics, leading him to correct the poetic and spontaneous expressions of some Spanish mystics. "It would be a very serious mistake to take the expressions of a passionate soul as a criterion to discern spiritual phenomena and as a rule to deduce doctrines and rules of conduct,"[25] he stated. Such corrections made it difficult for the common reader, for whom scholastic debates might appear alien. In *Mystical Theology*, Fernández Concha's evolution towards Thomism is almost complete. He cites and comments on various texts by Aquinas. As Jiménez reminds us, the true and fundamental inspiration of all his work was a genuine and well-assimilated Thomism, which provided the key to mystical problems.[26] Therefore, the Spanish Carmelite Samuel de Santa Teresa praised his work this way: "I would like to know how many mystical theologies are superior, not only in America, but in Europe itself."[27]

Anthropology

Fernández Concha's last book, *Of Man in the Psychological, Religious, and Social Order*, is an immense work of more than fourteen hundred pages. According to the review by ecclesiastical censor, Rafael Vergara Antúnez, it aimed to defend the faith and objective morality in a world where the struggle against Catholicism had been placed in an arena of reason and science. The work provides the educated reader with a set of anthropological and philosophical observations that sought to make apologetics capable of stopping the impulses of liberalism and secularism. In the words of Fernández Concha: "I made this book in order to attract to religion men of a certain age, men already educated, scholars, intellectuals."[28] Vergara's opinion helps contextualize the book and refers to the importance of the author in the national philosophical context:

> The work of Mr Fernández Concha is one of the most important of its kind that has been published in Chile, not only for its intrinsic merit but also for the services it has to render men of hesitant faith...A book that deals with the truths of the philosophical, religious, and social orders that interest man was missing in order to get a truly enlightened faith, as it is convenient in the present times, when the struggle against Catholicism has been placed in the field of reason and science.[29]

Here, then, lies the contextual importance of Fernández Concha's work, explained as the desire to combat the rationalist theories of his time, which denied other certainties than the empirical-logical one by disregarding theological and metaphysical categories. In this sense, he is a scholastic who faces modern times by making a didactic synthesis worthy of his great intellectual talents.

As its title implies, the book is divided into three parts: (a) the first, which addresses cosmology and philosophical psychology and refers to the nature of body and soul, the different types of soul, and the special characteristics of the human soul; (b) the second, which deals with religion, faith, the essence of God, revelation, the divinity of Jesus, and the main Christian dogmas; (c) the third, which coincides with the second volume and focuses on humanity in the social order, including domestic, civil, and religious societies. All three were approached from the most orthodox Thomistic tradition.

The philosophy of law

Fernández Concha has been especially influential in the philosophy of law. In a speech in 1857, he suggested the best organization of legal studies, dividing the speech into three parts:

I. How the specialties of a science should be divided.
II. The methodical order in which its teaching should be arranged.
III. The way to present this teaching.

The core of his speech is based on the thesis that the first step in learning a field is to understand all aspects related to its order of ideas. He regretted that, in the six years of law school, students were not provided with ideas about the principles of law, their place among the sciences, their organization and geography, and criteria for justice. In other words, he demanded an introduction to law in general. At first, he suggested this new subject should replace the study of natural law. Although natural law formed part of his thinking about law, in his view the academic course had become a mere criticism of social institutions and had abandoned its true object.[30]

His speech maintains that the jurist should cultivate knowledge in the sources of philosophy, taking the very idea of law as a starting point. He later defined law as that "part of morality whose compliance cannot be left to the mere awareness of those bound by duty, and whose fulfillment demands that social good be made effective by the public force."[31] It was necessary to organize each specialty scientifically, so that each aspect revolved around a single center of gravity. Fernández Concha thought the essence of things is naturally preeminent and central; the contemplation of principles and the good organization of the different areas of law will enable the jurist to unite the historicity of positive norms with the justice immanent in nature. Hence, he insisted on the need for historical-legal studies as part of the legal curriculum.

The speech criticized the curriculum of 1853, which sought to deliver only practical or professional knowledge to lawyers while disregarding speculative skills. Baeza comments that his concern for the great principles of legal life brought him personally closer to José Victorino Lastarria,[32] a well-known public figure. Lastarria was a classical liberal[33] who opposed Fernández Concha many times. The resulting inclusion of an introductory course on law demonstrated the influence of Fernández Concha's lecture. It was republished and cited many times in introductory manuals on law in the nineteenth and twentieth centuries.

Many of these ideas were later developed in the book *Philosophy of Law*, which was also written as an introduction, according to its subtitle: "ready to serve as an introduction to the legal sciences." Consequently, this work appears linked to his induction speech. He later published a set of fifteen anonymous articles in the *Revista Católica* (1874) covering the topics that would form *Philosophy of Law*, published in 1881. The second edition was published in Barcelona in 1887 and 1888, in two volumes. A third edition appeared on the fiftieth anniversary of the author's death. It continued as an important work in the field. In the prologue to the 1966 edition, Hübner says "it is a masterly treatise...a classic work in the Spanish American legal literature...the most valuable treatise that has ever been published on the subject in the country, and one of the most important in our language."[34]

There were, of course, other similar works. José Joaquín de Mora's book was the first text on theoretical-juridical matters to be published in Chile in 1830, and it aimed at satisfying imperative teaching needs rather than carrying out deeper theoretical work. Andrés Bello also addressed topics related to natural law, but he left almost nothing written, and certainly his doctrinal approach contradicted the essence of Fernández Concha's starting point.[35]

To fully understand the sense, meaning, and value of this work in its intellectual context, it is necessary to consider its intellectual underpinnings. The natural law content of this work directly contradicted the doctrinal tendencies of its time. As mentioned previously, Fernández Concha, initially adhered to Suárez's thoughts, but he gradually changed his position to become Thomas Aquinas's full supporter. This change of attitude is comprehensively reflected in the works mentioned here. Crescente Errázuriz says that after being for a long time:

> a supporter of Suárez, whose works were constantly seen in his hands and where he sought a solution to any difficulty...he was compelled to study some topics from the source, from St. Thomas Aquinas; in the end his conversion became total, absolute, and his Thomism was even more enthusiastic than his Molinism [the philosophy of Luis de Molina] had ever been.[36]

This process covered both Aquinas's works and his commentators, as evidenced by the erudition and breadth Fernández Concha shows in his philosophical debates on Aquinas's disciples and imitators.

How did this shift in orientation happen? Before he joined the seminary, Fernández Concha's speculative knowledge consisted of what today we would call modern philosophy, that is, the contemporary philosophy of his time. Although he referred to Aquinas in his early works, he displays in these works not a thorough knowledge of Aquinas but merely ideas resulting from a tradition that was already headed into crisis. Nonetheless, at seminary he studied firsthand the Scholastic texts. This was a system of thought that shocked him, probably for conceiving the world as an orderly unit. Fernández Concha pursued these ideas rigorously. Within this context, his early approach to Suárez's thoughts seems to have been exclusively fortuitous and, as such, disappeared as he discovered solid foundations in other texts. Errázuriz shares this anecdote:

> At that time, Archbishop Casanova had commissioned Jorge Montes to study a catechism. In the middle of the debate, Montes leaned on Suárez to defend an opinion, to which our author answered with a gesture that showed the little value he gave him. Then Montes said "Were not you his enthusiastic admirer for many years?" "Yes," Fernández Concha replied, "I lost a lot of time."[37]

Hanisch noted that Fernández Concha's intellectual stance had already shifted in *Mystical Theology* because "he rehearse[d] new literary forms" and quoted a significant number of passages from St. Thomas Aquinas's work.[38]

Fernández Concha's *Philosophy of Law* is a treatise on natural law, together with elements of philosophical psychology and Thomistic ethics. Following his induction speech to the faculty of law, the introduction places science in its epistemological context, shows its importance, and justifies the methods employed. The first systematic issue is the human act, beginning with a simply remarkable explanation of the good and freedom. The text is brilliantly written for its clarity and argumentation, something rare among the multiple followers of Aquinas. After referring to imputability (the moral and legal responsibility for one's human actions), morality, and natural law, Fernández Concha fully addresses the nature and properties of law. He decisively chooses the primacy of objective law by stating:

> In order to understand fully the essence of law, it is not enough to know that law involves a relationship between two or more persons resulting from the lawful and inviolable power to act, which is one person's responsibility, and the moral necessity that weighs on others, who are not going to threaten the exercise of this function. It is also necessary to know the object on which the aforementioned relationship falls, because only this knowledge can make us aware of the existence of a right.[39]

Ultimately, the primacy of objective law is based on nature and discovered by reason, since it is by virtue of the dictates of reason that law imposes on us the obligation to act.[40]

His explanation of *epikeia* is particularly interesting for its clarity and rigor. Fernández Concha explains that *epikeia* is understood as a special interpretation of the law, which states that, because of its peculiar and extraordinary circumstances, a particular case is not included in the provision of law, despite the general and conspicuous terms of the law.[41] This understanding presupposes that human law is naturally imperfect, because it is brief and general and consequently incapable of taking cognizance of all possible cases. Here lies the core of natural law, against rationalism and legal formalism.

The book sharply and completely criticizes these systems' nature of morality by contrasting them with Thomistic thought. It also explains from a Thomistic viewpoint the difference and intrinsic relationship between morality and law. This part of the book once again shows Fernández Concha's deep understanding of the modern doctrines of his time. From the point of view of the nature of morality, he concludes that the general object of ethics is the correct order of free acts from which moral goodness derives. When this general object is divided into several particular objects, the different species of moral goodness found in free actions become evident. Among these different species are justice and the science that deals with justice, which is law. "As it turns out, legal science is nothing more than a branch of ethical science."[42]

In the second volume, Fernández Concha focuses primarily on individual rights, whether innate or acquired. Among the first, he describes the personal rights to freedom (or independence), association, life, and defense. His explanations of the last two are particularly outstanding. He defines the right to life as "the right we have that nobody attacks our own [life],"[43] describing this as an "indirect right": this does not mean having life under control but is the power to demand that others recognize its inviolability. Therefore, the absence of full control over one's own life also does not allow for suicide. In this sense, Fernández Concha also adopts the Thomistic approach, which solves a problem that had been discussed historically at length. St. Athanasius condemned suicide as a matter of principle. St. Gregory the Theologian praised some cases in the Old Testament but generally condemns it, as did St. Ambrose. St. Jerome is incoherent on the point, for he rejects it in Christians but praises pagan widows who prefer committing suicide to remarrying. Meanwhile, Origen of Alexandria and Dionisius claimed that Jesus committed suicide, though they considered that we should not be unnecessarily exposed to this practice. St. Clement of Alexandria is the only one who bluntly condemns it by arguing that Christians who commit suicide misunderstand martyrdom. Moral theologians of the fourth century usually followed the Neoplatonic propositions: they condemned it at first but admitted exceptions: fulfilling an order of authority (Socrates), avoiding shame, or as a result of cruel destiny. The doctrine was very unclear. In 348 the Council of Carthage condemned it, while the Donatists defended it, and in 381 the bishop of Alexandria decreed that prayers could not be said for people who committed suicide unless madness could be certified. St. Augustine stated what would become the official position of the Church: he who commits suicide is a coward incapable of facing adversity. It is vanity that induces it by placing importance on what others think of you. No circumstance excuses it, not even rape. After the fifth century, the position hardened against a more indulgent Roman stance until being distilled in St. Thomas's views, which Fernández Concha reproduced when he asserted that "such an attack is never legal: there is not and cannot be any circumstance, even among the most extraordinary, capable of justifying it or excusing it."[44]

Regarding the right of defense, Fernández Concha began from the principle that the innocent who has not committed any real and voluntary aggression must not be killed. Yet in the face of unlawful aggression, the possibility of defense arises, consisting only of the just "prevention and ending of aggression" without vengefulness.[45] He concluded that it is sometimes lawful to harm our neighbor—even to take his life—when that is the only way to defend our person or property, and provided that this defense is proportionate to the aggression and ceases as soon as actual or imminent harm ends.

Fernández Concha also dealt with property as an acquired right and with conjugal, political, and religious societies. He later revised these topics in his text about humanity from a more philosophical and less juridical perspective. The rest of the work, faithful to its stated intention of providing the student with an orderly, hierarchical, and unitary vision of law, is dedicated to the special parts of the science: administrative, criminal, procedural, and international law.

Conclusion

In the short time that Ibero-American countries were sovereign and independent nations, Fernández Concha's intellectual personality is one of the most notable in the history of Chile, a fertile land of historians, chroniclers, poets, and even jurists, but certainly not of great speculative minds. This is indeed the exceptional merit of Fernández Concha. His remarkable intellectual capacity and gift for surprisingly clear and interconnected argumentation make his texts almost unique in the national historiography of intellectuals. The impulse that his work gives to scholastic philosophy, and specifically ethical-juridical studies, has also played a key role in defining the curricula of the faculties of law of the two great universities of the country (the Universidad de Chile and Pontificia Universidad Católica de Chile) for decades after his death. Despite being criticized by some as outdated, his clear and lucid writings have an intellectual imprint to this day. From the point of view of Thomistic scholasticism in Chile, his figure is likely comparable only to that of a twentieth-century author, Fr. Osvaldo Lira, SS.CC., whose philosophical studies also went beyond the strictly legal field, as lucid and comprehensive explorations of speculative knowledge.

The rigor, undoubted erudition, and argumentative accuracy of Fernández Concha's works are enough for him to have become a leading figure in the Spanish-speaking world, at least in the field of the so-called *philosophia perennis*. In this sense, it is unfortunate that his works have not been republished, as a reappraisal of the Chilean intellectual tradition is necessary. If we were to condense to one great idea his specific contribution to legal thought in the Spanish American sphere, it would be that he played a major role in recovering classical thought during the nineteenth century. All he did he did with a teaching spirit. Ultimately, he proposed to explain clearly the Greco–Scholastic doctrine of nature as the foundation of being and the root of moral and legal action. This effort was paralleled in time by the rise of liberal and skeptical ideas. Fernández Concha's work is explained precisely by the needs and demands of his time. He approached classical topics by contrasting the prevailing doctrines of his time, in both Europe and Spanish America, which invariably took Europe as its philosophical source.

Notes

1 The incident known by this name was a disciplinary action by the Catholic Church and raised questions about the link between the Church and the state, which ended up producing a great division in Chilean politics.
2 *Anales de la Universidad de Chile*, Section 3, 45. On Egaña, see Chapter 4 in this volume.
3 Sánchez Gaete, *Historia de la Iglesia en Chile*, 590.
4 Cruz Ugalde, *Flor de Chile. O la historia de un alma, y el alma de una historia*, 6.
5 Ibid.
6 See Chapter 2 of this volume.
7 Hanisch, "Rafael Fernández Concha," 417.
8 Baeza Marambio, *Esquema y notas*, 139.

9 Cf. Professor Aníbal Bascuñán Valdés prepared the introductory note to the new edition of this text, in University of Chile, *Boletín del Seminario*, 335–50.
10 Hanisch, "Rafael Fernández Concha," 421.
11 Rafael Fernández Concha, *Anales de la Universidad de Chile* (Santiago, 1857), 142. Cited by Hanisch, 422.
12 Araneda Bravo, *El Arzobispo Errázuriz*, 57.
13 Hanisch, 428.
14 Ibid., 457–58.
15 Cruz Ugalde, 6.
16 Ayala Godoy, *Rafael Fernández Concha*, 72.
17 Fernández Concha, *Derecho Público Eclesiástico*, 124.
18 Ibid., 126.
19 Ibid., 130.
20 Ibid., 82.
21 The most-cited authors are St. Thomas Aquinas and St. John of the Cross. It seems the latter was an old pastime of Fernández Concha.
22 Hanisch, 444.
23 Fernández Concha, *Teología mística*, v.
24 Ibid., vi.
25 Ibid., 348.
26 Jiménez, "Rafael Fernández Concha," 524–25.
27 "De Santa Teresa."
28 Ayala Godoy, 53.
29 Vergara Antúnez, "Report on *Del hombre en el orden psicológico, religioso y social*," v–vi.
30 Fernández Concha, "Estudios Jurídicos," in *Anales de la Universidad de Chile* (1857), 133.
31 Fernández Concha, *Derecho Público Eclesiástico*, 142.
32 Baeza Marambio, *Historia de la Facultad*, 141.
33 Hurtado, "Lastarria y la filosofía."
34 Hübner Gallo, "Prólogo," in Fernández Concha, *Filosofía del Derecho*, ix–x.
35 Ibid., xi.
36 Errázuriz, *Algo de lo que he visto*, 172.
37 Ibid., 173.
38 Hanisch, 425.
39 Fernández Concha, *Filosofía del Derecho*, 1:91.
40 Ibid., 1: 116.
41 Ibid., 1:149.
42 Ibid., 1:35–36.
43 Ibid., 2:28.
44 Ibid., 2:29.
45 Ibid., 2:32–33.

Bibliography

Araneda Bravo, Fidel. *El Arzobispo Errázuriz y la evolución política y social de Chile.* Santiago: Editorial Jurídica, 1956.

Ayala Godoy, Hugo. *Rafael Fernández Concha.* Santiago: Talleres Gráficos "El Chileno," 1947.

Baeza Marambio, Mario. *Esquema y notas para una historia de la Facultad de Ciencias Jurídicas y Sociales de la Universidad de Chile.* Santiago: Talleres gráficos Valdés hnos., 1944.

Baeza Marambio, Mario. *Historia de la Facultad de Ciencias Jurídicas y Sociales de la Universidad de Chile.* Santiago: Imprenta Universitaria, 1944.

Cruz Ugalde, Félix. *Flor de Chile. O la historia de un alma y el alma de la historia.* Montevideo: Editorial Mosca Hermanos, 1944.

De Santa Teresa, Samuel. "Rafael Fernández Concha." *Revista Católica* 29 (1915): 127–33.

Domingo, Rafael and Javier Martínez-Torrón, *Great Christian Jurists in Spanish History.* Cambridge: Cambridge University Press, 2018.

Errázuriz, Crescente. *Algo de lo que he visto.* Santiago: Nascimento, 1934.

Fernández Concha, Rafael. *Derecho público eclesiástico.* Santiago: Imprenta del Correo, 1872.

Fernández Concha, Rafael. *Filosofía del Derecho.* Edited by Jorge Ivan Hübner Gall, Vol. 2. Santiago: Editorial Jurídica, 1966.

Fernández Concha, Rafael. *Teología mística.* Barcelona: La Hormiga de Oro, 1889.

Hanisch Walter, S.J. "Rafael Fernández Concha y su teología mística." In *Estudios en honor de Pedro Lira Urquieta.* Santiago: Editorial Jurídica, 1982.

Hurtado, Cristina. "Lastarria y la filosofía europea en el siglo XIX en Chile." *Cuadernos del pensamiento latinoamericano* 17 (2009): 254–65.

Jiménez Julio, S.J. "Rafael Fernández Concha y su Teología Mística." *Teología Espiritual* 6 (1962): 519–37.

Sánchez Gaete, Marcial. *Historia de la Iglesia en Chile.* Santiago: Editorial Universitaria, 2014.

Universidad de Chile. *Boletín del Seminario de Derecho Público de la Escuela de Ciencias Jurídicas y Sociales de la Universidad de Chile.* Santiago: Universidad de Chile, 1947–48.

Vergara Antúnez, Rafael. "Report on *Del hombre en el orden psicológico, religioso y social.*" In *Del hombre en el orden psicológico, religioso y social.* Santiago: Imprenta de Emilio Pérez, 1900.

20 Tobias Barreto de Meneses (Brazil, 1839–89)

Márcio Ricardo Staffen

Introduction

To understand Tobias Barreto de Meneses's political, academic, juridical, and religious role is to draw a parallel with the history of institutions, actors, and relevant powers in the formation of Brazil as a nation in its transit from the nineteenth century to the twentieth century. He was especially important in navigating the crisis between the imperial model, linked to Portuguese traditions, and the construction of the republic under the ideals of the late Enlightenment in an atmosphere of social ferment.

Tobias Barreto de Meneses was born on June 7, 1839, in the village of Campos (now called Tobias Barreto), in the current state of Sergipe (in northeastern Brazil), the son of a notary who became an absent father; his mother was of both European and African parentage. From childhood, Tobias was destined for academic studies, encouraged by his mother at home and studying Latin fervently from the age of fifteen. In 1861, in the state of Bahia, he explored the clerical vocation but found no success. Two years later, in 1863, he was admitted to the Recife Faculty of Law (currently part of the Federal University of Pernambuco), where he also immersed himself in sociology and cultural studies. During this time, he came under the influence of Germanism and evolutionism, both as a student and later while teaching in the chair of philosophy. In his Brazilian alma mater, he fought important legal-political debates with Castro Alves, Silvio Romero, Ruy Barbosa, and Joaquim Nabuco.

Among the conditions of his life as a student and, subsequently, as a professor at the Faculty of Law, Barreto lived for a time in the smaller city of Escada, in the countryside. He was at first frustrated by lack of advancement in his public career because of his lack of a clerical letter of support and his biracial origin (as both European and African). During this period, he plunged into Germanic studies and publications, including a German newspaper. Without doubt, this interior retreat gave his thought maturity and depth and greatly contributed to his successful return to Recife and to the faculty. There, he helped to establish what came to be known as the "school of Recife" in the Faculty of Law, (subsequently nicknamed the "House of Tobias"). Barreto and those he influenced were critical of the philosophical positivism of Comte and other French writers, although

Barreto advanced a version of positivism. Drawing inspiration from German thought, Barreto defended secular thinking and the monism of Ernst Haeckel, who was an early proponent of Darwinism. Yet this thinking did not prejudice his Christian faith, which he preserved until the end of his life because he considered it an important paternal inheritance.

An extraordinary critic, speaker, and jurist, Barreto did not have the same success as a poet or deputy in the Provincial Assembly. However, he found room for the maturation of his ideas by joining the literary movement of Condorism—a school of the third phase of Brazilian Romanticism inspired by humanist and social themes and by the struggle for abolitionist ideals, to which Castro Alves also belonged. At the end of his life, Barreto was left bankrupt, a condition that affected him greatly in the last days of his life. When he died in Recife, on June 27, 1889, he left nine children. As a posthumous tribute, he became the patron of chair number thirty-eight in the Brazilian Academy of Letters.

Although he was not directly involved in the acts leading to the Proclamation of the Republic on November 15, 1889, his postulates, ideals, and teachings are found in the works of Joaquim Nabuco, Ruy Barbosa, Quintino Bocaiuva, and Benjamin Constant, especially manifested in their questioning of positivism and their advocacy of the abolition of slavery, the secularity of the state, and liberalism.

Born in a period when Latin America endured many emancipatory rebellions, Tobias Barreto in his youth experienced fluctuations in national politics between liberals and conservatives, the constancy of the executive power in the person of the emperor, the anguish of slavery, international conflicts, experimentation with national industrialization, the arrival of immigrants and, on the eve of his death, certainty about the collapse of the empire in a military *coup d'état*.

Tobias Barreto's behavior in this context offers the most complete and consistent portrait of a period of strong institutional oscillations and tensions in Brazil. The largest and most populous country in Latin America, it aimed to establish itself as a state and advance along the path to modernity, yet the nation was linked to and founded on conservative, even reactionary pillars. In this respect, the criticisms that Tobias Barreto produced are the apex of his contribution, illustrating his personality and the posture he assumed throughout his life: a man of great intelligence—a ruthless critic, patriot, extrovert, scholar, and architect of ideas. Tobias Barreto de Meneses did not hesitate to get involved in heated debates or discussions.

This trait also exemplified the behavior of the Christian jurist, who, while criticizing the Church, aimed to emphasize the dynamics of progress, limiting the tradition of the Catholic religion in Brazilian lands, yet intending to remain true to the faith.

On the Brazilian state

For the best comprehension of Tobias Barreto's contributions to his time and place, as well as his enduring influence, it is imperative to understand the foundations of the Brazilian state. The state claims to be based on the following criteria: (a) the nature of the relationship between the state and civil society, that is, the public-private relationship; (b) the way in which the authority exercises power; (c) the derivation of power; (d) the degree of legal recognition of freedoms; and (e) the existence of a constitutional text.[1] By Continental European standards, the fact is that the reality in Brazil has peculiar and specific features.

Not only did the form of Portuguese colonization bring its own attributes to the Brazilian state project, but the assimilation of the Indigenous population and Europeans constituted cultural and institutional peculiarities. The distribution of land, income, and public concessions during colonization formed *real estamentos*, or estates. The need to maintain national unity, especially the territorial integrity of a country that extends as far as a continent, also required ingenious and specific state structures. Sustaining an economic model by means of a slave regime created its own nuances. Being the only monarchy in the Americas also required creativity, especially because the emperor remained hereditarily linked to Portugal.

One cannot lose sight of the understanding of the state's use of Brazilian lands and wealth as a commercial activity, perhaps as a capitalist company. This was not a modern, rational, and industrialized capitalism but a particularly political capitalism, that is, one in which the state "intervenes, plans, and directs the economy as much as it can, taking into account the particular interests of the group that controls it, the *estamento*."[2] This economic activity was thus promoted in a space of fluidity and volatility of the rules of the game. Between the advent of Europeans to South America and the end of the Vargas government (1945), the historical strength of the nation endured in the prolonged persistence of a patrimonial structure, which resisted the full capitalist experience[3] and, with it, the matrices of modernity. In this scenario, predominating at the apex of the pyramid of administrative power was the *estamento*, or estate, which progressively became bureaucratized from its basis in the aristocracy, first through accommodation and then by formal structure.[4] This bureaucratic power developed from a mix of practical improvisations aimed at preserving the convenience and enjoyment of wealth, concessions, and position of the private estates. As a result, there was constant confusion between public and private spaces. Brazil operated under a quite different model from the classical understanding of the modern state, which maintains a distinction between the public and private.

Brazil gave bureaucracy potentially unrivaled importance, but with Brazilian bureaucratic precepts. In other words, the bureaucratic system implemented in Brazil led to and continues to drive the formalistic aspect of the state. The national bureaucratic paradigm is an adaptation to maintain the state's foundations, especially regarding the predominance of technical expertise. The neutral, technical, bureaucratic functioning of the government and public administration (*Berufsbeamtentum*, or professional civil service) came to rely on a "political caste" of civil servants (*Beamtenstand*). The theorizing behind this bureaucracy was applied first to the colony, then, later, to the empire and the republic.[5]

The state, for its part, kept the people in constant dependence and controlled lethargy. As a consequence, appropriating the discourse of Barreto's contemporary Joaquim Nabuco, the Brazilian paradigm of the state was a vacuum construction, whose basis was principles, not facts; whose material was ideas, not individuals; whose situation was the world, not the country; whose inhabitants were future generations, not the present.[6] It should be emphasized that the construction of the Brazilian state, which does not fit perfectly with modernity, and which passes by with a confusion of characters, but which remains faithful to the *estamentos*, persists in feeding a complex standardizing and centralizing machine at the national level. The human element becomes increasingly distant under the model of absolute sovereignty. Constant reforms manipulate the constitutional text and jurisdictional activity. Technique subverts the bureaucracy. But the territory is preserved for the state's convenience.

As this chapter demonstrates in more depth, however, Tobias Barreto's thinking includes a peculiar perspective on the relation between state policy and the Church in the formation of the Brazilian state. For Barreto, in short, the genesis of the Brazilian state avoided religious conflicts. In Brazil, the Catholic Church did not form a caste, did not have privileges, did not form resistance, and had no concerns about heresies.[7] Thus, the process of constituting the Brazilian state had not brought about a national conversation about religion until Barreto's time. The adoption of Catholicism as the official religion of the empire, as prescribed by the Imperial Constitution of 1824, did not demarcate a victory or a conquest but the institutionalization of something unquestionable. However, Barreto's criticism of the Church and government came from this scenario—out of the confusion between the roles of the Church and the state arising from the notion of religion as a public distribution or from the consequences of manipulation of the state's authority over the Church.

Topics of Tobias Barreto's thought

Despite his biracial origin, which was a source of recurring racial prejudice; despite having been born in the northeastern countryside (*sertão*), a place previously chosen as a refuge for runaway slaves; despite an education unaligned with the traditional axes of the empire—despite all this, Tobias Barreto as an academic, jurist, and critic challenged the main stigmas reigning in Brazilian society, so that his successes pour out of unlikely contexts. To a large extent, his intellectual makeup was owing not only to his personal attributes but also to the debates at the Recife Law School and its openness to dialectics, which did not conform to the bureaucratic aspect of state services after independence.

Tobiastic thought influenced and guided the vanguard of reformist debate in Brazil in the decade that began in 1870, a period when the national culture underwent great ferment, leaving behind the conservative anesthesia that prevailed in the empire. The elders of 1870 brought about a time of questioning. In this setting, Barreto's wide-ranging exploration of authors and intellectual currents led him not only to innovate in relation to the so-called schools of thought and ideological matrices but also to bring essential changes to the prism through which the nation viewed the Brazilian context, making it more adaptive to concepts from abroad.

The realism that Barreto presented sometimes borders on pessimism. According to Arnaldo Sampaio de Moraes Godoy, this attitude is unique to those who experience the vicissitudes, idiosyncrasies, and storms of life, who know that between the candor of the promises of metaphysics and the accidents of real life lies a distance that, after traveling, imprints the true meaning of existence through sacrifices, privations, and trials.[8] Not by chance, Barreto is thought of as the Baruch Spinoza of Brazilian thought, given the content of his criticism, his wit, the evolution of his research in conformation with the evolution of science, and his fearless battle against the scientific ignorance of state agents.

In politics, Barreto criticized the tendency to concentrate and personalize power, a tendency inherent not only to the people who hold it but also to the culture and institutions already in place. He demonstrated the mechanisms used by the national monarchy to seize nonpublic spaces. He anticipated the reasons why the monarchy would succumb to a republic in the near future, even with a culture that would not be exactly republican. In addition, while engaging in politics as a deputy, Barreto observed the superficiality of public debates and their marginal role in resolving latent problems.

As a poet, polemicist, and critic, Barreto drew on eclectic sources of thought, from Kant to Marx; confronted gender issues in defense of women at the university; spoke out about the anguish of structural racism in Brazil; and denounced the authoritarianism of the emperor. By various means, he attacked the problem of Brazilian social backwardness and the relative apathy in demanding changes, even after the European and American revolutionary uprisings (in the north and in the south). He asserted:

> It is important not to forget that in the production of our evils the complicity of the people is to a great extent present. In the balance of historical impartiality, I do not know what weighs more, whether the abuses of power or the neglect of freedom.[9]

With his philosophical positions, Barreto inaugurated a school of thought in Brazil. This was not his only contribution, however. He advanced a view of positivism (though fiercely critical of August Comte's philosophical positivism), introducing it into the academy under the bias of monism and culturality. Analysis and monism are the basis of tobiastic theorizing. At the fore of the vanguard, Tobias Barreto critically positioned himself with regard to determinism, freedom, nature, and culture. But he did not take up such movements just to study them; he went beyond, mirroring them to Brazilian culture, including the Catholic tradition in Brazil versus the Catholic religion.

With regard to the Catholic religion specifically, Barreto was born Catholic but criticized the Church throughout his academic career. As a conservative, he noted the central cause of institutional and social ills. For him, the Church's alliance with imperial absolutism was a minor problem, because it kept the governing patrimonialism active. Instead, he directed his criticism most sharply against using the Church of faith as a condition of intellectual domination, by which the Catholic tradition as it crystallized in Brazil did not correspond to the Catholic religion emanating from Rome.

As a man of faith, Tobias Barreto questioned the prevalence of vicars who nourished in themselves the political, bureaucratic, and *estamental* spirit, but who did little in apostolic and social works. In his judgment, the Brazilian Church made an abysmal mistake in repudiating abolitionism while remaining blind to the secularization of the state. Confirming his view of how faith suffered in the Catholic Church of the time, he leveled a blast against the utilitarianism of the Church in Brazil: "human nature protests against the miseries and narrowness of environmental reality."[10] The problem was in the skin-deep, non-visceral religiosity that the Church in Brazil produced, making use of syncretisms and exercising contempt through dogmas and orthodoxies. Tobias Barreto made an astute distinction between Brazilian Catholicism and Roman Catholicism, as he pointed out that what was forbidden in Rome was practiced by clerics in Brazil.[11] From this scenario emerged the Religious Question concerning the lay and ordained religious folk who participated in Masonic rites, which were strongly condemned by Bishop D. Vital of Olinda on the basis of the ultramontanism of Pius IX. One of the fuses that triggered the proclamation of the republic on November 15, 1889, as Tobias Barreto had already anticipated, materialized from this question.[12] Even with the clear and unequivocal content of the criticisms directed at Brazilian Church Catholicism, Tobias Barreto did not put his Christian faith in question. His maxim, when he was admitted as a professor at the law school in Recife, was that "faith is not disputed."[13]

Tobias Barreto: The Catholic jurist

Tobias Barreto was a jurist, teacher, musician, philosopher, poet, journalist, and polyglot. Above all, however, Tobias Barreto was a seducer—a seducer by word and oratory. In spite of his academic and legal qualities, Barreto emerged in the Brazilian university scene as a fruitful connoisseur of the French, English, Russian, Greek, Latin, Italian, and, above all, German languages. Tobias's Germanism marked his life and was responsible for the diffusion of German philosophy and law in Brazil, beginning, above all, with his works developed at Recife. German was minimally known in Brazil, however, even among academics. For this reason, many despised his use of it, thinking that "to speak in German is to say nothing."[14]

This intellectual Germanism attached to Barreto's name augmented the place of the Recife Law School in the vanguard, in whose midst an intellectual revolution materialized, substantiated in the criticism of national institutions and the mode of producing, interpreting, and applying law there. By escaping from the axis of education and French thought emanating from the University of Coimbra, in Portugal, which the Brazilian aristocracy had made a traditional home for forming the national intelligentsia even after independence, Barreto was able to resolve national ills through lenses different from those used by the majority.

In consonance with this intellectual ammunition, Barreto also aimed his attack against the faculties of law, for whom the mere reproduction of knowledge, of mechanical instruction of knowledge, was paramount. Instead, Barreto proposed that the true function of the faculties would be realized with their becoming a laboratory, a place of experimentation, true workshops of knowledge.[15] In his view, educational institutions should, at heart, turn to theoretical questions based on rational data, on higher studies.

Tobias Barreto filled a void by exemplifying a model for the Brazilian jurist at the time—knowledgeable about texts, professional in deportment, lawyerly, and blending in oneself the philosopher, the master of general ideas, the embodiment of concepts, the discoverer and articulator of current paths of thought. Up to that point, the process of intellectual liberation had operated in a fragmented manner, by means of sparse and sometimes contradictory readings. It lacked a system. The intellectual tradition in Brazil lacked a vision that brought humanity and nature into harmony or articulated the way in which these two realities complemented each other, communicated and moved, since dualism was dead, taken over by unilateralism.[16]

According to Clóvis Bevilaqua, a graduate and professor at the Recife Law School, responsible for the text of the Civil Code of 1916, one finds in Tobias Barreto's works the effort to redefine natural law in Brazil, ignoring it in favor of humanism, culture, and the monist project:

> Tobias's campaign against natural law is one of the most brilliant parts of his work. It is necessary to beat a hundred times and repeat a hundred times, he exclaims: Law is not a child of heaven, it is simply a historical phenomenon, a cultural product of humanity. *Serpes nisi serpentem comedit non fit draco*, the serpent that did not devour the serpent does not become a dragon. The force that does not overcome the force is not made Right; Right is the force that killed the force itself.[17]

The problem with natural law, Barreto insists, is that by mirroring law with theology, in form and background, legal thought resisted the changes that had taken place in the natural sciences, which could not be neglected, such as in the works of Charles Darwin and Rudolf von Ihering.[18] For the jurist Tobias Barreto, all the sciences had broken "the primitive poetic envelope; law alone does not want to come out of its mythological shell."[19] And so, in an indicative passage of culturalist thought,[20] critical of the perception of a transcendent right, he writes:

> I only have to face the three modern conceptions of the idea of law...: the monism of today's German school, the system of Schopenhauer's will, and Charles Darwin's Darwinian selection. Some people confuse monism with

> pantheism. These are fundamentally opposed ideas. While pantheism says that everything is God and substantiates the divinity in matter, monism says that everything is one and does not remember God, because God is not admitted in science. God can be the object of our worship, but not of our discussions. God in science plays the same role as the number 9 in arithmetic operations; he is excluded.[21] What our organs do not perceive, and what is not susceptible to observation, does not go before science. Now, here is the difference between pantheism and monism. Everything is one; every system I adopt has been made concrete.[22]

Law needs to satisfy the problems of its time and the claims that are cultivated from reality. Barreto repudiated the idea that the juridical is linked to cosmic revelation or to the metaphysics of Thomist/Augustinian thought. To believe this would result in asserting that human existence can support injustice, and that law is not interested in changing the status quo.

To Barreto, natural law seemed true foolishness because it included no concept of revelation. Faced with this scenario, he configured the existence of a science of law beyond the notion of natural law. To advance this thought, Barreto fought for the jurist to be no longer the honor guard before the emperor's throne. The jurist could no longer restrict himself to defending and promoting the status quo of the bureaucratic *estamento* inherited from the House of Avis and Bragança. Instead, the meaning of legal science must be conditioned by political aspiration.

This tobiastic formula materialized the conditions for opening critical paths for propositions. Through his legal science, Barreto aimed not to influence by means of reductionism the same vices, errors, and dysfunctionalities. It would not be enough to criticize the state, the national aristocracy, Brazilian Catholicism, the systems of thought, and entrenched conservatism. The possibility of change began with the rescue of humanity through monism, cultural dynamism, and evolution; without these, there would be a mere repetition of the same old systems.

Undeniably, the influence of Barreto marked generations as well as institutional logic. It was Barreto's responsibility to insert law into the currents of nineteenth-century evolutionism, showing the relationship of complementarity in the systems of social rules of conduct and organization. Among these systems, the law stands out, since in law desires, pretensions, morality, sociabilities, prohibitions, and judgments take shape—true artistic creations, because they result from deliberate human acts of creativity.

The school supported by Tobias Barreto provided a turning point, worthy of Copernicus, to project light on realms ranging from political economy to criminal law, from ecclesiastical law to commercial law. In Hermes Lima's interpretation of the work of Tobias Barreto, law, morals, and religion were considered cultural processes through which artistic selections were made—that is, selections deliberately designed and sought after, because without such processes the selection would follow the "so-called natural march of things," a God-given march, at the mercy of brute force, undisciplined. When Tobias spoke of legal Darwinism and characterized law as the "force that killed the force itself," he did not use empty, rhetorical phrases, but employed phrases in which he framed the concept of law within the more general concept of evolutionism.[23]

Illustrative of his particular conception of the jurist is one of his last epistles, to his friend and colleague from academia, Silvio Romero:

> When in your story you deal with me, I ask you to try to make it clear, in all objectivity, by means of dates, that it was I who first opened a new intuition of law to these people. Emphasize this. It's a capital issue for me today.[24]

In this sense, Tobias Barreto, like other jurists of different times and ages, anticipated the transition from an inadequate legal model—one with excessive and ineffective attachment to current rules with no correspondence to factual demands—to a new model of rationality and modern institutional attributes. Thus, Tobias Barreto is for Brazilian legal science the equivalent of Bartolo de Sassoferrato (1313–57) for Continental European law.

Final considerations

Tobias Barreto was a man of science, far ahead of the time in which he lived. If he were among us today, he would probably criticize the metaphysics of the dominant legal reasoning in Brazil, its creeping superficiality and lack of reflection. He would certainly keep as a motto a memorable passage: "One thing is made principle; other things are made principles." He would also be likely to air his frustration with having more than a million lawyers in one country and approximately eight-hundred legal courses in operation, while there remains continuing injustices, deprivations, violence, and exclusions from various ways of life. We multiply, import, adapt principles and references, as if references and presuppositions were given, made according to the laws of abiogenesis, coming from a raw material, lifeless, and not constructed.

In addition to criticism, Tobias Barreto presented new legal, philosophical, political, social, and institutional paths for a nation under construction. With humility and courage, he made his contribution at a time of multiple needs. He was able to demonstrate how to extract solutions and virtues from problems and vicissitudes. This observation can be reaffirmed from the way his analysis of law, state, and religion always focused on possibilities of optimization *pro homine*.

In fact, Tobias Barreto de Meneses made a name for himself not only by his resilience and ability to overcome adversities of all kinds, culturally constructed over centuries, but especially by having, in the words of Graça Aranha, emancipated Brazil. From Recife, Tobias Barreto emancipated Brazilian law, generating a Brazilian legal thought, although it still needed much for its development. As a legacy, Tobias Barreto demands of Brazilian jurists that they keep their thinking in keeping with their time.

Notes

1 Volpi, *Libertà e autorità*, 26–27.
2 “intervém, planeja e dirige o mais que pode a economia, tendo em vista os interesses particulares do grupo que o controla, o estamento”: in Goyatá Campante, “O patrimonialismo,” 153.
3 Caldeira, *Mauá*.
4 Faoro, *Os donos do poder*, 823.
5 Ibid., 825.
6 Ibid., 832–33.
7

> And that’s why I have my sympathies for the intransigent popes. I like a Julius II, of whom a chronicler of the time used to say: il papa é (there the old Italian). I like a Flavius V, of whom the Italian sage said, etc. (more Italian) and thus quoted about ten intransigent popes and the respective Italian authors, etc. And know this, Mr. Dr. (Tobias continues) that I am not one of those who kiss the popes’ sandals; no, I understand that it is so foolish (with heat) to believe in the pope who promises him eternal bliss in heaven; how foolish is he who believes in the king, who promises him the kingdom of justice on earth” (Bravos, prolonged applause). Then Bandeirinha blessed himself three times and José Higino grumbled, calling Tobias a heretic.
>
> (Barreto, *Estudos de direito* I, 261)

8 Sampaio de Moraes Godoy, *Tobias Barreto*.
9 “[I]mporta não esquecer que na produção de nossos males figura em grande parte a cumplicidade do povo. Na balança da imparcialidade histórica, não sei o que pesa mais, se os abusos do poder, ou os desleixos da liberdade”: Barreto, *Estudos de direito* I, 383.
10 “protesto da natureza humana contra as misérias e as estreitezas da realidade ambiente”: in Lima, *Tobias Barreto*, 187.
11 Ibid., 161.
12 Barreto, *Vários escritos*, 168.
13 Barreto, *Estudos alemães*, 274.
14 “Falar em alemão é nada dizer.” In Veiga, *A Escola do Recife*, 45.
15 Barreto, *Estudos de Direito*, 1:54.
16 Lima, *Tobias Barreto*, 207.
17 Cited in Bevilaqua, *História*, 542.
18 Sampaio de Moraes Godoy, *Tobias Barreto*, 37.
19 “o primitivo invólucro poético; só o direito não quer [queria] sair da sua casca mitológica.” In Barreto, *Estudos de Direito*, 1:52.
20 Reale, *Horizontes*.
21 “Casting out nines” can be any of a number of procedures in arithmetic sometimes used to check for errors.
22 Barreto, *Estudos de Direito*, 2:53.
23 Lima, *Tobias Barreto*, 212.
24 Barreto, *Vários escritos*, 318.

References

Barreto, Tobias. *Estudos alemães*. Rio de Janeiro: J.E. Solomon; Sergipe: Editora Diário Oficial, 2013.

Barreto, Tobias. *Estudos de Direito*. Campinas: Bookseller, 2000.

Barreto, Tobias. *Estudos de Direito*, Vol. 2. Rio de Janeiro: J.E. Solomon; Sergipe: Editora Diário Oficial, 2012.

Barreto, Tobias. *Vários escritos: Publicação póstuma dirigida por Sílvio Romero*. Rio de Janeiro: Laemmert, 1900.

Bevilaqua, Clóvis. *História da Faculdade de Direito do Recife*. 3rd ed. Recife: Editora Universitária da UFPE, 2012.

Caldeira, Jorge. *Mauá—o empresário do império*. São Paulo: Companhia das Letras, 1995.

Faoro, Raymundo. *Os donos do poder. Formação do patronato político brasileiro*. 3rd ed. Rio de Janeiro: Globo, 2010.

Goyatá Campante, Rubens. "O patrimonialismo em Faoro e Weber e a sociologia brasileira." *Revista Dados* 46, no. 1 (2003): 61–89.

Lima, Hermes. *Tobias Barreto. A época e o homem*. Rio de Janeiro: Companhia Editora Nacional, 1939.

Reale, Miguel. *Horizontes do Direito e da História*. São Paulo: Saraiva, 1956.

Sampaio de Moraes Godoy, Arnaldo. *Tobias Barreto. Uma biografia intelectual do insurreto sergipano e sua biblioteca com livros alemães no Brasil do século XIX*. Curitiba: Juruá, 2018.

Veiga, Gláucio. *A Escola do Recife*, Vol. 3, book 1. Recife: UFPE, 1989.

Volpi, Mauro. *Libertà e autorità. La classificazione delle forme di Stato e delle forme di governo*. 4th ed. Turin: G. Giappichelli, 2010.

21 José Manuel Estrada (Argentina, 1842–94)

Agustín Parise

Introduction

Catholics and liberals in Argentina and other Latin American countries challenged each other during the final decades of the nineteenth century. José Manuel Estrada played a fundamental role within this context and advocated for his ideals through prolific writings, legislative efforts, and teaching. He offered a solid historical and constitutional grounding to these endeavors and gained a place of prominence among his contemporaries. Estrada was active for thirty years during a pivotal time in Argentine history, when cultural and socioeconomic changes were taking place during the reuniting of the province of Buenos Aires with the rest of Argentina and the consolidation of the nation-state. Interest in the life and work of Estrada faded with time, and his legacy is now, regrettably, somehow neglected or at least not fully explored. Yet Estrada was a member of a vigorous generation that started to shape the consolidation of an Argentine identity, and thus he merits renewed attention.[1]

This chapter aims to redirect attention to this fundamental actor in the interplay of law, religion, history, and society in the southern part of the Americas. The chapter first offers biographical information on Estrada while attending to his place within the local tradition and offering a brief overview of his works. Second, the chapter focuses on two main pillars in the life and work of Estrada—his study of history and constitutional law. Third, the chapter reflects on the place of Christianity as it influenced these two pillars of Estrada's work. The chapter then offers some concluding remarks.

An apostle of freedom[2]

Estrada is properly placed among the great men and women in Argentine history who organized and led the country while shedding light on its past. Interest in Estrada's life and work has shifted from unconditional praise to indifference. Even when it could be claimed that his endeavors were not suitable for the progress of his time, he fought to defend his ideals and opened the way to deeper study of history, constitutional law, and political science. He was an educator with many abilities and talents. It has been said that Estrada did ordinary things in an extraordinary manner and was a kind of secular apostle.[3] As early as 1862, Estrada pointed out that he wrote with the "sincerity of a Catholic and of a republican."[4]

Biographical sketch

José Manuel Estrada was born in Buenos Aires, Argentina, on July 13, 1842, and died in Asunción, Paraguay, on September 17, 1894. His family strongly endorsed Christianity and had gained prestige and wealth over the generations. His great-grandfather was the Spanish viceroy Santiago de Liniers (1753–1810), and two of his brothers were Santiago Estrada (1841–91) and Ángel Estrada (1840–1918). José Manuel was a member of the elite of Buenos Aires; he married Elena Esteves Saguí in 1868, and they had three sons and two daughters. His life offers a mosaic of activities and interests, including roles as orator, journalist, writer, historian, educator, statesman, and politician. It is worth noting that he never enrolled as a student at a university, though he received a solid humanist formation at the prestigious Convent of St. Francis in Buenos Aires. Estrada was a *rara avis*: well read, with solid philosophical and theological formation, superior intelligence, and a religious zeal that pushed him to seek answers to the main questions faced by humankind. Indeed, Estrada had all the fundamental skills: knowledge of science, use of logic, lively imagination, and warmth of heart. He had a rich vocabulary and the ability to trigger emotions. He conveyed his thoughts well in writing and orally, and his education led him to blend his love for freedom with his love for religion.[5]

Estrada had many interests. He was a key member of a constantly evolving intellectual community in the River Plate region, where locals interacted and blended with foreigners. For example, as a journalist, writer, and publisher, he established and directed a number of journals and newspapers (e.g. *Revista Argentina*, 1868; *El Argentino*, 1873; *La Unión*, 1882), and with Lucio V. Mansilla (1831–1913) he was one of the founders of the cultural association called the Círculo Literario (1864). As a statesman and politician, he was a member of the Constitutional Convention (1871) of Buenos Aires, a member of the House of Representatives (1886), plenipotentiary minister to Paraguay (1893), and cofounder (and first president) of a Catholic political party (Unión Católica, 1885). As an educator, he taught history at the Normal School of Buenos Aires (1865), was head of the General Department of Schools (*jefe del Departamento General de Escuelas*, 1869), director of Normal Schools (1874), and a teacher at the renowned National School of Buenos Aires (*Colegio Nacional de Buenos Aires*, 1869), where he was also appointed rector in 1876. Estrada also taught at the university level, holding the chair of constitutional and administrative law at the University of Buenos Aires (1875). He never worked in the private sector.[6]

Estrada was a militant Catholic. His faith played a fundamental role in his life; he pondered social problems and showed particular care for the poor. In one of his earliest works, in 1862, Estrada rebutted Lamarckian evolutionist attacks against Catholicism.[7] In that context he stated:

> Christianity, while transforming the warrior into the man of law, removes the bloody knife from the priest and erases from his lips the oracles of the Pythoness, to communicate words of eternal life, and to turn him into the angel of consolation and the minister of charity.[8]

Estrada's place in the tradition

Modern Argentina took form during Estrada's life. The Argentine economy prospered during the last decades of his life, reaching the first place among Latin American countries. He was a central figure as the country entered the twentieth century, and was praised by his contemporaries, including Miguel Cané (1851–1905), Pedro Goyena (1843–92), and Paul Groussac (1848–1929). Estrada was born under the dictatorship of Juan M. de Rosas (1793–1877), who ruled Argentina with absolute power, and a constant quest for freedom shaped Estrada's life. He claimed that freedom was found in nature,[9] and he was known as the "Apostle of Freedom."[10] He advocated for a regime of civil and political freedom, yet under a social order in which justice would fully prevail.[11] Religion played an important role in that quest for freedom, and in the words of Estrada in 1862, "Catholicism is the seed of freedom."[12] In his mature life, he was considered an outstanding figure of the legislature and a new type of politician who opposed the administration of Julio A. Roca (1843–1914), while remaining a Catholic.[13]

Estrada's thought may be contextualized within the development of the philosophical discourse of the River Plate region. During the Spanish period, scholasticism prevailed and advocated for a philosophy that followed the dogmatic principles of the Catholic Church. Enlightenment ideas then percolated toward the end of the Spanish period. Utilitarianism also received attention during the time of Bernardino Rivadavia (1780–1845). Historical Romanticism, a liberal movement opposing the scholastic tradition, was welcomed at the time of Rosas, as exemplified in the work of Esteban Echeverría (1805–51). Philosophical eclecticism, as in the works of Victor Cousin (1792–1867), eventually found a place in the region, mainly in Buenos Aires. The French ideals of the 1830 Revolution eclectic, Saint-Simonian, and romantic—were challenged by followers of scholasticism who tried to harmonize Christian values with the new mentality of the time by advocating mainly for the spirituality and immortality of the soul. This last effort found a forum in the life and work of Félix Frías (1816–81) and of Estrada.[14]

The Apostle of Freedom reacted against the ideals of the Enlightenment, naturalism, and rationalistic immanence. For Estrada, life in society had to be connected and subordinated to morals and the eternal principles of Christianity. Furthermore, religion was necessary for freedom, and freedom was necessary for religion. Thus, four main passions ruled his life: God, church, republic, and freedom. He was further referred to as a "secular tribune of Catholicism" and as an "apostle of Christ"; he was considered a victim variously of the dictatorship of

Roca, of the secular liberalism of the end of the century, or of a Masonic conspiracy.[15] In 1862, Estrada wrote:

> Rationalism does not recognize the law, curses sacrifice, [and] precludes progress on the basis of individual unerring and absolute and supreme domination of *ego*. Consequently, it is the negation of every principle of society, of every notion of order, of every republican form, of every civilization, [and] of all hope. That is why we say [that] there is no republic beyond Catholicism.[16]

He further claimed, on that same occasion:

> Our faith as Catholics and republicans has driven us to defend those two great causes attacked by rationalism, because this absurd [ideal], similar to cancer, devours everything, and is the poison that destroys all hope and embitters all hearts, without relieving pain, preventing danger, offering comfort, or drying a single tear.[17]

In similar lines, Estrada concluded that "there is an abyss between the rationalist and the Catholic; yet between man and man, Jesus Christ has placed the unbreakable bond of love."[18]

Estrada was the leading Catholic to oppose the prevailing liberalism in Argentina at the end of the nineteenth century.[19] His own writings eloquently depicted his ideals. For example, he claimed in 1878 that "the century of liberalism misunderstands freedom and the causes and results of its fatal and obstructed mistake."[20] Further, in 1883, Estrada stated that liberalism "destroys the economy of the supernatural, [and] destroys all elements of dignity and peace within society."[21] One year later, Estrada similarly stated:

> [T]he century of liberalism is the century of Pius IX and Leo XIII. If liberalism is for the church the element of pain in the present century, its element of glory lies in those two great pontiffs, and in the fullness of their apostolic power, and in the extension, in the purity, and in the unity of the Christian community.[22]

Likewise, at the peak of the conflicts between the Church and liberals (described below), only a few days later that same year, he stated, "Anti-Christian liberalism has martyred peoples more ferociously than all tyrannies, always temporary, dreaming of owning the land; while it persecutes and abhors society, as it persecutes and abhors the Holy Church of Christ."[23] These statements by Estrada strongly endorse religion; radical liberalism, in his view, threatened society.

Secular liberalism had gained ground by the end of the century in Argentina as it was welcomed in Europe, mainly in France, and in the Americas in neighboring Chile and Uruguay. Liberalism was Estrada's main challenge. He faced, however, the additional divide between secular and Catholic liberalism. Following European liberal Catholics, in his youth Estrada tried to combine liberal and Catholic tenets. In fact, he could be placed within the tradition of Christian liberalism. Later, in the 1880s, he noted that both tenets could no longer fully cohabit, being incompatible.[24] Historian Ricardo Rojas (1882–1957) pointed to that divide in Estrada's life, claiming that his works were of special interest because he had an ideological position that combined the liberal and the democrat within Christianity.[25]

Estrada offered two approaches to culture, one national and the other Catholic. On one hand, he promoted national culture beginning in his youth. For example, the activities of the Círculo Literario enabled Estrada to explore cultural elements of the River Plate region. In this environment, Estrada and Mansilla aimed to foment harmony among the enlightened actors of Buenos Aires within the framework of cultural life. They sought to reconcile interests and practices, and they extended invitations to people of diverse political leanings. It was a call to cohabit in heterogeneity, even though the project would soon fade away. Within this context, Estrada was able to offer a network for newcomers, such as Groussac. On the other hand, also beginning in his youth, Estrada was a promoter of Catholic culture. He was able to transform the existent structures of Argentine Catholicism by supporting a network of associations that served in the political struggles of that time. In his later years, he was able to create new expressions of Catholic culture through important political positions. Even when he could be deemed conservative by many, he reshaped cultural elements, with a special focus on Catholic culture toward the turn of the century.[26]

Works

Estrada was prolific, and his works are vast and diverse. Research on the *opera* of Estrada benefited from the efforts of his son, Alberto, who gathered the writings of José Manuel into twelve posthumously published volumes of his collected works (*Obras completas*). The content of those volumes illustrates that the life of Estrada was indeed a mosaic of activities and interests.[27] As Edwin M. Borchard (1884–1951) pointed out to English-language readers, volumes six through eight are of special interest for legal studies, since they enclose his seminal writings on constitutional law.[28] The richness of the twelve volumes confirms that Estrada gained an undisputed place in the cultural life of Argentina. In addition, his work led to well deserved recognition. For example, the Argentine Academy of Letters and the Academy of Law and Social Sciences of Buenos Aires established chairs to honor him. Likewise, Professor's Day in Argentina is celebrated on September 17, the anniversary of his death, to commemorate his life and work; he is remembered as a model for educators. Several schools are named after him, and sculptures of him are found across the country. Events related to Estrada were covered by the press, both from Argentina and beyond, well into the twentieth century. For instance, the unveiling of a bust in Buenos Aires was reported in France by the newspaper *Le Gaulois* in 1927.[29]

Estrada's works evolved across more than three decades. He wrote about the discovery of America (and received an award) at age sixteen; on evolutionism at age nineteen; on Catholicism and democracy at age twenty; and on the history of Paraguay at age twenty-one. He was inclined to engage in debate, was an enthusiastic teacher, and was considered an eloquent and superb orator, all traits reflected in his writings. Scholars tend to count as his primary works his lessons on Argentine history (*Lecciones sobre la historia de la República Argentina*, 1868) and his *opus* on Catholicism and democracy (*El Catolicismo y la Democracia*, 1862), together with his exposition on the tyrannical regime of Rosas (*La Política liberal bajo la tiranía de Rosas*, 1873) and his materials on constitutional law (*Curso de Derecho constitucional*, starting in 1877). Estrada likewise published writings on education, literature, religion, and legislation. As a gifted orator, he presented several of his main works first as lectures. In his work, Estrada took sociological approaches that were deemed interesting when compared with the approaches taken by others in Latin America at that time. Furthermore, his *opera* triggered many works by others. His writings were studied by scholars in Argentina and beyond, as would be expected from the life and work of a seminal thinker.[30]

These works can be divided or grouped into two categories. On one hand is his primary output. This includes his historical studies and his constitutional law course. On the other hand are his miscellaneous pieces. Many of these were shorter contributions, first formed as improvised speeches and dealing with diverse topics ranging from the benefits of charity to the merits of the law of civil marriage.[31] Again, each entry in the two categories was a tile or *tessera* of the colorful mosaic of activities and interests of Estrada. Together they helped to depict fully the views and ideals of the Apostle of Freedom during the second half of the nineteenth century. Furthermore, each of these tiles is a fundamental tool to contextualize the activities of Estrada as a specific actor, at a specific time, in a specific place.

Main pillars

The life and work of Estrada can be best explored by attending to two main pillars. Among Estrada's many interests, his devotion to history and constitutional law was fundamental, and these interests were amalgamated into the place of Christianity in his life.

Estrada was a constitutive figure of Argentine culture. Guided by his Catholic faith, he established his political structure on the need for and preexistence and supremacy of individual freedom. He used his religious and philosophical ideas to strengthen that structure, blending them with political and legal ideas. Divine law prevailed over natural and positive laws, according to Estrada, since divine law offered rules that were eternal and supreme. He had an axiom: freedom, innate in humans, was necessary for the fulfillment of their privileged destiny. This approach entailed welfare; hence, it seemed to fall within the utilitarian tenets of Jeremy Bentham (1748–1832). Estrada considered a broad spectrum of thought when elaborating his ideals, contextualizing such ideas within legislation, history, traditions, customs, comparative law, natural law, and divine law. Resulting from Estrada's political and historical method, this approach was unknown to previous constitutional scholars in Argentina.[32]

Estrada taught, cared for education, conveyed knowledge, and invited students to think. He aimed to educate in a broad sense— to shape a concrete civic conscience in citizens and to trigger a sense of commitment and responsibility. He pointed to the problems of the schools in Buenos Aires in his report on elementary education (*Memoria sobre la educación común en la Provincia de Buenos Aires*, 1870) and to a woeful lack of training for instructors. There were no such studies at that time in Argentina, and he offered in-depth insights and information. He advocated for religious education, rejecting atheist schools. He opposed secular education and advanced this position in public in his writings in *La Unión*. Estrada was consequently removed from the position of rector and teacher at the Colegio Nacional (1883) and later from his chair at the University of Buenos Aires (1884). Those dismissals gained the attention of the press in Argentina and beyond. Students visited Estrada at his home to offer their support and to reject the second removal, and he delivered a speech stressing that teaching had always been his main concern.[33]

History

Estrada had a passion for history. He offered lectures and courses on Argentine history, later edited into several monographs. He also incorporated historical remarks and insights generally into his work.[34] In 1877 he advocated for the relevance of history by stating:

> Woe to the people who forget! Those from whose heart the memory of their benefactors disappears, like sepulchral inscriptions that erase the living in passing: those from whose conscience disappears hatred towards the great evil, like the fire of a torch extinguished in the abominable wave![35]

These words elegantly and poetically stressed the importance of history.

Estrada was an advocate for historical research. He benefited from the contents of archives, though scholars have pointed out that his own work would have benefitted from greater use of archival sources.[36] It should be noted, however, that in 1865, Estrada criticized the "poor conditions of our archives and the poverty of our libraries."[37] Through his own use of archival sources, Estrada offered systematization to Argentine history. He was perhaps the first to do so.[38]

Estrada's early historical output focused on Argentina and the region. Other writings displayed a broader scope by examining the Americas beyond Argentina. In his early works, Estrada addressed the idea of progress as a means to observe the evolution of society. Progress, for Estrada, tended toward the perfection of humankind, not just in a material sense or a sense of well-being. Progress was also a law of humanity and of history that affected the political sphere. In his later years, he no longer wrote systematic historical works. It seems he had left behind his romantic optimism and acknowledged the damage that ideologies and sectarian interests could inflict on society.[39]

The historical writings of Estrada attracted followers through the emotions they triggered. Bartolomé Mitre (1821–1906), the renowned Argentine historian, encouraged Estrada to develop his historical studies and granted Estrada access to his library. In 1865, Mitre viewed Estrada as a promising historian. Estrada worked as historian and sociologist, and although his writings could be considered lacking in scientific rigor, they reflected his efforts to depict reality.[40]

Estrada joined a school of historians with philosophic tendencies and promoted this approach in the Americas. With Mariano A. Pelliza (1837–1902) and Vicente F. López (1815–1903), Estrada welcomed European influences, such as the works of François Guizot (1787–1874).[41] Members of this school sought a philosophical view of history, occasionally neglecting archival research in favor of ideological interpretations. With that approach, Estrada aimed to understand the philosophy of Argentine history. In 1866, in a letter to Vicente G. Quesada (1830–1913), Estrada stated that "observation applied to history and philosophy of history is the initial formula of the method in the modern school."[42] In that same letter, he suggested that historians should attend to social and moral aspects to chart the path of society's progress. This philosophical approach was not fully able to offer an erudite apparatus or a clear organization of arguments. The past was recalled by means of broad lines and an interpretative tone. Accordingly, some scholars objected that the work of Estrada was tainted with subjective interpretations and literary style, neglecting any meticulous use of sources. For example, his lessons on Argentine history and his exposition on the tyrannical regime of Rosas offered a philosophical synthesis of the past. Philosophic tendencies could interplay with Christian ideals, and Estrada found a common ground for religious faith and political creed.[43]

Estrada began his studies of history at a very early age, with his account on the discovery of America. In the 1860s, he started to focus on Argentine history. He took an erudite approach in his early years and expressed concern about the state of the conservation of documents and repositories in Argentina. He likewise referred to the value of history as it reconstructed the past by the systematic study of sources. Midway through the 1860s, Estrada traced historical events by looking at the activities of seminal actors. Law is a social science subject to mutation, after all. The actors who trigger those changes are often identifiable, and the reconstruction of the activities of the main actors behind those changes creates a legal and cultural repository for future studies. Estrada focused on actors who participated in social struggles. His writings during the last years of the 1860s show his movement from an erudite approach to history to one attempting to capture and interpret the relation between past, present, and future. He moved toward this school of historians with philosophic tendencies and assimilated new ideas from history (for example, Hippolyte Taine, 1828–93), from classics (for example, Charles-Louis de Montesquieu, 1689–1755), and from positivism (for example, Auguste Comte, 1798–1857). He aimed to unveil the interplay between society and politics; and his study of Rosas, already in the following decade, offered an example of that interplay. He was very critical of the period of Rosas, yet always considered such events as the result of political and social dynamics.[44] Estrada claimed:

> Nobody ignores or denies that Rosas was a tyrant persecutor of the law in all its forms, was methodically cruel and popular by calculation, and was surrounded by mysteries due to the [infliction of] fear and [by being] arrogant. In addition, nobody ignores the terrors that he spread, the demoralization that he gestated, and the cowardice that he exploded. Yet Rosas was a social product, logical despite being abominable, [and that] is something not only generally ignored but also denied by publicists and poets claiming a patriotism that was lost by misleading views. I was very young when he succumbed; but childhood has a special aptitude to convey deep emotions; and I remember the popular jubilation of February 3, 1852.[45]

In his eyes, Rosas was a logical social product of his time.[46]

Argentine history merited special attention. In 1866, Estrada began delivering his lessons on Argentina, first published in installments in a journal and then as a consolidated monograph, among the first of its kind in Argentine historiography. This popular work may have influenced other books used to teach history in Argentina and beyond. Although not erudite, Estrada's lessons traced the evolution of Argentine society. He identified topics that required attention. In his lessons, he offered a passionate account of events and communicated them with the enthusiasm of an apostle.[47] In 1868, in the introduction to this work, Estrada pointed out:

> I have tried to guide [the] teaching toward the most useful and to reduce it to the indispensable, having in mind to explain the Argentine revolution. In order to understand [that revolution], it is necessary to study all antecedents and traditions of society…I have dispensed with all details [that might be deemed] necessary to write the history but [that were] detrimental to teach its philosophy [in a] brief way and with clarity.[48]

Erudite expositions should not be expected from these lessons. Ideas were presented only in an outline and not explored in depth. The lessons excelled in offering enlightened summaries and accurate analyses: they helped to trace historical processes.[49]

Estrada's historical output may be approached from the perspective of religion. His historical endeavors offered a new amalgam of Catholicism and liberalism. After all, Estrada considered Catholicism a fundamental part and pillar of Western history. Nonetheless, his historical works have been minimized or at least considered of limited relevance from a Catholic standpoint. This disregard may stem from his criticism of the Jesuits in a work from 1865, among other reasons.[50]

Constitutional law

The life and work of Estrada were constructed on a solid pillar provided by constitutional law. His interest in this area of law stemmed from an early age: in 1859 he endorsed the Argentine Constitution of 1853 in his study of the confederation, *Signum Foederis: Efectos sociales y religiosos de la armonía*. In this short piece he addressed nationality and politics, including the merits of an American federation. As the title of the work indicates, that work also addressed the social and religious effects of harmony, indicating the place of religion in his early work. A national constitutional convention had met in the city of Santa Fe in early 1853, summoned by Justo J. de Urquiza (1801–70), and having representatives from the different Argentine provinces, excluding Buenos Aires, which had seceded from the rest of the provinces in 1852. The reuniting of the province of Buenos Aires with the rest of Argentina was accomplished in the constitutional reform of 1860 and aligned with the ideas of, among others, Frías and Miguel Navarro Viola (1830–90).[51]

Estrada continued writing on constitutional law. For example, in 1870, he published two articles on constitutional law in the *Revista Argentina*: one dealing with electoral systems and the other with suffrage. In the pages of *El Argentino* he published a number of articles on constitutional law, addressing the merits of the constitutional text, with a focus also on specific areas such as citizenship. In 1876, Estrada completed a study of comparative legislation. On that occasion he offered a comparison of the preambles of the constitutional texts of Argentina, Colombia, Switzerland, the United States, and Venezuela.[52]

Estrada's concern for constitutional law expressed itself in practice. In 1871, he joined the Constitutional Convention for Buenos Aires, participating actively in several sessions, mainly in those dealing with freedom of education and municipal regulations. Estrada argued that the municipal sphere was central to the political and social life of the free individual. The municipal sphere was paramount for democratic organization, and Estrada studied its historical background. During the sessions of the Constitutional Convention, Estrada also presented a project on oaths of office, and was likewise involved in sessions dealing with, among other topics, the death penalty and election of governors. The sessions offered Estrada an occasion to explore comparative legislation, since he shared comparative remarks on the legislation in Belgium, England, France, Prussia, and the United States.[53]

Higher education offered an important forum for Estrada to explore constitutional law. In 1875 Estrada was appointed professor of constitutional and administrative law at the University of Buenos Aires, upon the death of Florentino González (1805–74).[54] Estrada taught there for nine years, during which he wrote extensively on history and constitutional law. He modified the university course of study in the field significantly. He introduced a novel interpretation of the historical background to offer an approach based on historical precedents.

Estrada was not trained as a lawyer, and he did not subscribe to the exegetical approach prevailing in Argentina. Rather, he employed free explanations informed by historical events. The contents of constitutions should be studied in light of each nation's history, he argued. Customs and traditions also merited attention, together with the study of foreign law. In that sense, Estrada gave a more national perspective to constitutional law.

Estrada also has been credited with developing the study of political science in Argentina, and he applied political events and analysis to the study of constitutional systems. In his course, he focused on political processes rather than mere juridical aspects and offered an interpretation of the decisions of the Argentine Supreme Court. Consistent with his interest in comparative legislation and foreign law, Estrada had a good command of US constitutional law and of translations of several US authors. Nonetheless, when he engaged in comparative dialogues with the US Constitution, he did not worship its text blindly, unlike some earlier Argentine jurists.[55]

Estrada's tenets of constitutional law were conveyed orally at the University of Buenos Aires and were gathered later in writing by his students. His lectures on constitutional law were also lectures on history and morals, since they incorporated his knowledge of philosophy and history. Student notes (*Notes*) of his lectures were published in a single volume in 1895, then as volumes six through eight of the *Obras completas*; they were re-edited and published in three volumes in 1927. *Notes*, together with an earlier study by González, was one of only two monographs on the constitutional law of Argentina published during the nineteenth century in the structure of a treatise. This work by Estrada offered one of the most elaborated interpretations of the constitutional system and soon became a mandatory reference benefiting generations of students in Argentina and beyond. For example, numerous dissertations analyzed Estrada's tenets as presented in *Notes*, either subscribing to or rejecting his ideas.[56] In addition, his ideas on republican governments and federations were translated into Portuguese in Brazil,[57] and his expositions on the requirements for membership in Congress were studied in Bolivia.[58] His influence extended well into the twentieth century, since, for example, Juan A. González Calderón (1883–1964) referred to *Notes* in his seminal constitutional law text when addressing citizenship and naturalization.[59] In the French-language narrative, a 1932 report on modern constitutions included *Notes*.[60] In English, Borchard included it in one of his well-circulated guides, stating that the work had "a leading place" among books that began as lectures delivered at universities.[61]

The content and structure of *Notes* merit special attention. The introduction to *Notes* considers the idea of freedom, a seminal building block in the life and work of Estrada.[62] The opening line of the introduction is, "all political science is contained in the idea of freedom."[63] A didactic work, it was divided into four parts: (1) declarations, rights, and guarantees; (2) government; (3) nation and provinces; and (4) organization of the national government. The work included multiple appendices, dealing with topics ranging from the death penalty to immigration, suffrage, sovereignty, freedom of education, and political rights of foreigners. Estrada advocated in *Notes* for democracy, justice, freedom, and the popular vote as the source of all powers. Making a novel contribution to this literature, Estrada incorporated decisions of the Argentine Supreme Court into the work. These cases explained the interpretation of the constitutional text. Estrada also pointed to US constitutional law to build on observations of North American jurists, and he incorporated historical accounts related to the different articles.[64] For example, when speaking of ownership, Estrada indicated:

> The right of ownership that our old legislation ensured, despite being deficient in many of its consequences, has been in the same way adopted in all constitutional statutes after 1870, and is formally guaranteed by Article 17 of the Federal Constitution.[65]

Estrada's intellectual ideas were linked to his political and religious understandings. For example, in his courses he conveyed that Christianity had enabled the development of ideas and political goals that inspired the full recognition of the inalienable rights of humankind. Estrada spoke openly against the administration of Roca at a time when the conflicts between liberals and Catholics were reaching a peak, and this stance led to his removal from his teaching position at the University of Buenos Aires.[66] Freedom, one of his main objectives, again took the main stage when he lost his position at the university. On that occasion of June 2, 1884, he stated that "from the splinters of the chairs destroyed by despotism, we will make stands to teach justice and to preach freedom!"[67]

Christianity

History and constitutional law were the two pillars of Estrada's life and work. Those pillars were embellished with mosaics of various interests held together by Christianity, which served, indeed, as an overarching bridge. Christianity was present in Estrada's activities from an early age. As a young man, he offered lectures on religion, theology, and history at the Society of St. Francis Solanus and at the Society of St. Francis Xavier. In 1862, he elaborated two early and important writings on the defense of the Church. One work, *El Génesis de nuestra raza*, followed seminal authors and provided his own interpretations to defend the Church. Another work, *El Catolicismo y la Democracia*, defended the social values of Catholicism while advocating for freedom and human dignity. Here Estrada advocated for Catholicism and for the republican system of government. From an early age, Estrada aimed to evangelize political and social actions. Freedom took the stage in his activities; the Christian state served to protect freedom.[68]

Subscribers to liberalism advocated for the separation of state and Church in Argentina during Estrada's lifetime. The formation of nation-states in Latin America was followed by a clash between Catholicism and anticlericalism. During the second half of the nineteenth century, tensions grew in the realms of education, marriage, funerals, and national symbols. The peak of these conflicts in

Argentina came in the 1880s and resulted in a gradual process of separation between the Church and the state. The Church in Argentina had a different institutional, economic, and social structure than the Church in other Latin American jurisdictions. It faced several reforms at a national level that restricted ecclesiastical influence in the public sphere.[69] Even when the Argentine Constitution of 1853 stated in Article 2, in an ambiguous manner, that Argentina supported the Catholic faith, important steps toward separation were taken when secular laws were enacted, mainly beginning in the 1880s. Accordingly, a law on civil marriage was adopted in 1888, together with laws on the civil registry that were adopted in 1884 and 1898. Civil marriage was introduced by means of Law 2,393 of 1888. Since then, only civil marriage has been recognized by the state, while ministers of the Church would be prosecuted if they celebrated religious marriages without a copy of the civil marriage act being produced before them. Estrada saw these secular laws as further proof that the state marched against liberty and against civil freedom. This view was not new for Estrada; he had already rendered an opinion on the relationship between state and church in the Argentine Constitution of 1853. On that occasion, he argued critically that the Argentine president's right of patronage (*derecho de patronato*) meant that the Church was subject to the civil powers in certain matters, such as the appointment of authorities, and therefore presented a limitation on religious freedom.[70]

Events related to the clash between the Church and state illuminate Estrada's approach to liberalism. The institutional development of many ecclesiastical jurisdictions in Latin America, together with the percolation of Enlightenment ideas, to be followed by the reception of liberal doctrines, triggered a clash between Church and state. Militant Catholics found inspiration in the *Syllabus of Errors* of Pius IX (1864), and several events occurred in Argentina within that context. For example, Frías established the Catholic Club in 1877, as a forum to react to the thundering advances of liberalism. Estrada was welcomed into that forum and was invited to deliver several lectures. During the turbulent year of 1848, Frías was in France, where he found inspiration for the creation of a Catholic press and of secular organizations. The newspaper *La Unión* served as another tool to react against liberalism and gained a strong reputation in Argentine journalism.[71]

The curricula of education at primary schools offered further significant points of conflict between Catholics and liberals, and as an educator and public servant, Estrada was well versed in education. In the 1880s President Roca, who had originally found support in the Church, clashed with Catholicism and was drawn towards Masonic and secular–liberal movements. Reactions against the Church began to occur during Roca's first presidential term, and Estrada accepted the challenge to advocate in favor of religion. Law 1,420 of 1884, on primary education, was debated in the National Congress in the early 1880s. The debates addressed the place of religion in the curricula as liberals explored the possibility of eliminating religious teaching from public schools. Catholics circulated petitions against the legislative draft, and a thousand women marched to the National Congress to oppose enactment of the law. By 1883, Estrada's writings had taken on a radical tone, and this shift eventually triggered his removal from his teaching positions.[72] Estrada felt his ideals were being threatened at that time, and he stated in a more belligerent tone that the "time has come to sell the tunic and buy the sword."[73]

The conflict between Catholics and liberals moved Estrada into the legislative and political arena. The two main pillars of history and constitutional law continued to play a fundamental role in shaping his activity. By then, Estrada was considered a "champion of Catholic causes;"[74] he served as president of the reorganized Catholic Association (1883) while it reached out to all Argentine provinces. This association grew in membership, drawing significantly from the influential upper classes. In 1885 Estrada helped establish the Unión Católica, a political party that entered into a coalition with other parties. It successfully placed representatives in the National Congress, including a seat for Estrada, who was able to represent Catholic constituents. By the late 1880s, Estrada had developed a political profile and joined public demonstrations by Catholics;[75] he was a political Catholic. For example, in 1888, when debating the law of civil marriage in the National Congress, Estrada proclaimed:

> We ask you to reject that [civil marriage] bill: to reject it for the love of freedom! That you reject it for love to the country! That you reject it for the sake of civilization! We ask you to back away from the disastrous path to which a destructive policy leads you: that you consolidate, in the social realm of Jesus Christ, the future of the republic, just, vigorous, and noble; and we say to you, finally: be reconciled with the truth, and the truth will set you free![76]

Estrada believed that men and women lived in society, and that politics always entailed a theological component. Within this context, Estrada pointed to the vulnerability of some constitutional tenets such as electoral freedom and provincial independence.[77] In 1890 he stated, "I come to associate with your generous efforts, with my notorious badge of Catholic citizen…in these dark days when only a ridiculous shadow remains of the constitutional freedoms."[78] Constitutional law, history, and Christianity were present in Estrada's activities during the turbulent years in which Catholics and liberals clashed in Argentina.

Concluding remarks

José Manuel Estrada played an active role during the last decades of the nineteenth century in Argentina, a period of great contest between Catholics and liberals. This chapter has explored Estrada's life as a mosaic of interests in which he performed as orator, journalist, writer, historian, educator, statesman, and politician. The chapter also places Estrada within the local tradition—during a period when modern Argentina was shaped. He was a leading Catholic to oppose Argentina's prevailing liberalism at the end of the nineteenth century. His extensive *opera* evolved during three decades and can be divided into his primary output and his miscellaneous pieces.

Two main pillars supported the life and work of the Apostle of Freedom — history and constitutional law—and each pillar informed his actions. Estrada's passion for history led to a number of lectures and courses on history, later edited into several monographs. He was a member of a school of historians with philosophic tendencies, presenting a philosophical view of history while neglecting erudite expositions. He had an active interest in constitutional law but did not limit himself to writing on the topic, as he also advanced his legal doctrine through lectures. His constitutional law course led to a seminal publication and influenced the field throughout the region and across generations.

Christianity linked the two pillars of Estrada's life and work. From an early age, he tied his activities to religion. Later, the Apostle of Freedom experienced the buffeting efforts of the subscribers of liberalism who advocated for the separation of state and the Church in Argentina. The clash between Church and state during his lifetime unveiled his ideals and efforts in dealing with liberalism. Active in debates on civil marriage and on changes to the curricula at primary schools, Estrada was pushed by conflicts between Catholics and liberals into the legislative and political arena that ultimately led to his removal from his teaching positions.

Christianity, history, law, and society were omnipresent in his life and work. As a very prolific publicist, a passionate teacher, and an engaged legislator, Estrada thought and wrote, studied and wrote, observed and wrote—as the contents of his collected works demonstrate.[79] He seems to have been self-aware of his role as a constitutive figure of the culture of his time in Argentina. Toward the end of his life, on April 13, 1890, perhaps already reflecting on his legacy, he claimed that there was an obligation to be accountable for acts of perseverance and courage, since "God will require it from us, he who judges human judgments, vanishes like smoke the ambitions of the proud, reigns, by law, over the courageous people who love and serve justice."[80]

Notes

1 Altamira, "José Manuel Estrada," 291; Bruno, "José Manuel Estrada," 90; and Torrendell, "Presentación. José M. Estrada," 9, 16.

2 Héctor P. Lanfranco, among others, referred to Estrada as an apostle of freedom. See Lanfranco, "La cátedra de Historia y de Derecho Constitucional," 70.

3 Lucero, "La filosofía política y de la historia de José M. Estrada," 105–06, and Tanzi, *José Manuel Estrada*, 137.

4 José M. Estrada, "El Catolicismo y la Democracia," in *Obras completas*, 115.

5 Altamira, "José Manuel Estrada," 292, 294–95; Auza, "Racionalismo y tradicionalismo en el Río de la Plata," 112; Bruno, "José Manuel Estrada," 87; Cutolo, *Nuevo Diccionario biográfico argentino*, 2:715; Garro, "José Manuel Estrada," in *Obras completas de José Manuel Estrada*, 1:vi; Torrendell, "La política educativa en el pensamiento de José Manuel Estrada," 7–13; Torrendell, "Presentación," 13, 16; and Ventura Flores, "Vida del apóstol de la libertad argentina," 177–78.

6 Bruno, "Biografía e historia de los intelectuales," 25–26; Bruno, "José Manuel Estrada," 87–88; Bruno, *Pioneros Culturales de la Argentina*, 83; Cárdenas, *Los ideales de José Manuel Estrada*, 249; Cutolo, *Nuevo Diccionario*, 715; Ramos, *El Derecho público de las provincias argentinas*, 2:76; Tanzi, *José Manuel Estrada*,

29–33, 35–40; Torrendell, "Presentación," 15–16; and Ventura Flores, "Vida del apóstol," 180–81, 183, 195.

7 Torrendell, "Presentación," 12, 16; and Ventura Flores, "Vida del apóstol," 179.

8 José M. Estrada, "El Génesis de nuestra raza," in *Obras completas*, 1:4. See also, Novoa, "The Dilemmas of Male Consumption in Nineteenth-Century Argentina," 782–83.

9 Bruno, *Pioneros culturales*, 96; Lucero, "La filosofía," 135–36; and Novoa, "The Dilemmas," 782.

10 Lanfranco, "La cátedra," 70.

11 Ventura Flores, "Vida del apóstol," 200.

12 José M. Estrada, "El Catolicismo y la Democracia," 139.

13 Bruno, *Pioneros Culturales*, 106; and *Congreso de 1886*, 128.

14 Cosmelli Ibáñez, *Historia cultural de los argentinos*, 463–64.

15 Bruno, *Pioneros Culturales*, 97; and Lucero, "La filosofía," 137.

16 José M. Estrada, "El Catolicismo y la Democracia," 249.

17 Ibid., 281.

18 Ibid., 282.

19 Torrendell, "Presentación," 16–17.

20 José M. Estrada, "La libertad y el liberalismo," in *Obras completas* 12:160.

21 José M. Estrada, "El Pueblo ante el liberalismo," in ibid., 11: 600–01.

22 José M. Estrada, "Lucha y victoria," in ibid., 11: 621.

23 José M. Estrada, "Discurso pronunciado en la Asociación Católica de Socorros Mutuos el 13 de noviembre de 1884," in ibid., 12: 434.

24 "Biografía," in Estrada, *La Política liberal bajo la tiranía de Rosas*, 8; Educadores Argentinos, "José Manuel Estrada (1842–1894)," available at: https://www.educ.ar/recursos/70949/jose-manuel-estrada-1842-1894; and Torrendell, "Presentación," 17–18.

25 Rojas, "Noticia preliminar," in Estrada, *La Política liberal bajo la tiranía de Rosas*, 14.

26 Bruno, "El Círculo literario (1864–1866)," 167; Bruno, "Paul Groussac," 77; and Bruno, *Pioneros culturales*, 98, 105.

27 Alberto Estrada, "Advertencia del editor," in *Obras completas de José Manuel Estrada*, 12:vi; and López Olaciregui, "Ideales cristianos y democráticos de Estrada," 204. See the brief chronological overview of the work of Estrada in Alberto Estrada, "Dos palabras del editor," in *Obras completas de José Manuel Estrada*, 11:vi–ix.

28 Borchard, *Guide to the Law and Legal Literature of Argentina, Brazil and Chile*, 45.

29 *Le Gaulois: littéraire et politique*, March 16, 1927, 2.

30 Altamira, "José Manuel Estrada," 292–93; "Biografía," 8; Cárdenas, *Los ideales*, 138, 249; Lanfranco, "La cátedra," 71, 75; and Recasens Siches, "El Pensamiento filosófico, social, político y jurídico en Hispano-América," 89.

31 López Olaciregui, "Ideales cristianos y democráticos," 205–06.

32 Bruno, *Pioneros culturales*, 67; Dana Montaño, "El concepto de libertad civil y la libertad política según José Manuel Estrada," 164–65, 172, 177; and Stokes, "Review," 1226.

33 Altamira, "José Manuel Estrada," 295; Bruno, *Pioneros culturales*, 91; Cárdenas, *Los ideales*, 71; Linares Quintana, "The Etiology of Revolutions in Latin America," 265; Tanzi, *José Manuel Estrada*, 29, 31–32; Tanzi, "La enseñanza del Derecho constitucional en la Universidad de Buenos Aires," 101; and Ventura Flores, "Vida del apóstol," 182–84, 191.

34 Bruno, "José Manuel Estrada," 88; and Bruno, *Pioneros culturales*, 68.

35 José M. Estrada, "La Tiranía de Rosas," in *Obras completas*, 12:143.

36 Lucero, "La filosofía," 166; and Ventura Flores, "Vida del apóstol," 181.

37 José M. Estrada, "Ensayo histórico sobre la Revolución de los Comuneros del Paraguay en el Siglo XVIII," in *Obras completas*, 1:285.
38 Lucero, "La filosofía," 166.
39 Cárdenas, *Los Ideales*, 155; and Torrendell, "Presentación," 25–26.
40 Altamira, "José Manuel Estrada," 293; Bruno, *Pioneros culturales*, 73; and Cárdenas, *Los ideales*, 155.
41 Bruno, "José Manuel Estrada," 88; Barager, "The Historiography of the Río de la Plata Area Since 1830," 593; and Lucero, "La filosofía," 152.
42 José M. Estrada, "Los P. P. Gervasoni y Cattaneo," in *Obras completas*, 5:613–14.
43 Bruno, "José Manuel Estrada," 88, 92; and Lucero, "La filosofía," 151–52.
44 Bruno, "José Manuel Estrada," 90–91, 93, 95, 98–100; Garro, "José Manuel Estrada," xvii; Parise, "Comparative European Experiences," 411; and Torrendell, "Presentación," 11.
45 José M. Estrada, *La Política liberal bajo la tiranía de Rosas*, in *Obras completas* 4:11.
46 López Olaciregui, "Ideales cristianos y democráticos," 208.
47 Bruno, "José Manuel Estrada," 101; Cárdenas, *Los ideales*, 117; and Lucero, "La filosofía," 165.
48 José M. Estrada, "Advertencia," in *Obras completas* 2:v.
49 Tanzi, *José Manuel Estrada*, 24.
50 Bruno, *Pioneros culturales*, 74–75; and Torrendell, "Presentación," 27.
51 Cárdenas, *Los ideales*, 11; Cutolo, *Nuevo Diccionario*, 715; Garro, "José Manuel Estrada," xi; Tau Anzoátegui, *La codificación en la Argentina*, 340; Ventura Flores, "Vida del apóstol," 179; and Zorraquín Becú, "Las fuentes de la Constitución de 1853," 210.
52 José M. Estrada, "Comparación de los preámbulos de las Constituciones de Suiza, Estados Unidos, Colombia, Venezuela y República Argentina," in *Obras completas* 8:390. See also, Tanzi, *José Manuel Estrada*, 44, 48–49; and Tanzi, "La enseñanza," 97.
53 Educadores argentinos, "José Manuel Estrada (1842–1894)"; Mouchet, "Florentino González," 83; and Tanzi, *José Manuel Estrada*, 45, 47–48.
54 The administrative law component was neglected in the curriculum. Mouchet, "Florentino González," 92; and Tanzi, "La enseñanza," 97.
55 Lanfranco, "La cátedra," 72, 75; Rowe, *The Federal System of the Argentine Republic*, vi; Tanzi, *José Manuel Estrada*, 50–51; Tanzi, "La enseñanza," 98, 100; and Zimmermann, "Translations of the 'American Model' in Nineteenth Century Argentina," 397–98.
56 Bruno, *Pioneros culturales*, 103; Vedia, *José Manuel Estrada*, 22; Martínez, "Introducción," in José M. Estrada, *Curso de Derecho constitucional, federal y administrativo*, vii; Miller, "The Authority of a Foreign Talisman," 1544; and Tanzi, "La enseñanza," 98, 100.
57 Barbalho, *Constituição Federal Brasileira*, 23.
58 Carrasco, *Estudios constitucionales*, 2:156.
59 González Calderón, *Derecho constitucional argentino*, 2:227–28.
60 Dareste et al., *Les Constitutions modernes, Amérique*, 5.
61 Borchard, *Guide to the Law*, 126.
62 Tanzi, "La enseñanza," 98. The introduction was part of his inaugural lecture at the *Colegio Nacional* in 1869. Tanzi, *José Manuel Estrada*, 36.
63 José M. Estrada, "Curso de Derecho constitucional—Tomo Primero," in *Obras completas* 6:1.
64 Altamira, "José Manuel Estrada," 294; Tanzi, *José Manuel Estrada*, 50–51; and Tanzi, "La enseñanza," 99–100.
65 Estrada, "Curso de Derecho constitucional," 191.
66 Rodríguez Varela, "Epílogo—Saldo positivo de las controversias del ochenta," 255; Sambrizzi, *Los ataques de 1884*, 59–60; Tanzi, *José Manuel Estrada*, 52; and Tanzi, "La enseñanza," 100.

67 José M. Estrada, "Despedida a sus alumnos de la Facultad de Derecho el 21 de junio de 1884," in *Obras completas* 12:382.
68 Cárdenas, *Los ideales*, 13–14; López Olaciregui, "Ideales cristianos y democráticos," 212; and Tanzi, *José Manuel Estrada*, 61–62.
69 Castro, "Los católicos en el juego político conservador de comienzos del siglo XX (1907–1912)," 33; and Egüés, "Las ideas políticas en el constitucionalismo argentino del siglo XIX," 61.
70 Altamira, "José Manuel Estrada," 300–01; Bruno, *Pioneros culturales*, 88; Cháneton, *Historia de Vélez Sársfield*, 2:335–36; Levaggi, *Manual de historia del Derecho argentino*, 2:136; Lo Prete, "The Protection of Religious Freedom," 678; and Torrendell, "Presentación," 17–18.
71 Bruno, "José Manuel Estrada," 87; Bruno, *Pioneros culturales*, 69; Dell'Oro Maini, "La contienda entre católicos y laicistas," 78; Gallo and Leo, "Una tea incendiaria. Iglesia y Estado en la Convención de Buenos Aires de 1860," 145; Lida, "La Iglesia católica en las más recientes historiografías de México y Argentina," 1408; and Torrendell, "Presentación," 14, 17–18.
72 Bruno, *Pioneros culturales*, 90; Cutolo, *Nuevo Diccionario*, 715; Lee B Kress, "Argentine Liberalism and the Church under Julio Roca, 1880–1886," 325, 330; Rojas, "Noticia preliminar," 25; Tanzi, *José Manuel Estrada*, 81; and Torrendell, "Presentación," 14. See generally, Sambrizzi, *Los ataques de 1884*.
73 López Olaciregui, "Ideales cristianos y democráticos," 214.
74 Kress, "Argentine Liberalism," 324–25.
75 Bruno, *Pioneros Culturales*, 94; Cutolo, *Nuevo Diccionario*, 715–16; Rojas, "Noticia preliminar," 24–25; Torrendell, "Presentación," 15; and Ventura Flores, "Vida del apóstol," 191.
76 José M. Estrada, "Matrimonio civil," in *Obras completas* 12:627.
77 Auza, "Racionalismo y tradicionalismo," 120; and Kress, "Argentine Liberalism," 335.
78 José M. Estrada, "Discurso pronunciado en el 'Frontón de Buenos Aires', en el Meeting de la Unión Cívica el 13 de abril de 1890," in *Obras completas* 12:687.
79 Vedia, *José Manuel Estrada*, 6.
80 Estrada, "Discurso pronunciado en el 'Frontón de Buenos Aires'," 690–91.

References

Altamira, Pedro G. "José Manuel Estrada." *Revista de la Facultad de Ciencias Económicas* 3, no. 3–4 (1950): 291–302.

Auza, Néstor Tomás. "Racionalismo y tradicionalismo en el Río de la Plata: Gustavo Mienlli–José Manuel Estrada." *Teología* 73 (1999): 99–121.

Barager, Joseph R. "The Historiography of the Río de la Plata Area Since 1830." *Hispanic American Historical Review* 39, no. 4 (1959): 588–642.

Borchard, Edwin M. *Guide to the Law and Legal Literature of Argentina, Brazil and Chile.* Washington, DC: Government Printing Office, 1917.

Bruno, Paula. "Biografía e historia de los intelectuales. Balance y reflexiones sobre la vida cultural argentina entre 1860 y 1910." *Literatura y Lingüística* 36 (2017): 19–36.

Bruno, Paula. "El Círculo Literario (1864–1866): un espacio de conciliación de intereses." *Prismas* 16, no. 2 (2012): 167–70.

Bruno, Paula. "José Manuel Estrada (1842–1894) y su obra histórica en la Argentina de las décadas de 1860 y 1870." *História da Historiografia: International Journal of Theory and History of Historiography* 8, no. 17 (2015): 86–104.

Bruno, Paula. "Paul Groussac. Hombre de Cultura y 'Renán Quejoso de su Gloria a Trasmano.'" *Revista de Historia de América* 139 (2008): 61–133.

Bruno, Paula. *Pioneros Culturales de la Argentina: Biografías de una época*. Buenos Aires: Siglo Veintiuno, 2011.

Cárdenas, Manuel A. *Los ideales de José Manuel Estrada*. Buenos Aires: Eudeba, 1979.

Carrasco, José. *Estudios constitucionales*, Vol. 2. La Paz: González & Medina, 1920.

Castro, Martín O. "Los católicos en el juego político conservador de comienzos del siglo XX (1907–1912)." *Desarrollo Económico* 49, no. 193 (2009): 31–60.

Cháneton, Abel. *Historia de Vélez Sársfield*, vol. 2. Buenos Aires: Editorial La Facultad, 1937.

Congreso de 1886: Siluetas parlamentarias. Buenos Aires: El Nacional, 1886.

Cosmelli Ibáñez, José L. *Historia cultural de los argentinos*. Buenos Aires: Troquel, 1975.

Cutolo, Vicente O. *Nuevo Diccionario biográfico argentino: (1750–1930)*, Vol. 2. Buenos Aires: Editorial Elche, 1968.

Dana Montaño, Salvador M. "El concepto de libertad civil y la libertad política según José Manuel Estrada, maestro argentino del siglo XVIII." *Revista de Estudios Políticos* 79 (1955): 161–80.

Dareste, François R., et al. *Les Constitutions Modernes, Amérique*. Paris: Recueil Sirey, 1932.

Dell'Oro Maini, Atilio. "La contienda entre católicos y laicistas." In *La Política del Ochenta*, edited by Romero Carranza, et al., 67–115. Buenos Aires: Club de Lectores, 1964.

Egüés, Carlos. "Las ideas políticas en el constitucionalismo argentino del siglo XIX. Un aporte metodológico." *Revista de Historia del Derecho* 24 (1996): 45–62.

Estrada, José Manuel. *Curso de Derecho constitucional, federal y administrativo*. Buenos Aires: Compañía Sud-Americana de Billetes de Banco, 1895.

Estrada, José Manuel. *Memoria sobre la educación común en la Provincia de Buenos Aires*. La Plata: UNIPE Editorial Universitaria, 2011.

Estrada, José Manuel. *Obras completas de José Manuel Estrada*, Vol. 12. Buenos Aires: Librería del Colegio, de Pedro Igón, etc., 1899–1905.

Estrada, José Manuel. *La Política liberal bajo la Tiranía de Rosas*. Buenos Aires: Librería La Facultad, 1927.

Gallo, Ezequiel, and Mariela Leo. "Una Tea Incendiaria. Iglesia y Estado en la Convención de Buenos Aires de 1860." *Desarrollo Económico* 51, no. 201 (2011): 135–47.

Garro, Juan M. "José Manuel Estrada. Nota biográfica." In *Obras completas de José Manuel Estrada*, Vol. 1, v–civ. Buenos Aires: Librería del Colegio, de Pedro Igón, etc., 1899–1905.

González Calderón, Juan A. *Derecho constitucional argentino: Historia, Teoría y Jurisprudencia de la Constitución*, Vol. 2. Buenos Aires: J. Lajouane & cia., 1918.

João Barbalho. *Constituição Federal Brasileira—Comentários*. Rio de Janeiro: Typographia da Companhia Litho-Typographica, 1902.

Kress, Lee B. "Argentine Liberalism and the Church under Julio Roca, 1880–1886." *The Americas* 30, no. 3 (1974): 319–40.

Lanfranco, Héctor P. "La cátedra de Historia y de Derecho Constitucional en la Facultad de Derecho de Buenos Aires y sus primeros maestros." *Revista del Instituto de Historia del Derecho* 8 (1957): 63–81.

Levaggi, Abelardo. *Manual de historia del Derecho argentino*, Vol. 2. Buenos Aires: Depalma, 1987.

Lida, Miranda. "La Iglesia católica en las más recientes historiografías de México y Argentina. Religión, modernidad y secularización." *Historia Mexicana* 56, no.4 (2007): 1393–426.

Linares Quintana, Segundo V. "The Etiology of Revolutions in Latin America." *Western Political Quarterly* 4, no.2 (1951): 254–67.

Lo Prete, Octavio. "The Protection of Religious Freedom by the National Constitution and by Human Rights Treaties in the Republic of Argentina." *Brigham Young University Law Review* (2009): 673–95.

López Olaciregui, José M. "Ideales cristianos y democráticos de Estrada." In *La Política del Ochenta*, edited by Romero Carranza, et al., 203–19.

Lucero, Ignacio T. "La filosofía política y de la historia de José M. Estrada." *Cuyo* 13 (1980): 135–67.

Miller, Jonathan M. "The Authority of a Foreign Talisman: A Study of U.S. Constitutional Practice as Authority in Nineteenth Century Argentina and the Argentine Elite's Leap of Faith." *American University Law Review* 46 (1997): 1483–572.

Mouchet, Carlos. "Florentino González, un jurista de América: Sus ideas sobre el régimen municipal." *Journal of Inter-American Studies* 2, no. 1 (1960): 83–101.

Novoa, Adriana. "The Dilemmas of Male Consumption in Nineteenth-Century Argentina: Fashion, Consumerism, and Darwinism in Domingo Sarmiento and Juan B. Alberdi." *Journal of Latin American Studies* 39, no. 4 (2007): 771–95.

Parise, Agustín. "Comparative European Experiences in Legal History and Constitutional Law (19th–20th Centuries)." *Historia Constitucional* 18 (2017): 411–17.

Ramos, Juan P. *El Derecho público de las provincias argentinas, con el Texto de las Constituciones sancionadas entre los años 1819 y 1913*, vol. 2. Buenos Aires: Facultad de Derecho y Ciencias Sociales, 1916.

Recaséns Siches, Luis. "El pensamiento filosófico, social, político y jurídico en Hispano-América." *Revista Mexicana de Sociología* 6, no. 1 (1944): 85–121.

Rodríguez Varela, Alberto. "Epílogo—Saldo positivo de las controversias del ochenta." In *La Política del Ochenta*, edited by Romero Carranza, et al., 221–80. Buenos Aires: Club de Lectores, 1964.

Rojas, Ricardo. "Noticia Preliminar." In *La Política liberal bajo la tiranía de Rosas*, 13–31. Buenos Aires: Librería La Facultad, 1927.

Romero Carranza, Ambrosio, et al., eds. *La política del Ochenta*. Buenos Aires: Club de Lectores, 1964.

Rowe, Leo S. *The Federal System of the Argentine Republic*. Washington, DC: Carnegie Institution of Washington, 1921.

Sambrizzi, Alejandro. *Los ataques de 1884: Un corte visceral en la lucha entre católicos y liberales durante la primera presidencia de Julio Argentino Roca*. Buenos Aires: Editorial Dunken, 2011.

Stokes, William S. "Review." *American Political Science Review* 38, no. 6 (1944): 1226.

Tanzi, Héctor J. "La enseñanza del Derecho constitucional en la Universidad de Buenos Aires." *Revista de Historia del Derecho "Ricardo Levene"* 31 (1995): 91–143.

Tanzi, Héctor J. *José Manuel Estrada (1842–1894): Apóstol laico del catolicismo*. Buenos Aires: Ediciones Braga, 1994.

Tau Anzoátegui, Víctor. *La codificación en la Argentina (1810–1870): Mentalidad social e ideas jurídicas*. Buenos Aires: Imprenta de la Universidad, 1977.

Torrendell, Carlos H. "La política educativa en el pensamiento de José Manuel Estrada." Licentiate Dissertation. Buenos Aires: Facultad de Filosofía y Letras, Pontificia Universidad Católica Argentina, 2005.

Torrendell, Carlos H. "Presentación. José M. Estrada: una escuela personalista, democrática y participativa" In *Memoria sobre la educación común*, 9–40. La Plata: UNIPE Editorial Universitaria, 2011.

Vedia, Enrique de. *José Manuel Estrada*: *Conferencia publicada el 16 de julio de 1904 en el Colegio Nacional de Buenos Aires*. Buenos Aires: Coni Hermanos, 1904.

Ventura Flores, Eduardo. "Vida del apóstol de la Libertad argentina." In *La Política del Ochenta*, edited by Romero Carranza, et al., 177–201. Buenos Aires: Club de Lectores, 1964.

Zimmermann, Eduardo. "Translations of the 'American Model' in Nineteenth Century Argentina: Constitutional Culture as a Global Legal Entanglement." In *Entanglements in Legal History: Conceptual Approaches*, edited by Thomas Duve, 385–425. Frankfurt am Main: Max Planck Institute for European Legal History, 2014.

Zorraquín Becú, Ricardo. "Las fuentes de la Constitución de 1853." *Revista de Historia del Derecho* 16 (1988): 209–47.

22 Miguel Antonio Caro Tobar (Colombia, 1843–1909)

Eduardo Herrera and M.C. Mirow

Miguel Antonio Caro Tobar is one of the most outstanding Colombian humanists, politicians, and jurists of the second half of the nineteenth century. His extensive activity and the variety of his work make it very difficult to study and understand him without taking into account the different facets of his life. Caro was a grounded man, full of ideas, who made marked contributions to several fields. His well-known political action, his journalistic activity, his studies in philosophy, and his vision of the state require us to study him as a whole to appreciate his important legal legacy. Despite not having studied law, he was, without doubt, a constitutionalist and legal expert.[1] His contributions to the consolidation of Colombia as a state governed by the rule of law was a decisive step in the construction of the Colombia we know today.

Biography

Caro was born in Bogotá on November 10, 1843. He died sixty-six years later, on August 5, 1909. Son of the poet, thinker, and conservative philosopher José Eusebio Caro Ibáñez and Blasina Tobar Pinzón, he was part of a household completed by his brother, Eusebio, and sister, Margarita. The family atmosphere and the traditions in which he grew up were decisive in the formation of his spirit and character. His strong personality, unwavering Catholic faith, firm political convictions, love of literature, and vocation for public service were characteristics that left indelible personal traits. Caro's education alternated between the rigorous school education of the time and the personal instruction he received in the house of his paternal grandfather. To these he added his own rigorous studies in the available classical literature of the period.[2] He perfected his skills in English, Latin, and Spanish. He acquired at the same time a wider and educated vision of the world and society. He immersed himself in the reading of the ancient classics, the Golden Age of Spanish literature, and German philology. He displayed at a very early age his journalistic skills and political combativeness. Indeed, Caro's public life began as a journalist in defense of his ideals. Behind this writer, one observes the nascent jurist and politician seeking the true dimension of human thought and behavior.

Fully immersed in intellectual life, he prepared himself to face political life. He was convinced that his knowledge must be placed at the service of nobler ideals and his country. In 1867 Caro decided to run for the Congress of the Republic with the endorsement of the Conservative Party, founded by his father. He was elected deputy to the House of Representatives, returning to Congress for a second time as a representative and finally as a senator, in the twilight of his public life, in 1903.

From 1868 onwards, Caro's political and intellectual life began to take on greater proportions. He openly opposed philosophical positivism and used his knowledge in the service of the principles of freedom and order.[3] He began a fruitful correspondence with various political and intellectual leaders in Spain and abroad. The following year, he took part in the creation of the Colombian Academy of Language, and that same year he founded *El Tradicionista*, a newspaper of the Catholic Party in which he expressed his political ideas. Around this time, in full intellectual maturity and already initiated into public life, he married Ana Narváez. He was thirty years old.

By 1881 Caro was a recognized politician and man of letters both nationally and internationally. He was director of the National Library of Colombia and adviser to the board of directors of the Conservative Party. At the end of 1883, Rafael Núñez was elected president for the second time. Caro observed the political panorama while waiting for what was to be his new role in this important period of Colombia's history. He was nominated to the National Council of Delegates that was to draft the Constitution of 1886. Here he sought to put into practice what he believed should be the model of the state born of the Hispanic and Catholic matrix. His participation in and contribution to this assembly were decisive. When the sessions of the Constituent Council were over, he was appointed a member of the Council of State. In 1892 he saw his name raised in candidacy for the vice presidency of the republic in elections with Rafael Núñez again as the presidential candidate. They won the elections, but when Núñez declined to take office because of poor health, Caro stepped in as acting president, and on Núñez's death in 1894, Caro assumed the presidency and exercised it until the end of the constitutional period.

In 1897 Caro decided not to accept the presidential candidacy for a new term, and he withdrew from public activity. In 1902 he practiced as a lawyer for a short period in the defense of some prisoners in cases involving human rights violations. In 1903 he obtained the chair of constitutional law at the School of Law of Bogotá. In 1905 Caro retired permanently from public life, and he died on August 5, 1909.

Humanist

"Caro is the symbol of humanism in Colombia. Colombian humanism is everything; it is the most representative expression of Colombia."[4] These three statements will be understood in their full dimension if we carefully analyze Caro's work in the humanities. These included literary criticism, the study of classics, poetry, translation, philological studies, and studies of the Spanish language.

Caro belongs to the generation of Latin American intellectuals of the second half of the nineteenth century who emerged to restore the humanities in their native lands, and he became an outstanding humanist in the region. Caro rejected the liberal and materialistic capitalist model then associated with Anglo-Saxon society that confronted the human and spiritual values associated with Hispanic and Catholic culture.

His humanistic formation began in his youth. He was born into a family in which the study of Latin authors was normal. He inherited his father's love of letters,[5] and he learned from his maternal grandfather the basic rules of versification and the first fundamentals of Spanish and Latin.[6] He received classes in Latin, Greek, and English; he corresponded in English, Latin, and Spanish.[7] From translations of Virgil to his versions of Catullus and Propertius, Caro continued to work with Latin. Caro's translation of *The Aeneid* was considered by Marcelino Menéndez y Pelayo to be the best Spanish translation of his time.[8] José Manuel Rivas Sacconi divides Caro's humanistic work into four major themes that correspond with his intellectual evolution. These include the study of Spanish grammar; the translations of Roman authors, culminating in the translation of Virgil and commentaries; critical works on themes of classical literature; and his own writings of verse and prose in Latin until the end of his life.[9]

Caro's philosophical formation goes far beyond that of a knowledge of scholastic philosophy. He received from an early age a grounding in the defense of the Christian speculative tradition. He went beyond the classics of this theological doctrine and deeper into the reading of authors and works of his time. Was Caro a philosopher? The answer is not easy. Scholars of Caro disagree on this point, and he left behind no philosophical treatise compiling his thought in this field. Monsignor Rafael María Carrasquilla, who knew him very well, praised Caro as one of Colombia's foremost philosophers.[10] For his part, Caro's biographer Jaime Jaramillo Uribe stated: "Caro is without a doubt the most solid intellectual personality the country has produced. If he had devoted himself to philosophy, he would have produced perhaps the most important work in America."[11] Edgar Sanabria laments that Caro, while intellectually brilliant, left no purely philosophical work.[12] Finally, Carlos Valderrama Andrade, perhaps the most important biographer and scholar of Miguel Antonio Caro in general, considers that, in order to catalogue him as a philosopher, we must do so with a broad spirit, because although he had a clear concept of philosophy and was a rigorous student of this science, he did not leave a defined system of structured ideas.[13]

Although Caro's intellectual work is imbued with philosophical content, his writings directly on this subject are few. His philosophical orientation is defined through his criticism of utilitarianism and empiricism. Jaime Jaramillo Uribe places Caro's thought in the orbit of Cartesian rationalism, Thomism, and Scottish philosophy.[14] His philosophical studies sustained his juridical thought, and one can observe the influence of this study in his legal philosophy and general philosophy and in his practical application of constitutional law.[15] As a realist, he recognized the existence of a natural physical order and a metaphysical one with an inseparable moral relationship:

> It should be noted that the judgments we make about good and bad, even in the physical order, have a moral character, involve the idea of good in general, and, although confusing, bring the idea of relations between that physical order and morality; [these judgments] raise the notion of duty.[16]

The religious foundation of thought and action

Caro's rigorous and deep religious conviction makes it impossible to understand his political thought and his concept of law if we do not study his Christian faith. Caro's work—somewhat limited in philosophy but broad in politics and full in law—is grounded in his spiritual convictions, his life as a believer, and his desire to serve society from a Christian perspective. Caro's attitude implies loyalty in his convictions, unity in thought, and coherence of action with his firm religious beliefs.[17] To draw out the essence of his religious convictions, Caro believed and always defended that:

> Religion and only religion can awaken a feeling or an attitude of generosity towards the pain and misery of one's neighbor, a characteristic that can be seen in the Catholic field of charity.[18]

Caro's concept of religion is based on this: "Christianity harmonizes man's faculties, illustrates his reason, moves his will, and orders his feelings."[19]

With this approach, Caro focused on ethical motives and viewed religious belief as the essence of morality, because religion touches the concrete reality of humanity. His concern was to imprint a Christian character on society, and, to this end, he advocated a moralization of human activity, both individual and social, in accordance with God-given human dignity. Caro saw the Church as a divine institution and a set of human and social realities.[20] The Church on this level of transcendence was also predestined for teaching and participating in public life beyond the merely spiritual: "It is the maker of men and the integrator of people."[21] Its relationship with the social, political, and juridical order is of great importance because it reminds civil authority of its duties and "also recognizes the rights that correspond to it as a power instituted by God, with its own faculties for the well being of society."[22] In the field of philosophy of history, Caro censured those who, forced by sociological zeal, did not see the determining factor of religion in the development and future of humanity. It was religion that made it possible for humans to realize the virtue that in turn is at the basis of every stable social organization.[23]

Political action: the "Regeneration"

Caro's political activity began in 1871 with his permanent collaboration with the national press and continued until 1904, when he retired from public life. Carlos Valderrama Andrade differentiates four great periods in Caro's life that allow us to identify the principles that guided his political activity. The first period extended from 1871 to 1876, when Caro, in open ideological opposition to the radical liberalism then triumphant in the United States of Colombia, aligned his political ideology with the Christian tradition of Colombians. This was the most controversial and significant moment in Caro's political activity, when he structured his political thought to guide his future actions. The second period began in 1877 and includes Caro's journalistic production between 1882 and 1891. This work coincided with the consolidation of the 1878 Regeneration Movement, the founding of the National Party in 1882, and the approval of the Constitution of 1886.[24] The third period covered the years Caro served as vice president and president of Colombia, from August 1892 to August 1898. These were culminating years in which, as a statesman, he produced documents of great legal and political interest.[25] The fourth and last period occurred between the end of his presidential term and his death in 1909, although he retired from public life in 1904. During this period, he consolidated his political legacy, even though his legal legacy was the Constitution of 1886.[26]

The ideological currents of the Regeneration found political and legal application in the creation of the National Party and in the approval of the Constitution of 1886. The Regeneration was an ideological movement led by Rafael Núñez that culminated in the reorganization of the republic as a unitary state, the promulgation of the Constitution of 1886, and a concordat with the Holy See in 1887. The Regeneration was characterized by legal, political, and economic reforms in the country. Caro was a part of this movement from its creation until 1898, when it ceased to exist. Caro was its most ardent defender, its principal ideologue. Under the National Party, he developed the movement's legal and political actions as explored in this chapter.[27]

From 1871 to 1876, two events marked Caro's political life: the short run of the newspaper *El Tradicionista*[28] and the unfulfilled project of founding the Catholic Party.[29] As early as 1869, in the *Study on Utilitarianism*,[30] he summarized his views:

> Order, Justice, Perfection: these conceptions that constitute the idea of good cannot subsist in an indeterminate, abstract state; they manifest the need for an identical and intelligent soul of creation, supreme reason of the spectacle in which we are actors and spectators. We do not realize the type of the perfect; we aspire to it with incessant longing. We do not see it; however, we conceive it existing, realized. Well, it is an abstract idea to which we are attracted by a more rational and just feeling of attachment, as, coming out of its abstraction, it becomes personalized in God. Order, goodness, beauty are guidelines which, by illustrating themselves, make up that holy name.[31]

Thus, Caro was in favor of establishing deep links between religion and politics. All political doctrine, he said, contains moral principles that come from religious truths.[32] That which emanates from God permeates all human activity:[33] "Political doctrines are derived from moral principles and moral principles from religious truths…So true is it that as theological beliefs are altered, the idea of law and rights is altered at the same time."[34]

This relationship establishes the foundation of political and legal principles. Christian values give humanity the ability to fight against any form of injustice and tyranny. Caro analyzed the two-party system that filled the Colombian political space: the secular liberal and the conservative, which is based on the Christian doctrine of the individual in society. This classification of the Colombian political parties and Caro's adherence to conservatism follow ideological affinity more than the content of political philosophies. This approach had to be followed by political action. Caro wrote:

> To govern is to educate. But all education presupposes rights and duties: preconstituted notions about right and wrong, what should be sought and what should be avoided…He who imposes laws is subject to a prior law which points out his rights and duties to the very attempt to legislate.[35]

The mission of governments is to educate and legislate according to the natural law.

This discussion about morality and politics had in its background the controversy around utilitarianism as a support for liberal radicalism. Caro observed that, in general, morality and utility go hand in hand, and as a consequence of this union the good is also useful, although the opposite cannot always be said. In this connection, Caro made a distinction between what he called "men of utility" and "men of the school of law": the former despise morality in the interests of utility, while the latter, starting from "a respect for morality, come to the end of complete and true utility, even if they give this utility only a secondary value."[36] According to Caro, men of utility seek it while hoping that justice will come later, but justice does not come at last, because it is not a consequence but a principle. Men of the law seek justice first and then receive utility in addition.[37] In this vein, he maintained that public confidence is based on morality and suitability, which are backed up by solid principles that guarantee the future of peoples.[38]

His legal legacy: the Constitution of 1886

Having established the importance Caro gave to political action, one may outline the guiding legal principles of this action. First is the relationship of thought, action, and word:

> The unlimited right to the use of the word implies the equally unlimited right to the use of action; because the word is nothing more than the expression, just as the act is the execution of the same thing—the thought. [39]

If the word must be absolutely free, human action must be absolutely free.[40]

A second fundamental principle of Caro's juridical legacy is the distinction between natural law and positive law. This distinction begins with the recognition of an equal law that exists for both individuals and society, which is above human legislation, and which he called (we call) natural law. Positive laws presuppose the existence of that natural law and must be recognized by both the ruler and society as prior and superior. Historically, this natural law appears entangled in human legislation, but it always remains unchanged as the foundation of social organization in the hope of recovering "its native splendor."[41]

The third and final part of Caro's legal legacy is his understanding of the relationship between freedom and interests and between truth and justice. Here he opposed the principles of the liberal school and those of traditionalism. He made a clear distinction:

> Political science contains a moral part that is derived from religious truths and a solely scientific part that is derived from knowledge of natural laws.[42]

At the heart of this reasoning is Caro's rejection of the principle of utility, which he combated in more than one writing.[43]

Concerning politics and philosophical criticism at this time in his public life, Caro already showed his interest in political debate and in the questions of state that would lead him to become a protagonist in Colombian public life a few years later. "A bad constitution is better than arbitrariness and disorder," he would say in 1872, in a letter to Rafael Núñez on constitutional hermeneutics.[44]

Caro was convinced that things of the spirit weigh heavily on political activity. He believed that the public man who does not know them is incapable of achieving high positions in civil society because he lacks noble instincts and disinterested action. Because of this conviction, Caro rejected out of hand the mercantilism he saw as a consequence of the spirit that had invaded the age and regretted that politicians had so easily given in to it. The bases of the constitutional reform that Caro later presented to the Council of Delegates, convoked by President Núñez in 1885, did not establish that the government must profess a certain religion, but they recognized the principles and action of Catholicism to set out indispensable elements for the organization of the state. Catholicism was, in Caro's words, shared by "almost all Colombians."[45]

One might think that Caro was not sensitive to the shock of the publication of the *Communist Manifesto* of 1848, since his struggle against utilitarianism occupied his intellect and political action. Nonetheless, a careful reading of his writings shows that he perceived the world's agitation from communist theory and did not fail to see outbreaks of this ideology in the Colombian political struggle. For this reason, it is interesting to see how he posed the problem of people and politics, framing it as a struggle for political power to seek the transformation of society. Caro separated the consideration of struggle as a human phenomenon and posed the problem in the following terms.[46]

Accepting the fact of inequality and trying to seek harmony is the mission of "men of order," who oppose those "men of revolution" who reject inequality and try to subvert the established order of their society. Societies change, but the interests will always be the same according to the law within a conception of humanity and history guided by divine providence. Thus, Caro was aware of the interests pushing the social process in Europe and America toward a radical atheistic liberalism. His intellectual and political response was to defend the Christian social order through legislation that would protect it. He proposed the freedom associated with the unity of the individual and society and with order and progress that resulted from a peace free from class struggle.

This position explains Caro's reservations about notions of absolute popular sovereignty, because he held that "as an absolute principle it means that the people...have all social power." And he concluded: "If the people do not have this right, then not all power belongs to them." Here, Caro was concerned about the differing views on the origin of social power. His understanding of Christian doctrine led him to conclude that this power must come from God. An opposing view, supported by the socialism of the time, asserted that such power was solely and exclusively from the people.[47]

Caro believed that civil society was distinct from the citizens and the authority that governs them. Along this line, he defined society as:

> a moral entity, with its rights and duties, and it is not enough that the individual fulfills his or her own for it to have fulfilled its mission, because it is not the individual. Society derives all its characteristics from man; society exists because man is by nature sociable; man and society are contemporaries; society is the man in his collective existence.[48]

Elsewhere, he sought a definition of civil government that, consistent with this statement and in consequence of his ideological position, allowed him to assert that government must always be *de jure* and therefore humanly and spiritually legitimate. Law was not simply a human word but has implications of subordination to natural law. For those who hold positions in public administration, this understanding had serious consequences: it was a matter of complying not only with human laws but also with natural and divine law. The important thing is the doctrinal systems and not the form of government, a secondary matter in the organization of the state.

Caro also had much to say about political parties. He considered them to be the way political action takes shape. Considering the party Caro intended to establish, he thought that parties should be characterized by their monolithic unity, in which all members adhere to the guidelines of the leadership that proposed them. Nonetheless, for Caro, this union would be seen as an immoral interest, because it would keep the citizenry irremediably divided.[49]

Caro's doctrinal position was clear. He recognized a traditionalist school as both a political expression and a legal foundation. He defined this school as the application of "Christianity to society," whose characteristic note would be adherence to ancient traditions that would become international under strong bonds of fraternity, whose "inspiration associates men with each other."[50]

From 1885 on, Caro became fully involved in the political enterprise promoted by Rafael Núñez. The identification with Núñez's political ideas led Caro to write extensively, in press articles and private documents, about the principles of political philosophy. Seeking strong legal foundations, Caro sought by the creation of the National Party to bring together conservatives and liberals who shared his political ideology.

Núñez and Caro appeared as protagonists of this process from the appearance of the Regeneration to the Constitution of 1886. They gave shape to the reforming ideas and set them in motion through their political activities. Núñez was the inspiration and the ideological promotor of Regeneration and the man who conceived the National Party, the instrument of the Regeneration's effort to give the country a new political organization. Caro was the author of the basis of the reform and the draft of the constitution approved in August 1886. Caro's thinking at that moment contributed to the construction of Colombia's institutional charter.

On Núñez's initiative, the Regeneration appeared on the Colombian political scene as a reaction to the Constitution of 1863. Caro saw two defects in the legal system under the Constitution of 1863 that made its modification indispensable: first was the clash among the three sovereignties (individual, regional, and national) that the legislator recognized as absolute without reconciling them; second was the constitution's traits of religious intolerance and anticlericalism. For Caro, the former made it inapplicable and the latter unjust and tyrannical.[51]

Going deeper into the problems that arose from the Constitution of 1863, Caro thought that the Regeneration tried to overcome them by ensuring a new legal and political structure based on order and peace. Caro sought to move past the revolutionary period, which had marked Colombia's evolution since the beginning of the nineteenth century, to a state of law that would give stability, development, and growth to the nation. He pointed out that, in the face of disorder, there were only two paths: either a dictatorship that would impose itself on the regions and subject the citizens to its will; or legislation and government guided by a collective movement of will under the rule of law and reason.[52] Regeneration was the second and most convenient way by which the country would find its path out of a deep crisis caused by revolutionary and anarchic law that deprived the central authority, legitimately constituted, of the power to sanction regional authorities and citizens.[53] By 1891, Caro noted that the Regeneration had succeeded in providing Colombians a level of peace, tranquility, and guarantees for the enjoyment of individual and social rights and progress for all citizens.[54]

The Regeneration responded to the needs of the republic at a particular time and was constrained, as any political movement in any modern democracy, by respect for the will of the majority. Its program was simple and found support from the political class and common citizens. Its main aspects included political centralization and administrative decentralization, Christian education, and the promotion of national work for the well-being of citizens. It achieved its sought after reconciliation of political parties in what was called the National Party.

Caro viewed the Constitution of 1886 with institutional esteem. A product of the Regeneration, the constitution was presented as a legitimate, useful, and necessary norm to solve the crisis that threatened the dissolution of Colombia. It was an effective tool to achieve peace, strengthen social harmony, and procure the social order for citizens. The constitution and its implementation were the work of Núñez[55] and Caro, who, in addition to drafting the text, later brought its provisions into effect as president. Núñez deeply admired Caro's moral rectitude. Trained in Comtian and Spencerian positivism, Núñez was a political analyst who united these philosophical positions as "integral humanism and skepticism," establishing two opposing philosophies in the same ideology. He was not a theorist of Colombian political thought, and yet his permanent direct contact with European political movements made him one of the Colombian politicians who greatly disseminated these ideas in Colombia during the second half of the nineteenth century.[56]

Caro, in contrast, offered a different political profile: he was a man of study, a humanist, an intellectual, a "systematic thinker,"[57] who, in keeping with his sense of duty to his country, devoted himself to public service in the best, and perhaps most difficult, years of his life. He was the architect of new institutions. Indeed, most of the documents emanating from the National Constituent Council are attributed to him. Caro's thought is found throughout the constitutional text that reflects his doctrine of what a state should be.

Fundamental features of the Constitution of 1886 include national unity, religious freedom, rights for all with prevalence of the common good over the particular, a republican system, stability of the government and presidential authority, political centralization, and administrative decentralization. The National Council of Delegates also resumed the national religious vocation that had been interrupted in 1863, invoking again in the preamble the name of God as the supreme source of all authority. The constitution gave the nation the name Republic of Colombia, organized it in a democratic manner, and sought understanding and mutual collaboration with the Church.

That the Colombian nation was reconstituted in the form of a unitary republic meant that the states of the old federal union assumed a new juridical identity without sovereignty. Caro called them departments and gave them autonomy, which, although initially restricted, was strengthened at the same time as the new constitutional process was consolidated. Caro and the 1886 constituents understood this principle of political centralization and administrative decentralization as a national reality. They attempted to institutionalize this reality through law and to regulate it through the state and its government. Colombia was henceforth a single state, a single nation, comprising an ethnic and cultural diversity that would be strengthened over time, as reinforced in the constitutional reforms after 1886 and invigorated, already with a vocation for permanence, in the new Colombian Constitution of 1991.[58]

In the celebration of the centenary of the Constitution of 1886, on August 5, 1986, President Belisario Betancur said:

> The permanence of our Constitution of 1886, after the experiments of the nineteenth century, indicates that it interprets the feeling of Colombians, that

> we look at it as an element of our unity and our concord. It can already be considered the patrimony of the nation and not of a person or a party, because, having passed the time of its authors, it has become the patrimony of other generations until it becomes genuinely national. The reforms made to it by Congress, the interpretations made of it by the Court, the Council of State, and its analysts from multiple and antagonistic positions, and the customs that we build around it show that our Constitution is capable of orienting national life despite the mutations in historical circumstances and even in the theory and practice of democracy, elaborated in stages from the Greek polis.[59]

The Constitution of 1886 was the most important event in the political and legal sphere of Colombia's nineteenth-century republican history. Together with the Constitution of 1991, it put an end to a turbulent past of internal struggles and unresolved controversies about the reorganization of the state. The Constitution of 1886 also opened a stage of stability and institutional reorganization around more realistic, pragmatic principles in line with Colombian history and traditions. It established essential principles that have made it possible to maintain the nation's legitimacy for more than a century. Confirming the power of cohesion and continuity of this earlier constitution, the Constitution of 1991 projected and maintained its postulates for the construction of the modern, pluralist, and democratic Colombian state of the twenty-first century.

The preamble to the Constitution of 1886 reveals how five essential points concerning the nation and the organization of the state were resolved.[60] First, it adopted a republican system. Second, it took on a particular political and moral philosophy. Third, it designated the very source of constituent power. Fourth, it invoked the title that gives it legitimacy. Fifth, in using the name Republic of Colombia, it determined that Colombia—a name that subsisted as a historical denomination—assumed the republican system of national unity for all Colombians, who form a single people and enjoy, by that very fact, a single sovereignty.

Furthermore, through the preamble, the constituents invoked, in addition to the authority of God, the authority of the territorial entities they represented. This invocation of authority asserted the legitimacy of the new legal order as the express will of the nation by approving and endorsing the basis of the new legal order and the moral reason for the political act of the constituents. The constituents sought to ensure justice, freedom, and peace for Colombians and all residents in the territory of the state. These phrases sought to express true principles through the supreme remote source and the immediate reason for political authority. The preamble provided the legitimacy of the act being carried out and the reasons to ensure the ultimate goal of the state. This aim was to guarantee to those who make up the state the exercise of responsible freedom, with duties and obligations, within a legal framework that guarantees life, property, and the free exercise of fundamental rights.

Caro, who had already been a representative to the Chamber of Congress of the Republic in 1864, 1868, and 1876, returned to parliamentary activity once the new constitution was issued and sanctioned by the executive on August 5, 1886. The National Council of Delegates continued to exercise the functions of the constituent body and held legislative power until July 20, 1888, when the Congress of the Republic would be elected, according to the provisions of the new constitution. The work of the National Council of Delegates was then reduced to reporting and a small number of bills. As far as reports are concerned, a good number concern expropriation and return of church property, while others of lesser importance validate acts of the executive, secret ballots, and the political, administrative, and municipal regime. Legislative texts include Law 32 of 1886 on literary and artistic property, a bill establishing the capitals of the departments, and others on amendments to the bills of reforms to the regulations of the chambers, on popular elections, and other legislative changes. Caro was a distinguished advocate of returning to religious institutions the property seized by liberal radicalism.[61]

Regarding congressional oversight of governmental acts, Caro considered that this should be limited to the time when the acts were made and in relation to administrative acts already effectuated.[62] Establishing capitals of the departments, Caro said:

> The territorial division corresponds to Congress, although with the limitations established by the Constitution. The designation of the capitals of the departments is naturally linked to the territorial division and, since the designation appears neither among the restrictions placed by the Constitution on the power of Congress to legislate on the matter, nor in the powers of the departmental assemblies, it is clear that the Legislative Council can and must today determine the capitals of the departments of the Republic.[63]

From 1888 on, Caro was marginalized from the direct political struggle and devoted his efforts to a series of works of legal and economic interest, primarily as a member of the Council of State. Caro opined on this institution within the governmental context:

> It is a consultative body of the government and an auxiliary one, the preparation of the legislative work, inasmuch as this preparation corresponds to the executive power, and also (if the law so provides) in the decision of litigation brought in administrative matters, inasmuch as these cases can be distinguished and separated from those that are the jurisdiction of ordinary justice. It is a body that moves with the degree of freedom that the Constitution grants it, but always within the orbit of the executive power, hierarchically organized.[64]

As a member of this advisory body, Caro participated in drafting several bills, including the criminal, judicial, and mining codes, the law of civil procedure, and laws pertaining to the general railway and public education. He also presented reports and legal concepts on expropriation,[65] chaplaincies,[66] vacant land, the concordat, freedom of the press, and the regulation of the monetary system. He also addressed uncultivated lands, relations of the Council of State with the congress, and the authorization of extraordinary expenses when the legislative chambers were in recess. In 1892, he occupied the presidency of the Council of State, but because of his candidacy for the vice presidency of the republic, his incumbency in this position was brief.

Conclusion

The predominant characteristic of Miguel Antonio Caro's personality was his humanism. It was the mainstay of his spirit. He filled his life with literature, law, research and teaching, family, journalism, poetry, religion, and philosophy—all pointing to his personal form of political action. For several decades of the nineteenth century, Caro was the dominant figure in Colombian politics and intellectual life. His legal and political contributions were definitive in the construction of the national conscience.[67] With his work and the institutional and ideological transformations that he promoted, he gave shape to political and legal structures that continue into the present in Colombia.

Caro's thought was supported by philosophy and religion, and these formed the basis for his political action and his legal conception of the state. His religious faith provided the foundation of his doctrine and the ideas with which he defended the model of the state. He believed that this model of the state corresponded to the historical reality, tradition, and immediate political moment of Colombia.

In the legal field, Caro's most important contribution was the Constitution of 1886. He drafted its language and was the spokesperson for the Regeneration movement. The Constitution included a set of rights of the citizens and duties of the state. It established the institutions that would develop these rights and duties and put them into practice. In this way, Caro provided full maturity to an incipient and unstable state that was still unsettled after independence. Caro's work did nothing less than consolidate Colombia as a free and sovereign nation.

Notes

1 He did not have an academic degree, but in view of his work as a humanist, philosopher, journalist, legislator, and jurist, he was awarded the degree of Doctor of Arts and Jurisprudence at universities in Chile and Mexico. He was also a convinced Hispanist, and in 1896 he was decorated by the Spanish government with the Great Cross of Isabel the Catholic for his neutrality in the War of Independence of Cuba.
2 Rivas, "Miguel Antonio Caro Humanista," 119ff.
3 Caro, Caro, and Gómez, *Obras completas de Miguel Antonio Caro* 1:7–271, 294–351, 426–556, and 577–82.
4 Rivas, *El latín en Colombia*, 410.
5 Classical study is evident in the poetical works, political thought, and philosophy of Miguel Antonio's father, José Eusebio Caro. Cf. M.A. Caro, *Obras completas*, vol. 2.

6 In 1850, José Eusebio Caro went into political exile, and Miguel Antonio, then six years old, went to live in the house of his paternal grandfather, who had an extensive library. Cf. V.E. Caro, *La juventud de don Miguel Antonio Caro*, 7–8 and 15–16.
7 Rivas, "Miguel Antonio Caro," 119, and V.E. Caro, *La juventud*, 10–15 and 30–36.
8 These translations were first published by Imprenta de Echeverría Hermanos in Bogotá in 1873. For Menéndez y Pelayo's assessment, see letter of April 6, 1879, in M.A. Caro, *Epistolario de don Miguel Antonio Caro.*
9 Rivas, "Miguel Antonio Caro," 119ff.
10 V.E. Caro, "Miguel Antonio Caro," in M.A. Caro, *Obras poéticas de don Miguel Antonio Caro. Sonetos-Cantilenas*, xiv.
11 Jaramillo, "Tradición y problemas de la filosofía en Colombia," 66.
12 López, "La Labor filosófica de Miguel Antonio Caro," 53.
13 Valderrama, "Estudio preliminar," in M.A. Caro, *Obras*, 1: xxi.
14 Jaramillo, "Tradición y problemas," 66.
15 Ibid., 395. There is a debate about whether Caro could be characterized as a Thomist. Perrier, "El renacimiento de la filosofía escolástica," 109; Suárez, "Miguel Antonio Caro," en *Escritos*, 351–52. Andrade, "Estudio preliminar," in M.A. Caro, *Obras completas*, 1: xxiv.
16 Ibid., 1:294.
17 Valderrama, "Estudio," in M.A. Caro, *Obras completas*, 1: xxxv.
18 M.A. Caro, "Non in solo pane vivit homo," 1–3.
19 M.A. Caro, "El Darwinismo y las misiones," 1098–107.
20 M.A. Caro, "Clericalismo y fanatismo," 1495.
21 M.A. Caro, *Obras completas*, 1: xlii.
22 Ibid., 7:280.
23 Ibid., 3:293–94.
24 Valderrama, "Estudio preliminar," in M.A. Caro, *Escritos políticos*, xvii.
25 Ibid., third series, xix.
26 Ibid., fourth series, xx.
27 Herrera, "Miguel Antonio Caro, Pensamiento y acción política," 47ff. For the intellectual and political origins of this movement, see Baquero, et al., "Miguel Antonio Caro, Semblanza de un jurista."
28 Valderrama, introduction and notes in *El centenario del Tradicionista*.
29 Valderrama, "El Partido Católico," in M.A. Caro, *Obras completas*, 1:751–60.
30 *Estudio sobre el utilitarismo* was published in Bogotá in 1869 in the press run by Foción Mantilla. There is no other edition. Cf. M.A. Caro, *Obras completas*, 1:7–270.
31 Ibid., 1:78.
32 M.A. Caro, "Principios y Hechos," *Escritos políticos*, first series, 1–10. Article published in number 7 of *La Unión Católica* of Bogotá, August 6, 1871, no. 7.
33 M.A. Caro, "Muerte de Ezequiel Rojas," *Escritos políticos*, first series, 279–87. Article published in *El Tradicionista* 3/3, no. 214, August 26, 1873.
34 Cf. Caro, *Escritos políticos*, first series, 1–10.
35 Caro, *Estudio sobre utilitarismo*, in *Obras completas*, 1:141.
36 Valderrama, "Estudio," in M.A. Caro, *Escritos políticos*, first series, xxixff.
37 M.A. Caro, "El utilitarismo Práctico," *Escritos políticos*, first series, 123–24. Article published in *El Tradicionista* 1/2, no. 26, April 30, 1872.
38 M.A. Caro, "El Tradicionista y la Secretaría de lo Interior," *Escritos políticos*, first series, 52–62. Article published in *El Tradicionista* 1/1, no. 9, January 2, 1872.
39 M.A. Caro, "Libertad Liberal," *Escritos políticos*, first series, 147. Article published in *El Tradicionista* 1/3, no. 57, July 16, 1872.
40 Ibid., 148.
41 Valderrama, "Estudio sobre el utilitarismo," in M.A. Caro, *Escritos políticos*, first series, xxxi.

42 M.A. Caro, "La Escuela Liberal," *Escritos políticos*, first series, 11. Article published in *La Unión Católica*, no. 8, August 13, 1871.
43 M.A. Caro, "Cosas del doctor Rojas," *Escritos políticos*, first series, 181. Article published in *El Tradicionista* 1/4, no. 81, September 10, 1872.
44 M.A. Caro, "Contestación al señor Núñez," *Escritos políticos*, first series, 196–204. Article published in *El Tradicionista* 1, no. 111, appendix, December 13, 1872.
45 M.A. Caro, *Estudios Constitucionales y Jurídicos*, first series, 12–15 and 23–80.
46 M.A. Caro, "La Lucha," *Escritos políticos*, first series, 245. Article published in *El Tradicionista* 2/1, no. 146, March 15, 1873.
47 Valderrama, "Estudio preliminar," in M.A. Caro, *Escritos políticos*, first series, xxxviii.
48 Ibid.
49 Caro, *Escritos políticos*, first series, 342. Article published in *El Tradicionista* 5/1, no. 471, February 18, 1876.
50 Valderrama, "Estudio preliminar," in M.A. Caro, *Escritos políticos*, first series, xliii.
51 M.A. Caro, "Historia y Filosofía," *Escritos políticos*, second series, 33–46. Article published in *El Conservador* 1/4, no. 83.
52 M.A. Caro, "Política Nacional," *Escritos políticos*, second series, 290–97. Article published in *La Nación* 3, no. 227, December 8, 1887.
53 M.A. Caro, "Actualidad," *Escritos políticos*, second series, 289. Article published in *La Nación* 3, no. 219, November 11, 1887.
54 Cf. M.A. Caro, "República Bartolina," *Escritos políticos*, second series, 470–84. Article published in *La Prensa* 4, no. 75, November 4, 1891.
55 For Núñez and the Constitution, see Liévano, *Rafael Núñez*, 279–81.
56 Jaramillo, *El pensamiento colombiano en el siglo XIX*, 261–62.
57 Ibid.
58 See, generally, Samper, *Derecho público interno de Colombia*, 369.
59 Betancur, *Antecedentes de la Constitución colombiana de 1886*, vol. 10.
60 Uribe, *Las constituciones de Colombia*, 2:971.
61 M.A. Caro, *Obras completas*, 7:110–14 and 108–06.
62 Ibid., 103–06.
63 Cf. *Proyecto de ley por el cual se fijan las capitales de los departamentos*, in *Diario Oficial*, February 16, 1887 (Bogotá: Imprenta Nacional).
64 M.A. Caro, Obra *completas*, 4: xviii.
65 M.A. Caro, *Escritos políticos*, second series, 377–85.
66 Valencia, *El pensamiento constitucional de Miguel Antonio Caro*, 170.
67 Suárez, *Elogio del señor doctor don Miguel Antonio Caro*, delivered October 12, 1909, at the Academia Colombiana de Historia; Cf. M.A. Caro, *Obras Completas*, 2: xxiii.

References

Arismendi Posada, Ignacio. *Presidentes de Colombia 1810–1890*. Bogotá: Planeta, 1989.

Baquero, Johana A., Libia Andrea Castro, Adriana Romero, and María de la Paz Useche. "Miguel Antonio Caro, Semblanza de un jurista." In *Monograph for the Degree in Law*. Bogotá: Universidad de La Sabana, 2004.

Betancur Cuartas, Belisario. *Antecedentes de la Constitución colombiana de 1886*. Historia Extensa de Colombia. Bogotá: Plaza & Janés, 1988.

Bonilla, Manuel Antonio. *Caro y su obra*. Bogotá: Imprenta nacional, 1948.

Caro, Miguel Antonio. *Artículos y discursos*. Bogotá: Biblioteca Popular de Cultura Colombiana, 1951.

Caro, Miguel Antonio. *Borradores sobre la Constitución de 1886* [Drafts on the Constitution of 1886]. Bogotá: Archivo del Instituto Caro y Cuervo, 1886.

Caro, Miguel Antonio. "Curso de filosofía dictado como profesor en el Seminario de Bogotá en 1872." *Boletín cultural y bibliográfico de la Biblioteca Luis Ángel Arango* 5, no. 12 (1962): 1596–613.

Caro, Miguel Antonio. "El Darwinismo y las misiones." *Repertorio Colombiano* 1 (1887): 1098–107.

Caro, Miguel Antonio. *Epistolario de don Miguel Antonio Caro. Correspondencia con Rufino J. Cuervo y don Marcelino Menéndez y Pelayo.* Bogotá: Editorial Centro, 1941.

Caro, Miguel Antonio. *Epistolario de Miguel Antonio Caro y otros colombianos con Joaquín Rubio y Ors y Antonio Rubio y Lluch.* Bogotá: Imprenta Patriótica del Instituto Caro y Cuervo, 1982.

Caro, Miguel Antonio. *Escritos políticos.* Introduction, compilation, and notes by Carlos Valderrama. Bogotá: Imprenta Patriótica del Instituto Caro y Cuervo, 1990.

Caro, Miguel Antonio. *Estudios constitucionales y jurídicos.* Bogotá: Biblioteca Popular de Cultura Colombiana, 1951.

Caro, Miguel Antonio. "Non in solo pane vivit homo." *Anales de la Sociedad de San Vicente de Paul* 1 (1869): 1–3.

Caro, Miguel Antonio. *Obras poéticas de don Miguel Antonio Caro. Sonetos-Cantilenas.* Bogotá: Imprenta Nacional, 1929.

Caro, Miguel Antonio, ed. *Informe sobre los elementos de Ideología de Tracy, respuesta escrita en 1870 a consulta hecha por el Rector del Colegio de Nuestra Señora del Rosario* [Report on the elements of Tracy's ideology, response written in 1870 to a consultation by the rector of the College of Our Lady of the Rosary]. Bogotá: Imprenta Nacional, 1870.

Caro, Miguel Antonio, Víctor Eduardo Caro, and Antonio Gómez. *Obras completas de Miguel Antonio Caro.* Introduction, compilation, and notes by Carlos Valderrama Andrade. Bogotá: Imprenta Nacional, 1942.

Caro, Víctor Eduardo. *La juventud de Don Miguel Antonio Caro.* Bogotá: Minerva, 1981.

Caro, Víctor Eduardo. *Labores legislativas y estudios jurídicos.* Bogotá: Imprenta Patriótica del Instituto Caro y Cuervo, 1982.

Díaz, Marco A. *La vida de don Miguel Antonio Caro.* Bogotá: Instituto Caro y Cuervo, 1984.

Galvis, Ligia. *Filosofía de la Constitución colombiana de 1886.* Bogotá: Lucía de Duguerra, 1986.

Hernández, Cecilia. *Miguel Antonio Caro, diversos aspectos de un humanista colombiano.* Bogotá: Biblioteca Nacional, 1943.

Hernández Norman, Isabel. *Miguel Antonio Caro, vida y obra.* Bogotá: Instituto Caro y Cuervo, 1968.

Herrera, Eduardo. "Miguel Antonio Caro, Pensamiento y acción política." PhD dissertation, Pamplona, 2008

Jaramillo, J. "Tradición y problemas de la filosofía en Colombia." *Ideas y Valores* 3, no. 9–10 (1954): 58–82.

Jaramillo Uribe, Jaime. *Antología del pensamiento político colombiano.* Bogotá: Banco de la República, 1970.

Jaramillo Uribe, Jaime. *El pensamiento colombiano en el siglo XIX.* Bogotá: Planeta, 1997.

Liévano Aguirre, Indalecio. *Rafael Núñez*. Bogotá: Biblioteca Colombiana de Cultura, 1977.

López, L. "La Labor filosófica de Miguel Antonio Caro." *Cultura Universitaria* 2 (1947): 53.

Nieto Arteta, Luis Eduardo. *La Regeneración y la organización nacional de Colombia*. Bogotá: El Áncora, 1987.

Olano, Hernán Alejandro. *Constitucionalismo histórico*. Bogotá: Temis, 1998.

Perrier, Joseph Louis. "El renacimiento de la filosofía escolástica." *Revista del Colegio Mayor de Nuestra Señora del Rosario* 12 (1916): 109.

Pombo, Manuel Antonio and José Joaquín Guerra. *Constituciones de Colombia*. Biblioteca Popular de la Cultura Colombiana, Vols. 1–4. Bogotá: Ministerio de Educación Nacional, 1951.

Porras Troconis, Gabriel. "Caro Razonador." *Boletín del Instituto Caro y Cuervo*. Bogotá: Instituto Caro y Cuervo, 1948.

Rivadeneira, Antonio José. *Historia Constitucional de Colombia*. Bogotá: Horizontes, 1978.

Rivadeneira, Antonio José. *El latín en Colombia: bosquejo histórico del humanismo en Colombia*. Bogotá: Instituto Caro y Cuervo, 1949.

Rivas Sacconi, José Manuel. *Miguel Antonio Caro humanista*. Bogotá: Imprenta Nacional, 1947.

Sáchica, Luis Carlos. *La Constitución colombiana (cien años haciéndose)*. Mexico City: Universidad Nacional Autónoma de México, 1982.

Samper, José María. *Derecho público interno*. Bogotá: Voto Nacional, 1887.

Sierra Mejía, Rubén. *Miguel Antonio Caro y la cultura de su época*. Bogotá: Universidad Nacional de Colombia, 2002.

Suárez, Marco Fidel. "Miguel Antonio Caro." In *Escritos*. Bogotá: Arboleda & Valencia, 1914.

Tascón, Tulio Enrique. *Historia del Derecho constitucional colombiano*. Pereira: Litoalfa, 2000.

Torres García, Guillermo. *Personalidad política de Miguel Antonio Caro*. Madrid: Ediciones Guadarrama, 1956.

Uribe Vargas, Diego. *Las constituciones de Colombia*. Madrid: Cultura Hispánica, 1977.

Uribe Vargas, Diego. *Evolución política y constitucional de Colombia*. Madrid: Instituto de Derecho Comparado de la Universidad Complutense de Madrid, 1997.

Valderrama Andrade, Carlos. *Un capítulo de las relaciones entre el Estado y la Iglesia en Colombia*. Bogotá: Instituto Caro y Cuervo, 1986.

Valderrama Andrade, Carlos. *El centenario del Tradicionista, datos para la biografía de Miguel Antonio Caro*. Bogotá: Instituto Caro y Cuervo, 1972.

Valderrama Andrade, Carlos. *Discursos y otras intervenciones de Miguel Antonio Caro en el Senado de la República 1903–1904*. Bogotá: Instituto Caro y Cuervo, 1985.

Valderrama Andrade, Carlos. *Miguel Antonio Caro y la Regeneración: apuntes y documentos para la comprensión de una época*. Bogotá: Instituto Caro y Cuervo, 1997.

Valencia Villa, Alejandro. *El pensamiento constitucional de Miguel Antonio Caro*. Bogotá: Instituto Caro y Cuervo, 1992.

Zuleta Álvarez, Enrique. *La iniciación filosófica de Miguel Antonio Caro*. Lima: Universidad Mayor de San Marcos, 1968.

23 Fernando Vélez Barrientos (Colombia, 1847–1935)

Victor M. Uribe-Uran

Birth, family background, and historical context

Colombian jurist Fernando Vélez, a renowned private law expert, was born in Hatoviejo (today's Bello), a municipality neighboring Medellín, the city where he would grow up. In 1826, two decades before his birth, Medellín had become the capital of mountainous and industrious Antioquia, a legendary province in the west of the country. This province's celebrated prosperity derived from consecutive cycles of gold mining, coffee growing, and early industrial ventures, especially textile mills. Vélez's life spanned the second half of the nineteenth century and the first three decades of the twentieth century, a period of intense political turmoil, dramatic socioeconomic change, and major cultural transformations in both his province and the South American nation as a whole.

During those years, for instance, when Vélez was just a child, the country, known at the time as New Granada, experienced a short-lived progressive military coup (1854). It was supported by groups of impoverished artisans that took over Bogotá, the nation's capital, asking for economic protection to save their small artisanal industries and workshops. When he was a teenager, the country went through a civil war (1860–62), in which the rebel leader, colorful General Tomás Mosquera, eventually seized power and went on to introduce political federalism, renaming the nation the United States of Colombia. Replacing the country's old constitution in 1863, and displaying authoritarian tendencies, Mosquera paradoxically undertook other radical liberal reforms with considerable impact. Even though Mosquera himself was forcibly removed from power in 1867, the impact of his reforms, including the elimination of the death penalty, the expulsion of the Jesuits, and a frontal attack on the properties of the Catholic Church, lasted over two decades (early 1860s to mid-1880s). Later, when Vélez was in his thirties, two more civil wars occurred, in 1876–77 and 1884–85. The former, a conservative rebellion against secularizing educational reforms, placed Vélez's native Antioquia at one of the conservative epicenters of the dispute. The latter war brought about the end of the liberal era and marked the implementation of a deeply conservative regime (*la regeneración*) under a new, centralist constitution (1886). Then, when he was in his late forties and early fifties, there were a short-lived liberal revolt (1895) and a prolonged and devastating civil war

(1899–1902), tellingly named the "Thousand Days War," in which over an estimated hundred thousand people died. The casualties included one of Vélez's six siblings, Eduardo, the youngest of his two brothers.[1] The year following the end of hostilities, a separatist movement encouraged and supported by the United States ended up with the secession of the province of Panama, which became an independent country in 1903 and the site of a strategic interoceanic canal guarded by the northern empire whose interests it was meant to serve. Finally, an external war with neighboring Peru (1932–33) took place as Vélez, then over eighty years old and residing in Europe, was nearing the end of his life.

Not surprisingly, during Velez's life his politically tumultuous nation bore four different names and had as many as four different constitutions.[2] Interestingly enough, except for a few journalistic pieces on constitutional issues, rather than turning the stormy public law scene facing his country into an object of study, he made private law his passion. In later years, in one of his main books, he actually claimed that private law norms were not only the most numerous but also "the most interesting."[3] Further, although active in public office at the regional and national level and politically engaged, unlike his sibling Eduardo he never joined the military fray but concentrated instead on public service, litigation, law teaching, and academic production. Before examining these various aspects of his life, it is worth pausing first over a few of the changing economic and cultural features of his time.

Like Colombia's politics, the country's economy changed considerably during Vélez's life, especially because of the construction of an export-centered railroad system. With fragments ranging from four to fifty-four kilometers, several of which were laid in Antioquia, the rail system connected highlands with the country's main waterway, the Magdalena River, and eventually reached the Caribbean Sea. A related development was the increase of the agrarian frontier through the internal occupation of temperate lands in or bordering Antioquia to the south. This massive and legendary movement of pioneers, widely known as *la colonización antioqueña*, led to the expansion and consolidation of the country's coffee export economy. Another important economic transformation besides railroads and agrarian expansion was the implementation and growth of a variety of industries, especially breweries, food-processing enterprises (chocolate factories and mills processing grains, in particular), textile mills, and small soap-making, candle-making, earthenware, and shoe-making factories. Antioquia was central to several of these processes, and Vélez, who continued to reside in the province and whose surviving brother, Lucrecio, was a partner in a small textile factory in the early 1900s, certainly witnessed the material changes brought about by industrial growth. He also must have experienced related labor turmoil. Some of these transformations had an impact on his family's economic outlook, his own legal practice, and even his worldview and that of others around him.

These material changes were accompanied by major cultural shifts. Initially, until Vélez's midlife, the shifts involved a rising liberal and secular outlook on life, growing inclination to practical rather than speculative endeavors, and the celebratory, outward-facing, and materialist attitude typically attached to societies experiencing economic prosperity. Eventually, though, the backlash took the form of deepening Catholicism, a revival of conservative Hispanism, and a growing inward-looking and authoritarian approach to life, which would characterize the "Regeneration" political regime dominant during the second half of Vélez's adult life (1886–1930). Of the two cultural approaches, Vélez seems to have embraced the former, exhibiting a somewhat liberal disposition, though perhaps far from radical. It is unclear, though, whether, as some sources claim, he joined Catholic organizations such as the Asamblea Católica de Antioquia or was a member of the nationalist faction, the most progressive, of the Conservative Party.[4]

Education, marriage, and career

Despite the Catholic background of his family, typical of many, if not all, Antioqueño households in those days, Vélez's formative years may have contributed to his moderately liberal inclinations. His father, Manuel Vélez Arango, was a well-to-do merchant and moneylender about whose personality or businesses we know little. Fernando's younger brother, Lucrecio, besides becoming a poet, writer, and journalist, also became a prosperous merchant, banker, and textile entrepreneur.[5] Having worked as a scribe in one of the local courthouses from about 1866 to 1869—right around the time when some of Mosqueras's liberal reforms were taking the country by storm—Fernando Vélez studied in Medellín's public college, the recently reorganized Colegio del Estado, later the University of Antioquia. Lucrecio (whose literary pseudonym was "Gaspar Chaverra"), three years his junior, also attended. Their four sisters (Filomena, María Luisa, Dolores, and Ana María) likely underwent domestic and religious training typical for women and, in any case, were not eligible to receive college education at the time; their brother Eduardo was likely too young for it.

The colegio was directed then by Roman de Hoyos, an experienced jurist, former appeals court judge, congressman, notary (an influential occupation in civil law countries), and the state's former *procurador*, or inspector general. Vélez probably took a variety of courses that Hoyos is known to have offered, including criminal law, civil law, judicial evidence, Roman law, and international law. Although the governor of the province, then called the Sovereign State of Antioquia, was the conservative and pious politician Pedro Justo Berrio, the school appears to have imparted at least a handful of progressive classes, including on political economy, one of the subjects Vélez himself would teach in the future. Judging by the defiant content of the newspaper the republican students in Velez's cohort printed (*La Esperanza*), in which they mocked and harshly criticized their professors, they seem to have been fairly unruly and iconoclastic.[6]

On making a public presentation on the notion of free will (*libre albedrío*), a concept central to both scholastic theology and legal contracts,[7] and answering a series of unspecified oral questions formulated by three examiners, Vélez graduated as a Doctor of Jurisprudence and Political Sciences in late 1869. Governor Berrio attended in his capacity as director of public instruction. Two years later, the *colegio* was renamed Universidad de Antioquia. That same year, in 1871, Vélez, who was then twenty-four years old, competed for public office for the first time and won a seat as delegate to the state legislature. Under the federal regime in place at the time and according to the state's provincial constitution (1864), this administrative and legislative body met every two years for about sixty days. Its main functions were to approve the state budget, administer state properties, regulate the formation and operation of the provincial militias, issue amnesties and pardons, elect justices to the state court of appeals, designate the state inspector general, supervise the appointment of some of the state's civil servants, and issue laws relevant to provincial affairs. Vélez was re-elected twice more, in 1873 and 1875. Since this was not a full-time occupation, it is very likely that Vélez spent part of his time practicing law.

In 1875, at age twenty-eight, Vélez married Elena Margarita Lalinde Santamaría, daughter of a wealthy landowner, planter, and architect from Medellín. The couple had two children—a girl, Marava, and a boy, Hernán. The same year of his marriage, for the first time Vélez became a professor at his alma mater, at least briefly. According to a newspaper from his native town, a few years later, sometime between 1880 and 1883, he spent time in Paris, presumably in the company of his wife. He may have taken advantage of the trip to learn French, gather and study civil codes and law materials on his own, and travel throughout Europe for pleasure.[8] The fragmentary records we have indicate that he taught again at the Universidad de Antioquia beginning in the late 1880s or early 1890s and continued to do so seemingly for decades afterward. His main course offering was civil law, but he also appears to have taught—at least occasionally—commercial law, political economy, and international law.[9] In the 1880s, he served twice more (1882 and 1888) as representative in the province's legislative assembly, and did so a final time in 1894. By then, the assembly had expanded powers under the state's new constitution (1877), including the appointment of provincial judges, prosecutors, notaries, and even the university's president and his deputy. At the dawn of the decade of 1890, Vélez published two major academic works and had an active legal practice, even representing the national government in major lawsuits involving international parties.

Major academic contributions, ideas, and legal practice

Vélez's first major publication, released in 1890, was a coauthored annotated edition of the *Colombian Mining Code*. His coauthor was a gifted former student of his, Antonio José Uribe Gaviria (1869–1942), who had graduated as a lawyer at the age of twenty, a year before the release of the *Colombian Mining Code*, and shortly thereafter became a professor of Spanish literature, rhetoric, and history at Universidad de Antioquia, his alma mater. Soon to become one of the most important jurists of his generation, young Uribe Gaviria was probably viewed by Vélez as a most-gifted pupil—one worth partnering with. Their publication's subtitle revealed the content and some of the purposes behind their work:

> a listing of the mining laws from the nation and Antioquia, an instruction to notify and declare mines and request their concession, templates to accomplish all of this, laws additional to the code, official resolutions on some disputed aspects involving these matters, and a table of the notaries and offices of registry in Antioquia.[10]

Prefaced by a reminder to readers about the significance of mining in Colombia, the excessive number of laws enacted after the respective code, and the unfortunate fact that the code's official edition was incomplete and had been sold out, the authors presented the publication as a complete and most valuable historical compilation, with an analytical index and abundant cross-references. They regretted, though, not having been able to compile mining laws in every province of the country. In any case, the book was indeed a comprehensive publication of both legislative and administrative mining norms, meant to serve the practical needs of lawyers, state employees, and claimants of mines.

The volume contained three parts. The first was a historical summary of mining laws from Spanish colonial times to the present, with a chapter exclusively devoted to the historical laws for Antioquia, along with updated and amended practical instructions. The instructions were an improved version the authors modeled after *instrucciones sobre minas* that the secretary of the treasury in the state of Antioquia had issued in hopes of standardizing methods and procedures soon after the region's code was released, while providing models of petitions and related administrative decisions. The second part was a transcription of the nation's mining code of 1887 (which was itself a copy of Antioquia's original mining code of 1867), followed by an analytical index organized by key words. The third part contained a copy of related laws and administrative orders from 1875 until 1889.

Valuable as a systematic compilation, perhaps the book's most original contribution appeared in its first twenty-four pages. Guided by a concern over whether mines belonged to the private owner of the land where they lay or rather with the state, the authors examined a variety of norms issued over the course of two hundred years, from the late seventeenth to the late nineteenth century. This section of the text was a chronological summary of mining laws, starting with the general ones found in the Spanish *Novísima Recopilación* (1805) and continuing with those specific to America, available in the *Recopilación de Indias* (1681). Then the authors surveyed laws issued in 1823 and 1829 in independent Colombia (New Granada); mining ordinances from 1783 from colonial Mexico (New Spain), applicable in Colombia by default; and a series of statutes enacted through the nineteenth century in Colombia.[11] As they discussed the main issue regarding ownership, they paid attention to a number of related aspects, including leasing contracts, concessions, and mechanisms of declaration of the existence of a mine.

Likely to have been a cherished reference work at the time for mining in Antioquia (where it was published) and elsewhere, the book went through a second, expanded and amended, edition in 1905. This was prepared by Fernando Vélez alone because Uribe Gaviria, having finished a stint as the country's minister of public instruction (education), was sent as a special envoy (*enviado extraordinario y ministro plenipotenciario*) to Chile, Argentina, and Brazil, and thus was not available to work on the text.[12] Vélez apologized that in the absence of his academic partner, and because of his own multiple occupations, particularly work on the fourth volume of his civil-law treatise, he had produced an edition "not as good as was to be desired." Still, he made sure to present it as a "notably expanded and amended" version of the earlier text, containing the additional mining laws enacted after 1888, a new section on both relevant judicial decisions, and more than fifty-eight additional executive resolutions on mining matters.[13]

Just the year after the first edition of his mining code, Vélez published perhaps his best known and most widely cited work, which positioned him as a precursor of legal history in Colombia. His modestly titled book *Datos para la historia del Derecho nacional* (*Data for the history of national law*), released in 1891, became a standard reference material for legal historians.[14] Vélez argued that, while the book was not specifically a history of the nation's law, its purpose was to start "gathering and ordering" basic documents for the benefit of those qualified to undertake the task of writing such a history one day. Despite the alleged limitations of his text, he went on to suggest that his book could serve in the meantime as a basic manual to teach Colombian legal history in all colleges. He lamented that law schools did not teach anything other than the current laws and thus deprived future attorneys of historical knowledge concerning previous laws, both public and private. He confessed that his original purpose was to concentrate on private law exclusively, but that, though the bulk of the book's chapters actually deal with it, ultimately he decided to add information on criminal and constitutional law. Similar to what he did in his *Mining Code*, he apologized for not having been able to incorporate information on the legislation of each of the former "sovereign states" but at least managed to address that of his native Antioquia, hoping other jurists would undertake similar works in each of the nation's provinces. While the book's first part was about Colombian law, the second part, almost a hundred pages, or a third of the entire text, indeed surveyed three decades of substantive legislation in Antioquia (*derecho antioqueño*), from 1856 to 1886.

Vélez organized the book's first part on Colombian law (*derecho colombiano*) thematically. Its first or preliminary chapter was about "internal public law," and the next sixteen chapters dealt with a series of discrete, mainly private law themes: slavery, Indians, the state's patronage over the Church, ecclesiastical jurisdiction, civil laws, marriage, primogeniture, concessions, "public, vacant, and derelict properties, and treasures," probate for foreigners, chaplaincies and ecclesiastical mortgages, "interest rates, loan forgiveness, and extension of deadlines for payment," eminent domain, commercial law, "scribes, notaries, and offices of registry," mining law, and criminal law. A final chapter addressed legal compilations in Colombia and described the way each was structured. Each section began with a discussion of the Spanish legal background (*antecedentes*) and continued with a survey of national law following a strict chronological sequence. The author paused over, and used as subheadings, the various years when there were relevant laws on the respective subject, and gave a list providing a short, mostly descriptive, summary of each. Believing that political events did not belong in his text, he refrained from narrating them. He also refrained from giving any opinions but instead stuck to factual information on even sensitive subjects, such as ecclesiastical immunity.[15] Occasionally, though, he ventured some analytical or interpretive observations that revealed some of his worldview.

Vélez, for instance, deemed slavery a "barbaric institution" and rejected the idea that gradual abolition had been needed to avoid a retroactive application of the law trampling on *derechos adquiridos* (acquired rights, or entitlements). In his opinion, no particular entitlements that violated human rights (*derechos de la humanidad*) were legally defensible (30–31). While addressing laws on Indigenous communities, he followed matter-of-factly the dominant legal language of the time, referring to them as savages in need of being civilized (47–48). In reference to marriage, "the foundation of family…and society," he stressed its enormous (*grandísima*) importance (89). For the most part, however, he seems to have made a concerted effort to keep himself from venturing any value judgments or ideological statements, sticking instead to empirical descriptions of a somewhat dry and technical nature.

In the portions of the text dedicated to civil law, Vélez displayed his comparative knowledge concerning, in particular, various civil codes around the globe. In addition to comparing the Colombian and the earlier Chilean codes, arguing that the former was a copy of the latter and that there were but minor differences between the two, he referenced the codes of Argentina and Mexico and those of Germany's Saxony, as well as various regions of Switzerland, such as Fribourg, Glaris, Soleure, and Zurich. He probably had gathered some of these codes during his European sojourn and may have read them all in French. He claimed that the arrangement of all of these was relatively similar to the Colombian and Chilean codes. Other codes, though, had a rather different thematic division. This was the case, he explained, of those of Austria, Bolivia, France, Italy's Ticino, Portugal, Serbia, and the Swiss cantons of Baden, Bern, and Lucerne. He elaborated briefly on the differences (86).

The second part of the book, concerning Antioquia's laws, followed a division relatively similar to that in part one, starting with a chapter on internal public law and continuing with eleven more on such topics as slavery, Indians, communal lands, and marriage. Overall, Vélez highlighted that the region's 1867 mining code, adopted twenty years later for the country as a whole, represented the most original component of Antioquia's law (227). As encyclopedic in nature as the book's first part, the portion on Antioquia maintained Velez's consistently descriptive and empirical tone. The entire book closed, in fact, with a list of norms and an appendix listing all of the laws issued at the national level in the year prior to its publication. This sealed its condition as a true historical legal directory, a virtually indispensable reference work.[16]

While building his academic profile, Vélez became involved in politics, too. The year after the publication of his historical manual, he served in the national House of Representatives as an alternate delegate for Antioquia. He appears to have been present during the opening session, became a member of the House's committee on civil and judicial affairs, and participated in the discussion of various bills.[17] Shortly thereafter, he served as secretary of the interior for the governor of Antioquia. One source claims he did so twice, in 1893 and 1895, under two separate governors, one of whom (Julian Cock Bayer), while serving as a justice in the local appeals court a couple of years earlier, had coauthored a laudatory preface for Vélez's historical manual. This source and others claim that Vélez served as interim governor for at least three months in 1894.[18]

While it has been difficult to corroborate such assertions, it is clear that by the 1890s, as he taught law, published his first books, participated in politics, and once more gained a seat in the Antioquia Assembly (1894), Vélez had an active law practice. It seems that Fernando Vélez became an attorney for members of the local elite of Medellín, then a rather small city with barely forty thousand inhabitants. Among his earliest cases, for instance, appears to have been the testamentary succession of Juan Ignacio Jaramillo, one of the founders of Envigado, a municipality neighboring Medellín. However, the best known of his legal interventions, though a failed one, concerned his representation of the Colombian government in the arbitration in London of a noisy legal dispute with the British company Punchard, McTaggart, Lowther & Co. The dispute, which took place in 1895, involved the breach of a contract for financing and constructing a portion of Antioquia's railroad that had been suspended, years before, due to civil war. The expectation under the new contract was that construction would resume and be completed between 1892 and about 1896, but the construction did not occur. An arbitration tribunal had to settle the matter. Probably to shape public opinion in their favor, each of the two parties published their lengthy legal briefs and filed separately before the tribunal.[19] Despite Vélez's articulate intervention, apparent diplomatic pressure from the British Government, in cooperation with a Colombian national interested in receiving a hefty commission, led to Colombia and the Department of Antioquia ultimately losing the case and paying an indemnification of forty thousand British pounds and sixty percent of the arbitration costs.[20]

By 1896, the Colombian Society of Jurisprudence, established in late 1894, designated Fernando Vélez as one of its corresponding members (*socios correspondientes*).[21] Notably, this occurred even before he had started to publish his magnum opus, a multivolume treatise on Colombian civil law. The book's nine volumes appeared between 1898 and 1911.[22] Apparently, to focus on his legal practice and the academic work he had decided to undertake, Vélez left politics and public service altogether in 1898. He even allegedly turned down a seat on the Colombian Supreme Court during these years. Over the next decade, except during the period of the Thousand Days War, he released volume after volume at a regular pace, almost one every year.

In the prologue to the second edition of his extensive study, Vélez suggested that his main objective was to compile legal doctrine and judicial decisions concerning all possible aspects of the Colombian Civil Code. The code, adopted nationwide in 1873, had been modeled after the Chilean one, drafted by renowned Venezuelan jurist Andrés Bello. Fernando Vélez explained that given that the code had been in place for just about two and a half decades, Colombians had not yet managed to accumulate as much doctrine and jurisprudence as, for instance, the French had accumulated for nearly a century. Therefore, he thought that it was quite difficult to reach definitive and well-informed conclusions. He regretted that, in the meantime, the diverse array of juridical opinions from both lawyers and judges would continue to make legal transactions complicated and might even lead to the "ruin" of families embarked on litigation. Still, judicial decisions from appeals courts had begun being published with some uniformity for the first time a few years earlier, and lawyers had also started to produce relevant studies. Vélez took advantage of this development to take the first steps toward a more comprehensive approach to the code. These steps consisted of summarizing available legal opinions in the hope that, one day, accumulated knowledge would be plentiful to formulate "fixed" rules on the application of every piece of the code.[23]

Volume one of Vélez's civil-law treatise included an introduction with basic definitions; comments on the goals of positive law ("to conserve social order" and "ensure public happiness"); references to "morality, legal history, and political economy," considered as the main "sciences auxiliary to jurisprudence"; and observations on legal divisions or branches. The two main divisions consisted of international and national law. Each contained two main subcategories—public and private. The national public law included political or constitutional law, administrative law, and criminal law. The national private law, in turn, was divided into civil, commercial, and procedural law. Finally, the introductory section went over a historical summary of Colombian law, identifying four periods—colonial, early republican, federal, and central. For obvious reasons, this part of the work relied extensively on Vélez's own historical manual.[24] Thereafter, the treatise gave a detailed overview of the Colombian Civil Code, chapter by chapter and article by article, including cross-references addressing related laws. For the most part, Vélez followed an exegetical method and, along the way, cited extensively a handful of doctrinal texts, not only from Colombia but also primarily from Chile, where the Colombian Civil Code had its roots, and France, the main source of civil codifications worldwide.[25] He also included references to judicial decisions from Chilean and Colombian tribunals, several of the latter being courts in Vélez's native Antioquia.

The year after the publication of the last volume of the first edition of his massive civil law treatise, Vélez, along with students and faculty from the Universidad de Antioquia, launched the *Revista de Estudios de Derecho*. Students appear to have been leading members of the editorial staff and seemingly more active than the faculty themselves in drafting articles and managing the publication. One of those students, Francisco Cardona S., was in fact the publication's first president. As it turns out, he was just midway through his legal studies. Three years after the publication had been launched, his mentor, Fernando Vélez, published a short notice in it praising the law thesis with which Cardona had just graduated, and in which he had recommended reforms to the Colombian mining code.[26] Other than a couple of such notices, Vélez did not contribute much to the *Revista* but continued to be busy with litigation and teaching. It is likely that through the former he accumulated sufficient material fortune to make it possible for him to move permanently to Europe with his family by the late 1910s. He settled first in Manchester, England, and then in Paris. Little is known about his occupation and life there apart from the fact that in the mid-1920s, he published a second edition of his main civil law work.

A decade and a half after the first edition published in Medellín, the second edition of *Estudio sobre el derecho civil colombiano* appeared in Paris, where the author seems to have resided at the time. Vélez completed this edition with the assistance of Luis Angel Arango, a lawyer, former state official, and banker. Because Vélez had moved to Europe years before, his new academic partner must have contributed to updating the work with the inclusion of laws enacted after the Colombian Civil Code took effect, in particular some from the late 1890s until 1926. In his characteristically apologetic tone, Vélez lamented any possible errors and insisted that the inspiration to complete the treatise was not his conviction of possessing vast juridical knowledge, nor was it the wish to make a profit, but rather his desire to "serve his fatherland."[27] Vélez would remain in Europe until the end of his life; he died in Rome in July 1935, when he was eighty-eight years old.

Conclusion

Colombian jurist Fernando Vélez contributed significant works to the fields of mining law, legal history, and civil law. Rather than being a deep and creative legal thinker, he was probably more than anything else a meticulous legal compiler and commentator of a positivist vein. Naively convinced that, over time and on the basis of gradual accumulation, jurists in Colombia and other countries would eventually reach scientific agreements about the meaning and interpretation of legal norms, thus overcoming hermeneutical disagreements and reducing litigation to a minimum, he devoted his life to helping his home country advance in such a chimerical and utopian direction. His intellectual production is, in any case, pioneering and deservedly awaits further study. His life beyond academia, even his overall political ideology, also remains somewhat mysterious and worth pursuing.

Notes

1 Arango Mejía, *Genealogías de Antioquia y Caldas*, 495–96; Vélez Guerra, *Moscas de todos los colores*, 231.
2 At the time of Vélez's birth and up until 1858, it was named Confederación Granadina. From 1858 to 1863, the country was called Nueva Granada. It became

the United States of Colombia from 1863 to 1886. Finally, it was renamed the Republic of Colombia in 1886. This was the name it had when Vélez died abroad, in 1935. Between 1847 and 1935, the country enacted constitutions in 1853, 1858, 1863, and 1886. A transitional constitutional regime was implemented in 1861, and a major constitutional reform took place in 1910. See Valencia Villa, *Cartas de Batalla*.

3 Vélez, *Datos para la historia*, xiii.

4 See Melo, *Historia de Antioquia*, 134; Escobar Vélez, "Fernando Vélez Barrientos"; Mejía Cubillos, *Diccionario biográfico*.

5 On Lucrecio Vélez's life, career, and literary production, see Vera Pabón, "Gaspar Chaverra"; see also Mejía Cubillos, *Diccionario biográfico*.

6 Robledo, *Universidad de Antioquia*, 136–40, 234.

7 Vélez rightly deemed it "the main source of all legal obligations." Vélez, *Datos*, 83.

8 Martinez Lobo, "Fernando Vélez Barrientos," *Bello Comenta*, 13 (2006).

9 Robledo, *Universidad de Antioquia*, 147, 159. Although some biographical pieces had him teaching "for forty years," he does not appear among the list of active faculty in subsequent years, say 1882 or 1888, but reappears in 1890. Ibid., 174, 182, 184. See Castaño, "Fernando Vélez," esp. 18, 20.

10 Vélez and Uribe, *Código de Minas Colombiano*.

11 They appeared listed under key years, in particular 1834, 1836, 1844, 1847, 1858, 1860, 1868, 1870, 1873, 1876, 1886, 1887, and 1888.

12 Uribe not only had rapidly climbed the political ladder but also had reached academic prestige through the publication in 1899 of a volume on civil law coauthored with prominent French civil-law expert Edmond Champeau.

13 Vélez and Uribe, *Código de Minas Colombiano*.

14 See references, some of them critical, in Aguilera, *Legislación y el derecho*, prologue; Means, *Underdevelopment and the Development of Law*, 278–79; and Mirow, *Latin American Law*, 130, 195. See also López Medina, *Teoria impura del Derecho*, 119, 131. I thank Matthew Mirow for these valuable references.

15 Vélez, *Datos*, 7, 63. References hereafter are noted parenthetically in the text.

16 It earned him designation as a full member (*académico numerario*) of Antioquia's Academy of History in 1904, shortly after the very foundation of the Academy. See Castaño, "Fernando Vélez," 20; and Mosquera Ruales, "La metamorfósis de Clio," 62.

17 Colombia, *Anales de la Cámara de Representantes*, August 3, 1891, pp. 1–2, 90, 98.

18 This is claimed in the website of a school in Bello, the city of Vélez's birth, that carries his name. See biography by Mesa y Posada. That Vélez was acting governor is also held by Castaño, "Fernando Vélez," 19; and Mejía Cubillos, *Diccionario biográfico*, 227.

19 See Vélez, *Alegato*; and *Ferrocarril de Antioquia*.

20 On the role of Colombian intermediary Santiago Pérez Triana, see Correa Restrepo, "El Ferrocarril de Antioquia," 157, 158.

21 Sociedad Colombiana de Jurisprudencia, *Anales de Jurisprudencia*.

22 Vélez, *Estudio sobre el Derecho civil colombiano*: Vol. 1 (1898) and Vol. 2 (1899) were "on persons"; Vol. 3 (1904) "on property and their use and usufruct"; Vol. 4 (1905) and Vol. 5 (1906) "on successions and donations"; Vol. 6 (1908) , Vol. 7 (1909), Vol. 8 (1910), and, Vol. 9 (1911) "on obligations in general and contracts."

23 Velez, *Estudio sobre el Derecho civil*, 1: Prólogo.

24 Ibid., 1:1–17.

25 The Colombian authors and works cited included Manuel J. Angarita's *Comentarios a la Ley 153*, *Codificación nacional*, and *Suplemento a la codificación*

nacional; Adolfo León Gómez's *Prescripciones y términos legales*; Fernando Garavito's *Jurisprudencia colombiana*; Antonio José Uribe's *Estudio sobre las servidumbres* and *Jurisprudencia de la Corte*; and Nicolás Esguerra and Juan Lucas Caballero's *Estudio sobre la tradición de inmuebles*. The Chilean works included Enrique Cood and José Clemente Fabres's *Explicaciones de Código Civil*; Enrique C. Latorre's *Memorias y discursos*; Robustiano Vera's *Código Civil*; Eulojio Piñera's *Jurisprudencia*; and Jacinto Chacon's *Exposición comparativa*. The French authors and works were, among others, Frédéric Mourlon's *Repetitions Écrites sur le Code Napoléon*; Gabriel Baudry-Lacantinerie's *Précis de droit civil*; Charles Aubry and Christoph Rau's *Cours de droit civil français*; Charles Demolombe's *Cours de Code Napoléon*; and Frantz Despagnet's *Droit International Public*.

26 See Vélez, "Informe del Sr. Presidente de tesis." See also idem., 3/23–24 (1915): 647–48, and idem., 3/25–26 (1915): 645. The *Revista* kept publishing concepts by mentors concerning the theses submitted by their students for graduation. See, for instance, Vélez, "Dr. Florencio Arango F.," Ibid., 3/25–26 (1915): 681–82.

27 Vélez and Arango, *Estudio sobre el Derecho civil colombiano*, 1: Prólogo.

References

Aguilera, Miguel. *La legislación y el derecho en Colombia: sinopsis histórica desde la conquista hasta el presente*, Vol. 14 of *Historia Extensa de Colombia*. Bogotá: Ediciones Lerner, 1965.

Arango Mejía, Gabriel. *Genealogias de Antioquia y Caldas*, Vol. 2. 2nd ed. Medellín: Imprenta Departamental, 1942.

Castaño, Ociel. "Fernando Vélez: Una vida consagrada al estudio del derecho." *Estudios de Derecho* 60 (2002): 17–27.

Colombia. Congreso. Cámara de Representantes. *Anales de la Cámara de Representantes*. Bogotá: Imprenta Nacional.

Correa Restrepo, Juan Santiago. *Ferrocarriles y tranvías en Antioquia*. Bogotá: CESA, 2012.

Escobar Vélez, Edgar Guillermo. "Fernando Vélez Barrientos. Miembro fundador de la Academia Antioqueña de Historia e insigne jurista bellamita." *Repertorio Histórico de la Academia Antioqueña de Historia* 103, no. 17 (2008): 22–26.

Ferrocarril de Antioquia. *Alegato de Conclusión que Charles Talent Spencer Apoderado especial de los señores Punchard, McTaggart, Lowther & Co. de Londres Presenta al Tribunal de Arbitramento*. Bogotá: Imprenta de La Luz, 1985.

López Medina, Diego. *Teoría impura del derecho. La transformación de la cultura jurídica latinoamericana*. Bogotá: Legis, 2009.

Martinez Lobo, William. "Fernando Vélez Barrientos." *Bello Comenta* 13 (2006).

Means, Robert C. *Underdevelopment and the Development of Law: Corporations and Corporation Law in Nineteenth-Century Colombia*. Chapel Hill: University of North Carolina Press, 1980.

Mejía Cubillos, Javier. *Diccionario biográfico y genealógico de la elite antioqueña y Riocaldense*. Pereira: Editorial Red Alma Mater, 2010.

Melo, Jorge Orlando. *Historia de Antioquia*. 2nd repr. Medellín: Suramericana de Seguros, 1991.

Mesa y Posada, Samuel Arturo. "Dr. Fernando Vélez Barrientos," available at: https://iefervelez.jimdo.com/50-a%C3%B1os/biograf%C3%ADa-dr-fernando-v/

Mirow, M.C. *Latin American Law: A History of Private Law and Institutions in Spanish America*. Austin: University of Texas Press, 2010.

Mosquera Ruales, Luis Efraín. "La metamorfosis de Clío. En torno a las transformaciones sobre la investigación y escritura de la historia en Antioquia." MA thesis, Universidad de Antioquia, Medellín, 2017.

Robledo, Emilio. *La Universidad de Antioquia: 1822–1922*. Medellín: Imprenta Oficial, 1923.

Sociedad Colombiana de Jurisprudencia. *Anales de Jurisprudencia* 2, no. 13–14 (1897): 255.

Valencia Villa, Hernando. *Cartas de Batalla. Una crítica al constitucionalismo colombiano*. Bogotá: Universidad Nacional de Colombia, 1987.

Vélez, Fernando. *Alegato que Fernando Vélez, apoderado del Gobierno, presenta al Tribunal de Arbitramento que debe dirimir las diferencias relativas a los contratos sobre el Ferrocarril de Antioquia celebrados con los señores Punchard, McTaggart, Lowther & Co*. Bogotá: Imprenta Nacional, 1895.

Vélez, Fernando. *Datos para la historia del Derecho nacional*. Medellín: Imprenta del Departamento, 1891.

Vélez, Fernando. *Estudio sobre el Derecho civil colombiano*, Vo. 9. Medellín: Imprenta del Departamento, 1898–1911.

Vélez, Fernando. "Informe del Sr. Presidente de tesis. Medellín, 21 de Mayo, 1915." *Revista de Estudios de Derecho* 3, no. 23–24 (1915): 647–48.

Vélez, Fernando, and Antonio José Uribe. *Código de Minas Colombiano. Concordado y Anotado*. Medellín: Imprenta del Departamento, 1890; 2nd ed., corrected and enlarged, Medellín: Imprenta de "La Verdad," 1905.

Vélez, Fernando, and Luis Ángel Arango. *Estudio sobre el Derecho civil colombiano*, Vol. 9. 2nd ed. París: Imprenta París-América, 1926.

Vélez Guerra, Eduardo. *Moscas de todos los colores: Barrio Guayaquil de Medellin, 1894–1934*. Medellín: Editorial Universidad de Antioquia, 2006.

Vera Pabón, Ricardo. "Gaspar Chaverra, una *rara avis* de la literatura Antioqueña." *Huellas de la Ciudad. Revista del Centro de Historia de Bello* 13, no. 15 (2014): 47–55.

Part II

Twentieth-century jurists

24 Antonio Sánchez de Bustamante y Sirvén (Cuba, 1865–1951)

Juan Bosco Amores Carredano

Biographical introduction

Antonio Sánchez de Bustamante was born to Juan Manuel Sánchez de Bustamante y García del Barrio and María Dolores Sirvén Borrás in Havana on April 13, 1865, and was christened in the parish of Santo Cristo del Buen Viaje in Havana. He was the couple's seventh child. All of his older siblings died very young, but two girls, Virginia and Amelia, and his brother Alberto followed him.

His father was born in Elguera, near Santander (Spain), and came to Cuba in 1835, at the age of seventeen, earning a living by working in a grocery store owned by some relatives. Juan Manuel attended the medical course at the University of Havana, gaining top marks, then going on to hold the chair in anatomy there for thirty years while working as a surgeon; in 1882 he was appointed the university's vice-chancellor. In 1878, Juan Manuel joined the Partido Unión Constitucional and was elected senator of the kingdom for the province of Pinar del Río in 1879, moving with part of the family to Madrid. He returned to Cuba when he was made vice chancellor, but he died of tuberculosis a few months later. He was decorated by the Spanish Government with the Order of Charles III and was a firm defender of Cuba's remaining under Spanish sovereignty. He left a substantial inheritance to his children. Their mother, María Dolores Sirvén Borrás, from Havana, came from a family of sugar cane growers of middling wealth.[1]

Antonio and his siblings grew up in a well-off, cultivated family environment, guided by humanistic and Christian values.[2] Antonio's education took place in Cuba and Madrid. In Havana, he attended the prestigious Belén College, run by the Society of Jesus, and achieved excellent results there. He began his secondary school education in Havana, but in late 1878, when his father was elected senator, Antonio and his younger brother accompanied him to Madrid, where Antonio finished his secondary studies with top marks at the Cardenal Cisneros School in Madrid, the most prestigious school in the country.[3]

In 1880–81, Antonio joined the law school at the Central University of Madrid but returned to Havana with his father the following year, continuing his law studies at the University of Havana. He graduated with top marks in 1884, when he was only nineteen. Two years later, he obtained a doctorate in civil and canon law, and in 1887 he was appointed assistant professor of philosophy of law, ecclesiastical discipline, and canon law at the University of Havana.[4]

That same year, despite being still legally a minor, Antonio was granted a license to work as a lawyer and joined the Havana Lawyers' Circle (a professional association of jurists), where he presented publicly for the first time on February 3, 1885, gaining the admiration of the audience.[5] During this period, he opened a legal practice that largely focused on mercantile law; this was to become one of Havana's leading practices, with over one hundred employees. Also in 1885, Antonio married Isabel Pulido Pagés. The middle-class Havana-born daughter of a Cantabrian immigrant, she and Antonio had three sons.[6]

From an early age, Antonio became involved with Havana's public charities. In 1890 he was appointed to the committee of the local mount of piety—a kind of institutional pawnbroker operating as a charity, with roots in the Renaissance. Soon Antonio gained an appointment to the Provincial Charity Committee and the General Hospital of Our Lady of Mercy, a Cuban medical institution founded in 1886 that was furnished with the most advanced equipment of the time. He combined all these activities with the defense of the Real Casa de Beneficencia y Maternidad de La Habana, a traditional charity that assisted poor women in the city and its environs.[7]

He also became involved with specialized journals, such as *Revista General de Derecho* and *El Foro*. The latter published his first article for the general public: "Comentarios a la nueva ley de enjuiciamiento criminal" ("Comments on the criminal prosecution law" 1883). He would return to this topic in cooperation with José Antonio González Lanuza and José Antonio Frías in the *Revista General de Derecho*. Other articles published by this journal included "*Estudios prácticos de derecho mercantil*" and "*El contrato de comisión en nuestro Código de comercio*" ("Practical studies of commercial law" and "The commission contract in our code of commerce," February and May 1885), in which he explained technical aspects of the new commercial law by means of practical examples. All this activity earned him an excellent professional reputation as a lawyer, lecturer, and writer. Bustamante's wish was to become a university professor, like his father. He wanted to specialize in international law; some of his education had taken place in Europe, and he was aware of the increasing importance that this branch of legal studies had acquired there in the preceding decade.[8]

In 1891, when he was barely twenty-six years old, he was appointed professor in public and private international law at the University of Havana; this was the second such professorship created in Spanish territories, after one created at the Central University of Madrid. His first book as professor, *El orden público: estudio de Derecho internacional privado* (*The public order: study of private international law*), was published in 1893.[9] He joined the International Law Institute in 1895, and by 1896 he had published *Tratado de Derecho internacional privado* (*Private international law treatise*).[10] Soon afterward, he received permission to undertake an academic trip to Europe. He traveled through France, Germany, and Italy, getting in touch with European academies and institutions with interest in public and private international law. He attended the first conference organized by the International Law Institute, held in Geneva in 1899. Both there and in Brussels he met the Spanish and American delegates that had just signed the Treaty of Paris (December 10, 1898), which brought the Spanish–American war to an end.

Soon afterward, Sánchez de Bustamante was summoned by his Habanero colleagues to return to Cuba, which was then under American administration (1899–1902). The assembly, which was in the process of writing the constitution of what would become the first Cuban Republic, was the center of heated debates; in this context, Sánchez de Bustamante firmly supported the Platt Amendment, which in his opinion was the only way for Cuba to become a prosperous, pacific, and, ultimately, sovereign nation.[11]

After the foundation of the republic in 1902, Sánchez de Bustamante was elected senator for the province of Pinar del Río for an eight-year term. Reelected in 1910, he abandoned the chamber in 1916. Owing to the violent swings in Cuban politics during these years, his work as a senator was intermittent rather than continuous.

The new republic joined the family of independent nations during a period marked by the belligerence of empires. In this context, and using Spanish colonial possessions as a launching pad, the United States had grown enormously to assume a position as a new imperial player. Developments in communications, navigation, and weaponry called for a new international code to guarantee the coexistence of nations within this emerging order; nineteenth-century law and diplomacy had to adapt to a changed international setting.

On his return to Cuba, Sánchez de Bustamante was able to lend his knowledge to the creation of a modern republic, always within the limits set by the first Cuban constitution. From the outset, he applied the principles of legal science in all matters in which his consultation was required, which were generally related to international law, a subject he taught at the university almost up to his death.

In 1903 Bustamante was appointed President of the Foreign Relations Committee in the Senate. The first task allocated to this committee was the confirmation of the commercial treaty between Cuba and the United States, the so-called Cuban–American Treaty of Relations. Against the arguments of critics, including the famous liberal politician Manuel Sanguily or the President of the Congress, Salvador Cisneros Betancourt, a hero of independence—who believed that the treaty made Cuba excessively dependent in economic and political terms—Sánchez de Bustamante presented rational and legal arguments for the reliability of the relationship with the United States and the convenience of keeping close business links with the Americans; this would allow the economy to improve and would facilitate the normal development of republican institutions, guaranteeing their independence and sovereignty. Eventually, these arguments gained the upper hand, and the treaty was signed; one of the most significant features of the treaty was the low price paid for Cuban sugar in the American market.[12]

In those years, the Foreign Relations Committee of the senate closed other deals, such as the Agreement Between the United States and Cuba for the Lease of Lands for Coaling and Naval Stations, by which Cuba ceded territories in Guantanamo Bay and Bahía Honda to the United States for the installation of military and naval bases; the Treaty of Relations with the United Kingdom (1904); and the Extradition Treaty with Spain (1905).

The serious civil conflicts faced by the island led the Cuban president, the conservative Tomás Estrada Palma, to disband parliament in 1906 and request that the United States enforce the Platt Amendment, which granted the United States authority to intervene in Cuba. Cuba was subject to US intervention until 1908. Despite these threats to independence, Sánchez de Bustamante continued with his frantic activity; alongside the diplomat Gonzalo de Quesada and the politician Manuel Sanguily, he became part of the Cuban delegation to the Second Peace Conference celebrated in The Hague in 1907.[13] The presence of Cuba in this conference could be nothing but symbolic, but it displayed the island's commitment to independence, despite the Platt Amendment and the interventionist activities of the United States in Central America and the Caribbean at that time.

The conference returned to the issues, such as disarmament and international arbitration, that had been debated at the first peace conference of 1899—also held in The Hague. This time, however, the conference was attended by forty-four nations, some from Latin America and Asia, as well as from Europe, and the United States. Pacifist ideals were behind the attempt to create new rules and conventions based on the law of nations (*ius gentium*) together with private and public international law. Although the conference made little progress concerning the disarmament of the Great Powers, an arbitration committee was created—a direct precedent to the Permanent Court of Arbitration constituted in The Hague in 1921—that included Sánchez de Bustamante as a member.[14]

In 1909, after the American withdrawal, political life in Cuba went back to normal; Sánchez de Bustamante resumed his work in the senate in the 1910 Parliament, now representing the Havana province. He participated in two committees—foreign relations and justice. In 1913, acting as spokesman of the Foreign Relations Committee, he presented a legal proposal for the construction of a monument to the victims of the explosion of the battleship *Maine*, to be erected in New York. During the 1914 Parliament, he argued in favor of creation of two separate courts for civil and administrative cases in Havana.[15]

In this same year, the Cuban Chamber of Representatives passed the Divorce Act. The publication of the associated regulations (and thus, effectively, the implementation of the act) was delayed for four years, owing to the social controversy caused by the legal text. The bitter parliamentary confrontations triggered by the act even forced the President of the Chamber, José Antonio González Lanuza, to resign. Sánchez de Bustamante, who had been absent from Cuba for a time, did not take part in the controversy. In 1912 he was a founding member of the American Institute of International Law, funded by the Carnegie Endowment for International Peace, supported by US Secretary of State Robert Bacon and the jurists James Brown Scott (United States) and Alejandro Álvarez (Chile). Later, Sánchez de Bustamante initiated the Cuban Society for International Law.

In addition to his international activity, Sánchez de Bustamante continued lecturing in international law at the University of Havana. His lectures were attended by many of the most prominent Cuban politicians and lawyers of the following generation. He continued to be actively involved in his legal practice in Havana and was appointed as a board member of the Cuban Cane Corporation, the largest sugar company in the island, participated in by some of the main financial groups in the United States.[16] From 1904 onwards, he was also Dean of the Lawyers' Professional Association of Havana.

Owing to these enterprises, his participation in senate activities became rarer. Most of his speeches were concerned with technical rather than political issues and were related to criminal, mercantile, and civil law. As a general rule, he requested that the bills under discussion be more precisely phrased. In this regard, his contribution to the development of the legal system of the young Cuban republic is undeniable.[17] Although his knowledge and prestige made him a key player, he tried to stay aloof from internal political conflicts. As pointed out by one of his admirers, the diplomat and historian Manuel Márquez Sterling: "His policy aimed not to engage in politics and not to interfere with the work or passions of other people."[18]

Although he abandoned his senate seat in 1916, Sánchez de Bustamante continued collaborating with the conservative government of Mario García Menocal whenever his advice on international law was requested, as in the government's legal suit with Dragados, an Anglo-American company. In 1911 this company was granted an exclusive government contract for the maintenance of the Cuban ports, but a new government decided in 1916 to rescind the contract. Based on strictly legal arguments, Sánchez de Bustamante advised the government not to pay the compensation demanded by the firm.[19]

On April 7, 1917, Cuba declared war on Germany in solidarity with the United States, which had declared war against Germany the previous day. (Cuba would follow the United States in declaring war on Austria-Hungary that December.) The government's purpose was to clearly display Cuba's position and to prevent Germany from getting any support on the island, for instance in the use of its harbors or coasts. President García Menocal placed an embargo on the property of German citizens who worked against the interests of the United States, and Sánchez de Bustamante was appointed chair of the committee created for this purpose. The European War ended just over a year later, and the Cuban jurist was present at the historical peace conference in Paris.

During this visit to Europe, Sánchez de Bustamante was very active. After the signing of the Armistice that led to the creation of the League of Nations and the Permanent Court of Arbitration in The Hague, on September 14, 1921, the Cuban jurist was appointed as a judge of the Permanent Court of International Justice in The Hague—a role that he performed without interruption until 1945.

Other public and private initiatives had Sánchez de Bustamante's support. The National Academy of Arts and Humanities was founded in 1910, with Sánchez de Bustamante as its first president. The institution was attached to the secretary of education but acted autonomously, granting scholarships and organizing public exhibitions and talks, as well as awarding the yearly National Grand Price for Arts and Letters.[20]

The peak of Sánchez de Bustamante's prestige coincided with the celebration of the Sixth International Conference of American States, or Sixth Pan-American Conference, convened in Havana in January 1928. Sánchez de Bustamante chaired the conference, and attendees included American President Calvin Coolidge and the President of Cuba, Gerardo Machado.[21] The program included issues related to American international law—for instance, intellectual property, nationality, women's rights, and maritime security. The organizing committee invited all university lecturers to attend the debates, which came to an end on February 20. The conference passed the International Private Law Code, also known as the Bustamante Code, which was published as an appendix of the final declaration of the conference, the Treaty of Havana.

Cuban President Gerardo Machado used the success of the conference to promote his reelection. His nationalistic discourse during his presidency (1924–28), and the palpable success of his economic policies, earned him increasing popularity,[22] leading his supporters in the senate to propose a constitutional reform to allow him to run for a second term. In order to legitimize this project, Machado invited Bustamante to chair the constitutional committee that was convened in April 1927 to endorse the proposal. In addition to his undeniable prestige in Cuba and abroad, other reasons lay behind this invitation. First, the reformist proposal had been signed by several political parties, and a legal reelection of Machado was the best chance for keeping political peace and dispelling the ghosts of previous conflicts that had led to American intervention on the island. Second, Bustamante's legal practice represented several of the main companies in the Cuban–American trade, which would clearly benefit from Machado's reelection. Third and ultimately, his commitment to the government was reinforced by the support provided by Cuban institutions to the success of the Sixth Pan-American Conference.

Against the instructions that he had been given, Bustamante's hand became obvious in the changes introduced to the government's proposal, especially concerning the technical precision of the legal terminology, a lifelong obsession of Bustamante's. Finally, however, the text was passed, and Machado, after the new constitution came into effect, was reelected in 1928 for a six-year term with the support of the three main parties.[23]

Despite being criticized for aligning himself with Machado's government, Sánchez de Bustamante's prestige did not overly suffer. He continued lecturing and traveling abroad whenever his position in the International Court in The Hague demanded it. His students at the University of Havana were to continue to be guided by the humanist, pragmatic, and Americanist spirit of this pioneer of international law.

The International Private Law Code or the Bustamante Code

The International Private Law Code, also known as the Bustamante Code, proposed a common code for private international law across the whole of the

American continent. Although designed by Sánchez de Bustamante, the code incorporated many elements from earlier initiatives. The first step was taken with the signing of the Treaty of Montevideo by several South American countries in 1889. This code tried to address national differences in civil, mercantile, and penal matters. The long period of economic and commercial development that the continent had undergone, which was also associated with the arrival of large contingents of migrants, raised the need for the various national legal systems to reach common ground on many issues. The main difficulties, when it came to putting things into writing, were the differences between advocates of the principle of domicile and those who argued that the scope of individual and state initiatives should be framed by the principle of nationality.[24]

In 1906, during the Third Pan-American Conference, held in Rio de Janeiro, Bustamante was part of the legal committee entrusted with drafting international private and public legal codes. In 1912, after the foundation of the American Institute of International Law, the committee presented an extradition treaty and organized several subcommittees, two of which convened in Montevideo and Lima and dealt with private international law. The Montevideo subcommittee focused on such issues as the legal rights of foreigners, and family and inheritance law. However, the doctrinal differences of the delegates (domicile versus national principle) prevented an agreement from being reached. The Lima subcommittee presented a project about civil and commercial law, court jurisdiction, and disagreements in the application of criminal law.

In 1923 the Fifth Pan-American Conference, in Santiago de Chile, took positive steps regarding the codification of international law after the aim of achieving a common public international legal code was abandoned. Efforts focused thenceforth on reaching a consensus concerning private law. While it was difficult for states to yield in matters of sovereignty and national interest, thus making any agreement concerning public law an arduous matter. When it came to private law agreement was easier; states were keen on safeguarding the activities, especially trade, of their subjects based in other countries. The conference decided to commission a code that could deal with all these questions.

Sánchez de Bustamante's active role in the meetings held by different international legal bodies in both America and Europe made him one of the foremost specialists in international law worldwide. As such, he served on a committee entrusted by the International Academy of Comparative Law, convened in Geneva in 1924, with the task of codifying private international law. This attempt was unsuccessful owing to the complicated political conditions in Europe during the interwar period. At the same time, however, the American Institute of International Law created a four-expert committee with the same purpose, and here Bustamante played a key role. Within the framework of this latter committee, he deployed his vast knowledge and experience to draft legal formulas that would be acceptable to all countries in the region, including the United States. In the following year, Bustamante published the Spanish and French versions of the result of these efforts, *Proyecto de Código de Derecho internacional privado.* In 1927 the permanent committee of American jurists met in Rio de Janeiro to analyze this project,[25] and the text, with some modifications, was passed by the Sixth Pan-American Conference; by 1930, the project had been ratified by fifteen countries (although some of those still had reservations in specific matters).[26]

The enactment of the Bustamante Code created some expectations that a general consensus concerning the codification of international law could be reached, but a number of countries—including Colombia, Paraguay, Argentina, and Uruguay—did not ratify the agreement owing to differences in their understanding of civil law (marriage and divorce), and stayed within the terms of the Treaty of Montevideo of 1889. Concerning the United States, the power of each state to legislate in matters of private law, within the constitution but in a context that gave great prominence to consuetudinary law, made the ratification of the code especially difficult.

Based on his broad knowledge, beginning with the classical authors of the Salamanca school (Vitoria, Suárez), and his Christian education, Sánchez de Bustamante was convinced that people and nations made up an international community with shared features and ends. This universal stance was reflected in his code, which was built on the premise that difference is not necessarily the same as antagonism.

The Bustamente Code is divided into four books or sections. The first deals with civil law issues such as nationality, domicile, family, marriage and divorce, adoption, and inheritance. The second focuses on mercantile law, contracts, exchange instruments, sea- and air-borne international commerce, and extraterritorial legal personas of mercantile societies, among other topics. These two opening sections were the most widely accepted among American jurists and legislators. The third book addresses criminal matters, and the fourth addresses procedural issues, the jurisdiction of courts of law, and extradition. Bustamante tried to use very general principles, to ensure that they could be accepted by as many countries as possible.

Concerning civil law and the scope of state and individual initiative, the code allowed for both nationality and domicile principles to be applied. The signatories of the Treaty of Montevideo recognized only the domicile principle in these issues. Concerning inheritance, the code contemplates the possibility of properties bequeathed being located in more than one country; geographical dispersion could lead to endless legal suits. In order to avoid this problem, and to simplify the management of inheritance, the code establishes the legal unity of all the property involved, and the application of a single law: the national law of the subject or that of the domicile of the assets. With regard to contracts, the code settles on the laws of the country where the case is judged. Concerning marriage, the code yields to national laws, except when religious marriage is concerned. In this regard, the code allows countries that give preference to religious marriage to choose not to recognize the validity of civil marital status bestowed on their nationals in a different country. Regarding divorce, the code applies the domicile principle and gives the state the possibility of recognizing divorce acts and the remarriage of divorced persons celebrated abroad, as far as the causes of the divorce are contemplated in the legislation of the state where it was granted. At this stage, divorce was legal in Cuba and the United States; in other countries, it was allowed under certain conditions, but in most Latin American countries it was not possible at all.

Concerning commerce, the Bustamante Code establishes the legal unity of international transport. No distinction is made between passenger and freight transport; transport should be considered a single act, regardless of whether it moves freight or people through one or several states. Assets, whether real estate or movable property, are subject to the law of the territory where they are located.[27]

With regard to the legal status of mercantile societies operating abroad, the code establishes that they must assume the limitations set forth by local legislation, for reasons of public order, especially in the following particular circumstances: first, the issuance of shares or bonds by mercantile societies, which must be governed primarily by public interest and the protection of the rights of third parties that may purchase and exchange them; second, societies that deal with activities of a special nature and are thus subject to a special legal framework; and, third, money-issuing banks, because the operation of these institutions is closely linked to the exercise of national sovereignty. The code has been variously labeled as "scientific" in its dispositions, "conservative" with regard to local legislation, and "liberal" insofar as it facilitated the development of international commerce.[28]

The code was published in different languages and became a part of law faculty syllabi in all of Latin America and much of Europe. This was Sánchez de Bustamante's main contribution to the peaceful coexistence of nations. His *Textbook of Private International Law* conveys the ideals that underlie his whole career.

> A universal texbook that covers a uniform international legislation still looks like a difficult thing. However, the fact that we already have one of a nearly continental scope, and that efforts in the right direction are being made everywhere, may turn this scientific chimera into something more solid. Private international law aims, like pretty much every branch of jurisprudence, for the well-being and happiness of humanity; in order to avoid conflict and barriers to people's personal and economic dealings, the general principles on which the limits of the legal jurisdiction of states rest must be universally defined and accepted. Pan-American codification is the first step, even if universal consensus is still a faraway ideal; working for this ideal, we shall render the world a real service.[29]

The Sixth Pan-American Conference was the zenith of Bustamante's prestige and career. Machado was ousted from the presidency by a revolution in 1933, bringing down the whole Cuban political system and culture. This was the beginning of a revolutionary decade that also reached the university lecture halls, where a wide range of ideological positions crystallized. However, Bustamante's legacy remained, as he continued teaching new generations in the classroom and via the sessions (regular courses and lectures) of the Cuban Society of International Law.[30]

With the election of Franklin D. Roosevelt as President of the United States in 1932, a new stage in the relationship with Cuba began. The Monroe Doctrine, which was perceived as giving priority to US interests, was set aside.[31] A new treaty signed by the United States and Cuba in 1934 canceled the Platt Amendment. The era of military intervention seemed to have been relegated to the past. Pan-American ideals were adapting to a new era, and in this regard the ratification of the Bustamante Code was an important guarantee for economic investment, the free movement of people, and the security of contracts signed by citizens of different countries.

Sánchez de Bustamante died in Havana on August 24, 1951, at the age of eighty-six. The University of Havana declared three days of official mourning, and the funeral was attended by the country's leading personalities.[32] The death of the leading jurist and professor united the Cuban political class, many of whose members had been through the lecture halls of the law school. Amazingly, they were able to put their differences to one side for a few days in order to pay homage to the professor. On August 25, the *New York Times* published an obituary note from the American Institute of International Law, of which Bustamante had been a founding member in 1912; alongside other prominent colleagues, it was pointed out, Sánchez de Bustamante had played an instrumental role in lending prestige to the discipline of international law in the Americas. Several Latin American newspapers, such as *La Nación* and *Clarín* in Argentina, also published obituaries stressing his long and successful career.[33]

The poet Gastón Baquero, a member of the National Academy of Arts, defined Sánchez de Bustamante's legacy in a few words:

> He belonged to a class of university professors that did not need revolutions to get chairs, and he always had the honesty to match his deeds to his words. He knew about what he taught and he taught about what he knew, out of respect for himself and for what the students expected of him.[34]

A colleague who knew him well said of him:

> In his private life, Dr. Bustamante's urbane manners and kind and genial disposition rendered him a typical representative of the cultured Cuban gentleman. His conversation was graced by the same simplicity of diction and clearness of statement which characterized his writing, and his personal charm attracted his host of friends as much as his upright character and his vast store of knowledge.[35]

Academic production

Bustamante's participation in international bodies and his long academic trajectory resulted in a substantial academic contribution. His first publication,

Comentarios a la ley de enjuiciamiento criminal vigente en Cuba (1883), was followed by many others throughout his career, not to mention the successive editions of the International Private Law Code, which was translated into multiple languages. From an early stage of his career, he published actively in both Cuban and international legal journals, such as the article "El Canal de Panamá y el derecho internacional," published by the *Revista de Derecho Internacional y Legislación Comparada* (Brussels, 1895) soon after he joined the International Institute of International Law. In 1896 he published the *Manual de Derecho internacional privado* (*Textbook of private international law*) in Havana, shortly before leaving for his first European trip.

Most of his works were published during the twentieth century. *La segunda conferencia de paz reunida en La Haya en 1907*, a chronicle of the debates that took place during the Sixth Pan-American Conference, was published in Madrid in 1908. Other oft-cited academic works include *La autarquía personal. Estudio de Derecho internacional privado* (Havana, 1914), where he expresses what would be for him the principle on which private international law is based:

> the idea of a zone or region of law in which one can freely be himself indicates also that this power does not result from a concession from another sovereign entity, but comes from the particular situation and the exigencies of the one who enjoys them.[36]

In addition, further popular works include: *El tribunal permanente de Justicia* (Havana, 1925); *La nacionalidad y el domicilio, estudio de derecho internacional privado* (Havana, 1927); *El mar territorial* (Havana, 1930), a scientific study of territorial seas and riparian rights; the monumental works, *Tratado de Derecho Internacional Privado* (four volumes, Havana 1931) and *Derecho Internacional Público* (five volumes published in Havana between 1933 and 1938), also published as abbreviated editions for students, were fundamental texts for students in many law schools in Latin America. Sánchez de Bustamante was granted honorary doctorates by Columbia University, Universidad de San Marcos, in Lima, and the Sorbonne, in Paris.

Notes

1 Le Roy y Gálvez, "El Dr. Juan Manuel Sánchez de Bustamante," 89–117. Also: Archivo Histórico Nacional de Madrid (AHN), Ultramar, 4669, Exp. 53.

2 Alberto Sánchez de Bustamante y Sirvén was an obstetrics professor at the faculty of medicine in Havana and director for many years of the *Revista Cubana de Medicina*. See AHN, Ultramar, 263, Exp. 33.

3 His subjects included the humanities (Latin, Greek, religion, universal and Spanish history, oratory and poetry, French, psychology, and logic) and positive and natural sciences (arithmetic, geometry, chemistry, and physics), as well as physiology, hygiene, and basic agriculture; see school records for the issuing of the title of "bachiller" to Antonio Sánchez de Bustamante y Sirvén, in AHN, Universidades, 7345, Exp. 8.

4 AHN, Ultramar, 49, Exp.10.

5 His dissertation was titled "Close codicils in our Legal System," *Revista General de Derecho* 33 (1885). AHN, Ultramar, 49, Exp.13.
6 All of his sons studied law at Havana. Two of them took over the legal practice, which in the 1950s fell to Antonio's grandson, Antonio Sánchez de Bustamante y Montoro, who was also philosophy professor at the University of Havana: see Jiménez, *Las empresas de Cuba* 149–50.
7 Hidalgo Valdés, *La Real Casa de Beneficencia de La Habana.*
8 The International Law Institute was founded in Ghent, Belgium, in 1873.
9 Sánchez de Bustamante, *El orden público: Estudio de derecho internacional privado* (Havana: Imprenta La Universal, 1893).
10 Sánchez de Bustamante y Sirvén, *Tratado de Derecho internacional privado* (Havana: Imprenta La Universal, 1896).
11 An example of the so-called Roosevelt Corollary, which directed US foreign policy towards Latin America and the Caribbean in the opening decades of the twentieth century, the Platt Amendment was introduced as an appendix in the constitution of the First Cuban Republic. According to this amendment, Cuba had its sovereignty to acquire debts with European nations curtailed, and the US Government reserved the right to intervene if the property of its citizens was considered to be in danger. See Torriente, *Cuba en la vida internacional.*
12 Zanetti, *Cautivos de la reciprocidad*, 87–92.
13 Gonzalo de Quesada y Aróstegui, a lawyer trained in the US, was one of the founders of the Cuban Revolutionary Party in New York, a member of the Constitutional Assembly, and later Cuban ambassador, first to the US and then in Berlin, where he died in 1915. Manuel Sanguily, another member of the Constitutional Assembly, was the first president of the Cuban Senate, Secretary of State in 1910–12, and Secretary of Government in 1915–17. Sánchez de Bustamante, *Informe relativo a la Segunda Conferencia Internacional de la Paz reunida en El Haya en 1907.*
14 Torriente, *Cuba, Bustamante y el Tribunal Permanente de Justicia Internacional.*
15 Senado de la República de Cuba, *Memoria*, 86–92.
16 Pérez Jr., *Cuba and the United States*, 140.
17 Primelles, *Crónica cubana*, 113.
18 Manuel Márquez Sterling, "Prologue" to Torriente, *Cuba en la vida internacional* (1922).
19 Primelles, 167.
20 Chacón y Calvo, "Don Antonio Sánchez de Bustamante y Sirvén."
21 The First Pan-American conference was held in Washington, DC, in 1888. Cuba first attended this meeting at the Third Conference, held in 1906 in Rio de Janeiro. The following conferences were organized in Buenos Aires (1910), Santiago de Chile (1923), and Havana (1928), under the chairmanship of Sánchez de Bustamante.
22 Zanetti, 101–06.
23 Costa, *Imagen y trayectoria del cubano en su historia*, 171–76.
24 Schoenrich, "Dr. Antonio Sánchez de Bustamante."
25 Sánchez de Bustamante, *La Commission des jurisconsultes.*
26 The signatory countries were Cuba, Panama, Dominican Republic, Brazil, Peru, Bolivia, Ecuador, Venezuela, Chile, Guatemala, Haiti, Costa Rica, Nicaragua, Honduras, and El Salvador.
27 Samtleben, *Derecho internacional privado en América Latina.*
28 Caicedo Castilla, "Desarrollo, orientaciones y porvenir del Derecho internacional privado en América."
29 Sánchez de Bustamante, *Manual de Derecho internacional privado.*
30 Gutiérrez y Sánchez, "El Instituto Americano."

31 For a perspective on the impact of the Monroe Doctrine on the Cuban Society of International Law, presided over by Sánchez de Bustamante, see Roig de Leuchsenring, *La doctrina Monroe*.
32 Peraza y Sarausa, *Personalidades cubanas*, 1:174–75.
33 Baquero, "Bustamante," 157–59.
34 Ibid., 158.
35 Schoenrich, 749.
36 Penfield, Review of *La autarquía personal*.

References

Baquero, Gastón. "Bustamante." *Anales de la Academia Nacional de Artes y Letras* 35 (1951): 157–59.

Caicedo Castilla, José Joaquín. "Desarrollo, orientaciones y porvenir del derecho internacional privado en América." *Revista de la Universidad Nacional* (1945) 2: 105–20.

Chacón y Calvo, José María. "Don Antonio Sánchez de Bustamante y Sirvén." *Anales de la Academia Nacional de Artes y Letras* 35 (1951): 149–53.

Costa, Octavio. *Imagen y trayectoria del cubano en su historia*. Miami: Ediciones Universal, 1994.

Gutiérrez y Sánchez, Gustavo. "El Instituto Americano y la Sociedad Cubana de Derecho Internacional." *Revista Contemporánea* (1917) 1: 27–41.

Hidalgo Valdés, Leyma. *La Real Casa de Beneficencia de La Habana. Luces y sombras de una institución (1764–1865)*. Barcelona: Linkgua, 2006.

Jiménez, Guillermo. *Las empresas de Cuba*. Miami: Ediciones Universal, 2000.

Le Roy y Gálvez, Luis Felipe. "El Dr. Juan Manuel Sánchez de Bustamante y García del Barrio, en el 150 aniversario de su nacimiento." *Cuadernos de la Salud Pública* (1969) 42: 89–117.

Penfield, Walter S. "Review of *La Autarquía personal: Estudio de Derecho Internacional Privado*, by Antonio S. de Bustamante." *The American Journal of International Law* 8, no. 4 (1914): 948–50.

Peraza y Sarausa, Fermín. *Personalidades cubanas*, Vol. 1. Havana: Ediciones Anuario Bibliográfico cubano, 1957.

Pérez Jr., Louis A. *Cuba and the United States*. Athens: University of Georgia Press, 1997.

Primelles, León. *Crónica cubana (1915–1918)*. Havana: Editorial Lex, 1955.

Roig de Leuchsenring, Emilio. *La doctrina Monroe y el pacto de la Liga de las Naciones*. Havana: Imprenta Siglo XX, 1921.

Samtleben, Jürgen. *Derecho internacional privado en América Latina: teoría y práctica del Código Bustamante*. Buenos Aires: Depalma, 1983.

Sánchez de Bustamante y Sirvén, Antonio. *La Commission des jurisconsultes de Rio de Janeiro et le Droit international*. Paris: Cadoret, 1928.

Sánchez de Bustamante y Sirvén, Antonio. *Informe relativo a la Segunda Conferencia Internacional de la Paz reunida en El Haya en 1907*. Havana: Imprenta La Moderna Poesía, 1908.

Sánchez de Bustamante y Sirvén, Antonio. *Manual de Derecho internacional privado*. Havana: La Mercantil, 1943.

Sánchez de Bustamante y Sirvén, Antonio. *El orden público: estudio de derecho internacional privado*. Havana: Imprenta La Universal, 1893.

Sánchez de Bustamante y Sirvén, Antonio. *Tratado de Derecho internacional privado.* Havana: Imprenta La Universal, 1896.

Schoenrich, Otto. "Dr. Antonio Sánchez de Bustamante." *The American Journal of International Law* 45, no. 4 (1951): 746–49.

Senado de la República de Cuba. *Memoria de los trabajos presentados en el VI período ordinario 1913–1914.* Havana: Imprenta y Papelería Rambla, 1915.

Torriente, Cosme de la. *Cuba en la vida internacional.* Havana: Imprenta Pi y Margall, 1922.

Torriente, Cosme de la. *Cuba, Bustamante y el Tribunal Permanente de Justicia Internacional.* Havana: Imprenta Rambla, Bauzá y Cía, 1922.

Zanetti, Oscar. *Cautivos de la reciprocidad.* Havana: Universidad de La Habana, 1989.

25 Víctor Andrés Belaúnde (Peru, 1883–1966)

Martín Santiváñez Vivanco

Introduction

Víctor Andrés Belaúnde Diez Canseco was a man of his time. The reformism of liberal democracy that influenced the society of 1900 was accepted overwhelmingly by the leading class of Peruvians and the learned sectors of Latin America. Profoundly indebted to Spanish Regenerationism and the Generation of 1898,[1] Belaúnde learned from the most common sources of the *intelligentsia* of his day. He created for himself a synthesis of knowledge that applied to the Peruvian reality. A connoisseur of culture and politics, he focused on the practice of diplomacy and international law. First and foremost, he was a Christian realist,[2] a down-to-earth man of faith.

After his return to Roman Catholicism in his thirties, his legal, philosophical, and political reflections—and, of course, his vital practice—were anchored in the *philosophia perennis*, focusing on developing his theory of a living synthesis and foreseeing, in the geopolitics of the Cold War, the prelude to globalization which would reshape international relations and law. Today, in a globalized society characterized by the speed of commercial, military, and cultural transactions, the living synthesis theory that he proposed, based on his understanding of racial mixing, gains new brio. A process that is slow and progressive by nature, racial mixing now in effect becomes, thanks to global interdependence, a steady and permanent event of increasing speed. Racial mixing, so vital to Belaúnde's thinking, is no longer an exception to the rule but a natural imperative. Globalization favors this process.

Considering this *novus ordo seclorum*, in which immigration redraws the physiognomy of the nations, Belaúnde's propositions maintain an interesting validity. During his life, as a good intellectual, Belaúnde defended the need for reviewing concepts over and over again, adapting them to a specific political order. The ghost of anarchy and coups encouraged an *entente cordiale* between the old-guard socialists and the Indigenous Caesarism that was now triumphant in large areas of the Andean geography. Foreseeing possible harmful consequences of blind and proactive imitation, Belaúnde preferred defending hybrid and original models that would adapt to a concrete space and time. This is the only way to understand the birth of his living synthesis as a corollary to a patriotic and functional *Belaundiano* realism, an approach respected by almost all Catholic Peruvian intellectuals from the second half of the twentieth century and the beginning of the twenty-first century.

Biographical information

Víctor Andrés Belaúnde was born in the city of Arequipa on December 15, 1883, in a mansion located on Moral Street, number 316.[3] He was the son of Mariano Andrés de Belaúnde y de la Torre and Mercedes Diez Canseco y Vargas. Víctor Andrés was the product of two Arequipa families that traced their lineages to the conquest of Peru.[4]

When Víctor Andrés Belaúnde was born, Peru was in the midst of the War of the Pacific (1879–83). Arequipa, the most important city in the south of Peru, was then occupied by invading Chilean troops due to the powerlessness of its inhabitants. The occupation of the Chilean army humiliated the national population, particularly the proud citizens of Arequipa, formerly the cradle of uprisings on behalf of liberty in light of dictatorial power or colonial oppression. Although Belaúnde's mother took shelter in the monastery of Santa Catalina, she was at home for the birth of the new family member.

During his first years, Belaúnde lived in the old family mansion, surrounded by his loved ones and protected by his large family. Indigenous servants in his household contributed significantly to his education, as from his early years he personally experienced the social segmentation that characterized Peru and the strong racial mixing that was developing at the time. His family's peace, constantly evoked over time, reflected a country that, despite the problems of wealth distribution, had a common future. The racial diversity of Arequipa's society would allow Belaúnde to develop the social and emotional intelligence that would characterize him throughout his life. Years later, Arequipa—as he remembered it from his childhood—would represent for him the paradigm of the city synthesis of cultures and races.[5] This natural context prepared Belaúnde for his future reflection on the destiny of Peru as a nation.

His hometown and his membership in a family with a stately past[6] had a crucial influence on the young Belaúnde. The philodemocratic character of Arequipa would be decisive in his political vocation. Years later, in the maturity of his thought, he would recall his beloved city in books and conferences, with these beautiful and nostalgic words:

> My old city, my old house, sunny landscape under the blue dome. Boulevard of willow trees, iridescent wheat fields, white quarries of volcanic lava that your children carved to decorate the majesty dawn of your temples; crystalline water that looks like air; transparent and subtle air that looks like ether, mystic alleys, love-dating bars, procession parade, *yaravi* [Andean song] echoes, low note bells for the day of the dead, maddening ringing of the bells of the civil militia; arches and columns of the Roman forum, granite stand for revolutions; square of elections and executions; old cathedral full of light

> and resonant with the notes of the organ, in the days of pain and joy, where among its towers, due to the open space, the summit of the tutelary volcano stands as a giant frontispiece.[7]

The Belaúnde-Diez Canseco marriage resulted in eight children. A family with many descendants, bourgeois, and land-owning, the Belaúnde-Diez Cansecos were part of Arequipa's elite. Three of his siblings—Juan, Francisca, and Francisco—died young. Other siblings would marry into middle-class comfort, while his brother Rafael would father a future president of the republic, Fernando Belaúnde Terry.

Belaúnde came from a line of outstanding men of national significance. José María Corbacho, a leader of Pereuvian independence, was an uncle by blood of Belaúnde's grandfather, Pedro Diez Canseco. On his maternal side, Belaúnde descended from General Pedro Diez Canseco, president of the republic in 1863–64. Other notable relatives of Belaúnde included Francisco Javier de Luna Pizarro, hero of the independence, later archbishop of Lima, and an uncle by blood of Belaúnde's maternal grandmother, Margarita de la Torre. His maternal grandmother's surname, de la Torre, harked back to Juan de la Torre y Díaz Chacón, the founder of Arequipa and one of the thirteen of the Isla del Gallo who conquered Peru in the seventeenth century. This famous four-line verse is attributed to de la Torre: "*Pues Señor Gobernador, miradlo bien por entero, que allá va el recogedor y aquí queda el carnicero.*" ("Well Mr. Governor, look well and completely; there goes the picker and here stays the butcher"). These verses attracted the enmity of Francisco Pizarro, who ordered de la Torre's exile. According to Raúl Porras Barrenechea, when another person confessed to the authorship of the four-line verse, Pizarro, conqueror of Peru, who had punished de la Torre, asked him to come from Santo Domingo, designated him a leading member and councilor of Arequipa, and granted him a parcel of land in Maguana.[8]

The Belaúndes were natives of Tacna. Juan Francisco Belaúnde and Pedro José Belaúnde moved to Arequipa in the eighteenth century. The Belaúnde surname is of Basque origin, and it apparently means "big crow" in Basque. Manuel Antonio de Belaúnde Obaldía was born in the town of Madaria[9], Álava (Spain), on September 4, 1729, and died on March 4, 1783.[10] He was the first of that lineage to come to Peru, and he served as a magistrate and royal ensign of Arica, a position that also included the title of general of the infantry. This latter title was of exceptional importance because of the connection of that harbor with the Audiencia of Charcas. The young magistrate married María de las Mercedes López de la Huerta y Ossorio, daughter of Ramón López de la Huerta y Calante, who was also a magistrate. The family had connections to Castile and Navarre. On the other hand, the López de la Huerta lineage was related to the widely known noble houses of López Calante and Machín y Garma, situated in the valley of Trucios.

Belaúnde's home and the weight of ancestry decisively influenced his destiny. With deep-rooted family values and a love of the land, Belaúnde had a spiritual fineness that allowed him to recall at crucial moments of his life what he had internalized for many years. He learned not only his first words in his paternal house but also the values that would govern his public and family life. His home had a definite influence in the formation of his character and his perception of life. He had a strong character and a coherent life of permanent quest. Belaúnde's personality was forged at home, and these experiences decisively influenced his approach to debates about being Peruvian.

The Catholic education of his early years was also instrumental when Belaúnde returned to religion after a period of liberalism. His early education was at home and at the neighborhood school of a Mrs. Chávez. However, he received significant and lasting formation from the Lazarist priest Hipólito Duhamel.[11] Father Duhamel was a great connoisseur of his homeland, France, and a loyal devotee of French literature. He was also well versed in Hispanic culture and sought to awaken in his students a sincere devotion to Spanish classical literature without neglecting their religious formation. This priest left a lasting legacy with the people in Arequipa. In the light of various problems of the diocesan seminary, Father Duhamel founded a new seminary to carry out more effective instruction. The new seminary was housed in a section of the old Jesuit cloister that looked onto San Juan de Dios Street, in front of the hospital and the church of that name. Belaúnde studied in the same location in a school named San Vicente de Paúl. This school later moved to San Agustín Street, with a view of a riverside landscape often recalled by Belaúnde in his memoirs.

In that school, founded by a foreign priest, Belaúnde immersed himself in a life full of religious piety and the challenging study of Latin. He read texts such as *La Historia Sagrada*, *De viris illustribus* by Cornelio Nepote, or *Epistulae ad familiares* by Cicero, as well as works by Livy, Tacitus, and Sallust. This early humanistic education prepared him to become, in time, one of the most important Peruvian scholars of Western Latin culture.

Belaúnde learned French by reading passages from Bossuet, Chateaubriand, and Pascal, as well as Delavigne's study of poetry. He took pleasure in the prose of Chateaubriand's work *Le génie du christianisme*. As a deep connoisseur of French pedagogy, Father Duhamel required an exercise every Thursday called "topic development." On that day, the lessons would be set aside, and the students focused on developing a suggested topic by dividing it into items or paragraphs and trying to use logic to introduce their ideas. This rigorous education subsequently allowed Belaúnde to defend, with precise logic and language, Peruvian positions in international forums. Furthermore, to maintain a comprehensive education, Father Duhamel organized frequent trips to aesthetically or historically significant places in the city and its surroundings.

Belaúnde and the Constituent Assembly of 1931

After a period of agnostic liberalism fostered by his admission to the National University of San Marcos, Belaúnde returned to Catholicism. The leaders of the new party Acción Republicana, composed of intellectuals, professionals, and disciples of Manuel Vicente Villarán, organized the opposition against President

Augusto B. Leguía. The leaders of this new party did not consider Belaúnde or his brother Rafael for leadership positions, because a new generation of leaders took over the center-right. The American Popular Revolutionary Alliance (APRA) had emerged as the promoter of new ideas of the left. The Peruvian Communist Party was already taking its first steps. Politicians from the early 1900s were excluded because of their stigma of "civilism" or "plutocracy."

Belaúnde joined the Commission of Jurists. Presided over by Manuel Vicente Villarán and under the Supreme Resolution of August 7, 1931, the commission prepared the draft of a new political constitution. The members of the commission were Toribio Alayza Paz Soldán, Carlos García Gastañeta, José León Barandiarán, Ricardo Palma, Emilio Romero, César Antonio Ugarte, and Luis E. Valcárcel, all renowned jurists prepared to provide Peru with a modern and functional constitution. Although José Gálvez, a member of the National Board of Governors, offered Belaúnde the position of minister of external affairs in August 1931, he declined. He aspired instead to join the next Constituent Assembly.

The Board of Governors organized the elections, and the candidates for president were Luis Miguel Sánchez Cerro, agent of the revolution against Leguía, and Víctor Raúl Haya de la Torre, APRA's candidate. Members of the 1900s generation, such as Belaúnde, joined the Alianza Política Descentralista (Descentralist Political Alliance), founded by Amadeo de Piérola, son of ex-president Nicolás de Piérola. This group and Acción Republicana (Republican Action) proposed José María de la Jara as their candidate, a member of the 1900s generation and a renowned journalist inspired by *arielismo*, a current of thought that valorized Latin America's Christian and Indigenous spiritual heritage. Luis Fernán Cisneros was in charge of the campaign, but upon his arrival in Lima, he was booed by a large crowd of supporters of APRA and Sánchez Cerro, an evident sign of their electoral preferences.

Belaúnde traveled to Arequipa to visit his mother after a long period of exile and political persecution caused by the Government of Leguía. Upon his arrival in his hometown, he tried to gather the supporters of La Jara. He managed to give a conference on social issues, but illness foiled his plans to speak in favor of La Jara. In any event, Sánchez Cerro was more appealing to Arequipa, as he had initiated the revolution against Leguía. Support for La Jara was minimal in Arequipa, where only the APRA and military candidates gained support.

The Catholic party of Arequipa requested financial support from Belaúnde to announce his candidacy for the Constituent Assembly. Belaúnde responded that he lacked funds, but he gave them authorization to use his name to launch the campaign. They did so, and he was unexpectedly elected representative of the minority.[12] In the opinion of José Pareja Paz Soldán, Belaúnde was "the most relevant personality of the Constituent Assembly of 1931."[13] Despite that fact, he had to confront most of the members' arrogance in a lonely and desperate battle. La Unión Revolucionaria (Revolutionary Union), the party of President Sánchez Cerro, was awarded eighty-three seats for deputies; APRA won twenty-nine; and the main decentralizing powers of the south, Cusco and Puno, joined by independent forces, added up to thirty-three.

As a member of the Constituent Assembly, Belaúnde confronted the majority representing Sánchez Cerro and APRA's radicalism. He advocated for the interests of the Church in a firmly anti-Catholic Assembly. The supporters of Sánchez Cerro included José Matías Manzanilla, Víctor J. Guevara, Manuel Jesús Gamarra, Alfredo Herrera, and Carlos Sayán Álvarez. APRA's deputies included Luis Alberto Sánchez and Manuel Seoane. There were only four socialist members of the Assembly, including the prominent Luciano Castillo and Hildebrando Castro Pozo. These, together with the representatives of the decentralizing faction, whose most important members were Erasmo Roca and Francisco Pastor, added up to thirty-three deputies. Of the total number of 145 deputies, 115 had been elected by a majority and thirty by a minority, Belaúnde among the latter.

The Assembly settled on December 8, 1931, to perform simultaneously its constituent and legislative functions. From the very beginning, it was impossible for the APRA and the minority to reach an understanding; the opposition did not manage to consolidate. The draft constitution written by the commission presided over by Manuel Vicente Villarán was rejected by both the majority and the APRA members of the Assembly.

The APRA proposed the right to vote for youths, unionized women, illiterate people, and the army. Belaúnde opposed the right to vote for youths because he considered that their involvement in politics without proper preparation would jeopardize their education. With regard to women's suffrage, he claimed the need to consider not only unionized women but also all women without exception. This opinion was unfortunately ignored, and women were bestowed only the right to vote in municipal elections. Years later, Belaúnde's initiative was widely accepted, and women accessed universal suffrage.

Belaúnde opposed giving the vote to members of the army because soldiers should be independent and nonpartisan. Despite support for this stance in the Assembly, his proposal was rejected. He also advocated for a bicameral parliament, presenting relevant trends and a comparison of constituent law, while explaining that unicameral systems existed only in small countries with counterbalances of referendum or dissolution. He advocated for the need to create a "functional senate" that would forestall a potential dictatorship by a single-chamber parliament, a form of totalitarianism as dangerous as the presidential system. He criticized the budget imbalance and ineffective economic policies, issues that worsened the political crisis.

Despite slow progress, the Government of Sánchez Cerro, through the cabinet of Francisco Lanatta, the Prime Minister, applied the Law of Emergency in Congress during the first days of January 1932. Breaking into Congress, law enforcement officials arrested and deported the APRA deputies. The Law of Emergency imposed by the government led to a permanent and intolerable state of exception by abolishing individual guarantees and violating parliamentary immunity. Freedom of the press was abolished, and a great number of opponents to the regime were deported. Belaúnde stood up for parliamentary immunity and unity during the sessions on February 20 and 21. He did not hesitate to yield the floor to Manuel Seoane to speak in their defense during the siege by the policemen who supported Sánchez Cerro.

Upon the mutilation of Congress, the minority members abandoned the Congress for that day as a sign of political protest. Belaúnde returned to the University of Miami to resume his teaching. Instead of acknowledging Sánchez Cerro's dictatorship or collaborating with APRA's revolutionary and sectarian methods, he waited for an agreement among the minority to define their position.[14]

His summer conferences in Miami concluded, he went back to Peru, determined to resume his teaching at the Pontificial Catholic University. The political situation in Peru was serious, however; Sánchez Cerro had suffered an attack. In Lima, Belaúnde was visited by the apostolic administrator of the Lima Archbishopric, Monsignor Holguín, who urged him to rejoin the Constituent Assembly to defend the concordat between the Catholic Church and the state as well as the freedom of education, an essential freedom for the existence of the Pontificial Catholic University.

To safeguard relations between the Church and state, Belaúnde attempted to create a balance between protection of the Church and the necessary social freedoms by introducing an innovative position of Catholicism on social reform. For Belaúnde, separation between the state and the Church implied persecution and hatred toward Catholicism, Peru's main religion. Therefore, he opted to highlight the unifying role of Catholicism in Peru as a spiritual connection to foster national cohesion. Under the wing of the Catholic Church, Belaúnde attempted to create a balance between his return to faith and the issue of *peruanidad*.[15]

The overall balance of Belaúnde's parliamentary journey is positive. His interventions were realistic and accurate. He advocated for the autonomy of the judicial branch, then compromised on an appointment mechanism led by the executive branch. Furthermore, he proposed the election of members of the Supreme Court by the Congress from lists of three candidates from competent entities such as the bar association, law schools, and the Supreme Court itself. When addressing Indigenous issues, he stated the need to grant such communities state lands and large estates that were unworked or misused. During this process, he suggested respecting the legal nature of the lands and encouraging technical improvements and legal protection. Regarding public education, he supported its technical aspects instead of the ideological education proposed by the left parties. He hoped to protect education from political influences and to instead educate all youths from elementary school through middle school with an emphasis on technical education to achieve an efficient working class, dedicated to the country's modernization. Belaúnde sought to develop the capacity of production in Peru throughout its population. Belaúnde also advocated placing the work of budget development in the executive branch, in lieu of granting such authority to Congress. Thus, it was necessary to establish a National Economic Council based on the faculties outlined in the Weimar Constitution for this purpose.

When conflict with Colombia occurred in 1932–33, prompted by the Leticia Incident and dispute over territory in the Amazon rainforest, Belaúnde reiterated his request for a national unity cabinet to present a unified political front in moments of crisis. During this border-related incident, he joined the Diplomatic Commission as well as the Commission of the Constitution.

In the Constitutional Assembly, Belaúnde had heated discussions with Luis Alberto Sánchez, Manuel Seoane, and José Matías Manzanilla. The murder of President Sánchez Cerro and the new government of General Benavides in April 1933 marked the beginning of a new chapter in Belaúnde's life.

Belaúnde's international journey: *Sub Specie Humanitatis*

Belaúnde was one of the last survivors among the constitutional delegates who signed the Charter of the United Nations in 1945, and from that moment to his death, he was intensively involved with the UN. He was president of the Peruvian delegation to the annual General Assemblies held from 1948 to 1966. He presided over the General Assembly in 1959, and he was assigned to the Security Council in 1955 and 1956. He was designated president of the Peruvian delegation for the first time in the early stages of President Manuel A. Odría's government, and he attended the second half of the Second Assembly held in New York in April 1949. From that date until his death, he presided over all Peruvian delegations attending the General Assembly.[16]

He gave his last speech before the United Nations General Assembly's Special Political Committee just hours before his death. In that speech, he recalled his role as signatory delegate in the Charter of the United Nations and, therefore, his capacity to express precisely the thoughts of the organization's founders regarding the functions of the General Assembly. Peace, Belaúnde stated, should not fall on the shoulders of the Security Council, which cannot focus on the direction of world politics while demanding servility from the weakest countries. He claimed that the importance of the United Nations, making it superior to the League of Nations, was that the UN allowed the much-expected involvement of the United States. For Belaúnde, world security and peace should be based on justice, and the function of the Charter of the United Nations was basically to maintain world peace.

Belaúnde stated his trust in the capacity of a young organization like the United Nations to stop world conflicts, and he identified two fundamental elements in the UN. The first was legal-ethical, involving selfless and impartial cooperation from the member nations. This atmosphere, infused with moral consensus and respect for given ethical principles, was the weaker countries' best weapon to fight the imperialist ambitions of powerful nations. The second element was the political and coactive element, involving agreement among the powers of the world. Such agreement experienced severe crises reflected in various vetoes imposed by the Security Council.

For Belaúnde, the organization's survival required an emphasis on the legal–ethical element, which was to be applied by most countries not sharing an imperialist vision of power. Latin American countries played an exceptional role in this task, he said, as they tried to gather the weakest blocs to stand up for global interests. In Belaúnde's opinion, Latin American countries had advocated for their existence and their global relevance since the founding of the United Nations.

Beginning in 1948, Belaúnde advocated for the admission of new members to the organization, working for the Good Offices Commission and as its president. New members were to be introduced or recommended by the Security Council and approved by the General Assembly as stipulated in Article 4 of the Charter of the United Nations.[17]

In 1965 Belaúnde defended the nonintervention principle, declaring it one of the most valuable Latin American contributions to public international law. During the Nineteenth General Assembly debates, the USSR introduced a draft statement regarding the nonintervention principle that would condemn American interventions in Vietnam and the Dominican Republic. As a suggestion to the Latin American group, Belaúnde decided to propose the development of a draft based on the continent's diplomatic tradition. Belaúnde was designated leader of the task force charged with drafting a resolution stating that the nonintervention principle is essential to the fulfillment of the mission and principles of the United Nations. The nonintervention principle would ensure equality, sovereignty, and peaceful coexistence for all nations. As a resolution, the document stipulated that all nations were obliged to refrain from direct or indirect intervention into the internal and external affairs of other nations, and noted that such obligation was a requirement for peacekeeping. He also emphasized the duty of respecting a population's rights to self-determination.

In December 1956, by the end of his term in the Security Council, Belaúnde had been designated president of the council twice and president of the first political commission. The president of the General Assembly was then to be a Latin American, and a strong movement for the designation of Belaúnde as president began. Belaúnde had given up his own candidacy in 1951 to make room for the Mexican candidate, Luis Padilla Nervo, who was eventually elected. In 1955, Latin American countries reached an agreement stating that no diplomat occupying a position within the United Nations would be able to apply for the presidency. As Belaúnde was a member of the Security Council, he abstained from participating in the elections, and the Chilean candidate, José de la Maza, was elected. Belaúnde then became the candidate representing Peru, and he competed against the Bolivian candidate, Víctor Paz Estenssoro, who was involved with the United Nations and, therefore, left the competition. To guarantee unanimity, Belaúnde was not formally introduced as a candidate until 1959, to avoid interference with the prospects of the Lebanese candidate, Charles Malik.

Belaúnde effectively carried out his duties as the president of the Fourteenth General Assembly of the United Nations. His presidency was announced in the afternoon of September 16, 1959, and he won by an overwhelming eighty-one out of eighty-two votes, where the only vote not in his favor was vitiated due to an error in writing "Peru" instead of his name. He was the first president of the General Assembly elected with full unanimity.[18] In his inaugural speech, he stated:

> I want to see the support from Peru to the United Nations' mission reflected in our work and in our efforts to serve with enthusiasm…Past generations lived with the false and presumptuous mark of the will to power; now humanity wishes only to live under the will of justice.[19]

Belaúnde's conciliatory style of government aroused admiration throughout the world. He became one of the most respected leaders in the United Nations through his warmth and ardent defense of the weakest countries. His term ended with a closing session of the Fourteenth General Assembly, which extended until 4 AM on December 14, 1960. During this session, Belaúnde ensured that Turkey and Poland reached an agreement regarding one of the Security Council vacancies corresponding to Eastern Europe, each country occupying the position for one year instead of the usual term of two years. At 4 AM Belaúnde gave his closing speech, describing the body as an "Assembly of Peace," in accordance with the wish he expressed during his assumption of office. In this General Assembly, different topics were discussed relating to Tibet, the French nuclear trials in the Sahara, the use of space for peaceful purposes (a topic brought up for the first time), and the independence of Algeria. To wrap up his final speech, he stated: "We must work for all these issues to be considered from the general point of view of humanity. Our motto is *sub specie humanitatis*."[20]

At the end of the session, members of the Peruvian delegation gathered at the president's office to make a toast honoring Víctor Andrés Belaúnde, who left with José Pareja Paz-Soldán almost at dawn. Thus, he concluded his brilliant term as President of the United Nations, the most relevant position he occupied in his life. Alongside Javier Pérez de Cuéllar, who served as Secretary General of the United Nations (1982–91), Belaúnde was one of the two greatest honorable personalities in the history of Peruvian diplomacy.

Six years after concluding his term as President of the United Nations General Assembly, and again on December 14, he gave a speech in the Special Political Committee of the United Nations General Assembly, the last speech of his life. After the speech, he attended a lunch offered by the representative of Italy, and later he went with his wife and the Peruvian delegation secretary, Jaime Cáceres, to the studio of the painter Mario Agostinelli, who was working on a portrait of Belaúnde's wife.

By the afternoon, after this event at the United Nations, he returned to his apartment at the Embassy House, at the corner of 2nd Avenue and 47th Street, where his wife and Rosa de la Fuente, a family friend, waited for him. While he was talking to them, he suddenly felt pain. "This pain is so weird, Teresa, I have never felt it before. Is this a spasm?" he managed to say before collapsing unconscious. The doctors only arrived to confirm his death. A priest from the nearby Church of the Holy Family, gave him the last sacraments, as Belaúnde had always wished.

The next day, Thursday, December 15, 1966, the UN General Assembly paid special tribute to him, an event that opened with the words of the president, Afghan Ambassador Abdul Rahman Pazhwak. In his homage, he recalled Belaúnde's eloquence when speaking about world peace awareness, and several delegates emphasized Belaúnde's interest in progress and solidarity among the nations as well as his strong advocacy for the principles which inspired the creation of the United Nations. The delegate from Spain, Manuel Aznar,[21] highlighted the way Belaúnde filled his expressions with conviction and ardor, inspired by significant concerns and worries which turned him, in the opinion of Aznar, into a representative of Western culture's universality.

Conclusion

Víctor Andrés Belaúnde was part of the generation of the 1900s, a generation that emerged into academic and public life around 1904, with the publication of the book *De litteris* by Francisco García Calderón. Among the personalities from this generation, Belaúnde was an advocate for the literary current called *arielismo*, inspired by the writer José Enrique Rodó, who supported the return to idealism in his book *Ariel* (1900), which contrasted Latin American spiritualism of Shakespeare's Ariel with the Anglo-Saxon materialism represented by Caliban. Until then, no Peruvian intellectual generation had made a collective effort to restore the glory of Peru through moral introspection and the passionate and objective study of national reality.

Belaúnde's great contribution to the analysis of Ibero-American political thinking lies in his theory of living synthesis. The first reference to this concept is found in his 1904 thesis, *La filosofía del derecho y el método positivo* (*The philosophy of law and the positive method*). Beginning in 1914, with his famous speech "La crisis presente" ("The current crisis"), Belaúnde appealed to the dialectal notion of thesis-antithesis-synthesis. In 1917, in a conference in the Student Federation, Belaúnde used the concept of synthesis to analyze Peru as a whole. It was, however, during his refutation of José Carlos Mariátegui, captured in the book *La realidad nacional* (*The national reality*, 1931), that Belaúnde, addressing the "land issue," referred to national synthesis and to Peru as a synthesis. This approach placed in opposition the imperialist thesis and the pro-Indigenous antithesis. *La síntesis viviente* (*The living synthesis*), the book in which Belaúnde directly addresses the conceptualization of a living synthesis, is named after this idea. Published in Madrid in 1950, the book was reprinted in Lima in 1993 by the National Commission for the Centenary of Víctor Andrés Belaúnde and the Pontificia Universidad Católica del Perú, through the Instituto Riva-Agüero, as part of volume six of *Obras completas*, together with another important book on his synthetic thinking (*Palabras de fe*), first published in 1952. Belaúnde stated that Peru is the living synthesis of two great traditions: Hispanic and Indigenous.

This synthesis, in turn, shapes a new *mestizo*, open, and inclusive tradition. Peruvian people are, essentially, the heirs of two cultures. In Belaúnde's view, there is an "embracing" culture (Hispanic) and an "embraced" culture. The superior values of the embracing culture infuse and determine the new synthesis. In this case, the superior values based on the Peruvian identity and emotions (*peruanidad*) are determined by Christian ethics. The Christian ethos is the essential element for national cohesion, as it represents a stronger bond than race, which is always a possible bond. Therefore, race itself does not shape *peruanidad*. Despite this fact, the physical factor should not be left aside, that is, land and race on which the embracing culture was based, since *peruanidad* would not exist without these physical elements. Both the spiritual element and the physical elements are essential for the creation of nationality, even though the Christian ethos is of greatest importance because it allows the fusion of traditions into a new and exceptional being. In spite of the superior value of the physical element, synthesis is impossible without it.

Belaúnde expected that Peru would face what he called "national deviations." These would lead to the breakup of the living synthesis and the consequent disbandment of national cohesion. They include radical deviation, supported by Manuel González Prada, who intended to associate *peruanidad* with a nonexistent religious matter. The Jacobinism of González Prada's theory was closely related to the positive and scientific deviation of Comte and Spencer, as it supported the supremacy of science over spirit. Despite everything, the most relevant deviation which Peru had to face during the twentieth century was shaped by Marxism. Based on the notions of dialectics and the clash between classes, Marxism intended to establish a disbanding project, advocating for a concept of nation based on racial-ethnic communism. Belaúnde opposed this fratricidal theory from the very beginning. He was convinced that Marxism would destroy national unity and would dissolve synthesis through the exaltation of the physical element.

Belaúnde based his political and legal thinking on the social doctrine of the Catholic Church. He held the belief in an objective reality. He accepted absolute values that had to fight against synthesis-deviating and relativism-based metaphysics. This battle was also waged at the political level. In this sense, politics is an extension of a metaphysical confrontation. The nation's problems must be addressed by applying the principle of solidarity in the social scope and the principle of subsidiarity in regard to state action. Belaúnde was a sincere advocate for the middle class. In his opinion, the middle class represented the economic basis of the nation, and its needs must be met by any governmental program.

The destiny of Latin America is to become the meeting point of all races of the world, creating, as the Mexican writer José Vasconcelos stated, a cosmic race. Latin racial mixing is a spiritual and transcendent ethic. The favorable and necessary racial mixing will always be subordinated to the subjective racial mixing, to the axiological synthesis. In this sense, Latin America is the mixture of two great traditions—Hispanic and Indigenous traditions enriched, in turn, with various cultures that, upon their arrival to the Americas, knew how to merge with a superior entity. Nowadays, Marxist Indigenism has altered that reality to create an Andean Leviathan seeking to impose a political uchronia, a racial dystopia. Latin America is the concrete evidence that a *mestizo* civilization is possible and that such racial mixing is, without a doubt, positive, original, and creative. The double unifying heritage, Hispanic and Indigenous, survives due to the vitality of Christian values. This produces a synthetic vitality that allows the process to continue and to confront successfully the uncountable social, political, and economic efforts to dissolve the Latin synthesis. In the third millennium, the synthesis extends to all civilizations and renovates the concept of Hispanidad.

Notes

1 The decisive influence of Spanish Regenerationism and the Generation of 1898 in Belaúnde's thought has been studied by Arroyo, among others. See Arroyo Reyes, "Entre el regeneracionismo y el Volksgeist."

2 Unlike the American Christian realism informed by Reinhold Niebuhr (1892–1971), Belaúnde's realism was always colored by an evolutionary traditionalism enunciated in *Meditaciones peruanas* (Peruvian meditations), more Hispanic than Anglo-Saxon: "Our goal won't be reaction and violence; it has to be evolutionary traditionalism, concentration, and vitalization." See Belaúnde, *Obras completas*, 2:110.

3 The most complete biography of Víctor Andrés Belaúnde was written by his disciple José Pareja Paz Soldán, *El maestro Belaúnde*. Nonetheless, the most extensive narrative of his life is still found in the two volumes of his memoirs: Belaúnde, *Trayectoria y destino*. In his memoirs, Belaúnde describes and analyzes the most important milestones of his life with a broad scope and graceful prose. Regarding his genealogy and Basque lineage, see the complete study of his family in Rey y Cabieses, "Linaje y vida de Víctor Andrés Belaúnde."

4 Belaúnde was baptized on the day of his birth by the parish priest of a Jesuit church, which is now destroyed. The priest was José María Carpenter, who later served as dean of Lima, auxiliary bishop of Lima, and titular bishop of Lorea. Belaúnde's uncle Pedro Antonio and his aunt María Diez Canseco were his godparents. He was named Mariano because he was born on the *Octava de la Inmaculada* (Octave of the Immaculate Conception); Andrés because it was his father's middle name; Víctor because of the book of saints; and Rafael because of his mother's special devotion to the Archangel Raphael. Some years later, his name Mariano Andrés Víctor Rafael would be reduced to Víctor Andrés.

5 For Belaúnde, Arequipa would always remain the paradigm of the mestizo city, the ideal city in a country of all races:

> In the Peruvian panorama, Arequipa has the character of the city synthesis. It is mountainous by geography and coastal from an ethnic and social point of view. It represents the union between the coast and the mountains; between the white, and the mestizo, and the aboriginal.

See Belaúnde, *Trayectoria y destino*, 1:13–15.

6 From the transcendent point of view of Belaúnde, Arequipa represented, as a city, the old Spanish adage: "All nobleman as the king, less money." In the same sense, see, Belaúnde, *Obras completas*, 1:63.

7 Cf. "Speech Delivered by Víctor Andrés Belaúnde in the Brazilian Academy of Letters in 1934," in García Belaúnde and Gonzales, *Víctor Andrés Belaúnde*, 240–51.

8 Porras Barrenechea, "La primera copla de la conquista," 183–89. Also Romero, *Los héroes de la Isla del Gallo*, 61. The reunion between Pizarro and Juan de la Torre is as dramatic as historical.

9 This small town in the Ayala Valley in Álava, an autonomous community of the Basque Country (Spain), lies along the road from Amurrio to Artziniega. The place has also been known throughout history as Obaldía, hence the second surname of the first Belaúnde in the Americas.

10 He was son of Martín de Belaúnde y Garay, who was born in Quejana, Álava, in 1699, and of María de Obaldía Salazar y Aldama, a native of Madaria, daughter of Joseph de Obaldía-Salazar and of Manuela de Aldama. They married on March 20, 1714, in San Clemente de Obaldía, in Madaria. Martín de Belaúnde y Garay was the son of Pedro Simón de Belaúnde y Aguirre, born in 1655 in Quejana, where he lived with his wife and Martín's mother, Dorotea de Garay y Ulibarry. Pedro Simón de Belaúnde's parents were Juan de Belaúnde y Ugalde, who was born in 1620, and Catalina de Aguirre y Urieta, who married in Respaldiza in 1645. Juan de Belaúnde was the son of Francisco de Belaúnde, who was born in 1850, and Casilda de Ugalde. Cf. Rey y Cabieses, "Linaje y vida de Víctor Andrés Belaúnde," 76.

11 This Brittany priest, educated in the discipline of seminars with the inspiration of St. Vincent de Paul, was destined to spread the gospel in China, accompanying Fr. Juan Gabriel Perboyré (1802–40), martyred in Ou-Tchang-Fou (China) for his faith and canonized on June 2, 1996 by Pope John Paul II. Fr. Duhamel managed to escape from persecution by receiving a wound to the neck that he exposed with modesty and as a testimony of his faith. Among his disciples were Juan Gualberto Guevara (archbishop of Lima and first cardinal of Peru), Emilio Lissón (archbishop of Lima) and Honorio Delgado (psychiatrist and Peruvian philosopher).

12 In that campaign he was, in the opinion of Basadre, "the faithful man on the scale." Cf. Letter from Jorge Basadre to Víctor Andrés Belaúnde, dated January 14, 1932 (VAB-E-0172).

13 According to Pareja Paz Soldán, Belaúnde's interventions in the Constituent Assembly can be classified as legal–constitutional and political commentaries connected to the parliamentary function. Then,

> In the first interventions, the most important ones were related to the involvement of citizens aged twenty-one or less in suffrage (two interventions), women's right to suffrage (two interventions), illiterates' and army members' right to suffrage; to the maintenance of a functional senate and its organization, and, after four extremely extensive and well-supported interventions, he succeeded to keep it in a labor-union form (corporativism); to administrative decentralization, focusing on it mainly according to the regions' economic features; to the relations between the church and the state (three interventions); to Indigenous issues; to public education; to the battle against the death penalty for political crimes, restricting it only to treason and aggravated homicide (two interventions); to the requirement of Peruvian nationality for priests to perform their functions; to the independence of the judicial branch and the designation of judges and magistrates. And he advocated for freedom of the press, but at the same time the responsibility of journals' publishers and editors. As for public education, he reaffirmed his position, adopted by him since 1914, about the need to encourage professional training, love for work, and the supremacy of land conquest in agricultural areas.

Cf. Pareja Paz Soldán, *El maestro Belaúnde*, 97–98.

14 As a sign of acknowledgement for his role in the Constituent Assembly, he was granted the right to join the Acción Social Católica de Arequipa. Cf. Letter from Juan Gualberto Guevara, director of Acción Social Católica de Arequipa, to Víctor Andrés Belaúnde, dated January 2, 1932 (VAB-E-0846). Guevara was named, in the end, archbishop of Lima and Peru's first cardinal.

15 Ever since his return to the Catholic Church, he stated, "I claim and proclaim the value of religion and faith": Belaúnde, *Obras completas*, 4:228.

16 Belaúnde divided the first twenty years of the United Nations into five stages: 1. Discussion and unanimous approval of the Charter of the United Nations in 1945; 2. From the beginning of the UN's work until the Korean crisis (1946–50), which he called the initiation and trial period; 3. From that crisis to the admission of new members (June 1950 to September 1955), paving the way to universality; 4. From the General Assembly to the Cuban missile crisis (1963); and 5. from the Cuban crisis to the present, with the bold attempt from the USSR to extend its influence to the Americas, which failed, revealing that the West would not lose the Cold War. One of the stages Belaúnde could not witness was the collapse of the Communist bloc and the end of the Cold War. Cf. Pareja Paz Soldán, *El maestro Belaúnde*, 147–48.

17 Article 4 states:

> Membership in the United Nations is open to all other peace-loving states which accept the obligations contained in the present Charter and, in the judgment of the Organization, are able and willing to carry out these obligations. The admission of any such state to membership in the United Nations will be effected by a decision of the General Assembly upon the recommendation of the Security Council.

See Charter of the United Nations, signed June 26, 1945 in San Francisco, at the closure of the United Nations Conference on International Organization, and effective October 24, 1945: www.un.org.

18 Raúl Porras Barrenechea, chancellor of the Republic of Peru, during his intervention in the general debate, said:

> We Peruvians are aware that, by electing Belaúnde, we have honored the men and the country significantly embodied by their ancient culture. By electing him unanimously, we have honored particularly one of the greatest architects of the United Nations, from the signature of the Charter of the United Nations up to present time, a narrator and prophet of his own destiny, apostle defending conciliation and understanding among nations, a man without enemies, as expressed by one of the interviewers of our premises, friend of the neighbour and the weak.

See Pareja Paz Soldán, *El maestro Belaúnde*, 173.

19 Speech given during the assumption of office of the president of the United Nations General Assembly: Belaúnde, *Trayectoria y destino*, 2:915–18.

20 Ibid., 930.

21 Manuel Aznar Zubigaray (1894–1975), grandfather of José María Aznar, ex-president of the Government of Spain. Aznar Zubigaray, journalist and diplomat, was managing director of the news agency EFE and Spanish ambassador to the UN. He always had good memories of Belaúnde: "By 1968 Fernando Belaúnde Terry, who was the nephew of the unforgettable Mr. Víctor Belaúnde, performed presidential functions." Quoted in Tanco Lerga, *Manuel Aznar*, 370. This is undoubtedly the most comprehensive biography of this interesting Spanish politician. He and Belaúnde were good friends and used to send each other letters in which Aznar calls himself a "Peruvian from Madrid" and Belaúnde a "Spaniard from Peru" and a "Basque from Lima." Letters from Manuel Aznar to Víctor Andrés Belaúnde, from April 17, 1958 to September 17, 1959 (VAB-E-0133).

References

Arroyo Reyes, Carlos. "Entre el regeneracionismo y el Volksgeist: el joven Belaúnde y la generación del 98." *Cuadernos Hispanoamericanos* 577–78 (1998): 299–312.

Belaúnde Moreyra, Martín, and Domingo García Belaúnde, eds. *Víctor Andrés Belaúnde. Epistolario político con Manuel Prado e Ismael Bielich.* Lima: Instituto Riva-Agüero, Pontificia Universidad Católica, 2009.

Belaúnde, Víctor Andrés. "La conferencia del doctor Víctor Andrés Belaúnde sobre la síntesis viviente y la filosofía de la cultura." *Mercurio Peruano* 208–09 (1944): 375.

Belaúnde, Víctor Andrés. *Libro jubilar de Víctor Andrés Belaúnde. En su octogésimo aniversario.* Lima: Mercurio Peruano and Pontificia Universidad Católica del Perú, 1963.

Belaúnde, Víctor Andrés. *Obras completas. Primera serie: El Proyecto Nacional*, Vol. 1, *El Perú antiguo y los modernos sociólogos y otros ensayos.* Lima: Comisión Nacional del Centenario de Belaúnde, 1987.

Belaúnde, Víctor Andrés. *Obras completas. Primera serie: El Proyecto Nacional*, Vol. 2, *Meditaciones peruanas.* Lima: Comisión Nacional del Centenario de Belaúnde, 1987.

Belaúnde, Víctor Andrés. *Obras completas. Primera serie: El Proyecto Nacional*, Vol. 3, *La realidad nacional.* Lima: Comisión Nacional del Centenario de Belaúnde, 1987.

Belaúnde, Víctor Andrés. *Obras completas. Primera serie: El Proyecto Nacional*, Vol. 4, *El debate constitucional.* Lima: Comisión Nacional del Centenario de Belaúnde, 1987.

Belaúnde, Víctor Andrés. *Obras completas. Primera serie: El Proyecto Nacional*, Vol. 5, Peruanidad. Lima: Comisión Nacional del Centenario de Belaúnde, 1987.

Belaúnde, Víctor Andrés. *Obras completas. Primera serie: El Proyecto Nacional*, Vol. 6, *La síntesis viviente. Palabras de fe.* Lima: Comisión Nacional del Centenario de Belaúnde, 1987.

Belaúnde, Víctor Andrés. *Trayectoria y destino. Memorias completas*, Vol. 2. Lima: Ediventas, 1967.

García Belaúnde, Domingo, and Osmar Gonzales. *Víctor Andrés Belaúnde. Peruanidad, contorno y confín. Textos esenciales.* Lima: Fondo Editorial del Congreso del Perú, 2007.

Muñiz Z., Carmen. "Bio-bibliografía de Víctor Andrés Belaúnde." *Anuario Bibliográfico Peruano* (1964–66):112–33.

Pacheco Vélez, César. *Ensayos de simpatía.* Lima: Universidad del Pacífico, 1993.

Pacheco Vélez, César. "Historia y crónica del tercer Mercurio Peruano (1918–1978)." *Mercurio Peruano* 496–500 (1988): 15–74.

Pareja Paz Soldán, José. *El maestro Belaúnde.* Lima: Instituto de Estudios Social-cristianos, [1968] 2008.

Porras Barrenechea, Raúl. "La primera copla de la conquista." *Mercurio Peruano* 169 (1941): 183–89.

Rey y Cabieses, Amadeo-Martín. "Linaje y vida de Víctor Andrés Belaúnde. Un peruano universal." *Junta Sabatina de Especialidades Históricas* 4 (2003): 73–111.

Riva-Agüero, José de la. *Afirmación del Perú. El Perú en su historia*, Vol. 1. Lima: Instituto Riva-Agüero, Pontificia Universidad Católica, 1960.

Romero, Carlos A. *Los héroes de la Isla del Gallo.* Lima: Librería e Imprenta D. Miranda, 1944.

Santiváñez Vivanco, Martín. *Víctor Andrés Belaúnde y la síntesis viviente.* Lima: Fondo editorial del Congreso del Perú, 2019.

Tanco Lerga, Jesús. *Manuel Aznar: periodista y diplomático.* Barcelona: Planeta, 2004.

26 José de la Riva-Agüero y Osma (Peru, 1885–1944)

José de la Puente Brunke

Biographical introduction

José de la Riva-Agüero y Osma is one of the most important Peruvian intellectual, political, and academic figures of the first half of the twentieth century. He was a humanist and polymath who exhibited sustained interest in the study of Peru and in defending the country's Christian roots through his investigations, teaching, and publications. He had a conscientious Catholic upbringing—the fundamentals of which he later questioned during his youth and early adulthood, influenced by diverse readings and the education that he received at the University of San Marcos in Lima, where positivism dominated. Afterward, he came back to embrace the Catholic faith. Given the historiographic, literary, and political importance of his work, the legal dimension of his thinking can at times be overlooked. The intent of this chapter is to highlight his extensive legal education and to underscore how juridical themes were a continuous concern in his academic work and his career.

Riva-Agüero was born in Lima on February 26, 1885, in the bosom of one of Lima's most distinguished aristocratic families, descendants of the first Spanish conquerors of Peru. From early childhood, he exhibited an unusual passion for reading, and in his school years he stood out because of his brilliance at the school managed by French priests of the Congregation of the Sacred Hearts of Jesus and Mary. Later he went on to study letters and law at the University of San Marcos, where he experienced a "deep spiritual change." He distanced himself from Catholicism and adhered to the positivist, relativist, and antimetaphysical doctrines that prevailed in the university.[1] At twenty years of age, he defended his bachelor's thesis in letters, titled *Carácter de la literatura del Perú independiente* (*Nature of the literature of independent Peru*, 1905). The presentation of that thesis was "quite an event," in the words of his peer Víctor Andrés Belaúnde, given that until then, a panorama of the development of nineteenth-century Peruvian literature had not been contemplated. Belaúnde himself proclaimed that the thesis was a sensation in the Hispanic American intellectual world (Miguel de Unamuno wrote a highly favorable review) due to its very broad scope and its reliable judgments, which revealed "top notch intelligence."[2]

La historia en el Perú (*History in Peru*, 1910) was his doctoral thesis in letters, and it marks the beginning of scientific historiography in Peru, according to unanimous scholarly opinion. In 1911 and 1912 he presented his bachelor's and doctoral theses in law, discussed below.

During his years as a university student in the first decade of the twentieth century, Riva-Agüero additionally began to express great political concern, which would persist until his death. This concern was shared by his contemporaries, known as the *novecentistas* (new centuryists). Indeed, Riva-Agüero's intellectual group is known as the "1900 generation," made up of young students who entered university around the year 1900.[3] They were born when the War of the Pacific (1879–83) was ending or in the years immediately following, and they grew up in the typical atmosphere of crisis of the period. Nevertheless, at the same time, by 1900 there was already some political stability in Peru, and the beginning of economic prosperity was noticeable—as in the broader Latin American context, where intense eagerness started to arise. As Luis Loayza affirms: progress, justice, and political democracy were seen as ideals within arm's reach, once the commotion of the founding republican century was overcome. In this way, the youth of the 1900 generation wondered about the future of Peru and about the country's viability. From abroad, they received decisive influence from the Uruguayan thinker José Enrique Rodó and his famous essay *Ariel*, for which they became known as *arielistas*. Rodó compared Latin America to the United States, and he declared that Latin Americans should not make the same mistakes as the overly crude and materialistic North Americans. Infused with idealism, *Ariel* warned the Latin American youth of the dangers that wealth could bring.[4]

In 1911 Riva-Agüero entered directly into the political discussion with the publication of a newspaper article against the government of President Augusto B. Leguía (1908–12). The article resulted in his arrest one night, bringing him great fame as a young leader. A year later he traveled around the southern Peruvian highlands for several months, an experience that sparked his later book *Paisajes peruanos* (*Peruvian landscapes*), which for many was his most important publication. This is the text that best expresses his interest in becoming familiar with and studying Peru: he combines reflections about geography, environment, archaeology, history, literature, and, above all, the social situation of the Indigenous population. The central message of the book concerns the need to integrate Peru, especially the coast and the highlands. It is a landmark in the history of Peruvian culture, given that until then, intellectuals had not studied Peru comprehensively in depth. Víctor Andrés Belaúnde described that trip as "a true patriotic pilgramage," and he linked it directly to the conviction that Peru's principal social problem was the "Indigenous problem." In their later political incursions, Riva-Agüero and Belaúnde wanted to address this problem with advanced reforms based on serious technical criteria, with the goal of not succumbing to stances that could be demagogic and inefficient.[5]

At the beginning of 1913, Riva-Agüero set out on his first trip to Europe, where he spent time in France, Belgium, Italy, and Spain until October 1914, when the eruption of the First World War forced him to return to Peru. During that European sojourn, he established important academic ties and was the Peruvian delegate to the Hispanic American Congress of History and Geography held in Seville.

In 1915 he decided to found a political party: the National Democratic Party. It was a project that included almost all of the members of his cohort, but it was unsuccessful because of various political circumstances. The founders of the party had resolved to initiate the political renewal of the country by bringing together young intellectuals and professionals. They had liberal ideas, but at the same time, they wanted to establish a link between history, tradition, and the present. Riva-Agüero—whom Belaúnde called a man "born to be a statesman and leader"[6]—was the indisputable leader of the party.

With President Leguía's coming to power a second time, in 1919, after a *coup d'état* following the election, Riva-Agüero began an eleven-year self-exile in Europe. He was accompanied by his mother and his maternal aunt, who both passed away on the old continent in the 1920s. There he dedicated himself to diverse historical and genealogical studies, and he bonded with European intellectual and social elites of the time. In Spain, he cultivated his ties to nobility and rehabilitated two noble titles that belonged to his family: marquis of Montealegre of Aulestia and marquis of Casa Dávila. During this European exile, as he came in contact with new Catholic trends in France, Italy, and Spain,[7] his return to the Catholic faith was maturing little by little, and he would make it explicit after returning to Peru. During that period, Riva-Agüero also developed a growing affection for fascism, as he valued the economic and social development that Italy achieved after the First World War, and he identified with Mussolini's nationalism and his rigid notion of order. At the time, Riva-Agüero himself noted that he was reactionary rather than conservative, inasmuch as it was necessary to recover "wholesome and noble" ideals from better times in order to overcome the "moral and intellectual decay" of his own era.[8]

Riva-Agüero returned to Peru in 1930 and soon made public his return to Catholicism. In that decade, he occupied various public offices, including dean of the bar association (1935–37), mayor of Lima (1931), and president of the Council of Ministers and minister of justice, instruction, devotion, and beneficence in 1933, in the government of General Óscar R. Benavides. Riva-Agüero occupied those ministerial roles for only a few months, renouncing them because of Congress's approval of the mutual-dissent divorce law. In 1935 he organized another political movement, Patriotic Action, which also had no electoral success. He was an active supporter of the nationalist faction in the Spanish Civil War, within the framework of his radical anti-communism.

Throughout the 1930s he delivered numerous speeches and wrote essays in which he exhibited his broad cultured learning and intellectual brilliance by dealing with very diverse topics. Often they involved reflections on the celebration of some ephemera. In this way, he dedicated works to the founding of Rome, to French literature and its influence on Hispanic culture, and to colonial Peruvian art, and he presented expert reflections about great cultural figures, such as

Goethe, Cervantes, Lope de Vega, and Alexander von Humboldt, among many others.

His public persona continued to be of the first order, although the political atmosphere of the time was quite different from the years prior to his self-exile in Europe. Socialist and communist ideas had gathered strength, along the lines of proposals by José Carlos Mariátegui and other political movements of leftist origins, such as APRA (the American Popular Revolutionary Alliance), a party founded by Víctor Raúl Haya de la Torre. For political reasons, Riva-Agüero began distancing himself from his alma mater, the University of San Marcos, and he continuously drew closer to the Catholic University, founded in 1917 by the French priest Georges Dintilhac, who was also a teacher at the Recoleta School, where Riva-Agüero had been a student. At the Catholic University, in 1937, he taught a well-remembered course about Inca Peru titled "Traditional Peruvian Civilization," which underscored his continuous interest in the Andean world. Moreover, in *Paisajes peruanos*, he had already affirmed that Cuzco was the "heart and symbol of Peru," and that the country of Peru was the creation of the Incas "as much as or more than of the conquerors." In the same pages, he affirmed that Peru's fortune could not be separated from the Indigenous population and that the country would sink or redeem itself with them.

His final long trip lasted two years, from 1938 to 1940, and it circled the world, following an invitation from one of Japan's cultural institutions. He first spent six weeks in California, visiting various universities, then spent three months in Japan, where he delivered seven conference lectures in French about various Peruvian topics. He then visited other Asian countries, including China and Singapore, before setting off for Europe by passing through Egypt and Palestine. On the continent, he visited France, Italy, Spain, Switzerland, and Portugal. Finally, he returned to Peru by passing through Cuba, Brazil, and Argentina.

Riva-Agüero spent his final years far from active political life, dedicating himself to reading and lecturing. He died in Lima on October 25, 1944. In his will, he left everything to the Pontifical Catholic University of Peru. His funeral was a mass demonstration of esteem from colleagues and disciples who identified with the ideals that he represented. Three years after his death, the Catholic University created the Riva-Agüero Institute in his home, in homage to his memory. The institute is a center for humanities research and overall an institution dedicated to the study of Peru in various facets.

Riva-Agüero and his contemporaries

Riva-Agüero and his contemporaries shared various concerns about Peru. Among the most important were national identity, the "Indigenous problem," Peru's position on the American continents, distrust of the influence of the United States, industrialization, and the need for a national project. They judged that the society of their time needed urgent reforms to achieve the "regeneration" of Peru.[9]

The vision of history held by this group of young people raised opposition to their teachers' opinions, especially that of Javier Prado, who, from his positivist and liberal conceptions, considered the Spanish legacy inherited by nineteenth-century Peruvians to be quite negative. Riva-Agüero and his contemporaries adopted a more favorable attitude toward Spanish heritage, influenced by Ricardo Palma's literary and intellectual output. This can be seen in Riva-Agüero's thesis *Carácter de la literatura del Perú independiente*, which advocates a less negative opinion of Spanish influence. Furthermore, one of his contemporaries, Ventura García Calderón, attributed a "national restoration" program to Riva-Agüero. While Javier Prado had proposed an assessment of the reality of Peru based on the negative legacy of the past, Riva-Agüero decided to do the opposite in 1905: to rescue and recover the historic past.[10] Regarding that period and its generation, Belaúnde affirmed that he connected with Riva-Agüero based on a mutual love for history and appreciation for tradition.[11] In addition, Riva-Agüero concerned himself with presenting the Indigenous population as a central part of Peruvian nationality. He held a modern vision that thus seemed very original in the face of traditional European conceptions of the non-Western world as savage or barbaric. The *novecentistas* understood that Peru's destiny was tied to solving the "Indigenous problem," and that the Indigenous population should be fully integrated into the country.[12]

Politics were very present for the youth of that generation. They understood politics to be a "critical deliberation" that should lead to a better organized state and modernization of the country, although they distrusted radical changes. Luis Loayza presents the hypothesis that the National Democratic Party was a serious attempt at creating a modern right in Peru, and that this endeavor was unsuccessful because of indifference from the traditional right, which opposed all modernizing changes, rather than because of an opposing radicalism.[13]

It was a generation that produced remarkable and innovative intellectual works, above all during their youth. It has been pointed out that what is surprising in these young people's work is not so much talent but other, less-frequent qualities: industriousness, patience, research techniques, and serenity in their conclusions. In this way, Riva-Agüero's first university theses and Francisco García Calderón's first books were "true overviews of Peruvian literature and history, of the situation in Peru or Latin America's past."[14]

The political events in Peru beginning in the 1920s prevented finalization of the regeneration that the *arielistas* proposed. As Loayza has pointed out, they were "a generation hindered by history's sharp acceleration." Loayza suggests that a key to understanding that generation is knowing that they were educated in a world that appeared to be permanently ordered but quickly disappeared during the chaos of the First World War and its subsequent series of crises. The Mexican and Soviet revolutions significantly unsettled this generation, which displayed merely a "prudent liberalism."[15] Individually, for the most part, they had extraordinary careers, but their generational project was unsuccessful. Contributing to this failure was the political and economic elite's lack of vision and commitment to the country—the elite did not support them—and the later appearance of other higher-profile political movements. It could be said that Riva-Agüero's cohort exemplified a lost opportunity, leaving undone a series of reforms that would have been crucial: their proposals sought to avoid a recurrence of the upheaval of the War of the Pacific by establishing a responsible and practical governing nucleus. They definitely intended to create a collective consciousness that would identify Peruvians as a nationality.[16]

Riva-Agüero's indebtedness to his university education

Riva-Agüero was a polymath, but juridical topics were present throughout his works, and he was a distinguished law student. In fact, on two occasions he won the annual university award in jurisprudence.[17]

In his legal and philosophical training at the University of San Marcos, at the beginning of the twentieth century, evolutionist and mechanistic perspectives dominated. Thus, in studying central concepts such as ethics, family, property, and law, the courses regressed—as Riva-Agüero himself explained—to the use of distant and primitive populations, with the pretense of fitting evolutionary processes to the disciplines and steering them toward predetermined ends, which often coincided with radical socialist positions.[18] The young Riva-Agüero, however, was philosophically voluntarist rather than liberal. Sociologically, he was a positivist, following the steps of his teacher Javier Prado, and a utilitarian, like Manuel Vicente Villarán.[19]

As for juridical–political ideas, Riva-Agüero contemplated the legal legitimacy of the coup d'état in his newspaper article titled "La amnistía y el gobierno" ("Amnesty and the government"), published on September 12, 1911, which caused a major furor. In the article, he asserted the illegitimacy of the government of President Augusto B. Leguía because of his repression of opponents and his inefficient policies. The article defended a group of people who had attempted to forcefully overthrow Leguía in 1909, and who for this reason were in prison. Fundamentally, Riva-Agüero declared that the law had shifted "from the formal legislation of the constituted regime to the social act of coercion." Thus, the 1911 article defended "coercive acts as means for maintaining legal order." He judged that in exceptional moments, revolutions were legitimate and necessary, and that the scope of law surpassed the order of legality. In other words, the juridical order stood above written law. In this sense, in the face of anarchy—which the legality of the written law could no longer uphold—revolution was an act of coercion that sought to preserve the juridical order. He defined Leguía's regime as an anarchy.[20]

In his two juridical theses, Riva-Agüero reflected on the origin and nature of law. He was a philosopher of law who considered himself an anti-metaphysical vitalist at that time, and therefore he did not believe in the idea of absolute justice, nor in the concept of absolute rights. Precisely in this context, he proposes that acts of coercion can be legal acts in certain circumstances. In his 1911 thesis for his Bachelor's Degree in Jurisprudence, titled *Fundamento de los interdictos posesorios* (*Basis for possessory interdicts*), Riva-Agüero explicitly exhibits his attachment to voluntarist doctrine by affirming that the ultimate basis of the sense of juridical themes is not in the law, but rather in a prior act of coercion. For Riva-Agüero "one's will in itself is a substantial element that always demands protection."[21] Furthermore, he literally ended up saying that all laws are types of coercion when he affirmed that a law pertains "to one of the types or expressions of coercion…to conscious and rational human energy, in a word, to human will."[22] In this way, the law would be the consequence and crystallization of coercion, and thus the basis for interdicts would be legal recognition of coercion.[23] In accordance with voluntarism, he defined justice as "the manner of coordinating desires in the coexistence of men."[24] Utilitarianism also appears in his thesis when he sanctions a primary act of coercion as being in accordance with general social interests. In other words, the "economic reason" complements the primary act of coercion. In this sense, consideration of social utility is fundamental. Therefore, he ends up saying that the greater social utility that revolutions may represent is precisely what justifies them. In this way, voluntarism and utilitarianism blend together in the legal justification of acts of coercion. Therefore, their legitimacy is broader than legality, and "every law is a coercion," with coercion originating from individual will.[25] He said it clearly in 1911 in the article against Leguía:

> The most extreme conservatism, the most rigid and strict authoritarianism, in certain cases has to recognize the legitimacy of the insurrection—socially equivalent to a private defense of the individual—at the risk of incurring tremendous absurdity…revolutions, which have been quite abused in Latin America, are nevertheless legitimate and necessary in exceptional moments, if countries do not wish to surrender, defenseless, to the blind discretion and despotic whim of their current leaders.[26]

In his defense of the juridical legitimacy of acts of coercion, Riva-Agüero exhibited a position in opposition to that of his teacher Alejandro Deustua, who—as the liberal that he was—opposed the use of coercion and any attempt to generate a political regime based on its use. For Deustua, only what was provided for in legislation was legal. From a philosophical point of view, the idea of coercion as a generator of law is intimately linked to voluntarism, and to authors such as Schopenhauer and Nietzsche. But these ideas should be joined to the historical pragmatism of Joseph de Maistre, one of the most important representatives of religious reaction in nineteenth-century Europe—and especially to one of his most important followers, the Spaniard Juan Donoso Cortés, who led Spanish reactionary thought of that century.

Donoso, a notable jurist and forensic orator, was initially a moderate liberal. Nevertheless, following the revolutions of 1848, he adopted a very decisive position opposing liberalism and modern representative regimes in general. Donoso aroused admiration from the young people of Riva-Agüero's generation. Donoso's positions led him to justify dictatorship in cases where legality was insufficient for salvaging society. In the face of the liberal position that identified law with legality, Donoso justified dictatorship when legality conflicted with the interests of society. That would legitimize society's resistance to legality through dictatorship when circumstances indicated its necessity.

While Donoso's positions definitively influenced Riva-Agüero, because he represented the anti-liberal religious reaction, Donoso was viewed with much caution in the liberal, positivist, and utilitarian atmosphere at the university in Lima. Thus, in his law theses, young Riva-Agüero supported his affirmation that "all law is coercion" by drawing on certain German authors, along with writings by Henri Bergson and the sociologist Gabriel Tardé and the voluntarist views of Schopenhauer and Nietzsche.[27]

In his thesis *Concepto del Derecho* (*Concept of law*, 1912), based on voluntarism and utilitarianism, Riva-Agüero continues to explain the legitimate character of coercion, but here he also exhibits positivist influences. Along the lines of voluntarism, he affirms that law is in principle an act of coercion. In this sense, he proposes the concept of "imposition." From utilitarianism he advances the notion of social utility or social interest. In this way, a leader or a group imposes itself, and if society consents to that imposition, the leadership is legitimized. But this legitimization ought to endure over time. Following Joseph de Maistre, Riva-Agüero affirms that law can be understood as a "durable imposition": by enduring, the coercion generates a type of equilibrium or status.[28] The positivist influence is notable when Riva-Agüero reveals his opposition to contractualism while explaining the origin of the state. In his view, the origin of the state was not in any contract; rather, it "emanates from the deepest part of nature and the laws of will." He ends up saying that the state is the creator of all rights, and that "against the state there are no rights," "when the law disappears, rights disappear"—affirmations inspired by both voluntarism and positivism. He denies the existence of an absolute right, and asserts that "legal power is the coercion of will above others, which is guaranteed and sanctioned by society."[29]

A few years later, in 1917, he posed a quite critical vision of positivism, considering it to have deteriorated into a "vulgar empiricism, and trashy and blind materialism," which denied spiritual components.[30] And on a later occasion—in 1934, when he had already recovered the notions of natural law from the Christian tradition—he referred to the "narrow positivism that then imprisoned me."[31] He recognized that he had received both idealist and positivist influences during his university education. "[I]n our adolescence we witnessed the combat between resurrected idealism and the hefty and crude positivist rearguard."[32] Later, he began to feel the influence of the thinking of Henri Bergson, a "logical coronation of all the mentioned contemporary tendencies."[33] In Bergson he saw the syncretism and reconciliation of various doctrines which combined the best of philosophical tradition with the postulates of modern sciences: "Their essential characters and undeniable tendencies are the supremacy of will over intelligence, glorification of ideals, justification of social activity and instincts, and therefore respect of the mystery and reverence of the past and loving confidence in the future."[34]

In this review of Riva-Agüero's legal stances, we cannot leave aside the *Declaración de Principios* (*Declaration of principles*) of the National Democratic

Party, which appeared in 1915. It was the product of his pen and makes up one of the volumes of his complete works. In the *Declaración*, he addressed issues of constitutional law—such as individual guarantees—and in this sense proposed reform of the *habeas corpus* law with the goal that the crime of arbitrary detention would not remain unpunished. In equal measure, the *Declaración* proposed the repeal of special press legislation, since a crime of opinion could not exist. The *Declaración* expressed absolute rejection of authoritarianism and autocracy, and in this sense advocated for an executive power that was not all-embracing but also did not remain defenseless before the legislative power. The *Declaración* defended presidential elections by direct suffrage, and it proposed no reelection of presidents until two entire subsequent terms had passed.[35]

Riva-Agüero's return to the natural law of the Christian tradition

When Riva-Agüero wrote his thesis about the concept of law, he was twenty-seven years old and had already distanced himself from the Catholic faith for several years. This distance lasted more than twenty years. His return to Catholicism was the result of a long intellectual process, as he publicly revealed in 1932 at age forty-seven in a famous speech delivered at the Recoleta School at its annual alumni lunch.[36] In this profession of faith, he expressed his "conscious, reasoned, and public adherence to the traditional doctrines that educated me and that are doubly precious for me, after having recovered them in a long and difficult struggle."[37] He accredited Nietzsche and his "unwholesome works" with infecting him with "their anti-Christian and antiascetical virus" that, united with "the indigestion of the most opposite and difficult philosophical systems," and in particular the "narrow positivist evolutionism," had brought him to formulate positions contrary to spiritualism and Catholicism.[38] Nevertheless, Riva-Agüero never adhered to philosophical materialism or atheism, given that the positivist and Kantian principles inculcated in him at the university "did not come quite to that."[39] He said that he was able to overcome his metaphysical and religious angst only with his return to a belief in a transcendent and personal God in the context of Roman Catholicism, given that neither in deism nor in Protestantism did he find relief.[40] Riva-Agüero's conversion coincided with the defense of realist metaphysics by important European intellectuals, as was the case—which Riva-Agüero commended—of the Italian Giorgio Del Vecchio, a former neo-Kantian and Dean of the University of Rome, who ultimately subscribed to Catholic doctrine.[41]

Following his return to the Catholic faith, Riva-Agüero demonstrated his juridical standpoints many times. In his inauguration speech as Dean of the Lima Bar Association, he defended the importance of the historical perspective when analyzing juridical realities, given that ignorance of history could drag along prior errors. He valued the fact that the comparative historical method was introduced into the juridical sciences in the nineteenth century. This allowed for understanding them as dynamic processes, which demonstrated society's evolution. He affirmed that the history of law warned about both the potential and the risks of legal systems. For that reason, he demanded adequate education in philosophy and history for judges, legislators, and lawyers, which he felt was key for the future of a nation.[42] He defended the study of Roman law and criticized prior movements that had scorned such study, given that Peruvian law had very clearly inherited it. In this sense, he exalted Andrés Bello's defense of the importance of the study of Roman law in the mid-nineteenth century in Chile. Similarly, he underscored the importance of canon law in a jurist's education. Roman law and canon law were two "centuries-old monuments." He spotlighted the great influence that canon law had had in the final period of Roman law, just as in medieval and modern times; and he highlighted how even contemporary procedural law has clear precedents in canon law.[43]

He judged that the republican Peruvian state had overreached in the issuance of laws, disregarding the example set by the Romans, who were restrained in issuing them. Like other Latin American republics, Peru had issued an extremely high number of laws—many copied from abroad and inapplicable, precipitous, or imprudent considering the real situation of Peru. He pointed out how "vigorous populations" placed greater importance on their own traditions and customs, which little by little ended up turning into solid laws.[44] He condemned the fact that in Peru, seduction by newness had prevailed:

> We, just like children, have been seduced continuously by what is new, unusual, adventitious, and alien. If we appreciated Peru because of reading its variegated collections of laws, from constitutional to administrative ones, we would conceive of a very confusing and inexact idea of its state.[45]

Concomitantly with his return to Catholicism, Riva-Agüero declared that he had come back to "respect the Catholic doctrine of absolute law or natural law," to which "historic and relative rights" ought to be subordinated. It is in this context that Riva-Agüero rectifies his juvenile vision of law as a coercion, or as a "coactive and constant mandate." In this way, he proposes that the law should be defined as a "rational mandate, and rational, coactive and durable," given that power ought to revolve around reason and common good.[46] Hence, Riva-Agüero defends transcendent natural law, which every individual recognizes with mere discretion. This natural law consists of few rules, which can generate many juridical modalities when it is applied.[47] In his commentaries about the works by Del Vecchio, he affirmed that "above the written laws there are superior unwritten laws that are innate in one's conscience and that generate the moral order."[48] He praised the Italian philosopher's efforts for "saving the principles of perennial law, essential and *a priori*, in the face of mere legal phenomenalism, historicist or positivist."[49]

Riva-Agüero not only described his legal principles but also defended them in the context of public Peruvian life. He did this to the greatest extent in the report that he presented in 1937 at the end of his administration as Dean of the Bar Association of Lima, when he laid out his critiques of the Civil Code passed the previous year, which replaced the first Peruvian Civil Code, from 1852. He declared that it was necessary to update the old code, but that he believed that having done what he considered a "total transformation" was an error, which in many respects diverged from "our legitimate Romanist and Castilian tradition."[50]

He was particularly critical of the reforms introduced around the topics of people and family. In agreement with his traditionalist spirit, he expressed that "with them [the reforms], we lose some of the scarce constitutive elements of the country."[51] His Catholic convictions were very present in his absolute rejection of divorce, which the code introduced in family law. He affirmed that illustrious non-Catholic thinkers and statists—including Hume, Goethe, Gladstone, and Theodore Roosevelt—had combated divorce. He pointed out that universal experience demonstrated that divorce was "a terrible scourge," given that it dissolved "the society's own cell." He judged that proposing to limit divorce to a few causes was naïve and futile, given that "its simple possibility determined its slow increase."[52] At the same time, he understood divorce to be a step toward later subversion of society, in which socialist and communist postulations would have an advantage: "Relaxation of the family is an inseparable part of the plan of subversion against inheritance, property, and all civilized regime...Consciously or unconsciously, divorcists work towards Bolshevization."[53]

Riva-Agüero believed that divorce deprived marriage of security, seriousness, and respectability; it sidelined marriage's important ethical and social character, and equated it to any old contract—"almost like a lease, as the sales [contract] is almost always irrevocable." Finally, divorce "tears down households and traditions."[54] Along the same line, he considered detrimental the code's provision for recognizing all children, given that it tended to unravel the family and discredit marriage.[55]

As for property, he remained vigilant against the diffusion of socialist ideas. He believed that the postulates of historical materialism reduced legal institutions to mere reflections of the production and distribution of wealth, which was seen as the only substantial reality in community life.[56] With respect to Indigenous communities, he insisted on not being fascinated by collective property, and in any case, insisted on family property. He pointed out that it was necessary to remain vigilant in the face of the aspirations of Peruvian leftists, who wanted to follow in the footsteps of Russia and Mexico and use communities to disseminate "rural socialism."[57]

He also referred to the "socialist dilettantisms" of the code, and to its "statist idolatry," by criticizing the codifiers for affirming that "the state is the source of all rights." Riva-Agüero believed this interpretation made the law arbitrary and tyrannical, given that it did not consider pre-state and non-state rights. In addition, he judged that the code included various provisions that attacked the rights of owners.[58]

In conclusion, Riva-Agüero declared that the Civil Code of 1936 weakened the family, property, and religion in dealing with "foundations of the nation" that had to be consolidated. This seemed especially important to him, considering that Peruvians were "tender and delicate," and therefore required solid laws so as not to break apart.[59]

Beginning with his return to Catholicism, his status as a Catholic was very present in the various aspects of his occupation, particularly in politics. In this way, in 1934 he discussed the political situation both in Peru and in the international realm, and underscored the values that he believed Catholics should defend. He set an important limit with respect to Hitler in Germany, and in particular with regard to racism: "[I]n order to not be racist like the German Nazis, it is sufficient for me to be Christian and remember the words of Saint Paul about the equality of humankind."[60]

He insisted that Catholics should firmly defend their principles, and he always saw Marxism as a great threat to society. Moreover, in the German case, he judged that the breeding ground for Nazism's rise to power was the centrist party's "ambiguous and detrimental" attitude, which was an "accomplice, accessory, and support" of the atheist and demagogic ambitions of Marxism. Based on the German case, he concluded that the political instability and social discord in other countries were due to the unsteady and unstable attitude of "lukewarm Catholics," ready to reach an agreement with enemies of religion.[61] He declared that he was not concerned that coherent Catholics would be considered a minority, given that "one of the most proven social laws is that resolved and organized minorities prevail over the greater number and create courses in history."[62]

In this sense, he was also concerned about the defense of educational freedom—invoked in various political constitutions in Peru—and in particular with the ability of the Catholic University to grow autonomously without the state attempting to establish a monopoly on public universities. In an article published in 1930, he warned of the dangers that could arise if freedom of instruction did not prevail in the university realm. In his view, it was crucial for people to have the right to education in a particular moral and religious environment, if they desired. If they were stripped of this right, it would be a more serious situation than the eventual stripping of their material goods, given that "more noble is conscience than patrimony."[63]

Among the juridical subjects about which Riva-Agüero posed ideas in the 1930s that differed from those of his youth was the position that he expressed in 1933 as president of the Council of Ministers, in favor of the judicial power's pursuit of "agitators" who attacked the government with expressions "incompatible with public decency."[64] On that occasion, he invoked application of the press law, repeal of which he had precisely requested in 1915 in the Declaration of Principles of the National Democratic Party, alleging that there were no felonies of opinion.

The juridical and intellectual legacy of Riva-Agüero

It is evident from what has been presented that—in his varied juridical studies of issues related to the philosophy of law, family law, property law, constitutional law, and the history of law, among others—Riva-Agüero underwent an ideological evolution in both his juridical and his political positions. Nevertheless, many elements of his earlier thinking can be found in his mature approaches—for example, his appreciation for tradition in understanding Peru. Similarly, his mature ideas about defense of order, authority, discipline, and hierarchy were already present in his writings as a youth, and they became more explicit later on.[65] His devotion and love for Peru are also permanent elements of his work through the concept of an integrated Peru, which understood the country to be predominantly *mestizo*.

Riva-Agüero represents a personality that reveals notable coherence between what he said and what he did, and great resolve in his behavior. He himself declared it: "Let us be sincere: let us do what we think and say what we feel. Let us not be fearful, timid, or crouched down."[66]

The transcendence and vastness of his work shine forth in the twenty-seven volumes of his *Obras completas*, published in Lima by the Riva-Agüero Institute. Reading the letters that he exchanged with countless public figures from the most diverse spheres allows us to value the varied dimensions of his personality and his work. He was definitely one of the greatest Peruvian thinkers of the twentieth century.

Notes

1 César Pacheco Vélez, "Nota preliminar," in Riva-Agüero, *Estudios de literatura peruana. Del Inca Garcilaso a Eguren*, vol. 2 of his *Obras completas*, xi.
2 Belaúnde, *Trayectoria y destino*, 1:333–34.
3 Planas, *El 900.*
4 Loayza, "Sobre el Novecientos," in idem, *Ensayos*, 228 and 280.
5 Belaúnde, 2:489.
6 Belaúnde, 2:826.
7 Pacheco, xi.
8 Gonzales, *Sanchos fracasados*, 127 and 136.
9 Ibid., 52.
10 Rivera, *Tradicionistas y maurrasianos*, 260–61.
11 Belaúnde, 1:278.
12 Gonzales, 95
13 Loayza, 280 and 317.
14 Ibid., 230.
15 Ibid., 232 and 331.
16 Gonzales, 216.
17 Rivera, 225.
18 Riva-Agüero, *Obras completas*, 26: 556–57. All references to quotes of José de la Riva-Agüero are from this work and are cited as "OC," followed by the volume number and separated by a colon from page numbers.
19 Rivera, 215.
20 Ibid., 216–17.
21 Ibid., 217–21.
22 OC 10:xxi.
23 Rivera, 219.
24 OC 10:xxi.
25 Rivera, 221–24.
26 OC 11:12.

27 Rivera, 227–36.
28 Ibid., 236–37.
29 OC 10:xxii–xxiii.
30 OC 10:166.
31 OC 10:235.
32 OC 10:167.
33 Ibid.
34 OC 10:169.
35 OC 11:37–40.
36 OC 26:31–39.
37 OC 26:31–32.
38 OC 26:32–33.
39 OC 26:34–35.
40 OC 26:36.
41 OC 10:305.
42 OC 26:555–56.
43 OC 26:561–63.
44 OC 26:570–71.
45 OC 26:571.
46 OC 26:559.
47 OC 26:560.
48 OC 10:xxv.
49 OC 10:295.
50 OC 26:726.
51 OC 26:734.
52 OC 26:743–44.
53 OC 26:744.
54 OC 26:745.
55 OC 26:752.
56 OC 10:306.
57 OC 26:757–59.
58 OC 26:760–61.
59 OC 26:766.
60 OC 10:229.
61 OC 10:229–30.
62 OC 10:230.
63 OC 10:175–77.
64 OC 10:207–08.
65 Gómez Acuña, "Ideología y política en José de la Riva-Agüero y Osma," 104.
66 OC 10:231.

Reference

Belaúnde, Víctor Andrés. *Peruanidad.* 2nd ed. Lima: Instituto Riva-Agüero, Ediciones Librería Studium, 1957.

Belaúnde, Víctor Andrés. *Trayectoria y destino. Memorias*, Vol. 2. Lima: Ediciones de Ediventas, 1967.

Gómez Acuña, Luis. "Ideología y política en José de la Riva-Agüero y Osma: breves apuntes e hipótesis de estudio." *Histórica* 23, no. 1 (1999): 79–109.

Gonzales, Osmar. *Sanchos fracasados. Los arielistas y el pensamiento político peruano.* Lima: Ediciones Preal, 1996.

Loayza, Luis. *Ensayos.* Lima: Editorial Universitaria, 2010.

Planas, Pedro. *El 900. Balance y recuperación*. Lima: CITDEC, 1994.

Riva-Agüero, José de la. *Carácter de la literatura del Perú independiente. Edición, prólogo y notas de Alberto Varillas Montenegro*. Lima: Universidad Ricardo Palma, Instituto Riva-Agüero, 2008.

Riva-Agüero, José de la. *La Historia en el Perú*. Tesis para el Doctorado en Letras. Edición facsimilar. Lima: Instituto Riva-Agüero, 2010.

Riva-Agüero, José de la. *Obras completas*, Vol. 27. Lima: Instituto Riva-Agüero, 1962–2018.

Riva-Agüero, José de la. *Paisajes Peruanos*. Lima: Sociedad Geográfica de Lima, Instituto Riva-Agüero, 2012.

Rivera, Víctor Samuel. *Tradicionistas y maurrasianos. José de la Riva-Agüero (1904–1919)*. Lima: Fondo Editorial del Congreso del Perú, 2017.

Wiesse Rebagliati, Jorge, ed. *Paisajes Peruanos, 1912–2012. José de la Riva-Agüero, la ruta y el texto*. Lima: Instituto Riva-Agüero, Sociedad Geográfica de Lima, 2013.

27 Manuel Herrera y Lasso (Mexico, 1890–1967)

Kif Augustine-Adams

Manuel Herrera y Lasso openly confessed an academic failing in the introductory lines to his first book, *Estudios constitucionales* (*Constitutional studies*) published in 1940. He did not like to write. He preferred by far the energy and immediacy of the spoken word. By that, the midpoint in his career, he had prodigiously offered the spoken word "in court and in the classroom" for twenty-five years and would continue to do so for another quarter of a century before his death in Mexico City in 1967. In Herrera y Lasso's view, words spoken with conviction embodied action in a way the written word—or at least a book written *sub specia aeternitatis*—did not.

Herrera y Lasso had in fact written extensively in other forms: his thesis to become a lawyer, a defense of religious freedom, an exposition on the autonomy of Mexico's federal district, and conference presentations on historical questions of government authority. He compiled these writings into *Estudios constitucionales*, which even then deviated from the platonic ideal for a book, finding cohesion as it did in Herrera y Lasso's authorship rather than in the usual thematic design of a monograph. *Estudios constitucionales* contained "fragments of [his] life in which Mexico has left a trail of anguished tears, indignant protests, and rebellious shouts."[1] Despite his lack of love for writing, Herrera y Lasso wrote consistently across five decades, returning repeatedly to central themes of Mexican constitutionalism: federalism, separation of powers, structures of government, the franchise, and religious freedom. He felt it his "patriotic duty" to bring his prolific writings together to publish them, "refined, completed, and polished," and thus to bequeath to Mexico "the offering of [his] spiritual patrimony."[2]

Although the ideal book form eluded him throughout his career, the power of the written word did not. His evocative prose in newspapers, journals, and essays spoke directly to people and contemporary problems. He addressed the challenges of government facing Mexican society as an attorney adviser to the office of the president of the republic; to the Chamber of Deputies, the lower house in the Mexican Congress; to the attorney general of the Federal District and Federal Territories; and to other government entities and cabinet officials. Herrera y Lasso's publication venues, forms, and style perhaps better approximate those of a public intellectual deeply engaged with the concrete issues of his era than those of an academic jurist theorizing abstractly, removed from the fray.

In the fortieth edition of his indispensable tome *Derecho constitucional mexicano* (*Mexican constitutional law*), Felipe Tena Ramírez—Mexican Supreme Court Justice, preeminent scholar of the Mexican Constitution in the twentieth century, and Herrera y Lasso's former student—characterized the work of his professor as part of the fundamental canon of Mexican constitutional law: "We must include the work of Manuel Herrera y Lasso, collected in part...and the rest dispersed in numerous newspaper articles, essays, and conferences, as it represents the most serious and impartial study of the Constitution in effect today."[3] While recognizing the seriousness and impartiality of Herrera y Lasso's written constitutional analysis, Tena Ramírez's commendation highlighted its dispersion and concomitant fragmentation, factors which complicate access and limit Herrera y Lasso's contemporary influence.

In a critique in 1993, Supreme Court justice Arturo F. Zaldívar Lelo de Larrea argued that "don Manuel Herrera y Lasso did not propose to elaborate a true doctrine defending the Mexican constitution."[4] Nonetheless, through careful exposition, Zaldívar identified within Herrera y Lasso's body of work "a solid and profound doctrine" that formed "an authentic theory of constitutional defense," a defense centered around *amparo* (protection of fundamental civil rights), federalism, and the separation of powers.[5] By 2017, a third Mexican Supreme Court Justice, José Fernando Franco González-Salas, disagreed profoundly:

> Paradoxically, notwithstanding the prestige that he enjoyed for at least two-thirds of the twentieth century, at present he is an author less and less cited in the curriculum, in the academy, and in constitutional law texts. Perhaps this paradox can be explained by the fact that don Manuel, a constitutionalist relevant to his day, in reality did not create doctrine, nor did he form or consolidate a "school" of constitutional law.[6]

Biographical information

Manuel Herrera y Lasso was born in 1890 in the city of San Luis Potosí, Mexico, to the mining engineer don Manuel Herrera y Raso and doña Guadalupe Lasso de la Vega y Villegas.[7] After his father's sudden death, when Herrera y Lasso was just shy of five years old, his mother raised him with tenderness and devotion, ensuring her youngest son a fine and deeply Catholic education. She sent him to primary school at La Divina Providencia, where his teacher, doña Guadalupe Vázquez Castillo, guided his moral development. At ten, he studied Latin and philosophy in San Luis Potosí's Seminario Conciliar, receiving the intellectual and spiritual guidance of Father José Bustamante and the Dominican friar Froylán Casquero. By thirteen, he had begun his high school studies (*preparatoria*) under the tutelage of professors Francisco Ávalos and José Undiano at the Instítuto Científico y Literario. Herrera y Lasso's love of learning and profound Catholic faith developed under the care of these earliest teachers, whom he honored by name for their formative influence on him. With the exception of Guadalupe Vázquez Castillo, whose name now graces a street in San Luis Potosí, their influence and contributions are otherwise largely lost to history. It is easy to imagine that Herrera y Lasso modeled his own fifty-year teaching career on their examples, along with those of his professors at the Escuela Nacional Preparatoria, in Mexico City, and his religious guides as a lay associate in the Society of Jesus, Fathers Méndez Medina and Pascual Díaz.

Herrera y Lasso's experiences as a law student at the Escuela Nacional de Jurisprudencia, in Mexico City, were less sanguine. Herrera y Lasso began his undergraduate law studies in July 1910, scant months before the nation erupted in revolutionary fratricide against the entrenched dictatorship of Porfirio Díaz. In 1911, Herrera y Lasso voted for Francisco Madero in the presidential elections as a balloted delegate for the Catholic Party. His political activism and leadership intertwined with his education when, as a third-year law student in 1912, he played a leading role in a student strike at the Escuela Nacional de Jurisprudencia. On their formal expulsion from the Escuela Nacional and ban from any institution of higher education in the Federal District, the student strikers founded a new law school, the Escuela Libre de Derecho (Free School of Law), with the support of a handful of prominent attorneys and jurists.

Popular renditions of the founding of the Escuela Libre de Derecho tend to simplify the event as rebellion against the dictates and politicization of Luis Cabrera, the fourth director of the Escuela Nacional de Jurisprudencia named in one tumultuous year. As Jaime del Arenal Fenochio argued, the reality was substantially more complex, with competing interests and values battling through ideas rather than by means of the revolutionary violence that swirled around them.[8] Other scholars note critically the Porfirian origins of the Escuela Libre de Derecho.[9] Herrera y Lasso gave the commemorative speech on behalf of students at the school's inauguration, his enduring relationship with it sustaining him throughout his life.

As a student at the Escuela Libre de Derecho, Herrera y Lasso studied under Agustín Rodríguez, Miguel S. Macedo, and his particular mentor, Emilio Rabasa, the eminent jurist and *científico*, whose constitutional writings sought to bridge Porfirianism and revolution. Herrera y Lasso received his law degree in 1915, the Mexican Revolution raging and structures of government in collapse, with a thesis he optimistically titled "Some Chapters of a Study on the Constitution," an analysis of the soon-to-be-defunct Constitution of 1857 and its historical antecedents. Although his thesis received high commendations from his professors, Herrera y Lasso published it only twenty-five years later in an updated form as the first section of *Estudios constitucionales.*

Herrera y Lasso's defense of Catholicism at the beginning of the Cristero Rebellion (1926–29) cost him dearly. In early February 1926, President Plutarco Elías Calles signed into law an act to enforce the anticlerical provisions in Articles 3, 5, 24, 27, and 130 of the Constitution of 1917. Violence erupted again. Catholics, particularly in central Mexico, resisted the closing of churches and religious schools, prohibitions on public worship, seizure of church property, and severe restrictions on priests. Herrera y Lasso resisted with the words of law. On February 23, 1926 he published on the editorial page of the national newspaper

Excelsior an opinion titled "The Closing of the Temple of the Holy Family. A Protest by Licenciado Herrera y Lasso." Herrera y Lasso argued in favor of religious freedom:

> Religious liberty, liberty of conscience, are essential to spiritual life in the same way that air is to physical life. No person, conscious of himself and his own personal responsibility, can tolerate limitations against these liberties, without endangering at the same time his right to live a noble life.[10]

On August 4, 1926, on behalf of the Defense League for Religious Liberty in Mexico, Herrera y Lasso debated President Calles's secretary of agriculture and development, Luis L. León, on "The Revolutionary Movement and Mexican Clericalism" and published a thirty-one-page memorialization of the debate. Herrera y Lasso assisted the Catholic episcopate in Mexico to draft proposed reforms to Articles 3, 5, 24, 27, and 130 of the Constitution of 1917 that would fortify the regulation of religious liberty and the function of religious associations. He sent the proposed reforms to both houses of the national legislature and published them in the press. Government patience wore thin. In January 1927 he was arrested and exiled to Cuba.

Reflecting back, decades later, Herrera y Lasso described poetically both longing and lesson in his banishment to Cuba:

> Never as in exile—exile which I lived for two years—does one love home more intensely. Distance embellishes and burnishes distant objects. Mountains lose their asperity in the uniform blue of a vast perspective.[11]

In Cuba, Herrera y Lasso continued to speak publicly and give interviews, never backing away from his religious commitment but also refraining from criticizing the Mexican Government. Early on, one interviewer complimented his restraint: "Mr. Herrera y Lasso understands moderation and discretion. He appears more a diplomat than a polemicist, and, even when we beg him, he declines to make declarations regarding the political condition of Mexico." Herrera y Lasso explained his behavior as patriotism: "He who does not accept the age in which he lives with all of its difficulties, with all of its shame, does not truly love his country."[12] As diplomatic efforts to end the Cristero Rebellion moved toward success, the Mexican Government allowed Herrera y Lasso to return home in February 1929. Return did not mean acquiescence on Herrera y Lasso's part. He immediately renewed his legal and political work with the Catholic episcopate to support the exercise of religion in Mexico.

In 1939, Herrera y Lasso joined with others to form a new conservative political party, Partido Acción Nacional (PAN), to offer an alternative to the increasingly hegemonic Partido Revolucionario Institucional (PRI). Consistent with Herrera y Lasso's personal faith, Catholic encyclicals regarding the rights and conditions of labor—*Rerum Novarum* in 1891 and *Qudragesimo Anno* in 1931—deeply influenced PAN's platform for social reform in Mexico. While

Herrera y Lasso campaigned in northern Mexico in the spring of 1940, the governor of Querétaro ordered his arrest. Herrera y Lasso spent three days in jail before national protest garnered his release.

In 1946, Herrera y Lasso stood under PAN's banner as a candidate for federal office from his home state of San Luis Potosí. When another candidate was named victor, Herrera y Lasso claimed fraud. Always the lawyer, Herrera y Lasso laid before the public and the electoral college the arguments and facts that supported his claim. His integrity and commitment to law demanded he fight for the truth. In the end, his arguments failed to persuade, but the next year, newly installed President Miguel Alemán, of the PRI (the party of all presidents of Mexico from 1929 to 2000), named Herrera y Lasso as a consulting attorney to the presidency. Herrera y Lasso never ran for political office again, but he continued in government service as an attorney, advising different entities for the rest of his life.

While still a law student at the Escuela Libre de Derecho, Herrera y Lasso taught in the sociology curriculum and as an adjunct to Emilio Rabasa in constitutional law. His co-teaching with Rabasa continued until, after Rabasa's death, in 1930, the Escuela Libre de Derecho honored Herrera y Lasso by naming him Rabasa's replacement in the constitutional law chair. As a professor, Herrera y Lasso preferred the Socratic method to straight lecture. He valued the "creative improvisation" that teaching required.[13] Moreover, he saw teaching as his calling, informed by his faith, flowing from "effusion of the mind, abundance of the heart, love of service...in sum, the love of charity that links man with man, brothers through the law of Jesus Christ."[14] He received numerous awards throughout his life, including the Honor Forense from President Ruiz Cortines and the title of honorary rector of the Escuela Libre de Derecho. In 1964, a full fifty years after he began teaching at the Escuela Libre de Derecho, he was named emeritus professor. He passed away in Mexico City on March 25, 1967, leaving behind his widow, Raquel Méndez Armendáriz, and daughter, Raquel Guadalupe Herrera Lasso Méndez.

Herrera y Lasso's scholarship

During his lifetime, Manuel Herrera y Lasso published two monographs: a first volume of *Estudios constitucionales* in 1940 and a second in 1964. Herrera y Lasso had gathered other of his writings into *Ensayos filosóficos* (*Philosophical essays*), published in 1968, shortly after his death. Additionally, Herrera y Lasso's daughter, Raquel, and Professor Jaime del Arenal Fenochio of the Escuela Libre de Derecho compiled many of his otherwise dispersed writings—essays, newspaper and journal articles, speeches—into two additional volumes: *Estudios políticos y constitucionales* (*Political and constitutional studies*) in 1986, and *Casa construida sobre roca: La Escuela Libre de Derecho y otros escritos* (*House built on rock: the Free School of Law and other writings*) in 2002.

All of Herrera y Lasso's monograph publications are collections of essays, conference contributions, and other writings rather than original publications organized around a central thesis or theme. In his prologue to *Estudios constitucionales* (1964), compiled as part of the fiftieth-anniversary celebrations of the Escuela Libre de Derecho and his own fifty-year association with it, Herrera y Lasso defended his unique career path in much the same way he had in the introduction to *Estudios constitucionales* (1940). A professor holding the chair in a particular subject (*cátedra*) would typically lecture to students and then publish the materials in a systematic consideration of the topic, such that teaching and scholarship became mutually constitutive endeavors in a published volume. Herrera y Lasso acknowledged that expectation—"friends and disciples asked for, hoped for" such a volume—but it was not an expectation that he would fulfill. Rather, collections of "studies" independent of his lectures, like the seventeen works in *Estudios constitucionales* (1964), provided a better guide to his teaching and constitutional thought than compiled lecture notes would have done.[15]

In the prologue to his *Estudios constitucionales* (1964), Herrera y Lasso provided a list of additional studies and unpublished writings that served as the guide for *Estudios políticos y constitucionales* (1986), compiled by his daughter, Raquel, and Professor del Arenal Fenochio and published as part of the seventy-fifth anniversary of the founding of the Escuela Libre de Derecho. Arenal Fenochio described the volume as containing thirty studies organized around nineteen themes including federalism, the powers of different branches of government, *amparo*, and election reform. The compilers provided an appendix identifying additional written work by Herrera y Lasso that had not been included in any of his previous collected works, including fifty-eight items previously published (many in the newspaper *Excelsior*), and approximately twenty-five unpublished items, such as speeches, letters, and class notes. Some of those writings became the book *Casa construida sobre roca* (2002) that Arenal Fenochio describes as reunifying Herrera y Lasso's literary, historical, spiritual, and humanist work, as well as his juridical and political studies. In 2003, Arenal Fenochio published an index to files containing Herrera y Lasso's voluminous professional work as a private attorney and a consulting attorney to Mexican entities.[16] A few of the documents in the files had been published in Herrera y Lasso's earlier compiled works. Arenal Fenochio transcribed the remainder for a volume that was never published, although he made the transcriptions available to the Supreme Court for its volume in honor of the centenary of the Constitution of 1917. The originals have been lost.[17]

During Herrera y Lasso's lifetime, journalists interviewed him, politicians countered his proposals, and jurists interrogated his ideas in nearly 150 newspaper articles, a list of which can be found at the end of *Estudios políticos y constitucionales*. Nonetheless, the secondary literature exploring Herrera y Lasso's constitutional legacy as a whole, rather than engaging in immediate debate, is somewhat limited in any form. Certain of Herrera y Lasso's ideas inspired the thesis of an aspiring lawyer or two, but nowhere near the volume prompted by other Mexican jurists similarly eminent in their lifetime.[18] Seasoned scholars occasionally reference his ideas in their work, but no one has yet analyzed his contributions to constitutionalism in Mexico in a book-length treatment.[19]

At the same time, no book-length biography of Herrera y Lasso exists, in Spanish or in English. The most readily available online secondary sources tend to be abbreviated, chronological, and hagiographic rather than in-depth, analytical, and critical. Exceptions include the research of Jaime del Arenal Fenochio and the chapter by Supreme Court justice José Fernando Franco González-Salas titled "Manuel Herrera y Lasso: Constitutional Lawyer by Calling and Professor by Passion," in a book celebrating the centennial of Mexico's Constitution of 1917, although the chapter also tends to be informational rather than analytical when presenting Herrera y Lasso's publications.[20]

None of Herrera y Lasso's compiled works are currently in print, nor did any of their publication runs exceed a thousand copies, a fact which helps explain their limited accessibility today despite the significant compilation efforts. Herrera y Lasso's books are not widely held by libraries outside of Mexico. The libraries in Mexico that hold them and related secondary literature do not participate in international inter-library loans. The books and some of the limited secondary literature are not available electronically. Access to both Herrera y Lasso's scholarship and secondary sources can be challenging—even impossible—for the twenty-first-century reader physically located outside of Mexico City.

Herrera y Lasso's constitutionalism

Throughout his writings, Herrera y Lasso returned repeatedly to fundamental questions of law and governance centered on sovereignty, federalism, separation of powers, structures of government, the franchise, and religious freedom. In Herrera y Lasso's political philosophy, God was sovereign, not the state. He admitted the concept of sovereignty in the international realm, one nation-state *vis-à-vis* another, but straight out rejected a nation's sovereignty over its people. Rather, "Man, by his very existence, has rights that are both anterior and superior to all political organization."[21] Herrera y Lasso identified a commitment to human rights as a fundamental principle of Mexican constitutional law dating back at least to the Constitution of 1842 and then beyond to France and its Declaration of the Rights of Man and of the Citizen (1789). Herrera y Lasso did not always explicitly foreground natural law in his analysis; its foundational influence, nonetheless, remains apparent, especially in Herrera y Lasso's identification of God as the true sovereign.

At the same time, Herrera y Lasso entered into a central debate of legal philosophy: the authority of law to oblige obedience. Herrera y Lasso noted that an imperative of democracy is the consent of the governed. Consent, tacit or expressed, undergirds law's authority. Without consent, "law lacks moral justification…law without moral justification is not law."[22] In other words, if positive law lacks moral justification, an individual is not bound to obey it because it is not actually law. Herrera y Lasso's argument, made in 1946, skirts another central issue of legal philosophy in the immediate aftermath of World War II: positivism versus natural law. While the explanatory power of natural law had faded in the early twentieth century, the Nazi regime revealed the tragic peril of an absolute commitment to positivism. Herrera y Lasso's argument, that law without moral authority is not law, rejected strict positivism.

Herrera y Lasso could, and did, speak in the language of natural rights that are based on the objective worth of human beings. He was at heart, however, a Thomist, committed to the natural law traditions of his Catholic faith. That religious faith infused the tone and tenor of a stirring call to resist tyranny, also made in 1946:

> Our existence is a constant process of self-creation. We are the author of our own destiny. Therefore, the strict obligation of all of us, on confronting the crisis that humanity currently suffers, is to oppose all despotism as it enslaves the constitutionalism that would liberate. That each of us—in thought and in action—defend at all costs the fundamental liberties of humanity, without which—I repeat and will repeat forever—life is not worth living.[23]

A constitution that protected the fundamental rights of people stood as the first line of defense against despotism.

Shortly before his death, in 1967, Herrera y Lasso wrote "Centralism and Federalism, 1814–1843," returning one last time to that crucible of Mexican nationhood: the always contested allocation of power between the states and the federal government. In a genealogy of constitutional ideas and principles set forth in early documents, he followed the meticulous method that characterized his earliest constitutional analysis in his 1915 thesis. To set the genealogy straight, he critiqued his beloved mentor, Emilio Rabasa, for various perceived errors in his constitutional analysis, but especially for failing to recognize God as the source of authority and guide to correct conduct. Despite impending blindness and death, or perhaps because of it, Herrera y Lasso concluded the legal analysis of "Centralism and Federalism" on a highly personal note, a note that in the end explained why he was a federalist. Herrera y Lasso bore testimony of his love for *patria*, Mexico as a nation, but more especially of *matria*, his natal state and city of San Luis Potosí, the bosom of his youth and religious faith. Although he had left San Luis Potosí at nineteen years old to study law in Mexico City, residing outside its embrace for well over fifty years, he could only be Potosino. San Luis was the home country of Herrera y Lasso's own mother; her memory represented to him the "very soul of the city."[24] By invoking *matria*, both literally and figuratively, Herrera y Lasso created an intensely personal and deeply religious image of Mexico's perennial challenge, centralism versus federalism, an image that resonated with the prime icon of Mexican national identity, the Virgin of Guadalupe. That resonance suggested a vision of federalism consistent with Herrera y Lasso's faith, the special place and respect for *matria*—the local—in the political construction of Mexico *patria*—the nation.

Herrera y Lasso was not without his critics, both as a professor and as a Catholic. His former student and heir to the constitutional law chair at the Escuela Libre de Derecho, Elisur Arteaga Nava, debunked a prevalent myth about Herrera y Lasso as a "holy Catholic saint," a myth Arteaga Nava himself professed to have believed.[25]

Arteaga Nava saw no demerit in his revelations of Herrera y Lasso's follies, his "love of alcohol and women," the inebriated class sessions when Herrera y Lasso "invited his students to the bar to hear his lectures." Rather, Arteaga Nava viewed Herrera y Lasso's less-than-saintly conduct as evidence of his full embrace of life, living without reproach or regret. Other scholars view Herrera y Lasso's Catholicism not through the lens of piety and orthopraxis, but as militant conservatism.[26]

Arteaga Nava's forgiveness of his former professor's moral foibles held no sway in the academic context where his criticism brutally undercut Herrera y Lasso's basic competence. Arteaga Nava considered Herrera y Lasso's inheritance of Emilio Rabasa's constitutional law chair, the same chair he himself would later hold, "a disgrace for the Escuela Libre de Derecho." In his view, Felipe Tena Ramírez or Gustavo R. Velasco, later a rector of the school, were more worthy of the chair, even though Herrera y Lasso "was considered the natural and direct heir of don Emilio Rabasa." Arteaga Nava savaged Herrera y Lasso's preferred Socratic teaching method, calling it a pretext for disordered, anecdotal, disastrous exposition. He considered Herrera y Lasso's written scholarship "far too baroque," distant from "the elegance and simple style of don Emilio." Nevertheless, Arteaga Nava conceded Herrera y Lasso's oratorical gifts, that same preference for the spoken above the written, that Herrera y Lasso had identified in his introductory lines to *Estudios constitucionales* (1940):

> He stood out as a great orator. In his time, no one else rose to his stature. When he stood up in court, his value was immediately apparent, his exposition slow, elegant, and measured. He smiled frequently. It seemed like he had learned his oratory pieces by heart. He never used notes.[27]

Arenal Fenochio conceded that Herrera y Lasso did not write much, but held that what he did write was "profound, original, and intelligent." Arenal Fenochio argued that Herrera y Lasso in fact surpassed Rabasa in many ways, particularly through "the specificity and concreteness of his legal analysis" and "his humanism." In Arenal Fenochio's view, Herrera y Lasso's humanism facilitated his engagement with "a rich variety of philosophic, historic, pedagogic, ideological, and religious themes" in ways that Rabasa could not and did not engage.[28] Most of all, in contrast to Rabasa, Herrera y Lasso's conservativism allowed him a more accurate vision of Mexican history, one "closer to the historic reality of the country."[29] Even Arenal Fenochio conceded, however, that Herrera y Lasso's supernal power lay in oratory rather than writing. With few recordings of Herrera y Lasso exercising his evanescent gift, his words now lie "frozen in the frailty of the typewritten versions," the best of his talent "lost from the moment he was silenced forever."[30] The ephemerality of the spoken word would limit appreciation for Herrera y Lasso's most persuasive self.

Whatever the medium of his persuasion, Herrera y Lasso's internal commitment lay with law above power, with constitutionalism above politics. Ending with biblical imagery, he expressed his view of the salvific force of law, fusing once again his two faiths:

> The law is a magnificent poem that reflects, like art and science, thought and spirit, the momentum and decision of men who have forged the country. Many have been the tempests, the waters have risen, appearing to inundate and destroy everything. Nonetheless, the ark floats above the flood.[31]

Law would save us all.

Notes

1 Herrera y Lasso, *Estudios constitucionales*, preliminary notes.
2 Herrera y Lasso, *Estudios constitucionales, Segunda serie*, 8.
3 Tena Ramírez, *Derecho constitucional mexicano*, 78.
4 Zaldívar, "La defensa," 319.
5 Ibid., 320–22.
6 Franco González-Salas, "Manuel Herrera y Lasso," fn. 111.
7 Biographical information comes primarily from Manuel Herrera y Lasso, *Estudios políticos y constitucionales*, 533–36 and other sources cited herein.
8 Arenal Fenochio, "Vasconcelos, Herrera y Lasso," 93–94; Arenal Fenochio, "La Fundación de la Escuela Libre de Derecho"; Arenal Fenochio, "Religión y política," 39–45.
9 Hale, "Edmundo O'Gorman," 16; Garciadiego Dantán, *Rudos contra científicos*, 137–94.
10 Herrera y Lasso, *Estudios constitucionales*, 101.
11 Herrera y Lasso, *Estudios políticos y constitucionales*, 74.
12 Franco González-Salas, "Manuel Herrera y Lasso," fn. 3 (citing Herrera y Lasso, *Ensayos filosóficos*, 15–16).
13 Herrera y Lasso, *Estudios constitucionales, Segunda serie*, 7.
14 Ibid., 9.
15 Ibid., 7.
16 Arenal Fenochio, "Las carpetas de dictámenes," 615–37.
17 Franco González-Salas, "Manuel Herrera y Lasso," fn. 47.
18 See, e.g., Quiroga Rivera, "El poder legislativo del Distrito Federal," and Alcántara Méndez, "Al César lo que es del César." See also Torres Mendoza, "La instauración de la reelección legislativa inmediata."
19 A sample of the limited citations to Herrera y Lasso outside of constitutional law texts include Dorantes Díaz, "Estado de excepción y derechos humanos," 377–94 (noting that Herrera y Lasso's ideas regarding fundamental rights are "little known in our country"); Medina, *Federalismo mexicano*; and Marván Laborde, "Reflexiones sobre federalismo."
20 Franco González-Salas, "Manuel Herrera."
21 Herrera y Lasso, *Estudios constitucionales, Segunda serie*, 19–20.
22 Ibid.
23 Ibid., 22.
24 Herrera y Lasso, *Estudios políticos y constitucionales*, 74.
25 Franco González-Salas, "Manuel Herrera y Lasso," fn 12 (quoting Arteaga Nava, "Tres grandes constitucionalistas," 161–66).
26 Hale, "Edmundo O'Gorman," 8; Urías Horcasitas, "Una pasión antirrevolucionaria," 609.
27 Franco González-Salas, "Manuel Herrera y Lasso," fn 12 (quoting Arteaga Nava, "Tres grandes constitucionalistas," 161–166).
28 Arenal Fenochio, "El humanismo jurídico," 44.
29 Arenal Fenochio, *Hombres e historia*, 405, 421.

30 Arenal Fenochio, "Vasconcelos, Herrera y Lasso," 77.
31 Oropeza y Segura, "Recordando a don Manuel Herrera y Lasso," 616 (quoting Herrera y Lasso but providing no citation).

References

Alcántara Méndez, Jesús Rogelio. "Al César lo que es del César." Thesis, Mexico City: Centro de Investigación y Docencia Económicas (CIDE), 2006.

Arenal Fenochio, Jaime del. "Las carpetas de dictámenes, cartas y opiniones constitucionales de don Manuel Herrera y Lasso." *Revista de Investigaciones Jurídicas* 27 (2003): 615–37.

Arenal Fenochio. Jaime del. "La Fundación de la Escuela Libre de Derecho: Documentos." *Revista de Investigaciones Jurídicas* 11 (1987): 555–58.

Arenal Fenochio, Jaime del. *Hombres e historia de la Escuela Libre de Derecho*. Mexico City: Escuela Libre de Derecho, 1999.

Arenal Fenochio, Jaime del. "El humanismo jurídico en tres juristas mexicanos del siglo XX." *Revista de Investigaciones Jurídicas* 25 (2001): 37–78.

Arenal Fenochio, Jaime del. "Vasconcelos, Herrera y Lasso y la Escuela Libre de Derecho." *Revista de Investigaciones Jurídicas* 9 (1985): 71–102.

Arteaga Nava, Elisur. "Tres grandes constitucionalistas de la Libre de Derecho." In *Un siglo de aportaciones de la Escuela libre de Derecho*, edited by Eljandro Munive Paez and Juan Pablo Pamillo Baliño, 161–66. Mexico City: Escuela Libre de Derecho, 2002.

Dorantes Díaz, Francisco Javier. "Estado de excepción y derechos humanos. Antecedentes y nueva regulación jurídica." *Alegatos* 26, no. 81 (2012): 377–94.

Franco González-Salas, José Fernando. "Manuel Herrera y Lasso: Abogado constitucionalista por vocación y maestro por pasión." In *Lecturas de la Constitución: El constitucionalismo mexicano frente a la Constitución de 1917*, edited by Jesús Silva-Herzog Márquez and José Ramón Cossío Díaz. Mexico City: Fondo de Cultura Económica, 2017.

Garciadiego Dantán, Javier. *Rudos contra científicos: La Universidad Nacional durante la revolución mexicana*. Mexico City: UNAM, 1996.

Hale, Charles. "Edmundo O'Gorman y la historia nacional." *Signos históricos* 1, no. 3 (2000): 11–18.

Herrera y Lasso, Manuel. *Casa construida sobre roca: La Escuela Libre de Derecho y otros escritos* Mexico City: Escuela Libre de Derecho, 2002.

Herrera y Lasso, Manuel. *Ensayos filosóficos*. Mexico City: Editorial Jus, 1968.

Herrera y Lasso, Manuel. *Estudios constitucionales, Segunda serie*. Mexico City: Editorial Jus, 1964.

Herrera y Lasso, Manuel. *Estudios constitucionales*. Mexico City: Editorial Polis, 1940.

Herrera y Lasso, Manuel. *Estudios políticos y constitucionales*. Mexico City: Porrúa, 1986.

Marván Laborde, Ignacio. "Reflexiones sobre federalismo y el sistema político en México." *Política y gobierno* IV, no. 1 (1997): 149–66.

Medina, Luis. *Federalismo mexicano para principiantes*. Mexico City: Centro de Investigación y Docencia Económicas (CIDE), September 2009.

Oropeza y Segura, Mauricio A. "Recordando a don Manuel Herrera y Lasso en el vigésimo quinto aniversario de su fallecimiento." *Revista de Investigaciones Jurídicas* 16 (1992): 613–18.

Quiroga Rivera, Leopoldo Alberto. "El poder legislativo del Distrito Federal." Thesis for the title of attorney, Mexico City: Escuela Libre de Derecho, 1969.

Tena Ramírez, Felipe. *Derecho constitucional mexicano.* 40th ed. Mexico City: Porrúa, 2011.

Torres Mendoza, Daniel Alejandro. "La instauración de la reelección legislativa inmediata como medida fortalecedora del poder legislativo hoy de la democracia en México." Escuela Libre de Derecho, February 2018.

Urías Horcasitas, Beatriz. "Una pasión antirrevolucionaria: el conservadurismo hispanófilo mexicano (1920–1960)." 72 *Revista Mexicana de Sociología* 72, no. 4 (2010): 599–628.

Zaldívar Lelo de Larrea, Arturo F. "La defensa de la Constitución en el pensamiento de Manuel Herrera y Lasso." *Revista de Investigaciones Jurídicas* 17 (1993): 319–39.

28 Heráclito Fontoura Sobral Pinto (Brazil, 1893–1991)

Ernesto Pimentel and Paul Sekscenski

Introduction

In a country with a historical record of violating the right to due process, a humble man raised his voice in defense of those who had been served humiliating sentences without fair trials. He wanted authority to be based on authentic Christian values. As is the custom for addressing attorneys in Brazil, Heráclito Fontoura Sobral Pinto[1] was known as Dr. Sobral. Dr. Sobral was a distinguished human rights attorney, journalist, and Catholic intellectual from Brazil, where he was born, built his career, and lived his entire life. As often as possible, he also provoked the authorities in attempts to end their arbitrary use of power.

Biographical information

Heráclito Fontoura Sobral Pinto was born in the small town of Barbacena, in the interior, mountainous state of Minas Gerais, north of Rio de Janeiro and São Paulo. His father, Príamo Cavalcanti Sobral Pinto, worked for the Central do Brasil railroad; his mother, Idalina Fontoura Sobral Pinto, took care of the home. Soon after Heráclito turned one year old, his father was promoted to the job of station manager in another small town, Porto Novo do Cunha (now Além Paraíba), located on the Minas Gerais border with Rio de Janeiro state, and the family moved to a house just off the train station's courtyard. His parents, very devout Catholics, were responsible for the strong religious upbringing of their three children, of which Heráclito was the youngest. His father's best friend, Padre Carloto Távora, the local Catholic priest, was also a major influence on the child.[2] The young Heráclito loved going to Mass and assisting the priest, and he would continue to do this into his later years.

Heráclito obtained his primary education in Porto Novo do Cunha. In 1907, he and his older brother, Rubens, were sent to a Jesuit boarding school, Colégio Anchieta, in Nova Friburgo, RJ, about eighty miles northeast of the city of Rio de Janeiro. At Colégio Anchieta, then considered to be the best Catholic school in the country,[3] he earned a solid foundation in the social sciences, in French, and in Latin, as well as in religious matters: "the Truths of Dogmatic Theology and Moral Theology [were] indispensable in the life of a Catholic, as a family man, a professional man, and a man in public life."[4]

By the time Sobral completed his studies at Colégio Anchieta, in 1912, his father had retired from the railroad, and the family had moved to the city of Rio de Janeiro, then the nation's capital. The seventeen-year-old Heráclito joined his family in Rio and obtained a job in the telegraph division of the Brazilian Post Office and Telegraph agency, of which his friend Paulo Gomide was the director. With the money he earned from his work, Sobral entered the Faculdade de Direito, a law school, from which he earned his degree in 1917, specializing in criminal law. In 1919 he left his job at the telegraph agency to dedicate his efforts strictly to the field of law.[5]

After working in private practice for a few years, in 1924 Sobral was appointed by President Artur Bernardes, a fellow *mineiro*[6] to be the interim *procurador criminal da República.*[7] In that position, he acted as part of the harsh arm of the federal bureaucracy, carrying out actions against subversive groups and other enemies of the regime. Although somewhat limited by the law, the position held much power, and Sobral did not hesitate to wield that power, convicting anarchists, military conspirators, and laborers, sometimes sending them into internal exile on Brazil's inhospitable northern border with Guyana, deep in the Amazon rainforest.

Sobral Pinto was a man who liked order. He aggressively prosecuted some members of the group of young army officers, known as the *tenentes* (lieutenants), who on two occasions had attempted to topple Bernardes: first, in a rebellion at Fort Copacabana, in Rio de Janeiro, in July 1922—when Bernardes was still just the president-elect—and exactly two years later in a rebellion in the city of São Paulo. Some of these rebels subsequently carried out a two-year trek around Brazil, marching through various parts of the country in an ultimately unsuccessful attempt to garner popular support for their cause. The trek became known as the Coluna Prestes,[8] or Prestes Column, named after one of the rebel leaders, Luiz Carlos Prestes, a man Sobral would get to know very well in the future. In addition to his dislike for the *tenentes* because they opposed his benefactor, Artur Bernardes, Sobral also believed that the soldiers who had rebelled were undisciplined, as they had gone against the sense of order they should have acquired in their military careers.

About this time, a crucial twist took place in his biographical trajectory. In 1927 Sobral Pinto—who five years earlier had married a family friend named Maria José Azambuja—had an extramarital affair with the wife of Paulo Gomide, the friend and director of the telegraph division previously mentioned. The affair—or perhaps more precisely the fallout from the discovery of the affair—changed Sobral from a loyal government bureaucrat to a lawyer who dedicated his life to struggling for freedom and human rights.

The year before Sobral's affair, Brazil had elected a new president. In those years, the two large coffee-producing states often alternated the national presidency between them in a system informally known as *café com leite*, coffee with milk, representing São Paulo and Minas Gerais, respectively. As President Bernardes was from Minas Gerais, the then governor of São Paulo, Washington Luís Pereira de Sousa, was chosen to replace him for the 1926–30 presidential term. Before leaving office, Bernardes recommended that Sobral Pinto remain in the *procurador criminal* position permanently, and Luís accepted the recommendation. When people became aware of Sobral's extramarital affair, however, he wrote a letter to the new president stating that he did not feel dignified enough to be the "public accuser" for the country. President Luís accepted his resignation and dismissed him from his position.[9]

After his dismissal, Sobral Pinto felt guilty and ashamed. To sort out his thoughts, he fled to the ranch of an acquaintance outside the city of Rio de Janeiro. Ultimately, his wife, Maria José, discovered where he was and went to the ranch to bring him home. Knowing his strong Catholic faith, Maria José, as well as some of Sobral's friends, suggested he speak to the bishop of Rio de Janeiro, Dom Sebastião Leme. The bishop absolved Sobral of his sins and told him to read *The Confessions* of St. Augustine, in which that Church Father discussed his own youthful transgressions. The talk strengthened the relationship between the two men, a relationship that endured for decades, as Sebastião Leme went on to become a cardinal, and Sobral Pinto became a prominent defense attorney. For their part, Heráclito and Maria José remained married for sixty-five years—until Maria José died, in 1987. She reportedly never referred to her husband's infidelity, and the couple raised seven children together.[10] Religiously tormented with the moral fault he had committed, Sobral was determined to lead a very ethical and ascetic life.

An avid reader, Sobral delved into the writings of St. Augustine as well as other Catholic authors, such as St. Thomas Aquinas, and he often used references to their works in his own work and writings. Always a devout Catholic, this man who had been a proactive agent of the arbitrariness of state power now discovered new ways to apply the truth of Jesus Christ above all transient institutions.

The affair itself may have faded from the public's attention but for the following incident. On September 22, 1928, as Sobral was leaving the Livraria Catolica, he was confronted by a highly agitated Paulo Gomide. In one hand Gomide held a whip; in the other, he brandished a love letter that Sobral had written to Gomide's wife. The two men fell to the ground in fisticuffs, and a passerby had to break up the fight. Sobral fled back into the bookstore to await the arrival of the police. His daughter, Gilda Sobral Pinto, has stated that her father never forgave himself for the scandal.[11]

The events surrounding the extramarital affair and its very public exposure—as the incident with Gomide was reported in most of Rio's newspapers—coupled with Sobral's own incapacity to forgive himself, led the still-young attorney to maintain an earlier decision to avoid any job in government and to embark on a very different career path. He borrowed office space in Rio de Janeiro and returned to private practice as an attorney. Some of his cases involved human and civil rights violations. As the national political environment changed, this work would grow, keeping him very busy over the following six decades—especially during the two periods of dictatorship Brazil experienced in the twentieth century: the Estado Novo of Getúlio Vargas (1937–45) and the twenty-one years of military rule after 1964.

Just as Sobral Pinto's life was undergoing drastic changes at the end of the 1920s and early 1930s, Brazil itself was also experiencing major upheavels. In an election held in March 1930, Julio Prestes was declared the winner over Getúlio Vargas. Although the results were questioned as fraudulent, initially Vargas decided not to contest them. In July of that same year, however, Vargas's former running mate in the March election, João Pessoa, was assassinated. Although the killing was later shown to be unrelated to the election, the event turned out to be the linchpin to what has gone down in history as the Revolution of 1930, and by the end of October of that year, Getúlio Vargas was installed as the provisional president of the country. He would remain in power for fifteen years.[12]

After the failure of the Prestes Column, Luís Carlos Prestes lived for some time in exile in Bolivia, but eventually made his way to Europe, ending up in Germany. By this time he had become a communist, and he met up with Arthur Ernest Ewert, aka Harry Berger, a member of the international communist organization—the Comintern—which had plans to take over the world. Prestes and Ewert had studied methods to bring about a communist takeover in Brazil, and they traveled to Prestes's home country sometime in 1935 to execute their plan. Part of the plan was to stir up domestic support for the takeover, and between November 23 and 27 of that year, uprisings were instigated in army bases in the cities of Natal, Recife, and Rio de Janeiro. But just as the Prestes Column had failed to garner support among the Brazilian people in the late 1920s, so this new attempt at rebellion also failed. Both Prestes and Berger were arrested.

After being turned down by a number of other attorneys, the Brazilian bar association asked Sobral Pinto to defend both Prestes and Berger, and despite his strong religious and anti-communist beliefs, he accepted the challenge. In some respects, defending Prestes and Berger was an impossible task, especially given the fact that neither man fully denied the main charges against them. Sobral concentrated his efforts on bettering the absolutely deplorable conditions in which his clients were held prisoner.

In an effort to assist Prestes and Berger, Sobral researched thoroughly, and he discovered a court case in which a man had been jailed for beating his horse to death. In addition, President Vargas had issued a decree, in 1934, in favor of the better treatment of animals, which stated:

> All animals in the country are under the protection of the State...[and] anyone who—either in a public or private location—mistreats animals will incur a fine...and a jail term of 2 to 15 days, whether said person is or is not the owner of the animal.

Maltreatment was considered to be any situation in which animals were maintained "in unhygienic conditions, or in locations that impede their respiration, their movement, or their rest." This fit his clients' situation almost perfectly. Shouldn't men be treated as at least equal to animals?

In addition to his own legal work, Sobral solicited the assistance of the Catholic bishop with whom he had spoken years earlier following his extramarital affair. Sebastião Leme, in 1930, had been raised by the pope to the level of cardinal and now had a close relationship with senior members of the Vargas government—including President Vargas himself. Cardinal Leme accepted Sobral's request and intervened for his former confessant's clients. Prestes and Berger were ultimately convicted and sentenced to lengthy prison terms—more than thirty years for the former and sixteen years for the latter. Through Sobral's persistence, however, the conditions of their incarceration did change at least partially for the better.

The sentence could have been even more severe. Sobral Pinto's line of legal actions sought to denounce the absence of the right to a fair defense as well as violations of human rights. Additionally, he argued that the accusations of multiple offenses were a mistake and that, therefore, the prosecution should consider only a single crime that would be linked to his clients' belief in communism and the dictatorship of the proletariat.[13] Luís Carlos Prestes, however, and his mother, Leocádia Prestes—who took an active role in his defense—refused the latter argument, saying that it was not a question of preaching authoritarianism: "Leocádia wrote Sobral that none of her son's manifestoes had called for the dictatorship of the proletariat."[14]

He was already the attorney of Luís Carlos Prestes when the case of Elza Fernandes became public in November 1940, four years after her death. Prestes authorized the killing of—in his own words—"a girl, a minor, who lived in obscurity." A comrade of the party, Elza Fernandes, a codename for Elvira Cupello Colônio, was arrested but then released by the police in an attempt to use her as bait to attract other members of the Partico Comunista do Brasil (PCB). Prestes guided his fellow members of the party to think about a possible crucial decision—that of eliminating one person for the sake of the party. He fired off words, full of macho values, asking his men not to be "fainthearted people, incapable of a decision, frightened in the face of responsibility."[15] The woman was strangled in 1936 by men associated with Prestes to save others they considered more important to the party and its cause.

With the trial of Prestes and Berger, the new legal mission of Heráclito Foutoura Sobral Pinto had begun. Sobral Pinto remained true to his conservative views despite his defense of communists, but he would now concern himself with the rights of citizens vis à vis state authority. Sobral received much criticism for his defense of Prestes and Berger. He had given special attention to the criticism of a close woman whose opinion was very important—his sister. A good summary of his thinking is found in the letter he wrote to his sister, Natalina, on January 11, 1937, thus before the horrible story of Elza became public. He explained his reasons for accepting the case as follows:

> Failing, in these conditions, to sponsor Luiz Carlos Prestes's cause would, Natalina, be an attempt against Christian charity. No one honored of being a Christian has the right not to extend his helping hand to someone, especially those who, like Luiz Carlos Prestes, find themselves insulted, reviled, and driven out of the lives of their fellow men.

In 1955 the country underwent another election for the highest office in the land. Sobral supported the candidate of the conservative União Democrática Nacional (UDN), Juarez Távora, a former *tenente* born in a small town of the state of Ceará. The two parties that had been founded by Getúlio Vargas, the Partido Trabalhista Brasileiro[16] and the Partido Social Democrático (PSD), joined forces to support the candidacy of the governor of Minas Gerais, Juscelino Kubitschek, who was also supported by the now-banned Brazilian Communist Party.

Kubitschek's running mate in the 1955 election was one of Getúlio Vargas's former ministers of labor, João Goulart, who many believed had close ties to the communists. Efforts were made to preclude the Kubitschek-Goulart ticket from participating in the electoral process. Despite having supported the UDN candidate, Sobral Pinto was instrumental in counter-efforts, in favor of democracy. Along with others, Sobral created the Liga de Defesa da Legalidade, whose "specific objective was to fight for the realization of the October 3rd elections that year and guarantee the inauguration of the elected, whoever they may be."[17]

Juscelino Kubitschek was very appreciative of Sobral Pinto's efforts in fighting for the legality of the election, and after he became president and an opening became available for a seat on the Supremo Tribunal Federal, he offered the position to Sobral. Sobral, however, turned down the offer, saying,

> It is a temptation from God, and I hope I have sufficient strength to resist. It has always been my dream—as an attorney and as a law professor—to be selected for a position on the Supreme Court. I cannot, however, accept something that will appear as though it was offered in exchange for a favor. It was not a favor, but only the defense of the law.[18]

In December 1968, soon after President Artur da Costa e Silva decreed *Ato Institucional Número Cinco* (AI-5) which, among other measures, denied *habeas corpus* rights to prisoners deemed to be dangerous to the country, Sobral himself was arrested. Although the seventy-five-year-old attorney was not physically abused in the ordeal, he was held in custody for a few days. While being processed at an army barracks, Sobral learned from the local commandant that he had been arrested because he worked to get communists released from prison. Sobral told the commandant that his comment was ignorant because it is the duty of judges, not attorneys, to order prisoners' release—if the judges verify abuses of power revealed by attorneys.[19]

Although he had initially favored the *coup d'état* that brought the military to power in 1964—because he agreed that João Goulart was too close to international communism—Sobral eventually defended numerous clients arrested by the military. As often as possible, he also provoked the authorities in his attempts to end their arbitrary use of power. Former President Juscelino Kubisthek and Carlos Lacerda, a famous journalist and politician, were both harshly persecuted during those hard times, yet Sobral defended each, saying, "There will be democracy in Brazil only when these two public men can stand in a public square in every corner of the country and plead their cases for the votes of their fellow citizens."[20]

In the 1984 political campaign of Diretas Já—a movement calling for direct presidential elections—the Brazilian people witnessed eighty-year-old Sobral Pinto in an encounter with the new generation. As told by his granddaughter, the filmmaker Paula Fiuza, her grandfather spoke to a crowd of over a million people, reminding them that *they*—the people—were the source of state power. Then he asked for the restoration of the first article of the first paragraph of the Brazilian Constitution: "All power emanates from the People, and in their name it should be exercised."[21]

Thought as ground for action

One of Sobral Pinto's best friends, until his tragic death in a drowning accident in 1928, was Jackson de Figueiredo, who had converted to Catholicism in 1918. Figueiredo was also friends with the archbishop of Rio de Janeiro, Sebastião Leme, as well as Leonel Franca, a Jesuit scholar who had been one of Sobral's roommates at Colégio Anchieta. Sobral Pinto and Jackson de Figueiredo had met while both were part of the Ministerio da Justiça in the Artur Bernardes government. They would often take long moonlit walks with other friends on the sidewalk along Ipanema Beach, discussing the events of the day as well as philosophical topics.[22] Jackson de Figueiredo was the role model for the generation of Catholic intellectuals associated with the Dom Vital Center, the organization he had founded in 1922. His materialistic perspective was deeply modified through personal interactions with Raimundo de Farias Brito, a philosopher from the state of Ceara, who lived in Rio de Janeiro beginning in 1909 and taught logic at Colégio Pedro II, a prestigious secondary school created by the imperial government in 1837.

A republican, Farias Brito had become greatly disillusioned with the type of republic established in Brazil in 1889, to the point of no longer believing in it. His writing featured a way to approach a subject in which the methodical affirmation of skepticism is the foundational grounding from which to arrive at the truth. A strong follower of metaphysics, partially based on the work of the German philosopher F.W.J. von Schelling, Farias Brito also criticized the positivism that had been the intellectual underpinning of many of the republic's founders. The scholar was a jurist who adhered to philosophical spiritualism with the goal of widening the comprehension of human thinking. He approached metaphysics as a means for the transcendence of reason in confrontation with experience, arguing that the existence of the spirit could not be contradicted by the empirical world. For him, we must value moral action in its intentionality, both free and creative. In his main work, *A Finalidade do Mundo* (*The purpose of the world*),[23] Farias Brito states that the principle of goodness could be a major historical actor. Sobral Pinto embodied at least some of Farias Brito's teachings, whether by coincidence or indirect influence.

For Figueiredo, the intellectual disciple of Farias Brito, socialism, liberalism, scientism, and Protestantism were not attractive choices, nor was he involved in masonry—even though Farias Brito had been a Mason. The Dom Vital Center published the periodical *A Ordem*, begun by Figueiredo in 1921. It supported the work of lay Catholic intellectuals under the leadership of Figueiredo. The social-democratic thinking of the group came from Alceu Amoroso Lima, also known by the pseudonym Tristão de Ataíde, who believed that the divisions between left and right were historical, given that politics is always subject to change. Such divisions might even be transient. Sobral Pinto's own trajectory demonstrates that his generation of intellectuals read a broad range of authors. There was a fluidity of ideas, constant dialogue, and conversions between large varieties of concepts.[24]

The first contribution of Sobral Pinto that one encounters on the online digital archive of *A Ordem* is "O Realista Político," published in 1929. The article is one of a series of tributes to his friend, Jackson de Figueiredo, who had died the year before. Sobral's intellectual background was conservative, distancing himself from fascist movements, such as the *Integralismo* of Plínio Salgado[25] and the populism of Getúlio Vargas. At the same time, Sobral Pinto was strongly opposed to any type of thought that came close to materialism.

In praise of Figueiredo, Sobral asserts that his friend wished to see control of the monopoly on violence exercised by civilians as opposed to the nation's military. It is essentially an idea about the rule of law more connected to authority than to democracy. While stressing that Figueiredo did not oppose freedom of the press, Sobral acknowledged that his friend did favor measures to control publications that practiced "harm, defamation, and insults."[26] He also emphasized Figueiredo's fear of the "mob," condemning policies made by "low popular passions" that destroyed rulers. Sobral also condemned the concentration of power in one central governing body. Figueiredo's leadership motivated the young Sobral Pinto in a sound realism infused with plenty of Brazilianness. He abhorred liberalism.[27]

Spiritualism was the doctrine that drove the governments of Brazil to a level absolutely beyond the ambitions of individual leaders.[28] The Catholic intellectuals who made up the Dom Vital Center opposed the militaristic foundation of the republic in 1889, while also regretting the separation of Church and state as established by the Constitution of 1891.[29] They believed that in order to guarantee that an authority will not be overpowered, it needs to command a mystical respect. Sobral wrote that according to his teacher and friend Figueiredo, "It is through force that authority is respected and loved."[30] Hence, in order for an authority to be of significant value to a society, it needed to be oriented by a perfect power, that is, by God. One should not, however, think that Sobral was a monarchist. Although he believed that the Catholic Church had lost much by its separation from the state, he was a republican who believed that public welfare could be protected only if it were grounded in religious morality, even in relation to the law and legal sciences.

"A Crônica Política," the political column that Sobral Pinto wrote between March 1931 and October 1933 in *A Ordem*, was a pretext to developing deductive rationales based on doctrinaire hypotheses, then testing those hypotheses in the real world. For Sobral Pinto, happiness did not come from rationalism. Rather, he believed, it came from spiritualism reconciled with faith and reason.[31]

Barreto Filho's essay "A Geração de Problemáticos"[32] takes the thought of Sobral Pinto into account. It analyzes the differences between capitalism and communism, seeing communism through the prism of a perfect world as a necessity for it to work. Barreto Filho also denies the argument that overcoming unhappiness is natural; that is, happiness is not attained by the spontaneous choice of the mind. Progress is a conscious action, yet just as human beings seek progress, they also seek revenge. Barreto Filho saw the Catholic Church as a synonym for a strong civilization.

Sobral Pinto also gave courses about communism and an introduction to law at the Dom Vital Center. In addition to having a strong emphasis in favor of the state, *A Ordem* addressed the coming together of owners, workers, and consumers. Under the guidance of Sobral Pinto, therefore, a militant brand of Catholicism developed which, while not rejecting reason, defended a type of spiritualism similar to that which had been philosphically defended by Raimundo de Farias Brito. In this way, it is possible to understand the strong influence of the members of the Catholic Dom Vital Center on the intellectual life of Brazil. Far from expressing a rigid connection to only the right or upper-class citizens, their views encompassed the entire philosophical spectrum, united by the idea of being engaged in the social and political life of the country.

At this same time, the Dom Vital Center started a student organization known as the Ação Universitária Católica (Catholic University Action, AUC), which included in its bylaws a full gamut of actions that could be taken by militants of the movement, establishing many possible interventions in society. The interventions ranged from the intellectual provocation of religious debates at universities to taking social action directly. One of the organization's goals was to "closely keep up with the public's problems—especially the problems of the proletariat."[33]

The AUC's bylaws did not include the democratic election of its president as one of its directives; it left up to the diocesan authorities the power to select a person for the office who had earned a diploma in any high-level area with more than one year of experience since the completion of his formal training or education. Similarly, a hierarchy of authority overrode everything else in the movement's organization. Unlike representative democracies, the term of office for the organization's president was lengthy. The president of the Rio de Janeiro district, for example, was elected to serve for six years.

Except perhaps from a European perspective, subjects concerning the history of the founding of the United States were not on the list of courses and debates at the Dom Vital Center. The goal was to flee from the US system, which was not regarded in its complexity, as well as from Bolshevism. Instead, Catholicism was seen as the proper solution for Brazil, a Brazil firmly rooted in Western civilization.

The values of Sobral Pinto were European, with full respect for a medieval and neoclassical type of authority. His ideas did not converge well with the doctrines of the Federalist Papers and a broader history of democracy in the United States. While that democracy is based on transparency and the public responsibility of public officials, Sobral Pinto believed in the strict obligations toward moral authority of public servants, and that only those who live up to its name could be called an authority. "Character, morality, order, discipline, work, authority, and law became strictly rational ideas, stripped of all that could place them within anything divine emanating from a Creator, a Lord of Everything."[34]

Although Sobral Pinto criticized the idea of a republic based on rationalism, this does not imply a total rejection of the legal traditions of the United States, the nation that inspired the Brazilian republic inaugurated in 1891, the Estados Unidos do Brasil. In defending a parochial judicial character in the acquisition and administration of goods, Sobral used the United States system of laws. He referred to legal pluralism to argue that canon law was a "regulator of the sacred rights"[35] according to the legal order established in 1891, in which the newly inaugurated framework coexisted with the medieval Christian system. "The proclaimers of the Brazilian republic, in destroying the empire and substituting it with a new system, wished to install a true democracy on Brazilian soil," and "toward that end, they looked to the great republic that was the bold pioneer of democratic institutions in this hemisphere."[36]

The inspiration for the above explanation is from a French source that Sobral Pinto had read to interpret the Brazilian circumstances at the time. Along with Latin, French was widely adopted by the educated elite of the Empire of Brazil. Its use lasted for decades into the twentieth century. The quote is from the book *L'Église catholique et la liberté aux États-Unis*,[37] published in 1892 by Camile de Meaux, the Viscount of Meaux. This French author oscillated between the center and the extreme right, but always decisively in favor of peace as well as an end to the exile laws of his country. He was the director of La Diana, a cultural association that promoted the study of history and archeology, and as such, he had more than a superficial view of the past.

In the second chapter of his book, which was about the development of Christian cults in the United States, he drew attention to the crimes of Europeans when he wrote, "The Indians were nearly destroyed before they were enlightened."[38] And in a later part of the book, he wrote that African Americans were "transported by them [the Europeans] to the new continent," and immediately "they were equally exploited and oppressed." If the Indians and black people still hoped for the promise of enlightenment, "the destruction of one race and the degradation of the other are a burden and a plague for the entire American civilization." Similarly, the Catholic thought espoused by the intellectuals of the Dom Vital Center inaugurated activism that, especially in later years, experienced oscillation between the political right and left.

In 1931, trying to find arguments based on European history, Sobral Pinto advocated for the use of a judicial system like that of the United States.[39] The European legal system had disintegrated in 1914 after the beginning of World War I, he argued, and the judicial system of the United States was a natural evolution that fortunately flourished as a result. It is a weird statement, and probably not entirely correct, but he emphasized this milestone of World War I repeatedly until his death. It seems a false impression. The US judicial system predated World War I by more than a century, so it did not arise from the war. It is not clear what effect, if any, the war or the undisciplined chaos brought about by that war had on the US judicial system. But the US system appeared to be a cure for what he identified as a breakup of order. For Sobral Pinto the common reasoning of the jurist had been recognized in light of a judicial review of the laws. He considered it revolutionary for the institutions. The problem for him was that the necessary reforms did not maintain the Christian tradition.

The attitude of Sobral Pinto the attorney was always in favor of supporting the coherent values of Christianity in society, as he well explained in what he wrote about the Berger case in 1937:

> Criminal or innocent, rich or poor, political ally or adversary, the incarcerated deserves to have his spirituality preserved by states which call themselves Christian. Public powers that maintain prisons must remain permanently capable of distinguishing this constant and embedded feature, which the crime may have caused to fall asleep but never to disappear: that spirituality, this sacred glimmer, is ingrained in the human flesh.[40]

In 1948, in the face of what he saw as the persecution of communists in Brazil, Sobral Pinto perhaps saw the United States differently—especially from the days when he was part of the Artur Bernardes administration. As his biographer Johnn W.F. Dulles explained:

> After [President] Dutra's party, the PSD, worked in Congress for the passage of a law project, introduced by Senator Ivo d'Aquino, declaring all PCB mandates extinct, Sobral, at the request of Prestes, produced a study for protecting the mandates.[41]

At the same time, Sobral felt that the archdiocese of Rio should not have supported President Dutra, as he believed this to be a betrayal of the workers.

A colorful anecdote offers a telling insight into this genius from Barbacena. When he was detained in Goiânia by the military one day after the declaration of the AI-5, in 1968, an army officer told him that AI-5 was decreed in order to establish a democracy *à Brasileira*—in the Brazilian style. Sobral retorted that there was no such thing as "a Brazilian democracy." He said that he was familiar with *peru à Brasileira*—a dish of turkey served in a Brazilian style—but that democracy is universal, without any adjectives.

Far from being just an amusing anecdote, this story demonstrates the consistent theoretical thinking of this prominent human rights attorney, journalist, and university professor. Sobral did not always develop his ideas in academic environments, but he did so through his essays, his articles, and, especially, the many letters he wrote over his long life. Fragments of his texts show him to be a coherent thinker with ideas that evolved over time, without ever straying from the political spectrum of a conservative defender of the rule of law, authority, and morality in support of order.

On April 1, 1977, using powers given to Brazilian presidents by the AI-5 decreed nine years earlier, President Ernesto Geisel—the penultimate of five army generals to hold the office of president during the twenty-one years of military rule after 1964—issued a new series of arbitrary decrees that came to be known as the *Pacote de Abril.* This "April Package" was basically a set of constitutional amendments that, among other measures, gave the executive branch the power to appoint a number of unelected federal senators and to have state governors indirectly elected, by electoral colleges, as opposed to directly by the people.[42]

Prior to issuing this new set of decrees, President Geisel gave a speech, basically outlining what was to come in this new package, and the speech was published in the *Jornal do Brasil.* Over the days following the speech, just before the April Package was decreed, Sobral Pinto wrote a letter in response to the president's speech. He said that Geisel had reiterated the xenophobic doctrine of militarism; that it was a move toward further authoritarianism and a break with Western judicial tradition. He was strong and direct:

> It is not possible, Mr. President, that you plan to use—for a civilized country such as Brazil—a system built on acts that revoke the constitution, permanently in some cases and sporadically in others. According to this model, if it even deserves that name, whenever the executive decides to change laws that have been voted upon by the national Congress—as the Institutional Act #5 of December 13, 1968, allows—and, your Excellency, this is done without any type of judicial control, as your decision allows, then—by decree—the executive power would be authorized to change any laws whenever it felt it convenient to do so, and base it on Institutional Act #5.[43]

Sobral completed his statement by saying, "such a system, Your Excellency, which causes instability, uncertainty, and fear, cannot be raised to the level of being a Brazilian model." In the second half of the 1970s, Sobral Pinto was in a sound position to criticize the military regime. He had shown that its discourse was fallacious:

> I was and am a man of order; I was and am a man of the law; I was, I am, and I always will be a man of rights, a man who wants to instill justice in the heart of my homeland.[44]

The Catholic University of Minas Gerais asked the already famous activist for a monograph, something that might support an academic award that the faculty was about to create, the Sobral Pinto Medal. The lecturer sent the school copies of newspaper articles, telegrams, and letters that composed *Lições de Liberdade* (*Lessons of freedom*). The book was published in 1977 and shortly afterward it went out of print. A new edition appeared the next year. Sobral Pinto was ready for the competition for the Premio Juca Pato, an award given annually to the "intellectual of the year" by a writers association in São Paulo. Another candidate was Gilberto Freyre, someone who had published numerous books over his lengthy career, with three publications in 1978 alone. Dr. Sobral had been much less dedicated to literary production than the famous sociologist, and some believed the judges were leaning towards Freyre. This changed, however, "when the Women's Movement for Amnesty came out for Sobral on account of his 'struggle for liberty and his moral qualities.'"[45] In addition, as Dulles wrote: "Eduardo de Oliveira, a well-established poet, declared: 'As a black writer, I vote for the intellectual Sobral Pinto...who never hesitated to place his talent in defense of the oppressed, among whom are a majority of the Afro-Brazilians.'"[46] It is not possible, however, to state that Sobral Pinto was always sensitive to specific issues of Afro-Brazilians, nor to those of women. Concerning the latter, for example, Dulles highlighted: "The most important role of women, he argued, was the one they carried out in the family at home."[47]

Born in a bucolic region of an interior state of Brazil, Sobral Pinto developed his ideas in a deceptively simple universe, a world whose existence he attributed to the historical environment before the tragic events of 1914. In an interview granted in his later years, when asked what advice he would give to young people—especially young attorneys — he said:

> I had known a legally organized world, but after World War I, all that changed. Violence came into the world, and, because of it, we now see a world in which law no longer works, where there is no respect for the law... This is a deadly, dangerous situation. Young attorneys must fight to get back to that pre-World War I conception of the law.[48]

Sobral Pinto, who said he did not believe in retiring, worked as an attorney up to his final year of life. In August 1991, he defended one of his sons in a labor dispute with a government office in Rio de Janeiro. He died in Rio on November 30, 1991, just a few weeks after his ninety-eighth birthday.

Conclusion

This narrative is undoubtedly about a controversial historical figure. As an ultraconservative Catholic, Sobral Pinto never adhered to the tenets of liberation theology, which he thought was a disguised form of Marxism, incompatible with the most authentic doctrines of the Catholic Church.[49] He also never expressed anything of substance identifying himself with Latin America. He was simply one of the most relevant figures among the group of Brazilian anti-materialist thinkers, and his advocacy was a tireless effort to defend the rule of law and democracy. Heráclito Fontoura Sobral Pinto was first and foremost a Brazilian patriot, and he believed in strong ties between Brazilian culture and the Christian values found in Western culture.

Notes

1 We are grateful for the information provided by Paula Fiuza. Moreover, we would like to acknowledge the help given by the scholar Leonardo Pinheiro, from Brasilia, where the library of the Federal Council of the Ordem dos Advogados do Brasil is located. According to Paula Fiuza, the Instituto Moreira Salles in Rio de Janeiro is the depositary of Sobral Pinto's correspondence as well as other documents from his personal collection. The institution has organized and catalogued the material for public consultation.
2 Dulles, *Sobral Pinto*, 2.
3 Dulles, *Resisting Brazil's Military Regime*, 3.
4 Dulles, *Sobral Pinto*, 4.
5 Scalercio, *Toda liberdade*, 14–29.
6 Someone from the state of Minas Gerais.
7 Dulles, *Sobral Pinto*, 5–6.
8 For the *Coluna Prestes*, see Macaulay, *The Prestes Column*; also Prestes, *A Coluna Prestes*.
9 Scalercio, *Toda liberdade*, 42–48.
10 Dulles, *Sobral Pinto*, 18–25.
11 Scalercio, *Toda liberdade*, 208.
12 On this period of Brazilian history, see mainly Bello, *History of Modern Brazil*; Burns, *History of Brazil*; Neto, *Getúlio: 1930–1945*; and Skidmore, *Brazil*.
13 Sobral Pinto, *Por que defendo*, 131–40.
14 Dulles, *Sobral Pinto*, 63.
15 Ibid., 98–99.
16 PTB, the Brazilian Labor Party—not to be confused with the later Partido dos Trabalhadores, or PT.
17 As source of general information, the authors of this chapter consulted entries available at https://cpdoc.fgv.br/ as is the case for Sérgio Lamarão, *FGV CPDOC*, 2009.
18 Caldeira, *Como Sobral Pinto se Tornou um Defensor de Presos Políticos*.
19 Dulles, *Resisting Brazil's Military Regime*, 141.
20 Scalercio, *Toda liberdade*, 267–68.
21 Fiuza, "Sobral Pinto," 2013.
22 Dulles, *Sobral Pinto*, 18.
23 Farias Brito, *Finalidade do Mundo*.
24 Velloso, "A Ordem."
25 Integralism itself, however, was recognized by the editors of *A Ordem*—for instance, in articles concerning the actions of Severino Sombra with the working class. According to Mônica Velloso (idem, 142): "As for the Integralist movement, the magazine assumes an attitude of veiled sympathy, never backing it openly." For more on the Anauê members, see Parente, *Anauê*.
26 Sobral Pinto, "O Realista Político," 310.
27 Ibid., 312.
28 Although he did not define the term, it is understood for the purpose of this chapter that the absolute is a perfect creation requiring power similar to a god. The omnipotence encompassed by sovereignty, whether individual or political, features the absolute for a political community. In totalitarianism, it compresses the space between humans, destroying their capacity to act and to begin. Lindsay, "Hannah Arendt." According to Lindsay: "What is clear, however, is that her [Hanna Arendt's] considerations of the problem of the absolute introduce an interpretive apparatus for considering political founding that pries apart the conventional associations of stability with 'conservatism' and novelty with 'radicalism.'" Ibid., 25.

29 Editorial Team of *A Ordem*, "Agonia Burguesa?"
30 Sobral Pinto, "O Realista Político," 313.
31 Sobral Pinto, "Crônica Política—De 18 de Março a 17 de Abril," 1931.
32 Barreto Filho, "A Geração de Problemáticos," 1931.
33 Ação Universitária Católica, "Estatutos da Ação Universitária Católica do Rio de Janeiro," 1931.
34 Sobral Pinto, "Crônica Política—De 18 de Março a 17 de Abril," 289.
35 Sobral Pinto, "A Personalidade Jurídica das Paróquias," 519.
36 Ibid., 513.
37 Meaux, *L'Église catholique*, 381.
38 Ibid., 37.
39 Sobral Pinto, "Crônica Política—De 18 de Fevereiro a 17 de Março," 225.
40 Sobral Pinto, *Por que defendo*, 73.
41 Dulles, *Resisting Brazil's Military Regime*, 7.
42 Skidmore, *Brazil*, 186.
43 Sobral Pinto, *Lições de Liberdade*, 179.
44 Sobral Pinto, *Não há justiça*, 1976.
45 Dulles, *Resisting Brazil's Military Regime*, 179.
46 Ibid.
47 Ibid., 3.
48 Sobral Pinto, *Mensagem de Sobral Pinto, Video on YouTube*, n.d.
49 This is supported by Sobral Pinto, *Teologia da Libertação.*

References

Ação Universitária Católica. "Estatutos da Ação Universitária Católica do Rio de Janeiro." *A Ordem*, 1931.

Barreto, Filho. "A Geração de Problemáticos." *A Ordem* (1931): 79–85.

Bello, José Maria. *A History of Modern Brazil, 1889–1964.* Stanford, CA: Stanford University Press, 1966.

Burns, E. Bradford. *A History of Brazil.* 3rd ed. New York: Columbia University Press, 1993.

Caldeira, Jorge. "Como Sobral Pinto se Tornou um Defensor de Presos Políticos" *SocializandoNoticiaseIdéias*, online journal, July 21, 2011, https://socializandonoticiaseideias.blogspot.com/2011/07/como-sobral-pinto-se-tornou-um-defensor.html.

CPDOC—Centro de Pesquisa e Documentação de História Contemporânea do Brasil. *FGV CPDOC*, 2017 https://cpdoc.fgv.br/.

Dulles, John W. F. *Resisting Brazil's Military Regime: An Account of the Battle of Sobral Pinto.* Austin: University of Texas Press, 2007.

Dulles, John W. F. *Sobral Pinto, the Conscience of Brazil: Leading the Attack against Vargas.* Austin: University of Texas Press, 2002.

Editorial Team of *A Ordem.* "Agonia Burguesa?" *A Ordem* (1931): 129–35.

Farias Brito, Raimundo de. *Finalidade do Mundo.* Rio de Janeiro: Instituto Nacional do Livro, 1957.

Fiuza, Paula. "Sobral Pinto Viu o Direito como uma Missão de Vida." *Conjur-Consultor Jurídico* 2013: https://www.conjur.com.br/2013-nov-02/entrevista-paula-fiuza-diretora-sobral-homem-nao-preco.

Lamarão, Sérgio. *FGV CPDOC*, 2009, http://www.fgv.br/cpdoc/acervo/dicionarios/verbete-tematico/liga-de-defesa-da-legalidade.

Lindsay, Adam. "Hannah Arendt, the Problem of the Absolute and the Paradox of Constitutionalism, or: 'How to Restart Time within an Inexorable Time Continuum.'" *Philosophy and Social Criticism* 43, no. 10 (2017): 1–36.

Macaulay, Neil. *The Prestes Column: Revolution in Brazil.* New York: New Viewpoints, 1974.

Meaux, Camille de. *L'Église catholique et la liberté aux États-Unis.* 2nd ed. Paris: Libraire Victor Lecofre, 1893.

Neto, Lira. *Getúlio, 1930–1945: Do Governo Provisório à Ditadura do Estado Novo.* São Paulo: Companhia das Letras, 2013.

Neto, Lira. *Getúlio, 1945–1954: De Volta pela Consagração Popular ao Suicídio.* São Paulo: Companhia das Letras, 2014.

Parente, Josênio Camelo. *Anauê, os Camisas Verdes no Poder.* Fortaleza: Universidade Federal do Ceará, 1986.

Prestes, Anita L. *A Coluna Prestes.* São Paulo: Brasiliense, 1990.

Scalercio, Márcio. *Toda liberdade é íngreme.* Rio de Janeiro: FGV Editora, 2014.

Skidmore, Thomas E. *Brazil: Five Centuries of Change.* New York: Oxford University Press, 1999.

Sobral Pinto, Heráclito Fontoura. "Crônica Política—De 18 de Fevereiro a 17 de Março." *A Ordem* (1931a): 223–34.

Sobral Pinto, Heráclito Fontoura. "Crônica Política—De 18 de Março a 17 de Abril." *A Ordem* (1931b): 286–97.

Sobral Pinto, Heráclito Fontoura. *Lições de Liberdade.* Belo Horizonte: Editora Comunicação, 1977.

Sobral Pinto, Heráclito Fontoura. *Mensagem de Sobral Pinto aos jovens.* Globo News. Video on YouTube.

Sobral Pinto, Heráclito Fontoura. "Não há justiça, diz Sobral Pinto." *Folha de São Paulo* (1976): 6.

Sobral Pinto, Heráclito Fontoura. "A Personalidade Jurídica das Paróquias." *A Ordem*, (1941): 510–20.

Sobral Pinto, Heráclito Fontoura. *Por que defendo os comunistas.* Belo Horizonte: Universidade Católica de Minas Gerais, 1979.

Sobral Pinto, Heráclito Fontoura. "O Realista Político." *A Ordem* (1929): 306–17.

Sobral Pinto, Heráclito Fontoura. *Teologia da Libertação: o Materialismo Marxista na Teoria Espiritualista.* Rio de Janeiro: Lidador, 1984.

Velloso, Mônica Pimenta. "A Ordem: uma Revista de Doutrina, Política e Cultura Católica." *Revista de Ciência Política* (1978) 21: 117–60.

29 Julio Tobar Donoso (Ecuador, 1894–1981)

Álvaro R. Mejía-Salazar

The Republic of Ecuador has long been characterized as a Catholic nation. It is the birthplace of men and women who have, over time, come to be held as symbols of Christendom, such as Saint Mariana de Jesús, Saint Narcisa de Jesús, Saint Hermano Miguel, and the Blessed Emilio Moscoso Cárdenas, SJ. From the realm of secular life, many other Ecuadorians have come to be seen as examples of Catholicism; it is within their daily lives, family activities, and professional work that they seek to embody the Kingdom of God on Earth. From transcendental public figures like President Gabriel García Moreno, who was responsible for consecrating the fatherland to the Sacred Heart of Jesus Christ, to the nation's ordinary people, who are committed to their faith, there are many Ecuadorians to whom I could refer as archetypes of devout Catholics. Among those, one of the most notable is Dr. Julio Tobar Donoso.

Tobar Donoso was one of the great scholars of Ecuador, taking an active role in all aspects of national life for most of the twentieth century. While a noted legal expert, diplomat, historian, and professor, he was first and foremost a Catholic. Tobar Donoso was an exponent of an intellectual Catholicism, fully devoted to dogma. He wrote entire volumes in which he expounded upon and explained the social doctrine of the Catholic Church; he researched and informed the public on the history of the Ecuadorian Church and defended the fundamental role that it played in the nation's birth, consolidation, and progress. Although in his diplomatic life he would come to endure horrible setbacks, he faced them with Christian serenity. In his professional practice, he was always keen to put Christian values above any worldly whim, and he came to be known as a legal scholar and virtuous magistrate of the highest court of the Ecuadorian justice system. In his personal life as well, he was always attuned to his religious philosophy and affiliation. This was yet another of the many virtues that filled out the exemplary person that he was and further buttresses his reputation as a representative figure of what it means to be a Christian person, especially in today's world.

Biographical information

Born in Quito, Ecuador, on January 25, 1894, Julio Tobar Donoso completed his elementary education in schools closely related to the Church. His charisma was pointedly reinforced by the Jesuit education that he received at San Gabriel School. He was twelve years old when the miracle of Our Lady of Sorrows occurred, an event witnessed by several of his classmates. This holy event sent waves not only through the student body of his Jesuit school but through the city and the entire country as well. Not even the liberal government in power at the time was able to dampen the uplifting presence of Saint Mariana.[1]

Tobar Donoso was involved in social issues from a very young age. While still a schoolboy, he became part of the Catholic Workers' Guild, over which he would later preside. While in high school, he began to write for gazettes—*El Republicano* (*The Republican*), *El Porvenir* (*The Future*), and *La Corona de María* (*The Crown of Mary*). This work was a product of his friendship with the revered priest Father Manuel José Proaño, SJ, who was a spiritual mentor to Tobar Donoso and instilled in him the unbending responsibility of being a Catholic intellectual.[2]

Tobar Donoso studied law in Quito at the Central University of Ecuador, and in 1915, while still a university student, he joined the Conservative Party. He continued polishing his skills as a writer, and one of his student essays, "Observaciones sobre la quiebra de los deudores solidarios" ("Observations on the bankruptcy of joint and several debtors," 1916), was published in the *Anales de la Universidad Central de Ecuador* No. 40 (*Annals of the Central University of Ecuador* No. 40). On March 7, 1917, he successfully completed his final exams to receive the degree of juris doctor from the Supreme Court of Justice of Ecuador seven days later. His thesis was titled "La letra de cambio, su forma y capacidad para obligarse por ella" ("The bill of exchange, its format, and ability to be bound by it").[3] In that same year, his study about the immunity from seizure enjoyed by family estates was published in the *Revista de la Sociedad Jurídico Literaria* (*The Journal of the Legal Literary Society*), twelve years before the issue was ever addressed in the national constitution.[4] After graduation, Tobar Donoso took a job as legal adviser at the Banco Hipotecario del Ecuador (Mortgage Bank of Ecuador). [5]

In 1918 he joined the Sociedad Ecuatoriana de Estudios Americanos, an organization which in 1920 was elevated by the legislature to the National Academy of History of Ecuador. On joining the group, he gave a speech titled "Las segundas elecciones de 1875, luego de la muerte de Gabriel García Moreno" ("The second elections of 1875, after the death of Gabriel García Moreno"), which was published in volume one, number two, of the society's gazette. That year he also joined the Congregation of the Knights of the Immaculate Conception[6] and published *Génesis y antecedentes de las ideas sociales cristianas* (*Genesis and background of social Christian ideas*). In 1923 he published *García Moreno y la instrucción pública* (*García Moreno and public education*); the second edition was printed in 1940. In 1924 he published *El Obispo de Botren Dr. José Miguel de Carrión y Valdivieso* (*The Bishop of Botren Dr. José Miguel de Carrión y Valdivieso*), as well as *Relaciones entre la Iglesia y el Estado Ecuatoriano* (*Church–state relations in Ecuador*). He was a member and president of Catholic Action, in close collaboration with his longtime friend Archbishop Manuel María Pólit. In 1925 he edited *Desarrollo constitucional de la República del Ecuador* (*Constitutional development of the Republic of Ecuador*); its second edition came out in 1936. In 1926 he published a series of biographies of celebrated nineteenth-century Catholics in a newspaper called *La Defensa* (*The Defense*). These biographies were published together in 1928 in an anthology titled *Figuras del catolicismo social* (*Figures of Social Catholicism*) .[7] In 1928 his comments on a proposed education law were published in the press.

The Ecuadorian Academy of Language inducted Tobar Donoso as a member in 1929. To become a formal member, he had to give a speech, which he titled "La oratoria política en el Ecuador" ("Political oratory in Ecuador"). He was then welcomed into the group by the legal scholar Clemente Ponce. In that same year, he published *El Ilmo. and Rvdo. Sr. Dn. Ignacio Checa y Barba*, and the following year he edited *Por la libertad de enseñanza* (*For the freedom of education*).[8] Between 1930 and 1937, he became the most vocal defender of the rights of the Church in his editorials, which were published in important newspapers and magazines. In these editorials, he expounded upon the doctrine of Pope Leo XIII, the guiding role of the Catholic Church, and the mission of Catholics in furthering labor causes. In other words, he developed Christian democratic content and principles.

In 1933 Tobar Donoso reviewed many of the files held in the archives of the Office of the President in Quito, along with those in the Ministry of Government, the Ministry of Foreign Affairs, the Congress, the Curia, and several convents. This work resulted in a book titled *La Iglesia ecuatoriana en el Siglo XIX* (*The Ecuadorian Church in the nineteenth century*), which he edited in 1934. The next year, he left his job at the Banco Hipotecario del Ecuador after being named legal adviser and member of the Ministry of Foreign Affairs Advisory Board. He was entrusted with the negotiations that led to execution of the *Modus Vivendi* in 1937, an international treaty that to this day governs relations between the Catholic Church and Ecuador.

Appointed as minister of foreign affairs by President Manuel María Borrero in 1938, he found time that year to publish *Los orígenes constitucionales del Ecuador* (*The constitutional origins of Ecuador*). In November of the same year, he presided over the Ecuadorian delegation to the Eighth Pan-American Conference in Lima. Tobar Donoso was at the helm of the Ecuadorian Chancery in 1941 when Peru invaded Ecuador, and he remained in that post during the war that followed. While he was minister, he edited *Exposición del Ministro de Relaciones Exteriores a los Cancilleres de América* (*Exposition by the minister of foreign affairs to other American foreign affairs ministers*), a book intended to buttress Ecuador's diplomatic image across South America. His diplomatic expertise was valued by several successive presidents of the republic, and following his first appointment in 1938, by Manuel María Borrero, he continued as minister of foreign affairs under presidents Aurelio Mosquera Narváez (1939), Carlos Alberto Arroyo del Río (1939), Andrés F. Córdova (1939), Julio Enrique Moreno (1940), and Carlos Alberto Arroyo del Río once again (1940).[9]

In January 1942 Tobar Donoso presided over the Ecuadorian delegation at the Pan-American Summit of foreign ministers, held in Rio de Janeiro. On January 29 of that year, Ecuador and Peru signed the Rio de Janeiro Protocol. On one hand, the protocol put an end to the war between the two nations, which had become progressively worse since 1941, but on the other hand, it sliced away large sections of Ecuadorian territory in the coastal and Amazon regions. In reference to this somber period in Tobar Donoso's life, Rodolfo Pérez Pimentel has commented:

> On returning to Quito, Francisco Chiriboga Bustamante said to him: "It is a shame you signed that; we wanted to make you president." Tobar responded: "I have sacrificed my own ambitions for the nation's continued existence." The fact of the matter was that Tobar Donoso was correct, since the reality of the situation was difficult to face. There were not enough weapons to defend the borders, and two provinces were occupied by the Peruvian military, which was threatening to overtake the city of Guayaquil. Worst of all, our army was disorganized and reckoning with defeat. With World War II on the international stage, nations of the American hemisphere paid little attention to our problem. On the diplomatic front, through the Herrera-García Treaty of 1890, Ecuador had recognized as Peruvian soil everything that it had on the left bank of the Amazon River. On signing the protocol, Tobar established a new border that ensured the nation's existence. [10]

Popular opinion, however, did not share that view of the protocol, and Tobar Donoso suffered a level of repudiation so unprecedented that he wound up resigning as foreign minister soon after returning to Quito. From then on, he lived quietly with the insolence of ill-wishers and demagogues who accused him of showing too much weakness in signing the protocol, without their realizing that the only true weakness had lain in the republic itself and its beaten-down army. The wise Aurelio Espinosa Pólit, SJ, with whom Tobar would later undertake an ambitious educational project that I will address further in this chapter, remarked with his characteristic Christian benevolence about the repudiation to which Tobar Donoso fell victim:

> When people are unable to judge such intricate events for themselves, they are not responsible for the injustices that they commit, particularly when they are insidiously misled. But in cases like this, who engenders the evil, if not such misled people? Nothing is more degrading than that cowardly injustice that implicates innocent parties in that which is attributable to a phantom guilty party. It would constitute a patriotic effort to help the Ecuadorian people to understand the disastrous error that constituted blaming our 1941 misfortunes on a man who did everything humanly possible to prevent them, and who heroically sacrificed his own fortunes to stop a temporary disaster from spelling the end of our nation. When the true history is finally revealed, and people come to understand the reality of what happened

> at that most terrible hour, when the country's very survival was at risk, and how, faced with the threat of brute force, that risk was averted through the split-second decision to surrender; once people understand the agony that a patriotic soul had to endure to decide to make such a cruel sacrifice, and the unprecedented courage needed to take on such immense responsibility... only then will people come to understand just how much the Ecuadorian nation owes to Dr. Julio Tobar Donoso.[11]

At the end of 1942, Tobar Donoso's writings appeared in *Dictámenes jurídicos acerca del problema ecuatoriano-peruano, dados por ilustres internacionalistas americanos* (*Legal opinions on the Ecuadorian-Peruvian issue, offered by celebrated American international specialists*), which was published in a two-volume set. During that same year, he published the book *Cooperativas y mutualidades* (*Cooperatives and mutual institutions*), in which he explained why such systems were so useful to the development of the country's most disadvantaged social classes. In 1943 he became a founding member of the Ecuadorian Cultural Institute and actively collaborated with Father Aurelio Espinosa Pólit, SJ, to publish several works. His voluminous book *La invasión peruana y el Protocolo de Río de Janeiro* (*The Peruvian invasion and the Rio de Janeiro Protocol*) appeared in 1945.

The following year, he became a member of the Comité de Caballeros (Knights' Committee), which advocated for freedom of education, and he received the Great Cross of the Order of St. Gregory the Great from the Vatican. That year, too, he worked with the Quito Catholic University exploratory committee, traveling to Bogotá to learn about the experiences of their Javerian University. On November 4, 1946, Tobar Donoso, along with Espinoza Pólit, founded the Universidad Católica, taking the helm of its school of law. In 1947 he published his *Estudio sobre límites ecuatoriano-peruano* (*Study on Ecuadorian-Peruvian borders*), and the next year he wrote *Apuntes para la historia de la educación laica en el Ecuador* (*Reflections on the history of secular education in Ecuador*). [12]

Elected president of the (now defunct) Ecuadorian Institute of Hispanic Culture in 1951, Tobar Donoso produced a spate of important works over the next few years, editing the book *Elementos de la Ciencia Política* (*Elements of political science*) in 1951,[13] publishing one of his most important works, *La Iglesia, modeladora de la nacionalidad* (*The Church: carving out nationality*) in 1953 (receiving an award for it from the Quito Municipality), followed by *Derechos y deberes de los patronos y trabajadores del campo* (*Rights and duties of rural employers and workers*) that same year, and then in 1954 editing the book *Evolución de las ideas pedagógicas en el Ecuador* (*Evolution of ideas on pedagogy in Ecuador*), which provided information about pedagogy during the colonial, republican, and modern periods through 1953. In 1956, he published *El pensamiento jurídico de Pío XII* (*Legal thought of Pope Pius XII*).

Tobar Donoso was appointed in 1959 as judge of the First Courtroom of the Supreme Court of Justice of the Republic of Ecuador, the nation's highest court.[14] The following year, he wrote several prologues and introductory pieces that appeared in the amazing *Biblioteca Ecuatoriana Mínima* (*Minimum Ecuadorian Library*), put together following the failed Eleventh Pan-American Conference, which was supposed to be held in Quito in 1961. He edited *Lenguaje rural en la región interandina del Ecuador* (*Rural language in the inter-Andean region of Ecuador*) in 1961 and followed that the next year with a biography of Pedro Gual, a Venezuelan lawyer and diplomat.

Elected president of the Ecuadorian Supreme Court of Justice in 1965, he was opposed by the military dictatorship at the time and he was forced to resign. That year, he was appointed as director of the Ecuadorian Academy of Language, and in 1968 he was again elected president of the Supreme Court of Justice of Ecuador.

When he left his position as judge of the First Courtroom of the Ecuadorian Supreme Court of Justice in 1970, he left behind twelve volumes of rulings. Named professor emeritus of the Catholic University School of Law in 1972, he left behind teaching and the deanship, a post that he had held since 1949. Continuing his writing, however, in 1974 he edited *Las instituciones del período hispánico, especialmente en la Presidencia de Quito* (*The institutions of the Hispanic period, especially in the Office of the President of Quito*), and in 1976 he published a voluminous work with the biographies of *Los Miembros de Número de la Academia Ecuatoriana muertos en el primer siglo de su existencia* (*Members of the Ecuadorian Academy who died during the first century of its existence*). His last book appeared in 1979: *El tratado de Guayaquil de 1829* (*The Treaty of Guayaquil of 1829*).[15] Tobar Donoso suffered chronic bronchitis during his last years of life and died with no declared cause on March 10, 1981 at the age of eighty-seven.

The attorney

The legal bibliography attributed to Tobar Donoso is extensive and comprises both books and essays. His work focused on topics in the areas of commercial law, political law, territorial law, and diplomacy, along with employment law, and social law. Some of his most important works are: *Desarrollo constitucional de la República del Ecuador*, *La junta consultiva del trabajo* (*The Labor Advisory Board*, 1926), *Cooperativas de consumo* (*Consumer cooperatives*, 1926), *Los socios de las cajas rurales* (*Members of rural savings banks*, 1926), *Hacia la sindicalización obrera* (*Towards worker unionization*, 1932), *Los orígenes constitucionales del Ecuador*, *Exposición del Ministro de Relaciones Exteriores a los Cancilleres de América*, *Cooperativas y mutualidades*, *Estudio sobre límites ecuatoriano-peruano*, *Elementos de la Ciencia Política*, *Derechos y Deberes de los patronos y trabajadores del campo*, *La doctrina Uti Possidetis* (*The Uti Possidetis Doctrine*, 1957–58), *Derecho Territorial Ecuatoriano* (*Ecuadorian territorial law*, 1961), *El Modus Vivendi con la Santa Sede*, and *El tratado de Guayaquil de 1829*.

It is clear that Tobar Donoso had a wide range of interests in law. While he began with a focus on commercial and international law, his interest in Catholic social doctrine inspired him to delve into issues related to employment law and the study of cooperatives. This led him to apply several of the most important

Christian theories throughout his professional life without losing the grasp on objectivity so direly needed by attorneys. He was never small-minded in any area of his life, but on the contrary, he was always mindful to share his knowledge and ideology with anyone who sought it out and, in general, with society at large through his numerous published works.

One should remember that Tobar Donoso was born shortly before the radicalization of atheist and Masonic liberalism in Ecuador, so it is not striking that, in his adulthood, he was convinced of the need for a university in which Catholic charisma would be the emblem of professional training for young people, particularly for those studying law. It was this conviction that led him, along with Father Aurelio Espinosa Pólit, SJ, to found the Catholic University of Quito, which later was recognized as the Pontifical Catholic University of Ecuador. Tobar Donoso himself explained this spirit of education:

> Catholic universities cannot be considered as mere laboratories of sterile, useless science that, in its own haughtiness, isolates itself from life and relinquishes its responsibility to direct it. No! Catholic universities are a means for perfecting and improving Christian conscience, a living machine for the formation of genuine intellectual and moral aristocracies which, to elevate their own thinking through vigorous preparation for creative action, and because of their conviction and energy for faith as well as the variety and unconquerable efficacy of their methods, are called on to transform, through Christian sensibility, the very face of their nations.

Here, Tobar Donoso held the post of law school dean for twenty-five years, piloting the faculty to be recognized as the best legal program in the country for many decades. Tobar Donoso imprinted on the school's very essence his firm belief in student, professional, and personal excellence. Francisco Salazar Alvarado, one of his students, has remembered him this way:

> Day after day, we watch as the illustrious dean walks through the old classrooms with his demanding yet peaceful gaze. His daily work consists of attending and guiding students through their problems and difficulties. We watch him sternly and calmly stand before his classes with the serenity of a man of science whose foundations are built on granite. He is unflappable against the whipping winds of the world and shows no fears when facing life's twists and turns. His serenity is one that can be experienced only by those whose feet are firmly planted on the ground by their own humanity, but whose thoughts have been tightly tethered to God himself. Political science, which serves as the most important foundation of legal studies, is entrusted to his scholarly teaching. His work is not a mere text of vulgar content, but rather a treatise on political law that is the result of mature, profound meditation, summarizing schools of thought and theories that have spread out across that which is the science of the state. He has a definitive command of the subject of constitutional law, with deep understanding of

> everything related to Ecuadorian territorial law, along with profound knowledge of international law and sociology, athough I could easily continue listing more areas here.[16]

As mentioned above, besides his noteworthy professional, doctrinal, and teaching work, Julio Tobar Donoso became a magistrate of the Supreme Court of Justice of Ecuador, where he was on the bench for twelve years, twice elected president of the highest court in the land in 1965 and 1968. As a judge, he was highly respected, and his writing on jurisprudence was prolific, including the volume *Doctrina sobre Derecho Sucesorio* (*Doctrine on the law of successions*, 1968). His long period serving on the nation's court was characterized by his honesty and mastery of laws when called upon to administer justice. One of his contemporaries, another prominent attorney and professor, Dr. Guillermo Bossano Valdivieso, described Tobar this way:

> Called upon to wield justice, he served on the Supreme Court of Ecuador. What rulings, what upright thinking, depth, and profoundness in concepts, what knowledge of our laws, what breadth of spirit to lay out the argument, fully study it, and give to each person that which is rightly their own.[17]

Another prominent magistrate of the Supreme Court, Dr. Gonzalo Zambrano Palacios, referred to Tobar Donoso's time as a judge this way:

> We could say that, at first, his presence on the Supreme Court provoked expectations. No one doubted his mental acumen and his vast, diverse scholarship. However, everyone was waiting to see how the new justice would rise to the challenge before him. Dr. Tobar was not only up to this incredible responsibility that had been assigned to him; he went above and beyond the calling, engaging with lawyers and judges having a great depth of scholarship and experience…It is gratifying to say that Dr. Tobar Donoso's presence on the Supreme Court of Justice also gave judges and magistrates, along with legal professionals and those appearing before the court, the opportunity to have direct contact with the man and become enraptured by his finesse and exquisite, perfected discourse. When faced with him, one immediately had the sensation of unforgettable and delightful dehiscence.[18]

In this way, Julio Tobar Donoso forged a legacy in legal doctrine, university professorship, and the judiciary. Without a doubt, his most important contribution to the legal field was the foundation and consolidation of one of the nation's most important law schools, which even today continues to mold excellent attorneys.

The Catholic intellectual

Julio Tobar Donoso was a Catholic man first, then an intellectual. His faith guided his life and the many activities that he undertook throughout it. His intellectual work reflected his clear decision to study and disseminate Catholic ideology. He published studies of Catholic doctrine and Church history so prolifically that his publications on these topics outnumber even those on legal subjects. In fact, his first writings on Church doctrine and history appeared early in his youth and were related to denominational matters. History tells us that he began buying books at seven years of age, and his personal library eventually totaled 23,226 books and journals (today preserved by the Society of Jesus).

His endless hours of reading and archival research enabled him to become a prolific author of Catholic subject matter. Some of his most important works related to Catholic doctrine include the following: *Génesis y antecedentes de las ideas sociales cristianas* (1918), *Acción social católica* (1926), *San Francisco de Asís, reformador social* (1926), *Figuras del catolicismo social* (1928), *El catolicismo, filosofía suprema de la solidaridad* (1932), *Teología de un prodigio* (1934), *La soberanía de la Iglesia* (*The sovereignty of the Church*, 1936), *Neutralidad o irreligión* (*Neutrality or irreligion*, 1936), *Catolicismo social* (1936), *Los Hermanos de las EECC y la renovación pedagógica en el Ecuador* (*The friars of Christian schools and pedagogical reform in Ecuador*, 1938), *González Suárez, defensor por excelencia en el Ecuador de la libertad de la Iglesia* (1944), *Estudios religiosos* (1944), *El P. Matovelle y la acción social en el Ecuador* (1946), *La Eucaristía, sacramento de unidad* (1949), *La Iglesia modeladora de la nacionalidad* (1953), and *El pensamiento político de S.S Pío XII* (1957). The theories expounded in these works did not lie alone as mere rhetoric, since Tobar Donoso was an activist of faith. He worked tirelessly as a member of the Third Order of San Francisco, as well as of the Mariana Congregation of Knights of the Immaculate, never missing their biweekly meetings. He was also a Salesian cooperator and member of the Conference of St. Vincent de Paul.[19]

Some of his most outstanding titles on Church history are: *El R.P.F. José Primo Betancourt* (1918), *El Dr. Pedro José de Arteta* (1918), *Benedicto XV* (1922), *El obispo de Botren, Dr. José Miguel de Carrión y Valdivieso* (1924), *El cardenal Gibbons* (1926), *San Francisco de Asís* (1926), *El ilustrísimo y reverendísimo Sr. Dr. Ignacio Checa y Barba* (1929), *La tradición mariana del Ecuador desde la conquista hasta el año 1906* (*The Mariana tradition of Ecuador, from the Conquest to 1906*, 1931), *La Iglesia ecuatoriana en el siglo XIX* (1934), *El primer centenario del nacimiento del padre Proaño* (*The first centenary of Father Proaño*, 1935), *Un religioso insigne, el R.P. Manuel Fez Córdova* (1936), *El R. P. José María Le Gouhir y Raud S.J.* (1940), *El Ilmo. señor Borja Yerovi* (1949), *Santa Mariana de Jesús* (1950), *El milagro de Isabel La Católica* (1951), *Centenario glorioso: Los Jesuitas en el Ecuador* (1951), *Pío XII, terciario franciscano* (1953), *Una aurea página mariana en el Ecuador* (*A golden Mariana page in Ecuador's history*, 1954), *La soberana del Ecuador* (*She who watches over Ecuador*, 1954), *Un nuevo mapa de las misiones ecuatorianas* (*A new map of Ecuadorian missions*, 1955), *A la más alta gloria* (*To the highest glory*, 1970), and *La diócesis de 1845 a 1851* (1979).

In the end, it was impossible for him to separate his faith from his profession, which led him to produce important studies in which he made a deep analysis of the legal aspects of the Church as well as the connection between earthly and divine powers. His most representative works on this subject include: *Relaciones entre la Iglesia y el Estado Ecuatoriano* (1924), *El problema religioso, la próxima Constitución y los católicos ecuatoriano* (1925), *El primer concordato ecuatoriano* (1932), *El Modus Vivendi y la enseñanza libre* (1938), *Relaciones entre la Iglesia y el Estado ecuatoriano* (1938), *Las personas eclesiásticas en el Ecuador* (1951), *El pensamiento jurídico de S.S Pío XII* (1956), *La reclamación de los obispos chilenos de 1956 y la reforma del Código Civil ecuatoriano* (*The claims of Chilean bishops of 1956 and reforms to the Ecuadorian Civil Code*, 1956), *S.S Pío XII y los concordatos* (1958), *Iglesia y Estado en las primeras constituciones de la Gran Colombia* (1961), *El Modus Vivendi con la Santa* (1961), *La Constituyente de 1945 desde el punto de vista religioso* (1971), and *La política religiosa del presidente Roca* (*The religious policy of President Roca*, 1972).

Tobar Donoso's erudition is absolutely clear, as is his inclination toward the development and diffusion of ecclesiastical issues. To this day, he continues to be one of the Ecuadorian laypersons who have contributed the most to the study of Church affairs, especially its social doctrine and history in the Republic of Ecuador. His prose is neat and elegant, and his ideas are well supported and explained. At a time when the intelligentsia was practically required to be atheist, Tobar Donoso wrote many volumes on Catholic issues. On this matter, he wrote in the preamble to his book *La Iglesia ecuatoriana en el siglo XIX*:

> Truthfulness and impartiality do not mean glacial indifference, nor do they require abandonment of one's convictions. No sensible historian should, nor can ever, drown the voices of the soul, stifle the cry of condemnation and protest that injustice spontaneously rips from the chest of every well-born man. Such a story, in which the writer's spirit was absent, would be good for morally fallow people. Not here; this book contains the beating heart of a faithful Catholic who places his love for the church of Jesus Christ above all other loves, and for whose pen faith is at once the lighthouse and northern star.[20]

In what may well be one of his most famous works, *La Iglesia, modeladora de la nacionalidad*, Tobar Donoso took on the task of demonstrating the decisive influence of Catholicism in shaping what today we know as the Ecuadorian nation. Tobar Donoso showed the Church's role in "nation building" through its participation in organizing the first towns after the Conquest and its evangelization, which included Indigenous peoples in the new, mixed-race societies and offered the Indigenous protection by prelates, which lay in clear distinction from the mistreatment such peoples had suffered at the hands of their landowner bosses. The Church also undertook evangelization missions in the territory's eastern rainforest, founding and maintaining hospitals, schools, and universities. Tobar Donoso also focused on the role of the Church in developing the arts and, therefore, the direct responsibility that it had on the nation's cultural treasures. He ended by highlighting the Church's role in the nineteenth century in the emergence of a new regime following independence and the consolidation of the republic, from both a social and an educational perspective.[21]

Tobar Donoso's contribution to people's understanding and valuing of the Church's contribution to society and the Ecuadorian state, from its colonial roots to its consolidation as a sovereign republic, was fundamental during a period when attacks on faith perniciously disfigured an institution that had gone above and beyond its calling and, in reality, was fundamental to the existence of the Ecuadorian nation as we know it. The significance of this book was such that Pope John Paul II, in his speech on January 30, 1985, at the Church of the Society of Jesus, in Quito, said, "Given the high human values of this nation, having the seal of the Christian faith, it is only correct to remember your illustrious compatriot who defined the church as a force that served to carve out Ecuadorian nationality."[22]

On the issue of sociopolitical philosophy, Tobar Donoso's commitment to the Church's social doctrine was absolute. As mentioned, he published several works focused on the analysis and communication of Christian social philosophy, with a special emphasis on the reality of workers. This is evidenced by the fact that from a young age he became involved as an intellectual in the Catholic Workers' Guild. Tobar Donoso called for the active implementation of Catholic ideals in solving the economic problems of workers, without accepting the possibility of eschewing that responsibility and demonstrating apathy. He opted for the opposite of indifference: the indispensable urgency of social action, seeking out youth to take on the vocation of those efforts. In his book *Catolicismo social*, he put together a set of social articles inspired by the Catholic ideal. His conservative conviction led him to severely criticize the excesses of economic liberalism and communist socialism. In this book, Tobar Donoso stated:

> The church fights economic liberalism and socialism: against the first, because with its deleterious principles, it has been the cause of social problems, given the trust placed in the value of freedom, which at one point was seen as the panacea of all the world's ailments; and against the second, because with its imagined utopia, it attempts to violate social facts and accommodate them to a schoolyard fantasy, to make them a religion, containing the ocean of human destiny within the narrow borders of Earth, promising an impossible happiness that is not its to offer…Justice and charity: these are the two areas of leverage that the church uses to achieve social reform. The church, unlike liberalism or individualism, does not believe that freedom is sufficient to cure the ailments of humanity and to reconcile, through the spontaneous and automatic play of conflicting interests, the rights of capitalists and workers.

The social direction that Tobar Donoso proposed was always firmly based on the authenticity of a Christian life, which, rooted in love among all people, is gradually reinforced in the framework of justice and morality. Tobar Donoso always put his pen at the service of the Church, as an author, a speaker, an attorney, a statesman, a professor, and a historian. He served the Church in his various positions as a layman in Catholic and national public institutions, where he was adept at preaching a rectilinear, balanced approach, obeying both earthly and divine rules, always espousing the idea that "the only sadness fitting to earthly life is the matter of not being saintly." As Iñigo Salvador put it:

> Dr. Julio Tobar Donoso was a Christian in every sense of the word, as he so demonstrated during the thirty-nine years in which he stoically carried the cross, forgiving and even loving his opponents; helping to educate openly Catholic youth during the twenty-five years of his professorship and deanship at the Faculty of Jurisprudence of the Catholic University; writing treatises and using his wisdom to teach on social law inspired by the doctrine of the church. However, his most important action consisted of bearing witness to his faith during his eighty-seven years of life, always in keeping with the words of Christ that the Pontifical Catholic University of Ecuador, which he helped to found, took as its motto: *Eritis mihi testes* [Be my witnesses].[23]

Conclusion

Julio Tobar Donoso's life and legacy are admirable from a variety of perspectives. Few men are able, during their time on this Earth, to contribute so much to society in so many ways in the areas in which they have been involved. The multifaceted nature of Tobar Donoso and the abundance of his activities in every area of his life, always acting smartly and with integrity, undoubtedly make him one of the great Ecuadorian figures of the twentieth century. As an attorney, he completely distanced himself from any petty exercise of the craft, always endeavoring to share his knowledge through the prolific publication of legal books and articles, in which he made deep dives into the study of institutions, principles, and laws. He was aware of the need for law to be practiced in accordance with Christian values as the only mechanism to ensure that such a noble profession would not transform the administration of justice into a commercial good. He also wrote and lectured about the ethical principles of the profession. This way of feeling and conceiving law led him to become one of the most active figures in founding and establishing a Catholic university in Ecuador—a country which, at that time, had only public universities, often characterized by a clear liberal and atheist dogmatism. This massive initiative, successfully achieved in 1946, resulted in a university that continues to provide excellent education under a broad, inclusive Catholic ideology. Lawyers trained in its classrooms continue to enroll in subjects that instill the ethical values inspired by Christian teachings, just as Tobar Donoso once envisioned.

While perhaps his work as a legal scholar and educator of legal science constituted the most transcendental and memorable contributions that he made to Ecuadorian society, another major contribution by Tobar Donoso was his work as a judge in the nation's courts. By exercising the magistracy in the highest court of Ecuador, he brought to fruition his musings on the need to apply the law without losing sight of Christian iusnaturalist values. His rulings were considered fair in their substance and spotless in their form. He was valued as a prudent judge who was able to materialize the maxim of "giving to each that which is his." These professional achievements, added to his pure and dignified honesty, adorned Tobar Donoso with a coherency that is achieved only by great men.

Diplomacy, which was the activity to which he dedicated a large portion of his life, brought him the greatest distaste he would experience in his lifetime. He was responsible for representing his country internationally in the gloomiest part of the nation's history of international relations, following an iniquitous invasion by its southern neighbor, which wanted to take over Amazonian lands with oil reserves and ended up overpowering the Ecuadorian military and putting the country's very stability at risk. Tobar Donoso took on this serious and historic role with the integrity and responsibility that it merited. Practically forced to sign a protocol that cut off a good part of Ecuador's eastern territory, he achieved peace and guaranteed the nation's survival, but the enormous sacrifice that this action entailed was wholly uncomprehended by the Ecuadorian public. For many years he bore public opprobrium, often of the crudest sort, because of his decision. He responded to these unjustified offenses with biblical meekness, fulfilling the Christian mandate to turn the other cheek.

Julio Tobar Donoso not only put his intellect at the service of law but also used his keen mind to delve more deeply into the knowledge and communication of Christian doctrine, both on small matters and in the most important issues of the Catholic Church's social doctrine. He was one of the primary scholars of issues relating to the Church in Ecuador, with a methodological imprint of the sciences, elevating Christian thought to levels of twentieth-century intellectuality without straying from accessible language and understandable prose. In other words, he was ever diligent in ensuring that his musings on denominational matters would be available to all types of readers, from ordinary people to eminent scholars. I would characterize him, if I may, as a secular evangelist of contemporary Christian subject matter.

Julio Tobar Donoso was a man committed to his faith, with superlative intelligence that he knew how to employ to benefit Ecuadorian society, both in earthly and divine aspects. His life and his works unmistakably show him to be one of the great Christian legal scholars of Latin America.[24]

Notes

1 Flor Vásconez, "Julio Tobar Donoso," 36.
2 Pérez Pimentel, "Julio Tobar Donoso," 404.
3 Rumazo González, "Homenaje fúnebre," 24.
4 Tobar Donoso, "El patrimonio inembargable."
5 Salazar Alvarado, "Julio Tobar Donoso," 20.
6 Flor Vásconez, 41.
7 Moreno Proaño, "Julio Tobar Donoso," 108.
8 Rumazo González, 24.
9 Salazar Alvarado, 4.
10 Pérez Pimentel.
11 Salazar Alvarado, 7.

12 Moreno Proaño, 112.
13 Flor Vásconez, 48.
14 Pérez Pimentel, 405.
15 Moreno Proaño, 116.
16 Salazar Alvarado, 10.
17 Bossano Valdivieso, "Homenaje del Ateneo," 32.
18 Flor Vásconez, 45.
19 Ibid., 77.
20 Tobar Donoso, *La Iglesia ecuatoriana en el siglo XIX*, 7.
21 Tobar Donoso, *La Iglesia, modeladora de la nacionalidad.*
22 John Paul II, "Meeting with the cultural world in the Church of the Society of Jesus."
23 Salvador Crespo, "Julio Tobar Donoso," 111.
24 The final version of this paper was supported by the Simón Bolívar Andean University, Campus Ecuador, and its Research Committee.

References

Bossano Valdivieso, Guillermo. "Homenaje del Ateneo a Tobar Donoso." In *Homenaje póstumo al Dr. Julio Tobar Donoso.* Quito: Editorial Voluntad, 1982.

Flor Vásconez, José Joaquín. "Julio Tobar Donoso." In *Homenaje póstumo al Dr. Julio Tobar Donoso.* Quito: Editorial Voluntad, 1982.

John Paul II, Pope. "Meeting with the cultural world in the Church of the Society of Jesus," https://w2.vatican.va/content/john-paul-ii/es/speeches/1985/january/documents/hf_jp-ii_spe_19850130_mondo-cultura.html.

Moreno Proaño, Agustín. "Julio Tobar Donoso: historiador." In *Julio Tobar Donoso, centenario 1894–1994.* Quito: Editorial Mendieta, 1994.

Pérez Pimentel, Rodolfo. "Julio Tobar Donoso." In *Diccionario biográfico ecuatoriano.* Guayaquil: Universidad de Guayaquil, 2001.

Rumazo González, José. "Homenaje fúnebre de la Academia de la Lengua." In *Homenaje póstumo al Dr. Julio Tobar Donoso.* Quito: Editorial Voluntad, 1982.

Salazar Alvarado, Francisco. "Julio Tobar Donoso." *Biblioteca Ecuatoriana Clásica.* Vol. 32. Quito: Corporación de Estudios y Publicaciones, 1995.

Salvador Crespo, Íñigo. "Julio Tobar Donoso: testigo de su fe." In *Julio Tobar Donoso, un estilo al servicio a Dios y la Patria.* Quito: Offset Ecuador, 1984.

Tobar Donoso, Julio. *La Iglesia ecuatoriana en el siglo XIX.* Quito: Editorial Ecuatoriana, 1934.

Tobar Donoso, Julio. *La Iglesia, modeladora de la nacionalidad.* Quito: La prensa católica, 1953.

Tobar Donoso, Julio. "El patrimonio inembargable." *Revista de la Sociedad Jurídico-Literaria* 18: 49. Quito: Sociedad Jurírico Literaria, 1917.

30 Tomás Darío Casares (Argentina, 1895–1976)

Juan Cianciardo and Marcelo Fernández Peralta

Biographical introduction

Tomás Darío Casares was a jurist who excelled in various fields. As a judge, he oversaw the direction of the Argentinian Supreme Court of Justice during a particularly turbulent period of its history characterized by threats to its independence. As a teacher, he was confronted with the task of defending iusnaturalism before the appeal of positivism and other fashionable trends. Examples of his success include, but are not limited to, exemplary court judgments and work but also a series of philosophical, legal, and theological training courses that were the foundation on which the Catholic University of Argentina and other Catholic universities across the country would later be built. This biographical piece addresses and develops certain aspects of his life, his work as a judge, and the fundamental lines of his contributions as a philosopher.

Casares was born in Buenos Aires, Argentina, on October 25, 1895 in a traditional Catholic family. He lost his mother at a very young age and was primarily raised by his aunt. At the age of twenty-five, he married María Martha Giménez Zapiola. They had nine children, whom they raised in a highly disciplined manner. From a very young age, he demonstrated his proactive character by participating in Catholic groups, such as Ateneo de Estudiantes Universitarios, Colegio Novecentista, Acción Católica Argentina, and others. He was cofounder of *Criterio*, one of the first Argentinian Catholic magazines, which continues to publish today. However, one of his more significant achievements as a young man was the foundation of the Cursos de Cultura Católica (Catholic Culture Courses). This materialized into one of the most important centers for Catholic laypersons as a response to the deficiency in training of Catholic laity in the face of the growing appeal of atheism and liberalism. Many disciplines were studied at the Cursos: philosophy, the history of the Catholic Church, holy writings, and more. For this reason, the classes became very popular among the Catholic youth who attended them. Some of the most renowned Catholic authors of the period visited Argentina to give lectures in the Cursos. Among them were Garrigou Lagrange, Tristán de Athayde, and Jacques Maritain, who happened to brighten those days at the Cursos.

The significant influence of the Cursos on an entire generation of remarkable Catholic intellectuals is indisputable. Through them was channeled their concern for preserving the principles of Catholicism in the face of the new ways of thinking, which put in serious doubt the foundation of the faith and the ability of Catholics to cope with criticism. Their principal publication, *Ortodoxia* magazine, affirmed that the Catholic Culture Courses "were born and exist to promote the life of intelligence under the sign of faith, in the bosom of the [Catholic] Church, depository of the truth."[1] This group of restless young people took up the challenge with the conviction of playing a role of great importance, convinced that something had to be done and that they were responsible for that change. Of course, the task was not for nothing; it had a purpose, as José María Medrano clarifies: "the Cursos and their works were not always looked upon with equal sympathy in the various Catholic environments, both ecclesiastics and laity."[2]

Among this group of renowned young Catholics—Atilio Dell'Oro Maini, Rafael Ayerza, Faustino Legón, and Samuel Medrano—Tomás Darío Casares stood out. Faithful to his austere and humble style, he expressed in his "Reflections on the Condition of Intelligence in Catholicism" that "courses were born from the awareness that the Catholic generation had of their intellectual poverty, and that the root of that poverty was the divorce of faith from intelligence."[3] The intention was to know God in order to love Him. This is how Casares himself expressed it in his inaugural speech of the school year on May 10, 1933:

> So that the exercise of intelligence in freedom is carried out without detriment of obedience, it must come from the inner life and lead to it: it should always be, through all the possible ways, knowledge of God that moves to love of God.[4]

Despite the low profile cultivated by Casares, his action as director of the Cursos was well highlighted. Indeed, under his management, the range of the Cursos was expanded from their initial lessons of philosophy, Church history, and holy scripture to include a significant number of seminars that covered other areas of knowledge:

> the library was increased, a bookstore service was created; they were interested in the liturgy; they founded a school of philosophy, a so-called Convivio for the cultivation of letters and arts, [and] a department of folklore; and books and magazines were published.[5]

Special attention should be drawn to the university section, which was the seed from which the Argentinian Catholic University would eventually grow. This transcendent fact was pointed out by the rector at the time, Monsignor Octavio Nicolás Derisi, whose doctoral thesis was directed by Casares. In his inaugural speech, Derisi said, "In the Catholic Culture Courses…some of perhaps the best

Argentinian Catholic intellectuals from that generation have been formed, and thus naturally it has evolved into our Argentinian Catholic University."[6]

The tireless work of Casares, as director of the courses, was recognized not only by his local colleagues but by Jacques Maritain himself, who, during his visit to Buenos Aires, said that Casares was the "right man in the right place."[7] According to one of the most important commentators, Carlos Massini Correas, Casares can be considered "one of the main architects of the renewal of Catholic thought in Argentina."[8]

His academic career was prolific. In 1917, he received a law degree at the University of Buenos Aires, and just two years later he received a PhD in Jurisprudence for his work "La Religión y el Estado" ("Religion and State"). He also taught at the University of Buenos Aires, teaching not only in the law college but also in the philosophy college. Furthermore, he was Dean of the Faculty of Humanities at the University of La Plata. Embodying the spirit of the Cursos, he co-founded the Argentinian Catholic University (UCA), where he was dean of the law college. He taught philosophy of law for many years and eventually conducted the Institute for Knowledge Integration. In his last years, he retired from public life, appearing only occasionally, whenever he was invited, mostly by the Argentinian Catholic University to give a lecture or to be honored.

As for his judicial career, it was not until 1920 that he began occupying minor positions. In 1937 he was appointed judge of the civil forum, and in 1939 judge of the National Civil Chamber. There he gained praise for his well-reasoned and accurate decisions from many specialists, such as Raymundo Salvat, one of the most important jurists in Argentinian history.

In 1944, after Judge Luis Linares's resignation, Casares was appointed judge of the Argentinian Supreme Court. These were particularly difficult times for Argentina because of the deep political changes that were occurring. Thus, he had to work with two totally different compositions of the court. From 1944 to 1947 his fellow judges were prestigious liberal jurists. As the figure of Juan Domingo Perón was growing, so was the confrontation with the Supreme Court. The struggle ended when all the judges except Casares were fired. This was one of the most embarrassing institutional moments in Argentina's history, as the charges made against the judges seemed to be compliments rather than criticisms, demonstrating that the underlying reason for the removal of the judges was political and not technical. The new judges were associated with the government of Perón, and they did not hide that affiliation. In this atmosphere, it is remarkable that Casares remained independent, regardless of who retained political power. His tools for doing so were the large number of dissents and solitary votes. Nevertheless, independent of the composition of the court, Casares remained coherent in thought in his writings and academic life. It should come as no surprise that his stance cost him many subsequent problems.

One of the saddest episodes in Casares's life happened in June 1955, when violent groups that had been attacking and burning churches decided to assault the Buenos Aires Cathedral while many people, including Casares and his family, were there. During this confrontation, he was both strong and determined in his efforts to avoid damages not only to the people within the building but also to the building itself. Instead of being praised for courage, however, he was unreasonably criticized. This incident illustrates how difficult the political situation was at the time. It was so intense that three months later, Perón was overthrown by a military coup, and the entire Supreme Court was dismissed. Casares had enough prestige that he was given the opportunity to resign. Not wanting special treatment, however, he rejected the offer and was subsequently fired along with the other justices. He passed away on December 28, 1976.

Casares as a judge

Casares left a very important legacy as a judge of the Supreme Court. He joined the Court in mid-1944, during the presidency of Edelmiro J. Farrell (1944–46), the second president of the military government following the coup d'état of June 4, 1944. As noted above, in 1947, with democracy restored and President Juan D. Perón in office, Congress removed all the judges except Casares, who continued until Perón was overthrown in 1955. During the democratic period, in which the Supreme Court was characterized by a "close adherence to the regime and unity of opinion,"[9] Casares showed not only erudition but also courage to remain independent. In fact, he did not hesitate to include in his opinions references to God and to his Catholic beliefs. In some cases he did so following the majority decision; in others, he made individual or dissenting statements.[10] Altogether, he was responsible for eighty-five dissents and twenty-two solo opinions.[11]

According to Sacristán, Casares's contributions as a judge can be divided into two fundamental categories: first, the most notable public law cases that relate to specific matters, which include: (a) the unionization of professionals; (b) the validity of de facto legislation; (c) the designation, removal, and transfer of judges; (d) the comparison between arbitrators and judges, and the nature of the disciplinary decisions taken by the bar associations; (e) the implementation of the Constitution for times of peace and war; (f) the need to introduce the action of protection as a guarantee of rights; and (g) the criteria for the interpretation of legal texts. In all of these matters, Casares produced "judicial disagreements," which today in Argentina are "part of the history of each of the respective cases." All of these votes "are a sign of an education meant to last and to encourage powers as a legislative competence."[12]

Second, Sacristán continues, there is a group of decisions issued by Casares in cases of patrimonial content or administrative-economic law, which involved: (a) currency; (b) several aspects of administrative contracts; (c) property rights; (d) state responsibility; and (e) the requirement of previous payment in order to have access to an appeal against fines imposed by the administration. According to Sacristán, it is perhaps in this second group of cases where Casares had to confront the dominant individualism of the time. In the following paragraphs, we examine some of these cases in more detail.

The Sambuco case[13] involved a question of whether a pension for a supervening disability should be paid to a military man as a result of illness or physical defects suffered in the course of service. According to the relevant law, if the injuries suffered by the soldier were serious enough to prevent him from carrying on with his career, his remuneration was to be raised to the next higher rank from the one he held at the time of the incident.

The majority of the court upheld the claim. Casares, however, issued a dissenting opinion, in which he referred to "the spirit of the law." In his opinion, the legal text required extreme care in analyzing "the circumstance of the episode in which the military man became disabled." The event in which the individual became disabled, Casares continued, "cannot be considered from any point of view analogous to an action of war, nor did it result in an attitude of the individual that in peacetime service can lead to an extraordinary promotion." Furthermore, Casares asserted, the medical studies carried out in the case showed that the functional loss of the member of the individual's body was relative. For all these reasons, invoking his desire to avoid a resolution "of irritating injustice," which would occur if situations that were clearly different were put on an equal footing, he rejected the claim for the integration of the pension into the next higher grade.

The common good was another central concept in Casares's decisions. He was concerned with distinguishing it from the utilitarian concept of calculating the sum of individual goods. This is why, in the case of the Banco Provincia de Buenos Aires, he said that "there can be nothing in the institutional life of the nation but the nation itself."[14] The bank had claimed exemption from payment of taxes on transactions with foreign financial institutions on the grounds that a law released it from that obligation. The majority of the court upheld the claim. Casares filed a dissent. He stated that granting the demand would imply leaving aside "principles concerning the nation's tax power of unwavering application in all circumstances because they refer to the exercise of powers inherent to sovereignty." His stand in the case was coherent with his vision of the common good, which he considered to be a "right-obligation" of each person. And in the Quilmes case,[15] he ruled that inviolability of private property is not more important than an urgency dealing with the social interest. To avoid criticism from liberals, Casares clarified that this decision did not intend to affect individual rights. On the contrary, he said that by protecting social interests, the authority protected individual interests as well, as persons individually considered could achieve their aims only in society. It was clear that Casares's notion of rights could not be separated from duty, as two sides of the same coin.

His notion of authority is remarkable too. In the case of Cámara de Apelaciones del Norte,[16] Casares said that the condition of legitimacy of the political power was that it was performed for the common good and according to the law. It should then come as no surprise that for Casares, the validity of positive law was contingent on its compatibility with natural law. In the Mayer case, this way of thinking led him to conclude that the norms given by the military, nondemocratic government remained valid until they were substituted by other norms.[17] This was a polemical decision—one which ultimately brought him much criticism.

Special attention should be brought to his concept of law as well. In the case of Municipalidad c/ Compañía Primitiva de Gas,[18] Casares concluded that a law could be declared unconstitutional not only when it is not in accordance with the constitution but also when it is substantially unfair. In the Merck Química case,[19] he defined his concept of war as fair if it intends to restore order. However, war cannot take place without an adherence to the human dignity inherent to natural law. This concept of dignity, as a consequence of humanity being created in the image of God, was central to Casares's decisions.

Finally, in the case of San Miguel,[20] he voted to extend the protection of the action of *habeas corpus* to other constitutional rights, such as liberty of expression. This case is so important that it is considered the first antecedent of the Act of Protection of Constitutional Rights in Argentina.

Casares as a teacher and scholar

Casares was not only a judge but also a legal philosopher. He dedicated himself to this discipline as both a scholar and a professor. As a scholar, he made his best-known contribution with the book *La justicia y el derecho* (*Justice and Law*), which has had three editions. The last one, from 1973, has important additions and changes in comparison to the first two, which were very similar to each other. In what follows, we concentrate on some of the fundamental ideas of that work, in order to offer some brushstrokes of the most original aspects of Casares's jurisprudential ideas. In fact, we are convinced that an exhaustive analysis is neither attainable nor necessary for the purpose of this chapter. Casares is a convinced Thomist, and we concentrate on those aspects in which he had an impact, going beyond what Thomas Aquinas developed.

A first aspect worth highlighting is Casares's legal philosophy. The purpose of his legal philosophical proposal did not vary throughout its long trajectory. It consisted, in his own words, in affirming

> the principle of the subordination of the juridical to the moral, of the moral to the metaphysical, and all temporal ordering of human conduct to an eternal order. It is a question of showing that the sense of right can only give it a complete understanding of human spiritual structure and destiny; and that, consequently, perfection of the law must be ordered, through its extrinsic and social purposes, to the spiritual perfection of humanity.[21]

Casares's proposal conflicted with the contemporary, fashionable ideas of the day. The prevailing thought at the time was that of Kelsenian positivism, which hinged on the rigorous separation between law and morality. Such positivism, in turn, was one of the consequences of the epistemology of modernity. Modern scientism replaced the idea of truth by that of accuracy and transformed the application of the scientific method under the condition of the possibility of rational knowledge. This point of view did not leave room for practical reason: reason either was theoretical or was not reason. In Hume's words, when persuaded of these principles, a reader who visits libraries and comes across books on metaphysics or ethics would have no alternative but to throw them into the fire, because there would be nothing there but falsehood or deception.

If ethics is not a science, if there are no cognizable moral truths, and if law is, on one hand, the "object of the virtue of justice" or, on the other hand, "that which is just," then it is not easy to assert the scientific nature of law. Precisely to avoid this risk was the aim of the Kelsenian project: the proposal of separating law, morality, and politics had the purpose of affirming legal science as a true science according to modern canons.

In this context, Casares faced a double challenge: to affirm the scientificity of morality, on one hand, and to affirm the scientific autonomy of law on the other. This challenge explains why his core work is divided into two parts, one dedicated to justice and the other to law. In the third edition, he introduced a third part, "Plenitud del derecho y la justicia," (*The plenitude of law and justice*) originally published in the journal *Universitas*. Two of the most interesting ideas in this book are explored next.

A right dissociated from justice is unfounded

For positivism, the foundation of law can never be moral. If it were, this would imply a "naturalistic fallacy," in which there is an undue derivation of law from the duty to be. The content of the law may or may not coincide with morality—the law can have any content. However, any coincidence between morality and law should never concern the jurist. The lawyer, like the judge, must focus only on the law that is, regardless of its correspondence with the ideal right. Faced with these ideas, Casares emphatically affirms the connection between law and justice. In his opinion, if that connection did not exist, the law would be meaningless. For this same reason, an unjust positive standard cannot "be legal"; it is legal insofar as it is just. That is:

> Attributing legal status to an unjust positive norm is as much as admitting the existence of an unfounded law, since the foundation of the law requires a reference to the norm, by which the law is expressed, to the reason with which it is expressed, by virtue of which its obligatory nature is imposed on the conscience of the persons governed by it. And that reason holds in all cases, regardless of the conception for which the legal order is proposed and carried out. For the foundation is always in the first principles; and in the practical order, the ends play the same role as principles in the speculative. Discernment of the truth of a speculative proof contains a reference to the latest instance to the first principles. Therefore, the proof will be true if we do not admit contradictions. The establishment of the authority of a precept of moral order requires a definitive reference to the human end of life. The precept will have the authority of a moral mandate if it is oriented toward that supreme end.[22]

According to Casares, law without foundation is, ultimately, indistinguishable from violence.[23]

Throughout all of Casares's work are numerous references to law as a term with multiple meanings. According to Casares, the word "law" refers both to the positive legislation of a particular place and time and to what must be given to a person to satisfy the demands of his nature as a human being. Failure to differentiate these and other possible meanings potentially leads to many problems.[24]

On observation, the fact that the word "right" represents varied realities leads to a double challenge. First is the challenge of analytical differentiation. Here, planes of analysis are distinguished according to the object of the analogy that the author refers to. Second is the challenge of determining the central analogy that could potentially serve as an ordering criterion or source of sense for the different analogues.

Roscoe Pound emphasized that it is the univocal rather than analogical search for a single meaning for law that is the root of deep theoretical disagreements.[25] Carlos Santiago Nino, on the other hand, emphasized the need to shed light on the perspective from which each of the participants in a debate refers to the law.[26] In his opinion, differences around the concept of law do not come from a lack of light; rather, the differences emerge within the dialogues, in which the opponents use the same words with different references. Like Casare's efforts, both opinions support the plausibility of referring to the law by clarifying the contextual legal reality it refers to. Moreover, this thought has evolved over time. Initially, it did not include the analogues to the law.[27]

Justice is a virtue and resides in the will, even though it presupposes knowledge

Following Aquinas, Casares defined justice as a virtue: "Justice is a virtue, and only as such is its authentic essence apprehended and its relationship with law determined." Justice is a virtue that consists in giving to each what is his own: "It is a habit by which Aquinas defines this virtue with perpetual and constant will. As such, each one is given his right. And following this line of thought, right is the object of justice."[28]

Casares's true vocation was law, and virtue provides a perspective from which to consider it. This virtue resides in the will, not in intelligence. However, like all the other virtues with which it shares this characteristic, its exercise presupposes a certain discernment or knowledge. It is the knowledge of that which is one's own, which must be given to the one to whom it belongs. Casares points out that this knowledge is certainly provided by law, although only in the first instance.

On the second level, although Casares does not say so with these words, the knowledge of what is just is based on understanding that what is disposed of does not transgress the content of another law, the natural law. On the third level, the knowledge that what is just, as known in the law, is also just as what is due presupposes the knowledge that the human being has a special dignity.

As for the second plane, Casares develops it further in the following passage:

> The intellectual discernment to which we have referred intends to interpret not only the text of the law when it comes to applying it, or the popular

> will—mere fact—but the very substance of the legal relationship itself: that is, its essential reason (and not the circumstantial reason, such as the fact that the law says it or the majority wants it) by which something must be recognized as someone's or given to someone.[29]

Finally, "The Fullness of Justice" is the title of Chapter 3 of *Justice and Law*. According to Casares:

> Considering only what would be the coexistence of human beings without religion, without piety, without observance, without friendship, without gratitude, without liberality, without equity, there is evidence that the only positive right, maintained by the coercion of the state with respect to external conduct, does not order humanity, and that ultimately this legal regime would be unsustainable. It is also evident that the living effectiveness of law, its true sovereignty, its own virtue, can be achieved only in the coexistence of people who—while not universally and not always practicing it—recognize it as a potential part of justice in their category of virtues; that is, they recognize the law as moral duties ordered to the perfection of the justice. In order that the practice of law on the part of persons is not deficient, it is not what has been erroneously given as its definition: a "minimum of ethics"; it is necessary that the conscience submitted to it tends to transcend the limit of the obligations that law imposes. Whoever is only willing to do more than what is due in justice will not even do what is due. Treating the totality of legal life with the same criteria as the fulfillment of a contract will lead to contracts not being fulfilled, even within the minimum limits of the extrinsic obligations that they expressly impose.[30]

This paragraph synthesizes perhaps one of the most controversial aspects of Casares's legal philosophy. His opposition to the Kelsenian proposal to separate conceptually the law from the moral led him to affirm the subordination of law to the moral, in line with other proposals of his time. However, it should be noted that subordination is not to be confused with subalternation. Against this moralization of the legal phenomenon, Michel Villey, in France, and Carlos R. Sanz, in Argentina, among other authors, wrote years after Casares did.[31] The risk of making morality the object of law is to promote an illegalization of sin, as impossible to achieve as it is potentially harmful to important aspects of the common good (privacy, intimacy, freedom of conscience, and religious freedom). To say that law is necessarily connected to morality is not to deny it scientific autonomy, either in its sources or in its method and object.

Notes

1 *Ortodoxia* No. 1 (July 1942).
2 Medrano, *Los iniciales "Cursos de cultura católica,"* 10.

3 Casares, *Reflexiones sobre la condición de la inteligencia*, 7.
4 Casares, *Los cursos de cultura católica*, 10.
5 Medrano, *Los iniciales*, 11.
6 Derisi, *La Universidad Católica*, 15.
7 Lasa, *Tomás Darío Casares*, 38.
8 Massini Correas, "In Memoriam Tomás Casares," 267.
9 Leiva, "Tomás Darío Casares."
10 Sacristán, "El juez Tomás D. Casares y el Derecho público."
11 Leiva, "Tomás Darío Casares."
12 Sacristán, "El juez Tomás D. Casares," 1.
13 "David Sambuco c/ Nación Argentina," *Fallos de la Corte Suprema de Justicia de la Nación*, 201:45 (1945).
14 "Banco Provincia de Buenos Aires," *Fallos* 201:142 (1945).
15 "Tranvías Eléctricos S. A. y Balneario de Quilmes c/ Municipalidad de Quilmes," *Fallos* 204:496 (1946).
16 "Acordada sobre la creación de la Cámara de Apelaciones del Norte," *Fallos* 201:243 (1945).
17 "Municipalidad de Buenos Aires c/ Mayer, Carlos," *Fallos* 201:249 (1945).
18 "Anders, Carlos y otros, Farnelli, Gaspar, Kamp, Germán," *Fallos* 204:435 (1946).
19 "Merck Química Argentina S. A. c/ Nación," *Fallos* 211:162 (1948).
20 "San Miguel, José S. s/ recurso de amparo," *Fallos* 216:606 (1950).
21 Casares, "Derecho y ley," in Casares, *La justicia y el Derecho*, 7.
22 Ibid., "Advertencia."
23 Ibid.
24 Ibid.
25 Cf. Pound, *An Introduction to the Philosophy of Law*, 115–20; and Pound, "The Theory of Judicial Decision," 940.
26 Nino, *Derecho, moral y política*, 21–45.
27 As Casares himself acknowledges in the second edition of his main book (cfr. Casares, "Derecho y ley," in *La justicia y el Derecho.*
28 Casares, *La justicia y el Derecho*, Chapter 1.
29 Ibid.
30 Ibid., Chapters 3, 6.
31 Villey, specifically, condemned the existence of a contemporary confusion between law and morality, which in his opinion would be found in the basis of the identification of law with positive law, and would have its historical origin in a process that would unite the Stoics with some of the ideas of the Second Scholastics and with the ideas of the modern school of natural law. See Villey, *Filosofía del Derecho*, 53–57, 70–87. See also Sanz, "Algunas reflexiones sobre el derecho y la justicia."

References

Casares, Tomás Darío. *Los cursos de cultura católica*. Buenos Aires: Cursos de Cultura Católica, 1933.

Casares, Tomás Darío. *La justicia y el Derecho.* 3rd. ed. Buenos Aires: Abeledo Perrot, 1973.

Casares, Tomás Darío. *Reflexiones sobre la condición de la inteligencia en el catolicismo.* Buenos Aires: Cursos de Cultura Católica, 1942.

Derisi, Octavio Nicolás. *La Universidad Católica en el recuerdo.* Buenos Aires: EDUCA, 1983.

Fallos de la Corte Suprema de Justicia de la Nación. Publicación a cargo de la Secretaría de Jurisprudencia del Tribunal. Buenos Aires: Corte Suprema de Justicia de la Nación, n.d.

Lasa, Carlos Daniel. *Tomás Darío Casares. El pensamiento y la obra de un jurista y filósofo cristiano.* Buenos Aires: Gladius, 1994.

Leiva, Alberto D. "Tomás Darío Casares, un jurista católico en la Corte Suprema de la Nación Argentina." *Revista de la Cruz del Sur* 3, no. 4 (2013): 11–31.

Massini Correas, Carlos Ignacio. "In Memoriam Tomás Casares." *Idearium* 2 (1976).

Medrano, José María. *Los iniciales "Cursos de cultura católica."* Buenos Aires: Dunken, 2015.

Nino, Carlos Santiago. *Derecho, moral y política.* Buenos Aires: Siglo 21, 2014.

Pound, Roscoe. *An Introduction to the Philosophy of Law.* New Haven: Yale University Press, 1922; 2nd ed. revised, 1954.

Pound, Roscoe. "The Theory of Judicial Decision." *Harvard Law Review* 36 (1923): 802–25.

Sacristán, Estela. "El juez Tomás D. Casares y el Derecho público. Aportes desde el Máximo Tribunal." *El Derecho* 263 (2015): 812–28.

Sanz, Carlos Raúl. "Algunas reflexiones sobre el derecho y la justicia." *Sapientia* 69 (2013): http://bibliotecadigital.uca.edu.ar/repositorio/revistas/algunas-reflexiones-sobre-derecho-justicia.pdf.

Villey, Michel. *Filosofía del Derecho.* Barcelona: Scire Universitaria, 2003.

31 Pedro Lira Urquieta (Chile, 1900–81)

Cristián Villalonga

Biographical introduction

Pedro Lira was one of the most renowned legal scholars and humanists of mid-twentieth century Chile. A committed Catholic law professor who followed the Conservative Party, he was directly connected to the political and religious challenges of his time, involving questions about social justice, the separation of Church and state, and the Second Vatican Council.[1] Some of those events provide the keys to understanding his contribution to legal scholarship and, perhaps, the course of his life.

Indeed, a relevant part of Lira's work in the humanities and private law exceeds the scope of this chapter. Nonetheless, his relentless reflections on law and social affairs constitute, to a great extent, a particular form of engagement with Catholicism after *Quadragesimo Anno* (1931). Pius XI's encyclical warned against the perils of both unrestrained capitalism and socialist collectivism, setting the ground to rebuild the modern social order according to the Christian concept of human dignity.[2] This ecclesiastical document, among others, subtly oriented Lira's approach to legal issues. In this light, Lira is an exceptional example of how socially conservative Catholic jurists made sense of the rise of the welfare state in Latin America, as he oriented his scholarship in terms of the ecclesial magisterium and a dialogue with neoscholastic thought.

After a brief biographical introduction, this chapter attends to the core of Lira's intellectual contribution by addressing three aspects of his work: a) his view of the fundamentals of the legal system, which tries to reconnect Catholic natural law tradition with modern society; b) his claim to adapt nineteenth-century liberal legislation according to the new social order proposed by the social teachings of the Catholic Church; and c) his reassertion of law as moral reasoning into public governance.

A son of an aristocratic family of Santiago, Pedro Lira was born in 1900. He received a Catholic education, first in the German lyceum administered by the Society of the Divine Word. After a year of military service, he entered the School of Law of the Catholic University of Chile, where he worked in the library and attended classes of prominent law professors influenced by the social teachings of the Catholic Church, such as Roberto Peragallo and Alfredo Barros Errázuriz.

These influences were deepened during a trip to Europe in 1925 as a representative to the Catholic Youth Congress in Rome and to the University of Paris.[3] He was granted the Tocornal Award as the best law graduate of his cohort in 1925 and was conferred a law degree by the Supreme Court a year later.

Throughout this period, Lira became involved enthusiastically in the National League of Catholic Students (in Spanish, ANEC), taking part in a remarkable generation of conservative young Catholic students who attended university immediately after the First World War (for example, St. Alberto Hurtado and Eduardo Cruz-Coke).[4] Within that association, he also became familiar with the authors of the French Catholic intellectual renaissance (among them Charles Péguy and Léon Bloy) and neoscholasticism.[5] The league also allowed Lira to participate in the polemics about secularization during Arturo Alessandri's liberal presidency, which separated the state and the Church definitively.[6] Representing the league, he addressed the president of the republic in 1925, asserting that "societies fail when they do not consider religious ideas in the public sphere."[7] Polemics on the religious identity of the country continued during the next decades, becoming critical to understanding Lira and other members of his generation.[8]

After graduation, Lira continued to engage with ANEC, establishing the *Revista de Estudios Católicos* (*Catholic Studies Journal*, 1930) and leading debates in academic meetings and newspaper articles. Like many other young intellectuals linked to ANEC, Lira felt sympathy for the natural corporatism proposed by Pius XI's *Quadragesimo Anno*.[9] Considering Lira's academic interests in the possible direction of a new social order, the minister of finance and the University of Chile in 1935 commissioned him to study corporatist organizations in Belgium, Germany, and Italy. Already a young law professor by this time, Lira traveled to Europe to observe this phenomenon. He asserted that there was a great similitude between Chile and Belgium, where there was a coalition of Catholic, liberal, and socialist individuals who supported spontaneous associations. In line with Pius XI, he showed skepticism about the wide-ranging corporatist systems of Italy and Germany, which were organized by strong centralized governments.[10]

Lira joined the Conservative Party as a Catholic alternative to secular liberalism, Marxism, and fascism. In 1934 he published *El futuro del país y el Partido Conservador* (*The future of the country and the Conservative Party*), advocating a genuine institutional pathway that would take into consideration the national tradition, which both refused violence and reconciled order and progress.[11] Although his activities were mostly devoted to law and humanities, he continued to engage in partisan politics across the following decades. He was elected to the Conservative Party's board in the late 1940s and devoted significant effort to avoiding the separation of traditionalist and social-Christian factions, which perhaps was one of the most important debates within the Catholic constituency by the mid-twentieth century.[12]

Lira also assumed important professional responsibilities. As soon as he began his career, he joined the State Defense Counsel, the public agency in charge of the judicial representation of the state, then one of the most prestigious settings for law practice. There, he litigated major cases for almost forty years.

Between 1936 and 1939, he was also appointed chief manager of the Workers' Insurance Fund, an organization devoted to promoting social welfare under the Ministry of Health.[13] These activities provided him with firsthand knowledge of the social question, concerning economic justice for the laboring classes, and the new administrative laws that challenged the previously dominant *laissez-faire* economic policies.[14] At the same time, such experiences granted him a significant amount of prestige among his peers, and he became a well-reputed attorney in private practice. From 1936 until 1962, he was elected repeatedly as a member of the general board of the Chilean Bar Association.[15]

Besides politics and practice, he was very active in teaching law. In the early 1930s, he was appointed professor of civil law at the Catholic University and at the University of Chile, continuing that activity until the late 1960s. In 1948, he also taught a class in legal philosophy at the Catholic University for a brief period. Lira performed an outstanding role as director of the Law School of the Catholic University several times during the 1930s and 1940s and finally as dean from 1950 to 1968.[16]

Pedro Lira was a prolific author, and his scholarship constituted an important point of reference for Chilean private law by the mid-twentieth century. Among his works are *El régimen de aguas en Chile* (*The water law regime, with Lorenzo de la Maza*, 1936), *El Código Civil y el Nuevo Derecho* (*The Civil Code and the new law*, 1944), *La partición de bienes* (*The partition of property*, 1948), *El Código Civil y su época* (*The Civil Code and its epoch*, 1956), and tens of other books and articles. In all of those writings, Lira employed a general humanist approach that included the social teachings of the Catholic Church, canonical authors of the Western tradition, and comparative law.[17]

He did not limit his scholarship to the law, however. Like Andrés Bello, who constantly served as his ideal model of a scholar, Lira was a humanist who wrote extensively about diverse nonlegal topics ranging from history to literary criticism and linguistics. Several of his works—like *Felipe II, Newman y Balmes* (1940), *Andrés Bello* (1948), and *Sobre Quevedo y otros clásicos* (*On Quevedo and other classics*, 1958)—were published in Spain, Chile, and other Latin American countries. Commenting on the first of these works, Gabriela Mistral—a Nobel Laureate in literature—asserted,

> Professor Pedro Lira has decided bravely to understand and to live his epoch, and despite his warm tenderness towards tradition, he follows the religious crisis of the world closely as if he were a biologist analyzing the precious fabrics of a beloved body, that is the beloved body of his time.[18]

During the last three decades of his life, Lira experienced both difficult moments and, at the same time, the peak of his career. In 1956, his wife—with whom he had three daughters—passed away. He overcame this profound loss through his cheerful personality, his constant piety (which included daily Mass), and the reading of St. Theresa of Avila's mystic texts.[19] During those years, Lira also threw himself into participation in multiple academic associations, such as the Hispanic

Institute for Culture, the Chilean Academy for History, and the Chilean Society of Language.

In 1963 President Jorge Alessandri appointed Pedro Lira as ambassador to the Holy See during the Second Vatican Council. There, he received the bishops' delegations coming from Chile and followed the ecclesial debates closely, informing national authorities about them.[20] In general, his writings reveal that he looked at the Council with hopefulness, criticizing traditionalist groups that disregarded some of its results. "How the Church's spirituality has won! What an extraordinary development the Church has had in our century! How this is easily forgotten by those who solely look at formalism!" he wrote later.[21]

After his return to Chile, in the middle of a mounting political conflict during the Cold War years, Lira received various awards and homages. In 1967 he was elected to the Law and Social Sciences Academy of the University of Chile. Meanwhile, the Catholic University of Chile published a volume of works honoring him in 1970, and the Chilean Academy of Language officially celebrated its former secretary with an homage in 1972. He also received the Queen Isabella Award, bestowed by the Spanish Government, in 1973. After the mid-1970s, Lira's health deteriorated gradually, forcing him to leave his numerous activities and take refuge in his family, until his death in 1981.

On natural law, religion, and modern society

Like other jurists of his time, Lira tried to reconcile the permanency of some fundamental legal values, such as respect for human dignity, with the necessity of revisiting legal institutions during the rise of the welfare state. He received part of his legal education within the intellectual tradition of neo-Thomist natural law revived by Leo XIII's *Aeterna Patris* (1879), which exerted a strong influence in Latin America during the first half of the twentieth century.[22] That tradition emphasized the relevance of perennial moral principles, whose incorporation into statutes bestowed validity to positive norms. Nevertheless, he also was an attorney, practicing within a positivist legal culture, who observed how the Great Depression and the increasing technological and political transformation of the period led to an incentive to review the socioeconomic system. Lira resorted to neoscholastic authors (for instance, Rafael Fernández Concha, Luis Mendizábal, Victor Catherin) to face this intellectual dilemma, attempting a reconciliation of tradition and modern society.

In several of his texts, Lira asserted again and again that law was a moral discipline whose object was to adjudicate in the classic sense (*suum cuique tribuere*).[23] Lira thus subscribed to neoscholastic conceptions affirming that, although legal adjudication was a sort of practical reasoning, it significantly rested on natural order manifested through permanent ends and principles that rule social life.[24] For legal scholars, such an order provides the only possible ground to approach positive law. He explained:

> If we do not count on a general and accurate notion of what society and the state are, about what are their ends and human purposes…it is impossible to

> give an opinion of the legal system or of a statute. We would simply lack a compass to navigate the sea of the law.[25]

In an account of Western legal history, Lira asserted that Christian religion had provided the keys to understanding such an order during several centuries, serving as a sort of moral sustenance of the law. Following the Spanish Catholic apologist Jaime Balmes, he affirmed that Christian faith had had an indirect impact on the culture of corrupt Roman society, instilling moderation in pagan jurists like Ulpian and Papinian and in the empire's legislation after Constantine. Although maintaining an older conceptual scaffolding, this influence would have been perceptible in the broader idea of equity, in the protection of marital progeny and slaves, and in women's legal status, among others subjects.[26] By the same token, Lira admired the rise of Christendom in the late Middle Ages—which produced a reelaboration of law impregnated with religious spirit—and the Spanish legislation of the colonial period that was highly engaged with the protection of indigenous people.[27] All of these contributions showed how Christian beliefs were at the very core of Western culture in general and of Spanish law in particular.

According to Lira, the continuity of the Christian spirit was a realistic enterprise within modern society. Although he was always linked to neo-Thomist thought, several of his works exhibit admiration for jurists and lawmakers of the Catholic Enlightenment and mainly for Andrés Bello's contribution to the private legislation of nineteenth-century Chile.[28] Perhaps by employing a misleading philosophical interpretation of rationalism, Lira explained that the jurists associated with the Catholic Enlightenment intended not a break but a continuity with the core of the Western moral tradition. They would have been simultaneously conservative and progressive scholars because they prompted modern legal reform respecting some elements of the natural law tradition.[29] Describing the intellectual legacy of Bello and Gaspar Melchor de Jovellanos, Lira summarized:

> What was their conception of man, society, and the world? Without hesitation, we can answer: the Christian conception, the old and realist doctrine delivered by Aristotle and baptized by Saint Thomas Aquinas.[30]

For Lira, the Chilean civil code drafted by Andrés Bello offered a clear example of how Christian morals, previous legal development, and the modern world could be harmoniously reconciled at a precise moment in history. Lira affirmed that Bello's "clear mind understood plainly that religion was the necessary ground of all true progress," and a secure ground for moral and social life itself.[31] Moreover, he recognized that Bello was able to integrate several key aspects of the Spanish legal tradition with other European innovations that maintained basic standards of natural law, such as regulation in the realm of marriage and family. Thus, the adaptation of enduring principles to a new context explained the success of the civil code and its acceptance in other Latin American countries.[32]

After modern secularization, however, social adherence to the conception of a natural order seemed problematic to Lira. Like many other young Catholics of the 1930s, he thought that Western civilization had experienced the end of its spiritual unit— a perception that was amplified by the separation of the Church and the state in Chile. In line with the writings of Jaime Eyzaguirre, Alfredo Bowen, and Eduardo Frei—who also published their reflections in the *Catholic Studies Journal*—the idea of spiritual crisis that had a significant impact on the law was a topic that appeared very early in Lira's work.[33] He asserted that people had abandoned their religious ideals, which were gradually replaced by individual preferences. Meanwhile, jurists and lawyers had reduced the discipline of law to a mere technical knowledge, separating law from its moral foundations. Subsequently, society had lost the meaning of justice and accentuated a veneration for violence.[34] At the same time, he criticized modern legal philosophy (for example, Kant and positivism), avowing that this would have been unable to provide an alternative orientation for the law at a substantive level.[35] As a result, he averred, the modern mind had produced a true legal crisis:

> Justice and the law are not satisfied by being fixed in legal texts; they require and need social consciousness, and when in such a consciousness the idea of justice is eclipsed, the functioning of the legal system is reduced to a sterile and annoying mechanism.[36]

However, Lira assumed implicitly that this crisis of the modern legal mindset—characterized by the lack of a clear concept of justice and a mismatch between social expectations and legal texts—was not a permanent situation. In his later works, written after the late 1950s, he expressed assurance that seeds of hope lay behind the disorientation and the political conflict of the period. For example, he admitted that the Catholic Social Code of Malinas would have inspired labor legislation and that the Universal Declaration of Human Rights, an undeniable confirmation that Christian doctrine, was exerting an enormous influence upon modern law.[37] Besides validating such sources, this assertion should not be surprising; Lira was imbued with neo-Thomist theories that admitted the idea of a natural order but that, by the first half of the twentieth century, were also intermingled with the modern language of rights.

Adapting the law after *Quadragesimo Anno*: property and contract

An essential part of Lira's scholarship was related to adapting private law to the guidelines proposed by *Quadragesimo Anno*. Although the Conservative Party looked at the encyclical with some degree of suspicion, Lira and the young social Christians of the 1930s found it an important stimulus for intellectual and political mobilization. The document profoundly inspired them, since it laid the groundwork needed to reestablish an authentic Christian social order that valued the function of natural associations and replaced liberalism. At the same time, the encyclical attempted to balance solidarity and human dignity, addressing the very core of the social question: the injustice of social relations as a moral issue.[38]

Within the legal realm, Lira agreed with the pope's condemnation of individualist liberalism. Despite the significant accomplishments of nineteenth-century legislation, he affirmed that individualism constituted a pitfall of the civil code and other statutes that must be remediated. From his standpoint, justice does not address only commutative relations, because that approach would reduce human relationships to market interchanges. Rather, justice also implies what everyone owes to the community and what the community owes to its members, particularly to the weak and poor (that is, legal and distributive patterns of justice as found in Aristotle). This last focus would comprise what the pontifical language of the encyclical identifies as social justice. Hence, Lira appropriated classic philosophy and praised *Quadragesimo Anno* for forming a complete ideal of justice that considered a broader conception of the common good of society.[39]

Following this analysis, Lira looked on the legal reforms of the welfare state with enthusiasm. In *The Civil Code and the New Law* (1944), he reviewed how the regime of welfare statism had gradually restructured the legal system during the first half of the twentieth century, adopting the spirit of social justice already described. Bearing in mind his years as head of the Workers' Insurance Fund and his experience as attorney at the State Defense Council, he provided a favorable appraisal of several such reforms, including patrimonial protections for illegitimate offspring and for married women, the expansion of torts and insurance to labor activities, and the different public and private corporations established during those decades.[40] It is in his views of property rights and contracts where we can best observe his effort to reconcile natural law and recent changes to legislation. In concrete terms, he employed arguments of the neo-Thomist tradition—like the distinction between essential and accidental elements of human private property and the moral character of law—to orient his scholarly approach to these matters and to sustain his vision of public economic order. [41]

Under the influence of Georges Ripert's study of French legislation, Lira delivered a complete account of the transformation of ownership by the first half of the twentieth century. He considered that the way the civil code dealt with property meant true progress because it ended the precapitalist limitations on conveyances and assured the owner's entitlement to make free use and alienation of assets. Nevertheless, he also underscored that the new statutes had gradually imposed public encumbrances on property to face urgent social needs and the increasing requirements of the administrative state (for example, regulations on the rents of dwellings, the expropriation of underused agricultural lands to establish productive farms, and the state's price-fixing powers).[42] Prior to such changes, legal theory would have lagged behind. Lira was aware that limitations on property were consistently supported theoretically by authors like August Comte and Léon Duguit, who considered that ownership performed a social function and that proprietors have specific duties to contribute to the commonwealth.[43] For him, such theories seemed proficient in explaining the new social character of property since the turn of the century but did not offer a clear explanation about the boundaries of those limitations. For that reason, he attempted a more satisfactory reformulation according to the ecclesial magisterium.

Although most of the conservative *cadres* initially thought that the reforms mentioned above had a socialist aim, Lira considered that a well-understood and moderate take on these restrictions to property rights was compatible with the Spanish legal tradition and the social teachings of the Catholic Church. After all, the idea of public interest itself was already associated with the traditional conception of ownership in medieval legal texts such as *Las Siete Partidas*, which indicates that a property owner must use his or her belongings according to God's word and the law.[44] Furthermore, the same moral connotation was present in the ecclesial doctrine that dealt with the social question. Referring to that last point, Lira affirmed:

> The problem [of property rights] has a particular interest for the defenders of natural law. We understand it in the traditional and Christian way. Leo XIII's teachings already addressed the topic. But it has been Pope Pius XI, in his encyclical *Quadragesimo Anno*, who clarified the issue. He adopted an eclectic position. He does not admit either an absolute version of property rights or their abolition.[45]

To reconcile the defense of private ownership and its contribution to the commonwealth, Lira resorted to the neoscholastic distinction between essential and accidental elements of private property. On one hand, he described what he called human property, a sort of ownership that consisted of the estate and chattels that the owner employs for his and his family's sustenance. Even though its extent could be relatively variable, as long as it rested on the productivity of the owner's estate and the social condition of the family, Lira emphasized that this ownership required lawmakers' strong protection, with minimal or no taxes and limitations. "This property must be observed as a concrete expression of natural law regarding ownership and, accordingly, as an absolute and inviolable good," he insisted.[46] On the other hand, Lira alluded to superfluous ownership, which consisted of all that exceeded human property. This latter form of ownership did not rest upon natural law, and, consequently, "the greater or lesser extension and limitations on it depend on the state's convenience and the necessities of the social order."[47] Since the burdens on this last form of ownership arose from social utility, the state could freely impose them. If the limitation did not affect human property, he asserted, the matter lay outside the sphere of natural law and was properly within the bounds of political power.[48]

In a similar vein, Lira descriptively and normatively analyzed the limitations imposed on contract by the welfare state. In the civil code, theories of will governed contract formation and several related subjects, such as the enforcement of covenants and the rules related to fraud, mistake, and duress. Parallel to the right to manage and to dispose of private property, the code originally envisioned few limits on the freedom of contract, usually considering social customs and public order. However, Lira underscored that several statutes and judicial decisions had gradually undermined such an individualistic understanding of contract law since the 1920s. Although the legal structure of the civil code had remained mostly unaltered on this matter, lawmakers passed numerous limitations on free will for humanitarian and political reasons (for example, standard form contracts or the new regulations of labor relations). In other cases, courts had prevented injustice by more elastic reasoning that went beyond theories of will, like regarding a flexible approach to contractual enforcement in the face of unforeseen circumstances.[49]

For Lira, these changes to contract law did not just reflect new political and economic ideas. Behind those regulations and remedies lay deep reasons of justice, such as the release of the weaker party from a contract to prevent exploitation, safeguards to fair bargaining and just price, and simply the defense of a broader notion of public interest. He thought that most reforms introduced to contracts in the context of the welfare state embodied an attempt to provide a robust moral ideal in the life of the law.[50] In this thinking, Pedro Lira asserted that he followed Ripert's work *La règle morale dans les obligations civiles* (*The moral rule in civil obligations*), "which does not depart from the traditional Christian concept delivered successfully among us by Rafael Fernández Concha," the noted intellectual representative of Thomist legal philosophy in Chile.[51]

Lira presented several cases to demonstrate how the recent statutory or judicial restrictions to free will evinced a moralizing purpose. The example of the abuse of rights, for instance, clarifies this point. Lira described how new legislation in several countries forbade the exercise of a right when such exercise had the determined goal of harming another person and granted compensation under the rules of torts to the person harmed. Courts had expanded such restriction regarding contractual rights and obligations on the grounds that covenants must be performed in good faith. Most liberal jurists rejected these judicial decisions as an intrusion of moral opinions into the law. For Lira, however, these objections to this new legal development were theoretically weak.[52]

Following Fernández Concha's work, Lira employed arguments from the neoscholastic tradition to endorse the banning of abusive exercise of a right. To determine whether an act is legal or illegal, we must make a moral judgment. This does not mean denying the role of will, but it entails a legal analysis in a broader and more genuine spirit. From that perspective, a licit act must be honest in all its aspects, even regarding its motivations. After all, the law is a part of moral reasoning associated with the virtue of justice. Accordingly, the owner or holder of a contractual right is submitted to moral considerations. For instance, a creditor must collect a debt if his own family has a need but must try to avoid doing so if it would cause the debtor's ruin. He summarized this point, explaining:

> the banning of the abusive exercise of a right goes beyond the strict legal province. It invades the moral field effectively. This is one of several means to incorporate moral considerations into the law. In this sense, we should look at it favorably.[53]

On legal expertise and its relation to the common good

Throughout his academic life, Pedro Lira was concerned with the ethical character of law and its place in contemporary society. Both his first article, published when he was a student in 1923, and his last legal work, published in 1967—*En Defensa del Derecho* (*In defense of the law*)—constituted true apologies for the role of legal expertise in contemporary society.[54] For him, the law was a particular sort of moral reasoning that must perform a central function in public governance, particularly in the context of the welfare state, where some corporatist arrangements sought to rectify the pure forces of the market and the bare political will. From his perspective, law constituted a pathway to introduce justice into the state's action, allowing it to fulfill its goal of the common good.

Lira's writings affirmed that legal expertise that integrates moral reasoning must be preferred to other alternatives for mobilization and decision making. In the course of the populist and authoritarian movements of the 1930s, for example, he harshly criticized people's trust in violence instead of law and formal institutions.[55] Over time, he also refused the dogmatic positivism that characterized Latin American legal culture, which was consolidated along with strong executive authorities and growing bureaucracy. "A jurist cannot be merely a skillful technician who writes or explains legal text with his cleverness. He must try to translate his moral ideals into the law."[56] Similarly, Lira stressed that economists and sociologists, who began to constitute a rising technocracy, would never replace legal professionals in producing norms. Only lawyers could provide a moral orientation to lawmaking and translate political decisions into precise legal prescriptions.[57] To sustain his point, Lira assigned several virtues to the law and legal professionals; true jurists are trained in thinking about justice and proceed with a clean spirit, without the passions that characterize politicians.[58]

This view of law in governance should not be read outside the context of Lira's time and political ideas. Under the influence of the encyclicals *Quadragesimo Anno* and *Pacem in Terris*, as well as Luigi Sturzo and Balmes's writings, he admitted pursuing the notion of a Christian social order. A key aspect of such a conception was determined by a view that the common good was the goal of the state, a view that distinguished conservative politics from class struggle, individualism, and other partisan aims. Paraphrasing St. Thomas Aquinas, Lira accepted that the common good was an adequate form of social organization that maintained peace and justice and sought the maximum material and spiritual well-being of every member of the community. In other words, the common good was in part a manifestation of justice, and chiefly what pontifical texts label social justice. He admitted that although the common good corresponded to the ancient ideal of good government in Aristotle and medieval texts, the Church's social teachings—*Pacem in Terris*—had adjusted such a formulation to fit the modern language of citizens' duties and rights.[59]

Lira's emphasis on a conception of legal expertise that integrated a traditional version of moral reasoning was suited to the earlier idea of the common good and the challenges of the welfare state. First, this view of law tried to match Thomist philosophy consistently, maintaining coherency with the overarching religious and political assumptions of the ecclesial magisterium. Second, this view also provided flexible intellectual tools for adapting legal institutions, favoring a harmonious and nonconflictive social organization according to Christian moral norms and corporatism. His justification of how public economic order must prudentially restrict property rights and contracts, explained above, provided an enlightening example of this point. Third, Lira recognized that law has a moral effect on the constitution of Christian society, performing a transcendental function in human spiritual improvement. Following Ripert, he asserted that law must follow a specific format of Christian morality, which, "by its particular conception of the ends of humanity in this world, impose a variety of rules that do not simply look to secure respect for others, but also aim to enhance the soul of humanity."[60] Thus, at least theoretically, his version of legal expertise attained even the spiritual facets of the common good.

From the 1930s to the 1960s, the decades when Lira concentrated his legal scholarship, none of these affirmations of legal expertise and the common good were merely an accepted guiding principle, mere entelechy. Rather, they addressed a deep political conflict about the course of the socioeconomic order and its consequences in the realm of law. The tenor of his writings confirms that Lira felt overwhelmed by technological and political change, underpinning a legal crisis that had carried out, amid chaotic legislation, the loss of a shared conception of justice. Nevertheless, he also saw an opportunity to advance different legal reforms, such as revision of the civil code and the reorganization of public legislation. Lira thought of legal reform as a particular contribution of juridical expertise in the building of a new social order, which reconciled the necessities of the modern world and the "Christian principles of natural law."[61]

Concluding remarks: a Catholic jurist before the welfare state

Certainly, Pedro Lira stands out as one of the most relevant Catholic jurists of mid-twentieth century Chile. His oeuvre was perhaps diffuse and sometimes confusing, without reaching the heights of other scholars who wrote during the preceding decades. His works did not constitute a legal monument such as Luis Claro Solar's civil law treatises, nor do they reveal Rafael Fernández Concha's philosophical depth.[62] But taken in full measure, Lira emerges as a unique figure who represents an explicit dialogue between the ecclesial magisterium and legal science to face the challenges of the welfare state. Besides leading the Catholic University School of Law for almost two decades, he was a remarkable jurist in several senses.

While Lira was not the only member of his generation attempting to reconcile Catholicism and the modern world (within the humanities, several other authors were moved by *Quadragesimo Anno* and the project to establish an authentic Christian social order during the 1930s and 1950s), however, he was exceptional within the realm of law. Several of his writings presented a comprehensive interpretive account that advanced this inquiry into legal history and legal philosophy. He asserted the core of a moral–legal tradition that was deeply embedded in Christianity, bolstering the religious character of that tradition. By alleging a continuity between this tradition and the origins of Chilean law, Lira sought to reaffirm the religious identity of the country and to correct the flaws of liberal legislation according to Pius XI's guidelines. In this sense, he looked at social and legal modernity with frank optimism, without Catholic traditionalism's sense of tragic decay or the Chilean Christian Democrats' revolutionary sign.[63]

On a broader canvas, Lira also proposed a relatively systematic justification of the public economic order imposed during those decades. He asserted that the state, motivated by public interest and moral reasons qualified prudentially, might limit property rights and freedom of contract.[64] Other jurists of this time, Catholics and non-Catholics, supported the emergence of the welfare state and its reform of the legal system. Nonetheless, almost all of them admitted plainly the dominant secular ideas of the period—such as Duguit's social function of property—or alluded to the Church's teachings very loosely.[65] Although still fairly immersed in dogmatic expertise that characterized Chilean legal culture, only Lira engaged genuinely with neoscholastic arguments and the ecclesial magisterium to analyze such transformation within the sphere of private law.[66] In this way, he not only supported the legal reforms of the welfare state but also sought to limit them according to the Christian concept of human dignity.

Finally, Lira defended a particular form of legal expertise that integrated dogmatic analysis with moral reasoning, asserting that knowledge of the justice of social affairs has an unrivaled place in governance. He thereby differed from the plain secular positivism that dominated the legal culture of his time. Instead of merely accepting statutes as a firm truth, Lira was very prone to look at neoscholastic ethics to assess legislation and to promote legal reform. Such a view of the law in governance matched the ecclesial teachings of the common good as the foundation for a nonconflictive and well-regulated society, and it was instrumental for the corporatist logic that sought prudentially to limit economic liberalism and collectivism. Thus, Lira was a clear exponent of the Christian social–conservative politics of the mid-twentieth century and was also an uncommon scholar.

In spite of his unusual opinions *vis-à-vis* the dominant legal culture of his time, Lira enjoyed major academic stature and exerted significant influence on Chilean legal development. He was one of the first law professors to address a legal crisis caused by political conflict and to speak about a public economic order to regulate property and contracts. His works also foresaw several of the legal problems that emerged at the end of the twentieth century, such as the perils of the state's price-fixing powers and the legal implications of the widespread breakdown of family ties. Although he did not establish a school of legal thought, his classes and texts influenced several noted lawyers and legal scholars who have followed similar intellectual paths to the present day. Hence, it is not surprising that some decades after his death, he is still remembered as a great "jurist, humanist, and wise Christian man."[67]

Notes

1 Ugarte, "Pedro Lira, Jurisconsulto, Humanista y Sabio Cristiano."
2 Pius XI, *Quadragesimmo Anno.*

3 Sánchez, *Pedro Lira Urquieta*, 11–36.
4 Ibid.
5 Pereira, *El Partido Conservador*, 55.
6 Andes, *The Vatican and Catholic Activism in Mexico and Chile*, 35.
7 Valenzuela, *Pedro Lira 1900–1981*, 22.
8 Hurtado, *¿Es Chile un país católico?*
9 González Cañete, *Una revolución del espíritu*, 123, 155–68.
10 Pereira, *El Partido Conservador*, 120–21, 124.
11 Lira Urquieta, *El futuro de país y el Partido Conservador*, 13.
12 Pereira, *El Partido Conservador*, 235, 246. Botto, *Catolicismo Chileno*, 275–335.
13 Sánchez, *Pedro Lira Urquieta*, 72–75.
14 Lira Urquieta, *El código civil y el nuevo derecho*, 8.
15 Sánchez, *Pedro Lira Urquieta*, 72–79.
16 Ibid., 47–69.
17 Ibid., 88–93. Ugarte, *Pedro Lira*, 15–33.
18 Mistral, "Pensamiento de América."
19 Lira Urquieta, *Lecturas Consolatorias*.
20 Carrasco, *Cartas del Presidente Jorge Alessandri*.
21 Lira Urquieta, *Crónicas de Roma*, 11.
22 Kunz, *La Filosofía del Derecho Latinoamericana en el Siglo XX*, 51–64.
23 Lira Urquieta, "La crisis del Derecho," in Lira Urquieta, *Temas Universitarios*, 90.
24 Lira Urquieta, "Concepto y fin del derecho."
25 Lira Urquieta, *El código civil y el nuevo derecho*, 10.
26 Lira Urquieta, "La influencia del cristianismo en el derecho privado," in *Temas Universitarios*, 56–68.
27 Ibid., 70. Lira Urquieta, "La educación en las Leyes de Indias."
28 Lira Urquieta, "Jovellanos y Bello," in *Temas Universitarios*, 333–73. Lira Urquieta, *El Código Civil Chileno y su época*.
29 Lira Urquieta, *El Código Civil Chileno y su época*, 69, 102.
30 Lira Urquieta, "Jovellanos y Bello," 350.
31 Lira Urquieta, *El Código Civil Chileno y su época*, 102.
32 Ibid., 103.
33 González Cañete, *Una Revolución del Espíritu*, 117–25.
34 Lira Urquieta, "La crisis del Derecho," 82–83, 91, 93.
35 Lira Urquieta, "Concepto y fin del derecho," 13–16.
36 Lira Urquieta, "La crisis del Derecho," 84.
37 Lira Urquieta, "Grandes líneas de la legislación contemporánea." Lira Urquieta, "El pensamiento filosófico-jurídico de Ripert."
38 González Cañete, *Una Revolución del Espíritu*, 139, 143. Andes, *The Vatican and Catholic Activism*, 1.
39 Lira Urquieta, "Concepto y fin del derecho," 25–26. Lira Urquieta, "La Justicia Social. Conceptos y Aplicaciones," in *Temas Universitarios*, 153–81.
40 Lira Urquieta, *El código civil y el nuevo derecho*.
41 Lira Urquieta, "La Justicia Social," 174.
42 Ibid., 171, 175–92.
43 Ibid., 172.
44 Ibid., 167.
45 Lira Urquieta, *El código civil y el nuevo derecho*, 194.
46 Ibid., 196–97.
47 Ibid., 196.
48 On the different types of properties, Lira asserted that he followed the Dominican scholar García Pérez. Ibid., 197.
49 Ibid., 230–52. For a general view on this process, see Gordley, "Contract, Property and the Will."

50 Lira Urquieta, *El código civil y el nuevo derecho,* 256.
51 Ibid., 10. Ripert, *La règle morale.* Fernández Concha, *Filosofía del Derecho o Derecho Natural.*
52 Lira Urquieta, *El código civil y el nuevo derecho,* 280.
53 Ibid., 281.
54 Sánchez, *Pedro Lira Urquieta*, 89.
55 Lira Urquieta, "La crisis del Derecho," 83–84.
56 Ibid., 95.
57 Lira Urquieta, "En Defensa del Derecho," 119. Lira Urquieta, *El código civil y el nuevo derecho*, 10.
58 Lira Urquieta, "En Defensa del Derecho," 120. Lira Urquieta, *El código civil y el nuevo derecho*, 10.
59 Lira Urquieta, "La Noción de Bien Común."
60 Lira Urquieta, "La crisis del Derecho," 93–94.
61 Lira Urquieta, *De la necesidad de refundir y modernizar nuestra legislación*, 17–18.
62 Fernández Concha, *Filosofía del Derecho.* Claro Solar, *Explicaciones de derecho civil chileno.*
63 Lira Urquieta, "Pio XII y el mundo moderno."
64 Lira Urquieta, "La Justicia Social," 174.
65 Mirow, "Origins of the Social Function of Property in Chile."
66 I refer exclusively to private law, since constitutional law scholars José María Cifuentes, Carlos Estévez, and Alejandro Silva Bascuñán were closely associated with Christian ideals during the same decades. García, *Tradición Constitucional de la Pontificia Universidad Católica de Chile.*
67 Ugarte, "Pedro Lira."

References

Andes, Stephen J. C. *The Vatican and Catholic Activism in Mexico and Chile: The Politics of Transnational Catholicism 1920–1940.* New York: Oxford University Press, 2014.

Botto, Andrea. *Catolicismo Chileno: Controversias y Divisiones (1930–1962)* Santiago: Finnis Terrae, 2018.

Carrasco, Sergio. *Cartas del Presidente Jorge Alessandri con los embajadores en la Santa Sede (1959–1964).* Santiago: Pehuén, 1994.

Claro Solar, Luis. *Explicaciones de derecho civil chileno y comparado*, Vol. 17. Santiago: Imprenta Roma, 1898–1944.

Fernández Concha, Rafael. *Filosofía del Derecho o Derecho Natural*, Vol. 2. Santiago: El Correo, 1877–81.

García, José Francisco. *Tradición Constitucional de la Pontificia Universidad Católica de Chile, Vol. I (1889–1967).* Santiago: Ediciones Universidad Católica de Chile, 2018.

González Cañete, Diego. *Una revolución del espíritu. Política y esperanza en Frei, Eyzaguirre y Góngora en los años de entreguerras.* Santiago: Centro de Estudios Bicentenario, 2018.

Gordley, James. "Contract, Property and the Will: The Civil Law and the Common Law Tradition." In *The State and Freedom of Contract*, edited by Harry Scheiber, 66–87. Stanford, CA: Stanford University Press, 1998.

Hurtado, Alberto. *¿Es Chile un país católico?* Santiago: Ediciones Splendor, 1941.

Kunz, Josef. *La Filosofía del Derecho Latinoamericana en el Siglo XX*. Buenos Aires: Losada, 1951.
Lira Urquieta, Pedro. *El Código Civil Chileno y su época*. Santiago: Editorial Jurídica de Chile, 1956.
Lira Urquieta, Pedro. *El código civil y el nuevo derecho*. Santiago: Nascimiento, 1944.
Lira Urquieta, Pedro. "Concepto y fin del derecho." *Revista Universitaria* 2 (1951): 13–27.
Lira Urquieta, Pedro. *Crónicas de Roma*. Santiago: Editorial Andrés Bello, 1969.
Lira Urquieta, Pedro. "En Defensa del Derecho." *Anales de la Facultad de Ciencias Jurídicas y Sociales, Universidad de Chile* 7 (1967): 106–136.
Lira Urquieta, Pedro. "La educación en las Leyes de Indias." *Estudios*, 145–46 (1945): 13–22.
Lira Urquieta, Pedro. *El futuro de país y el Partido Conservador*. Santiago: Splendor, 1934.
Lira Urquieta, Pedro. "Grandes líneas de la legislación contemporánea." *Revista de Derecho y Jurisprudencia* 54 (1957): 91.
Pedro Lira Urquieta. *Lecturas Consolatorias*. Santiago: Imprenta Chile, 1957.
Lira Urquieta, Pedro. *De la necesidad de refundir y modernizar nuestra legislación*. Santiago: Imprenta Chile, 1957.
Lira Urquieta, Pedro. "La Noción de Bien Común." *Anales de La Facultad de Ciencias Jurídicas, Políticas y Sociales, Universidad Católica de Chile* 17–18 (1963–1964): 41–59.
Lira Urquieta, Pedro. "El pensamiento filosófico-jurídico de Ripert." *Revista de Derecho y Jurisprudencia* 56 (1959): 42.
Lira Urquieta, Pedro. "Pio XII y el mundo moderno." *Finnis Terrae* 9 (1958): 12.
Lira Urquieta, Pedro. *Temas Universitarios*. Santiago: Nascimiento, 1945.
Mirow, M.C. "Origins of the Social Function of Property in Chile." *Fordham Law Review* 80 (2011): 1183–217.
Mistral, Gabriela "Pensamiento de América." *El Mercurio* (1943): 3.
Pereira, Teresa. *El Partido Conservador. Ideas, figuras y actitudes 1930–1965*. Santiago: Vivaria, 1994.
Pius XI. *Quadragesimmo Anno: Encyclical Letter on Constructing the Social Order*. New York: Paulist Press, 1939.
Ripert, Georges. *La règle morale dans les obligations civiles*. Paris: Librairie générale de droit, 1935.
Sánchez, Elena. *Pedro Lira Urquieta*. Santiago: Pontificia Universidad Católica de Chile, 1989.
Ugarte, José Joaquín. "Pedro Lira, Juriconsulto, Humanista y Sabio Cristiano." *Revista Chilena de Derecho* 31, no. 1 (2004): 11–38.
Valenzuela, Alejandra. *Pedro Lira 1900–1981. Álbum biográfico*. Santiago: Origo, 2006.

32 Arturo Enrique Sampay (Argentina, 1911–77)

Susana T. Ramella

Intellectual and political formation

Arturo Enrique Sampay was one of Argentina's most prestigious jurists of the twentieth century for the Justicialist Government. This chapter aims to show the deep Catholicism that runs throughout his numerous philosophical and juridical works and in his presentations as a constitutional representative in 1949. Special emphasis is given to the influence of Aristotle and St. Thomas Aquinas on Sampay's thought and to the events that led Sampay to these sources. He was one of the most important proponents of social constitutionalism, deeply informed by neoscholasticism and Catholic social doctrine.

Sampay was born on July 28, 1911 in Concordia, province of Entre Ríos, and died in La Plata, Buenos Aires, on February 14, 1977. His grandfather Enrique and his great uncle, the priest Carlos Sampay, were both Basques who arrived in Argentina in 1861. Carlos, a professor at the Colegio Secundario in Concepción del Uruguay, province of Entre Ríos, greatly influenced Arturo in his philosophical, religious, and political ideas. Carlos induced him to study Latin and introduced him to St. Thomas Aquinas's *Summa Theologiae*, which left an imprint on all of Sampay's later writings and political actions.[1]

At a young age, Sampay joined the Unión Cívica Radical (UCR) political party, founded in 1891 by Leandro N. Alem, who was succeeded by Hipólito Irigoyen after Alem's death in 1896. This political party questioned the political parties of the "notables," or wealthy persons who guided Argentine destiny until 1916. In that year, Hipólito Irigoyen assumed the Presidency of the Nation and governed for two periods (1916–22 and 1928–30), until his government was overthrown by a military *coup d'état* led by General Agustín P. Justo. Sampay adhered to the party's most nationalist and popular vein. For example, he defended to President Irigoyen the nationalization of oil exploitation proposed by General Enrique Mosconi, then general director of Yacimientos Petrolíferos Fiscales.

Sampay studied law at the School of Law of the University of La Plata, province of Buenos Aires, when intellectual turmoil and great political changes forced him to face a renewed legal world. "The new philosophy, with roots in the ideas of Franz Brentano, was being fed by the ancient philosophy. A return to St. Thomas and Kant (among others) was happening."[2]

Completing his legal studies, Sampay traveled to Europe. This trip afforded him new juridical perspectives through the great personalities he met, like Dietrich Schindler, a disciple of Hermann Heller, and with Gerhard Leibholz.[3] These experiences led him away from the juridical positivism he had learned during his studies at La Plata and introduced him to analyzing constitutional order and relations in the context of their social reality. This was the beginning of his sociological and epistemological realism. While in Paris, he attended courses taught by Louis Le Fur and the discussions of Jacques Maritain. In Milan, Monsignor Olgiati introduced him to the philosophy of law. Through this learning, Sampay widened his knowledge and prepared himself for his own intellectual production. As I have written elsewhere,[4] Sampay's early thought was especially dedicated to analyzing the state and its transformations.[5]

At the same time, he began his political militancy. He left the Unión Cívica Radical of his youth and joined the Peronist Party, afterward named the Justicialista Party. He was first government adviser during the intervention of Juan Atilio Bramuglia in the province of Buenos Aires (1945), and then public prosecutor during the government of Colonel Domingo Mercante. He was then elected as a member and informing member of the Convención Nacional Constituyente of 1949. Through this political participation, he united his speculative and philosophical reflections about the state with action within the state.

Through a trial immersed in political matters, Sampay was removed as public prosecutor, but no illicit act was proved against him.[6] This action led to his exile first in Paraguay and then in Uruguay. In solidarity, Pablo A. Ramella wrote to him:

> This saddens me deeply for you and for the revolution that is now under trial in one of its most outstanding exponents. The powerful oil consortiums, instruments of the imperialism which you so accurately condemned, are now taking their revenge.[7]

The draft of the Constitution of 1949 established articles on the organization of wealth, on the intervention of the state, and on the nationalization of minerals, oil, and other energy sources—all matters that annoyed these consortiums. In addition, the conflict between Perón and the Catholic Church had begun, and this presented an intolerable state of affairs for Sampay.

Sampay's life ran its course during the twentieth century, when Argentina was affected by world events such as the two World Wars, in 1914–18 and 1939–45, and the economic crisis of 1930, with resultant *coups d'état.* One coup occurred in 1930, at the beginning of the great economic depression that affected the entire world. There was another *coup d'état* in 1943 and another in 1945, at the end of the Second World War. This last one, after the situation was stabilized, led Sampay to enter politics. The following years witnessed further *coups d'état*, in 1955, 1962, 1966, and 1976. The last was among the bloodiest, during which thousands were assassinated.

Sampay's Catholic thought

Sampay's works contain profuse bibliographic references to jurists, constitutionalists, and philosophers. It would be quite a feat to name all of them, but they include the outstanding thinkers of ancient times, the middle ages, and contemporary and modern times. He referred to them to question their ideas as well as to adhere to them. Sampay's works before his Peronism and afterward refer to Catholic thought extracted from authors and constitutions as a base for establishing constitutional rights. He constantly referred to St. Thomas, Aristotle, papal writings, and Catholic juridical works to sustain his thought and argument. In addition, he was well versed in Latin, French, and Italian, so he could read many authors in their original language. He admired most of all Aristotle and St. Thomas.

Relying on Aquinas, Sampay wrote that the "corruption of justice has two causes: the deviousness of the knowing, who falsify right judgment, and the violence of the powerful, who subvert that which is fair." Sampay adds,

> According to what we know, no one has ever pointed more exactly to the causes of social injustice. Also, together with the respect and promotion of human rights—thoroughly determined by the Declaration of the United Nations Assembly on December 10, 1948—the creative freedom of people must be stimulated.[8]

Sampay's prolific bibliographic production centered fundamentally on the Argentine constitutions or statutes from the nineteenth and twentieth centuries.[9] He compared these Argentine works with other foreign constitutions or legislations as a way to endorse his thinking or to question his conclusions. Sampay analyzed constitutional law from the perspective of legal history. The state and human rights are present in his works, which are broadly dedicated to defending the rights of those who are defenseless. This approach led him also to question the world economic system as it was accepted or rejected by Argentina throughout different periods and governments.

The state and rights

The realist theory and idealist theories about the state

For Sampay, rights correspond to all human beings, not just to the privileged social classes. During the nineteenth century, the privileged classes made law and promulgated constitutions without the participation of the poorest sectors of society, the workers and the defenseless, who were excluded from the most elemental rights.

In Sampay's work, he looked to several American and European constitutions, such as the Mexican Constitution of 1917, which incorporated social rights. Based on these and other works, he introduced important proposals at the Constituent Convention of 1949. Supported by all the Justicialist members of that Convention,[10] Sampay urged the introduction of social justice into the Constitution because, he said, "it is the application of the principles of legal justice to economic and social matters provoked by the intrinsic injustice of modern capitalism. By social justice must be understood the justice that ordains the reciprocal relations of social groups."[11] He added, "to satisfy their own needs, they depend closely on one another,"[12] and he enumerated several situations—salary, land and urban leases, and consumer goods—that are governed by social justice and not by commutative justice. As Juan Fernando Segovia has elegantly expressed it,

> Right, for Sampay, far from being a fragment of reality polished and modified to look at from the entire reality, right is a dimension of human life not connected with all the other realities that may be discovered or can be said of humankind.[13]

Indeed, the idea of the just and the right encompasses a wide spectrum. After considering numerous foreign and Argentine authors in their conception of humanity or (as Sampay expressed it) in their "philosophic anthropology," he explained that "happiness is the condition of the person when the individual enjoys vital health, owns that which frees him from material needs, and practices the intellectual virtues acquiring truth as the moral virtues proceed in accordance to what is good."[14] Thus, Sampay required consistency between constitutional prescription and constitutional reality.

Aristotle and Aquinas were the most important bases of Sampay's thought. His works *Introducción a la Teoría del Estado* (*Introduction to the theory of the state*, 1951) and *Carl Schmitt y la crisis de la ciencia juridical* (*Carl Schmitt and the crisis of juridical science*, 1965) are critical of idealist theories. Therefore, these works situate Sampay's ideas about realist theories with particular focus on legal philosophy and epistemology. The object in both theories was to show the antithetical stands between the idealist and realist theories of the state in order to supplant the idealist theory with the realist. Idealist theories were "an arbitrary limitation of the epistemology upon which they are based."[15] Sampay was aware that such thinking precluded knowing the reality of the state. Instead, Sampay adopts an Aristotelian-Thomistic theory as preparatory background to a realist epistemology for apprehending the ontology of the state as "an order ordained in itself."[16] The first chapter of the *Introduction* begins with the philosophy of the state in Aristotle and Aquinas, and Sampay adopts the Christian philosophy of the Middle Ages whose "Summa was elaborated by the genius of St. Thomas, who accepted from Aristotle his realist metaphysic of the state, based in social and political human nature."[17]

After these introductory remarks, Sampay developed a critical history of modern idealist theories of the state and considered these approaches in crisis. He distinguished these main theories for their "disrealization of the state" and their juridical method in the cases of Geirg Jellinek, Max Weber, Wilhelm Dilthey, Léon Duguit, Hans Kelsen, and Raymond Carré de Malberg.

He also addressed phenomenological approaches to the state in Edmund Husserl, Max Scheler, and Hermann Heller. In regard to Heller, Sampay noted that he was the greatest exponent of this position. Heller's disciple Gerhard Leibholz took a similar approach, but in their quest for a realist theory, they also fell into an idealist position with the idea of "recovering the real object of the theory of the state," using the epistemology of Dilthey and Hegel. Thus, they came in the end to a "voluntary conditioning of political knowledge, and therefore their realist design was frustrated from the first steps."[18] Sampay also questioned the speculative agnosticism of Marxism.

The fundamental question was whether one may or may not know reality. Like all those addressing this subject, Sampay inquired into which discipline—politics, sociology, law, or history—is the most appropriate to attain true knowledge of the state. For him, the theory of the state provided systematic knowledge and offered "the exercised knowledge of that political reality so that in an ulterior moment, it is valued through the normative principles of political science."[19] Thus, scientific knowledge was gained from the theory of the state as a scientific discipline, aided by political science, the sociology or theory of society, which could be synthesized as follows:

> the subject of the study of the theory of the state...as the self political organization of the entire society, with the inclusion of imperfect societies...and the conflicting social sectors that struggle within society for the possession of the government, as well as their real relations, in religious and political matters, with other perfect communities, as are respectively the church and the international community of the other states.[20]

Although criticizing the epistemology of modernity, Sampay did not greatly separate himself from the belief of isolated compartments of different disciplines that fail to capture the unity of knowledge or to strictly perceive the interconnections of disciplines, thus hindering selection of only one discipline as the appropriate method for knowing the state. The same can be said of the uncertainty that new epistemological trends posed in the works of Ricoeur, Gadamer, and Prigogine.[21]

Sampay's work held the juridical thinking of Carl Schmitt at a distance, and he made clear that his ideas did not embrace Schmitt's approach.[22] Schmitt was part of the National Socialist Party during the Nazi regime, between 1933 and 1936, from which he later moved away because of SS threats. Because Sampay had written about Schmitt, he was greatly criticized, and his thinking was associated with Schmitt's work and, through this, with National Socialism. Hence, in the second publication of his work on Schmitt, in 1965, he provided the following clarification:

> I believe that if this work had been better known, some jurists of the Río de la Plata would not have committed the mistake of identifying the political and juridical conception of Carl Schmitt with the system of ideas which I

> adopt, as my acceptance of the natural right places me further away from Carl Schmitt than near him.[23]

For this reason, Sampay questioned the idea of the domain of the rule of law over the domain of humanity.[24]

The idea of natural right fed into all of Sampay's juridical thinking as he turned away from the logicist or decisionist positivism of Kelsen and Schmitt. Sampay wrote that there are "those who accept that the only right is the positive right established by a competent governmental instance, and we are opposed to it, revealing its falsehood and the annihilating effects it has for human dignity and freedom."[25]

The work is a history of the theories of the state, criticizing not only Schmitt but also those already mentioned. Sampay praised Maurice Hauriou for his realist theory and found it concordant with his own thinking. Nevertheless, he observed "that the theory of Hauriou gets obscure because of the nomenclature created purposely by the author, but it is classic in the sense that it is based on Aristotelian Thomistic metaphysical thought." He further defended Hauriou:

> I must once and for all give testimony, that he treasures social reflections accumulated in the *Summa Theologiae* that have been most helpful…I must confess that not only have I taken from him my best inspirations, but I extracted as well the formula needed to not commit gross mistakes.[26]

Sampay questioned Schmitt for disqualifying neo-Thomism this way: "He does not highlight what it adopts, but disqualifies it flatly because its philosophical substantiation is in Aristotelian metaphysics accepted by St. Thomas."[27] Sampay continued his objections because of Schmitt's belligerence toward Catholicism. Indeed, though Sampay recognized that Schmitt came from Catholicism and had written a work about it, he believed that Schmitt sought to destroy Catholicism.

Gadamer says that Aristotle cannot be properly identified with the *jusnaturalism* of later times. He not only takes into account the constancy of the natural right and the alterability of the positive right, acknowledging the idea of an inalterable right, but he (Aristotle) limits it expressly to the gods and declares that among men not only the positive right but the natural one as well is inalterable.[28] In truth, it is difficult to adopt thinking from the third century BC to a "realist" theory of the twentieth century.

The right to property and its social function

The Irish Constitution, a Catholic document, inspired Sampay to write about the right to property for the individual and the social function of property. Article 43 of the Irish Constitution states:

> The State acknowledges that man, in virtue of his rational being, has the natural right, antecedent to positive law, to the private ownership of external

> goods. The State accordingly guarantees to pass no law attempting to abolish the right of private ownership or the general right to transfer, bequeath, and inherit property. The State recognises, however, that the exercise of the rights mentioned in the foregoing provisions of this Article ought, in civil society, to be regulated by the principles of social justice. The State, accordingly, may, as occasion requires, delimit by law the exercise of the said rights with a view to reconciling their exercise with the exigencies of the common good.

With this language in mind, Sampay stated:

> Whoever possesses property deals with goods that do not belong to him in an absolute way; therefore, he cannot dispose of them as he pleases, as he has a function to fulfill that is oriented to the Common Good...Property performs a double function: it satisfies an individual goal fulfilling the needs of the owner, and it accomplishes a social goal orienting its benefits toward the community. Property and external goods are a service of the Common Good."[29]

When drafting provisions of the Constitution of 1949, Sampay returned to the subject of property. This constitution reformed Article 17 of the Constitution of 1853 that acknowledged then, and still does today, the inviolability of property, even though the Constitution of 1949 was abrogated. After this statement about absolute property, the Constitution of 1949 added: "Private property has a social function, and is consequently subjected to the obligations that the law establishes for the common good." In this regard, Sampay expressed:

> The owner—the concept belongs to St. Thomas Aquinas—has the power of administration and just distribution of the benefits yielded by the exterior goods that he owns...[H]ence the property fulfills its double task: it satisfies a personal goal covering the needs of the owner, and a social one moving the rest toward the community. This is why the reform of the constitution consecrates, together with the guarantee of the personal function of property, the enforceability of the social function that is its concern...and that makes of this institution the building block of the new Argentine economic order."[30]

The right to intimacy: "the private actions of humankind"

Sampay was suspicious of the Constitution of 1853 and its predecessors because many of their drafters did not respect Catholic principles, the basis of Argentine culture since the colonial period. Instead, drafters imposed an agnostic model belonging to the nineteenth century. Thus, Sampay wrote:

> This Constitution [of 1853] was rendered by our liberal bourgeoisie of the nineteenth century, composed by proprietors and intellectuals where the

> former saw in the exercise of economic freedom a means to increase their businesses, and the latter a means to promote social progress...fully joining the movement of European capitalism.[31]

In *The Legal Philosophy of Article 19 of the National Constitution*, Sampay reviews the legal antecedents of Argentina's Constitution. He traces the sources back to 1813 and the draft presented by Bernardo de Monteagudo, a member of the Sociedad Patriótica y Literaria, who expressed that "what is not forbidden by the law cannot be prevented, and no one will be forced to do what it does not prescribe" (Article 194), an idea found in the Constitution of Venezuela of 1811. Similarly, the Estatuto Provisional of 1815 stated: "The private actions of men that do not offend the public order in any way or do not harm a third person, are only reserved to God, and exempted from the authority of the magistrates" (Article 112).

Sampay considered Antonio Sáenz the principal author of this article in the Constitution of 1819. Sampay praised him and noted Sáenz's skills as an illustrious jurist influenced by the teachings of the University of Charcas, where Sáenz taught. He "spread the philosophy of St. Thomas and through it the principles of the Greco-Roman legal culture." Similarly, instruction at the Colegio San Carlos in Buenos Aires, founded by Sáenz, was "consistent with the doctrine of St. Thomas."[32]

This constitutional article was maintained in the Constitution of 1853 and remains in force with the same number, Article 19, even in the constitutional reform of 1994, as follows: "The private actions of men that do not offend the order and the public moral in any way and do not harm a third person, are only reserved to God and exempt from the authority of the magistrates."

Sampay made it clear that "at the end, God shall judge for breaking the moral order," a principle he traced from Ulpian, Greek philosophy, and Aquinas.[33] For him, the constitutional public moral order meant

> the moral part that rules the actions referring to the order of the community...[J]ustice is the virtue causing and preserving said order, therefore Aristotle states that 'justice is a matter for the polis, because justice is the political order,' and adds, 'not damaging a third person.'[34]

Once more he quoted Aristotle, who considered that the judge acts as "if the legislator himself were present, as he would have so declared or...would have so legislated."[35]

Sampay said that Article 19 "condenses the universal juridical philosophy formulated from the great paradigms of our civilization's ideas." He compared it with the Constitution of the United States, noting that "the enumeration of certain rights carried out by this Constitution should not be interpreted as a denial or undermining of other rights belonging to the people." Therefore, Sampay understood that the same legal philosophy found in Article 19 of the Argentine Constitution recognized that God is our supreme legislator.[36] Another author commented on Sampay's study this way: "This work, as all of his other works, is a solid and elegant juridical and philosophical piece in which no words are in excess or lacking."[37]

"Democracy is a Christian creature"

Sampay's works addressing the history of the national constitution or collecting Argentine constitutions from 1810 to 1949 were always grounded in his Catholic thought, with special emphasis on the works of Aristotle and Aquinas.

When Sampay referred to the political principles in the Dogmatic Part of the Constitution, he sought to avoid differences between the Argentines based on race, because "our country acknowledges as doctrinal content the life and teachings of Jesus Christ, estimated as the world 'Logos' and the answer to the natural human yearning for values." He added the phrase transcribed in the above heading, "Democracy is a Christian creature." He then quoted President Harry Truman, who, when he addressed Pope Pius XII, noted that the United States is a "Christian nation" and criticized the Nazi Holocaust. The answer of the pope was, "There exist today social injustices and racial injustices between men and groups boasting of having a Christian civilization."[38] In this way, Sampay pointed at the contempt held in the United States at ethnic groups different from the "white people" who claimed superiority. When referring to the family, Sampay insisted that only the Christian conception provided freedom, equality, fraternity, and justice.[39]

In his constitutional thought, Sampay also relied on Vincenzo Lanza, who promoted a form of Christian philosophic anthropology. In the realm of education, he deferred to Aristotle, saying that within national pedagogy, education was properly part of the constitutional sphere. To endorse the economical and spiritual policy of the constitution, Sampay did not quote Jacques Maritain in his works, even though they had similar views. Both grounded their work in Aristotle and Aquinas, and they both combated liberalism and totalitarianisms.

After criticizing Hitler and Stalin, as the root of the "absorption of humanity by the state," Sampay shared with Lenin the belief that "moral neutrality at school is an occidental hypocrisy," while moving this idea into a Catholic perspective by quoting Pius XI's Encyclical *Quadragesimo Anno*. "The truth, whoever expresses it, belongs to the church as depositary of the truth."[40] In accordance with both Aristotle and Lenin, Sampay said that to ensure the permanency of political regimes, educational content matching the regime was of the utmost importance. "The most useful laws are useless…if citizens are not trained and educated in the political regime, democratically if the constitution is democratic and oligarchically if the constitution is oligarchic."[41]

Given that Sampay praises Lenin in this work, a person supposedly at his ideological antipodes, and in other works quotes Marx, Fernando Segovia states that "Sampay moves from Thomism to Marxism." Further on, Segovia insists that Sampay "parted from the original Thomism that had been his starting point," and that his Thomism "was amputated and turned to procommunism."[42] Such assertions appear to have been based on the amplitude of power Sampay gave to the state. Nonetheless, to commend aspects of a particular school of thought does not mean to adopt that ideology or school of thought. At that time, states were moving to either communist or liberal models. For example, in the United States, after the crisis of 1929 and the beginning of the Great Depression, the New Deal established by President Franklin Delano Roosevelt imposed an economic policy with state intervention that departed from an earlier model of liberalism. The same can be said of the work of John Maynard Keynes. For example, his *The General Theory of Employment, Interest and Money*, published in 1936, challenged the dominant paradigm. Both examples sponsored forms of state intervention to avoid unemployment and poverty occasioned by this great economic crisis.

Sampay's comments at the Constitutional Convention of 1949 shed light on his approach to this topic. Sampay stated that to justify major state intervention and to criticize the neutral state of liberalism in the economic, labor, and social arenas, Keynes and the New Deal criticized the preceding system as "a regulatory and controlling administration…that is, intervention in favor of the powerful."[43] Instead, Sampay proposed state intervention to favor the lowest social classes. Such ideas do not make Sampay a Marxist. It was a time when states embraced political economy to solve unemployment and poverty. It was a very different time from the present, when, as Bauman says, the state is in crisis as it is supplanted by multinational companies.[44]

Final considerations

Words of Gadamer are particularly telling here. He stated,

> A hermeneutically formed conscience has to show itself receptive from the beginning to the alterity of the text. But this receptivity does not presuppose 'neutrality' facing things or self-cancelling, but includes a nuanced incorporation of its own previous opinions.[45]

The same happens with the thought of Sampay as he moved away from and questioned the idealist, liberal, agnostic theories belonging to legal positivism and rationalist *jusnaturalism*. He placed himself in a school of natural rights in which every human being is considered without differences of wealth or poverty and in all times and places. Here, Sampay's thought flowed from Aristotle and Aquinas.

Sampay criticized idealist theories for making rights a matter of the state. Instead, he viewed natural rights as the substantiation of a strengthened state. Nevertheless, Sampay considered rights as inalienable and preceding the state. At the Convention of 1949, he appealed to incorporate the common good, natural human rights, and social rights for the well-being of people as state goals, while strengthening the links between the state and the economy.

Husserl examined the character of epistemological controversies between idealism and realism, between subjectivity and objectivity.[46] Evidently, idealists based all on human reason; the realism of Sampay was sustained by God. This is the substantial difference separating him from pure rationalism. Sampay understood that realist theory depended on neither subjectivity nor the abstractions that he criticized in idealist theories. He constructed a theological rather than a philosophical hermeneutic.

The importance of Sampay's idea of natural rights found in constitutions and the state was not embraced on the international level until later. This development occurred after the end of the First World War and mostly after the Second World War, when international institutions adopted human rights within powers superior to individual states. International human rights were subsequently ratified by states, limiting their own jurisdiction. This path often incorporated Sampay's discourse of natural rights as overcoming the power of the state.

Notes

1 Data on Sampay's formation in the work of González Arzac, *Sampay y la constitución del futuro.*
2 In regard to this moment of renewal in the Argentine universities through the influence of Kelsen's logical normativism and neo-Thomist currents, see Tau Anzoátegui, *Las ideas jurídicas.*
3 In a letter to Pablo A. Ramella, Sampay comments that "as a young man I met Leibholz, who was recommended to me by Hermann Heller's widow." La Plata, Sunday, Feb. 15, 1970. In Pablo A. Ramella archive in author's possession.
4 Ramella, "Arturo E. Sampay. El derecho natural y el Estado."
5 Sampay's works on the state are detailed at the end of the article.
6 At the end of Mercante's governmental period, Carlos Aloé, officer of the Argentine army, began a period of political intolerance against Mercante and Sampay, the cause of Sampay's dismissal as public prosecutor. For Aloé's opposition, and especially for the radical party, this was a political persecution. Cf. Camara de Diputados, Legislatura de Buenos Aires, 4th Sesión Ordinaria, June 26, 1953. Archive of Pablo A. Ramella, letter from June 30, 1952.
7 Archive of Pablo A. Ramella, letter from June 30, 1952.
8 Sampay "¿Qué Constitución tiene la Argentina y que constitución debe tener?" The quote from St. Thomas Aquinas is *Expositio super Job ad litteram*, Cap. VIII, 1, edición leonina, lines 50/52.
9 See references for this chapter.
10 It must be said that the members of the convention from the Partido Radical had retired from the convention because the senate had not achieved a quorum to declare the need for a reform. This is why these reforms were sanctioned only by the Justicialists.
11 Sampay, *La Constitución Argentina de 1949*, 48.
12 Ibid.
13 Segovia, "Aproximaciones al pensamiento jurídico político."
14 Sampay, *Constitución y pueblo*, 77.
15 Sampay, *Introducción a la Teoría del Estado*, 13.
16 Ibid., 14.
17 Ibid., 24.
18 Ibid., 194.
19 Ibid., 372ff.
20 Ibid., 375.
21 Cf. Ricoeur, *El conflicto de las interpretaciones*; Gadamer, *Verdad y Método*, vol. 1; and Prigogine, *El fin de las certidumbres.*

22 In regard to the thinking of Schmitt and Sampay, see Rodriguez Rial, "Carl Schmitt y el estado de derecho como forma política."
23 Sampay, *Carl Schmitt y la crisis de la ciencia jurídica*, 9.
24 Ibid., 14.
25 Ibid., 9.
26 Ibid., 34, Hauriou's work cited is *Principes de droit public.*
27 Ibid., 36.
28 Gadamer, *Verdad y método*, 390.
29 Sampay, "El derecho internacional de la Paz en la Constitución de Irlanda"; Idem., "La doctrina tomista de la función social de la propiedad en la Constitución Irlandesa de 1937," quoted in González Arzac, *Sampay y la constitución del futuro*, 27, 28.
30 Speech given in the Convención Nacional Constituyente, Session of Feb. 15, 1949. Diario de Sesiones, 189, in Sampay, *La Reforma Constitucional*, 45.
31 Sampay, *Constitución y pueblo*, 102.
32 Sampay, *La filosofía jurídica*, 13–14.
33 Ibid., 28.
34 Ibid., 38.
35 Aristotle, *Nichomachean Ethics*, cited in ibid., 46.
36 Sampay, *La filosofía jurídica*, 49.
37 Letter of Pablo A. Ramella to Sampay from San Juan, Argentine Province, Nov. 18, 1965.
38 Sampay, *La Reforma Constitucional*, 55.
39 Ibid., 60.
40 Ibid., 65.
41 Sampay, *La Constitución Argentina de 1949*, 151 and 156.
42 Segovia, "Aproximación al pensamiento jurídico y político de Arturo Enrique Sampay," 183, 189–91.
43 Sampay, "Informe del despacho de la mayoría de la Comisión Revisora de la Constitución en el Debate en general," in idem., *Las Constituciones de la Argentina (1810/1972)*, 490.
44 Bauman and Bordoni, *Estado de crisis.*
45 Gadamer, *Verdad y método*, 136.
46 Ibid., 132. In a similar sense also rescuing Gadamer's thought: Carlos María Cárcova:

> Positivism first, and the analytical currents later on, represent more a continuation than a rupture in regards to the jusnaturalist conception, as long as they ground this order in a matrix that is also of a formal and abstract nature." See Cárcova, "Jusnaturalismo vs Positivismo jurídico.

This is why he considers that Kelsen himself, different from what Sampay thinks, bases his pure theory in axiomatic principles.

References

Baumann, Zygmunt, and Carlo Bordoni. *Estado de crisis.* Buenos Aires: Ed. Paidós, 2016.

Cárcova, Carlos María. "Jusnaturalismo vs positivismo jurídico: un debate superado." *Revista de Ciencias Sociales* 39 (March 1996). Available at http://www.saij.gob.ar/carlos-maria-carcova-jusnaturalismo-vs-positivismo-juridico-debate-superado-dacf010073-1996-03/123456789-0abc-defg3700-10fcanirtcod.

Gadamer, Hans-Georg. *Verdad y Método*, Vol. 1, *Fundamentos de una hermenéutica filosófica*. 5th ed. Salamanca: Ed. Sígueme, 1993.

González Arzac, Alberto. *Sampay y la Constitución del futuro.* Buenos Aires: Ed. Peña Lillo, 1982.

Hauriou, Maurice. *Principes de droit public.* 2nd ed. Paris: Sirey, 1916.

Mirow, M.C. "Léon Duguit and the Social Function of Property in Argentina." In *Léon Duguit and the Social Obligation Norm of Property: A Translation and Global Exploration*, edited by Paul Babie and Jessica Viven-Wilksch, 267–285. Cham: Springer, 2019.

Prigogine, Ilya. *El fin de las certidumbres.* Santiago, Chile: Ed. Andrés Bello, 1996.

Ramella, Susana T. "Arturo E. Sampay: el Derecho natural y el Estado." *Revista de Historia del Derecho* 36 (2008): 285–308.

Ricoeur, Paul. *El conflicto de las interpretaciones. Ensayos de hermenéutica.* Buenos Aires: Fondo de Cultura Económica, 2003.

Rodriguez Rial, Gabriela. *Carl Schmitt y el Estado de Derecho como forma política. Un diálogo con Arturo Sampay y Norberto Bobbio.* Available at https://revistas.uchile.cl/index.php/RDH/article/view/48440.

Sampay, Arturo E. *La Argentina en la revolución de nuestro tiempo.* Buenos Aires: Ed. Pampa y Cielo, 1964.

Sampay, Arturo E. *Carl Schmitt y la crisis de la ciencia jurídica.* Buenos Aires: Ed. Abeledo Perrot, 1965.

Sampay, Arturo E. *La Constitución Argentina de 1949.* Buenos Aires: Ed. Relevo, 1963.

Sampay, Arturo E. *Constitución y Pueblo.* Buenos Aires: Ed. Cuenca, 1973.

Sampay, Arturo E. *Las constituciones de la Argentina (1810/1972) Recopilación, notas y estudio preliminar de Arturo Enrique Sampay.* Buenos Aires: EUDEBA, 1975.

Sampay, Arturo E. "El derecho internacional de la Paz en la Constitución de Irlanda." *Revista de Derecho, Jurisprudencia y Administración* 37, no. 9 (1939): 257–59.

Sampay, Arturo E. *Estudios de Derecho público, constitucional, de gentes y eclesiástico.* Buenos Aires: Ed. Politeia, 1951.

Sampay, Arturo E. *La filosofía del Iluminismo.* Buenos Aires: Ed. Depalma, 1944.

Sampay, Arturo E. *La filosofía jurídica del Artículo 19 de la Constitución Nacional.* Buenos Aires: Ed. Bibliográfica Argentina, 1965.

Sampay, Arturo E. *Ideas para la revolución de nuestro tiempo de la Argentina.* Buenos Aires: Ed. Juárez, 1968.

Sampay, Arturo E. *Introducción a la Teoría del Estado.* Buenos Aires: Ed. Politeia, 1951.

Sampay, Arturo E. ¿Qué Constitución tiene la Argentina y qué constitución debe tener? En Ministerio de Justicia y Derechos Humanos, Presidencia de la Nación." *Revista Derecho Público* 3, no. 9 (2015): 3.

Sampay, Arturo E. *La Reforma Constitucional.* La Plata: Ed. De Biblioteca Laboremus, 1949.

Segovia, Juan Fernando. "Aproximación al pensamiento jurídico y político de Arturo Enrique Sampay; Catolicismo, Peronismo y Socialismo Argentino." *Anales de la Fundación Francisco Elías de Tejada* 13 (2007): 165–92.

Segovia, Juan Fernando. "Peronismo, Estado y Reforma Constitucional, Ernesto Palacio, Pablo Ramella y Arturo Sampay." *Revista de Historia del Derecho, Instituto de Investigaciones de Historia del Derecho* 32 (2004): 347–441.

Tau Anzoátegui, Víctor. *Las ideas jurídicas argentinas.* Buenos Aires: Ed. Perrot, 1977.

33 Rafael Antonio Caldera Rodríguez (Venezuela, 1916–2009)

Carlos García-Soto

Introduction

Rafael Caldera is one of the most well-rounded personalities of Venezuela's contemporary history. Statesman, founder of a political party, parliamentarian, president of the republic, president of international organizations, jurist, essayist, and university professor, he combined these dimensions to bring together political action and academic reflection.[1] Caldera studied, taught, interpreted, and legislated with a transcendent vision of the human person and social sensibility, infusing his political and legal work with clear Christian views. This chapter highlights how and why Rafael Caldera can be considered a Christian jurist with a Christian sensibility in understanding and applying the law.

Biographical information

Rafael Antonio Caldera Rodríguez was born in San Felipe, the capital of the state of Yaracuy in Venezuela, on January 24, 1916, and died in Caracas, Venezuela, on December 24, 2009, after ninety-three years of life and more than seventy years serving Venezuela. Son of Rafael Caldera Izaguirre and Rosa Sofía Rodríguez Rivero, he married Alicia Pietri Montemayor in 1941, with whom he had a family of six children. He received an intense Christian formation during his childhood and gave to his own family the same example of life and Christian education that he had received from his parents.

He earned his high school diploma at San Ignacio School, in Caracas, in 1931, where he received education from the Jesuits. At school, Caldera developed an extraordinary sensibility for social problems of the country. After graduating from high school, Caldera enrolled in the Central University of Venezuela, where he participated actively in student politics.

Caldera's university experience was decisive in his subsequent activity. There he began to build his political leadership, and there he acquired the academic training that later allowed him to be a politician in the noblest sense of the expression and a jurist who rendered invaluable services to his country. In fact, Caldera was linked to the university all his life as a highly disciplined professor across various subjects.

Between 1932 and 1934, Caldera acted as secretary of the Central Council of the Catholic Youth of Venezuela, where he began his friendship with several of the main Christian democratic leaders who would later be key figures in various Latin American countries, such as Frei Montalva from Chile, Calderón Vega from Mexico, Mario Polar from Peru, and Venancio Flórez from Uruguay. As a student, Caldera was an important figure in the Federation of Students of Venezuela (FEV). In 1936 he left the FEV and, along with other colleagues, founded the National Union Student (UNE). Caldera was recognized from that moment as a young political leader. In 1935, at just nineteen years of age, Caldera won the prize given by the Venezuelan Academy of Language, with his biography of Andrés Bello, the great Latin Americanist, who became a model of civility that Caldera himself would follow.

In 1936 Caldera was appointed Deputy Director of the National Labor Office (created in February, 1936), an office in which he took a leading role in drafting the Labor Law of 1936. Labor conflicts began to have a significant importance in the country, to the point that in 1936 there was a very important strike by workers in the oil sector. These activities were key in his future work in the labor field. More than fifty years later, he actively promoted the first reform of this law and its regulation, both passed in 1990. He was appointed as the first representative to the International Labor Office (ILO) in Venezuela.

In 1939 he graduated from law school and earned his PhD in Political Science, *summa cum laude*, from Central University of Venezuela. Carracciolo Parra León, a very distinguished law professor, became one of his mentors in his university career. Caldera's thesis entitled *Derecho del Trabajo* ("Labor law") became the textbook used by generations of students and lawyers and gained importance even outside of Venezuela.

From the moment of completing his education, Caldera placed his political career as his main occupation. Caldera was an example of Christian politician in Venezuela, serving as one of the founders of the Venezuelan democracy and as one of the most important politicians of the country for decades. Caldera held the post of attorney general of the nation in 1945 and 1946, and he was a key member of the National Constituent Assemblies that drafted Venezuela's constitutions of 1947 and 1961. He served as a national deputy three times (in 1941–44, 1959–64, and 1968–69), and was president of the Chamber of Deputies and vice president of the Congress in 1959–62. He also served twice as a senator (1974–94 and 1999–2000) and presided over the Inter-Parliamentary Union between 1979 and 1982. Twice he was elected president of the republic (1969–74 and 1994–99), both times without the support of the congressional majority. It is widely recognized that Rómulo Betancourt and Rafael Caldera were the builders of the Venezuelan democratic system that functioned between 1958 and 1998.

An essential aspect of the political work of Rafael Caldera was his effort to promote a Christian democratic party in Venezuela and to inspire Christian democratic organizations throughout the world. He founded the Social-Christian Party (COPEI) in 1946 and presided over the Christian Democratic Organization of America (ODCA) from 1964 to 1968, and over the Christian Democratic World

Union in 1967 and 1968. Caldera is recognized worldwide as one of the main promoters of Christian democracy during the twentieth century.

Caldera was not only a politician interested in the social problems of Venezuela. He also served the country through his university teaching. As an academic, Caldera was professor of juridical sociology and labor law at Central University of Venezuela from 1943 to 1968 and at Andrés Bello Catholic University from 1953 to 1968. He was awarded the doctorate *honoris causa* and honorary professorships at more than forty universities around the world. Elected to membership in Venezuela's Academy of Political and Social Sciences in 1953, to the position of his late adoptive father, Tomás Liscano, Caldera also became a member of the Venezuelan Academy of Language in 1967. He presided over the Venezuelan Association of Sociology and the Venezuelan Institute of Labor Law. As an author, he published a number of very important books, articles, essays, prologues, and other publications.

According to the personal characteristics that many have ascribed to Rafael Caldera, it is relevant to understand that he was not only a politician but also an academic. Caldera was able to engage in intense activity as a politician, serving the country in a variety of ways and playing an essential role in Christian democratic activities around the world. In the same way, Caldera was an academic with a wide range of intellectual interests, from the study of the Spanish language to the study of Venezuelan history, becoming the most important authority on labor law in Venezuela for decades.

A Christian conception of the person and of its social dimension

As noted, Rafael Caldera received an in-depth Christian education. He made an effort to unravel the core of the social doctrine of the Catholic Church, and he studied this doctrine beginning at the university and for the rest of his life, as is reflected in many of his essays, speechs, and books.

Rafael Caldera's political and legal understanding makes the human person a central character, as the nucleus of all government actions. This perspective referred not only to the person in his or her individual condition but also in the sphere of the person's social undertakings. In this view, the influence of the social doctrine of the Catholic Church would be decisive.[2] From this perspective, Caldera was clear about how the religious dimension of the human person reached both the individual side and the social side. On the importance of the religious reality of the person in social life, he wrote:

> The most virulent explosions of atheist materialism have not succeeded in extirpating religious sentiment from people's souls. Their [atheists'] leaders have come to distrust their methods of militant antireligiousness and have officially recognized the existence of religion, finally coming to the same thesis of secular liberalism, cornering in the temples the manifestations of worship by which they want to distill a state religion. It's useless. The religious exists

> within the social and cannot ignore the great questions that anguish the people, just as those who ignore life's religious aspect cannot know social reality.[3]

From this point of view, Caldera understood that religion is a constitutive part of human nature and that spirituality is a crucial aspect of the social order, even when it is not easy to see the reason for some events in history.

In fact, Caldera clearly expressed why he believed that divine Providence played a fundamental role in history. He reflected such beliefs in a passage from a speech made on January 1, 1999, weeks before his second term as president of the Republic of Venezuela ended:

> The "mysterious presence of God in history we call Providence," according to the insuperable definition coined by John Paul II, is expressed in respect to the freedom of choice. The Almighty, in his infinite wisdom, knows the causes and consequences of each act of human will and offers the actors the possibility of obtaining, with their free performance, the greatest benefit in the ethical and material orders. [4]

Such conceptions were decisive in Caldera's political and legal work.

The influence of the social doctrine of the Church in Caldera's ideas and actions

In his political work, Rafael Caldera defended the social doctrine of the Catholic Church whether he was part of the political opposition or a member of the government. His work as constituent, legislator, professor, author, and lawyer was also infused with the notion that every person should be protected, and there are several examples of his oral and written expressions on these subjects. He approached his recurrent area of legal work—labor law—from a perspective in which the rights of workers should be respected and protected.[5] In his book *Derecho del Trabajo* (*Labor law*) he emphasized the importance of the social doctrine of the Church, explaining that the social doctrine of the Church is the application of the norms of Christian morality to the problem of each era. He reasoned that Catholic social doctrine responds to the nature of the different social problems in every epoch.[6]

One of Caldera's sons, Rafael Tomás Caldera, a philosophy professor, notes that his father's conception of work was deeply influenced by such ideas:

> For Rafael Caldera, the social fact of work is the cornerstone of life in society and, therefore, of the realization of the person. The adequate regulation of labor relations, a work that cannot be treated as a commodity since it is always an act of the person, is of paramount importance in the development and harmony of societies. [7]

In fact, from his privileged position as a Christian democratic leader of worldwide authority, Rafael Caldera would come to be recognized as a defender and disseminator of the proposals of the social doctrine of the Church in international policy. He was an insistent defender of the concept of international social justice as a call for solidarity among people. It is not of small importance that he was invited to be a keynote speaker at the ceremony to commemorate the twentieth anniversary of Pope Paul VI's encyclical *Populorum progressio* in the Synod of Bishops on March 24, 1987, in front of the College of Cardinals and Pope John Paul II.[8] Abdón Vivas Terán concludes that the set of postulates that derive from the social doctrine of the Church permeated the ideas and actions of Rafael Caldera and were integrated indissolubly in his mind and heart.[9] We will see how these ideas came to fruition.

Politics and Christianity in the ideas of Rafael Caldera: Christian democracy

It is widely recognized that one of the main problems regarding the links between politics and religion is the necessity of differentiating the roles of each institution in every subject. For Caldera it would be highly important, on one hand, to take on political work based on a social and Christian conception of the person and of society. But, on the other hand, he would always be very clear that the Catholic Church, to which he was faithful, could neither be involved in nor be an instrument of supporting or defending a political position. At the inauguration of the First Inter-American Catholic Congress for Integral Human Development, while he was president of the Republic of Venezuela, he summarized these ideas well:

> I also come as a ruler to say that, in the midst of the imperfections of life, in the midst of the difficulties that reality establishes, nothing would be more pleasing to my spirit than having acted as a Christian in the exercise of authority. That is why I have endeavored to forgive, to dialogue, to tolerate, to respect, to announce sincere intentions of friendship with countries with which it would be easy to show a negative and infertile demagoguery, and to open roads to all the people of the world. But I know at the same time the tremendous danger that exists when a government intends to assume the representation of a thought of such universal magnitude as Christian thought. Governments pass; the church and Christianity remain. Governments represent concrete efforts to exercise authority in the life of communities; Christianity represents much more. That is why I want to say here, in the most sincere way, that nothing is more intimately my desire than not compromising Christianity in any way by the temporary action of my government.[10]

The political ideology that Caldera would adhere to, then, would be Christian democracy, and the approaches of Christian democracy would guide all of his political work. He became one of the most important exponents of that doctrine. Indeed, he dedicated one of his books to summarizing the essence of Christian democracy as an ideology: *Especificidad de la Democracia Cristiana*

(*The specificity of Christian democracy*), which became a fundamental text on the subject. In it, he sums up what Christianity means for a Christian democrat in political and social work:

> By calling ourselves Christians, we are holding the primacy of morality—the idea that any problem of political-social order is entangled in a moral question that should not be dispensed with. That politics is not a simple art of convenience but a maintenance of attitudes, an exercise of behaviors that, like everything related to human behavior, are subject to the ethical order, an empire that cannot be subtracted. Precisely when social Christian thought is analyzed, there is an affirmation that for some represents something trivial, but which, in our view, has a great importance: the social problem is, above all, a moral problem.[11]

These statements are significant. Caldera insists on this fundamental aspect of Christian democracy: social problems are not just technical problems to be solved through mere economic or organizational techniques. On the contrary, Caldera's thought and political work stand upon a fundamental consideration: that social problems are, above all, moral problems, which must be solved through the prism of Christian morality. Such ideas would also influence Caldera's legal work. Indeed, insofar as Caldera saw a moral core in social problems, he also observed the need to solve legal issues with a moral sense of justice.

A jurist with a Christian conception of the law

Just as Caldera's conception of politics was impregnated with his Christian conception of the person, so too was his legal work oriented toward the protection of the person from a Christian perspective. In this sense, it is not a coincidence that Caldera chose labor law as the main field of study. By the time Caldera began working as a lawyer and law professor, the so-called "social question" was a fundamental matter in which basic problems of the social order were debated. It was rightly considered that the worker should be subject to special protection by law. Labor law, from that perspective, was seen as an instrument for the protection of workers' rights and as an instrument to ensure peace in society.

Thus, for example, in a speech during the Third Latin American Congress of Writers in Caracas, on July 3, 1970, Caldera stated:

> As a man of law, I would like my life to contribute to the realization of the legal system in what is its most noble attribute, in the conquest of peace, in fruitful exchange, in respect for the human person, in the presence of higher standards that must govern coexistence.[12]

The outcome of such aspirations is described by Alfredo Morles Hernández, a prominent professor of commercial law in Venezuela:

> A devout Catholic of sincere faith, he frequented and made friends with some of the highest dignitaries of the Catholic Church, including popes like John Paul II; he was always interested in the social thought contained in encyclicals and other ecclesial documents, which he studied, analyzed, exploited, and disseminated. Jurist and iusnaturalist, his ideological position was not unreflective.[13]

As a university professor, Caldera would study the different schools for the interpretation and application of law. His way of studying and exercising law would be clearly influenced by his moral conceptions, based on the Christian faith.

It was natural, therefore, for Rafael Caldera to consider the conception of law from a broader perspective than that of reductionist positivism:

> That the law is power; that the law stems solely from the state; that laws are no more than their content was taught in the last century by the highest authorities of juridical science, and it is still taught by the professors of our professors. It was a period of spiritual crisis. Souls were tired from searching, deprived of faith, of the fundaments of the moral life, seeking refuge in a distressing pragmatism. Renowned personalities of undeniable worth elevated the "fetishism of the laws" to the supreme cult of the jurist; in the comments and justifications of the written norm, in the Spenglerian "philology of juridical texts," they sought comfort for disoriented and skeptical minds. Fortunately, this crisis is already passing. It is positivism that, in turn, has entered a decisive crisis. It becomes more important to satisfy the "need for idealism" that Charmont called for in the first ten years of this century. Such a need for idealism, such a reaction against positivism, is accredited to the philosophy with progressive strength. The newest aphorisms consecrate the revolt of facts against the code, the impotence of the laws, the crisis of the modern juridical conscience, the phenomenon, in the end, of a juridical rebirth over the ruins of the laws originally considered perfect, but later found incapable of solving the fragile schematization of norms.[14]

Such a perspective of the law, then, would turn Rafael Caldera into a jurist who would reason with necessary scientific rigor while also acknowledging the philosophical foundation of the law. In other words, Caldera would not reduce the solution of juridical problems to simple logic or technical reasoning.

In the same way that Caldera felt that political problems should not be solved with merely technical criteria, he also concluded that legal problems must be solved from an ethical perspective without the expectation that the mere application of the law, as dictated by the state, is sufficient. As Rafael Tomás Caldera wrote:

> This is why the epithet "integral" is fully justified in his condition as a jurist. Caldera is not a mere legal technician, a specialist in a specific branch or legal field that serves a practical purpose. He is a man of the law, who seeks the

> realization of justice and, with it, the instauration of a way of life that values freedom, private property, family, education, work, and social security.[15]

As noted previously, it should not be considered a mere coincidence that Caldera chose labor law as his field of study and work from his youth. There he would find the scope to provide legal solutions to important social problems from a Christian perspective.

In Caldera's work as a professor and author of studies on labor law, this conception of law had very practical applications around the concept of "social justice."[16] As Caldera himself concluded:

> This idea of social justice implies in each national community, within the domestic sphere, the abandonment of the relationship of arithmetic equalities characteristic of commutative justice, and the establishment of proportionalities that rest on the capabilities and possibilities of each person. It is proper for the laws derived from social justice to establish inequalities in what each person is obliged to do, in order to seek, through regulatory methods, the restoration of the effective equality of rights, so that social reality demands more from him who has more and does not establish a regime of arithmetic equalities. Thus, in relations between capital and labor, social justice imposes increasing burdens on capital in order to restore labor rights. Within the tax regime, especially with regard to direct tax, social justice welcomes the principle of "progressivity" instead of simple "proportionality," so that the powerful economic classes bear the greatest weight of the expenses demanded by society; it seeks to convert the state, through taxes, into an instrument of distributive justice that demands more from those who have greater resources, to attend through services of various kinds to the needs of those who have the greatest need.[17]

Social doctrine of the Church, Labor Law, and morality as the foundation of politics and law

As we can see from the above, Rafael Caldera's multifaceted personality comprises three interrelated aspects: his conviction about the relevance of the social doctrine of the Catholic Church, the importance of a correct understanding and application of labor law, and the need for fundamental political action and solution of legal problems from a moral foundation. These foundations guided him in his political and legal action in the drafting of constitutions in Venezuela.

Rafael Caldera's transcendence in the constitutional configuration of Venezuela is based on his participation in the fundamental act of drafting the constitutions of 1947 and 1961. In the constitutional processes that gave rise to these constitutions, Caldera was one of the most powerful and persuasive voices, and his ideas were collected in many texts of those constitutional assemblies. In the most sensitive moral issues that arose in those constituent debates, Caldera participated actively, defending the dignity of the human person, promoting the recognition and protection of rights (such as those related to religious freedom and education), and promoting a consistent social organization with the nature and dignity of the human person.

From this point of view, the transcendent conception of the person that Rafael Caldera infused into his political and legal work would have very particular manifestations in his work as a constituent—both in the National Constituent Assembly that gave rise to the Constitution of 1947 and in the National Constituent Assembly that gave rise to the Constitution of 1961.[18] Many subjects of those constitutions were expressly contemplated in the proposals made by Caldera in the constituent assembly debates. From the norm of judicial control of administrative acts, to the normative principles of the tax system, to everything related to the right to work and other social rights, all were drafted largely according to ideas promoted by Caldera.

Among those ideas, several that stand out reflect his Christian vision of the person and society. For example, in the debate on education in the National Constituent Assembly that gave rise to the Constitution of 1947, he made very clear his conception of the act of freedom that implies the acceptance of faith:

> By the way, and in reference to the phrase used by Representative Lander about dogmas that in his view could inhibit the very meaning of education, know that religious dogmas are accepted by an act of freedom of conscience; that man never feels freer than when, in the use of that very freedom of conscience, he proclaims these dogmas and recognizes himself subservient. But the new kind of dogma is very different, and is intended to be imposed by relying on the material sovereignty of the state, because the church has no armies, the church does not have public power, the church speaks to conscience, while the state is an organization that, by its very nature, involves the maintenance of an army and police and forces that impose themselves over art.[19]

On another occasion during discussions in the National Constituent Assembly, Caldera insisted, in regard to the right to religious freedom:

> We also believe that in the field of guarantees, the guarantee of religious freedom must be stated without any more restrictions than those imposed by morality and public order...We do not believe that it is in accordance with the structure of a modern state to maintain norms that subject the religious experience of people to a guardianship, often ill-intentioned, of the state.[20]

On the other hand, nothing less than the protection of human life from conception was introduced by the constituent Rafael Caldera in the process that gave rise to the Constitution of 1961, a rule that is largely maintained in the Constitution of 1999.

Conclusion

This chapter has summarized essential features of Rafael Caldera, not only as a fundamental Christian politician for the understanding of contemporary Venezuela, but also as a Christian jurist who understood the value of law in society and studied, interpreted, legislated, and applied the right from his own Christian vision of social life. Thanks to his multifaceted nature, this Christian jurist was able to project his influence on Venezuelan law in a variety of ways: as a writer of constitutions, a legislator, an executor of the law from his post as president of the republic, a professor and author of *Derecho del Trabajo*, and even as a lawyer who exercised his profession with a Christian vision of the person and social life. As Abdón Vivas Terán states:

> We maintain that this Christian faith was, surely, the powerful force that Rafael Caldera always demonstrated possessing through his long, vital work to develop a dizzying rhythm as a builder of public, social, intellectual, academic, pedagogical, family works, whose accumulated total is certainly overwhelming.[21]

He was a Christian jurist in the strictest sense of the term.

Notes

1 See Suárez, "Caldera, Rafael," 588–89.
2 On how the young Rafael Caldera was finding perspective from which to assume his commitment as a Christian politician, see Rafael Tomás Caldera, "Hombre de fe," 18–21. Rafael Caldera made important reflections on the personal demands that Christianity implied in his speech "La Hora de Emaús."
3 Caldera, *Moldes para la fragua*, 312.
4 Cited by Rafael Tomás Caldera, "Hombre de fe," 27.
5 Rafael Caldera would choose labor law as his main area of juridical work, precisely because it focuses on the employment relationship. See Cartay Ramírez, *Caldera y Betancourt*, 60. Caldera's book *Derecho del Trabajo* compiles several writings where he exposes many of his concerns about the employment relationship from the perspective of the social doctrine of the Catholic Church.
6 Caldera, *Derecho del Trabajo*, 47–48. In this sense, Ramón Vinke summarizes that

> in the Labor Law of 1936 the influence of the social doctrine of the church was felt. As a student of the San Ignacio School, run by the Jesuit fathers, the student Rafael Caldera had participated in the effervescence produced by the encyclical *Quadragesimo Anno*, promulgated by Pope Pius XI on May 15, 1931, on the fortieth anniversary of the encyclical *Rerum Novarum* of Pope Leo XIII, with which a decisive impulse to the social doctrine of the church was given. As leader of Acción Católica [Catholic Action], Rafael Caldera attended, in 1931, at the Archbishop's Palace in Caracas, a tribute to Bishop Salvador Montes de Oca, who returned triumphantly from exile and spoke—on that occasion—of social issues. As leader of Acción Católica, Rafael Caldera also had traveled—alongside two companions—to Rome, to participate in a Latin American student Catholic congress, where he heard the social teachings of the church from the lips of Pope Pius XI himself.
>
> (Vinke, *El Dr. Rafael Caldera*, 23)

7 Rafael Tomás Caldera, "Presentación," in *Rafael Caldera, jurista integral*, 10.
8 See Vivas Terán, "Rafael Caldera y la inspiración cristiana," 32.
9 Ibid., 34.
10 Cited by Rafael Tomás Caldera, "Hombre de fe," 21–22. In regards to such statements, Rafael Tomás Caldera concludes,

> it is a clear position, also expressed very clearly. But the Christian will always be a mystery perhaps for those who do not have faith. Caldera, a man of faith, has known how to rely on Providence to go forward in the midst of difficulties, misunderstandings, and setbacks, with the certainty that the effort in that struggle made sense.
>
> ("Presentación," in Vinke, *El Dr. Rafael Caldera*, 6–7)

In another essay, Rafael Tomás Caldera concluded:

> With the clarity of these approaches, then, we should not be surprised, on one hand, by the persistence of carrying out the Christian social doctrine through political action and, on the other, the attempt not to involve the Catholic Church in political positions in any way. This presumes, at the same time, a respect for the transcendence of the revealed truth that cannot be reduced to a political program in a determined time and place; and the presumption that only in Jesus Christ and in his message does the human being find the guidance and strength to carry out existence with meaning and value.
>
> ("Hombre de fe," 21)

11 Caldera, *Especificidad de la Democracia Cristiana*, 84. In this book, Caldera sums up the elements that Christian philosophy provides to the political doctrine of Christian democracy: (i) affirmation of the spiritual, (ii) the ethical foundation of politics, (iii) the dignity of the human being, (iv) the primacy of the common good, and (v) the perfectibility of civil society. He also expands on the key premises defended by the Christian democrats:

> these ideas that move all Christian democrats, in every country in the world, to defend the democratic state; pluralism; community solidarity; the development of humanity and of all people; international integration; the concept of community property and the regulation of individual property in such a way that it serves a social function; harmony between social classes; renovation and social change; strengthening of the family, the municipality, of trade union organizations; the ethical meaning of the political life, so the realist position does not reduce the moral norms to a pragmatic position; the realization of a new order inspiring social justice, nationally and internationally—all of this, in my view, qualifies the contribution of the Christian Democratic element within our political conception.
>
> (Caldera, *Especificidad de la Democracia Cristiana*, 109)

12 Cited by Morles Hernández, *Rafael Caldera, jurista integral*, 47.
13 Ibid., 19–20.
14 Caldera, *Hacia el renacimiento del Derecho*, 12–13. During the discussions of the National Constituent Assembly that gave birth to the Constitution of 1947, Caldera said: "The principle of obedience to the laws of the state is inherent to the sovereignty, but it is also inherent to the democratic conception of political life, to the fundamental concepts of Christian civilization, the principle that the laws of any state cannot violate the power of conscience…The laws of the state must stop before the fundamental reduction of the guaranties of the human person." Cited by Oliveros Villa, *El derecho de libertad religiosa en Venezuela*, 127. For more details regarding Caldera's conception of the importance of respecting the state of law, see Aguiar Aranguren, "Rafael Caldera y el Estado de derecho en Venezuela."

15 Rafael Tomás Caldera, "Presentación," in *Rafael Caldera, jurista integral*, 10.
16 His book *Derecho del Trabajo*, which was his doctoral thesis, was a pioneering work on that subject in Venezuela. The text later became a fundamental bibliographic reference not only in Venezuela but throughout Latin America.
17 Caldera, *Especificidad de la Democracia Cristiana*, 103–04.
18 Regarding the constitutional thoughts of Rafael Caldera, see Álvarez, "Fundamentos del pensamiento constitucional de Rafael Caldera."
19 *Diario de Debates*, National Constituent Assembly, March 10, 1947, 533. On other statements and reasoning made by Caldera regarding the discussion of religious freedom in the National Constituent Assembly, see Oliveros Villa, *El derecho de libertad religiosa en Venezuela*, 98ff.
20 Cited by Oliveros Villa, *El derecho de libertad religiosa*, 109.
21 Vivas Terán, "Rafael Caldera y la inspiración cristiana," 48–49. See also, Caldera Pietri, *El compromiso con el ideal.*

References

Aguiar Aranguren, Asdrúbal. "Rafael Caldera y el Estado de derecho en Venezuela." In *Rafael Caldera: estadista y pacificador*, edited by Arráiz Lucca, 79–112. Caracas: Ediciones B-Fundación Konrad Adenauer-Universidad Metropolitana, 2016.

Álvarez, Tulio Alberto. "Fundamentos del pensamiento constitucional de Rafael Caldera." In *Rafael Caldera: estadista y pacificador*, edited by Arráiz Lucca, 113–36. Caracas: Ediciones B-Fundación Konrad Adenauer-Universidad Metropolitana, 2016.

Arráiz Lucca, Rafael, ed. *Rafael Caldera: estadista y pacificador. Centenario de su nacimiento 1916–2016.* Caracas: Ediciones B-Fundación Konrad Adenauer-Universidad Metropolitana, 2016.

Caldera Pietri, Andrés. *El compromiso con el ideal: el siempre joven Rafael Caldera.* Caracas: Fundación Tomás Liscano, 2016.

Caldera, Rafael. *Derecho al Trabajo.* Caracas: Cyngular, 2017.

Caldera, Rafael. *Derecho del Trabajo.* Buenos Aires: Editorial El Ateneo, 1984.

Caldera, Rafael. *Especificidad de la Democracia Cristiana.* Caracas: Dimensiones, 1987.

Caldera, Rafael. *Hacia el renacimiento del Derecho.* Caracas: Tipografía La Nación, 1942.

Caldera, Rafael. "La Hora de Emaús." Speech delivered at Ciudad Universitaria de Caracas, in the International Catholic Conference Series before the 11th Bolivarian Eucharistic Congress, December 4, 1956.

Caldera, Rafael. *Moldes para la fragua.* Buenos Aires: Editorial El Ateneo, 1962.

Caldera, Rafael Tomás. "Hombre de fe." In *Rafael Caldera: estadista y pacificador*, edited by Arráiz Lucca, 17–28. Caracas: Ediciones B-Fundación Konrad Adenauer-Universidad Metropolitana, 2016.

Caldera, Rafael Tomás. "Presentación." In Vinke, *El Dr. Rafael Caldera, hombre de la Patria y de la Iglesia*, 5–7. Caracas: La Iglesia en la Venezuela Republicana, 2010.

Caldera, Rafael Tomás. "Presentación." In *Rafael Caldera, jurista integral*, edited by, Alfredo Morles Hernández, 7–9. Caracas: Editorial Jurídica Venezolana, 2017.

Cartay Ramírez, Gehard. *Caldera y Betancourt. Constructores de la Democracia.* Caracas: Dahbar, 2017.

Morles Hernández, Alfredo. *Rafael Caldera, jurista integral.* Caracas: Editorial Jurídica Venezolana, 2017.

Oliveros Villa, Pedro. *El derecho de libertad religiosa en Venezuela. Estudio histórico jurídico.* Caracas: Academia Nacional de la Historia, 2000.

Suárez, Naudy. "Caldera, Rafael." *Diccionario de Historia de Venezuela.* Caracas: Fundación Polar, 1997.

Vinke, Ramón. *El Dr. Rafael Caldera, hombre de la Patria y de la Iglesia.* Caracas: La Iglesia en la Venezuela Republicana, 2010.

Vivas Terán, Abdón. "Rafael Caldera y la inspiración cristiana de su acción política." In *Rafael Caldera: estadista y pacificador*, edited by Arráiz Lucca, 29–54. Caracas: Ediciones B-Fundación Konrad Adenauer-Universidad Metropolitana, 2016.

34 Óscar Arnulfo Romero y Galdámez (El Salvador, 1917–80)

Rafael Domingo

Introduction

A Christian martyr for the gospel of social justice, and a man of deep spirituality and great ethical stature, Óscar Romero, Archbishop of San Salvador during years of brutal government and paramilitary repression, is a towering figure in the recent history of El Salvador and Latin America. Since his murder on March 24, 1980, while he was celebrating the Eucharist, his legacy and cultural influence have only grown. For decades, in life and after it, he was controversial and often manipulated, branded as both a communist and a conservative, as a provocateur of the Salvadoran civil war (1980–92), and a leader of people's liberation and human rights. Many political, military, and ecclesiastical authorities inside and outside his country harshly criticized Romero's attitude and behavior. Salvadoran oligarchs denounced him repeatedly, but not so the hundreds of thousands of peasants who confirmed as true what Romero wrote about his own mission: "The ministry that God has given me is, like the one given to Moses, to lead our people to the Promised Land."[1]

It is now widely accepted that Romero was the "voice of the voiceless," an advocate of the "violence of love," and a champion of human rights in the struggle for social justice. He devoted himself completely to preventing the tragic civil war in his long-suffering country and to defending and protecting the poor. Not a politician, Romero became the cornerstone of Salvadoran political life. Not a professional theologian, Romero marked Latin American theology of the twenty-first century. Not a lawyer, Romero was an indefatigable defender of social justice. As a martyr and as a patriot, he preferred to die for God and his country rather than condone a repressive government that abusively violated the most basic human rights of the poor.

In 1998 life-size statutes of Archbishop Óscar Arnulfo Romero and other twentieth-century figures who died for their faith—including Martin Luther King Jr., Maximilian Kolbe, and Dietrich Bonhoeffer—were unveiled in Westminster Abbey's main entrance in London. Years later, Romero's statue was included in the Human Rights Porch of the National Cathedral in Washington, DC. In 2010 the United Nations General Assembly proclaimed March 24 as the International Day for the Right to the Truth Concerning Gross Human Rights

Violations and for the Dignity of Victims, in recognition of Romero's role in defending the human rights of the most vulnerable populations.[2] In 2015 and after Romero's cause languished for years in the Vatican bureaucracy, the Catholic Church beatified Romero during a multitudinous Eucharistic celebration in San Salvador that brought together more than 250,000 people.[3] Three years later, in October 2018, Pope Francis canonized Romero along with Pope Paul VI in St. Peter's Square. This coincidence was not accidental. Paul VI was, for Romero, a good shepherd, a teacher, and an inspirer.[4]

Many books have been written about Romero, and many remain to be written. So far, three biographies stand out: the pioneering and well-documented biography in English written by James R. Brockman;[5] the first-hand account written in Spanish by Jesús Delgado, Romero's private secretary;[6] and the recent biography written in Italian by Roberto Morozzo della Rocca, based on the archive of the Archdiocese of San Salvador and on Romero's personal papers.[7] A revised short version (without footnotes) of Morozzo's biography was published in English in 2015.[8] For the last two years of his life, Romero's diary constitutes a wonderful account and source of inspiration.[9] Recently, Michael Lee and Matthew Phillip Whelan offered two interesting and knowledgeable approaches to Romero's theological legacy. Lee highlights Romero's relevancy in the understanding of the Church's mission of in today's world, and Matthew Phillip Whelan focuses on Romero's Catholic social teaching in the area of land reform.[10]

Biographical information

Óscar Arnulfo Romero y Galdámez was born on August 15, 1917, in Ciudad Barrios, a municipality in the department of San Miguel in El Salvador, near the Honduran border. He was the second of the eight children (one of whom died at birth) of Santos Romero, the local telegraph operator, and Guadalupe de Jesús Goldámez. Like their neighbors in the town, the family had neither electricity nor running water in their home. At the age of four, Óscar was struck with polio, which affected his ability to move and speak for some months. Romero received his elementary education both in the public school (for the first three grades) and with a private teacher. He then was apprenticed to a carpenter. In 1930, he entered the minor seminary in San Miguel, run by the Claretians. To pay part of the expenses of the seminary, he spent one summer working in the Potosí gold mine, located a few miles from Ciudad Barrios.

In 1937, the year his father died, Romero went to the national seminary run by the Jesuits in El Salvador, but in the middle of the year, Romero's bishop sent him to Rome. In the Eternal City, he lived at the Latin American College and studied at the Gregorian University, where he received a Licentiate in Theology in 1941 and began a doctorate on the ascetic theology of the Spanish Jesuit Luis de la Puente (1554–1624). On April 4, 1942, he was ordained as a priest in the college chapel. The words he wrote in his diary in February 1943 are a good summary of his high spiritual aspirations at that time:

> In recent days after reading some of Father La Puente at the curia, principally his *Life of Father Álvarez*,[11] the Lord has inspired in me a great desire for holiness. I have been thinking of how far a soul can ascend if it lets itself be possessed entirely by God. It is a shame to waste such precious time and such valuable gifts.[12]

During World War II, in August 1943, Romero left the bombed city of Rome without completing his doctorate, summoned home by his bishop. Romero, however, was not able to arrive in El Salvador until December 1943—as passengers coming from Italy to Cuba, Romero and his colleague and friend Rafael Valladares were suspected of being enemy aliens and sent to a prison camp. After being recognized as clerics by a Cuban priest and spending time in hospital to recover, they were freed.

Romero's first assignment as a priest was in Anamorós, a small village in the La Unión area of El Salvador. In 1947, Romero moved to San Miguel to be the secretary of the bishop and pastor of the city parish of Santo Domingo. He was also the rector of the minor seminary, the editor of the diocesan newspaper, the promoter of an Alcoholics Anonymous group, and the leader of the committee for the completion of the construction of San Miguel's Cathedral Basilica of the Queen of Peace. On June 8, 1967, he was appointed secretary of the Bishops Conference of El Salvador and moved to San Salvador. One year later, in May 1968, he also became the secretary of the Central American Bishops' Secretariat (*Secretariado Episcopal de América Central* or SEDAC). Working unceasingly, Romero sometimes weakened his health, resulting occasionally in natural exhaustion.

On June 21, 1970, Romero was ordained bishop and became auxiliary bishop of El Salvador. His episcopal motto, "Think with the Church," drawn from the spiritual exercises of Saint Ignatius, reflected Romero's sentiments of moral and doctrinal union with Rome. During these complicated years for the Catholic Church, in the aftermath of Second Vatican Council, Romero sought for a more cautious interpretation of the pronouncements of the Council and the Conference of Medellín.[13] He had difficult relations with the diocesan clergy and with a group of young Salvadoran Jesuits who actively defended a controversial political theology of liberation. In 1972 he was named rector of the interdiocesan seminary, which was closed by the Bishops' Conference a year later owing to financial problems.

In 1974 the Holy See appointed Romero bishop of the diocese of Santiago de María, covering the territory of the department of Usulután, in the southeast of the country, and a small part of the department of San Miguel, including his hometown, Ciudad Barrios. Before being installed as a bishop by the papal nuncio on December 14, 1974, Romero went to Rome to thank Pope Paul VI for his appointment.

As a diocesan pastor, Romero developed a very intense activity of visiting the poor, preaching in the most remote corners of the dioceses, and spending time with and promoting the unity of the clergy. He opened some church buildings for use by hundreds of laborers as shelters during the fall harvest and ordered the churches to provide the workers with hot meals at night. He saw firsthand the suffering of the poor *campesinos* and how they were often paid below the officially required minimum. He denounced in a pastoral letter the treatment of the laborers who harvested coffee in the area.[14] On May 18, 1975 the Vatican named Romero consultor of the Pontifical Commission for Latin America, under the auspices of the Congregation for Bishops. This allowed Romero to experience the government of the Catholic Church at the highest level of the Roman Curia.

The massacre of Tres Calles, in the city of San Agustín, Usulután, had a deep impact on Romero. On Saturday, June, 21, 1975 at 1:00 AM, National Guard officers entered Tres Calles and cold-bloodedly murdered four members of the Ostorga family (José Alberto, José Alfredo, Hector David, and Jorge Alberto) and their neighbor Santos Morales, all alleged to be part of a subversive organization.[15] Romero visited and consoled the relatives of the victims, celebrated the Eucharist for them, and protested in person before the local commander of the National Guard. The officer, however, incriminated Romero, telling him: "Cassocks are not bulletproof."[16] Some days later, Romero wrote a private letter to the president of El Salvador, Colonel Arturo Armando Molina, in the name of the voiceless poor, requesting a full investigation and indemnification of the victims' families. The government, however, did not investigate the incident.

Archbishop of San Salvador

On February 3, 1977, the Holy See appointed Romero as the new archbishop of San Salvador to replace Bishop Luis Chávez y González. Romero had been the favorite of the apostolic nuncio to El Salvador, Emanuele Gerada, but not of Chávez himself, nor of many Salvadoran diocesan priests. They preferred the longtime auxiliary bishop, Monsignor Rivera, whom they considered to be closer to the poor and to the spirit of Medellín. The government and the wealthiest families in the country respected Romero and supported his candidacy—as did the Vatican, although this would change.[17] Romero was installed on February 22 in a modest ceremony in the church attached to the seminary of San José de la Montaña, amid strong political and social tensions. He chose to live with great austerity at the Divine Providence Hospital, known as *El hospitalito* (the Little Hospital), run by Carmelite sisters.[18]

Two days before Romero's installation, General Carlos Humberto Romero (1924–2017), won the presidential elections, which were marred by accusations of voting fraud. Popular protests of the electoral fraud followed, and the government responded with violence. On February 28, the security forces opened fire against the crowd in the Plaza de La Libertad, killing dozens of civilians. Two months later, on May 1, security forces fired again at protesters in a public demonstration at the Metropolitan Cathedral (*la matanza de la Catedral*—the slaughter at the cathedral).

In the months around Romero's installation, the government had started an intimidation campaign and persecution against the Catholic Church. The oligarchy and the military forces saw a potential threat in some priests who had become leaders among the landless laborers and were trying to organize them to confront Salvadoran social injustice. The oligarchs and the military accused the Catholic Church of meddling in political affairs and inciting peasants against the government. Some priests were arrested and some foreign priests were deported or denied entry into the country, but at that point, no priest had been killed. On March 12, 1977, however, the Salvadoran Jesuit Rutilio Grande, Romero's good friend and confidant, was murdered along with an elderly man, Manuel Solórzano, and a young boy, Nelson Lemus, while traveling in a jeep toward El Paisnal.[19] A passionate preacher, Fr. Rutilio Grande worked hard with peasants and helped them to organize and advocate for human rights. Right-wing extremists branded him a communist and, consequently, a target for shooting. The beatification of Fr. Grande and his two lay companions was approved by Pope Francis on February 21, 2020.

The assassination of Rutilio Grande shocked Archbishop Romero. It was not only the slaying of a beloved priest and friend, a leader of Christian work with the poor, but also the confirmation that the killers served the interest of the Salvadoran oligarchy. Advised by his priests, Romero adopted two controversial momentous decisions. First, he suspended the Sunday Masses on March 20 throughout the whole archdiocese and celebrated only one Mass in the cathedral as a sign of unity, grief, and protest for the assassination of Fr. Rutilio Grande and the persecution of the Church. The decision drew criticism from some ecclesiastical authorities, especially the apostolic nuncio. However, more than 150 priests joined the Mass as celebrants, and more than one-hundred-thousand people attended the liturgical celebration.[20] Second, Romero decided not to participate in any official governmental ceremony until the government led a serious investigation of the murders. In fact, Archbishop Romero did not attend General Romero's inauguration on July 1, 1977.

The two measures were taken as a challenge to the government. On May 11, 1977, death squads killed another priest, Alfonso Navarro, along with a young parishioner, Luis Torres, at the rectory. This assassination took place in revenge for the kidnapping and murder of the foreign minister, Mauricio Borgonovo Pohl, by the left-wing paramilitary organization Liberation People's Forces. The oligarchy believed that some revolutionary priests supported that organization. Some days later, on May 17, two-thousand soldiers occupied Aguilares to intimidate the population. Many civilians were tortured and killed, and the military desecrated the Blessed Sacrament at the parish church, which was used as a barracks. In 1978 and 1979, repression intensified with the murders of thousands of people, including four more priests. "Be a patriot: kill a priest!" was the statement that appeared in many advertisements, posters, and billboards.

Romero spoke out forcefully: "The church is not involved in politics, but when politics touches the altar, the church defends the altar."[21] He denounced the disappearances, tortures, killings, and crimes from his cathedral pulpit during his Sunday homilies that were always transmitted over radio and heard by thousands of Salvadorans. His sermons became the best and most popular report on human rights abuses in his country. Romero demanded justice and recompense for atrocities committed by security forces or paramilitary organizations. As a result, Romero's reputation grew considerably among the people, especially the priests, who initially had opposed him. He established a legal aid office (Socorro Jurídico) that documented hundreds of kidnappings, tortures, and murders carried out by the armed forces and paramilitary groups. He also condemned the atrocities of partisan warfare. Personally, he was convinced that the guerrillas would disappear once the repression ended.[22]

In the hopes of preventing a civil war, on October 15, 1979, young officers led a bloodless military coup and deposed General Romero. Some well-intentioned and reform-minded civilians were involved in the new government which was called the Revolutionary Government Junta. Archbishop Romero understood the coup as a peaceful and necessary governmental change to stop corruption, violence, and social injustice. He harbored some hope that the new government would contribute to the resolution of the deep conflict that polarized the Salvadoran society.[23] However, the opposite happened. Although the junta denounced the killing of *campesinos*, the National Guard, the police, and the death squads continued committing thousands of brutal criminal atrocities. The junta was weak, and while it made some efforts to improve the situation—for example, by land reform—it could not control the military and the oligarchy.

Government repression grew in part through help from the United States, which considered the Salvadoran government a US ally in the context of the Cold War.[24] On February 17, 1980, Romero wrote, and read publicly during his Sunday homily,[25] a letter to US President Jimmy Carter to try to avoid "greater bloodshed." He appealed to Carter's Christian convictions and asked him (1) to "forbid that military aid be given to the Salvadoran government," and (2) to guarantee that the US government "will not intervene directly or indirectly, with military, economic, diplomatic, or other pressures, in determining the destiny of the Salvadoran people."[26] The letter had a great global media impact. However, it was not well received by either the White House,[27] which began diplomatic conversations with the Vatican, or, of course, by the Salvadoran oligarchy, which again responded violently. One day later, the archdiocesan radio transmitter that Romero used to broadcast his homilies was blown up, and two days later, a bomb exploded at the Central American University, run by the Jesuits.

Romero's last days

Romero was very conscious that his life was in constant danger. He received death threats from the right and the left, and abundant slander.[28] The Vatican suggested that he leave the country, but he rejected the offer. He had already accepted martyrdom as a spiritual option to express his faith in God and his love of his country. As he wrote in his diary during a trip to Rome:

> I also visited Saint Peter's Basilica again, and...I asked for great faithfulness to my Christian faith and the courage, should it be necessary, to die as those

> martyrs died, or to live a consecrated life as those modern successors to Peter did.[29]

A personal testimony written during a spiritual retreat he made with some priests in February 1980 confirmed how close he felt to death during his last weeks: "I find it hard to accept a violent death that, in these circumstances, is very possible."[30] In addition, he added a personal consecration to the Heart of Jesus: "So, too, I place under His loving providence all my life and accept with faith in Him my death, however difficult it may be."[31]

Emotional fear of death and desire to live in no way diminished his confidence in the non-violent struggle against repression. Rather, the opposite—the strength in his condemnation of repression grew. On March 23, 1980, his Sunday homily lasted almost two hours. Romero was probably bolder than ever before. At the end of his sermon, he made his famous appeal to the National Guard and the police, which many interpreted as triggering Romero's death sentence:

> Brothers: you are of part of our own people. You kill your own campesino brothers and sisters. Before an order to kill that a man may give, God's law must prevail: Thou shalt not kill! No soldier is obliged to obey an order against the law of God. No one has to fulfill an immoral law. It is time to take back your consciences and to obey your consciences rather than the orders of sin. The church, defender of the rights of God, of the law of God, of human dignity, of the person, cannot remain silent before such abominations. We want the government to understand seriously that reforms are worth nothing if they are stained with so much blood. In the name of God, and in the name of this suffering people, whose laments rise to heaven each day more tumultuous, I beg you, I beseech you, I order you in the name of God: Stop the repression![32]

The high military command considered the appeal subversive and incendiary. Romero's death was already sentenced. The next day, Monday, March 24, 1980, while celebrating the funeral Mass on the first anniversary of the death of Sara Meardi de Pino, in the modest chapel of the Hospitalito, Romero was struck by a single gunshot and died within minutes.[33] Romero was standing behind the altar about to start the offertory. He had just ended the homily with these prophetic words:

> May this body immolated and this blood sacrificed for humans nourish us also, so that we may give our body and our blood to suffering and to pain—like Christ, not for self, but to bring about justice and peace for our people.[34]

If blood bathed Romero's death, so, too, it bathed his funeral. The funeral Mass took place in front of the Metropolitan Cathedral on March 30, 1980. Television images of the immense crowd that filled the square are preserved.[35] In the middle of the ceremony, several bombs exploded and snipers opened fire, killing dozens of people in the midst of terror, confusion, and blood. The funeral was interrupted, and Romero was hurriedly buried in the crypt of the cathedral.

Romero's death and funeral marked a turning point in the recent history of El Salvador. In 1980, more than twelve-thousand people were killed. The escalating violence soon turned into a civil war in the international framework of the Cold War. More than seventy-five thousand Salvadorans died in the fighting, most of them victims of the military and its death squads. However, the war could not kill Romero's legacy.

Romero's legacy on social justice

Romero did not develop an original theological thought of his own. He was not a professional theologian. He tried simply to live in accordance with the Gospel during the dramatic situation of El Salvador in his time. His thinking was, therefore, predominantly practical and experiential, manifested as it was in his pastoral letters, homilies, and speeches. Romero's Christian convictions, doctrine, and ideals remained firmly rooted in the Catholic tradition interpreted in the light of the Second Vatican Council and the most recent magisterium of the Catholic Church.[36] In particular, Pope Paul VI's teaching clarified Romero's own reflections, as he himself recognized.[37]

Some scholars say that there are two different Romeros: one conservative, before the death of Fr. Rutilio, and a new one, much more progressive, after Rutilio's murder.[38] Martín Baró probably exaggerated when he affirmed that the road from Aguilares (where Fr. Rutilio was assassinated) was to be Romero's "road to Damascus."[39] Sobrino, although more cautious, has also overemphasized Romero's *conversion*.[40] Recently, Michael Lee has understood Romero's conversion or "radical transformation"[41] as a "seeing anew" and a "coming home" in the sense of a profound understanding of "the gravity of social sin and the response that it demanded from him."[42]

Romero himself denied any tumbling conversion: "I would not speak of conversion, as many call it...because I have always been devoted to the people and the poor."[43] My own view is that Romero's life was gradually evolving without any kind of break or rupture with the past. His understanding and experience of his own mission as a pastor, and his constant updating of his moral judgment on the Salvadoran situation in light of new events and circumstances, marked the rhythm of Romero's continuous spiritual growth without a disruptive conversion. Of course, the assassination of Rutilio Grande played a decisive role in that spiritual process and was relevant to his changing moral judgment about the Salvadorian situation.

Romero understood his pastoral mission as deeply religious and not political: "This is my greatest concern, namely, to build with Christ, to build a church according to the Heart of Jesus."[44] And a church according to the Heart of Jesus is in character with a church absolutely involved in the cause of the poor and social justice in action. On the other hand, Romero changed his moral judgment and, as a result, his behavior toward the government, as long as he was convinced that the persecution of the Church and the repression of the peasants was supported by the Salvadoran authorities. He came to the conclusion that the Catholic Church, and he as the highest authority of the Church in El Salvador, could not remain silent and could not abstain from condemning the brutal atrocities committed by a repressive government, which included the slaying of priests. Neutrality was not a moral option in that situation—neutrality implied a way of collaborating with a repressive government, and therefore an unacceptable complicity with crime. For Romero, raising his voice was not a political decision but a moral and deeply evangelical decision:

> Our voice as pastor of the archdiocese seeks only to be an instrument in the hands of Christ so that he can speak to his people today. We want to be faithful to the gospel, and we are aware of the consequences which that can bring.[45]

According to Romero, the triumph of Christianity in El Salvador, and not the political fight, would bring peace to his beloved country—and to talk about Christianity was to talk about a person, Christ, who is the incarnated Truth. For Romero, truth was the driving power of peace because only truth can unite people among themselves and with God. Four main ideas support Romero's theology of social justice.

The political dimension of the faith.[46] For Romero, faith and politics are united but should not be identified with each other. When faith identifies with politics, faith is tainted and freedom is enslaved. On the other hand, faith isolated from life in the world is not true faith. According to Romero, faith should inspire and illuminate politics, but Christian faith and political activity must not become confused and entangled with each other. When that happens, it is easy to "substitute for the demands of the faith and Christian justice the demands of a particular political organization."[47] In a practical way, Romero defends the notion that political organizations can expect the Church to advocate for civil rights. No organization, however, even if Christian in inspiration or name, can require that the Church become the direct means of propaganda for political purposes.

Integral liberation. Romero believed that Christian liberation is more complete and deeper than any other political, social, or economic liberation. Christian liberation involves the person as a whole and, therefore, implies a truly spiritual and salvific dimension.[48] For this reason, simple structural changes cannot provide complete Christian liberation. Human beings cannot produce their own liberation. Liberation comes from Christ, the Redeemer.[49] The fact that Christ says that his reign does not belong to this world (John 18:36) does not mean that

> Christ is isolated from the power of earth. It means that he will use a different basis, a religious basis, to judge the consciences of political leaders and of the rich (and of the poor also), judging them from the eschatological and transcendent perspective of God's reign.[50]

Christian liberation, centered on the Kingdom of God established by Jesus Christ, fosters a deep desire for justice in love and demands a conversion of heart and mind.

The violence of love.[51] Romero defended a constructive dynamism of non-violence and excluded violence (except in case of self-defense), considering it unchristian and unscriptural, ineffective, and out of keeping with the dignity of the people.[52] Romero did not believe in violent solutions. He believed "in only one violence, that of Christ, who was nailed to the cross."[53] The revolution of Christ is a revolution of love. It is the revolution to establish a civilization of love. But a civilization of love "that did not demand justice of people would not be a true civilization. True love begins by demanding what is just in the relations of those who love."[54] Love gives plenitude to all human duties. With love, justice becomes a brother's embrace. Without love, laws become inhuman, repressive, cruel.[55]

Christian preferential option for the poor.[56] Like Jesus, the Church was sent to bring good news to the poor. The Church has incarnated herself in the world of the poor, giving them hope. Therefore, she is firmly committed to the evangelization of the poor and to their defense and protection. This preferential option for the poor is not an expression of particularism or sectarianism, but a manifestation of the evangelical mission of the Church, which is universal in character. This option is not discriminatory at all since it does not exclude anyone. Even the rich must become spiritually poor to share with the poor the benefits and graces of God's kingdom. The poor

> are the ones who make up in their own bodies that which is lacking in the passion of Christ. And for that reason, when the church has organized and united herself around the hopes and anxieties of the poor, she has incurred the same fate as that of Jesus and the poor: persecution.[57]

This preferential option for the poor cannot be reduced to ideological categories nor become a source of sociological conflict. It is spiritual and evangelical, but with important social and political implications.

Conclusion

A patriotic Salvadoran of strong fortitude and high Christian ethical values and ideals, Archbishop Romero advocated for a form of Christian humanism based on the Gospel and the magisterium of the Catholic Church, especially the Second Vatican Council. Following the tradition of the prophets, he denounced extortion, injustice, and corruption. He defended human rights and social justice in a country wounded by political, military, and paramilitary crime. Romero understood that the denunciation of brutal governmental atrocities was not a political issue, but a necessary requirement to establish the Kingdom of God on Earth. Romero advocated for the non-violent defense of justice inspired by love, forgiveness, and social participation. The preferential option for the poor was at the heart of his pastoral mission and action.

Romero spoke with profound moral authority, absolutely deprived of all political power, and detached from any self-interest. His main weapon was his own moral authenticity. His message was as resounding and accurate as it was annoying to the political parties and factions of the left and right. Romero felt the loneliness of the leader and was often misunderstood and misinterpreted by political, military, and ecclesiastical authorities. As repression became firmly fixed in El Salvador, Romero was ever more resolute in his denunciation of the government's cruel attitude and more demanding of the urgent need for nonviolent social change. His moral judgment on the Salvadoran situation was clear and forceful: the desirable Church–state cooperation to develop the common good in society must never lead to any kind of complicity with crime and repression. Only the truth liberates.

Romero's theological reflection on social justice, sealed with his own martyrdom and based on his preferential option for the poor, constitutes a great contribution to the ideal of Christian justice and the international implementation of human rights in our globalized world. The figure of Romero, martyred for his commitment to social justice and the poor, deserves universal respect.

Notes

1 Letter to Ernestina R., November 26, 1979, in Romero, *The Church Cannot Remain Silent*, 15.

2 Further information is available at: http://www.un.org/en/events/righttotruthday/

3 See BBC News: http://www.bbc.com/news/world-latin-america-32859627. See the ceremony at: https://www.youtube.com/watch?v=Hssxhk4Izeo

4 On January 28, 1980, Romero wrote in his diary:

> "I felt a special emotion on praying at the tomb of Paul VI. I remembered so many things from his conversations with me, in the visits in which I had the honor and the blessing to be admitted to a private audience."

See entry for January 28, 1980, in Romero, *A Shepherd's Diary*, 464. See also, Romero, "The Church and the Popular Organizations: Third Pastoral Letter," in Romero, *Voice of the Voiceless*, 99.

5 Brockman, *Romero: A Life.*

6 Delgado, *Óscar A. Romero.*

7 Morozzo della Rocca, *Primero Dios. Vita di Óscar Romero.*

8 Morozzo della Rocca, *Óscar Romero: Prophet of Hope*. See also Wright, *Óscar Romero and the Communion of the Saints*; and Clarke, *Óscar Romero: Love*

Must Win Out. Important information about Romero's life and bibliography is also available at the website of the Archbishop Romero Trust, http://www.romerotrust.org.uk/ See also the website of the Kellogg Institute of the University of Notre Dame, https://kellogg.nd.edu/archbishop-Óscar-romero#tab-297.

9 See Romero, *A Shepherd's Diary*, hereafter *Diary.*

10 Lee, *Revolutionary Saint: The Theological Legacy of Óscar Romero*; and Whelan, *Blood in the Fields: Óscar Romero, Catholic Social Teaching, and Land Reform.*

11 Puente, *Vida del P. Baltasar Álvarez.*

12 Romero, *Diary of Rome*, 4 February 1943, quoted by Brockman, *Romero*, 38–39. The diary was discovered by Romero's biographer and friend Jesús Delgado. See Delgado, "Romero: Un joven aspirante a la santidad."

13 The Medellín Conference was the second meeting of Latin American bishops held in Medellín, Colombia, in 1968. The conference marked a change in the Latin American Church, denouncing unjust social structures and embracing the concept of the "preferential option for the poor." See an English version of the conclusive document of the conference, available at: http://www.povertystudies.org/TeachingPages/EDS_PDFs4WEB/Medellin%20Document-%20Poverty%20of%20the%20Church.pdf

14 See Brockman, *Romero*, 55; and Wright, *Óscar Romero and the Communion of the Saints*, 34.

15 Shortly after the massacre, a boy of Tres Calles was tortured, executed, and found down from the unpaved road leading away from Tres Calles. See Clarke, *Óscar Romero: Love Must Win Out*, 64.

16 See Clarke, *Óscar Romero*, 65.

17 On the difficulties with the Vatican, see Maier, "Erzbishof Óscar Romeros Kirchenkonflikte."

18 See the website: http://www.hospitaldivinaprovidencia.org/index.php/es/hospital.

19 On the relationship between Romero and Rutilio, see Brackley, "Rutilio and Romero."

20 See Romero's homily and justification of the single mass at: http://www.romerotrust.org.uk/sites/default/files/homilies/one_mass.pdfhttp://www.romerotrust.org.uk/sites/default/files/homilies/one_mass.pdf

21 See Óscar Romero, Homily, May 8, 1977, available at: http://www.romerotrust.org.uk/sites/default/files/homilies/churchs_mission.pdf

22 See Morozzo della Rocca, *Óscar Romero: Prophet of Hope*, 205.

23 On the relation between Romero and the Junta, see Delgado, *Óscar A. Romero*, 163–69.

24 See LeoGrande, *Our Own Backyard*; Crandall, *The Salvador Option*; and D'Haeseleer, *The Salvadoran Crucible.*

25 See Óscar Romero, Homily, February 17, 1980, available at: http://www.romerotrust.org.uk/sites/default/files/homilies/poverty_beatitudes_strength.pdf.

26 See the letter reproduced in Romero, *Voice of the Voiceless*, 188–90.

27 See further information in Lee, *Revolutionary Saint*, 139.

28 See Romero, *Diary* January 4, 1979; June 1, 1979; September 7, 1979; November 5, 1979; February 23, 1980; March 10, 1980.

29 Ibid., May 3, 1979.

30 See Delgado, *Óscar A. Romero*, 190: "Me cuesta aceptar una muerte violenta que en estas circunstancias es muy posible."

31 Ibid., 191: "Así también pongo bajo su providencia amorosa toda mi vida y acepto con fe en Él mi muerte, por más difícil que sea."
32 The homily is available at: http://www.romerotrust.org.uk/homilies-and-writings/homilies/church-service-personal-community-and-transcendent-liberation
33 To date, no one in El Salvador has been prosecuted for Romero's assassination. The assassins were members of the death squad led by the soldier and politician Roberto D'Aubuisson (1943–92). For further information about the assassination, see Eisenbrandt, *Assassination of a Saint.*
34 Last homily of Archbishop Romero on March 24, 1980, available at: http://www.romerotrust.org.uk/sites/default/files/homilies/final_homily_of_archbishop_romero.pdf
35 See images at: https://www.youtube.com/watch?v=EN6LWdqcyuc&has_verified=1
36 See, in the same vain, Morozzo della Rocca, *Óscar Romero*, 221.
37 Romero, "Third Pastoral Letter," in *Voice of the Voiceless*, 99.
38 See López Vigil, *Monseñor Romero*, xiii. On Romero and conversion, see Lee, *Revolutionary Saint*, 44–85.
39 Ignacio Martín Baró, "Óscar Romero: Voice of the Downtrodden," in Romero, *Voice of the Voiceless*, 6.
40 See Sobrino, *Archbishop Romero*, 9: "I believe that the murder of Rutilio Grande was the occasion of the conversion of Archbishop Romero—as well as being a source of light and courage to follow his new path."
41 Lee, *Revolutionary Saint*, 69, 195, and 176–88.
42 Ibid., loc. cit.
43 See interview in March 1979 by Juan Rodríguez, quoted by Morozzo della Roca, *Primero Dios*, 152 and 392. See Amato, "Introduction," in Romero, *The Church Cannot Remain Silent*, xxiii.
44 Óscar Romero, Homily, September 3, 1978, available at http://www.romerotrust.org.uk/sites/default/files/homilies/cross_in_life.pdf
45 Letter to Roberto M.C., November 14, 1977, published in Romero, *The Church Cannot Remain Silent*, 15.
46 See, Romero, "Lovain Address: The Political Dimension of the Faith from the Perspective of the Option of the Poor," in Romero, *Voice of the Voiceless*, esp. at 182.
47 Romero, "Third Pastoral Letter," 100.
48 See Romero, *Diary*, April 9, 1978, 32.
49 Romero, Homily, December 1, 1977, available at: http://www.romerotrust.org.uk/sites/default/files/homilies/to_mothers_for_disappeared_children.pdf
50 Romero, Homily, January 14, 1979 available at: http://www.romerotrust.org.uk/sites/default/files/homilies/baptism_epiphany_of_messiah.pdf
51 See Romero, *The Violence of Love*.
52 See Romero, "The Church and Popular Political Organizations," Third Pastoral Letter of Archbishop Romero, co-authored by Bishop Arturo Rivera y Damas, Bishop of Santiago de María, Feast of the Transfiguration, August 6, 1978; Romero, "The Church's Mission amid the National Crisis," Fourth Pastoral Letter of Archbishop Romero, Feast of the Transfiguration, August 6, 1979, number 68–83.
53 Óscar Romero, Homily, November 20, 1977, available at: http://www.romerotrust.org.uk/sites/default/files/homilies/christ_prophet_priest_king.pdf
54 Óscar Romero, Homily, April 12, 1979, available at: http://www.romerotrust.org.uk/sites/default/files/homilies/love_law_of_new_covenant.pdf

55 Óscar Romero, Homily, September 10, 1978, available at: http://www.romerotrust.org.uk/sites/default/files/homilies/a_prophetic_sacramental_loving_church.pdf
56 See Romero, "Lovain Address, 177–87. See also Óscar Romero, Homily, February 17, 1980, available at: http://www.romerotrust.org.uk/sites/default/files/homilies/poverty_beatitudes_strength.pdf
57 See Romero, "Lovain Address," 182.

References

Brackley, Dean. "Rutilio and Romero." In *Monsignor Romero: A Bishop for the Third Millennium*, edited by Pelton, 79–99. Notre Dame, IN: University of Notre Dame Press, 2004.

Brockman, James R. *Romero: A Life*. 2nd. ed. Maryknoll, NY: Orbis Books, 2005.

Clarke, Kevin. *Óscar Romero: Love Must Win Out*. Collegeville, MN: Liturgical Press, 2014.

Crandall, Russell. *The Salvador Option: The United States in El Salvador, 1977–1992*. New York: Cambridge University Press, 2016.

Delgado, Jesús. *Óscar A. Romero. Biografía*. Madrid: Ediciones Paulinas, 1986.

Delgado, Jesús. "Romero: Un joven aspirante a la santidad." *Semanario Orientación, Arzobispado de San Salvador*, March 25, 2007.

D'Haeseleer, Brian. *The Salvadoran Crucible: The Failure of U.S. Counterinsurgency in El Salvador, 1979–1992*. Lawrence: University Press of Kansas, 2017.

Eisenbrandt, Matt. *Assassination of a Saint*. Oakland: University of California Press, 2017.

Lee, Michael E. *Revolutionary Saint: The Theological Legacy of Óscar Romero*. Maryknoll, NY: Orbis Books, 2018.

LeoGrande, William M. *Our Own Backyard: The United States in Central America, 1977–1992*. Chapel Hill: University of North Carolina Press, 1998.

López Vigil, María. *Monseñor Romero. Memories in Mosaic*. Translated by Kathy Ogle. Maryknoll, NY: Orbis Books, 2013.

Maier, Martin. "Erzbishof Óscar Romeros Kirchenkonflikte." *Stimmen der Zeit* 130 (2005): 198–210.

Morozzo della Rocca, Roberto. *Óscar Romero: Prophet of Hope*. Translated by Michael J. Miller. London: Darton, Longman and Todd, 2015.

Morozzo della Rocca, Roberto. *Primero Dios. Vita di Óscar Romero*. Milan: Mondadori, 2005.

Pelton, Robert S., ed. *Archbishop Romero and Spiritual Leadership in the Modern World*. Lanham, MD: Lexington Books, 2015.

Pelton, Robert S., ed. *Monsignor Romero: A Bishop for the Third Millennium*: Notre Dame, IN: University of Notre Dame Press, 2004.

Puente, Luis de la. *Vida del P. Baltasar Álvarez*. Edited by Camilo María Abad. Madrid: Atlas, 1958. Available at: http://www.cervantesvirtual.com/obra-visor/vida-del-p-baltasar-alvarez--0/html/.

Romero, Óscar. *The Church Cannot Remain Silent: Unpublished Letters and Other Writings*. Edited by Jesús Delgado, translated by Gene Palumbo and Dinah Livingstone. Maryknoll, NY: Orbis Books, 2016.

Romero, Óscar. *A Prophetic Bishop Speaks to His People: The Complete Homilies of Archbishop Óscar Arnulfo Romero.* Edited by the Romero Trust, Vol. 6. Miami, FL: Convivium Press, 2015–17.
Romero, Óscar. *A Shepherd's Diary.* Translated by Irene B. Hodson. Cincinnati, OH: St. Anthony Messenger Press; Montreal: Novalis, 1993.
Romero, Óscar. *Su Pensamiento*, Vol. 7. San Salvador: Publicaciones pastorales del Arzobispado, 1980–88.
Romero, Óscar. *The Violence of Love.* Edited and translated by James R. Brockman. Maryknoll, NY: Orbis Books, 1988.
Romero, Óscar. *Voice of the Voiceless: The Four Pastoral Letters and Other Statements.* Edited by Ignacio Martín-Baró and Jon Sobrino, translated by Michael J. Walsh. Maryknoll, NY: Orbis Books, 1985.
Sobrino, Jon. *Archbishop Romero: Memories and Reflections.* Translated by Robert R. Barr. Maryknoll, NY: Orbis Books, 1990.
Whelan, Matthew Phillip. *Blood in the Fields: Oscar Romero, Catholic Social Teaching, and Land Reform.* Washington, DC: Catholic University of America, 2020.
Wright, Scott. *Óscar Romero and the Communion of the Saints: A Biography.* Maryknoll, NY: Orbis Books, 2009.

Websites

The Archbishop Romero Trust: http://www.romerotrust.org.uk/.
Biblioteca Virtual Miguel de Cervantes: http://bib.cervantesvirtual.com/bib_autor/romero/dossier.shtml.
Kellogg Institute of International Affairs. University of Notre Dame: https://kellogg.nd.edu/archbishop-Óscar-romero#tab-297.

35 Germán Bidart Campos (Argentina, 1927–2004)

Santiago Legarre

Biographical introduction

Germán José Bidart Campos was born in Buenos Aires on December 9, 1927. He rose to be the most important Argentine constitutional scholar of all time, even as he always held his stalwart adhesion to the Catholic faith he professed. While he did so without any compromise whatsoever—he was to remain deeply faithful to his Christ-informed conscience[1]—he did not avoid controversy on that score, especially in his final days. He died of a heart attack at his home in Buenos Aires at the age of seventy-six, on September 3, 2004,[2] surrounded by a small group of friends and disciples.[3]

Bidart—as he was (and still is) typically called in Argentina, where multipart surnames like Bidart Campos are shortened to the first part—studied law as an undergraduate at the state university of Buenos Aires, known as UBA, which conferred on him the degree of *abogado* (similar to a Bachelor of Law) in 1949. He subsequently pursued a Doctorate in Law and in 1953 became a doctor at the age of twenty-five.[4] From that tender age, he began teaching law (and political science) in such a way that his teaching contributions would mold future generations of scholars and students. Moreover, he was not only a jurist but also a humanist,[5] and this was reflected in all of his scholarship. Formed in the scholasticism of the followers of Thomas Aquinas, Bidart complemented classical views of law and politics with those modern ones of Wilhelm Dilthey and of the Spanish thinker José Ortega y Gasset.[6]

Bidart was a strong adherent to natural-law theory, and he wrote a book on the value of justice and natural law, titled *Valor justicia y derecho natural*.[7] But he would add his own tweaks to the classical view of Aquinas and others in his tradition, under the influence of Max Scheler and his philosophy of value. Bidart's overall conclusion on this subject was that the idea of human rights is "the new natural law."[8] This particular position, regardless of its wording,[9] is not altogether different from the one held by the leading contemporary natural law philosopher in the English-speaking world, John Finnis,[10] who was to a large extent a contemporary of Bidart's. Even though Finnis visited Argentina three times (one of them while Bidart was still lingering), Bidart did not speak or read in English, and Finnis does not speak, and only reads some Spanish, so there was not much of an interaction.

It is not well known that Bidart was a very fine poet.[11] In 1977 he published in Mexico a book including sonnets in honor of the Virgin Mary,[12] a collection of which not many people are aware.[13] This work reflects, in endearing terms, his faith and love for Christ and his mother.

Surely Bidart inherited his humanism—this vision of law as something transcending the technical domain—partly from the only teacher whom he acknowledged as a master of sorts: Werner Goldschmidt,[14] a professor of conflicts of laws who was very interested in philosophy. Indeed, Goldschmidt coined "trialism" (*trialismo*), a legal–philosophical school that Bidart happily endorsed.[15] It consisted of a triple approach to law: sociological, normological, and axiological. This approach can be traced through all of Bidart's works, where he systematically and gladly acknowledges Goldschmidt's model and guidance.[16] Whatever Bidart is writing about, he always starts with facts, follows with norms, and wraps up with evaluation. I remember, incidentally, that on my first day of law school, there was a small poster at the entrance of the building informing of the death of Professor Goldschmidt, who had taught for decades at my school, the Pontifical Catholic University of Argentina (UCA). I later learned that only two persons outside the family had attended the wake: the one who told me this story (Guillermo Lozano, a junior lecturer of conflicts of laws)—and Bidart Campos. Shortly after Goldschmidt's death, in 1988, when Bidart had just turned sixty, I was lucky enough to have him as my own professor.[17] By then he had already taught as a chaired professor for decades. He also had been one of the first deans of UCA, from 1962–67.[18] The brief, ensuing recollections here are personal and go back to those days.

As there were only sixteen students in that constitutional law course, and as Bidart had a very close and warm demeanor, I have indeed many anecdotes, though of course I can include only a few because of space limitations. One thing to know about Professor Bidart Campos is that he wanted his students to call him by his first name, Germán,[19] which most of us, however, never did. We knew full well, even in our ignorance, that we were facing the most important Argentine professor of all time, and we did not want to spoil the magic. But the very fact that he would insist that we called him Germán says a lot about the person behind the persona: he was relaxed and informal[20] (although he would always dress in a suit in those days). In fact, it is in light of this relaxed manner that some of the controversies during his final years, to which I refer in the closing section, ought to be understood.

Bidart was an egalitarian through thick and thin. An anecdote of my days as a student illustrates this trait well. On the first day of class, he said,

> I have just been told that from now on students will not be allowed to smoke in class. On the other hand, we, professors, will be allowed to continue smoking in class. I will not have that disparity. I am a great smoker, but if you are not to smoke I shall not smoke myself.

Other than the likely shock the reader will experience by learning or, depending on the reader's age, recollecting, that smoking was allowed at all in such academic contexts, the point of this anecdote is to stress the fervent extent to which Bidart embraced equality, regardless of age or professional status.

Finally, I remember distinctly when he announced who would be, in his own view, his intellectual successor—whom he declared in one of his 1988 lectures to be "the new formula one of constitutional law." This was Professor Néstor P. Sagüés, who was then already a name in his own right and subsequently rose to be the star that Bidart had described, foreseen, and prophesied. Of course, in line with his informal tone, what Bidart said was: "The new formula one…is Néstor."

Major themes and contributions

As I noted earlier, Bidart began to write from a very tender age[21] and was always faithful to his vocation as a writer and as a scholar, favored perhaps by the circumstance of his remaining a bachelor until his death. He wrote dozens of books and hundreds of articles.[22] Just as important, as I was fortunate to attest, he was an amazing teacher.[23]

What were his major themes and contributions? From its inception, Bidart's academic production was not restricted to his main area of interest, which was, unquestionably, constitutional law. He wrote vastly on political science and held a chair of political science at UBA. He also wrote on international law of human rights, a field in which he was a pioneer and a vocal actor, even in difficult times of military dictatorships; and on social doctrine of the Church. Regarding the latter, he worried about the tensions between church doctrine and economic liberalism. He therefore devoted a whole book to exploring those issues, *La re-creación del liberalismo* (*The re-creation of liberalism*).[24] The long and the short of that extended essay highlights that for market economy to be compatible with the social doctrine of the Church, it ought to be tempered by social considerations—the way the Church suggested and still suggests.

But of course it was the discipline of constitutional law that mostly benefited from Bidart's wide-ranging contributions. I am quite tempted to share yet another personal anecdote that might throw some light on the way that discipline was (and still is) perceived and regarded in Argentina, though I fear that it might not be very different around the rest of the world. When I finished law school, I thought I would start teaching. The way it works in my country is that you approach your favorite professor and ask him if you could assist him. I had two favorites. One was Bidart, and the other was his nemesis, Jaime Luis Anaya, our professor of commercial law, a distinguished scholar, and a very fine person. I decided to choose Bidart, and I later became a professor of constitutional law (indeed, holding the very chair at UCA that he had held for many decades). Shortly after I was inducted into academia, as a teaching assistant under Bidart's aegis, I ran into Anaya in one of the corridors of the law school. He asked me point-blank: "So, Mr. Legarre, have you started teaching yet?" After I replied, he continued: "What are you teaching? Constitutional law, really? That is wonderful!

Although it is a true pity that we have lost you for the cause of the law." What he meant was that constitutional law is not law. Real law is commercial law, and private law in general—constitutional law is more like a bunch of moral ideas under the pretense of law.

I must say that Bidart did not do much to dispel what could have seemed a myth on the non-legal nature of constitutional law. On the contrary, he did not pay much attention to texts and norms, concerned as he was with ideas and values more than anything else. This is my own criticism to, and my reservation regarding, his constitutional theory. But then he shares that fault, alas, with most of my contemporary fellow constititutional scholars, for whom any preoccupation with norms has an old-fashioned ring of positivism. I find this rather absurd, as the position they depart from was Thomas Aquinas's rather than Kelsen's; but that story belongs to another book!

Considering once more his work in constitutional law, I would like to draw a clear distinction within his work; the distinction is chronological, but its importance goes beyond a matter of time. His first books on constitutional law—published for the first time in the sixties—were long, theoretical, learned, and full of footnotes (many of them, in dialogue with the leading European public law scholars).[25] In contrast, his work from the mid-eighties until the end of his life, starting with *Tratado elemental de Derecho constitucional* (*Basic treatise of constitutional law*),[26] was of a very different nature and style, marking a clear break and a beginning to what I consider a different phase in his academic life: addressed to any reader, including students; easier, simpler (but sometimes at the expense of the complexity of the issues involved); much shorter, unannotated. My preference was with what I could term "the first Bidart Campos." So once, when I was still his student and happened to meet him randomly at a bus stop—Bidart would use public transportation; perhaps it was part of his "anti-snob" demeanor; plus he probably did not have enough money for a daily taxi, as he was modest and did not earn much as a professor—I asked him: "Why this change?" that I had perceived in his work. He did not give me an answer but merely smiled.

Bidart had a short stint in public office, from 1967 to the early seventies. He was director of the Registro Civil de la Ciudad de Buenos Aires—the head of the office in charge of certain public registrations—and his book *Resoluciones y dictámenes del Registro Civil de la Capital Federal* (*Decisions and opinions of the Civil Register of the Federal Capital*) bears witness to his time there.[27] This stint lasted through more than one *de facto* government—which circumstance, it should be noted, was in tension with his reiterated criticism of such undemocratic regimes.

General appraisal and influence

Bidart's work is of lasting influence. The fact that, on the occasion of the tenth anniversary of his death, the most important study group of constitutional law in Argentina, the Asociación Argentina de Derecho Constitucional, published a festschrift in his honor in the official magazine of the group is telling.[28] Likewise, that same year of 2014, a big event to celebrate his memory was organized at the

University of Buenos Aires (UBA).[29] The event stressed the crucial role Bidart had during the dark years of the military dictatorship of 1976–83, when his voice was to constitutional law what the forerunner of Jesus, John the Baptist, had been to the desert.[30] It is noteworthy that one of the speakers at the UBA event openly criticized Bidart's Catholicism, both because the remark confirmed another comment that I noted earlier—namely, that Bidart was a stalwart Christian—but also because this critic (Professor Roberto Gargarella) affirmed that his criticism constituted an homage to Bidart's love for freedom of expression. I believe Gargarella was right in thinking that Bidart would have welcomed his peaceful dissent.[31]

Interestingly, and rightly, the UBA event also underscored Bidart's crucial role in highlighting the constitutional relevance of international law of human rights, which would be fully recognized in the constitutional amendment of 1994. One of the participants at the UBA event, Professor Susana Albanese, aptly showed Bidart's direct influence in that amendment regarding the constitutional ranking of the most important human rights treaties[32] and pointed out the relevance of one of his books on the topic, one which she had co-authored with him.[33]

Bidart had always held that all international treaties—whether human rights treaties or not—have a higher ranking than all laws of Congress. In this he followed a position held before him by Werner Goldschmidt (his only master, as I have noted), who had consistently criticized the case law of the Supreme Court to the contrary. In effect, our Supreme Court had held the "American position" that treaties and laws of Congress stand on the same level, and that the principle of *lex posterior derogat priori* ("a later law repeals an earlier one") applies equally to treaties and laws of Congress. The Argentine Supreme Court in 1992 overruled its own precedent and subscribed to the position that had been held by both Goldschmidt and Bidart,[34] namely, that treaties rank above laws of Congress, no matter their timing. Two years after this crucial decision, the 1994 Amendment to the Argentine Constitution incorporated this doctrine, and Bidart, who was actively involved as a jurist and adviser at the reforming constitutional assembly,[35] was generally credited as one of the intellectual authors of the new norm, which simply and clearly states that "treaties and concordats have higher standing than laws."[36]

Bidart was very interested in social issues and in the social aspect of the law,[37] all of which was informed by his Christian formation and conscience.[38]

Books would be published to honor him even during his lifetime.[39] His fame extended abroad, especially in Latin America, where he was well known and respected.[40] The number of scholars who requested and received from him a preface to their own books was enormous.[41] So, too, was the number of scholars and others to whom he dedicated his own books, which exemplified his warm affection for so many colleagues,[42] and the number of dedications to his Catholic faith as well.[43] I find it particularly interesting, concerning the latter, that one of his most important books—his *Tratado Elemental de Derecho Constitucional* (*Basic treatise on constitutional law*)— was dedicated to "María and Manuel, for an old debt of fraternal friendship."[44] It seems clear to me that he means Mary and Jesus, as there have been some saints in the Catholic tradition known for calling them María and Manuel.[45]

There are, at any rate, many more important ways to measure the general appraisal of his legacy. One of his disciples, Pablo Manili, wrote in a book titled *Maestros del Derecho constitucional* (*Great scholars of constitutional law*) that

> Germán produced a fundamental change in the way we view constitutional interpretation; he viewed the Constitution as a norm and underscored its normative force—by way of contrast with views that saw the Constitution as a catalogue of illusions and political declarations.[46]

Manili was largely right, the caveat being that by the time Bidart wrote, there already was a consensus around the idea that the constitution was a legal instrument. Indeed, as Dolabjian shows (when he contrasts European theory and practice), as early as in the late nineteenth century the normative force of the Argentine Constitution was largely in place both in the case law of the Supreme Court and in the doctrine of early writers such as José Manuel Estrada, Joaquín V. González, and Nicolás Matienzo.[47] Perhaps Bidart's greatest accomplishment on this score was to extend and apply the idea of normativity and of the normative force of the constitution to its first part, the one dealing with rights, typically called in Argentina the "Dogmatic Part."[48]

At a personal level, Bidart was widely considered a humble person.[49] Along the same lines, one of his students described him as meek.[50] Of course, these two adjectives used together bring to mind the words of Jesus Christ about himself.[51]

As I come now to a conclusion, I refer to something I briefly indicated above by way of introduction. In the final years of his life, Bidart was surrounded by a significant degree of controversy, especially regarding his purported interpretation and application of certain aspects of Catholic doctrine and mores. On the one hand, he wrote a couple of journal articles defending positions that seemed at odds with Christian (and even natural law) views. Although everything he wrote in those days ended up published in *El Derecho*, the journal of Pontifical Catholic University of Argentina (of which he had been the editor-in-chief for years), the single most important of those controversial articles apparently was found too shocking for that journal by the then editor-in-chief (Bidart's successor).[52] Bidart therefore decided to send the piece to *Jurisprudencia Argentina*—the secular competition of sorts. It was a case note advocating for the change of name for a transgender person.[53] Moreover, his apparent divergence with traditional Catholic teaching—never overt; always played down by Bidart himself—was not circumscribed to gender matters. The more recent, 2000 edition of his *Tratado Elemental de Derecho Constitucional* deals with topics such as privacy and drug abuse, and the constitutional right to freedom of association of homosexual persons, in ways which may seem removed not only from traditional Catholic doctrine but also from Bidart's own initial positions on such questions in previous editions of the same book.

On the other hand, there was an unfortunate incident in his personal life that drew the attention of the public in a negative way. One afternoon Bidart went to La Biela—a very traditional coffee place in the very traditional neighborhood of Recoleta—dressed in a sleeveless vest. One of the waiters told him that with such attire he could not stay at La Biela, and he was asked to leave the premises. That same day, very annoyed and offended, the professor sent a letter to the editor of the newspaper *La Nación* (which was promptly published, given the authority of the sender), in which he told the Argentine public what had happened at the Recoleta coffee house and complained of having been discriminated against, in breach of the Argentine Constitution. Immediately, a score of other letters followed, defending the right of the private company who owned La Biela to decide about their premises as they saw fit, criticizing Bidart, and regretting conduct that was considered by most readers not to be up to the standards that everyone had become used to expecting from him.

My own appraisal of the impact of these two developments in the general appraisal of the work of Bidart is that whether or not one approves, from a Christian perspective, of Bidart's take on the change of name of transgender persons (and other similar positions he adopted on analogous matters in the last years of his life, some of which I referenced earlier), or of the infamous incident of the sleeveless vest at La Biela, those are at most tiny spots that do not detract from the whole. Bidart Campos was a conscientious Catholic and a tremendous Christian scholar throughout. No one is perfect, nor was he. But his contributions to the study and teaching of constitutional law will remain forever high in the firmament of the great Christian jurists of Latin American history.

Notes

1 One of his disciples, Pablo Manili, rightly described him as a "fervent Catholic." Manili, *Maestros del Derecho Constitucional*, 20.

2 He is buried in the City of Lujan, by the grave of his mother. Lujan is the seat of Argentina's national shrine to the Virgin Mary, to whom Bidart was very devout. See Palomino Machego and Remotti Carvonell, *Derechos humanos y Constitución en Iberoamérica*, ii (with a picture of the grave).

3 This is Bidart's obituary in *La Nación*, an important Argentine newspaper and a reliable source: https://www.lanacion.com.ar/politica/murio-el-constitucionalista-bidart-campos-nid633570

4 His doctoral dissertation was titled "La democracia como forma de estado" ("Democracy as form of state"). For Bidart's biographical information, see this trustworthy webpage administered by the prestigious Konex Foundation: https://www.fundacionkonex.org/b1368-german_j_bidart_campos

5 Jiménez, "En memoria de Germán José Bidart," obituary in the Spanish newspaper *El País*. Ferreyra is of a similar view: Ferreyra, 258.

6 Rodríguez Varela, 3.

7 Bidart Campos, *Valor justicia y Derecho natural.*

8 The idea that Bidart equated natural law and human rights is Domingo Rondina's, at a commemorative event at UBA. I think Rondina was quite right; see Rondina, 255.

9 Finnis would not have accepted the wording "new natural law," however. See Legarre, "H.L.A. Hart."

10 Finnis's position on this topic was elaborated at lenght in his monograph *Aquinas: Moral, Political, and Legal Theory.*
11 Bidart Campos, *El aljibe.*
12 Bidart Campos, *El misterio de María.*
13 An exception is Alberto Rodríguez Varela, who underscored the existence and value of this book by Bidart. See Rodríguez Varela, speech in honor of Bidart at the Argentine Scientific Society, 4.
14 Rodríguez Varela, who knew Bidart for more than forty years, stated that Werner Goldschmidt was Bidart's "master and friend." Rodríguez Varela, speech in honor of Bidart Campos, 4.
15 Bidart even went ahead and quite early on wrote a philosophical monograph in trialistic key: *Filosofía del Derecho constitucional.*
16 See Dolabjian, "Sobre la fuerza normativa de la Constitución," 699.
17 In Argentina, usually two instructors take care of each group of students: a chaired professor and a so-called "adjunct professor". I was taught constitutional law by Bidart as the chair and by María Cristina Serrano as the adjunct. See her enlightening contribution to a festschrift for Bidart: "Doctor Germán J. Bidart Campos: Maestro y Amigo."
18 See Manili, *Maestros del Derecho Constitucional*, 1.
19 His disciple and former student Manili even calls him "Germán" in writing (which is even more striking but would have surely been liked by Bidart). Manili, *Maestros del Derecho Constitucional*, 6.
20 Serrano, "Doctor Germán J. Bidart Campos," 642.
21 Bidart Campos delivered the speech that earned him induction into the very prestigious Academia Nacional de Derecho when he was only twenty-seven.
22 For a rather complete list of Bidart Campos's books, in chronological order, see Ferreyra's "Creo en estas letras."
23 I find Cristina Serrano's description of his teaching style by far the best. Serrano, "Doctor Germán J. Bidart Campos," 641–42. I can relate, especially as she taught me in 1988 side-by-side with Bidart.
24 Bidart Campos, *La re-creación del liberalismo.*
25 Examples of such books are: Bidart Campos, *Derecho constitucional. Realidad, normatividad y justicia en el derecho constitucional*, and *Derecho constitucional del poder.*
26 Bidart Campos, *Tratado elemental de Derecho constitucional.*
27 Bidart Campos, *Resoluciones y dictámenes.*
28 See Asociación Argentina de Derecho Constitucional, "Liber Amicorum Germán J. Bidart Campos."
29 A summary of the different panels at the UBA ten-year anniversary event of September 10, 2014, can be found in *Academia. Revista sobre enseñanza del Derecho* 12/24 (2014): 251–59.
30 Ibid., 252. The analogy is mine.
31 Ibid., 253.
32 Ibid., 255, where Albanese explains the point made here in the text. See, too, Article 75, Section 22 of the Argentine Constitution, as amended in 1994, which reads as follows (in what is relevant):

> The following [international instruments], under the conditions under which they are in force, stand on the same level as the Constitution, [but] do not repeal any article in the First Part of this Constitution, and must be understood as complementary of the rights and guarantees recognized therein: The American Declaration of the Rights and Duties of Man; the Universal Declaration of Human Rights; the American Convention on Human Rights; the International Covenant on Economic, Social, and Cultural Rights; the International Cove-

nant on Civil and Political Rights and its Optional Protocol; the [International] Convention on the Prevention and Punishment of Genocide; the International Convention on the Elimination of all Forms of Racial Discrimination; the Convention on the Elimination of All Forms of Discrimination Against Women; the Convention Against Torture and other Cruel, Inhumane, or Degrading Treatment or Punishment; and the Convention on the Rights of the Child.

33 Bidart Campos and Albanese, *Derecho internacional, Derechos humanos y Derecho comunitario.*
34 Argentine Supreme Court, *Ekmekdjian v. Sofovich*, July 7, 1992.
35 Manili rightly points out that at the 1994 Constitutional Assembly, former Argentine president Raúl Alfonsín hired Bidart Campos as his consultant and adviser. Manili, *Maestros del Derecho Constitucional*, 2.
36 From Article 75, Section 22 of the Argentine Constitution, as amended in 1994.
37 A book he wrote well into his prime is tellingly titled *El orden socioeconómico en la Constitución*. See also Fessia, "Muere Bidart Campos."
38 One of his last books, published in 2003, is proof of this Christian conscience: *La Doctrina social de la Iglesia y el Derecho constitucional.* Little known, but very much in point too, is his earlier, historical essay *La Iglesia en la historia: su influencia en lo spiritual, social, cultural y político*, published in Mexico in 1977.
39 For example, the year before he passed away, one of his disciples, Víctor Bazán, celebrated Bidart by publishing *Defensa de la Constitución.*
40 An example is the book in his honor published in Peru two years before his death: Palomino Machego and Remotti Carbonell, *Derechos Humanos y Constitución en Iberoamérica*. See also Professor Horacio Rosatti's view that Bidart had an unparalleled impact in South America, in *Academia. Revista sobre enseñanza del Derecho* 12/24, 256.
41 I am one of them, and I can bear witness to the generosity and kindness of his introductory remarks to my first book: Legarre, *El requisito de la trascendencia.*
42 It would be difficult and pointless to try to mention them all, but I will just say here that as he approached the end of his academic production, he would dedicate one single book to a good number of people. For example, *La interpretación del sistema de derechos humanos* was dedicated to Alberto Antonio Spota, Humerto Quiroga Lavié, Juan Carlos Hitters, Osvaldo Gozaini, Adelina Loiano, Eduardo Oteiza, and Alberto R. Dalla Vía (all of them colleages or disciples) "for everything they have given me both academically and affectionately." *El derecho de la constitución y su fuerza normativa* was dedicated "In memory of Laura Esther Pico, Josefina Celina Anción, Rosa Esperanza Negri, Concepción Marquese, Lucilda S. de Lúgaro, Amelia P. de Echegoyen, María Inés D. de Bourda, Dolores P. de Tarsia, y Elena E. Lacourt." This trend of dedicating one book to many people, of course, increased the total number of those who got published dedications from Bidart.
43 *La re-creación del liberalismo, política y derecho constitucional* is dedicated to "the beloved memory of John Paul I"; *Valor justicia y Derecho natural* is dedicated to the first president of Pontificia Universidad Católica Argentina, Monsignor Octavio N. Derisi, "for his friendship."
44 Bidart Campos, *Tratado elemental de Derecho constitucional.* I hope the reader will not mind my noting that my own copy of the book has a handwritten dedication to me: "To Santiago, with much affection."
45 E.g., Josemaría Escrivá de Balaguer, who, during the Spanish Civil War, referred to Jesus as "Manuel." Although the war situation diferred from Bidart's, the two have in common the idea of "discretion." See Vázquez de Prada, *El Fundador del Opus Dei*, 188.

46 Manili, *Maestros del Derecho*, 6, with particular reference to Bidart's *El derecho de la constitución y su fuerza normativa*. As Dolabjian explains, it is in the European tradition where the normative force of the constitution is watered-down, at least in the founding conception (by way of contrast with the founding conception in the United States, which was the inspiration for Argentina). See Dolabjian, "Sobre la fuerza normativa de la Constitución," 658.
47 Dolabjian, "Sobre la fuerza normativa de la Constitución," 671–74.
48 Bidart recorded this idea in *El Derecho de la constitución y su fuerza normativa*, but even before that in *Teoría general de los derechos humanos*, one of the few books of his not to have been published by Ediar. I remember that Bidart shared with his students in class that he felt awkward about changing publisher for this book, which he did, he said, to try to reach a greater readership.
49 See Jimenez, "En memoria de Germán José Bidart." See also Bazán, *Defensa de la Constitución*, 9.
50 That was the word used by Professor Juan V. Sola in the tenth anniversary UBA event. See *Academia. Revista sobre enseñanza del Derecho*, 12/24, 254.
51 "Learn from me, for I am meek and humble of heart." Matthew 11:29.
52 Bidart's successor was, incidentally, Professor Jaime Luis Anaya, alluded to above in the text as my professor of commercial law.
53 Bidart Campos, "El cambio de identidad civil de los transexuales transformados."

References

Asociación Argentina de Derecho Constitucional. "Liber Amicorum Germán J. Bidart Campos (homenaje a 10 años de su desaparición física)." *Debates de Actualidad* 28, 208–09 (2014).

Bazán, Víctor, ed., *Defensa de la Constitución: garantismo y controles*. Buenos Aires: Ediar, 2003.

Bidart Campos, Germán J. *El aljibe*. Buenos Aires: Ediar, 1969.

Bidart Campos, Germán J. "El cambio de identidad civil de los transexuales transformados." *Jurisprudencia Argentina* 3 (1990): 103–11.

Bidart Campos, Germán J. *Derecho constitucional. Realidad, normatividad y justicia en el derecho constitucional*. Buenos Aires: Ediar, 1964/1966.

Bidart Campos, Germán J. *Derecho constitucional del poder*. Buenos Aires: Ediar, 1967.

Bidart Campos, Germán J. *El Derecho de la constitución y su fuerza normativa*. Buenos Aires: Ediar, 1995.

Bidart Campos, Germán J. *La Doctrina social de la Iglesia y el Derecho constitucional*. Buenos Aires: Ediar, 2003.

Bidart Campos, Germán J. *Filosofía del Derecho constitucional*. Buenos Aires: Ediar, 1969.

Bidart Campos, Germán J. *La Iglesia en la historia: su influencia en lo espiritual, social, cultural y político*, México: Editorial Tradición, 1977.

Bidart Campos, Germán J. *La interpretación del sistema derechos humanos*. Buenos Aires: Ediar, 1994.

Bidart Campos, Germán J. *El misterio de María en el pueblo de Dios*. Mexico City: Editorial Tradición, 1977.

Bidart Campos, Germán J. *El orden socioeconómico en la Constitución*. Buenos Aires: Ediar, 1999.

Bidart Campos, Germán J. *La re-creación del liberalismo, política y derecho constitucional.* Buenos Aires: Ediar, 1982.

Bidart Campos, Germán J. *Resoluciones y dictámenes del Registro Civil de la Capital Federal.* Buenos Aires: La Ley (Fedye), 1973.

Bidart Campos, Germán J. *Teoría general de los derechos humanos.* Buenos Aires: Astrea, 1991; new edition, 2015.

Bidart Campos, Germán J. *Tratado elemental de Derecho constitucional.* 1st ed. Buenos Aires: Ediar, 1986; and 3rd ed. Buenos Aires: Ediar, 2000.

Bidart Campos, Germán J. *Valor justicia y Derecho natural.* Buenos Aires: Ediar, 1983.

Bidart Campos, Germán J., and Susana Albanese. *Derecho internacional, Derechos humanos y Derecho comunitario.* Buenos Aires: Ediar, 1998.

Dolabjian, Diego A. "Sobre la fuerza normativa de la Constitución." In *Derechos humanos y Constitución en Iberoamérica*, edited by Palomino Machego and Remotti Carbonell, 655–710.

Domingo, Rafael and Beatriz Rodríguez-Antolín. *Reglas jurídicas y aforismos.* Cizur Menor: Aranzadi, 2000.

Ferreyra, Gustavo Raúl. "Creo en estas letras: sobre veinte proposiciones capitales de la teoría jurídica del Prof. Dr. Germán J. Bidart Campos."*Academia. Revista sobre enseñanza del Derecho* 12, no. 24 (2014): 269–72.

Fessia, Ricardo Miguel. "Muere Bidart Campos." Available at https://historiadeld erechounl.wordpress.com/2017/09/04/german-bidart-campos/.

Finnis, John. *Aquinas: Moral, Political, and Legal Theory.* New York: Oxford University Press, 1998.

Jiménez, Eduardo Pablo. "En memoria de Germán José Bidart." *El País* (Spain), September 24, 2004. Available at https://elpais.com/diario/2004/09/24/age nda/1095976807_850215.html.

Legarre, Santiago. "H.L.A. Hart and the Making of the New Natural Law Theory." *Jurisprudence: An International Journal of Legal and Political Thought* 82 (2017): 82–98.

Legarre, Santiago. *El requisito de la trascendencia en el recurso extraordinario.* With prologue by Germán J. Bidart Campos. Buenos Aires: Abeledo-Perrot, 1994.

Manili, Pablo L., ed. *Maestros del Derecho Constitucional.* Buenos Aires: Astrea, 2017.

Palomino Machego, José F., and José Carlos Remotti Carbonell, eds. *Derechos humanos y Constitución en Iberoamérica. Libro homenaje a Germán J. Bidart Campos.* Lima: Instituto Iberoamericano de Derecho Constitucional, 2002; 2nd edition, 2016.

Rodríguez Varela, Alberto. Speech in honor of Bidart Campos at the Argentine Scientific Society, August 19, 2003. Available at https://www.ancmyp.org.ar/user/files/Homenaje-a-Bidart-Campos-Rodriguez-Varela-2003.pdf.

Rondina, Domingo. "Celebratory remarks." *Academia. Revista sobre enseñanza del Derecho* 12, no. 24 (2014): 251–59.

Serrano, María Cristina. "Doctor Germán J. Bidart Campos: Maestro y amigo." In *Derechos humanos y Constitución en Iberoamérica*, edited by Palomino Machego and Remotti Carbonell, 641–44. Lima: Instituto Iberoamericano de Derecho Constitucional, 2002; 2nd edition, 2016.

Vázquez de Prada, Andrés. *El Fundador del Opus Dei*, Vol. 2. Madrid: Rialp, 2002.

36 Juan Larrea Holguín (Ecuador, 1927–2006)

Juan Carlos Riofrío Martínez-Villalba

Introduction

Bishop Juan Larrea exhibits many facets that could well define him as a humanist. He stands out through his love for God, for the poor, for history, for letters, theology, sports, painting, and—in what concerns us here—his passion for law. In this field he dealt with a wide range of topics: he was the first Ecuadorian to write a complete commentary on Andrés Bello's Civil Code that was enforced in several Latin American countries. He also devoted himself to constitutional law, to public and private international law, and to canon law—procedural and commercial. He was extremely prolific: sole author of almost three hundred books (of several sizes), co-author of fifty more, and author of hundreds of scientific articles and thousands of opinion articles, as well as creator of more than two-thousand paintings. Coming from the most proper background of Quito, from a family of ambassadors, he served as a lawyer at the best law firm in Ecuador, was a professor of countless subjects of law, a co-author of part of the Ecuadorian Constitution, promoter of several laws, and expert in border issues. The first Ecuadorian member of Opus Dei, he was also a priest, the first military bishop of Ecuador, and bishop of several dioceses. As if that were not enough, he participated in more than a thousand radio programs and as many short television programs.

We are still perhaps too close to his life to be able to weigh fully the influence he had on culture, politics, and law. In this chapter we will make only a brief study of him as a jurist, necessarily leaving aside other aspects of his life, such as his pastoral, social, and cultural work. For this chapter we will go to three types of sources: the autobiography and other writings that Bishop Larrea wrote about himself,[1] the few and brief biographies that third parties have written about him,[2] and the interview with him that I conducted during his life—together with the testimony of what I have been able to learn while living close to him from 1992 until his death on August 27, 2006.

Biographical information

Juan Ignacio Larrea Holguín was born on August 9, 1927, in Buenos Aires, while his father, Ambassador Carlos Manuel Larrea Rivadeneira (1887–1983), was carrying out a diplomatic mission in the city. His father, a Catholic believer, suffered a lot during the liberal revolution that swept Latin America at the beginning of the twentieth century, which left Ecuador's agreement with the Holy See groundless in the time of President Eloy Alfaro (died 1912). When Carlos Manuel saw that the diplomatic environment was more propitious, he managed the signing of a new treaty that put an end to that persecutory period of the Catholic Church. In 1937 he succeeded in signing the *Modus Vivendi*, which to this day governs relations between the Ecuadorian state and the Catholic Church. He had an extensive library covering historical, legal, technical, and cultural topics, and his Quito house was almost a museum, where paintings and sculptures of the best artists of the colony were exhibited. The life of the father would deeply mark what the son would become: his taste for reading and art, his breadth of interests, his concern for social and ecclesiastical questions, his faith, elegance in dress, and the delicacy and the influence that comes with it. In addition, the various diplomatic missions that his father carried out in Buenos Aires (1927, 1942, 1943), Bogotá (1932, 1951), Santiago de Chile (1927), Panamá (1940), Lima (1941), and Rome (1948) provided the son with a broad and cosmopolitan vision of the world that would remain fixed in his iron memory.

During high school, Juan Larrea showed preferences for literature, history, and philosophy. There he won the prize for best speaker for his speech on the question whether *¿La conquista española fue o no ventajosa para el indio ecuatoriano?* ("Was the Spanish conquest advantageous for the Ecuadorian Indian or not?" May 19, 1945), and he graduated with the highest honors.[3] His father proposed that he study philosophy in Paris; however, the turbulent history of the previous fifty years in Ecuador—where new divorce laws and agrarian reform had appeared, and where religion had suffered so much—left a mark on his soul, and that wound caused him to opt for a career in law.[4] In 1998 he stated that he had decided on his career

> from high school. My desire to study law was not so much to practice law in trials, even though I had to intervene in many, but above all I thought that it's much better to be a lawyer that could influence the drafting and correction of the laws of the country. Even when I was young, still in school, I realized that we needed some reforms, and my desire was to intervene in this. I must also thank Providence, because it has been possible for me to carry them out to a large extent.[5]

That is how he entered the Catholic University of Ecuador, newly founded in 1946 by the archbishop of Quito, Cardinal Carlos María de la Torre. "From the first day of university," he later said, "I assumed with passion the study of the law."[6] Among other teachers there he had Dr. Jorge Pérez Serrano as a professor, and he continued to study lofty history books on his own.[7]

Two years after Larrea began his university studies, his father was appointed ambassador of Ecuador to the Holy See, and the family moved to Rome. In the middle of 1948, Larrea enrolled in the Sapienza University of Rome, in the third level of law studies, managing to validate some subjects studied in Ecuador. The material environment of post-war Italian universities was not the most suitable for study: the citizens wanted to leave open the wounds of the war and, as a gesture of protest, had decided not to replace the windowpanes broken by the bombings just three years before. In classrooms, from October to January, the cold could drop below zero degrees centigrade. In those facilities, he heard from first-class teachers, such as the legal philosopher Giorgio Del Vecchio, the civil law expert Emilio Betti, and Roman law scholar Vincenzo Arangio Ruiz, whom he befriended. Betti even persuaded Larrea to deepen his studies of the Ecuadorian Civil Code, and Larrea took advantage of these joint studies to review the code that he had somewhat forgotten since leaving Quito.

In Rome, Juan Larrea met Opus Dei and frequented a poor residence where the founder of this institution, D. Josemaría Escrivá de Balaguer, lived.[8] Larrea considered this meeting to be one of the greatest opportunities of his life. In April 1949 a member of Opus Dei, Ignacio Sallent, explained to him in detail what was "The Work" (as Opus Dei is called): a new way to holiness without leaving the world, in the midst of professional tasks and the ordinary situations of life. He was not asked to wear a religious habit, nor to profess vows, but to offer his studies and his work, and to find God in everyday circumstances. On April 23, 1949, Juan Larrea asked for admission to Opus Dei as a numerary.[9] This decision would give Christian depth to his studies and his whole life. Losing no time, and without leaving his career at the state university, that same year he joined the newly founded Roman College of the Holy Cross. St. Josemaría had founded it a year earlier to offer intense training to the members of Opus Dei who had come from different countries to obtain an ecclesiastical doctorate; many of them would be ordained priests and return to their homelands. The Roman College was born without means: "you start as you can," said the founder.[10] The first class began with ten students, and by the time they finished there were only four. Juan Larrea joined six more students in the second class, in the 1949–50 academic year.

Thus, a year after arriving in Rome, Juan Larrea was enrolled in two universities at the same time: at La Sapienza, and at the Pontifical Athenaeum Angelicum, where he studied canon law. At first, he carried out these studies while living in his father's warm and comfortable home, typical of an ambassador. However, it soon happened that his father's diplomatic career changed course, and in 1951 he was transferred to London. After that, the son went to live in the *Pensionato* of St. Josemaría, a narrow guardhouse of the former Embassy of Hungary to the Holy See.[11] There the occupants lived in poverty: most slept on the ground,[12] studying without tables, sitting on the stairs or on their knees inside a hollow space under the terrace that was no more than five feet high. Despite the fatigue and the narrowness, the students undertook their studies in a heroic and brilliant way.

St. Josemaría had realized from the beginning the intellectual quality of Juan Larrea and knew how to get the best out of him. Consistent with his motto, "Whoever can be wise, we do not forgive him for not being,"[13] Juan was not forgiven for not being wise. Between 1951 and 1952, Larrea prepared two doctoral theses that he defended almost two days in a row. The first one, about state law, was at La Sapienza and dealt with "marriage in the concordat regimes": he wrote it in Italian and obtained the highest grade. The second one, on canon law, supervised by the Dominican father Severino Álvarez of the Angelicum, dealt with "the personality of the church in the *Modus Vivendi* celebrated between the Holy See and Ecuador" (some decades earlier, Ecuador had breached its concordat, and the new *Modus Vivendi* became the only possibility to acquire peace in the relationship with the Holy See); this second thesis also obtained the highest qualification. He wrote it in Castilian but included a twelve-page summary in Latin.[14] Larrea had chosen that subject at the suggestion of a teacher because he had a lot of firsthand information, but mainly because his father, Carlos Manuel Larrea, had in 1937 promoted the consummation of this treaty, and the son wanted to highlight what his father considered to be the greatest achievement of his diplomatic career.[15]

Larrea lived with St. Josemaría in Rome for three years, until July 1952.[16] Before Larrea left the city, St. Josemaría suggested that he should finish philosophical studies on his own and advance his theological studies in Spain. Finally, Juan Larrea arrived in Quito on October 6, 1952.

Barely stepping into the capital, he contacted Dr. Jorge Pérez Serrano, a former professor of his who ran the most prestigious law firm in the city,[17] where Larrea began working the day after the interview, and where he came to acquire great prestige as a lawyer. Then he presented himself to the dean of the faculty of law at the Catholic University, Dr. Julio Tobar Donoso, who was a friend of his father's. By fortunate coincidence, there was a vacancy in a discipline, and the semester had to begin immediately; the dean appreciated the visit, and Larrea joined the faculty as a teacher in that same month of October.[18]

As he needed a national title to practice, a few months after his arrival he was introduced to a new doctoral degree to obtain the title of Doctor of Jurisprudence and Lawyer of the Courts of Ecuador.[19] He passed the tests of eight subjects on national law, obtaining again the maximum qualification. This was the first doctoral degree obtained by a graduate at the Catholic University.

In this university, he taught various subjects for twenty-two consecutive years, fourteen of which he served as vice dean of the faculty of law. He delivered the entire long branch of civil law. He almost always taught private international law at the same time and also taught other subjects, such as Roman law[20] and religion. Furthermore, he taught international trade at the faculty of economics at the same university. He began as an assistant professor of civil law and soon became the head of the department. He maintained his academic vocation throughout his life, even after his priestly ordination. He also taught several courses at the Central University[21] (affiliated with the leftist party),[22] at the Academy of Diplomacy for three or four years, and at the Institute of Higher National Studies (IAEN) in territorial and international private law for ten years. During his stay in Ibarra and Guayaquil, he gave classes at the seminary. In this last city, he taught several civil law courses from 1989 to 1994 at the Santiago de Guayaquil Catholic University.[23] His spirit of spreading good doctrine was always about much more: he had a brief daily program on television and wrote twice a week for the newspaper *El Telégrafo* (*The Telegraph*).

During the 1960s and 1970s, Larrea taught his classes in the old-school style: he began classes on time by crossing himself and praying an Our Father or a Hail Mary, then saying two words—*Sedes Sapientiae* (Seat of Wisdom)—encouraging the students to answer, *ora pro nobis* (pray for us); then he gave a master class and finally opened a time for questions. His explanations were very clear and good, very similar to the doctrine of the Catholic Church, but he was more engaging. For example, during the first year, students would go through the first four volumes of his commentary on the civil code, advancing thirty or forty pages a day. Although the topic was serious, the students admired him and knew how to win his friendship.[24] Later, without lowering the level of excellence, he adapted his way of teaching to the modern times.

During the years from 1952 to 1962, Larrea acted in the courts and tribunals of Ecuador and in certain processes abroad.[25] From the beginning of his profession, he held numerous public offices.[26] He was secretary of the National Commission of UNESCO from 1953 to 1954; in 1955 he was appointed attorney of the National Social Security Fund; the following year he was tax attorney of the republic; electoral attorney from 1957 to 1961; and vice president of the Court from 1960 to 1961. He was also an adviser to multiple entities: the Presidency of the Republic, the Supreme Court of Justice, the Ministry of Foreign Affairs,[27] the Ministry of Agriculture, and the Permanent Legislative Commission of the National Congress.

But Larrea's prestigious professional career as a lawyer suffered a radical change in 1962, the year he was ordained as a priest. From then on, he stopped taking cases and dedicated himself to the priestly ministry.[28] In any case, he would never stop teaching, neither humanist nor legal studies, nor would he cease publishing. His prestige in the legal field became so high that on several occasions he had to return to the national[29] and international[30] courts, called by judges and arbitrators so that he could render his version as an expert in law. Shortly after his ordination, he began to receive several ecclesiastical appointments: that of counselor of Opus Dei (1966–69), auxiliary bishop of Quito (1969–75), coadjutor bishop of Ibarra (1975–78), bishop of Ibarra (1978–82), military bishop (1982–88), coadjutor bishop of Guayaquil (1988), and archbishop of Guayaquil (1989–2003). In 2003 he became archbishop emeritus of Guayaquil.

By 1965 Juan Larrea had already had a good career as a legal writer. That year, with René Bustamante Muñoz and Eduardo Burneo, he founded the Studies and Publications Corporation,[31] a company that has become the largest legal publisher in Ecuador. In Ibarra he founded the Seminary of the Diocese. In 1992 he inaugurated the Catholic Pedagogical Institute for teacher training, built with donations. Many other ecclesiastical and social projects can be counted among his achievements too.

Bishop Larrea also promoted numerous norms and reforms inspired by Christian principles, in favor of the rights of people, women, family, education, and religious freedom. We have details of some of these initiatives, but not all of them.[32] His legal advice counted so much that he was consulted on many occasions by parties on the right, center, and left for the approval of norms.[33] As Bishop Javier Echevarría said,

> he did not intervene in political matters despite having actively participated in politics, when he was younger. However, he knew how to give doctrine so that those who deal with public affairs could act responsibly, in service to citizens, Catholics or not.[34]

In my opinion, the most important norms that he promoted are the following:[35]

1) *Law 256 from 1970*,[36] which favored equality between men and women, and between all siblings, and which regulated other civil matters. Bishop Larrea wrote:

   > The Permanent Legislative Commission decided to entrust a special commission with the study of the necessary reforms to put the civil code in accordance with current legislation and, above all, with the Constitution of the Republic that came into force on the 25th of May 1967. The commission was integrated by Dr. Franco Costales Herrera, and for him I write this. I was responsible for the development of the project, which was reviewed in conjunction with Dr. Costales, during the months of November and December of 1969 and January and February of this year. In those four months of intense work, I wrote the explanatory statement that served as the basis for the discussion of the Legislative Commission.[37]...The Legislative Commission accepted most of the project but also introduced some modifications.[38]

   He added, however,

   > I should note with satisfaction that the commission welcomed with enthusiasm some proposed reforms, such as those aimed at facilitating the recognition of children, to equate the rights of husband and wife, to repress usury, to extend family patrimony, to extend the public domain to the underwater riches, etc.[39]

2) *Law 43 of 1989*,[40] which updated some aspects of the 1970 reform and made them accord with the Constitution of 1979 that introduced the legal regulation of de facto unions.[41] As Bishop Larrea points out:

   > The Legal Commission of the Ecuadorian Committee of Cooperation of the Inter-American Commission of Women—CECIM—delivered to the Secretariat of the Public Administration a draft of reforms to Book 1 of the civil code, and by order of the President of the Republic conducted a study and issued an opinion, which undoubtedly served for a re-elaboration of the project, which was presented to the National Congress, with an explanatory statement, signed by three Provincial Deputies—Doctors Anunziatta Valdés L., Floripa Mejía V., and Josefina

> Izurieta—in 1987. This project has served as the fundamental basis for Law 43, in which enough elements of another project have been introduced, presented to Congress by the distinguished jurist Dr. Carlos Feraud Blum.[42]

Larrea would later write a commentary[43] highlighting the positive aspects and observing the negatives of the law that, in part, originated in his works. Although he considered positive the intentions of the legislature proclaimed in the recitals, he stated that:

> unfortunately, instead of complying with the constitutional norm, the legislature has issued a new grievance to the Ecuadorian family, further easing divorce and establishing norms, some ambiguous and others clearly unjust, that you can easily predict will cause countless uncertainties, conflicts, and, ultimately, legal and moral damages to the family.[44]

3) The *reforms to the Constitution of 1994*, which corrected serious defects in the text and introduced new guarantees of rights. President Sixto Durán Ballén in 1994 appointed a commission of jurists and constitutionalists, including Bishop Larrea, to create a preliminary draft of the constitutional reform. The president endorsed the recommendations, almost without any change, and presented them to Congress, which discussed and approved them by blocks.[45]
4) *The Family Educational Freedom Act of 1994*[46] was sanctioned after a heated debate to enable each family to have access to the religious education of their choice (in Ecuador there are no religious classes in public schools). In addition, Larrea prepared more than four hundred professors of Catholic religion to face the demand that immediately resulted in the application of the law.[47]
5) *The 1978 agreement between the Holy See and the Republic of Ecuador on religious assistance to the armed forces and the national police*[48] regulates, in accordance with the provisions of the *Modus Vivendi*, the religious assistance of members of the armed forces and the national police. Bishop Larrea was appointed as the first military bishop of Ecuador in 1982, a position he held until 1988. In that last year, he promoted the Statutes of the Military Ordinariate or Military Bishopric of Ecuador[49] and the Regulation of the Military Bishopric of Ecuador, promulgated *ad experimentum*.[50] On behalf of the state, President Sixto Durán Ballén completed the missing regulation in 1996.[51] We see how the son completes here the work started by his father, the ambassador, who managed the *Modus Vivendi* that regulates church–state relations.[52]

He became a true expert on matters of international law. In addition to writing works referring to the subject, he participated in multiple conferences and international conventions on legal issues in Mexico, Colombia, Venezuela, Chile,

Peru, and Ecuador. For that reason, one can understand why he was frequently asked for his advice on these matters. Many times, he was a member of the Advisory Board of the Ministry of Foreign Affairs[53] and, for a period, president of the same ministry.[54]

At the end of his life, Bishop Larrea had accumulated many chairs, titles, and memberships. He was a member of the Hispano-Luso-American Institute of International Law, the Ecuadorian Academy of Language, the Royal Academy of the Spanish Language, the National Academy of the History of Ecuador (founded by his father with other historians), the Academy of Lawyers of Quito, and the Mariana Academy of Ecuador. He belonged to the House of Ecuadorian Culture and was a member of its Board of Directors (1974–76). Bishop Larrea also participated in countless diplomatic and international events. He was appointed Cavalier Knight of the Order of Malta. Yet despite all the bulky curriculum that could plunge anyone into vanity and pride, the virtue that most stood out in Bishop Larrea was his extreme delicacy and humility.[55]

In the mid-1990s, he was discovered to have cancer, which ten years later would cause his death. Even in those circumstances, he maintained the strength to fulfill his pastoral duties and write dozens of books. As mandated by the canonical norm, at the age of seventy-five Bishop Larrea presented his resignation to the archdiocese, which the supreme pontiff did not accept until the following year, in May 2003. From that moment, Bishop Larrea moved to live in Quito, where he carried out intense pastoral work and wrote dozens of legal and religious books.

He died on August 27, 2006. The Archdiocese of Guayaquil began the process of beatification on February 3, 2017. Because of his participation as an expert in international arbitration proceedings (especially in the ICSID), it has been proposed that, if he becomes beatified or canonized, he should be the patron of arbitrators.[56]

Major themes and contributions

Bishop Larrea wrote a lot with a very definite motive: to give doctrine, and to re-Christianize society. "We have to paper the world," I remember him saying to those present at a meeting, alluding to the task of giving a lot of good doctrine everywhere.[57] We do not know of another Ecuadorian writer who has been more prolific. Of the works that we have managed to register[58] so far, we count 261 books with him as the sole author (160 on law, 101 on humanities), not counting the numerous editions of several of them, many of which contain very substantial changes; thirty books of which he is co-author (in law); twenty-six book chapters (twenty-one in law, five in humanities); along with one hundred articles (ninty-eight in law, two in humanities). In all, seventy-five percent of the titles of Bishop Larrea were dedicated to law, while twenty-six percent were dedicated to ethics, theology, or the humanities in general. Data[59] about the level of impact of his writings indicate that his civil and constitutional works have the greatest number of citations. Of 1,563 citations, 866 citations refer to his comment on the Civil Code: 358 to the volume on property and possession, 323 to the *Manual elemental de Derecho civil del Ecuador* (*Elementary manual of Ecuadorian civil law*), and 185 to other works. In second place, the works on constitutional right are mentioned 250 times: 192 references to the book *Derecho Constitucional ecuatoriano* (*Ecuadorian constitutional law*), forty-five to the manual, and thirteen to other versions of the work. Third, there are 103 citations to the *Enciclopedia Jurídica Ecuatoriana* (Ecuadorian legal encyclopedia). The rest of his works have fewer citations.

Larrea's most famous work, to which he devoted forty years of his life (from 1965 to 2005), was *Derecho civil del Ecuador* (*Ecuadorian civil law*), where, in fifteen thick volumes, he commented on the entire civil code.[60] It is the first complete commentary on the civil code of Andrés Bello[61] made by an Ecuadorian, the principal text in practically all the universities of the country. It is his most cited work on Ecuadorian doctrine and jurisprudence, and the one that has most influenced provisions of the substantive code. Some volumes and many fragments of the work have the singularity of containing, to a certain extent, the *mens legislatoris* of some reforms proposed by Bishop Larrea himself, as, for example, the above-mentioned Law 256. Moreover, volume five, relative to the "the latest reforms" (1986),[62] contains part of the bill that he had proposed years earlier. His writings serve to reconstruct historically the will of the legislature.

After civil law, the second major area in which he stood out was constitutional law. He especially had luck with *La nueva estructura constitucional Ecuatoriana* (*The new Ecuadorian constitutional structure*), which won the 1969 Tobar Prize for his commentary on the 1967 Constitution. With the appearance of the Constitution of 1979 he updated his comments, prepared a constitutional history, and published the book *Derecho constitucional ecuatoriano* (*Ecuadorian constitutional law*, 1980). New updates came later, especially with the issuance of the Constitution of 1998, where the text of *Ecuadorian constitutional law* (1999) was printed in two volumes. An underlying idea in his work is that despite the numerous constitutions that Ecuador has had (more than twenty in two centuries), "the fundamental bases of the state have not changed in the most substantial way since the separation of Gran Colombia, that is from the year 1830":[63] there has been no second, third, or fourth republic as in France, Spain, and Germany, but, on the contrary, the country has maintained "an exemplary continuity in the fundamentals: independent state, unitary, republican, democratic, with a regime of presidential government, division of powers or functions, and a progressive recognition of guarantees and general rights."[64] In his last comments on the Constitution of 1998 he continued:

> One of the purest glories of our history consists of the progressive consolidation of human rights in constitutional texts. Almost without setbacks, gradually but constantly, we have been achieving a better formulation of the guarantees of freedom and equality of the inhabitants of the republic.[65]

This has created a historical pattern for developing the idea of a customary Ecuadorian *secundum constitutionem*.[66] Although he did not fail to observe certain setbacks and less accurate dispositions, the positive tone of his writings is admirable.

In the third place, his output related to international law has great merit, especially those works regarding relations with the Holy See and in private international law. We notice here the imprint of the ambassador father on the son. We saw how the concern of Ecuador's relations with the Church, broken by the liberal revolution and recomposed by Larrea's father, Carlos Manuel Larrea, with the *Modus Vivendi* of 1937, was an issue that occupied his mind from his childhood. His doctoral theses dealt with this issue,[67] and he wrote several books as well as seven chapters in different books and dozens of articles in scientific journals on these topics. The principal work that summarizes his thinking on the subject is *Derecho eclesiástico ecuatoriano* (*Ecuadorian ecclesiastical law*, 1983, with three editions). On the other hand, he was a professor of private international law for several decades, at the Catholic University of Ecuador and the IAEN, during which he published several updated editions of his *Manual de Derecho internacional privado ecuatoriano* (*Manual of Ecuadorian private international law*, the first edition is from 1962, the sixth from 1998); it is the most important and complete work in the country on the matter. For all this, Bishop Larrea was called to appear as an expert in law before several judges and tribunals abroad.

The most voluminous part of his output is his summaries of legislation, indexes with concordances, bibliographic lists, repertoires of jurisprudence and compilations that, as a whole, exceed one hundred volumes.[68] They have been very useful to practitioners of law, fundamentally before the advent of the computer age. Many of these works began as his articles,[69] but he later had some collaborators.[70] The materials were, at the time, the most systematized versions that existed with regard to Ecuadorian legislation. Before Bishop Larrea, lawyers used to prepare during their career a summary of the laws enforced in the country, which they tried to keep up with over the years. This practice ended with the works published by the Studies and Publications Corporation (CEP). Currently, the indexes and summaries of the legislation have been replaced, to a large extent, by computer programs with access to national regulations. In any case, jurisprudential repertoires continue to be very valid.

Finally, Bishop Larrea addressed many other topics. He made several investigations, publications, and speeches on the history of law, his main work being the *Historia del Derecho ecuatoriano* (*History of Ecuadorian law*, 2000), written with Dr. José Reig: Larrea was responsible for the republican era. Other works that stand out are his *Enciclopedia jurídica ecuatoriana* (*Ecuadorian Legal Encyclopedia*, 2005),[71] a project of eleven volumes that began when his cancer was already very advanced; *Asuntos sociales y religiosos* (*Social and religious affairs, seven volumes*, 1992–98); *Moral y política* (*Morality and Politics*, 1991); *Educación ética y cívica* (*Ethical and civil Education*, 1996); and a number of texts and articles on social issues and bioethics.[72] In all these matters one could appreciate the vision of ethics and Thomist law—from Larrea's Roman years he was a devotee of St. Thomas Aquinas and St. Albert the Great[73]—with the resolution of the most current issues.

Conclusion

As a humanist, Juan Larrea dealt with a wide variety of theological, cultural, ethical, and historical issues that gave him a broader perspective on his legal work. His books have circulated around the world, and many have been translated into several languages. In addition, he undertook major editorial initiatives that have been of great service to the practitioners of law, and numerous bills in favor of the person, women, family, education, and religious freedom.

He is, without a doubt, the most distinguished and prestigious Ecuadorian jurist, the one who has most influenced legislation and national doctrine, and the conception of civil law in the countries that share the civil code prepared by Andrés Bello. In the legal field, Larrea excelled especially for his contribution to Ecuadorian civil law. However, he also made notable contributions to constitutional law, private international law, and ecclesiastical law.

He completed the work begun by his father, Carlos Manuel Larrea, who achieved the subscription of *Modus Vivendi* between Ecuador and the Holy See. Bishop Larrea helped to apply this treaty, not only by writing legal works that give a notion of how to apply the provisions of the treaty, such as issuing regulations of the military vicariate when he was the military bishop, but also by promoting the sanction in Ecuador of the specific regulation in this matter.

Notes

1 The main sources are three: his private unpublished autobiography (see references; hereinafter *Autobiography*), the article "Dos años en el Ecuador (1952–1954)" (see bibliography; hereafter "Dos años"), and an unpublished paper in relation to his affairs entitled "Notas sobre la Universidad" that he wrote in Guayaquil on February 17, 2002 (hereafter "Notes").

2 The most extensive biographies are by Vázquez Galiano and Riofrío Martínez-Villalba; see references.

3 He was named "abanderado," a distinction that in Ecuador is granted to the best student of all courses. All texts are in Spanish in the original; translations are mine.

4 This is the opinion of Vázquez, *Juan Larrea*, 34 and 41–42.

5 Riofrío, "Entrevista."

6 Vázquez, *Juan Larrea*, 42.

7 Ibid., 29.

8 Cf. Larrea, *Autobiografía*, and "Dos años"; Riofrío, *Juan Larrea Holguín*, and Luis González Gullón, "Los años romanos."

9 Larrea, "Dos años," 115. "Numeraries" are members of Opus Dei who live in celibacy and, thus, are more available for the apostolic requirements. But like those members who can marry, they also work in their own professions and live like any other citizen.

10 Cf. Vázquez de Prada, *Fundador del Opus Dei*, 133.

11 Ibid., 102–18.
12 Testimony of Juan Larrea, Sum. 6025, collected in Ibid., 233, note 102.
13 Escrivá, *The Way*, no 332.
14 Cf. Vázquez, *Juan Larrea*, 73–74.
15 For Arregui, the latter was the main reason. Cf. Arregui, "Juan Larrea Holguín Pastor." However, it was not the only reason, nor the first in chronological terms. Cf. also, Larrea, *Autobiografía*, 11; and Larrea, "Monseñor Juan Larrea Holguín: 'Sigo Las Huellas De Mi Padre,'" where he cites other reasons.
16 Cf. Riofrío, *Personal Testimony*, Quito, 2-XI-2013; Vázquez, *Juan Larrea*, 85–91.
17 Cf. Pérez Pimentel, "Juan Larrea Holguín."
18 Cf. Larrea, "Notes."
19 Ibid.
20 As stated in his letter of May 31, 1955, he had to replace Professor Manuel Elicio Flor.
21 Cf. Larrea, "Notes." Larrea renounced continuing classes at the Catholic University, by letter of February 12, 1975, because of the new twists that the university was giving on theological issues. On other possible reasons for the resignation, see Salvador Crespo, "Juan Larrea Holguín y la Pontificia Universidad Católica."
22 Eduardo Mora Anda says that for "admirable irony, he was invited to teach at the Central University. The left party recognized the wisdom of the professor, who did not value the irrepressible authorities of the Catholic University": Mora Anda, "Personalidad de Juan Larrea," 127.
23 Cf. Larrea, "Notes."
24 On his way of teaching, cf. Flor Rubianes, Interview; Riofrío, *Juan Larrea Holguín*, 29–37.
25 Vázquez, *Juan Larrea*, 146–49, details his first clients and some cases he defended.
26 Cf. Puente, "Monseñor Juan Larrea."
27 Cf. Ayala Lasso, "Amistad," 156.
28 Cf. Vázquez, *Juan Larrea*, 211–12.
29 For example, in the gloss to Xavier Vidal Maspons (1985–86) and in the Filanbanco case (2003).
30 For example, in the case of the international arbitration of Duke Energy (2008) processed in Washington, DC, before the International Center for Settlement of Investment Disputes (ICSID).
31 About the foundation, cf. Puente, "Monseñor."
32 Ibid.
33 Bishop Javier Echevarría testified that before being a priest, he was active in a political party in Ecuador, and the members of the opposing party asked him to study and provide them with statutes for their organization. In addition, the leaders commented to the members themselves that they had asked Larrea precisely because they knew he was going to do it objectively, without trying to impose his judgment on those who thought otherwise about the approach that had to be focused on the exercise of public life in his country. Cf. Echevarría, "Mons. Juan Larrea Holguín: Un 'grande' en lo grande y en lo pequeño."
34 Ibid., N. 89. Such an attitude is what is to be expected of a bishop. It belongs to the mission of the Church "to issue a moral judgment even on things that affect the political order when the fundamental rights of the person or the salvation of souls demand it." (*Gaudium et Spes*, 76.5; Catechism of the Catholic Church, no. 2246).
35 In addition, there is evidence that he actively participated in many other regulations. Cf. Arregui, "Juan Larrea Holguín Pastor." He also advised the pro-life movements in preparation for the 2007–08 Constituent Assembly: one year

before the assembly, Bishop Larrea wrote a document that included the essential points that should be defended. He died shortly afterward.

36 Published in the Registro Oficial 446 of June 4, 1970.

37 Larrea, *Derecho civil del Ecuador*, Vol. 6, p. 9.

38 Ibid.

39 Ibid., 9–10.

40 Published in the Supplement of the Registro Oficial 256 on August 18, 1989.

41 The same that were the subject of Law 115 (Registro Oficial 399 of December 29, 1982).

42 Larrea, *Derecho Civil del Ecuador*, Annex Vol. 2, p. 568.

43 Ibid. The commentary would later be structurally integrated into the fifteen volumes of his work *Derecho Civil del Ecuador*.

44 Ibid., 575.

45 Cf. Larrea, *Derecho Constitucional*, 1:26.

46 The Law of Educational Freedom of Families in Ecuador (Law 69) was published in the Supplement to the Registro Oficial 540, dated October 4, 1994. It was abolished by the 4th Repellant Provision of the Organic Law of Intercultural Education (published in Registro Oficial-Suplemento 417, of March 31, 2011).

47 Regrettably, the new authorities abolished this law departing from a constitutional right to receive religious education.

48 Signed on August 3, 1978 (*Ecclesiastical Bulletin of the Military Bishopric of Ecuador*, 1 [1987], 1–10). Subsequently, the Agreement has been implemented through the Regulation of the Military Bishopric of Ecuador (Executive Decree 3565, published in the Registro Oficial 899 of March 7, 1996).

49 Published in the *Ecclesiastical Bulletin of the Military Bishopric of Ecuador* 2 (1988): 1–3.

50 Published in the *Ecclesiastical Bulletin of the Military Bishopric of Ecuador* 2 (1988): 11–17.

51 The regulation of the military bishopric in Ecuador was issued by Executive Decree 3565, which was published in the Registro Oficial 899 of March 7, 1996. We suppose that Mons. Larrea intervened in its redaction.

52 On what these norms have meant, cf. Dobronsky, "Vicariato Militar."

53 Cf. Mora Anda, "Personalidad de Juan Larrea," 128.

54 According to Agreement 82 of May 13, 1966, he was appointed member of the Advisory Board of Foreign Affairs, as Representative of the Cardinal of Quito. It is recorded in the minutes that on February 29, 1988, he was appointed chairman of the same board by a unanimous vote.

55 What is said is expressed in all of his biographies. In addition, cf. Oyarte Martínez and Oyarte Cienfuegos, "Entrevista a Monseñor Juan Larrea," 198.

56 See Perry, "*A Patron Saint of Arbitration?*"

57 Cf. Rodrigo-Mendizábal, "Columnas periodísticas."

58 We are still missing some texts. The list of his works is on the site www.juanlarrea-holguin.com.

59 See Google Scholar at https://scholar.google.com.ec/citations?user=ikhrhUkAAAAJ&hl=en) (accessed January 9, 2019).

60 The work of fifteen volumes has had four editions, plus an edition of six volumes; a compendium of eight volumes titled *Manual de Derecho Civil del Ecuador* has had two editions and another compendium of four volumes, plus three simplified editions, as well as posthumous updates by other authors. This does not count the digital editions. All these data can be found on the website www.juanlarrea-holguin.com.

61 The civil code drafted by Andrés Bello is in force, with slight variations, in Chile, Colombia, and Ecuador.

62 In later editions it was renamed "Comentarios a la Codificación del Código Civil de 1970 y posteriores reformas" (CEP, Quito, 2009).
63 Larrea and Tobar Donoso, *Derecho Constitucional*, 79.
64 Ibid.
65 Introduction to the *Political Constitution of the Republic of Ecuador of 1998* (Quito: CEP, 2002), 7.
66 In this sense, Riofrío "Constitutional custom."
67 As we saw, his theses dealt with "marriage in the concordat regimes" and "the personality of the church in the *modus vivendi* celebrated between the Holy See and Ecuador."
68 The list of these works is detailed at www.juanlarreaholguin.com.
69 Thus, for example, the "Concordancias y Jurisprudencia del Código Civil" published in the *Revista de Derecho*, between 1964 and 1967, in the following volumes and pages (volume and page numbers separated by colon): 1:141–47; I2:103–11; 3:64–73; 4:138–48; 5:122–34; 6:82–87; 7–8:189–98; 9:107–18; 10:119–24; and 12:114–24.
70 Until 1986 he bore only the weight of the production of all these repertoire books. Starting with volume 28, he helped in several volumes in the work of others credited as coauthors.
71 On the history of this project and its authors, see Riofrío, *Juan Larrea*, 44.
72 See the list of articles, book chapters, and texts at www.juanlarreaholguin.com.
73 Cf. Flor, *Testimony*, n. 93. On the Thomist vision of law, see Robalino Bolle, "Monseñor Juan Larrea Holguín."

References

Arregui, Antonio. "Juan Larrea Holguín, Pastor." *Congress of Law and Humanities.* Quito: Universidad de Los Hemisferios, 2016 (*pro manuscripto*).

Ayala Lasso, José. "Amistad con Juan Ignacio Larrea Holguín." *Colloquia, Academic Journal of Culture and Thought* 3 (2016): 152–57.

Dobronsky, Fernando. "Vicariato Militar." *Congress of Law and Humanities.* Quito: Universidad de Los Hemisferios, 2016 (*pro manuscripto*).

Echevarría, Javier. "Mons. Juan Larrea Holguín: Un "grande" en lo grande y en lo pequeño." *Colloquia, Academic Journal of Culture and Thought* 3 (2016): 1–6.

Escrivá, Josemaría, *The Way. Critical-Historical Edition*, edited by Pedro Rodríguez. Strongsville, OH: Scepter Publishers, 2010.

Flor Rubianes, Jaime. Interview with Juan Carlos Riofrío. November 21, 2013.

González Gullón, José Luis. "Los años romanos de Juan Larrea (1948–1952)." *Colloquia, Academic Journal of Culture and Thought* 3 (2016): 24–36.

Hautebert, Joël. "Registro civil y secularización. Comparación entre Ecuador y Francia." *Ius Humani* 5 (2016): 259–72.

Larrea Holguín, Juan. "Autobiografía." Post 1988. Quito: General Archive of Juan Larrea.

Larrea Holguín, Juan. *Derecho constitucional ecuatoriano*, Vol. 2. Quito: CEP, 2000.

Larrea Holguín, Juan. *Derecho civil del Ecuador*, Annex Vol. 2: *Commentary on Law 43 That Reforms the Civil Code.* Quito: CEP, 1989.

Larrea Holguín, Juan. *Derecho civil del Ecuador*, Vol. 6: *The Last Reforms.* Quito: CEP, 1970.

Larrea Holguín, Juan. "Dos años en el Ecuador (1952–1954): recuerdos en torno a unas cartas de San Josemaría Escrivá de Balaguer." *Studia et Documenta* 1 (2007): 113–25; Available at http://www.es.josemariaescriva.info/articulo/dos-anos-en-ecuador-281952-1954293a-recuerdos-en-torno-a-unas-cartas-de-san-josemaria-escriva-de-balaguer.

Larrea Holguín, Juan. "Monseñor Juan Larrea Holguín: 'Sigo Las Huellas De Mi Padre.'" *Hoy*, January 15, 1995. Available at http://hoy.tawsa.com/noticias-ecuador/monsenor-juan-larrea-holguin-sigo-las-huellas-de-mi-padre-20906.html.

Larrea Holguín, Juan. *Notas sobre la Universidad.* Quito: General Archive of Juan Larrea, February 17, 2002.

Larrea Holguín, Juan, and Julio Tobar Donoso. *Derecho Constitucional Ecuatoriano.* Quito: CEP, 1980.

Mora Anda, Eduardo. "La personalidad de Juan Larrea Holguín y el Derecho Internacional." *Colloquia, Academic Journal of Culture and Thought* 3 (2016): 125–32.

Oyarte Martínez, Rafael, and Hugo Oyarte Cienfuegos. "Entrevista a Monseñor Juan Larrea Holguín." *Revista de la Facultad de Jurisprudencia* 1 (1999): 197–211.

Pérez Pimentel, Rodolfo. "Juan Larrea Holguín." *Diccionario biográfico del Ecuador.* Guayaquil: Universidad de Guayaquil, 2005.

Perry, Sebastian. "A Patron Saint of Arbitration?" *Global Arbitration Review* (GAR), April 5, 2012. Available at https://globalarbitrationreview.com/article/1031249/a-patron-saint-of-arbitration.

Puente, Eduardo. "Monseñor Juan Larrea Holguín." *Congress of Law and Humanities.* Quito: Universidad de Los Hemisferios, 2016 (*pro manuscrito*).

Riofrío Martínez-Villalba, Juan Carlos. "Constitutional Custom and Supreme Values in Juan Larrea Holguín." *Congress of Law and Humanities.* Quito: Universidad de Los Hemisferios, 2016 (*pro manuscrito*).

Riofrío Martínez-Villalba, Juan Carlos. "Entrevista con Mons. Juan Larrea Holguín." *Revista Más* (1998): 20–24.

Riofrío Martínez-Villalba, Juan Carlos. *Juan Larrea Holguín. La amistad, la universidad y la investigación.* 2nd ed. Quito: Universidad de Los Hemisferios, 2016.

Riofrío Martínez-Villalba, Juan Carlos. "Larrea Holguín, Juan." In *Diccionario de Canonistas y Eclesiasticistas Europeos y Americanos*, Vol. 1, *1309 semblanzas del año 1000 al 2015*, edited by Manuel J. Peláez, 237–39. Saarbrücken: Editorial Académica Española, 2012.

Robalino Bolle, Isabel. "Monseñor Juan Larrea Holguín, el jurista." *Congress of Law and Humanities.* Quito: Universidad de Los Hemisferios, 2016 (*pro manuscripto*).

Rodrigo-Mendizábale, Iván. "Las columnas periodísticas de asuntos políticos en Mons. Juan Larrea Holguín." *ComHumanitas: Revista científica de comunicación*, 7 (2006): 1–11.

Salvador Crespo, Íñigo. "Juan Larrea Holguín y la Pontificia Universidad Católica del Ecuador." *Colloquia, Academic Journal of Culture and Thought* 3 (2016): 7–23.

Trueba Barahona, Álvaro. "Un personaje inolvidable." *Equinoccio. Series académicas* 4 (2006): 6–9.
Vázquez de Prada, Andrés. *El fundador del Opus Dei*, Vol. 1. Madrid: Rialp, 2003.
Vázquez Galiano, Antonio. *Juan Larrea: un rayo de luz sobre fondo gris*. Madrid: Palabra, 2009.

37 Carlos Alberto Menezes Direito (Brazil, 1942–2009)

Robert J. Cottrol

Introduction

A devout Catholic and prolific legal scholar, Carlos Alberto Menezes Direito served as a jurist at the highest levels of the Brazilian federal judiciary from his appointment to the Superior Tribunal of Justice in 1996 until his death in 2009 while serving on Brazil's highest court, the Supreme Federal Tribunal. His tenure on the federal bench came at a time when the South American nation had only recently returned to a state of full democratic governance. Since the overthrow of the Brazilian monarchy in 1888 and the establishment of the Brazilian republic in 1889, the nation had experienced alternate democratic and authoritarian regimes. But in 1985, with the end of the military government which had led the nation since 1964, something new appeared on the Brazilian political scene—a move toward a robust democracy as embodied by the new constitution adopted in 1988. Previous democratic governments had been limited because, while they had political representatives chosen by electors, the right to vote was restricted to people who were literate, and a significant percentage of Brazilian adults was thus disfranchised. This would not be the case after the adoption of the Constitution of 1988, which did away with the literacy requirement and opened the way for widespread public participation in the nation's governance.[1]

Brazil's democratization presented new challenges for the Catholic Church in its efforts both to preserve its interests and to advance its views of a just society. If in older, more authoritarian iterations of the Brazilian nation, the Catholic Church may have enjoyed a place of privilege as a moral authority, in the new, more democratic Brazil, the Church would have to struggle to make its voice heard against competing voices increasingly being raised by rival Protestant denominations and from the secular practices and ideologies coming from the worlds of business and the universities. The Church would also have its internal conflicts in the struggle between those faithful to the traditional authority of the Church and the more radical adherents of the new doctrines of liberation theology.

Menezes Direito was part of the Brazilian Catholic Church's effort to bring the Church's voice to that part of the public square which is law. The recipient of an elite secondary education, he came of age intellectually at the Pontifical

Catholic University of Rio de Janeiro (PUC). University life matched his temperament and interests; he became an avid scholar, not only of the law but of theology and science as well. He kept these intellectual interests throughout his career, persisting in his life as a teacher and scholar even as he served on the nation's two highest courts. He became most identified for upholding the Church's position and leading the dissenting side in a high court case involving embryonic stem cell research. Although he was on the losing side of the case, the clarity of his arguments and the strength of his scholarly presentation on Brazil's high court won widespread admiration.

Biographical summary

Carlos Alberto Menezes Direito served as a minister on Brazil's highest court, the Supreme Federal Tribunal (*O Supremo Tribunal Federal*), from his appointment by President Luis Inacio Lula da Silva on September 5, 2007, until his death on September 1, 2009. He was born in the city of Belém in Brazil's northern state of Para on September 8, 1942. Menezes Direito would become renowned in Brazil and internationally as both a jurist and a legal scholar. He was also recognized as a man with a deep commitment to his Catholic faith. His career, particularly his brief tenure on the South American nation's highest tribunal, came to reflect the tensions between these two commitments. Nowhere would this tension become more apparent than when Menezes Direito took part in the Brazilian high court's 2008 decision determining the legality of research on stem cells taken from human embryos.

The son of Luiz Nunes Direito and Carmen Menezes Direito, the future jurist and legal scholar attended secondary school in the late 1950s at the elite *Colegio Anglo Americano* in Rio de Janeiro, then Brazil's capital. At an early age, Menezes Direito displayed the kind of interest in writing, scholarship, and public issues that would later characterize his whole career. At Anglo Americano he was president of the Literary Society and founded the society's journal, *O Anglo*. He also gained prizes in oratory and classics at the school. But it was at the Pontifical Catholic University of Rio de Janeiro where Direito brought together what would become his two worlds, one as an advocate for the principles of the Catholic Church and the other as a scholar and later a jurist of the secular law. In Brazil, one takes one's first degree in law as an undergraduate, and Menezes Direito enrolled in the PUC Faculty of Law in 1961 after completing his secondary education. An education in the law at the PUC went beyond the standard law faculty curriculum in Brazil. Typically the first degree in law is a five-year program with courses in law and a brief exposure to the social sciences. The university's curriculum had these elements, but also included courses in theology and philosophy, exposing students at a university level to the Catholic Church's teachings.[2]

But Direito's activities at the university went far beyond the demands of the classroom in subjects secular and sacred. He was an active student, founding and acting as president of a student group offering assistance to imprisoned inmates, while also founding the University Solidarity movement. As an undergraduate, he participated in a seminar on international law at Oxford University. Immediately after receiving his Bachelor of Law degree in 1965, Direito enrolled in the PhD program of the PUC law faculty. While a student in the program, he did additional study in the fields of corporate law, banking law, and Catholic social doctrine. Drawn to the study of law and the protection of human rights, he explored that topic in a dissertation titled *O Estado Moderno e a protecao dos direitos do homen* (*The modern state and the protection of the rights of man*). He received his PhD degree in 1968 and published his dissertation as a book the same year.[3]

As a student, Menezes Direito was well regarded by the professors at the PUC. He received an offer to join the ranks of the university faculty even before receiving his doctorate. By the late sixties he had become a full-fledged member of the university's faculty. In the late sixties and early seventies he held a variety of faculty and administrative positions at the university: professor of constitutional law, professor of Church doctrine, and professor of legal institutions in the university's Department of Economics. In 1971 he was appointed Dean of the Center of Juridical Sciences and later, in 1972, vice-rector of the university. His appointments reflected his increasing prominence in the Brazilian legal academy in the 1970s. His first book, on the state and the protection of rights, was followed by a robust body of scholarship embracing fields as diverse as intellectual property, constitutional law, judicial reform, political science, administrative law, and medical malpractice. During the course of his career as both a legal scholar and jurist, Menezes Direito published more than nine books, eighteen book chapters, and well over seventy scholarly articles. He gained a high national and international profile as a participant in and organizer of international law conferences. These ranged far and wide and included conferences on Brazilian law and international conferences on law and human rights in Mexico, France, the United Kingdom, Chile, and Peru.[4]

Menezes Direito came of age politically at a time when Brazil was governed by a succession of authoritarian military presidents. He initially joined Brazil's Christian Democratic Party, which modeled itself after the Christian democratic parties of Europe and saw itself as a "third way" between parties of the right and parties of the left. Menezes Direito's early affiliation with the Christian Democratic Party reflected his general support for the Church's approach to social and political issues. In an address, "Christian Faith and Social Commitment," which he gave at the PUC in March 1982, Menezes Direito outlined what he believed should be the approach of the practicing Catholic and the Catholic University to the social problems then facing Brazil and other modern societies. His approach in many ways tracked the views of Pope Paul VI in his 1971 apostolic letter *Octogesima Adveniens* and Pope John Paul II in his 1981 encyclical *Laborem Exercens*. Menezes Direito's thinking appears to have been particularly influenced by the warnings of *Octogesima Adveniens* against the excesses of modern capitalism, with its unlimited competition and manipulation of the public through advertising. The pontiff's 1971 letter also cautioned against the anomie and isolation of modern society and the soulless pursuit of economic efficiency urged by classical liberalism. Pope Paul VI also warned against the totalitarian and violent tendencies of Marxism, with its materialistic tendency to deny the transcendent.[5]

Like the papal documents, Menezes Direito's address outlined a view of humanity and society sharply critical of both classical liberal capitalism and Marxism. For Menezes Direito, classical liberalism was to be criticized for destroying society's social fabric through the corrosive force of its competitive individualism. Unrestrained capitalism had created an urban proletariat alienated from the most basic of human needs. But Menezes Direito also attacked Marxist collectivism for creating societies incapable of satisfying humanity's needs. Marxism imprisoned the proletariat in a monolithic dictatorship of party rule that became a form of state capitalism administered by an irremediably anachronistic gerontocracy.[6]

That humanity in the latter part of the twentieth century often had a choice between two basically unsatisfactory alternatives was, Menezes Direito argued, particularly tragic, because the choice came at a time when the possibilities for satisfying both cultural and material human wants had never been greater. For Menezes Direito, the late twentieth century was also a time when humanity had never been more frustrated. It was an era when large numbers of people were thwarted in their aspirations and lived in soul-crushing isolation from others in society.[7]

In his address, Menezes Direito argued that the fundamental failure in the development of modern social policy stemmed from a failure to develop a proper view of humanity, one that relied on what he described as a "holistic anthropology," a human science that took into account the need for an "opening to the transcendent inherent in human beings." The Catholic scholar urged that the PUC take the lead in developing models for organizing society that avoided the pitfalls of both the classical liberal and Marxist models. Menezes Direito urged that Brazil itself was most in need of this "third way" approach to solving social problems. The South American nation was paying the price for not having eradicated poverty and, indeed, for permitting structural injustice and inequality. He likened going after poverty and deep-seated economic inequality as similar to a public-health program to vaccinate the poor; it would cost less to have a vaccination program and avoid an epidemic than to cure the epidemic after it had started.[8]

Menezes Direito concluded his lecture by stating that each Christian was required by faith to have social commitment. For the professor, social commitment was not just the title of the day's lecture but a demand at the core of Christianity. It was also, Menezes Direito argued, a reason to fight social, political, economic, racial, and cultural discrimination. He told his colleagues that a university would be pontifical and Catholic to the exact extent that it would take on social commitment. He noted that the Church had much to offer because its pastoral experience had made it an "expert in humanity."[9]

Menezes Direito's ideas about the Church would affect his outlook on life and public policy throughout his career. When the Christian Democratic Party went defunct, Menezes Direito aligned himself with the centrist Brazilian Democratic Movement. By the mid-1970s, his activities began to move beyond the university.

He practiced law before the local trial court, the Foro do Rio de Janeiro, and in 1979 was appointed chief of cabinet of the city government in Rio. Menezes Direito was also a member of the Council of Civil Society, which was supported by the PUC. The council was intended to be an organization which would publically represent the Church's views on matters of governance and social responsibility. Menezes Direito would serve in a number of positions with both the federal government and the government of the state of Rio de Janeiro, holding offices in the state's Ministry of Education and the federal copyright court, among other posts. In 1988 he was appointed as a trial judge in Rio's Tribunal of Justice. While on that court, he continued writing on a wide array of legal issues.

A full democratic government had returned to Brazil in 1985 with the election that year of José Sarney as president. Sarney succeeded Brazil's last military president, Joao Figueiredo. The South American nation adopted a new constitution in 1988. In a lecture titled "Constitutional Democracy in the 80s," Menezes Direito offered some cautionary notes concerning constitutionalism and democracy. Echoing some of the themes he had made in his talk on Christian faith and social commitment, Menezes Direito stressed the need for a greater public commitment to social justice and noted the great gulf between rich and poor in Brazil. He also stressed concern that the growth of governmental bureaucracy was taking funds that should be used to fight extreme poverty. The trial judge magistrate also called for citizen education to strengthen public respect for the rule of law.[10]

Menezes Direito joined the ranks of the federal judiciary in 1996. On June 27 of that year, Brazilian president Fernando Henrique Cardoso appointed him to the nation's highest appellate court for nonconstitutional issues, the Superior Tribunal of Justice, a court created by the Constitution of 1988. Cardoso, like Menezes Direito, was a member of Brazil's centrist Movement for a Democratic Brazil. Perhaps he also found the scholarly Menezes Direito an attractive nominee because, like Direito, Cardoso is a renowned scholar in the social sciences in his own right. It was on the Superior Tribunal that Menezes Direito would gain a reputation as a technocratic jurist with a detailed knowledge of Brazilian and foreign law.

Direito spent the next eleven years on the appellate court while continuing to teach at Rio's Pontifical Catholic University. He also became active as a member of the Union of Catholic Jurists. The organization, founded in 1994, had as its stated aim to introduce Catholic ethics into jurisprudence, judicial activities, and lawmaking. Menezes Direito's participation in the group would later raise questions about the extent to which his affiliation with the group may have led to his being unduly biased by the Catholic Church.[11]

On the tribunal, Menezes Direito was chosen as the relator, or presenter, for hundreds of the court's cases. The cases he presided over ran the gamut of issues before the appellate court in the late nineties and first decade of the twenty-first century. Two areas became special interests of his. The first was intellectual property, a reflection of his earlier expertise in copyright. The second was medical malpractice. The medical malpractice cases appear to have awakened in him an interest in biology and medicine and would lead him to write a number of scholarly papers on the area. He embarked on a program of self-study on various topics in biology and medicine and later noted that he had a particular interest in psychiatry.[12]

Menezes Direito's judicial opinions were constrained by the discipline of having to resolve cases before the court and the need to gain a judicial consensus for particular decisions. The Superior Tribunal's cases did not directly implicate Church doctrine, although Menezes Direito would later recall a case where he supported the rights of a couple that had not been formally married to be treated as a married couple for inheritance purposes. His views, like those of the Church and the Brazilian population more generally, seemed mainly supportive of the South American nation's return to democratic governance in the 1980s, including the adoption of a new democratic constitution in 1988.[13]

The real opportunity that the public and the legal profession had for gauging the jurist's views on issues of law and public policy came through his prolific writings on a wide range of topics. His writings reveal the Superior Tribunal minister as an engaged legal scholar, well versed in the international world of legal scholarship, jurisprudence, and social theory.[14] In the field of constitutional law and constitutional rights, Menezes Direito took an approach that many observers called conservative; his approach was cautious and pragmatic. In a 1998 essay titled "The Jurisdictional Contribution and the Effect of Declared Rights," he offered a cautionary note for fellow jurists and legal scholars on the subject of "third-generation rights." The notion of third-generation rights had gained considerable currency among international legal scholars in preceding decades. Third-generation rights are generally seen as community rights, including a right to have peace, a right to a clean environment, a right to development, a right to share in the common patrimony of humanity, and a right to communicate. The concept of third-generation rights had had a significant effect on Brazil's Constitution of 1988, which provides for, among other things, a right to human dignity and the eradication of poverty and marginalization.[15]

Menezes Direito's prominence as a jurist and legal scholar led to his appointment to the Supreme Federal Tribunal by President Lula in 2007. Menezes Direito seemed to many a somewhat curious choice for Lula, who was very much a man of the left. Lula had agitated quite fiercely against Brazil's military governments in the seventies and eighties and was elected as the leader of the nation's left-wing Workers' Party. Research by political scientists Mariana Llanos and Leany Barreiro Lemos indicates that Lula, who appointed more ministers to the Supreme Tribunal than any of his predecessors since the return to democratic government in 1985, appointed Menezes Direito in part because his affiliation with the Movement for a Democratic Brazil (PMDB), the strongest party in the senate, made confirmation more likely.[16]

The nomination caused something of a stir in the Brazilian press, as some reporters questioned whether Menezes Direito's religious views would influence his judicial decision-making. He was questioned in the senate on the legalization of abortion, a new law permitting stem cell research on human embryos, and legal protection for social movements, among other topics. He managed to avoid direct answers on the most contentious issues. When asked about abortion, he replied, "My Catholic faith, in which I have much pride, causes me to defend life with intransigence, but as a judge, I always comply with the law." In reply to a question about stem cell research, Menezes Direito replied, "Faith cannot limit science, and science cannot attack faith. There must be a convergence." When asked about social movements, particularly the movement of landless people to occupy and gain land, he noted that democratic societies needed social movements: "We cannot live without them."[17] On August 29, 2007, the senate approved Menezes Direito by a vote of sixty-one in favor of the nominee, two opposed, and one abstention. He took his seat on the court on September 5 of the same year.[18]

The questions about Menezes Direito's adherence to Church doctrine and the challenges his religious allegiances might pose for his role as a minister on Brazil's highest court were more than purely hypothetical concerns. Even as Menezes Direito was in the process of being nominated to the court and undergoing confirmation hearings in the senate, a case was making its way toward the Supreme Federal Tribunal that would bring the question of religious doctrine and the rule of law under the Brazilian constitution into sharp focus. The case would also highlight Menezes Direito's multiple roles as a committed Catholic, a national jurist and legal scholar, and a lay student of biology and medicine.

On March 24, 2005, Brazil's Congress passed legislation titled the Law of Bio-Security. Article 5 of the statute authorized the extraction of stem cells from human embryos developed during in vitro fertilization for scientific research. The statute specified that only embryos that were considered unviable or that had been frozen three or more years at the time of the law's passage could be used for research. The statute specified that researchers would require permission from the embryo's sperm and egg donors in order to conduct research. The Union of Catholic Jurists had lobbied heavily against the legislation. The law was to go into effect in October 2005. In May of that year, the nation's attorney general, Claudio Fonteles, moved to declare the measure unconstitutional because it violated the right to life and human dignity. Fonteles argued that these were the foundations of the democratic rule of law. Fonteles was criticized in the press as acting at the behest of the Catholic Church.[19]

The case came before the Supreme Federal Tribunal and its new minister, Menezes Direito, in May 2008. While a minister on the Superior Tribunal of Justice, Menezes Direito had previously written on issues of bioethics expressing skepticism concerning the claim that cloning could produce identical human beings, and arguing in favor of natural reproduction. The action challenging the constitutionality of the biosecurity law would draw on Menezes Direito's acquired knowledge in biology and medicine. For Menezes Direito and the other ministers, it also would pit the hope that embryonic stem cell research might provide a path for treatment of many debilitating diseases against the Catholic Church's firm belief that human life begins at conception. Menezes Direito would support the Church in his opinion, and in doing so he would win admiration even from his opponents for his arguments, which drew support from and in turn supported the arguments of the Church. The case helped cement Menezes Direito's reputation as a Catholic jurist.[20]

Brazil's Catholic Church and other interested parties presented their views to the high tribunal. In constitutional cases of significant gravity, Brazil's Supreme Federal Tribunal seeks public participation from concerned interest groups. Interest groups as well as individuals with recognized expertise in the relevant areas are invited to give oral amicus briefs, called *Palestras*, to the court, stating their views on the issues at hand. In the interest of transparency, proceedings of the Brazilian high court are filmed daily and made available on the Brazilian TV channel *Justicia*. These proceedings are available outside Brazil on YouTube. The procedure has the Supreme Federal Tribunal in effect presiding over national town meetings on key constitutional questions. The statements of the presenters, or *Palestrants*, in the stem cell case have been preserved on YouTube in a program made on July 29, 2011.[21]

Palestras were offered by a range of scientific groups and nongovernmental organizations. Brazil's National Conference of Bishops played a large role in supporting Attorney General Fonteles's challenge to the statute. The conference had published a book titled *Vida O Primeiro Direito da Cidadania* (*Life, the first right of citizenship*), which outlined the Church's point of view and was presented at the court's hearing.[22]

The first session considering the case was scheduled for May 5. Menezes Direito asked for a delay to further examine the issues. On May 28 and 29, 2008, the ministers of the court delivered their opinions. In significant cases the high court's ministers usually give their opinions orally. Menezes Direito did so in a measured, meticulous fashion. The Pontifical Catholic University professor reiterated the Church's teachings that human life begins at conception, and that to use stem cells in a way that resulted in the subsequent destruction of the embryos would be a complete violation of the right to life. The Supreme Court minister rejected the argument that personality was a requirement of human life, arguing instead that personality depended on life, not life on personality. Menezes Direito also argued for an alternative to using embryonic stem cells. He argued that adult stem cells held greater promise for beneficial results from scientific research. Throughout his opinion, he demonstrated the familiarity with the biological sciences that he had gained as an avid, self-taught student of the subject. Menezes Direito ended up on the losing side of the case, however. Six of the eleven ministers voted to uphold the constitutionality of the law. Four joined Menezes Direito in voting to declare the law unconstitutional.[23]

The detailed examination of legal and factual issues that Menezes Direito brought to the stem cell issue would be brought, a year later, to the issue of Indigenous rights. On August 27, 2008, the Brazilian high court heard the first of what would be three sessions on a dispute involving an Indigenous reserve, Raposa Serra do Sol, in the northern state of Roraima. The dispute involved, in part, the question of whether the inhabitants of the reserve—some nineteen thousand people of the Ingarico, Macuxi, Patamona, Taurepangue, and Uapixana communities—could exclude commercial rice growers from cultivating reserve lands. The issue of Indigenous autonomy on the reserve lands was made more complicated by the Brazilian Government's view of the Amazon region, where Roraima is located, as part of the national patrimony. The federal government also had security concerns, because the state of Roraima and the Indigenous reserve bordered the volatile nations of Venezuela and Guyana.[24]

Initial soundings of the eleven-member Supreme Federal Tribunal indicated that the court was divided among members who favored a strong reading of the 1988 constitutional provisions guaranteeing Indigenous land rights and cultural autonomy, and others favoring a more restrictive reading, and at least one inclined to give only minimal recognition to Indigenous rights. The August session ended without a ruling. A second session on the topic was scheduled for December.[25]

On December 11, Menezes Direito, in his initial vote, expressed his views. He noted that Indigenous land rights were a facet of the Constitution of 1988 and that those rights had not been recognized in the Constitution of 1967, promulgated under the military government. Menezes Direito argued for an approach that, while recognizing Indigenous rights, would nonetheless avoid conferring totally exclusive rights to the inhabitants of the reserve. Instead, the legal scholar and jurist laid out some eighteen conditions which he argued would balance the interests of the Indigenous inhabitants of Raposa Serra do Sol with those of the nation as a whole, particularly the nation's interest in the environment and national defense. Menezes Direito proposed, among other points, that the armed forces should have access to the reserve, and that recognition of Indigenous rights to the reserve should not be interpreted as interfering with the development of infrastructure, including the building of roads, transportation systems, and communication networks. He also put forward conditions that would protect the government's ability to build schools and hospitals on the reserve. His conditions included protection for the Chico Mendez Institute for the Conservation of Biodiversity and the Mount Roraima National Park, which was on reserve land. The conditions were adopted in the court's final decision.[26]

During his short but eventful tenure on the court, Menezes Direito was able to make an impact on the conduct of elections and the problem of crime in his home city of Rio. Ministers on the Supreme Federal Tribunal also serve as regular or substitute ministers on the Superior Electoral Tribunal (Superior Tribunal Eleitoral). They do this in conjunction with ministers from the Superior Tribunal of Justice. In 2008, while serving as a substitute minister on the electoral tribunal, Menezes Direito persuaded the court to order troops into Rio de Janeiro to protect the integrity of elections in the city. The city had been plagued with a large amount of violence due to narcotics trafficking and gang turf wars.[27]

Menezes Direito's time on the court proved to be short. He took medical leave in May 2009 when he underwent surgery for pancreatic cancer. He died of that disease on September 1 of that same year. The Supreme Court minister was survived by his wife, Wanda Direito, three children—Carlos Alberto, Carlos Gustavo, and Luciana Maria—and several grandchildren.[28]

Notes

1 Love, "Political Participation in Brazil," 3–24; Power and Roberts, "Compulsory Voting," 800–03.
2 *Supremo Tribunal Federal, Ministros*, 1–5.
3 Ibid.; Menezes Direito, *O Estado Moderno.*
4 Superior Tribunal de Justiça, *Coletânea de Julgados e Momentos Jurídicos.*
5 Menezes Direito, "Fé cristâ e Compromisso Social"; Paul VI, *Octogesima Adveniens*; John Paul II, *Laborem Exercens.*
6 Menezes Direito, "Fé cristâ."
7 Ibid.
8 Ibid.
9 Ibid.
10 Menezes Direito, "A democracia constitucional dos oitenta."
11 Freitas, "Ligado à Igreja."
12 "Entre a Fé e a Lei"; Menezes Direito, "A responsibilidade civil dos medicos"; "A responsibilidade civil em cirurgia plastica."
13 Consultor Jurídico "Direito À Herança: STJ reconhece união estável de 32 anos para partilha de bens," 20 de Agosto de 2003, 16h07.
14 See, e.g., Menezes Direito, "Breves notas."
15 Menezes Direito, "A prestaçâo Jurisdicional."
16 Llanos and Barreiro Lemos, "Presidential Preferences?," 91.
17 "Ministro do STF defende convergencia."
18 "Carlos Alberto Direito e approvado."
19 Luna, "From abortion to embryonic stem cell reseach," 173; *Supremo Tribunal Federal, Coordenadoria de Analise de Jurisprudência*, 134, hereinafter STF hearing.
20 Menezes Direito, "O Mistério da Vida e a Descoberta Do Código Genético."
21 Vivas, "Grandes Julgamentos do STF" (YouTube).
22 Luna, 173–74.
23 Ibid., 182–83.
24 Yamada and Villares, "Julgamento da Terra Indígena."
25 Ibid.
26 Ibid.; Matauura, "Direito indigena nasceu com Constituicao de 1988."
27 Ruberti, "TSE define atuacao."
28 "Morre, no RJ, o ministro Carlos Alberto Menezes Direito"; Pinho and Pinheiro, "Morre o ministro do Supremo Menezes Direito."

References

"Carlos Alberto Direito e Approvado Para o Cargo de Ministro do STF." *Senado Noticias*, Aug. 29, 2007.
"Entre a Fé e a Lei: Minha Fé Nunca Interferiu nos Julgamentos, Diz Direito." *Consultor Jurídico*, Sept. 2, 2007.
Freitas, Silvania de. "Ligado à Igreja, Ministro Deve Julgar Aborto." *Folha de S. Paulo*, Aug. 27, 2007.
John Paul II. *Laborem Exercens*, Sept. 14, 1981.
Llanos, Mariana, and Leany Barreiro Lemos. "Presidential Preferences? The Supreme Federal Tribunal Nominations in Democratic Brazil." *Latin American Politics and Society* 55, no. 2 (2013): 77–105.
Love, Joseph L. "Political Participation in Brazil, 1881–1969." *Luso-Brazilian Review* 7, no. 2 (1970): 3–24.

Luna, Naara. "From Abortion to Embryonic Stem Cell Research: Biosociality and the Constitution of Subjects in the Debate over Human Rights." *Vibrant: Virtual Brazilian Anthropology* 12, no. 1 (2015): 167–203.

Matauura, Lilian. "Direito Indigena Nascenu com Constituicao de 1988, Diz Ministro." *Consultor Jurídico*, Dec. 11, 2008.

Menezes Direito, Carlos Alberto. "Breves Notas Sobre o Primado da Constituição." *Revista de Direito Administrativo* 209 (1997): 19–41.

Menezes Direito, Carlos Alberto. "A Democracia Constitucional Dos Oitenta: transicao e consolidacao, [Brasilia] 1996. Cited in *Coletanea de Julgados e Momentos Jurídicos dos Magistrados no TFR e no STJ: Homenagem Póstuma* 61 (Ministro Menezes Direito), 17.

Menezes Direito, Carlos Alberto. *O Estado Moderno e a proteçâo dos diretios do homen.* Rio de Janeiro: Renovar, 2008.

Menezes Direito, Carlos Alberto. *Estudos De Direito Público E Privado.* Rio De Janeiro: Renovar, 2008.

Menezes Direito, Carlos Alberto. "Fe Crista e Compromisso Social." Speech at Pontifical University of Rio de Janeiro, Brazil, 1982.

Menezes Direito, Carlos Alberto. "O Mistério da Vida e a Descoberta Do Código Genético." Mesa Rodonda (Round table): Clonagem reprodutiva versus clonagem terapeutica: avancos e limites (Reproductive cloning versus therapeutic cloning: advances and limits. Brasilia, Superior Tribunal de Justiça, *Ensaios Juridicos*, S.D.

Menezes Direito, Carlos Alberto. "A Prestação Jurisdicional e a Efetividade dos Direitos Declarados." *Revista da EMERJ* 1, no. 1 (1998): 141–46.

Menezes Direito, Carlos Alberto. "A responsibilidade civil dos médicos, [Brasilia] 1996. Cited in *Coletanea de Julgados e Momentos Jurídicos dos Magistrados no TFR e no STJ: Homenagem Póstuma* 61 (Ministro Menezes Direito), 23.

Menezes Direito, Carlos Alberto. "A responsibilidade civil em cirurgia plastica." *Revista de Direito Renovar, Rio de Janeiro* 7 (1997): 11–19.

"Ministro do STF Defende convergência entre fé ciência e Evita polêmica E Evita Polmica." BOL, folHA.com 29/08/2007 16h16.

"Morre, no RJ, o ministro Carlos Alberto Menezes Direito." *Migalhas*, Tuesday, Sept. 1, 2009.

Paul VI. "Apostolic Letter." *Octogesima Adveniens*, May 14, 1971.

Pinho, Deborah, and Pinheiro Aline. "Morre o ministro do Supremo Menezes Direito." *Consultor Jurídico*, Sept. 1, 2009.

Power, Timothy J., and Timmons J. Roberts. "Compulsory Voting, Invalid Ballots, and Abstention in Brazil." *Political Research Quarterly* 48, no. 4 (1995): 795–826.

Ruberti, Irene. "TSE Define Atuacao de Tropas no Rio." *Veja*, Aug. 18, 2008.

Superior Tribunal de Justicça. *Coletânea de Julgados e Momentos Jurídicos dos Magisstrados no TFR e no STJ: Homenagem Póstuma: 61 Ministro Menezes Direito.* Brazil, 2012.

Supremo Tribunal Federal. *Coordenadoria de Analise de Jurisprudência DJe No. 96 Divulgaçâo 27/05/2010 Publicaçâo 28/05/2010 Ementario no. 2403-1*, 29/05/2008, "Ação Direta de Inconstitucionalidade 3.510 Distrito Federal.

Supremo Tribunal Federal. *Ministros: Carlos Alberto Menezes Direito*, 1–5.

Yamada, Erica, and Luiz Fernando Villares. "Julgamento da Terra Indígena Raposa Serra do Sol: todo dia era dia de Índio." *Revista Direito GV* 6, no. 1 (2010): 143–58.

Index

For Product Safety Concerns and Information please contact our EU representative GPSR@taylorandfrancis.com
Taylor & Francis Verlag GmbH, Kaufingerstraße 24, 80331 München, Germany

www.ingramcontent.com/pod-product-compliance
Ingram Content Group UK Ltd.
Pitfield, Milton Keynes, MK11 3LW, UK
UKHW022005180926
475701UK00003B/212
* 9 7 8 0 3 6 7 7 0 7 4 8 4 *